ADR, ARBITRATION, AND MEDIATION
A Collection of Essays

AuthorHouse™ UK Ltd.
1663 Liberty Drive
Bloomington, IN 47403 USA
www.authorhouse.co.uk
Phone: 0800.197.4150

© Chartered Institute of Arbitrators 2014.

All rights are reserved. No part of this publication may be reproduced, stored in a retrieval system or transmitted in any form or by any means, electronic, mechanical, photocopying, recording or otherwise, without the prior permission in writing of the Chartered Institute of Arbitrators. Enquiries concerning the reproduction outside the scope of the above should be sent to the Chartered Institute of Arbitrators.

While the Chartered Institute of Arbitrators, the publisher and the editors have used their best efforts in preparing this book, they make no representations or warranties with respect to the accuracy or completeness of the contents of this publication and specifically disclaim any implied warranties of merchantability or fitness for a particular purpose. No warranty may be created or extended by sales representatives or written sales materials. The advice and strategies contained herein may not be suitable for your situation. You should consult with a professional where appropriate. The opinions expressed in this publication are those of the contributors concerned and are not necessarily those held by the Chartered Institute of Arbitrators, the publisher and/or the editors. Neither the Chartered Institute of Arbitrators, the publisher nor the editors shall be liable for any loss of profit or any other commercial damages, including but not limited to special, incidental, consequential, or other damages.

The publisher has no responsibility for the persistence or accuracy of URLs for external or third-party internet websites referred to in this book, and does not guarantee that any content on such websites is, or will remain, accurate or appropriate.

ADR, Arbitration, and Mediation: A Collection of Essays
Edited by Julio César Betancourt and Jason A. Crook

ISBN: 978-1-4918-8664-9 (sc)
ISBN: 978-1-4918-8665-6 (hc)
ISBN: 978-1-4918-8666-3 (e)

Published by AuthorHouse 01/09/2014

ADR, ARBITRATION, AND MEDIATION
A Collection of Essays

Edited by

Julio César Betancourt and Jason A. Crook

authorHOUSE®

CONTRIBUTORS

Albert Jan Van den Berg
Andrew Bartlett
Andrew Tweeddale
Ann Brady
Arthur Marriott
Craig Pollack
Dame Hazel Genn
David E. Hollands
Derek Roebuck
Elina Zlatanska
Elizabeth Birch
Frank E. A. Sander
Geoffrey Gibson
Ian Richard Scott
Jan Paulsson
Jason A. Crook
John Griffiths
John Uff
Julian D. M. Lew
Julio César Betancourt
Karen Tweeddale
Karl J. Mackie
Karl-Heinz Böckstiegel
Lord Clarke
Lord Donaldson

Lord Dyson
Lord Goff
Lord Saville
Lord Steyn
Lord Phillips
Lord Woolf
Michael O'Reilly
Otto L. O. de Witt Wijinen
Peter Mason
Philip Naughton
Pieter Sanders
Robert Coulson
Roger Holmes
Simon Roberts
Sir Anthony Colman
Sir Anthony Evans
Sir Brian Neill
Sir Gavin Lightman
Sir Laurence Street
Sir Ronald Davison
Sir Roy Beldam
Sir Vivian Ramsey
Tony Willis
Warren E. Burger
Wolf Von Kumberg

In memory of H. C. Emery, F. Malcolm Burr, I. W. Bullen, A. Powells, and A. Stevens, founders of the Institute of Arbitrators

CONTENTS

FOREWORD xi
Lord Neuberger of Abbotsbury
President of the Supreme Court of the United Kingdom

INTRODUCTION xiii
Michael O'Reilly

ADR, ARBITRATION, AND MEDIATION: AN OVERVIEW xxi
Julio César Betancourt and Jason A. Crook

CHAPTER 1 ADR

Alternative Dispute Resolution in the United States: An Overview 1
Frank E. A. Sander

Alternative Dispute Resolution: Contemporary Developments in Britain 16
John Griffiths and Simon Roberts

Alternative Dispute Resolution in Practice 28
Karl J. Mackie

The Future of Private Dispute Resolution in the United States 36
Robert Coulson

Alternative Forms of Dispute Resolution: Strengths and Weaknesses 43
Philip Naughton

The Courts and Alternative Dispute Resolution 64
Ian Richard Scott

Alternative Dispute Resolution in Construction 83
David E. Hollands

ADR, Arbitration, and Mediation: A Collection of Essays

Alternative Dispute Resolution 91
Lord Donaldson

The Language of ADR 105
Sir Laurence Street

Report of the Committee on Alternative Dispute Resolution 121
Sir Roy Beldam

Windows on the World 141
Lord Goff

ADR in Civil Law Countries 152
Pieter Sanders

ADR: The Civil Law Approach 162
Otto L. O. de Witt Wijinen

Dispute Resolution in the 21st Century: Barriers or Bridges 174
John Uff

Dispute Resolution 2020 201
Sir Anthony Evans

Are Trial Lawyers Bad for ADR? 211
Geoffrey Gibson

ADR Developments within the European Union 229
Ann Brady

Mandatory ADR and Access to Justice 253
Arthur Marriott

Alternative Dispute Resolution: An English Viewpoint 279
Lord Phillips

Chartered Institute of Arbitrators

Online Dispute Resolution (ODR): What Is It, and Is It the Way Forward?..309
Julio César Betancourt and Elina Zlatanska

CHAPTER 2 ARBITRATION

Arbitration – Its Future – Its Prospects 337
Sir Ronald Davison

Using Arbitration to Achieve Justice 352
Warren E. Burger

Arbitration: The Six F's 361
Peter Mason

England's Response to the Model Law of Arbitration 369
Lord Steyn

The Problems Facing Arbitration in the European Union 398
Karl-Heinz Böckstiegel

The Arbitration Act 1996 and its Effect on International Arbitration 411
Lord Saville

Why Arbitration Will Be With Us Always 438
Albert Jan Van den Berg

Achieving the Potential of Effective Arbitration 447
Julian D. M. Lew

Client-Friendly Arbitration 472
Andrew Bartlett

Appeals from Arbitral Awards: Should Section 69 be Repealed? 484
Roger Holmes and Michael O'Reilly

ADR, Arbitration, and Mediation: A Collection of Essays

Commencement of Arbitration and Time-Bar Clauses 501
Andrew Tweeddale and Karen Tweeddale

Mediation in Arbitration in the Pursuit of Justice 516
Lord Woolf

Universal Arbitration — What We Gain, What We Lose 535
Jan Paulsson

CHAPTER 3 MEDIATION

The Central London County Court Pilot Mediation Scheme 559
Dame Hazel Genn

The Historical Background to the EU Directive on Mediation 565
Elizabeth Birch

The Future of Mediation in Europe 576
Wolf Von Kumberg

Mediation and its Future Prospects 581
Sir Brian Neill

The Myth of Modern Mediation 591
Derek Roebuck

Mediation: Big Bang, Steady State or Black Hole? 615
Tony Willis

The Role of the Mediation Advocate: A User's Guide to Mediation 634
Craig Pollack

Mediation: An Approximation to Justice 643
Sir Gavin Lightman

Chartered Institute of Arbitrators

Mediation and ADR: A Judicial Perspective 651
Sir Anthony Colman
The Future of Civil Mediation 659
Lord Clarke
A Word on 'Halsey v Milton Keynes' 671
Lord Dyson
Mediation 2020 684
Sir Vivian Ramsey

FOREWORD

The acronym ADR has only relatively recently become part of the common currency of the language of practising lawyers in the United Kingdom. But, of course, one form of alternative dispute resolution has been very familiar for centuries, especially in the field of commercial law, and that is arbitration. With the ever-increasing internationalisation of business and cross-border trade, coupled with the growing desire for privacy and party autonomy, arbitration has been growing. Further, partly because of electronic communication and electronic documentation, and partly because of enthusiasm for, and interest in, new procedures and approaches generally, arbitration is undergoing many innovations. In addition, arbitration has been the subject of relatively new legislation, which, although it re-enacts much of the previous law, includes quite a lot that is new.

These various developments and changes in the field of arbitration, coupled with the large sums and important issues which are so often at stake in them, mean that a new book providing a comprehensive overview on the topic from an authoritative source is not merely very welcome: it is positively needed by professionals involved in arbitration and their clients. It is hard to think of an organisation better qualified to sponsor such a book than the Chartered Institute of Arbitrators, with its enormous experience and authority in the field. It is also hard to conceive of a more impressive and well qualified group of contributors to such a book than the list of people who Julio César Betancourt and Jason A. Crook have included in this volume.

While arbitration represents familiar territory to lawyers, other forms of ADR are relatively new to mainstream UK lawyers. In the past fifteen years, from a virtual standing start, mediation has taken off exponentially. It has not only done so informally, as on e-Bay: it is playing an increasing part of the court procedure in civil and family cases. It is highly desirable that every dispute which can properly and fairly be resolved without going to court can be so resolved, particularly when the sums and other issues at stake are, in objective terms, small. Further, while it seems to me that it is a fundamental requirement of a modern democratic society that access to the courts should be available to everyone, the cost of litigation and cutbacks in legal aid mean that, at least for the moment, this is more of an aspiration than a reality. So long as this remains the melancholy reality, arbitration and mediation represent an almost constitutionally vital service.

This book is therefore to be welcomed for a second very important reason, namely because it provides expert guidance from highly qualified and expert individuals on the increasingly important topic of mediation and other newer forms of ADR. Not least because it is relatively new, flexible and very fast growing, mediation and associated forms of ADR are areas where authoritative guidance is essential. The Institute is historically connected only with arbitration, but with its reputation, and experience, and with the editorship of Betancourt and Crook, it is an ideal organisation to sponsor a book giving guidance from renowned people with real experience in the field.

Lord Neuberger of Abbotsbury
President of the Supreme Court of the United Kingdom

INTRODUCTION

The Institute of Arbitrators was established in London by a small group of professionals "to raise the status of Arbitration to the dignity of a distinct and recognised position as one of the learned professions." It was the first professional institute set up with the specific aim of promoting a system of dispute management outside the formal court structures. That was in 1915. Since then the Institute has been granted a charter, reinforcing its status, and is now the largest professional body for dispute settlement in the world, with a majority of its members overseas.

As we approach the Institute's centenary it is appropriate to take a few moments to consider how the world of dispute settlement and resolution has changed. The founding members would note a number of developments. They would surely have been gratified to see the spectacular growth of international commercial arbitration. They may have been surprised to see that mediation had been recognised as a distinct approach to dispute processes. They would perhaps have been pleased to see that the Institute's membership has not only grown in numbers but is also much more diverse — including, for example, many more women. On the other hand, some things have not changed.

First, the Institute has remained a learned society, and has through its journal published important, enlightening and entertaining articles. Secondly, its members have been committed to the improvement and development of dispute settlement and dispute resolution techniques — namely ADR, arbitration and mediation. The Journal, which initially focused almost entirely on arbitration-related matters, now deals with a wider range of matters and uses a longer title which more clearly expresses its mission: "Arbitration: the International Journal of Arbitration, Mediation and Dispute Management."

This present work is a selection of articles which have previously been published in the Journal and which reflect the Institute's focus on the improvement and development of dispute resolution. Julio César Betancourt and Jason A. Crook have examined the past thirty years' output from the Journal and have selected 45 articles which they consider important or representative. In this they have done an excellent job. The articles they have selected continue to be relevant, providing valuable insights for today's dispute resolvers.

As the editors point out in their Overview, we need to distinguish between dispute settlement and dispute resolution, as they define it. Dispute settlement is what a judge or arbitrator does: the disputants lay before the tribunal their competing arguments and the judge or arbitrator makes a decision which settles the dispute. In this sense ADR, if it is defined to include arbitration, employs techniques which overlap with the court system, although arbitration enjoys much greater flexibility and a commitment to party autonomy which state courts do not generally allow. However, resolution is a much wider concept. It includes where parties find a resolution — either through direct negotiation or through a third party mediator — to their issues.

These resolutions may not be perfect, but they have a number of advantages: they are agreed, so each disputant enjoys a degree of autonomy and, viewed from a purely utilitarian perspective, they usually represent a least damaging outcome on aggregate. Indeed, because the resolution is not constrained by the remedies that can be imposed by a court, it is possible to describe many resolution outcomes as win-win solutions.

Although the Institute's name reflects its original focus on arbitration which, in 1915, was the most recognised alternative to litigation, the past thirty years have seen various forms of ADR flourish. Of these, mediation has been the most prominent. We are reminded by Derek Roebuck in *The Myth of Modern Mediation* that mediation has ancient origins — as he puts it "everywhere and at all times, the most natural and pervasive means that humans have devised for managing disputes." Many of the articles selected argue that mediation should retain its flexibility and should not be constrained by set procedures. There is now a European directive (Directive 2008/52/EC) and some have argued for legislation — and Sir Vivian Ramsey in his piece *Mediation 2020* has even suggested a name for the statute: the Justice, Mediation and Dispute Resolution (Miscellaneous Provisions) Act 2020 — before warning us to think twice before going down this route. Although the term mediation tends to refer to non-evaluative assistance by the mediator, and this is the system enjoying widest support, we see in the articles published here a number of suggestions for non-binding evaluation. In a piece entitled *Alternative Dispute Resolution* published in 1992 Lord Donaldson, one of the eminent Masters of the Rolls and a supporter of the Institute, spoke of a scheme in which "the essential feature is the employment of a lawyer as a mediator who, at an early stage in the proceedings, listens to a 'run through' of the parties' evidence and contentions and expresses an impartial, but informed, view of the likely outcome if the matter went to trial. Whether or not the mediator's view is accepted, the result is that the parties begin to think settlement...". In this and in other views expressed by a variety of writers we see a number of proposals which have been considered alongside non-evaluative mediation.

As the reader continues to read Lord Donaldson's piece one encounters what may appear a surprising reaction. Having referred to a working party being set up under the chairmanship of a judge, Lord Donaldson says this: "ADR enthusiasts will be deeply disappointed [by the decision to set up a working party]. They will believe that the time for working parties is long since past and what is now needed is a little action. At the risk of appearing tiresome, I do not agree. ADR is a PR man's dream. It conjures up visions of a factor 'x' which will do for dispute resolution what it is said to have done for washing powders and petrol. The truth is that there is no factor 'x'. Indeed I rather doubt whether there is any such thing as ADR. It is simply an umbrella term or 'buzz word' covering any new procedure or modification of old procedures which one is able to think up." What Lord Donaldson was saying of course was not that ADR should not be used, but that it should not be considered as separate or apart from litigation but as part of it. I rather think that had Lord Donaldson been with us 20 years on, he may have taken a different view, or at least have expressed it in different terms.

One of the most cited articles from this selection — especially in relation to mediation — will no doubt be that by Lord Dyson in *A Word on Halsey v Milton Keynes*. As most readers will know, the English courts had prior to 2004 expressed a deal of support for mediation and there was a hope that an appellate court would state categorically that a party that refused mediation was likely to be penalised in costs. Such a statement coming from someone such as Lord Justice Dyson — as he then was — would have been invaluable to those promoting mediation. His reputation was as judge who looked the purpose of legislation; he had for instance been instrumental in setting construction adjudication on the right course, effectively rescuing the legislation from its poor drafting. However, mediation fans were to be sorely disappointed. In 2004, in the case of *Halsey* Lord Justice Dyson expressed the view that mediation should not generally be forced on unwilling parties. In the article *A Word on Halsey v Milton Keynes* — derived from the transcript of Lord Dyson's speech at the Chartered Institute of Arbitrators' 3rd Mediation Symposium — he says: "So, where do I stand six years on [from the decision in *Halsey*]? Well I am afraid that if anyone came here expecting some sort of Halsey recantation on my part then they will be disappointed." However Lord Dyson did go on to explain the decision further in a way in which supporters of mediation may have found encouraging, at least in part: "First, mediation is important and should be used in many cases but is not a universal panacea. Secondly, parties should not be compelled to mediate if they are truly unwilling to do so, and thirdly that adverse costs orders are an appropriate means of encouraging parties to use mediation." The article contains a valuable discussion of subsequent European jurisprudence, particularly regarding the European Court of Justice's 2010 case of *Rosalba Alassini v Telecom Italia* in which it decided that a pre-requirement to mediate before commencing litigation did not necessarily infringe rights of access to the courts. But the article reinforces the third point above, namely that the English court will retain a discretion to use costs sanctions where there has been an unreasonable refusal to mediate — and no doubt the point in issue is now where does one draw the line between reasonable and unreasonable refusals to mediate and what sort of costs sanctions may be appropriately levied. This discussion is important not only from an English perspective but will be viewed with interest by those framing rules and making submissions to courts around the world.

The articles on arbitration touch on a number of themes. Some promote the use of arbitration in a domestic context. Some provide useful reminders of the basics of arbitration, which can sometimes be taken so much for granted that they are forgotten. An example is Peter Mason's amusing article dealing with the six F's: fairness, firmness, formality, friendliness, flexibility, and being fast.

One theme that appears in a number of pieces relates to a key issue facing international arbitration: harmonisation. The United Nations Commission on International Trade Law (UNCITRAL) published its Model Law on Arbitration in 1985. It was the intention of UNCITRAL that it should become the basis of legislation enacted by states around the world. A question which arose in the late 1980s and early 1990s was whether or not England would adopt the Model Law. Although this question can be seen in terms of a domestic English decision, in reality it involved deeper questions about the willingness of jurisdictions such as England to approximate their laws to an international standard. The Journal published a number of speeches by those most closely involved in the process of delivering the philosophy and text of what became the 1996 Act. Lord Steyn's 1993 Freshfields Lecture, published by the Journal in 1994, for example, seeks to explain the decision not to adopt the Model Law. That explanation, with respect, was not entirely convincing at the time and has not become more convincing with the passage of 20 years. In an article by Lord Saville, immediately after enactment of the 1996 legislation, he also touches upon the reasons for not adopting the Model Law. He explained that there were three factors. First, in the Model law "there were a number of things which we could usefully adopt", but secondly, "in other respects the Model Law contained provisions which were considered to be inferior to our existing laws" and finally "The Model Law was not a complete Code and would in any event have to be supplemented." In retrospect, we see that the growth of other major arbitration venues, such as Singapore, has not been hampered by adopting the Model Law and enacting parallel provisions to supplement any perceived shortcomings. One might reflect that Lord Saville's statement "London is the acknowledged centre for international arbitration" might well be challenged today by a number of such jurisdictions.

But, whatever one's stance on the Model Law and its effect on the attractiveness of venues, we can all agree that these articles are of historical importance, written by those most closely involved in events at the time. Their re-publication will enable a new generation of ADR practitioners and students to consider them afresh. Although there is insufficient space in this brief introduction to refer to more than a handful of the essays, I hope that the few I have mentioned are sufficient to illustrate what a valuable resource this book provides and that this shallow dip has whetted the appetite to dive in deeper. It is in the articles read in full that one can best understand what the authors intended and benefit from the enormous experience which is shared in them.

As well as being of benefit to practitioners, this work will be particularly valuable to historians of our subject. Having such a breadth of learning in one location will also be of assistance to students, providing a platform for deeper and wider studies. One of the things we need to do is to encourage more undergraduate and postgraduate students to take ADR courses and this volume will provide a central text for such studies.

Finally, it is appropriate to mention three groups of people. First, I should briefly mention my fellow editors of the Journal during the relevant period — Alan Shilston and Derek Roebuck whose efforts have enabled this unique repository of articles. Secondly, we should thank the original authors whose time and effort in putting together these essays is hugely appreciated. And finally we should express our gratitude to the editors — Julio César Betancourt and Jason A. Crook — for their labours and diligence in putting together such a valuable resource.

Dr Michael O'Reilly
Editor of Arbitration

ADR, ARBITRATION, AND MEDIATION:

An Overview

Julio César Betancourt and Jason A. Crook

The notion of alternative dispute resolution (ADR) has received considerable attention in common law literature,[1] and the same can be said about the principal ADR categories:[2] *arbitration*,[3] and *mediation*.[4] ADR, in its broadest sense, refers to the idea of utilising a wide spectrum of mechanisms aimed at *preventing, managing, settling,* and *resolving* disputes. The expression 'alternative dispute *resolution*' is therefore a bit of a misnomer, in the sense that it does not accurately reflect the full extent of the concepts that are inextricably linked with the sentiments behind this notion, namely *dispute prevention, dispute management,* and *dispute settlement*.[5] ADR originally arose in reaction to the state's dispute-settlement system, litigation.[6] This system allows any person to either make or defend a claim in the state courts.[7] State courts are supposed to *settle* the cases that are brought to them by means of judicial decisions, but in practice the vast majority of these cases (over 90%) do not go to trial[8] and end up being disposed of by means other than full litigation.[9] This suggests that courts only decide a relatively small proportion of the number of lawsuits that are actually filed, and yet even so concerns have been expressed about court congestion, delays, and several other closely related problems. The idea of deploying ADR mechanisms is precisely 'to have courts more effectively doing those things that they are peculiarly fit to do, and have other [mechanisms such as] arbitration and mediation dispose of those cases that [do not] require the specialized expertise of courts'.[10] Arbitration, without a doubt, has proved to be one of the most effective methods of *settling* disputes, particularly within the international arena. Mediation, on the other hand, is an extraordinary way of *resolving* disputes. Such a distinction between settling and resolving disputes is important because the former is related to the theme of *third party decision-making*, whereas the latter has to do with the concept of *joint decision-making*.[11] By gaining an understanding of the concepts of *ADR, arbitration, and mediation*, students, lawyers, judges, businessmen, and others interested in preventing, managing, settling, and resolving disputes should be able to identify what is the most *appropriate*[12] way to deal with them. This may help to reduce the number of cases that are unnecessarily taken to the state courts, thereby avoiding 'swamping and paralyzing them with cases that do not require their unique capabilities'.[13] It may also allow courts to make a more 'appropriate use of state resources'.[14] And, most importantly, it may help the parties to employ the method that best suits their interests.[15] ADR mechanisms cannot be seen as a replacement for litigation.[16] Nor can they be seen as a panacea,[17] let alone as something *better than* litigation. In other words, ADR 'is not about being better than; it is about being in addition to'.[18] There are some cases that are particularly suited to court adjudication.[19] Thus, when it comes to deciding whether to make use of the state courts the issue is not simply "for or against" litigation,[20] but rather "is this case appropriate for litigation?" The so-called alternatives to the court system in general, and arbitration and mediation in particular, have contributed significantly to 'our general knowledge of dispute processing',[21] and may allow us to realise that 'no important function in a society [can ever be] performed by a single institution'.[22]

This publication is intended to provide the reader with an overview of the notions of ADR, arbitration, and mediation, and was inspired by the work of some of the most prominent individuals in these burgeoning fields. It contains a selection of essays originally published in the Chartered Institute of Arbitrators' journal over the last thirty years. Because these essays have been previously peer reviewed and scrutinised before publication, editorial changes have been kept to a minimum. Footnotes and other citations, for example, have been converted into references. Bulleted and numbered lists were incorporated into the main text and, where appropriate, short paragraphs have been merged with longer paragraphs. Thousands of pages of text have been consulted to produce the volume you now hold.

Our goal has been to produce a single work containing three broad chapters, something that would not have been possible without the efforts of many people. We would like to thank Elina Zlatanska for her tireless dedication and effort in helping compile and format the manuscript, and without whom this work would not have been the same. Thanks must also be given to Katriina Karvonen, Claudia Pharaon, Jackie Sears, Waj Khan, and Yvonne Hanly for their assistance. Finally, we are grateful to Professor Derek Roebuck, Dr Michael O'Reilly, the contributing authors, and the late Alan Shilston without whom this book would not have been published.

REFERENCES

1 See, for example, T. Carbonneau, *Alternative Dispute Resolution: Melting the Lances and Dismounting the Steeds* (Urbana: University of Illinois Press 1989); G. Applebey, 'Alternative Dispute Resolution and the Civil Justice System', in *A Handbook of Dispute Resolution: ADR in Action*, ed. K. Mackie (London: Routledge, 1991); A. Bevan, *Alternative Dispute Resolution: A Lawyer's Guide to Mediation and Other Forms of Dispute Resolution* (London: Sweet & Maxwell, 1992); M. Freeman, *Alternative Dispute Resolution* (New York: New York University Press, 1995); S. Meek, *Alternative Dispute Resolution* (Tucson: Lawyers & Judges, 1996); Edward Brunet & Charles Craver, *Alternative Dispute Resolution: The Advocate's Perspective* (Charlottesville: Michie, 1997); P. Rao & William Sheffield (eds.), *Alternative Dispute Resolution: What it is and How it Works* (Delhi: Universal Law Pub. Co., 1997); A. Pirie, *Alternative Dispute Resolution: Skills, Science, and the Law* (Toronto: Irwin Law, 2000); S. Ware, *Alternative Dispute Resolution* (St. Paul: West Group, 2001); T. Sourdin, *Alternative Dispute Resolution* (Pyrmont: Lawbook Co., 2002); J. Barrett, *A History of Alternative Dispute Resolution: The Story of a Political, Cultural, and Social Movement* (San Francisco: Jossey-Bass, 2004); A. Fiadjoe, *Alternative Dispute Resolution: A Developing World Perspective* (London: Cavendish, 2004); J. Grenig, *Alternative Dispute Resolution* (St. Paul: Thomson-West, 2005); A. Bongat, *The Art and Heart of Alternative Dispute Resolution: Mediation* (Quezon City: Central Book Supply, 2006); S. Ware, *Principles of Alternative Dispute Resolution* (St. Paul:

Thomson-West, 2007); Charles Chatterjee & Anna Lefcovitch, *Alternative Dispute Resolution: A Practical Guide* (London: Routledge 2008); J. Nolan-Haley, *Alternative Dispute Resolution in a Nutshell* (St. Paul: Thomson-West, 2008); M. Partridge, *Alternative Dispute Resolution: An Essential Competency for Lawyers* (Oxford: OUP, 2009); J. Crook, 'What is Alternative Dispute Resolution (ADR)?', in Julio César Betancourt (ed.) (London: Chartered Institute of Arbitrators, 2010); L. Coltri, *Alternative Dispute Resolution: A Conflict Diagnosis Approach* (Boston: Prentice Hall, 2010); Susan Blake, Julie Browne & Stuart Sime, *A Practical Approach to Alternative Dispute Resolution* (Oxford: OUP, 2011); Henry Brown & Arthur Marriott, *ADR Principles and Practice* (London: Sweet & Maxwell, 2011).

2 J. Auerbach, *Justice Without Law* (Oxford: OUP, 1983), 4; J. Sabatino, 'ADR as "Litigation Lite": Procedural and Evidentiary Norms Embedded Within Alternative Dispute Resolution', *Emory Law Journal* 47 (1998): 1296; J. Sternlight, 'Is Binding Arbitration a Form of ADR?: An Argument that the Term "ADR" has Begun to Outlive its Usefulness?', *Journal of Dispute Resolution* 1 (2000): 97; W. Smith, 'Much To Do About ADR', *ABA Journal* (2000): 64; R. Hogan, 'ADR: Adding Extra Value to Law', *Arbitration* 78 (2012): 247.

3 See for example, J. Coe, Jr., *International Commercial Arbitration* (New York: Transnational Publishers, 1997); H. Crowter, *Introduction to Arbitration* (London: LLP, 1998); M. Heleatt-James & Nicholas Gould, *International Commercial Arbitration: A Handbook* (London: LLP, 1999); G. Born, *International Commercial Arbitration: Commentary*

and Materials (The Hague: Kluwer Law International, 2001); E. Marshall, *Gill: The Law of Arbitration* (London: Sweet & Maxwell, 2001); M. Rubino-Sammartano, *International Arbitration: Law and Practice* (Boston: Kluwer Academic Pub., 2001); Julian Lew, Loukas Mistelis & Stefan Kröll, *Comparative International Commercial Arbitration* (The Hague: Kluwer Law International, 2003); John Tackaberry & Arthur Marriot, *Bernstein's Handbook of Arbitration and Dispute Resolution Practice*, vol. 1 (London: Sweet & Maxwell, 2003); John Tackaberry & Arthur Marriot, *Bernstein's Handbook of Arbitration and Dispute Resolution Practice*, vol. 2 (London: Sweet & Maxwell, 2003); P. Capper, *International Arbitration: A Handbook* (London: LLP, 2004); Andrew Tweeddale & Keren Tweeddale, *Arbitration of Commercial Disputes: International and English Law Practice* (Oxford: OUP, 2005); W. Park, *Arbitration of International Business Disputes: Studies in Law and Practice* (Oxford: OUP, 2006); Emmanuel Gaillard & John Savage, *Fouchard Gaillard Goldman on International Commercial Arbitration* (The Hague: Kluwer Law International, 2009); G. Born, *International Commercial Arbitration* (The Hague: Kluwer Law International, 2009); Nigel Blackaby et al., *Redfern and Hunter on International Arbitration* (Oxford: OUP, 2009); Simon Greenberg, Christopher Kee & J. Romesh Weeramantry, *International Commercial Arbitration: An Asia Pacific Perspective* (Cambridge: Cambridge University Press, 2011); M. Moses, *The Principles and Practice of International Commercial Arbitration* (Cambridge: Cambridge University Press, 2012).

4 D. Kolb, *The Mediators* (Cambridge: MIT Press, 1983); Jay Folberg & Alison Taylor, *Mediation: A Comprehensive Guide to Resolving Conflicts Without Litigation* (San Francisco: Jossey-Bass, 1984); M. Noone, *Mediation* (London: Cavendish, 1996); J. Macfarlane, *Rethinking Disputes: The Mediation Alternative* (London: Cavendish, 1997); H. Genn, *Mediation in Action: Resolving Court Disputes Without Trial* (London: Calouste Gulbenkian Foundation, 1999); K. Kovach, *Mediation in a Nutshell* (St. Paul: Thomson-West, 2003); C. Moore, *The Mediation Process: Practical Strategies for Resolving Conflict* (San Francisco: Jossey-Bass, 2003); A. Stitt, *Mediation: A Practical Guide* (London: Cavendish, 2004); K. Kovach, *Mediation: Principles and Practice* (St. Paul: West Group, 2004); Robert Baruch Bush & Joseph Folger, *The Promise of Mediation: The Transformative Approach to Conflict* (San Francisco: Jossey-Bass 2005); N. Alexander (ed.), *Global Trends in Mediation* (The Netherlands: Kluwer Law International, 2006); David Spencer & Michael Brogan, *Mediation Law and Practice* (Cambridge: Cambridge University Press, 2006); James Alfini et al., *Mediation Theory And Practice* (Newark: LexisNexis Matthew Bender, 2006); C. Menkel-Meadow, L. Love & Andrea Schneider, *Mediation: Practice, Policy, and Ethics* (New York: Aspen Publishers, 2006); L. Boulle, V. Goldblatt & P. Green (eds). *Mediation: Principles, Process and Practice* (Wellington: LexisNexis, 2008); N. Alexander, *International and Comparative Mediation: Legal Perspectives* (The Netherlands: Kluwer Law International, 2009); Dwight Golann & Jay Folberg (eds.), *Mediation: The Roles Of Advocate And Neutral* (New

York: Aspen Publishers, 2011) K. Aubrey-Johnson, *Making Mediation Work For You: A Practical Handbook* (London: Legal Action Group, 2012).

5   Cf J. Fleischer, 'One Size Does Not Fit All: Differentiating ADR Processes', *South Texas Law Review* 49 (2008): 1039.

6   P. Brooker, 'The "Juridification" of Alternative Dispute Resolution', *Anglo-American Law Review* 28 (1999): 3; R. Reuben, 'Constitutional Gravity: A Unitary Theory of Alternative Dispute Resolution and Public Civil Justice', *UCLA Law Review* 47 (2000): 962.

7   Cf L. Friedman, 'Litigation and Society', *Annual Review of Sociology* 15 (1989): 18.

8   Marc Galanter & Mia Cahill, '"Most Cases Settle": Judicial Promotion of Settlement and Regulation of Settlement', *Stanford Law Review* 46 (1994): 1339-1391.

9   Cf M. Galanter, 'Justice in Many Rooms: Courts, Private Ordering, and Indigenous Law', *Journal of Legal Pluralism* 19 (1981): 1-47; F. Sander, 'Alternative Methods of Dispute Resolution: An Overview', *University of Florida Law Review* XXXVII (1985): 1; James Guill & Edward Slavin, Jr., 'Rush to Unfairness: The Downside of ADR', *Judges' Journal* 28 (1989): 45; S. Keilitz, 'Alternative Dispute Resolution in the Courts', in *Handbook of Court Administration*, eds. S. Hays & Cole Graham, Jr. (New York, Marcel Dekker, 1993), 383; 'Access to Justice: Final Report', (London: HMSO, 1996), 15; Nancy Atlas, Stephen Huber & E. Wendy Trachte-Huber (eds), *Alternative Dispute Resolution: The Litigator's Handbook* (Chicago: ABA

Publishing, 2000), 17.

10 F. Sander, 'The Future of ADR', *Journal of Dispute Resolution* (2000): 5.

11 J. Burton, *Conflict and Communication: The Use of Controlled Communication in International Relations* (New York: Free Press, 1969), 171. B. Hill, 'An Analysis of Conflict Resolution Techniques: From Problem-Solving Workshops to Theory', *Journal of Conflict Resolution* 26 (1982): 115; J. Burton, cited by G. Tillett, *Resolving Conflict: A Practical Approach* (Oxford: Sydney University Press, 1991), 9. See also A. Pirie, *Alternative Dispute Resolution: Skills, Science, and the Law* (Toronto: Irwin Law, 2000), 42.

12 Davis & H. Gadlin, 'Mediators Gain Trust the Old-Fashioned Way — We Earn It!', *Negotiation Journal* (1988): 62; R. Ackerman, 'ADR: An Appropriate Alternative?', *Willamette Law Review* 33 (1997): 498; J. Henry, 'Some Reflections on ADR', *Journal of Dispute Resolution* 1 (2000): 63; C. Menkel-Meadow, 'When Litigation is Not the Only Way: Consensus Building and Mediation as Public Interest Lawyering', *Journal of Law and Policy* 10 (2002): 43.

13 F. Sander, 'Varieties of Dispute Processing' Federal Rules Decisions: Addresses Delivered at the National Conference on the Causes of Popular Dissatisfaction with the Administration of Justice (1976): 132.

14 A. Paterson, *Lawyers and the Public Good: Democracy in Action* (Cambridge: Cambridge University Press, 2012), 62.

15 Frank Sander & Stephen Goldberg, 'Fitting the Forum to the Fuss: A User-Friendly Guide to Selecting an ADR Procedure', *Negotiation*

Journal (1994): 49-68; Frank Sander & Lukasz Rozdeiczer, 'Matching Cases and Dispute Resolution Procedures: Detailed Analysis Leading to a Mediation-Centered Approach', *Harvard Negotiation Law Review* 11 (2006): 1-41.

16 J. Sternlight, 'Is Alternative Dispute Resolution Consistent with The Rule of Law?', *Depaul Law Review* 56 (2007): 573.

17 H. Edwards, 'Alternative Dispute Resolution: Panacea or Anathema', *Harvard Law Review* 99 (1986): 669.

18 W. Brazil, 'Court ADR 25 Years after Pound: Have We Found a Better Way', *Ohio State Journal on Dispute Resolution* 18 (2002): 94.

19 Jethro Lieberman & James Henry, 'Lessons from the Alternative Dispute Resolution Movement', *University of Chicago Law Review* 53 (1986): 433; C. Menkel-Meadow, 'Pursuing Settlement in an Adversary Culture: A Tale of Innovation Co-opted or "The Law of ADR"', *Florida State University Law Review* 19 (1991): 12.

20 C. Menkel-Meadow, 'Whose Dispute Is It Anyway?: A Philosophical and Democratic Defense of Settlement (In Some Cases)', *Georgetown Law Journal* 83 (1995): 2665.

21 J. Esser, 'Evaluations of Dispute Processing: We Do Not Know What We Think and We Do Not Think What We Know', *Denver University Law Review* 66 (1989): 499.

22 R. Cover, 'Dispute Resolution: A Foreword', *Yale Law Journal* 88 (1979): 912; Richard McLaren & John Sanderson, *Innovative Dispute Resolution: The Alternative* (Scarborough: Carswell, 1994), 1-1, 1-4.

ADR, ARBITRATION, AND MEDIATION
A Collection of Essays

CHAPTER 1

ALTERNATIVE DISPUTE RESOLUTION

CHAPTER 1

Alternative Dispute Resolution in the United States: An Overview

Frank E. A. Sander

Beginning in the late 1960s, American society witnessed an extraordinary flowering of interest in alternative forms of dispute settlement. Following a decade or so of virtually unabashed enthusiasm, serious questions and doubts are now beginning to be raised. In addition, we are slowly starting to accumulate some limited data concerning viable models and empirical effects, making this an opportune time for taking stock and exploring promising future directions. Initially, it is important to realise that current interest in alternatives to the courts is not a new phenomenon. Arbitration has been used to resolve commercial disputes for hundreds of years, and mediation was commonplace in religious communities in colonial New England (Auerbach, 1983). It appears, however, that alternatives are now being used more broadly than at any other time in American history. It may therefore be useful to speculate on the confluence of events that have led to the current renewal of interest in alternatives. The 1960s, it will be recalled, were characterised by considerable strife and conflict, emanating in part from the civil rights struggles and the Vietnam War protests. An apparent legacy of those times was a lessened tolerance and a greater tendency to turn grievances into law suits. While the reasons for this are not clear, surely one factor was the waning role of some of society's traditional mediating institutions — the family, the church, and the community. At the same time that our capacity to resolve disputes outside the courtroom was diminishing, the grounds for going to court were expanding. Initially, both state and federal legislatures were rapidly creating new causes of action to remedy some of our oldest woes, such as race and sex discrimination. Additionally, advances in technology increased the imposition of harm (in the form of chemicals and other toxic substances) while at the same time enhancing our capacity to detect and seek redress for such harm.

The net result of all these factors was the assertion of an increased volume of legal claims, many of which had not been previously recognised. Courts began to find themselves inundated with new filings, triggering cries of alarm from the judicial administration establishment. At the same time, judicial congestion, with its concomitant delay, led to claims of denials of access to justice. One response to these problems was a demand for more judges and more courtrooms; another was a search for alternatives to the courts. In part, this search was a product of disillusionment with courts as dispute resolvers in many types of cases (child custody disputes come quickly to mind); in part, it was a product of a growing mood of anti-professionalism.

This movement was also supported by contemporaneous intellectual developments. Over the past 15-20 years, cultural anthropologists have sought to apply to disputes in the United States their studies of dispute resolution in other cultures. At times, the influence of the cultural anthropologists has been indirect; at times, as with the transformation of the

Kpelle tribal moot into the neighborhood justice center, it has been direct (Danzig, 1973). Legal scholars, too, most notably the late Lon Fuller, were active in the 1960s and 1970s, in analysing the characteristics of various dispute resolution processes, such as mediation and arbitration, with a view to reaching useful conclusions about their strengths and limitations for particular types of disputes (Fuller, 1963, 1971, 1978).

The early interest in resolving disputes outside the courts received important support from a variety of sources. In the 1964 Civil Rights Act, Congress established the Community Relations Service to aid in the settlement of racial and community disputes. The Ford Foundation established the National Center for Dispute Settlement to bring to bear accumulated learning on dispute settlement in the solution of newly emerging disputes. Again with the help of the Ford Foundation, Ted Kheel, a noted labour arbitrator and mediator, set up the Institute of Mediation and Conflict Resolution in an attempt to apply to newer conflicts the techniques long successfully utilised in labour disputes. Finally, the Law Enforcement Assistance Administration (LEAA) took a firm interest in developing and testing alternatives, even if the required statutory nexus to the criminal justice system at times frustrated a wide-ranging approach. From this brief summary, there emerge four contrasting goals of the alternatives movement, each with its own constituency, namely (1) to relieve court congestion, as well as undue cost and delay; (2) to enhance community involvement in the dispute resolution process; (3) to facilitate access to justice; and (4) to provide more 'effective' dispute resolution. Quite obviously these goals may overlap and conflict. For example, measures aimed at relieving court congestion would take a very different form from measures designed to enhance community control over dispute settlement. The point is that in any particular situation it is essential to think clearly and precisely about the reasons for pursuing alternatives.

As regards the goal of relieving court congestion, the literature of dispute processing has made it plain that only a small proportion of disputes result in court filings, and only a similarly small proportion of the latter consume significant amounts of judicial resources. Disputes that cannot be readily adjusted through negotiation may be resolved by mediation or arbitration; of those disputes that do lead to a court filing, somewhere around 90-95% are settled without the need for a full-blown trial.

In view of this substantial winnowing-out process, it is unlikely that an expansion or more appropriate use of alternatives will significantly reduce still further the number of filings or the proportion of filing that lead to a full-blown trial. This is not to say that a cautious and informed use of ancillary mechanisms to screen (and stimulate the settlement of) court cases is not worth undertaking; on the contrary, such a programme appears to hold considerable promise. But the notion that a pervasive use of alternatives can hope to solve 'the court crisis' seems misguided.

One must be similarly skeptical regarding the communitarian goal of the alternatives movement. While the proponents of this goal view community participation in the dispute resolution process as a means by which a lost sense of community can be regained and community power enhanced, critics have questioned the feasibility of this goal in today's highly mobile American society. Moreover, if dispute settlement is to be a community function, unconnected to the justice system, funds to operate such programmes may be difficult to find. Finally, these programmes, which were stimulated by the perceived inadequacies of the justice system, will themselves give rise to comparable questions, such as how they can prevent denials of due process or the latent coercion that is implicit in group decision making. This, the principal promise of the alternatives movement would appear to lie in facilitating access to justice and providing more effective dispute resolution processes.

As one thinks about the goal of increasing access to justice, one is immediately struck by the paradox that providing more accessible means of dispute resolution may result in more disputes being brought forward to be resolved, thus further clogging the dispute resolution machinery and causing further delays. Today, some people who believe that they have legitimate claims do not assert those claims, choosing either to avoid the person they believe has wronged them, or simply to 'lump it' (as in 'like it or lump it').

With the advent of dispute resolution forums more accessible than the courts, such people may flock to those forums. Whether or not this result is desirable depends on the costs of providing alternatives, compared with the costs, real but difficult to measure, of having no means at all of resolving some grievances. The important thing to note is that there is a trade-off: the price of increased access to dispute resolution mechanisms may be a substantial increase in the number of disputes brought forward for resolution. It is also important to note that the goal of increasing access to justice is not necessarily met by providing access to a dispute resolution mechanism other than the courts. Indeed, one of the criticisms of the alternatives movement is that it serves to screen out of the courts some disputes that can be resolved effectively only by judicial intervention.

Hence, the access goal of the alternatives movement should be that of ensuring access to a dispute resolution mechanism that is appropriate for the dispute. This redefinition or clarification of the access goal of the alternatives movement both relates that goal to the goal of providing more effective or appropriate dispute resolution, and highlights the importance of the latter goal. The central question in implementing the latter goal is what dispute resolution process or combination of processes is appropriate or effective for resolving different types of disputes. Preliminarily, there would appear to be general agreement that an effective dispute resolution mechanism is one that is inexpensive, speedy and leads to a final resolution of the dispute. At the same time it should be procedurally fair, efficient (in the sense of leading to optimal solutions), and satisfying to the parties. Indeed, one of the notable contributions of the alternatives movement has been a renewed emphasis on process as a way of underscoring the importance of the values cited above. In addition to looking at outcomes, dispute resolution scholars now ask: Did each disputant have a fair chance? Given a specific outcome, what was the quality of the process? Were the parties satisfied with the process utilised? In short, how parties won or lost may often be as important as whether they did.

ALTERNATIVE DISPUTE RESOLUTION PROCESSES

Description

It may be useful at this point to consider the extent to which the various dispute processes further the values noted above.

The most common and familiar form of dispute settlement is bargaining or negotiation. Compared to processes utilising third parties, negotiation has the great advantage of allowing the parties themselves to control the process and the solution. If the parties cannot settle the dispute themselves, and bring in a third party, the critical question is whether the third party has power to impose a solution or simply to assist the disputants in arriving at their own solution. The latter process is commonly referred to as mediation; the former is referred to as adjudication, whether performed by a court or by a private adjudicator, known as an arbitrator. These three primary processes — negotiation, mediation, and adjudication — can, of course, be combined in a variety of ways, and one of the achievements of the alternatives movement has been the rich variety of hybrid dispute resolution processes it has spawned. For example, an adjudication-like presentation of proofs and arguments is combined with negotiation in the mini-trial, arbitration is combined with court adjudication in a procedure known as rent-a-judge, and mediation is combined with arbitration in med-arb. Other well-known hybrid processes are the ombudsman (which involves a mediator/investigator) and the neutral expert. These processes are further considered below.

Taxonomy

While no empirically validated determination of which process is appropriate for a particular dispute has yet been developed, a variety of considerations appear relevant. First among these is the relationship between the disputants (i.e., is the dispute between individuals with an ongoing relationship or is it the product of a single interaction, such as an automobile accident). In the former situation, it is important to have the parties seek to work out their own solution, for such a solution is more likely to be acceptable to them than an imposed solution, hence more long-lasting. Thus negotiation, or if necessary, mediation, appears to be a preferable technique in these situations. Another advantage of such an approach is that it encourages a restructuring of the underlying relationship so as to eliminate or mitigate the source of conflict, rather than simply dealing with each manifestation of conflict as an isolated event.

Another criterion is the nature of the dispute. Lon Fuller (1978) has pointed out that 'polycentric' problems are not well suited to an adjudicatory approach. These are allocational disputes, in which no clear governing guidelines for decision are available and where any particular solution has proliferating ramifications. One example of such a dispute, given by Fuller, is where two museums received a bequest of a collection of paintings in equal shares, with no directions for apportionment. The problem, as Fuller points out, is that the disposition of any single painting has implications for the disposition of every other painting, as each museum seeks a complete and well-rounded collection. For disputes such as this, a negotiated or mediated solution that seeks to accommodate the desires of the disputants is far better than any externally imposed solution.

Another important distinction is between novel disputes requiring a definitive precedent (and hence a court decision), and recurring applications of the same issue, which can be readily handled by some less-sophisticated and elaborate adjudicatory mechanism, such as arbitration. The amount at stake in a dispute has generally been thought significant in determining the appropriateness of a particular dispute resolution procedure. Indeed, the small claims court movement had as its premise that small cases are simple cases, and that therefore a pared-down judicial procedure was what was called for. Yet there is no necessary connection between amount in controversy and appropriate process. Quite obviously a small case may be complex, just as a large case may be simple. Thus, a more sensible approach would be to analyse disputes in terms of the novelty or complexity of the issues presented. Those disputes presenting novel or complex issues would be appropriately referred to a dispute resolution forum in which there was ample opportunity for the full presentation of evidence and argument; those presenting simpler or more routine issues would be referred to a more truncated procedure.

Speed and cost also appear to be relevant factors in determining the appropriate dispute resolution process. From the perspective of the disputants, if a speedy and inexpensive resolution is desired, then negotiation may be ideal since it requires no involvement of third parties. But if negotiation fails, simplified adjudication may be preferable to mediation, in view of the latter's emphasis on thoroughly probing the conflicts in the underlying relationship, rather than simply seeking to resolve the dispute. Alternatively, the parties might choose mediation, but advise the mediator that their goal was limited to dispute resolution, and did not encompass a wide-ranging effort to restructure their relationship.

Where public funds are involved, the public interest in the fisc must also be taken into account. From this perspective, even if the parties are unconcerned with the costs of dispute resolution, the state is, and should provide only that procedure which is appropriate in light of the relevant characteristics of the dispute. In the United States, this statement of the ideal must, of course, be qualified by such considerations (where applicable) as the constitutional right of access to the courts and to a jury trial.

Finally, attention must be paid to the power relationship between the parties. Where one disputant has notably less bargaining power than the other (e.g., a habitually deferential or financially naive wife dealing with her experienced businessman husband, or a pollution victim faced by a powerful corporation), an adjudicatory mode in which principle, not power, will determine the outcome may be preferable. In some situations, the mere availability of adjudication is important as leverage to bring the more powerful party to the bargaining table and to reduce inequalities of bargaining power. For example, a threatened challenge to the adequacy of an environmental impact statement may both bring the alleged polluter to the bargaining table and encourage it to take more seriously the claims of the pollution victim.

Applications

Both primary and hybrid processes have been used in a number of contexts, some for many years, others only recently. Arbitration, for example, has been used to resolve commercial disputes for hundreds of years, and to resolve disputes about the interpretation of collective bargaining contracts, at least on a large-scale basis, since the 1940s. Recently, arbitration has been used in a host of new areas, such as consumer disputes and medical malpractice claims. While a submission to arbitration is normally voluntary, and the outcome final and binding (except for limited judicial review), non-binding arbitration has been used in prison and other institutional disputes, where the authorities are unwilling to delegate total decision making power to outsiders. Compulsory, non-binding arbitration of cases filed in court, but falling below a fixed value (court-annexed arbitration) has also become increasingly widespread in recent years.

Mediation, which was used for many years to help employers and unions arrive at mutually acceptable contract terms, is today used in a wide variety of disputes, particularly among persons with an ongoing relationship. Indeed, California requires that all child custody disputes be mediated prior to judicial disposition.

Another type of interpersonal dispute frequently resolved by mediation is the neighbourhood squabble. There are now almost 200 neighborhood justice centers, which receive civil and minor criminal cases from court, prosecutors, or police (and sometimes on a walk-in basis), and which attempt to resolve those cases primarily by mediation. In addition to its use in interpersonal disputes, mediation has also been used to resolve large-scale public disputes involving a multiplicity of parties and interests. Among these are environmental disputes, disputes over the content of government regulations, and disputes over the allocation of public funds.

Many hybrid processes have also been used with considerable success. Med-arb, in which issues unresolved by mediation are submitted to arbitration, typically with the same person serving first as mediator and then as arbitrator, is used to resolve contract negotiation disputes between public employers and their unionised employees. Perhaps the most publicised of the hybrids has been the mini-trial, in which the lawyers for each party are given a brief period (typically no more than a day) in which to present the essence of their case to senior executives of both parties. After the presentation, the executives try to negotiate a settlement of the case, sometimes assisted by a neutral advisor who has heard the presentations. If settlement does not come about, the advisor provides the parties with his opinion of the likely outcome if the dispute were litigated, and sometimes that dose of reality helps to break the deadlock. The mini-trial has been utilised in a number of major inter-corporate disputes in recent years, and appears to have led to settlements in nearly all.

Perhaps the most valuable by-product of the recent resurgence of interest in dispute resolution has been the renewed interest in negotiation that it has stimulated. Obviously, negotiation as a means of dispute resolution long antedates the alternatives movement, and would stand as the pre-eminent mode of dispute resolution even without such a movement. Nonetheless, the interest in resolving disputes outside the courts has focused attention on negotiation as a basic means of dispute resolution. This is apparent in the number of 'how-to-negotiate' books that have been published in recent years, the spate of negotiation workshops and seminars, the appearance of scholarly works on negotiation, and the introduction of negotiation into the curriculum of law schools and business schools. Although it is too soon to tell, these developments may improve the practice of negotiation sufficiently that more and more disputes will be resolved by negotiation, with less and less need for third-party involvement.

Concluding Cautions

It would be inappropriate to conclude this brief survey of recent dispute resolution developments in the United States without at least summary reference to some of the critical questions that are now beginning to emerge. Detailed consideration of any of these issues would necessitate a callous disregard of the limited scope of this overview paper, and is in any event premature. But it does seem appropriate at least to take note of these questions by way of lending focus and direction to future research and inquiry relating to alternative modes of dispute resolution.

If the alternatives to adjudication have all the advantages claimed for them why are they not more widely used? Are there aspects of the legal system that deter the use of alternatives? Or does the lack of demand for alternatives reflect the fact that the alternatives movement is primarily a product of the self-interest of the alternatives providers, rather than an expression of the needs of alternatives consumers?

Is there an adequate empirical basis for the claimed advantages of the alternatives? How, for example, can one adequately measure the asserted advantages of mediation over adjudications? Is it possible to develop a sophisticated cost-benefit analysis of alternative processes?

Is there a risk that the availability of alternatives will shunt low and middle-income disputants to a form of second-class justice, consisting primarily of semicoerced compromise settlements, while the so-called first-class justice offered by the courts becomes available only to the rich and powerful? In thinking about this question, the reader should be aware that the neighborhood justice center clientele consists primarily of low-income disputants referred by courts and prosecutors as an alternative to criminal proceedings.

Is there a danger that mediation, with its emphasis on accommodation and compromise, will deter large-scale structural changes in political and societal institutions that only court adjudication can accomplish, and that it will thus serve the interests of the powerful against the disadvantaged?

To the extent that new modes of dispute resolution call for new practitioners, with skills different from those who practice in the judicial system, what steps should be taken to ensure that these practitioners have the requisite skills? Should there be regulation of the practice of dispute resolution similar to that of the practice of law? Can the alternatives movement survive success? If alternative dispute resolution processes become widely used, will they suffer from the woes common to other heavily-used institutions — increasing costs and delay, bureaucratisation and perfunctory performance?

In light of the prominent place of the courts in American society, and the free dispute resolution services provided by the courts, how can other forms of dispute resolution, even if more appropriate for a particular dispute, succeed in attracting users and adequate funding? Does the answer lie in integrating alternative dispute resolution processes into the public justice system? One model for public institutionalisation of alternative dispute resolution is the Multi-door Courthouse. This concept calls for a multi-faceted intake center where disputes are analysed according to their salient characteristics and referred to that process, or sequence of processes, most appropriate for their resolution. This proposal is now being tested under ABA auspices. The results of that experiment should help to tell us whether this idea is indeed a promising herald for more effective dispute resolution.

REFERENCES

* This article was originally published as F. Sander, 'Alternative Dispute Resolution in the United States: An Overview', *Arbitration* 52, no. 2 (1986): 123-127.

1. J. Auerbach, *Justice Without Law?* (Oxford: Oxford University Press, 1983).
2. J. Lieberman (ed.), *The Role of Courts in American Society: The Final Report of the Council on the Role of Courts* (St. Paul: West, 1984).
3. R. Danzig, 'Toward the Creation of a Complementary Decentralized System of Criminal Justice', *Stanford Law Review* 26 (1973): 1.
4. L. Fuller, 'Collective Bargaining and the Arbitrator', *Wisconsin Law Review* (1963): 3.
5. L. Fuller, 'Mediation: Its Forms and Functions', *Southern California Law Review* 44 (1971): 305.
6. L. Fuller, 'The Forms and Limits of Adjudication', *Harvard Law Review* 92 (1978): 353
7. J. Marks, E. Johnson, & P. Szanton, *Dispute Resolution in America: Processes in Evolution* (National Institute for Dispute Resolution, 1984).
8. US Department of Justice, *Paths to Justice: Major Public Policy Issues of Dispute Resolution* (National Institute of Dispute Resolution, 1984).

CHAPTER 1

Alternative Dispute Resolution: Contemporary Developments in Britain

John Griffiths and Simon Roberts

The general label 'alternative dispute resolution' embraces potentially an almost endless variety of forms. In this paper discussion is limited to two kinds of departure from state-sponsored adjudication. In the first, an essential characteristic of formal adjudication remains, in that the dispute is still taken to a third party for decision — but in a procedural environment chosen by the parties themselves. Here commercial arbitration is the example we consider. In the second, the power to make a decision is retained, so the efforts of third parties remain auxiliary to those of the disputants. Community and family conciliation provide the cases examined. In preparing this paper we have been conscious that, while there may be particular enthusiasm for alternative forms of dispute resolution at present, the advocacy and growth of such alternatives has a history as long as state-sponsored adjudication itself. Some procedures (commercial arbitration is an example) are well established and have long taken on a definite shape; others, such as family conciliation, represent only embryonic forms. We also recognise that the interest now shown here in alternatives to formal adjudication comes somewhat behind similar movements in the United States; so we are in the fortunate position to profit from recent transatlantic experience.

COMMERCIAL ARBITRATION

The main theme of this part of the paper is the extent to which the wishes of disputants as to the resolution of justiciable disputes (in particular, commercial disputes) are, and can be, accommodated by the law. In England, arbitration has long been an acknowledged and effective method of resolving disputes. No doubt this very fact may reflect a failure or deficiency in the system or practice of the courts adequately to provide for disputants either the remedies they desired or those means of achieving those remedies which the disputants felt was appropriate. On the other hand, the very toleration and recognition of arbitration as an alternative to litigation in the courts is itself evidence of the law's response to the desires of disputants.

Nevertheless, arbitration and the process of the courts are inextricably intertwined. This interdependence owes its existence partly to the jealous preservation by the courts of their jurisdiction. A rationale for this jealousy can easily be found in the possibility, and undesirability, of there arising an arbitral body of law separate and distinct from that of the courts, or, even, several such bodies, each peculiar to the trade or commodity in question. Such a development could also invite the arbitrators themselves, fortified by their known expertise and experience in the relevant trade or commodity, to rely upon their intuitive response to the merits of the case before them. Inevitably consequent on such practices would be uncertainty and injustice: the fallibility, even of arbitrators, requires adherence to a body of authority universally accepted within a system of law. Reliance on the unfettered instinct of an arbitrator would be unwise.

The dependence of arbitrations on court process has another reason. That is, the preference of the disputants themselves for the buttressing of their own agreement for arbitration by a developed and coherent legal system. To this extent, the interrelation, and means of resolution, themselves evidence flexibility in the law in responding to the wishes of disputants. Indeed, it is presumably partly because the disputants themselves wish it, that the courts have powers of enforcement of an arbitration, and have the right and duty to ensure that the arbitration is conducted in accordance with the requirements of natural justice. Similarly, while an arbitrator may, and often will, have considerable latitude as to procedure, he must apply the relevant legal principles as if he were a judge.

Historically, there have been statutory provisions and regulations relating to arbitrations from as long ago as 1698; however, the response to disputants' needs by the law has been imperfect. One major area of deficiency, prior to the passing of the 1979 Arbitration Act, was the extent to which the pre-1979 system, or the way in which it was operated, failed adequately to cater to disputants' needs. Prior to 1979, the losing party had a virtually absolute right of appeal in all cases where a question of law had arisen. There was always the possibility, therefore, of the prolongation of a dispute, far beyond its reasonable timespan, by the exercise of that right. The extent to which abuse of the right actually caused frequent and considerable delay is not clear. Nevertheless, the existence of the possibility must have been a deterrent to resort to English arbitration. Moreover, there were a number of developments which rendered the existing system unsuitable. In the 1970s, commercial disputes of a magnitude hitherto unknown, which were not well suited to resolution in the courts, were arising. Yet they involved issues of fact and law which were so complex and interrelated that their separation (by application to the courts for resolution of the legal questions) was both impracticable and undesirable. The arbitrations consequent on the embargo of the export of American soya bean meal were examples. Another important aspect was the fact that foreign organisations, while wishing to resolve disputes by arbitration according to English law in England, were reluctant to have the issues of the dispute so readily exposed to the scrutiny of English courts. This reluctance was perhaps particularly marked and understandable, in the trading agencies of sovereign states.

A third major concomitant deficiency was the increase in cost and delay (these being, of course, directly correlated in any event) resulting from the system and its operation. After all, among the major advantages of arbitration over litigation in the courts are speed — in that the disputants do not have to await a space in the court's lists — and cost — in that arbitrations may dispense with formalities. Even the advantages of London as a place for arbitration, being without par in its combined expertise in finance, banking, insurance, commodity markets — and, indeed, arbitration — were insufficient compensation, increasingly, for these difficulties.

The implications and operation of the 1979 Act have yet to be worked through fully, but the Act has done much to ameliorate the position. The much-reduced prospects of appeal — indeed, the difficulty of even obtaining leave to appeal — have reduced the uncertainty as to the finality of the arbitrator's award and thereby also removed many of the difficulties set out above. While there is still no obligation to provide a reasoned award (which was a further objection of some to English arbitration, for in some places an award without reasons cannot be enforced), the practice of providing one is more prevalent. At the same time, it is quite plain that arbitration really is intended to be more free of formalities: Lord Justice Donaldson (as he then was) stressed the absence of any technical requirements in the writing of an award (*Bremer Handelsgesellschaft v Westzucker* [1981] 2 L1.R. 130 and 132).

Nevertheless, these reforms are necessarily somewhat piecemeal and are not made on the basis of one coherent view of the interrelation between resolution by the courts and resolution by arbitration. For example, in that an agreement to go to arbitration rather than to litigate in the courts is consensual, the parties to it might be thought entitled to exclude the jurisdiction of the courts altogether. Yet they cannot.

However, the reason for this is that different disputants have different needs and desires as to how arbitration is to work out their disputes and to what extent they wish to retain resort to the courts. Inevitably, a statute cannot simultaneously reflect the inconsistent — often contradictory — wishes of disputants. That there has been change shows flexibility to the pressures of disputants' needs.

There are many other ways in which the law relating to arbitration could, nevertheless, provide more adequately for disputants. For example, cases could be heard in camera, and there could be edited judgments, in response to the desire of some disputants for privacy (over and above that to have justice to be seen to be done). There could be power to proceed with an arbitration in default of the appearance of the other party, or any other default, including the power to strike out wherever there has been delay and the interests of justice so require. There could be an option to exclude the right to judicial review. A court could have power to appoint an arbitrator where the arbitration agreement provides for a stranger to make an appointment, but he has failed to do so. On a reference to three arbitrators, the award of any two could be binding. There could be a right of consolidation where there is a string of interrelated arbitrations, provision for payment-in, and a rules committee like the Supreme Court Rules Committee. Arbitrators could allow the costs of foreign lawyers.

That these are possible is shown by their incorporation in the Arbitration Ordinance of Hong Kong. A further possibility reflecting the desires of many disputants, and included in the Hong Kong legislation, is provision for conciliation, the arbitration only to proceed on its failure, while protecting the disputants against any possible difficulties or embarrassment consequent on the failure of the conciliation. This must be a development which many disputants would welcome.

Indeed it is central to the resolution of labour disputes. The degree to which elaborate machinery for conciliation is required, whether the identity of the conciliator should be stipulated, and whether the conciliation agreement should be enforceable, are matters as to which, again, there will be wide divergence of disputants' views. The relative equality or otherwise of the disputants may be a guiding factor. Nevertheless, there are many other ways in which the law plainly does not provide for disputants' needs. The second major area is that it simply leaves out of account disputants who do not want, or cannot afford, arbitration on the scale and at the cost at which it is available. There is no option as to the scale of arbitration process available. There may indeed be an objection, that a two-tiered system might lead to a second class of justice being dispensed, for those choosing the second tier. But this is to adopt an absolute and rigid notion of justice, which is not one in any event necessarily dispensed at present. Lengthy and exhaustive enquiry may be obfuscatory. A crude light, albeit briefly shone, may be more illuminating.

The satisfactory resolution of disputes, subject only to the requirements of natural justice, must be dependent on the taking into account of those variables, the needs and resources of the disputants. It must be conceded that the law cannot comprehensively provide for infinite variety. However, plainly, it falls short of the potential it possesses for adequate account of such permutations.

EMBRYONIC FORMS

While the growth of commercial arbitration can credibly be presented as a simple struggle of disputants to disengage from the perceived constraints of formal adjudication, the characterisation of contemporary developments in the areas of community and family mediation is more complex. A notable feature of the position in Britain is the wide variety of sources from which the demand for institutional reform comes: from government, as a means of reducing the load of court business and as a way of handling 'tension' within particular communities; from utopian reformers anxious to bring dispute resolution procedures back to 'the people'; from professional groups, such as lawyers or family therapists, looking for business; and from grass-roots sources, disputants dissatisfied with what they are getting from existing agencies. We have to remember the possibly contradictory interest which these diverse viewpoints represent.

New forms of alternative dispute resolution have recently been advocated, and have now begun to appear, in two principal fields: general community conciliation and family conciliation. Agencies in the former category (there is one, for example, in the London Borough of Newham) claim to provide 'help' for a wide range of disputes. The precise nature of this intervention is not always clearly articulated in the prospectus, but in general it appears that assistance is of a mediatory character, a matter of promoting a negotiated solution rather than offering a third-party decision. Prospective business may cover such matters as minor crime, disputes between neighbours, disputes between suppliers of goods or services and their customers, disputes between members of different ethnic groups, and disputes between police and public. None of these agencies in Britain has been in operation long enough for a general assessment, but experience of similar projects in the United States suggests some pitfalls which might be avoided. American commentators seem to have agreed that such agencies are seldom 'successful' in the sense of satisfying their customers where there are large disparities of power between the two disputants. Such disparities arguably separate large commercial concerns and individual litigants, e.g., police and members of the public, employers and employees. In short, alternative agencies are most appropriate in a relatively egalitarian context. There also seems to be a consensus that the disputants themselves have got to want the new agency, and that the procedures introduced must 'make sense' to members of the community concerned. Such conditions are less likely to be met where the 'demand' comes from above, rather than from within the group(s) involved. There is a real danger that institutions imposed by government can come to represent an auxiliary tier of 'second class' justice into which certain categories of troublesome business will be filtered.

Agencies of community conciliation in Britain have been established too short a time for it to be clear whether these dangers have been avoided. However, institutions of 'family conciliation' are both more numerous and have been in operation for longer periods, some since 1979, so the shape of their development is more distinct. The broad objective of these agencies appears to be agreed. This is to assist with joint decision making by the parties themselves. They aim to help with the construction of an agreed solution, rather than by offering a decision from a third-party standpoint. These are not, therefore, processes of arbitration. However, the procedural forms encountered under this form of intervention are extremely varied, and there appears no clear consensus on a range of crucial questions.

First, while the kind of help extended to the parties clearly falls under the generic head of mediation, practices range from unobtrusive aids to communication to heavily directive forms of intervention. Mostly family mediators seem to conceive of their role as extending beyond that of the go-between (passing messages backwards and forwards between the parties) and the convener (setting up a forum in which the parties can meet). But beyond that little is clear. Some mediators appear to limit themselves to identifying options; some go further and offer an evaluation of available choices as they see them; others make active efforts to persuade the parties to accept a preferred solution, even putting pressure upon them to do so. Differences of view also exist as to whether it is appropriate for the mediator to intervene in protection of a weaker party or to safeguard the interests of children. All of these doubts really resolve themselves around the question of the extent to which power is to remain with the disputants themselves, or pass to a third party. Some argue that the essence of family conciliation is that, for better or worse, this form of dispute resolution should aim to yield a solution which the parties themselves have reached.

A second imponderable surrounds the relationship of family conciliation to the work of existing professional groups, notably lawyers, social workers, and therapists. Are family mediators to emerge as an autonomous group of specialists, or will they remain within existing professions? English lawyers have, on the whole, been much more reluctant to hold themselves out as mediators than their American counterparts, preferring to confine themselves to the roles of partisan (albeit one with a responsibility to the legal system itself), or adjudicator. However, the recent development of 'incourt' and 'court-related' schemes under which judges and registrars participate in, or at least supervise, mediation (often as a first step in disputes brought to court for adjudication) reveals one way in which lawyers are already becoming implicated in this form of alternative dispute resolution. There are obvious hazards in such arrangements, in that adjudicatory roles will tend to get muddled in the minds of disputants in a manner that may damage both types of process. Is it in anyone's interest that judges should come to be seen, even in a limited way, as promoters and managers of negotiation? Given the authority that judges rightly enjoy in this society, it can be argued that they are the wrong kind of people to offer unobtrusive help with joint decision making.

Were barristers and solicitors to overcome their present doubts as to the desirability of acting in mediatory, as opposed to partisan, roles, there remains the drawback that they also enjoy an authority which must diminish the freedom of many disputants to negotiate before them. Even if lawyers do not mediate, problems still surround their role in processes of family conciliation. Clearly, many who take their disputes before a mediator will want and need the advice and support of lawyers as skilled partisans. But should lawyers be 'there', directly supporting their clients when efforts at mediation are made, or should they confine themselves to giving advice in advance and then wait on the sidelines to help evaluate any potential agreement? If lawyers are directly involved in mediatory processes, many disputants will seek to use them as champions. Where they do so, the distinctive quality of joint decision making, as putting power back into the hands of disputants themselves, will be lost. Equally controversial is the proper relationship of family mediation to 'social work', 'counselling', and 'therapy.' It is notable that family therapists in Britain are already holding themselves out as possessing the skills necessary to train 'conciliators', as well as to act as conciliators themselves (see, for example, the current prospectus of the Institute of Family Therapy (London) Ltd). Here again, it seems desirable that proper boundaries be maintained between these different, if complementary, disciplines. Mediation and therapy are not the same, and should be performed on separate occasions by different people.

A tendentious argument is being advanced here. It is that family mediation should develop as a form of dispute resolution distinct from legal processes, and that only harm can come to both modes of resolution by relating them too closely to each other. Family mediation must also be distinguished from those forms of intervention associated with counselling and therapy. Mediators should be low-key figures, closer in image to the neighbour than the dominant professional. It follows, too, that while many disputants may choose to have their quarrels adjudicated upon; those who do not should be encouraged through the institution of mediation to retain as much of the responsibility for decision making as is possible. Finally, we argue that family mediation will only work where the parties wish to experience it, and where a relative equality of bargaining power is present. 'Power', of course, is found in many forms, and economic muscle on one side may be off-set by different forms of strength (e.g., physical control of the children) on the other. It follows from this last point that mediation should be addressed to the whole complex of matters demanding decision on family breakdown, rather than one isolated element (such as custody or access) alone.

* This article was originally published as Jonathan Griffiths & Simon Roberts, 'Alternative Dispute Resolution: Contemporary Developments in Britain', *Arbitration* 52, no. 2 (1986): 119-123.

CHAPTER 1

Alternative Dispute Resolution in Practice

Karl J. Mackie

Few people in the dispute-resolution world can be unaware of the explosion of 'Alternative Dispute Resolution' (ADR) as a new fashion in settling disputes. This 'new wave' has been most apparent in the US where litigation is a prominent means of business and social dispute-settlement, but interest in the practice of ADR has been growing in other countries.

The Workshop held at Nottingham was probably the first in the UK to explore the concept in depth across a range of areas of dispute — commercial, community, family, industrial relations. The aims of the Workshop were: (i) to establish what is going on in the UK; (ii) to help 'bridge the gaps' which exist between different sectors and institutions in dispute resolution, and between interested practitioners and academics; (iii) to consider international developments; (iv) to explore the education and training needs of practitioners, and (v) to identify some research directions in this emerging field. This report is a personal response to the experience of organising and participating in the proceedings. I believe the key issues raised in the Workshop can be described in terms of posing three questions about ADR, namely (1) Why ADR?, (2) Which techniques?, and (3) Whither ADR?

WHY ADR?

The key word here is 'alternative'. This implies a sort of minority, even nonconformist, approach. Clearly exponents of the concept had in mind alternatives to litigation. Yet this is a curious reversal of reality. Most disputes in society are settled by alternatives to litigation and always have been. However, the success of the concept is an indication that all is not well in the world of litigation — disputes involving litigation are becoming more frequent, more complex and potentially more damaging in terms of their costs and their impact on the parties and the community. Business in particular is threatened by a movement to 'mega-law' actions in inter-business disputes where processes of discovery and conflict expend major amounts of executive time and energy that can be more usefully directed to the business. When linked to the traditional formality of law, lawyers and courts, the outcome is delay, frustration and settlements which are often dissatisfying to both parties.

The ADR movement has therefore been propelled by a number of mixed motives, sometimes leading to confusion of interests and goals, and hence uncertainty about the appropriateness and value of techniques. The motives can be summarised as: (a) finding more efficient ways of resolving disputes, (b) finding processes where parties have more control of the process and outcome, (c) finding ways of relieving court congestion, (d) finding more 'just' ways of resolving disputes than the traditional adversarial system, (e) finding ways of involving the community to a greater extent in conflict settlement. It was apparent at the Workshop that there were different emphases in different sectors of dispute, arising from particular histories and traditions (procedures in industrial relations disputes, for example, compared with those in commercial disputes). However, there were also perceived common elements, for example, of sensitivity to the subtlety of the process and attention to the parties' underlying needs. Research reported by Professors Tom Tyler and Alan Lind of the US also clearly emerged in support of the fact that parties to disputes do tend to separate their judgments of the fairness of the process of a conflict-settlement procedure from those of the outcomes (win-lose) of that procedure. The stress in ADR on the importance of finding procedures appropriate to the dispute and the parties, was in that sense justifiable. This raises the issue of the techniques which are available and being used in ADR.

ADR — WHICH TECHNIQUES?

ADR as a concept has become closely associated with one of the newest techniques in the area — the mini-trial. This is a procedure 'structured to reconvert a legal dispute back into a business dispute.' It involves an agreement between companies in dispute for senior executives from each company to sit together to hear a relatively brief presentation of each organisation's case, following which they attempt to negotiate an agreement. There would also normally be present throughout a neutral 'expert' who can assist the parties to settle and who may if necessary give a legal or technical view of the merits of the case or likely litigation outcome. David Sutton of Allen and Overy spoke at the Workshop of the pros and cons of the procedure and of the attempt in one case in the UK to use the process. Elisabeth Wentworth of Baker and Mackenzie elaborated on the use of the process and other techniques in the area of technology disputes where the complexity of the emerging technology is in itself requiring the judiciary to reconsider their use of experts.

There are however many techniques available as alternatives to litigation, and many situations where the mini-trial (or litigation) would be an inappropriate process. Dr Tony Gibson gave a sparkling demonstration of his methods in the field of community planning, whereby the issue that might be in dispute can be resolved with a minimum of conflict by non-verbal means — by the use of simple models of the location and impersonal methods of expressing choices amongst the options available. One of the particular strengths of this process was the way it restored some power to the inarticulate who are normally edged out by the 'professionals' who take over planning issues. Similarly, sensitivity to the needs of the parties and the delicacy of relationships between them, and with third parties, was a key factor in both the family and industrial relations sectors, and not unknown in the commercial disputes field too! (Contributions here from the National Family Conciliation Council, the Newcastle Conciliation Project, ACAS and the Central Arbitration Committee, the British Columbia International Commercial Arbitration Centre, the Chartered Institute of Arbitrators and the *Zentrum fur Europaische Rechstpolitik* in West Germany.) Finally Rowland Williams spoke of the concept of concilio-arbitration which he has developed (a process of providing an expert opinion, with cost-penalties to improve its outcome in later litigation).

The Workshop confirmed the richness of the efforts that are taking place across many sectors to find appropriate models for handling conflict. (Not only the sectors mentioned above, but also in consumer disputes, financial services, and local authorities.) The crucial variable was not a fixation on any one system, but a recognition of the diversity of options available — prevention, conciliation, mediation, arbitration, med-arb, fact-finding, expert opinions, ombudsmen, court-annexed systems. At the same time, the core issues of gaining respect and influencing others were common to most systems. Tom Colosi, Vice-President of the American Arbitration Association, reminded us forcefully that perhaps the key skills underlying most dispute resolution by third parties were substantially based on skills found amongst effective negotiators.

WHITHER ADR?

If one can identify a weakness of ADR, it perhaps lies in the comments I have just made, but 'translated' into a sceptic's viewpoint. If the process is so rich and so variable in its aptness for disputes, couldn't a sceptic now turn round and re-describe this field not as an exciting portent of the future but as merely an unhelpful mish-mash of vague schemes and half-baked optimism with little substantial merit or applicability, and little likelihood of permanence? Couldn't the sceptic shake his head at the volcanic eruption of dispute-resolution centres in the United States — commercial, charitable, academic, legal — and dismiss this as merely a typical example of the crazy swings of fashion in a somewhat crazy culture (one which, after all, manages to combine a statistic of more psychotherapists and more lawyers per head of the population than any other country!)? Hot AIR rather than hot ADR, so to speak?

I have detected elements of this viewpoint amongst many businessmen, lawyers and arbitrators to whom I have spoken. And, of course, any dispute-resolution professional worth his salt will appreciate that there are always two sides (at least) to a story. The real weakness of the ADR movement has perhaps been its stress on the adjective 'alternative.' Take that away, however, and examine the evidence and one thing is clear. We are witnessing an era where dispute resolution per se, defined as systems of third-party intervention of all kinds, traditional and new, has been finding significant new sources of inspiration and energy. Wherever one looks one finds evidence of developing debates and action: the worldwide re-discovery of arbitration as a genuine alternative to litigation (rather than an imitation of, or a prelude to, litigation); the growth of the conciliation movement in family law work; the spread of new models of dispute/settlement in industrial relations along the lines of 'final-offer' arbitration and med-arb; the growth of offender reparation and mediation schemes in criminal justice; the expansion of arbitration and ombudsmen in the consumer disputes field; the proposals for ombudsmen in the media; the suggestions in the Lord Chancellor's Civil Justice Review of a major extension of the small claims arbitration system. Perhaps the strongest reminder at the Workshop that dispute resolution admits of many models was Michael Palmer's description of the country with the world's largest concentration of mediators — the Chinese system of community mediation committees handling over 80% of all civil disputes in China.

The upsurge of ADR has been compared to the development of Equity in the history of English law — a new system with more justice and flexibility emerged to compensate for an earlier system of dispute resolution that had become fettered by tradition and institutionalisation. However, the analogy breaks down in terms of the fact that current developments do not admit of one easy label. What we are witnessing is the increasing sophistication of dispute settlement procedures appropriate to a much more complex society. A consumer analogy is more appropriate than the historical legal one — the corner shop (court or Dispute Resolution Store) with its limited stock of products is being overtaken by the Dispute Resolution Supermarket with an array of prices and labels!

However, there are also cautions against this optimism. The widespread knowledge of ADR, alongside limited use, testifies to a degree of consumer confusion. It is not yet clear which systems give best value for money (nor how best to define value), and there is a degree of caution amongst consumers as to whether to try new products as against the tested-and-tried systems of arbitration and litigation. The traditionalism of lawyers and legal training also contributes to the slowness of change. This is nowhere clearer than in the world of inter-business disputes, where schemes of outside mediation, mini-trials, et cetera, are only slowly making headway.

If we do believe, therefore, that there is still considerable scope to develop more effective dispute resolution systems, how to achieve this? The future development of ADR, I suggest, lies in the following developments taking place: (i) an educational campaign to make users and practitioners more widely aware of the flexibility that can be brought into dispute-settlement techniques (this should not detract, however, from attempts to see that those who are currently deprived of real opportunities for access to the courts, can obtain such access); (ii) a call for users and institutions to be ready to experiment, to demonstrate a degree of courage in their activities and advice in this area, and in their readiness to learn from others' experiences; (iii) I believe developments will also depend on a degree of institutional support for initiatives in research and practice — in business and consumer disputes from the Lord Chancellor's Department, from employers' associations, in-house and outside lawyers, the Chartered Institute of Arbitrators, the Office of Fair Trading — and the many similar bodies in the various fields of dispute resolution; (iv) there is an important role for research in refining our knowledge of the various procedures, their effectiveness, efficiency and appropriateness in different contexts. (For example, when should an arbitration system be used in preference to an ombudsman system in consumer disputes?) (v) there needs to be progress towards more effective definition of the skills and training needs of those involved in third-party intervention and of those involved in tutoring such programmes. This is as true for the legal profession (where the emphasis in training tends to downplay knowledge even of arbitration as an alternative to litigation) as it is for others involved in disputes.

* This article was originally published as K. Mackie, 'Alternative Dispute Resolution in Practice', *Arbitration* 54, no. 4 (1988): 239-241.

CHAPTER 1

The Future of Private Dispute Resolution in the United States

Robert Coulson

Alternative forms of dispute resolution have become popular in the United States as a counter current against the floodtide of litigation which dominates the American economy. The United States suffers from an apprehension of legal claims, of the costs and delays that result from litigation in American courts. In recent years, thousand of eager young lawyers have been admitted to the practice. By the year 2000, the attorneys may exceed one million. With so many potential litigators, the future growth of civil court action is secure. The quandary for Americans is how to avoid being diverted and impoverished by litigation.

In recent years, American courts have devised new ways to encourage settlements, but little has been done to simplify the actual trial of cases. Court-annexed arbitration, settlement conferences and mock jury trials are some of the expedients used by courts to encourage settlements. But the outpouring of litigation continues, engaging attorneys in the time-consuming procedures required by court rules. Even though judges complain about their crushing caseloads, it would be a mistake to conclude that American judges will clear their calendars using such procedures. In any case, many are content to allow lawyers to set the pace, to drift down the languid byways of traditional court practice. Most lawsuits slumber in their assigned docket until they are settled. In fact, an overwhelming percentage of civil cases in American courts are resolved only by a negotiated settlement, often just prior to trial.

Private arbitration plays a major role in dispute resolution. Many thousands of arbitrations occur each year, mostly resulting from arbitration clauses in contracts; construction contracts, insurance policies, consumer warranties and other business documents. In 1987, 54,000 cases were filed with the American Arbitration Association.

Arbitration takes place when parties agree that their disputes will be channeled away from the courts. In the United States, the enforcement of arbitration clauses in commercial agreements is based upon the Federal Arbitration Act which confirms the right to settle disagreements by arbitration.

American courts encourage arbitration, liberally interpreting the law, emphasising the national policy in favour of private arbitration. Recently, there has also been an increase in the number of cases taken off the court calendar and submitted to arbitration by the parties because they are no longer willing to wait their turn.

Another private mechanism used in the United States is mediation, under which parties strengthen their negotiations by involving a professional neutral. Many American lawyers and some non-lawyers are offering such a service. Last year, the AAA arranged for thousands of mediations, particularly in resolving insurance claims. At present, mediation is unregulated. If mediators exercise restraint, providing an impartial service and allowing the parties to negotiate without compulsion, this situation may continue. If mediators begin to pressure parties into predetermined patterns of settlement, regulation may be required.

American judges have not yet reached a consensus as to their proper role in mediation. Should they actively participate? They are sometimes encouraged to do. But some judges are skeptical, thinking it more appropriate, perhaps safer, to allow litigation to take its normal course. American trial judges usually defer to the attorneys, offering help when help is requested, but not injecting themselves into the negotiations unless invited to do so.

Judges have more to do than preside over settlement conferences. They operate with broad discretion. If some judges mediate frequently, others will not. In any case, mediation has become familiar to American judges. Some mediate. Others encourage parties to use professional mediators. In general, American courts favour mediation because it settles cases.

Court-administered arbitration raises other questions. This is a mandatory but non-binding procedure. In recent years, many jurisdictions have adopted the system by court rule or by legislation. Parties are obliged to submit their case to an arbitration panel of lawyers before obtaining the right to a trial. The arbitrators evaluate the claim. If the evaluation is accepted by the parties, the matter is settled. If not, the case can be submitted to a trial *de novo*.

When properly designed and administered, court-administered arbitration resolves many pending cases. The system has become popular with some courts because it relieves the pressure on swollen calendars. Court arbitration has been hailed as a change for the better in court procedures, a cost-effective screening device. On the other hand, it can equally well be viewed as an admission that some American courts are no longer able to provide a prompt trial on the issues.

In view of the crushing burden upon American courts, particularly in the large urban areas where criminal cases claim first priority, it might be difficult to design a more effective system for handling large numbers of relatively minor civil disputes. Surveys carried out by the Institute for Civil Justice indicate that such programmes are popular with the parties who use them. Inexact though the arbitrators' evaluations may be, these tribunals provide an early opportunity for parties to present their evidence. The hearing brings adversaries together at a time when meaningful settlement discussions can take place, facilitating resolution by breaking the inertia that exists when lawyers limit their activity to exchanging documents.

A somewhat similar private system has been devised for encouraging the settlement of major economic issues. This is called the mini-trial. The parties involved, two major business corporations, for example, agree that their trial lawyers will make legal presentations on behalf of their clients at a structured, but informal hearing. Presiding will be senior executives from each corporation. Sometimes a neutral chairman may preside. The mini-trial gives the executives an opportunity to better understand the legal issues, and then to enter into meaningful, confidential negotiations. Frequently, a climate is created which encourages settlement.

Business executives in the United States sometimes rail against lawyers and litigation. But relatively few are prepared to take control of litigation away from their lawyers. Much of the drive for innovative dispute resolution techniques has come from house counsel. Senior managers may lecture their legal advisors about the high cost of litigation, but they seldom demand that a mini-trial or mediation be superimposed over the court process. Nor is this likely to change. Dispute resolution will continue to be relegated to the professionals.

But at least, in recent years, the notion of experimenting with alternative techniques has been validated. Many major US corporations have pledged to attempt to resolve their disputes privately.

American executives frequently encourage attorneys to try to settle cases, utilising professional mediators and mini-trials, attempting to increase early settlements. Arbitration is widely used in contracts and in industry-wide schemes to channel certain kinds of disputes out of court, exactly as is done in the United Kingdom.

Practitioners in private dispute resolution offer their services, designing and installing ADR mechanisms. Many are lawyers, serving as neutral experts rather than advocates. Some are retired judges. Law firms are gaining experience in this growing field and now offer private dispute resolution as a legal service.

Despite the growth in such services, litigation will continue to prosper in the United States, driven by cultural and economic forces. Teachers continue to instruct children that legal disputes should be decided in court and that people need a lawyer to deal with legal disagreements. American law schools continue to produce many thousands of lawyers, trained towards practice in the courts. Litigation will continue to be glamorised by the American media as a well publicised game of chance. Billion dollar verdicts exert their customary feeding frenzy. The mindset that for every injury there is a consequent liability seems well entrenched.

Private dispute resolution will play an important but supplementary role. The main engine, the old fashioned American court system, underfinanced, managed by judges, hobbled by the complexities of Federalism, criticised on all sides, will continue to be the centrepiece of the judicial system. Patched up on one side by administrative agencies, held together by plea bargaining of criminal matters, private settlements of civil claims, by court-annexed arbitration and other band-aid solutions, the courts will be called upon to provide their traditional public service.

Court reform is a long, dusty road, one that never ends. The business world won't wait. Private dispute resolution will provide alternative procedures. Some will be consensual, such as mediation, mini-trials and court-based evaluations. Others will be definitive, such as binding arbitration. Some alternatives will be created and installed by judges to cope with court congestion. Those created by the private sector will be energised by the market place. Together, public and private alternative dispute settlement will supplement the judicial system. But ADR will not replace traditional litigation. Efforts to improve the courts should never be abandoned.

REFERENCES

* This article was originally published as R. Coulson, 'The Future of Private Dispute Resolution in the United States', *Arbitration* 54, no. 3 (1988): 154-155, 172.

1 J. Resnik, 'Failing Faith: Adjudicatory Procedure in Decline', *University*

of Chicago Law Review 53 (1986): 494-560; O. Fiss, 'Against Settlement', *Yale Law Journal* 93 (1984): 1073.

2   United States Arbitration Act of 1925, 9 USC (1982); *Moses H. Cone Memorial Hospital v Mercury Construction Corp*, 460 US 19 (1983); L. Hirschman, 'The Second Arbitration Trilogy: The Federalization of Arbitration Law', *Virginia Law Review* 71 (1985): 1305.

3   R. Coulson, *Business Mediation: What You Need to Know* (New York: American Arbitration Association, 1987).

4   R. Peckham, 'The Federal Judge as a Case Manager: The New Role in Guiding a Case from Filing to Disposition', *California Law Review* 69 (1981): 770.

5   P. Ebener & D. Betancourt, 'Court-Annexed Arbitration: The National Picture', N-2257-ICJ.

6   Mini Trial Rules, AAA, 1986.

7   T. Lambros, 'The Summary Jury Trial and Other Alternative Methods of Dispute Resolution', FRD 103 (1984): 46.

8   A. Sarat, 'The Litigation Explosion, Access to Justice, and Court Reform: Examining the Critical Assumptions', *Rutgers Law Review* 37 (1985): 331.

CHAPTER 1

Alternative Forms of Dispute Resolution: Strengths and Weaknesses

Philip Naughton

Ten years ago ADR was almost unheard of in the US. I do not mean by this that lawyers and others had not found ways of resolving disputes outside court but there was no published precedent, no body or organisation to turn to, no recognised procedure. There were no fax machines either. Now we have not only found a way of letting everyone have twice as much paper in a form only half as legible, we have also a multitude of alternatives to regular litigation, a library of textbooks about how to use them and, at least in North America, an army of consultants, advisers and practitioners to help to put them into practice. How exportable are these new techniques? Do we need them? What can we learn from the American experience? Although the legal system in the US (with a federal system and a written constitution) differs in obvious respects from the English legal system, its origins are to be found in our legal history — and some of its disadvantages. But, whether or not our system provides satisfactory facilities for dispute resolution, the legal system in the US was perceived by many to be deeply unsatisfactory. In the US, the Corporate General Counsel is a powerful executive in most large corporations. For him, litigation is an expensive way of resolving commercial disputes which benefits only his brothers in private practice. General Counsel and Insurance companies have been the force behind many of the developments in ADR and remain the most numerous supporters of the Center for Public Resources in New York which was established to promote ADR and has achieved a great deal. More than 300 corporations, including many of the 'Fortune 500', have signed the 'CPR Corporate Statement' in which they agree that in the event of a dispute they will attempt to resolve it by negotiation or ADR before resorting to litigation. The consequent change of mood and the incorporation of similar statements in trading agreements has done much to foster the development and use of ADR. I note with interest the similar proposals by the Working Party of the Chartered Institute of Arbitrators to introduce into construction contracts an agreement which anticipates resolving disputes by ADR.

Over the last few years, the greatest growth in the use of ADR in the US may have been in the courts rather than through 'private' intervention. The courts have been forced to seek new methods of diminishing the dramatic congestion of court time in many jurisdictions. A number of factors have combined to create these difficulties. The American citizen has a traditional love of litigation. Delays are built into a civil dispute procedure which almost always involves a jury trial, a commensurately high appeal rate and, more recently, exceptional numbers of class and similar actions of which the most critical are actions involving exposure to asbestos. In San Francisco this spring, for example, I was told that of 35 courts available to hear civil actions, 19 were occupied with asbestos claims. But the courts have also come to recognise that the ADR settlement procedures were meeting a need not met by the court. It was realised that it was in the interest of both the court and the litigant to intervene early in the dispute to help the parties to recognise the strengths and weaknesses of their case and to be realistic about the true benefits of the ultimate outcome. I make this point now because I believe it is important to recognise that ADR only has a place outside the regular legal system of courts and arbitration rooms when these are failing to satisfy the needs of parties to disputes.

As a result, the courts have introduced voluntary and in some cases compulsory mediations or other settlement procedures at an interlocutory stage. Thus the parties may be required to attend a settlement conference with a judge or an independent mediator (often a local lawyer). Alternatively the court may put pressure on the parties to agree to non-binding mediation by a judge. Much depends on local policy. There can be spectacular successes although sometimes the intervention of the trial judge can be somewhat alarming. Unfortunately, the success of one of the earliest schemes in Michigan may have been undermined by a recent appeal decision that the court cannot use the sanction of an award of costs against a party who proceeds to trial and recovers less (or pays more) than a mediator advised was a proper settlement. I move on to examine the most widely used techniques.

MEDIATION

Mediation describes a process whereby each side to a dispute is brought together before a neutral mediator whose function is to assist the parties to come to a common position by joint open session and private caucus. In this process the mediator does not (or should not) at any stage express his own opinion — he or she is a catalyst. The same term is also used to describe 'non binding arbitration' (NBA) and the two techniques may be employed by the same person. But in NBA the neutral will give an opinion of the likely result if the issue were to proceed to trial or will at least tell the parties what he believes to be a proper settlement. I will discuss both techniques but I should introduce this section by recording the strenuous opinion expressed by the professional mediation companies that I have spoken to that the success of mediation is the result of the mediator not expressing an opinion. By remaining neutral, he can retain the confidence of all sides even when there is real ill feeling between them.

In the US there are at least four different types of organisation offering mediation services: (1) The non-profit making Center for Public Resources. It encourages corporations and lawyers to think of and use ADR, provides suitable people to mediate and to preside over mini-trials and administers those procedures. The panel from which their names are drawn is described by others as a 'Famous People Panel'. Its members are lawyers and retired judges distinguished by their position and status and have no training in mediation beyond their experience. The CPR is now in the process of creating local panels of 'slightly less famous people' in response to its growing success. The New York panel was published earlier this year; (2) The non-profit making American Arbitration Association (AAA). The AAA provides mediators from a nationwide panel of mediators and will arrange mini-trials. It will also undertake the administration of ADR procedures. Mediation under the auspices of the AAA is a pre-trial requirement of the courts in some states; (3) The 'rent-a-judge' organisations. These include Judicate Inc. which is a publicly quoted corporation and 'JAMS' (Judicial

Arbitration and Mediation Service). These companies provide retired judges to undertake non-binding arbitration or mediation. They are popular. The judge will normally be expected to give his opinion of the likely result of a trial. So it can be a 'dry run' for the parties; (4) The professional mediation companies. These companies offer the services of professional or semi-professional trained mediators who may be employed by the company. Not all these mediators are qualified lawyers but they will have a case load of up to 100 mediations and may actually mediate in 150 or more disputes in a year. So in time, they acquire enormous experience.

There are other organisations, including, I understand, mediation services offering to resolve quite serious legal disputes without the intervention or supervision of lawyers — including reaching divorce settlements. There is no regulation or control over any of these organisations. I am not too concerned about the use of an unqualified mediator — after all many arbitrators are not legally qualified — but arbitrators are subject to supervision by the courts and are normally members of professional bodies which set standards.

Let me describe the process of a true mediation in more detail. The following describes the methods of a specialist company but the pattern appears to be well established and used by almost all mediators who are not expected to give a decision or express an opinion of any kind. The parties agree to a mediation of a difference between them or, more commonly, one party approaches the mediation company to get a mediation going. A representative then contacts the other side inviting them to cooperate in a mediation. This is a marketing activity requiring some skill. The representative may be talking to a lawyer who looks upon this litigation as a meal ticket for years and out of the blue someone is offering to help settle it in the next two months. If the parties agree to mediate, the identity of the mediator, the venue and the total fees are agreed at this stage. The aim will be to hold the mediation within about six weeks of the first contact. The parties meet in appropriate accommodation which must have three rooms: one for open session, two for private caucuses. If there are more than two parties then, of course, there must be more rooms. If the matter is of substance then a day will be set aside, but further time may be needed. The mediator may have been provided with an agreed statement of principal facts or statements from each side, some documents and pleadings if litigation is already on foot.

Normally each party is represented by a lawyer who now presents his client's case in open session, usually lasting between thirty minutes and two hours. Thereafter the mediator meets with each party examining and highlighting with them the strengths and weaknesses of their case. He must not disclose what he learns from either side without consent. He carries offers from one side to another: engaging in shuttle diplomacy. The mediator does not express a personal opinion, does not reveal his assessment of the merits of each side's case.

Because the mediation process of itself is non-binding and entirely 'without prejudice' (which gives rise to interesting questions as to the extent of the privilege from subsequent disclosure which the meetings enjoy), it is necessary to record the agreement in contract form. A good mediator will achieve a settlement in more than 80% of the cases referred to him.

The selection and training of the mediator is at the heart of any discussion of ADR. I have to say that I am influenced by my own experience in watching and talking to experienced mediators. Good mediators normally are lawyers. But a knowledge of the law is in many ways subordinate to the ability to bring parties between whom there may be little trust to a common position. There is something almost magical in following the progress of a mediated settlement. At the beginning when each party puts its case in the open session, the opportunity for reaching a common position appears remote. One side wants more than the case could possibly be worth, the other side is offering less than anyone should accept. But slowly, through the caucus sessions, the parties come closer and closer. The mediator does not drive them or force them but he does keep them talking and does insist that each side addresses the points put against them. I suspect that the mediator's greatest skill may be in persuading the parties to think in terms of settlement and of the possibility that the case will settle. This takes time. A mediation I attended in San Francisco (which was the second meeting of the parties) began at 4.00 pm and went on until after midnight.

These skills are not learned overnight. The professional mediator will have received both theoretical and practical training. In a reputable firm this will include a course lasting a few days and sitting in on a dozen or so mediations. He will then be appointed to assist in mediations involving small sums or simple issues. But as a mediator may undertake up to 150 mediations in a year, his principal training is working experience and after a year or two that experience is considerable.

I have been impressed by how well mediations which looked hopeless actually worked. I was also impressed by the scale of some disputes which had been resolved by mediation. Not only very large cases involving millions of dollars but multiple disputes, such as the run-off of the asbestosis and other related claims against the Manville Trust (which I refer to again below) which may involve resolving or at least processing more than 100,000 claims. Dealing in multiple claims requires an organisation of some size with the administrative resources to support the handling of multiple claims. The businesses which I visited were small when compared with the bigger law firms but they did employ an administrative staff and employed or had access to mediators both at their head office and at other centres (which normally operated pursuant to a franchise agreement). As I have already hinted, they are successful not only because of their professional marketing of the service which they offer.

As suggested above, non-binding arbitration is really a dry run of an anticipated trial. It can be brought even closer to the uncertainties of trial in 'summary jury trials' where the court has had some success in providing actual jurors to hear in court presentations by the parties and to give advisory verdicts. But NBA is particularly the province of the 'rent-a-judge' organisations. Judges may not make good mediators because they are too willing to intervene and are trained to reach a conclusion on the merits but there are so many retired judges available and willing in the US that a substantial number of organisations now exist to sell their services. Indeed, there is a growing concern that too many judges may be retiring early in order to undertake lucrative employment as mediators. In a typical case the initial stages will be the same as in the case of a mediation. And the mediator will hear both sides in open session and then meet each party in caucus. But if the parties do not reach agreement at this stage the judge or mediator may express his opinion of proper settlement terms.

Although NBA may have been undertaken at the election of the parties it is often initiated by the court either voluntarily or pursuant to a mandatory procedure. Members of the American Arbitration Association and local lawyers are enlisted to assist the parties in settlement conferences. According to reports these achieve considerable success both because they bring the parties together and at least until recently because they are used as a means of awarding costs to one party if the matter does not settle but the mediator's award is more favourable to that party than the ultimate award of the jury.

One of the best known proponents of ADR in the US and a stalwart of the CPR, Kenneth Feinberg, has recently published an update of the procedure after undertaking some two dozen mediations. Some of these mediations were very large and involved many parties including action by Vietnam veterans affected by Agent Orange. His favoured procedure requires the mediator to intervene quite aggressively in the settlement procedure, offering what he perceives to be a proper settlement early in the process and resorting to quite forceful pressure on each party (even though the process is non-binding) in an effort to reach a settlement. Mr Feinberg's techniques appear popular even if some think his work is too result-orientated. According to one attorney reported in the Wall Street Journal "He sets off a little Atom Bomb and gets people out of the trenches."

All commentators agree that, whatever procedure is adopted, the selection of an able mediator is vital. And in talking to a predominantly British audience I am conscious of the fact that there are very few people here with any real experience of mediation in practice. Although there is one commercial mediation business established in England which I understand is now beginning to take off, it will not be used with any frequency unless lawyers suggest it and skilled mediators are in place to undertake it. But how are intending mediators to become skilled? Some of the 'famous people' of the CPR panel are in much demand and their skills have grown with their experience. But others, I suspect, are rarely called upon and their natural talents and experience as a lawyer or a judge may not equip them for the less aggressive tasks of a mediator. I must say that, having watched mediators in action, I am presently convinced that mediators need training and they need experience if they are to realise the opportunities for successful mediation.

I noted earlier that in the US there are no formal qualifications and no supervision of mediators. Not all are lawyers but many arbitrators are not lawyers and, some would say, the better for it. But at this time, when there is no great body of mediators — or persons claiming ability as mediators — it is worthwhile giving consideration to whether mediators should be licensed or should be members of some association. The AAA is heavily involved in ADR (Robert Coulson, its president, has written a very useful booklet on mediation). But with the greatest of respect to my present audience I am not sure whether arbitrators any more than judges necessarily make good mediators: they are expected to reach decisions on the merits whereas, at least in my view, a mediator's task is to bring the parties together without expressing his or her own view — easier said than done. But I would like to see some organisation, either particular to mediators or sympathetic to them, which sets some minimum standard and by which a client can expect his mediator to be recognised.

MINI-TRIAL

To summarise, a mini-trial is a structured settlement negotiation in which each party's advocate puts his best case to a forum which consists of decision makers from each side with power to settle the dispute and an (optional) neutral party after which the executives meet to endeavour to resolve their differences. It has had some famous successes which have given it some considerable publicity. The procedure should at least be considered in the course of any major litigation. The mini-trial has been much promoted by the CPR and although the procedure has been described in detail elsewhere it may be worthwhile to summarise the procedure.

The parties agree to a formal, but without prejudice, hearing. It can take place at any time in the progress of proceedings. Often it does not take place until after discovery. A 'core' bundle of documents is agreed. The hearing takes place before one executive decision maker from each side, together with a 'neutral', at least in many cases, whose task is limited to giving assistance when asked. Each party (in England and Wales) is represented by one counsel or solicitor who will make one main speech last one to two hours and will have a right to reply for not more than 20 or 30 minutes. Thereafter the executives first retire with their advisers and then meet together in the hope that each will have recognised some common ground.

They may call upon the neutral to help them in their appreciation of what has been said. Any agreement is thereafter formalised. The process may not be very different from the sort of round table settlement conference which may often take place during major litigation. But by formalising it the greater commitment of time and the quality of preparation which results tends to pay dividends.

Having had some personal experiences of the mini-trial as an advocate I think of it as a way of getting a message across to a manager or director on the opposing side. I can point out that a trial will involve identified risks and undermine the perceived strengths of my opponent's case. Although it does mean disclosing more of my hand than I would otherwise, before trial, such experience as I have of litigation drives me to conclude that there is rarely any real advantage in keeping one's cards close to one's chest until the last moment. It is our task as lawyers to resolve a dispute by the most effective means and that does not oblige us to submit it to adversarial combat fought out in accordance with ancient rules whilst garbed in ancient dress before one of Her Majesty's Judges or even in plain clothes before a member of this audience.

But in speaking to American lawyers with greater experience than me I learned of the failures as well as the successes. Arranging and running a mini-trial which will last one or two days, requires at least partial discovery and considerable preparation by the lawyers. It is quite expensive and time consuming. It is argued that much of the work is necessary for the preparation of the case for court, but one lawyer specialising in international arbitration, particularly with third world countries, has made the point to me that although he has tried mini-trials on three different occasions, none of them had been successful. Where there were skilled lawyers on each side final and binding arbitrations before eminent arbitrators could be prepared and heard within six to eight months of commencement of proceedings. Procedure was often informal, little notice being taken of prohibitions of hearsay when witnesses were scattered around the world and with minimal discovery — because no one was going to give honest discovery anyway. Why, he asked, delay trial and incur the expense of a mini-trial which is non-binding and may not resolve the dispute when it can be disposed of anyway in such a short period. This, perhaps takes me back to the point I made earlier — that alternatives are only necessary if traditional methods of resolving disputes are proving unsatisfactory — whether because of delay, expense or whatever.

I have come to the conclusion that it is important to have a neutral 'referee' in mini-trial proceedings. Centuries of mistrust of lawyers cannot always be dispelled by a smile and a hand-shake and unqualified executives need someone they recognise as neutral to help them particularly with legal points if they are to commit substantial sums on the outcome of the process.

THE PARTICULAR STRENGHTS OF ADR

Costs

Litigation is so expensive that in many of the cases in which the practising lawyer is involved, even when a claim is for hundreds of thousands of pounds, the costs of taking the difference between the parties to trial are disproportionate to the possible benefit. And the cost/benefit equation must include the often dramatic drain upon the management resources of a litigating company. There is often a substantial financial justification for exchanging a slightly less successful result for a substantial saving of costs. Mediation does save money. The process is relatively inexpensive, it is quick and it can take place early in the dispute. Although more expensive and time consuming, even the additional expense of a mini-trial may not be significant when set against the overall cost of major litigation.

Feeling Good

In my mind there is little doubt that a great attraction of all ADR methods but particularly mediation is the achievement of a result which tends to leave all sides feeling good. In my own limited experience, even when one or other party has initially been unwilling to agree to mediation, as the process has continued, the desire to reach a common position seems to take over all parties, particularly if they can be kept talking (there are similarities between the length and effect of these sessions and industrial wage negotiating sessions between employers and unions). The parties begin with a joint session at which they hear their case put in the most favourable light and thereafter they have the opportunity of explaining their case and their concerns to the mediator in private and knowing that he will carry their cause to the other side. I am impressed at the degree of trust reposed in young mediators by hardened trial lawyers. At the end of the session the participants feel that they have had their 'day in court' — which we all can recognise as a real need — and feel that their case has been put and been heard. So mediation, as it was put to me by a San Francisco mediator, 'drains the poison from the wound'. Concluded litigation often leaves at least one party feeling bitter and can sour relations between individuals and corporations for many years. The limitations of the process of mediation (or conciliation) or mini-trial are often outweighed by resolution of a dispute in a manner which leaves commercial, or social, relationships undamaged.

Multiple Claims

In the last few years alternative methods have been widely used to resolve multiple party proceedings, whether they be the result of disasters, defective drugs, labour disputes or environmental claims. The largest that I am aware of is the run-off of the claims to be met by the Manville Trust which are being handled by US Arbitration in Seattle but it has become common for multiple claims to be handled in this way. The removal of the adversarial process of trial and use of less formal more flexible procedures to handle large numbers of similar claims seems to suit the defendants to such claims, whether they be a single corporation or a group of insurers.

DISADVANTAGES

Discovery and Expert Evidence

It is often argued that it is not possible to settle complex litigation before discovery but that discovery is one of the greatest expenses of litigation and having been given the parties are too close to trial for alternatives to be of value. Elsewhere in this paper I have noted that the mediator can be very powerful. Able mediators are greatly respected. Once involved in a mediation, the parties tend to start thinking in terms of settlement. It must be acknowledged that in complex litigation the calculation of the true level of loss, particularly, may require most careful analysis of disclosed documents and expert evidence. If a mediation or mini-trial takes place without litigation or before discovery there must be a risk of agreeing a level of recovery which is substantially inaccurate. This must be the responsibility of those acting for the parties.

To some extent the problem can be avoided if witness statements are discovered early or if parties are required to plead evidence as well as fact. Movements towards early disclosure of each side's true case which are slowly taking place in court procedure and in the rules set down at least by particular arbitrators diminish the problem. Indeed, having granted power to all divisions of the High Court to require disclosure of witness statements it might be a valuable step towards early resolution of disputes to either require witness statements to be delivered after close of pleadings or at least at the same time as discovery. The same principle must apply to arbitration. But, at least in my experience, parties tend to be aware of damaging documents very early on in a dispute. The entire discovery process turns upon the honesty of the parties and their lawyers in revealing damaging documents. The lawyers of many countries and certainly some countries in South America and Africa really do not understand why one party should so help the other side prove its case. So I would propose that each side to an ADR process undertaken before discovery be obliged to disclose documents of which they are aware and which are likely significantly to affect the issues between the parties. And if it is intended to rely upon a document, any other document which might significantly affect its significance be disclosed. This process of 'core discovery' is quite similar to that often used by the Industrial Tribunals.

Enforcement

All forms of ADR, even those ordered by US courts are 'non-binding.' A mediated agreement, like any other form of settlement between the parties, is only enforceable as a contract and so must be drawn up as one unless it can be incorporated in a Tomlin order.

Admissions

A great deal has been written about whether privilege attaches to records of mediations or documents disclosed during the course of such procedures, particularly if litigation is not on foot. Concern is also expressed as to whether a mediator is a compellable witness in proceedings. This should be controlled by the terms of any agreement between the parties but it may be that a third party might wish to compel the mediator to attend other litigation as a witness of admissions. An interesting problem?

Other Problems

Throughout this paper I have referred to other matters which have to be taken into account. It will be difficult to find a mediator or neutral and to persuade the other side to participate. The expense of a mini-trial may be wasted. Indeed I would only advise this procedure if both sides genuinely wanted to attempt a compromise or where one party had reason to believe that the other side was being sheltered from reality by its legal advisers, for whatever reason.

GETTING STARTED

I should not give the impression that the US legal process has abandoned the resolution of disputes by trial or even that ADR is responsible for the settlement of a substantial proportion of disputes. It is often used and provides employment for an army of specialists if only because there is such a large total volume of litigation. Many trial lawyers know nothing about it. Many are deeply suspicious of the effect which it might have upon their revenue. On the other hand, almost all the development has occurred in the last ten years and the use of mandatory settlement procedures in the courts and the espousal of the CPR policy by so many major companies is beginning to affect attitudes quite fundamentally. In the US much of the pressure has come from corporations and insurers dissatisfied with the costs and delays of traditional litigation. The English system is more efficient although expensive. Arbitrators are very conscious of the need for rapid resolution of disputes. But 90% of cases settle before trial and, at least in my experience, most settle too late when much expense has been incurred and on no better terms than would have been available long before if the parties had been helped to talk to each other constructively.

The best way to facilitate alternative methods of resolving disputes between contracting parties is to include an 'ADR Clause' in the contract obliging the parties to attempt to resolve their differences by mediation or conciliation. There are many precedents available. In this way neither party loses face or appears in a position of weakness if a problem arises. If there is no ADR clause or if the dispute is not contractual, someone must start the ball rolling. I am told that in 80% of the cases mediated in the US, the mediator is approached by one party. The mediator, or the appropriate representative of his firm, then approaches the other side. In this way the mediator can put his case, demonstrate the absence of risk and the attractions of mediation without making the party that approached him appear exposed. It is often said that ADR methods will never work unless both parties really do want to settle. This may well be true of mini-trials which are less intimate and can provide some benefit to a party that is simply interested in discovering how the other side puts its case. But I suspect that even an unwilling party drawn into a mediation may find itself carried along by the momentum of the negotiation. I watched this happen in a class action mediation in San Francisco. It reflects the surprising (and slightly worrying) power of a good mediator.

In a recent discussion with a very experienced arbitrator I asked him how often he felt able to put pressure upon the parties at an early stage to negotiate a settlement. "Almost never", he told me. He explained how difficult it was to intervene in any way which might be seen to reflect anticipation of the result or to suggest that the parties should in any way compromise and by showing that he believed that one or other party could not succeed in full. Of course it might also cause problems if an offer had been made and rejected. But I recall that His Honour Judge Stabb would often call counsel into his room and press them to look realistically (shall we say) at the case. Eminent judges can intervene, it seems. Could the arbitrator make it a term of his engagement that he might require the parties to negotiate with the assistance of an independent mediator? And if this was accepted by the parties then, provided a mediator was to be had, would not this step be taken as being no more than a part of the procedure of the arbitration? In the High Court, it seems to me that the Masters, who already undertake so much delicate work, are well placed to perform a similar function.

The last problem which I will address is the term 'Alternative Dispute Resolution' itself, that is the description used to describe mediation, conciliation, mini-trials and similar procedures. Is it appropriate? Am I right (as I believe I am) that it should describe only those procedures in which the parties are not subjected to a binding decision in the event of their failing to agree and should, therefore, exclude arbitration? Indeed, is any objection to the phrase no more than a desire for a more English name for an American idea?

REFERENCES

* This article was originally published as P. Naughton, 'Alternative Forms of Dispute Resolution — Their Strengths and Weaknesses', *Arbitration* 56, no. 2 (1990): 76-82.

1 See 'A New Concept' by Kenneth Severn given at the conference 'New Concepts in the Resolution of Disputes in International Construction Contracts' 15 and 16 June 1989.

2 For a detailed description see 'Court Annexed Arbitration in the United States' by The Hon Richard Enslen delivered as one of the papers in the series 'Current Problems in Arbitration and Litigation' in 1988.

3 In *Tiedel v Northwestern Michigan College* (6th Cir 29 December 1988) it was held that the fee shifting rules which are a part of the famous 'Michigan Mediation' procedures are inconsistent with the general rule that each side bears its own attorney's fees.

4 Judge Enslen is a pioneer of this process and has presided over 79 of these 'SJT's' in his court.

5 See *Tiedel v Northwestern Michigan College* above.

6   K. Feinberg, 'A Procedure for the Voluntary Mediation of Disputes', *Litigation and Administrative Practice Course Handbook Series-Litigation* (1992), 179.

7   20 October 1988.

8   International Dispute Resolution Ltd, which is associated with United States Arbitration and Mediation Inc whose headquarters are in Seattle.

9   R. Coulson, *Business Mediation — What You Need to Know* (New York: American Arbitration Association, 1987).

10 See particularly the 'CPR Legal Program Mini Trial Workbook' and the CPR mini-trial video, which I believe was shown at the Institute's conference last year. But refer also to the paper on mini-trials by Mark Blessing given at this year's conference 'New Concepts in the Resolution of Disputes in International Construction Contracts' which describes the 'Zurich mini-trial.'

CHAPTER 1

The Courts and Alternative Dispute Resolution

Ian Richard Scott

At the fourth of BILA's annual conferences I spoke on the topic 'The Courts and Alternative Dispute Resolution.' I did so with some misgivings as I am no expert on this subject. However, as I explained on that occasion, the topic encapsulates several issues that have been troubling me for some time, both during the years I served on the Lord Chancellor's Civil Justice Review Body and afterwards. In doing a little work on them over the years I have encountered some mental blocks. I thought that if I had to gear myself up to talk about them at the conference I might be able to clear my mind.

Those who were at the conference will remember that I did not really give a lecture. Rather, in the space of over an hour, I rambled through twelve overheads. Some of the overheads contained, or at least hinted at, a great deal of information. After the event, I realised that I would not be able to reduce to readable form the territory I covered in my own, inexpert way. The overheads and the notes I used lie in a badly disorganised file at the back of a drawer. I rather hoped that the successive requests I received for an account of my lecture would disappear if I ignored them for long enough. However, that was not to be and eventually my conscience got the better of me. I realised I had to produce something that could be read at leisure.

What follows is not the transcript of a lecture and it is not a law article in the traditional sense. Rather it is a collection of notes strung out into narrative form. I have endeavoured to touch upon most of the points I made at the conference. In some instances I have found it very difficult to reduce to narrative form points made on some of the more exotic overheads.

THE ADR MOVEMENT

Shortly after the Second World War, some American legal writers became interested in what they called 'private ordering.' They were concerned with the ways in which individuals through their own efforts adjusted their relationships, for example, prospectively through contractual agreements and retrospectively through adjudicatory and other dispute resolving mechanisms. However, alternative dispute resolution, or 'ADR' as it is known in the judicial administration trade, did not attract much interest until the 1980s.

The literature on the subject has grown enormously. Contributions have come not solely or even primarily from practising and academic lawyers. Practitioners of other social sciences have been involved. Discussion has ranged from the highly theoretical to the intensely practical and across virtually every known boundary in the administration of justice and indeed beyond. Although the literature is enormous, much of it is unoriginal; the same points are made over and over again. Thus, the babble of voices is loud; it is also confusing and for one coming to the subject for the first time it is difficult to find a way in. Nothing I have to say about ADR is original; I have drawn upon several sources in the literature that strike me as being among the more substantial.

The use of the word 'alternative' causes us to ask 'alternatives to what?' What is meant, certainly in North America and this country, are alternatives to what could be called 'the traditional court process.' The movement towards developing alternatives to traditional adjudication attracts three, possibly four, different groups. There are: (1) those who seek alternatives to law itself or, at least, to particular parts of the substantive law (often landlord and tenant law and family law); (2) those who are disturbed by contemporary professionalism in law and who seek to 'de-lawyerise' dispute resolution (e.g., members of consumer movements and, increasingly, business men). The members of these two groups are of a radical mind and want to see traditional dispute resolving processes abandoned and new and different, not merely alternative, ones put in their place. Then there are: (3) those who want to see fairly modest reforms which will provide acceptable alternative judicial procedures for the less serious cases thereby helping to 'save' the courts (and their traditional procedures) for the cases that courts should really be concerned with (whatever they might be). The possible fourth group in the alliance consists of: (4) those (usually found in government) who want to see economies made in public expenditure on the administration of justice and who believe that ADR mechanisms might prove cheaper to run than traditional courts. The members of the last two groups are likely to see 'alternative' processes as being complementary rather than as replacing traditional methods. These four groups, or 'constituencies' as they are sometimes called, form an unlikely but powerful political (with a small 'p') alliance. You can see that the political alliance that has been built around ADR contains some pretty strange bedfellows. The search for alternatives has ranged far and wide, well away from the kinds of issues dealt with by courts and the processes used by courts. It has led to an examination of the resolution of disputes by irrational as well as by rational methods, for example by physical force and by the tossing of a coin. It has led to an examination of the ways in which decisions are made in the political process, for example, by voting and by legislation, and in the economic sphere, for example by the private market and by management in organisations. Indeed, the mixing up of decision-making processes with dispute resolving processes is one of the main causes for confusion in the literature.

THE RESPONSE TO WEAKNESSES OF THE TRADITIONAL COURT PROCESSES

Despite their differences, the members of the groups I have mentioned as being proponents of ADR agree that there is something wrong with 'traditional court processes.' This has lead to much greater thought being given to the precise nature of these traditional processes both in the common law (adversarial) and continental (inquisitorial) court systems. The alternatives proposed are normally based on some analysis of traditional processes and usually they give emphasis to particular aspects of these processes.

Inevitably, much of the substantive law of any legal system consists of principles and rules defining what, in law, constitute valid claims to compensation or redress of some other kind. Claims between individuals could be left unsettled but a legal system that failed to provide a method for the settlement of disputes would appear to be lacking in one of its primary duties; that is, to provide a means for the realisation of what the substantive law proclaims. If importance is attached to settling disputes, as it must be, it is necessary to establish methods for so doing. Preferably, the methods chosen must be ones about which there can be very little dispute. Happily, it is often possible to have almost complete agreement about a method for settling disputes when it is impossible to reach any sort of agreement about the rights and wrongs of a particular dispute itself (see Lucas, 'On Processes for Resolving Disputes' in Essays in Legal Philosophy (Summers ed. 1968) p. 180). Looking at this from the point of view of a lawyer one would hope that the mode of dispute resolution chosen should be the one that maximises the likelihood that specific resolution of disputed claims will accord with applicable law and relevant facts (Summers, 'Law, Adjudicative Processes, and Civil Justice' in Law Reason and Justice, Hughes ed. 1969, p. 174).

A trial at law is a second-level process for achieving the settlement of a dispute that, for one reason or another, could not be settled at the first-level (see Golding, 'On the Adversary System and Justice' in Philosophical Law, Bronaugh ed. 1978, p. 98). At the second-level a new factor in the form of a third-party is introduced. Conceivably, the third-party may play one of a number of different roles but the significant feature of a trial at law is that the third-party in the form of a court acts as an adjudicator. But, the process of adjudication also may take different forms. Trial at law is a special kind of third-party adjudication and many writers have attempted to isolate and describe its salient features. Insofar as there is agreement as to what these features are, it seems to be generally accepted that it does not matter whether a particular forum acts inquisitorially or adversarily; the essential characteristics of a trial at law do not require that one mode of proceedings be preferred to the other. Efforts have been made to describe the differences between inquisitorial and adversarial systems and the advantages and disadvantages of each have been staunchly championed and, on the other hand, rigorously criticised. Trial at law in the Anglo-American legal systems based on the common law is said to be adversarial. However, in common law systems, including England, there has been a move away from adversary procedures in certain areas (e.g., juvenile court and mental commitment proceedings) towards non-adversary and expert-administered processes (see Schur, Law and Society (1968) p. 198).

I have always been rather irritated by this debate as I always suspected that it was much more complicated than was made out. I have been much relieved since I read Damaska, The Faces of Justice and State Authority (1986) which is a magnificent work and which reveals the stupidity of those who, on the basis of a brief visit to France and a cursory examination of their court system, claim to be smitten by the so-called inquisitorial system and argue that we in this country ought to adopt aspects of it.

Many ADR writers, in analysing traditional common law court processes refer to characteristics enumerated by Professor Chayes in 1976 (Chayes, 'The Role of the Judge in Public Law Litigation 89 Harv. L. Rev. 1281 (1976)). He was concerned with the role of American courts in public law cases. He noted that many cases now being adjudicated are an amalgam of private and public interests; typically, such hybrid cases involve the application of government regulation to particular circumstances, or the attempt by one private party to constrain the activities of another based upon constitutional considerations or statutory policies.

Chayes said (*ibid* p. 1282) 'traditional adjudications' consist of the following five characteristics: (1) the lawsuit is bipolar; litigation is organised as a contest between two individuals or at least two unitary interests, diametrically opposed, to be decided on a winner-takes-all basis; (2) litigation is retrospective; the controversy is about an identified set of completed events: whether they occurred, and if so, with what consequences for the legal relations of the parties; (3) right and remedy are interdependent; the scope of the relief is derived more or less logically from the substantive violation under the general theory that the plaintiff will get compensation measured by the harm caused by the defendant's breach of duty — in contract by giving the plaintiff the money he would have had absent the breach; in tort by paying the value of the damage caused; (4) the lawsuit is a self-contained episode; the impact of the judgment is confined to the parties; if the plaintiff prevails there is a simple compensatory transfer, usually of money, but occasionally the return of a thing or the performance of a definite act; if the defendant prevails, a loss lies where it has fallen; in either event, entry of judgment ends the court's involvement; and (5) the process is party-initiated and party-controlled; the case is organised and the issues defined by exchanges between the parties. Responsibility for fact development is theirs; the trial judge is a neutral arbiter of their interactions who decides the questions of law only if they are put in issue by appropriate move of a party.

What is wrong with adjudication, specifically, with court adjudication? The identification of the failings of adjudication follow on from the characteristics identified by Professor Chayes and developed by other authors. This is familiar territory and we need not spend a lot of time on it but we should notice that reform proposals are always based on perceived weaknesses of adjudication and different reformers stress different weaknesses. Further, some of them are highly selective and perhaps wrong in some of the criticisms they make of adjudication.

The criticisms that have been made can be classified variously (see e.g., Paths to Justice: Major Public Policy Issues of Dispute Resolution, US Department of Justice Report of the Ad Hoc Panel on Dispute Resolution and Public Policy (National Institute for Dispute Resolution, January, 1984)). There are those that focus on cost, delay, access, participation, and on inappropriateness of forum (e.g., inadequate expertise, ineffective remedies). A particular and much-voiced criticism has been the divisive nature of traditional processes. It is argued that the processes are inappropriate where the parties concerned are in a continuing relationship.

So much for the failings of adjudication. What has been the response? We know that a lot has gone on. Developments can be listed under various headings (see e.g., Marks, Szanton & Johnson, Taking Stock of Dispute Resolution: An Overview of the Field, commissioned by the National Institute for Dispute Resolution (1981)). There are those concerned with reforming the courts (e.g., procedural reform, case management, diversion, settlement conferences, creating new forums (e.g., arbitration, ombudsmen, mediations), and with system change (e.g., no fault).

DISPUTE AND PROCESS CHARACTERISTICS

A simple list of activities in the dispute resolution field does not tell us much. It does not tell us much about the processes being used or the disputes with which they deal. A closer analysis is required. There are at least two ways of proceeding.

First, one could look closely at the various types of civil dispute that seem to exist and seek to tease out what seem to be their important characteristics or variables. This is likely to be a difficult endeavour because we will find it hard to know where to stop. Secondly, one could adopt a rather more practical approach and look for significant characteristics or variables among the processes that are currently used to resolve disputes, including traditional court processes. Let me try to give you the flavour of both approaches without going into too much detail, taking them in the order in which I have mentioned them.

Dispute Characteristics

A number of authors have adopted this approach; I will confine my remarks to the writings of two of them. Professor Emond starts by pointing out that disputes are not static but evolve as time goes by. He says that disputes may be 'characterised' under four headings (Emond, 'Alternative Dispute Resolution: A Conceptual Overview' 22 Kobe University Law Review (International Edition) (1988) pp. 10-15). These headings are: (1) the causes of the conflict, for example, whether arising through (a) supply and demand, (b) different perceptions of a situation (cognitive conflict), or (c) differences in values; (2) variations in the dimensions of conflict, for example, (a) complexity (multiplicity of issues and parties), (b) whether distributive or integrative (i.e., whether parties' interests are necessarily in opposition, the problem is integrative if a way out in which both can 'win' something may be found, e.g., by 'expanding the pie'), (c) significance of what is at stake (longevity of result, impact on others), and (d) what is in dispute (e.g., policy or facts); (3) the parties in dispute, that is, (a) the number of parties and their relationships, (b) whether corporate or not, and (c) whether capable of rationality; (4) timing, that is to say, whether the process is reactive or anticipatory (either seeking to avoid disputes or to structure and manage them in ways that minimise conflict.)

The second author I wish to draw to your attention is Professor Barton. His approach to dispute characteristics identifies eight variables (see (a) and (h) below) under three headings (see (i) to (iii) below) and he claims that they indicate the most important structural features possessed by problems calling for judicial 'solving' (Barton, 'Justiciability: A Theory of Judicial Problem Solving' 24 Boston College Law Review 505 (1983), p. 517). This approach may be sketched as follows: (1) the 'difficulty' of the problem, that is to say, (a) whether the problem is composed of 'simple' variables (i.e., no variable influences any other variable) or 'interactive' variables (i.e., where trade-offs exist among the variables that comprise the problem and a proper solution is an optimisation that considers all the intricate connections), (b) whether the decisional criteria for its solution are well-established or, rather, are unknown or disputed, and (c) whether decisional information or evidence is based on past, or future events; (2) the 'setting' of the problem, that is to say, (d) whether the relationship of the parties is 'simplex' or 'multiplex', (e) whether the dispute is 'private' or 'public', and (f) whether private resolution of the problem is feasible or infeasible; (3) the 'social concerns' associated with the problem, that is to say, (g) whether social consensus or 'dissensus' exists regarding the proper outcome of the problem, and (h) whether private resolution of the problem is socially desirable or undesirable.

Process Characteristics

Now turning to the more practical approach of attempting to identify process, rather than dispute characteristics or variables, what do we find? Well, the identification and description characteristics, or variables, of extant processes are now fairly well settled. The leading exponents of this are the American Professors Goldberg, Green and Sander. Under their influence several process characteristics have been identified. They are: (i) voluntary/involuntary, (ii) binding/non-binding, (iii) third party role, (iv) degree of formality, (v) nature of proceeding, (vi) outcome and (vii) private/public (see Goldberg, Green & Sander, Dispute Resolution (1985) p. 9). The volume of the literature on process characteristics is enormous and repetitive.

THE DISPUTE RESOLUTION CONTINUUM

Whether you begin with an analysis of disputes or an analysis of processes identifiable in the real dispute resolution world, sooner or later you are going to be driven to some classification of dispute resolution processes that is better than the list we looked at some time ago. Here, the process characteristics approach just mentioned is the key. Often, the role of the third party seems to be the critical variable. As Goldberg, Green and Sander have illustrated, you can divide dispute resolution processes into those that involve a third party and those that do not and those that do can be further divided according to the role that the third party plays. This leads us to the so-called dispute resolution continuum.

The terminology is not settled but sometimes it is said that there is a continuum and it starts with (i) negotiation and ends with (v) adjudication with (ii) mediation, (iii) conciliation and (iv) arbitration (in its various forms) in between (there are difficulties in defining and classifying arbitration, also sometimes mediation and negotiation are collapsed). Some authors add other processes to the continuum, either as quite separate mechanisms or as 'hybrids' combining aspects of the basic five processes. To take account of this we could add, after (i) to (v), a sixth category on the continuum labelled as 'hybrids.' Goldberg and his colleagues list as 'hybrids' (i) private judging, (ii) neutral expert fact-finding, (iii) mini-trial, (iv) ombudsman, and (v) summary jury trial. As I have already said, in analyses, of this type, the third party variable seems to be the predominant one.

Negotiation, mediation and conciliation are informal, non-coercive forms of dispute resolution. On the other hand, adjudication is a formal, coercive method (arbitration is best regarded as a form of adjudication). Where disputes may be adjudicated if all else fails, the other steps on the continuum are affected by that prospect. In these circumstances, negotiation, conciliation and mediation take place 'in the shadow of the law' and in the knowledge that coercive adjudication may be invoked eventually by one party.

If we look beyond the 'role of the third-party' variable to the other variables, we can produce a matrix by matching up the categories of process found on the dispute resolution continuum with the process characteristics (or variables) outlined above (see Goldberg, Green & Sander, Dispute Resolution (1985) p. 9). Here, my effort to reduce to narrative form some of the overheads I produced at the conference breaks down. The reader should imagine that the labels of the rows accord with the six process characteristics and the columns with the six categories of process.

This matrix enables us to say something about the various strengths and weaknesses on each of the dispute resolution mechanisms appearing on the dispute resolution continuum. Having identified the strengths and weaknesses of the various dispute resolution mechanisms we can start to think about the ways in which particular disputes might ideally be matched up with particular processes.

RELATIONSHIP BETWEEN DISPUTE RESOLUTION MECHANISMS: 'LITIGOTIATION'

Up to this point I have been assuming that the various dispute resolution mechanisms are as a practical matter quite separate and that the problem is to match the right dispute with the right process. Of course, you know and I know that the real world is not like that. For example, if we take the ordinary civil court case we will probably find that the parties will have engaged in negotiation, conciliation, or mediation processes in an attempt to resolve their problems. Further, after court process has been issued they may continue to engage in such efforts. It is obvious that the various forms of dispute resolution are not mutually exclusive; the concession that 'hybrids' exist illustrates this. The most obvious connection for those of us who are lawyers is that between negotiation and adjudication. As an American author Jonathan Marks has put it: "[o]n the contemporary

American legal scene, the negotiation of disputes is not an alternative to litigation. It is only a slight exaggeration to say that it is litigation. There are not two distinct processes, negotiation and litigation; there is a single process of disputing in the vicinity of official tribunals that we might call litigotiation, that is, the strategic pursuit of a settlement through mobilizing the court process. Full-blown adjudication of the dispute — running the whole course [to trial] — might be thought of as an infrequently pursued alternative to the ordinary course of litigation." However, 'litigotiation' is not always successful in resolving disputes and, further, even in the many cases where it is, it seems to be an unsatisfactory process.

Why should this be so? Marks, Green and Croom in Beyond Adjudication (1988) talk of the barriers that seem to exist to parties arriving at a settlement negotiated by them and their attorneys in 'litigotiation'. They say these barriers include: (i) emotional barriers, as where there is antagonism or lack of trust between the parties and/or counsel, or where parties and/or counsel are unable to evaluate or communicate rationally; (ii) communication barriers, as where one or both parties are unwilling to negotiate because of the risk of being perceived as weak, or where one or both parties are unwilling to be honest about settlement positions because of strategic considerations stemming from lack of knowledge of the other side's position; (iii) predictive barriers arising from different views of the law, the facts, and the likely adjudicatory outcome; (iv) representation barriers, as where the lawyer fails adequately to prepare the case or is inattentive to the case, or where economic incentives do not favour early resolution, and (v) external and situational barriers; for example, the parties may view the risk of uncertainty of a third party decision differently, as where a repeat institutional litigant faces few consequences from an adverse verdict but the individual litigant faces ruin; or the dispute may be linked to other disputes, as where the litigate/settle decision of a party is not limited to a single case. Supplementary processes (by which these authors mean particularly arbitration and mediation) annexed to the court process are designed to overcome these barriers.

CRITICISMS OF ADR

The ADR movement has had a fair wind. Virtue seems to be on their side. But some voices of criticism have been raised. Even members of the movement have wondered out loud why the movement has not had more success. There have been plenty of examples of ADR processes being introduced to deal with minor, small cases and one wonders whether they are going to be restricted to such cases.

Does ADR have a more important role to play? Are there dangers in giving ADR processes a wider role? If alternative procedures are to be designed for cases other than the most minor our experience in operating the existing, traditional processes should throw up a range of particular questions.

Professor Carrington, one of America's leading civil procedure scholars, has argued that answers need to be provided to the following questions (Carrington, 'Civil Procedure and Alternative Dispute Resolution' 34 Journal of Legal Education 298 (1984)): (i) What qualifications are to be expected of a 'dispute resolver' in the ADR system? How is neutrality and impartiality to be guaranteed? How are they to be selected and how removed? Are they to be professional or lay or is there to be a balance of both? (ii) If different 'resolvers' are to be used in different kinds of disputes, how are disputes to be channelled to the right dispute resolver? What is to be done about jurisdictional problems whether based on territory or subject-matter? (iii) If the ADR mechanism is intended to achieve decisions that conform to controlling law, how are dispute resolvers to be made accountable for their fidelity to that law without excessive 'legalism' creeping in? If they can 'forget about the law' and base their decision on 'equity, good conscience, et cetera.', how is reasonableness ensured? (iv) Is the ADR mechanism expected to adhere to any particular procedural norms? What are the consequences of procedural error? Would abolition of interlocutory appeals lead to ADR procedures becoming ineffective? (v) On what information are the decisions of the ADR mechanisms to be based? What are the consequences of 'relaxing' the rules of evidence? Are decisions to be based on mere assertions or on informal statements by parties? Is it proposed that the ADR mechanism shall have the effect of extracting information from disputants even though it might be against their interests? Above all, how does the ADR mechanism propose to get available information at reasonable cost? Who should pay? (vi) Might there be a need to control or deter misuse of the ADR process? What is to be done about protecting the system from hopeless claims, dilatory defences and perjury? Is there to be tort liability for abuse of process? How are advocates or 'representors' appearing to be disciplined? Are cost sanctions to be used? (vii) What are the prospects for the ADR mechanisms dealing fairly with impecunious disputants? Should there be a charge for the ADR service?

Who is to pay for interpreters, expert evidence, et cetera? Are we happy about moving the costs of litigation away from the parties on to the State? Are we confident that the State will pick up the bill, not only now but in years to come? (viii) Will the ADR mechanism effectively terminate disputes? What if a decision turns out to be mistaken, obtained by fraud, or contrary to law? What are to be the *res judicata* effects of an ADR decision, and what are to be the effects on nonparties? and, finally, (ix) Will the ADR mechanism have the power to compel obedience to its dictates? How will enforcement work? And to what extent can enforcement be varied or controlled by contract?

ADR enthusiasts are likely to dismiss these matters as being so much humbug and as flak put up by lawyers in an effort to prevent change. I do not think that they can be so easily dismissed. Indeed, I think the difficulty in answering them indicates the difficulties that have been encountered in extending ADR mechanisms beyond the smaller disputes.

PROSPECTS IN ENGLAND

If there is to be a break-through in England it seems to me that it will come in the form of new arrangements for pre-adjudication disposal of the more serious civil cases, that is to say, in the field of 'litigotiation.' There is a whole range of litigotiation techniques, some of them formerly regarded as separate dispute resolution techniques or as various 'settlement programs' (e.g., informal adjudication, early neutral evaluation (ENE), 'mini-trials' and pre-recorded video-tape trials (PRVTT)).

The further development of these techniques holds out the prospects of: (i) the saving of costs to litigants and the saving of court resources, (ii) the freeing up of lawyers' time enabling them to handle more cases, (iii) the increase of the incidence of 'mediate' rather than 'dichotomous' outcomes (enabling both sides to 'win' something), and (iv) the reduction of post-trial reviews and appeals.

English lawyers are beginning to dabble with these techniques. It will be interesting to see whether they receive encouragement from the major repeat players on the civil litigation scene, for example, from the insurance companies. Doubtless it will be said that lawyers have always emphasised the importance of negotiated settlements and that there is nothing new in litigotiation but the name.

However, I think that what is new is a shift of emphasis towards negotiation in the post-process phase and away from the 'preparing for trial' emphasis. This shift has brought about a new awareness of what lawyers have been doing all along and an interest in developing more sophisticated negotiating and settlement techniques.

I suspect that, in the past, the divided legal profession has retarded developments; one could not expect that barristers would be much interested in dispute resolution techniques for the more serious cases where those techniques deflected cases away from the courts. But now, things are beginning to change and it may be that the breaking down of the divisions within the profession will help.

In my view, lawyers, whether solicitors or barristers, should be selling themselves as the problem-solvers for parties locked in contentious cases and not simply as the hand-maiden of inexorable judicial processes. They should move themselves to the centre of dispute resolution processes and not be content to remain at the margins. Perhaps we are looking for a new kind of lawyer (and here I make what I think might be an original contribution to the ADR jargon), the 'advogotiator'.

* This article was originally published as I. Scott, 'The Courts and Alternative Dispute Resolution', *Arbitration* 56, no. 3 (1990): 176-182.

CHAPTER 1

Alternative Dispute Resolution in Construction

David E. Hollands

The traditional legal and administrative systems we depend on for resolving claims select winners and losers, often at the expense of the legitimate concerns of one side or the other. However if only one side 'wins', the losing party is likely to want to shift the conflict to another arena or seek revenge in an unrelated situation. Each party therefore has more to gain from a negotiated settlement, than from the imposed decision of a judge or arbitrator. Furthermore, disputes which depend on the interpretation of scientific or technical data have an additional need to deal wisely with uncertainty and with what is known about the natural and technical systems involved.

Alternative Dispute Resolution (or Amicable Dispute Resolution or Assisted Dispute Resolution, all of which abbreviate to ADR) offers disputants opportunities to participate in the process and empowers them to be creative in solving their own problems. It is well suited to disputes arising from construction contracts, where all parties are striving to complete challenging work on time and within budget and usually hope to work together again in the future. Parties usually report satisfaction with the outcome of ADR, and are more likely to accept the agreements they reach, because they are perceived to be fairer and easier to implement.

INTEREST-BASED BARGAINING

Disputants usually begin by concentrating all their energies on 'winning'. Even the word 'compromise' has a negative connotation, involving concessions, splitting the difference, loss to everyone, manipulation and an inferior outcome. However, dispute resolution should not be based on either winning or compromise, but on attempting to negotiate a settlement by interest-based bargaining which focuses on satisfying as many as possible of the important needs and interests of the parties. A good outcome usually improves relationships between the parties, and leaves them in a better position to deal with their differences in future.

The four characteristics of a good negotiated settlement are: fairness, efficiency, wisdom and stability. It is more important that an agreement be perceived as fair by the parties involved, than by an independent analyst who applies an abstract decision rule. Perceived fairness depends on participation. Therefore people problems (e.g., perception, emotion, ego, communication, et cetera) must also be dealt with.

A key element in interest-based bargaining is that all parties believe they will be better off by working in cooperation as problem-solvers than by competing or working independently. Parties who believe they can work together are usually able to do so. They try to adopt inter-personal styles that are more congenial than combative, more open and trusting than evasive or defensive, and more flexible (but firm) than stubborn. Needs have to be made explicit, similarities have to be identified, and differences recognised and accepted. Uncertainties have to be tolerated and inconsistencies unravelled.

The purpose of interest-based bargaining is not to question or challenge the other's viewpoint, but to incorporate it into the definition of the problem, and to attend to it as the parties search for mutually acceptable outcomes. The persuasive power of a negotiator depends in part on having fully heard the views, suggestions, and notions of what is fair of the other party before making any commitment.

NEUTRAL PARTY TO FACILITATE NEGOTIATION

During negotiation, information exchange may bog down into sterile repetitiveness, interpersonal relations between particular negotiators may interfere adversely, and misunderstandings may grow from faulty signals and inadequate interpretations. These barriers can be minimised by involving a neutral party (i.e., a facilitator, mediator, conciliator, referee, et cetera) to facilitate negotiation.

Particularly in disputes arising from construction contracts, where the decision of the engineer has already indicated a possible outcome, independent assessment of the evidence and the merits of the claims may be an important element in resolving the dispute. It may provide legitimacy, allowing each party to review the claim (possibly seeing things in a new light) and to retreat from its previously stated position. If the neutral party has knowledge of construction law and practice, his or her views on the probable outcome if the dispute proceeded to arbitration will be taken seriously. The neutral party might therefore provide a non-binding assessment of a matter in dispute (e.g., as may a conciliator in terms of NZS 3910: 1987), but should do so cautiously as the primary objective is for the parties to reach their own agreement.

It might be thought that a conciliator should not receive information which could not be disclosed to the other party, because of the danger of being influenced by it without the other party having an opportunity to make any comment or answer. However, the parties (and their various representatives and advisers, including the engineer) will all have their own private agenda, which may not be discussed at joint meetings. The conciliator might need to understand these private agenda, so as to assist the parties towards a solution to their problem. It may also be important to know about matters which are not directly relevant to the issues in dispute, but which are important in understanding why a party has particular concerns. For example, one party may have relationships or contracts with third parties, or other objectives, which would make some possible solutions to the dispute unacceptable, or other possible solutions more attractive. If aware of these extraneous concerns, the conciliator may be in a better position to encourage settlement by agreement. The neutral party therefore usually needs to be able to speak to each party separately, and to hear information which is to be kept from other parties. However, if agreement is not reached, the conciliator/mediator should not provide any non-binding assessment of the merits of the dispute that might be influenced by any such confidential information.

The neutral party (conciliator/mediator) in ADR must be acceptable to the parties, have credibility with them, and have their trust to participate actively in resolving their dispute. He or she should develop and implement a process which is appropriate to the specific circumstances of the dispute. The conciliator/mediator tries to compensate for the parties' deficiencies and supports the areas of strength. When disputants are hostile or overly emotional, the conciliator/mediator needs to deal with these feelings. When the problem seems intractable, the conciliator/mediator helps with analysis. When the parties make progress, the conciliator/mediator builds on it. When the parties are stuck on matters of principle, the conciliator/mediator splits or changes the issues. When the parties are stuck on positions, the conciliator/mediator shifts them to interests.

FUNCTIONS OF A CONCILIATOR/MEDIATOR

According to the circumstances, the functions of a conciliator/mediator may include some or all of the following: (1) educate the parties on the process and procedures involved; (2) assist with setting up protocols and with the convening, agenda setting, logistics and moderating of meetings; (3) bring about a change in the behaviour of the parties, merely by being involved and present at meetings; (4) assist in bringing any reluctant parties into the negotiations; (5) encourage and manage effective face-to-face communication, interaction and mutual understanding between the parties themselves (i.e., not just between their hired advocates, or legal or technical advisers); (6) keep discussions going, without jeopardising either party's basic bargaining position; (7) accumulate information from each party in a balanced way; (8) probe to uncover additional facts; (9) administer and act as 'banker' for any joint fact-finding studies; (10) provide analytical and problem-solving skills that are not available; (11) attempt to clarify information and interpretation, and encourage co-ordination between the parties; (12) provide the opportunity for each party to state its case, to the other party and to the neutral party, with an assurance of confidentiality;

(13) assist each party to identify its real interests and concerns and to review unrealistic expectations; (14) create a positive tone and maintain a discernible progress of the process; (15) communicate interests, concerns and proposals in understandable or more palatable terms; (16) have each party better understand the other party's views and evaluation of a particular issue, without violating any confidences; (17) suggest, clarify, interpret, reason, persuade and inform the parties about their dispute and its resolution; (18) offer an impartial appraisal of each party's case; (19) reduce the number of decisions to be made, and make the decisions easier to make; (20) put forward options that a party wants considered, but does not wish to suggest; (21) open discussions into areas not previously considered or inadequately developed; (22) help the parties to analyse their joint problem, narrow the issues, and develop objective criteria; (23) allow a party to retreat gracefully from a previously-stated position; (24) maintain each party's self-respect and satisfaction with the process; (25) help the parties to devise creative alternative outcomes, and negotiate their own mutually-acceptable settlement; (26) assist in checking that any proposed settlement meets the important interests and concerns of each party; (27) structure and prepare the preliminary draft of a settlement agreement; (28) assist in binding the parties to their agreement and monitoring its implementation; (29) assist with any future re-negotiation required, to deal with mistakes, unexpected changes or new factors.

GENERAL

There has been a tremendous growth in the use of alternative dispute resolution processes, to settle a variety of disputes. The key feature is that the parties do not give away the power to decide the outcome of their dispute. Parties and their legal advisers have indicated that they like conciliation/mediation, because it is usually more effective than litigation/arbitration in resolving a dispute, because the process is less stressful and the outcome is more amicable.

Conciliation/mediation forces earlier and greater involvement of the parties. This may be contrasted with litigation/arbitration, which can eliminate the parties as the lawyers take hold of 'their' case and translate real-world problems into abstract legal concepts and adversarial tactics. The parties will not necessarily find conciliation/mediation any easier. They can no longer merely deliver the dispute to their lawyers to handle, but must face up to increased participation. Lawyers may also need to readjust. Just as doctors do not always recommend surgery, lawyers should not always recommend arbitration/litigation. As in medicine, a less intrusive method often produces a more effective solution.

Conciliation/mediation is not an alternative to arbitration/litigation, but rather complements and depends on it. However, the parties, the lawyers and the neutral party must ensure that ADR does not become too formalised, and simply add one more layer of proceedings to the legal process. Arbitration/litigation can only deal with matters in dispute in terms of the contract from which they arise and based on the law. The outcome may also be uncertain, as evidenced by lawyers having opposing views as to who should prevail. Conciliation/mediation is neither constrained nor uncertain. It can deal with any or all matters affecting the parties (and their subcontractors, consultants, insurers, et cetera) and incorporate them into a more acceptable and better quality final outcome.

Disputants who emerge from conciliation/mediation with a sense that they have had their say, the issues came out, they were listened to and understood, the process was fair, and they participated directly in deciding the outcome, are more likely to comply with agreements they reached and rebuild their relationship. Properly used, conciliation/mediation is able to foster the settlement of disputes on a fair and amicable basis. For disputes arising from construction contracts, a technical conciliator/mediator can understand the issues and establish rapport to assist the parties in quickly and economically resolving their dispute.

* This article was originally published as D. Hollands, 'Alternative Dispute Resolution (ADR) in Construction', *Arbitration* 58, no. 1 (1992): 57-59.

CHAPTER 1

Alternative Dispute Resolution

Lord Donaldson

Last September the Law Society's working party on Alternative Dispute Resolution issued a report that was subsequently adopted by the Bar Council. It made a number of points which I can summarise as follows: (1) The small claims procedure in the County Courts had been a success and it was not recommended that any changes be made; (2) The same unfortunately could not be said of the remainder of the County Court jurisdiction, which was hopelessly uneconomic for the parties. The report also drew attention to the fact that where a hearing could not be completed within the day, the adjourned hearing might not take place for a considerable time. I would comment that this particular defect is already being tackled by the establishment of continuous hearing centres throughout the country, but the uneconomic nature of the proceedings remains an unacceptable feature; (3) There is considerable experience of court-annexed ADR in the United States, Canada, Australia and New Zealand. The essential feature is the employment of a lawyer as a mediator who, at an early stage in the proceedings, listens to a 'run through' of the parties' evidence and contentions and expresses an impartial, but informed, view of the likely outcome if the matter went to trial. Whether or not the mediator's view is accepted, the result is that the parties begin to think settlement; (4)

In England a high proportion of cases settle before trial, but they do so at a very late stage when most of the costs have already been incurred. The principal reasons for this state of affairs are late preparation by those representing one or other or both the parties and a belief that making the first approach with a view to settlement will be interpreted as weakness; (5) In the field of family law a variety of services are available in order to reach settlements with regard to children and financial matters; (6) Some system of court-annexed ADR should be introduced into the County Courts for claims above the small claims limit, it being the duty of the Judges and District Judges to identify which cases would be likely to benefit; (7) The report recommended a pilot scheme under which District Judges conducting pre-trial reviews would seek in appropriate cases to persuade the parties to submit to a non-binding and without prejudice hearing before a conciliator. For this purpose there should be what is described as 'core discovery'. As an alternative in more complex cases there could be mediation or a mini-trial after full discovery, but the report recommended that the pilot scheme should be limited to conciliation.

The report was sent to the Lord Chancellor with a request that such a pilot scheme be established. He expressed the view that to do so at this stage would be premature and that it would be better to wait until more was known of the effects of expanding the limits of the jurisdiction of the small claims procedure and of devolving heavier work from the High Court. He also drew attention to the fact that a general requirement was being introduced for the pre-trial exchange of witnesses' statements which would of itself bring forward the 'moment of truth', when the parties appreciated the strengths and weaknesses of their respective cases and began to think in terms of settlement. The report was sent to the Lord Chancellor with a request that such a pilot scheme be established. He expressed the view that to do so at this stage would be premature and that it would be better to wait until more was known of the effects of expanding the limits of the jurisdiction of the small claims procedure and of devolving heavier work from the High Court. He also drew attention to the fact that a general requirement was being introduced for the pre-trial exchange of witnesses' statements which would of itself bring forward the 'moment of truth', when the parties appreciated the strengths and weaknesses of their respective cases and began to think in terms of settlement.

Nevertheless the Lord Chancellor made it clear that he was very interested in the possibilities of court-annexed ADR and was setting up a departmental working party to study the matter, including the cost implications for his departmental vote. This working party would welcome any suggestions from the Bar, the solicitors' branch and others who were concerned to improve access to justice.

The report was also sent to the Judges' Council with the suggestion that a judge should be invited to chair a working party on ADR. This invitation was accepted and Lord Justice Beldam has agreed to act as Chairman. The terms of reference of his working party are 'To enquire into the possibility of promoting a system of court based alternative dispute resolution which would encourage and assist parties to litigation to resolve their differences without resort to a formal trial.' The membership consists of: Beldam, L.J. (Chairman), Anthony Scrivener, Q.C., Philip Naughton, Q.C., Christopher

Chandler (The Law Society), Jane Hern and John Davies (Secretary).

ADR enthusiasts will be deeply disappointed. They will believe that the time for working parties is long since past and that what is now needed is a little action. At the risk of appearing tiresome, I do not agree. ADR is a PR man's dream. It conjures up visions of a factor 'x' which will do for dispute resolution what it is said to have done for washing powders and petrol. The truth is that there is no factor 'x'. Indeed I rather doubt whether there is any such thing as ADR. It is simply an umbrella term or 'buzz word' covering any new procedure or modification of old procedures which anyone is able to think up. By the Judicature Acts of the 1870s, Parliament introduced sweeping reforms in the civil courts. They were not thought to go nearly far enough by the commercial community. The Judges of the Queen's Bench Division produced an ADR which they called the Commercial List. You will find details in Volume 1 of the Commercial Case Reports. In essence it involved a pre-trial review before the Judge in charge of the list within days of the service of the writ. He simply asked the parties what was the nature and extent of their disagreement, wrote it down in his notebook and fixed the trial for a few days later. I mention this only to illustrate that so called ADR is something which always has to have a context. The Commercial List was only successful because its procedures were tailored to the needs of a particular class of intelligent litigant. Whether you call the result ADR is immaterial. What is essential is that procedures should be tailor made for particular types of dispute. Before going further let me define a few terms which are bandied about in discussions on ADR: (1) DIY (Do It Yourself) Settlement. The parties settle the dispute between themselves without outside assistance; (2) Adviser-assisted Settlements. The legal or other advisers of the parties settle the dispute or assist in its settlement; (3) Conciliation. This is a process whereby a neutral third party listens to the complaints of the disputants and seeks to narrow the field of controversy. The Chinese word for a conciliator is said to be "A 'go-between' who wears out 1,000 sandals." This is the essence of his function. He moves backwards and forwards between the parties explaining the point of view of each to the other. He indulges in an onion peeling operation. He peels off each individual aspect of complaint, inquiring whether that aspect really matters. In the end he and the parties are left with a core dispute which, so much having been discarded under the guidance of the conciliator, at once seems more capable of settlement on common sense lines. Perhaps the most skilled practitioner of conciliation is ACAS (Advisory, Conciliation and Arbitration Service) operating in the field of industrial relations. In the 1970s, the NIRC (National Industrial Relations Court) ran it a close second; (4) Mediation. This is what a PR man would describe as 'conciliation plus.' The mediator performs the functions of a conciliator, but also expresses his view on what would constitute a sensible settlement. In putting forward this suggestion, which the parties will be free to reject, the mediator will in most cases be guided by what he believes would be the likely outcome if no settlement was reached and the matter went to a judicial or arbitral hearing; (5) The Mini-Trial. This is a different form of mediation designed to overcome a particular problem. There is a class of dispute, usually involving medium sized claims between large corporations, in which the lawyers tend to take over and the clients are not invited to concern themselves with the matter until the case comes on for hearing. Under the mini-trial procedure, at a much earlier stage the case is 'run through' in miniature before a neutral third party in the presence of executives of the parties. The theory, and I understand the practice, is that the experience, assisted by comments from the third party, concentrates the minds of the executives who come to realise that their best interests will be served by preserving good commercial relations and refraining from feathering the nests of the lawyers. A commercial solution soon suggests itself. (6) Rent-a-Judge. This is a system popular in the United States whereby a retired judge is engaged to conduct a private trial acting inquisitorially and, as it has been put, 'riding herd on the lawyers.' The end product is a settlement or a decision which in some cases is appealable to the appellate courts. The attractions for the retired judge are undeniable, but that is beside the point. This seems to me to be essentially merely a special form of arbitration with its own procedures. (7) Arbitration. This is litigation subject to four qualifications. It is private. It is subject to restricted rights of appeal to the courts. The parties have the privilege of choosing and paying for their own judge. The procedure is infinitely flexible, if the parties can agree on the procedure to be adopted or agree to the arbitrator determining what that procedure should be. Its flexibility is indicated by the range of procedures in fact adopted extending from the 'look-sniff' arbitration, familiar in the commodity trades, where there is no evidence other than the sample, no lawyers, no documents and no speeches, through documents — only arbitrations, which are surprisingly successful in the travel industry, to full blown arbitrations which are indistinguishable from a High Court hearing.

(8) Litigation itself. This needs no definition except to point out that it has either to include proceedings before statutory tribunals or such proceedings must be recorded as a separate category. I mention it for completeness and also in order to correct the impression that court procedures are inflexible. Given consent by the parties or imaginative exploitation of the inherent right of any judge to control the procedure in his own court unless prevented by law, procedures can be very flexible. For at least fifty years it was only the expressed or implied consent of the parties which enabled the Commercial Court to dispense with pleadings and the rules of evidence and indeed to bypass almost all the normal court procedures. (9) Ombudsmen. These are so heterogeneous in their powers and procedures that I can really only mention them as a method of resolving disputes. In saying this I do not mean to suggest that they do not perform a very valuable function.

The great divide in these categories is between consensual settlement, however achieved, and determination by third party decision, be that third party a judge, a tribunal or an arbitrator. If there is one thing above all others of which I am certain, it is that no one ever agreed to settle a dispute, if they thought that there was a more profitable alternative, whether that alternative was slogging it out in the hope of victory or dragging their feet in the hope that the disputes would go away. As a Judge I have found that the best way of assisting or inducing a settlement is to sow the seeds of doubt in the minds of both parties as to whether they have a more profitable alternative, i.e., whether they will win. Ideally you convince both that they are likely to lose, but this requires a higher order of judicial advocacy. The point which I am seeking to make is that all other avenues to settlement —

DIY, Conciliation, Mediation or whatever — have a better chance of success if the parties are acutely aware that the alternative is an imposed solution. For this reason I do not regard conciliation, mediation or any like process as an alternative form of disputes resolution. It should, where appropriate, be regarded as part of a process which, in the absence of agreement, will lead to an imposed decision.

If that is right, as I am sure it is, we should not be looking for alternative dispute resolution. Instead we should be seeking to improve the opportunities and the pressures towards a consensual settlement in the course of dispute resolution systems — courts, tribunals or arbitration — which in the last resort will impose a solution. In parallel with this, we should be seeking to simplify, and thus accelerate and render less expensive, the procedures involved. We should also be seeking to increase the number and diversity of tribunals, including courts and arbitral tribunals, capable of producing an imposed solution. This is not to say that I want to see more imposed solutions. Far from it. I want to see consensual settlements at the earliest possible moment. I do, however, want the threat of an imposed settlement to be ever present in the background as an aid and stimulus to such settlements. Indeed there is something to be said for bringing it into the foreground. If I listed ten cases for hearing before imaginary judges tomorrow, I would bet that five would settle — provided always that no one knew that the judges were imaginary.

All this sounds relatively simple, but of course it is not. The specialist statutory tribunals have the advantage of some degree of homogeneity in their workload. To this extent it is easier for them to evolve improved, which usually means simpler, procedures. However if costs to the disputant are to be contained or reduced, their procedures must be geared to the DIY litigant. Media comment notwithstanding, lawyers are worthy of their hire. What has to be appreciated is that most of the disputes coming before specialist tribunals, like other small claims, are not, or at least should not be, worthy of the lawyers.

In the case of the County Courts, where the work is far from homogeneous, the approach should be to have an utterly basic originating procedure which applies whatever the nature of the dispute. All you need at that stage is a simple form on which the Plaintiff indicates what he is complaining about and the Defendant gives his answer. It worked in the NIRC. It works in many of the tribunals. This should be followed shortly thereafter by a meeting between the parties in person before the District Judge for directions.

The District Judge (DJ) should be completely free to invoke whatever he considers to be the appropriate procedure for that particular dispute. By 'appropriate' I mean the procedure which will best and most speedily and economically identify and concentrate the parties' minds on the crux of the dispute and the strengths and weaknesses of their respective cases. In a case which justified the employment of lawyers and in which they were employed, he might call for pleadings. But it might be better in most cases if he himself settled and recorded the issues. He could then tell the parties to let the court and each other have a copy of relevant documents — discovery in a simplified form. He could ask questions and require and record answers — interrogatories in another form.

If it is a neighbour's boundary dispute, he may well conclude that it would be a waste of time to contemplate conciliation, but he might think it worthwhile to appoint a surveyor to inquire and report to the court. In a dispute which is matrimonial in character, conciliation would have much to commend it and he could head the parties in that direction. Indeed this would be true in most cases where the parties, whether by choice or circumstances, were involved in a relationship which would continue after the dispute had been settled. But always in the background would be the threat of an imposed solution.

What is required is a study of all the different types of dispute and a consideration of which is usually the most sensible, and thus economical, way of handling them. The result would be a collection of alternative standard procedures which would be invoked by District Judges, unless contra-indicated. But — and this is the vital qualification — unless the dispute is worthy of the expense of involving lawyers, the procedures must be capable of being described in simple language in an instructional booklet appropriate only to that particular procedure. If you buy a washing machine, nothing is more infuriating or confusing than to find that the users' manual covers a large number of different models with different instructions for each when you are only interested in one. So it is with disputes settlement. If you doubt it, look at the County Court Green Book through a layman's eyes. No doubt it will be objected that any such 'hands on' approach by the County Courts would call for a large number of additional District Judges, a prospect which would cause both the Lord Chancellor and the Treasury to shudder. Not so. Although many District Judges deal admirably with small claims under the small claims arbitration procedure, this is a waste of legally qualified resources. Someone else should be dealing with such disputes.

This brings me back to an idea which I floated at the Bar Conference in October 1989. 'Floated' is perhaps the wrong word, because it sank without trace. We have a great tradition in this country of voluntary service. Since World War II it has been weakened in the field of social services by the introduction of professionals. I think this is regrettable, but that is outside the scope of my subject tonight. In terms of the administration of justice, it remains as strong as ever and we have 28,000 Justices of the Peace (JPs) who give of their time to resolving disputes which arise under the criminal law. Why do we not expand this team of volunteers to cover the resolution of the smaller civil disputes?

Although I did not know it at the time, I have since learnt that there is such a system in Germany. Their civil JPs are known as 'Schiedsmänner.' They are official mediators rather than justices to the extent that they cannot impose a solution, but settlements, which occur in 50% to 75% of cases, are officially recorded, as is the fact that no settlement is achieved where this is the outcome. I would give civil justices a power of decision, because, as I have explained, I think that this would greatly increase the rate of consensual settlement. But even if they did not have this power, if the civil justices could give a binding decision on the facts there would be few cases which would go on for judicial decision by the County Court on the basis of the law applied to those facts. What we need to do is to persuade or remind responsible citizens that it is an honourable task to assist in settling disputes and a civic duty to do so. I would depart from the traditional approach to criminal disputes and divide civil JPs into specialist panels. Some would deal with retail trade complaints, others with those involving service industries, others with motoring accidents and yet others with landlord and tenant matters and disputes between neighbours. Which panel or panels a civil JP joined would depend upon his or her temperament and experience. A High Street trader would be a natural as one member of a panel concerned with retail trade disputes and it would be a great mistake to think that he would be biased in favour of traders. If experience of industrial tribunals is any guide, there is no bias, or if there is it will be against the group from which he comes. Neither employers nor trade unionists like to see their peers getting away with it and I am sure that this attitude would be found to be general.

Before I sit down, I should like to say a word about the dreaded matter of costs. Quite clearly we have to reduce the overall cost of litigation. We have to evolve much simpler procedures which make legal advice less necessary. When it is necessary, lawyers should consider telling clients how to do it themselves in cases in which this would be cheaper than the lawyers doing it for them. And where lawyers have to conduct the litigation, they should always be asking themselves 'Is this step really necessary? Is there a simpler and therefore cheaper way?' But that is not what I am on about. My concern is with the incidence of costs. The English system whereby the unsuccessful party pays all or most of the costs of the other party has much to commend it. But it can operate as a positive disincentive to settlement. The disincentive has two elements and I should like to see both reduced.

The first element relates to court fees. The threat of proceedings is an essential spur to settlement, but it is often necessary actually to begin them by entering a plaint or issuing a writ if the threat is to be credible. Once this has been done, the stakes have been raised. The plaintiff is then seeking to recover not only his claim, but the costs of bringing the proceedings. The defendant is then seeking to resist not only the claim, but recovery of those costs. As it seems to me, there is a strong case for remitting part of these fees if the dispute is settled and the proceedings withdrawn within a limited time of their commencement. The Treasury would have a fit, since court fees are meant to cover the running costs of the courts. However settlements save expense to public funds in the form of legal aid and, if there were enough of them, might well not only improve the service which the courts can provide for other litigants, but also enable court staff and even the number of judges to be reduced. Furthermore, although considerations of fairness may not move the Treasury greatly, it is a fact that in County Court proceedings the fee payable on the issue of the plaint is usually all that has to be paid until after the conclusion of the hearing. An early settlement means that the parties are not getting all or most of what they have paid for.

The second element relates to the liability for costs inter partes. The bottom line for a defendant is that he can make a payment into court or, where this is impossible because it is not a money claim, make an offer of settlement. If he does so and the plaintiff does not beat the payment in or offer, he will still have to pay the plaintiff's costs up to that time. He has a limited incentive to offer to settle at an early stage, because the plaintiff's costs will increase progressively, but it seems to me that he would have a greater incentive if his liability to the plaintiff was limited to a proportion of the plaintiff's costs, the proportion reflecting the speed with which the defendant's offer of settlement was put forward. I would like to see consideration given to a costs free period immediately following the issue of proceedings. The fact that proceedings had been issued would be a shot across the bows which would concentrate minds. On the other hand the stakes would not at once be raised making settlement more difficult. Theoretically parties already know that the longer they delay a settlement the more their potential liability for the other side's costs increases, but it does not seem to penetrate. If they were told "You have 1 month in which to settle without a costs problem, but if you delay you have an additional problem on your hands", I think that settlements might be encouraged. It could of course be made more sophisticated with a 25% potential liability in the second month ending with indemnity costs at the door of the court, but that does not affect the principle. My conclusion overall is that there is much to be said for delaying the introduction of pilot schemes until the problem has been studied more intensively and in more detail, but I am equally sure that this study must proceed with all speed. Meanwhile I hope that we shall hear much less of ADR as if, as such, it was a panacea for all our ills. What we need are improved and simplified procedures tailor-made for different types of dispute and 'hands on' case management by dispute settlers such as judges and arbitrators.

* This article was originally published as J. Donaldson, 'Alternative Dispute Resolution', *Arbitration* 58, no. 2 (1992): 102-106.

CHAPTER 1

The Language of ADR

Sir Laurence Street

An exposition of the language of ADR will, I believe, be of use in dispelling some of the fog that is beginning to cloud the whole field of dispute resolution. The fog has been generated by well-intentioned, but misguided, attempts, to introduce precision of terminology into a field that, by its very nature, does not lend itself to precision. The British Academy of Experts recently established a working party upon the language of ADR with a view to seeing if it is possible to make some recommendations in respect of the more commonly used expressions. The decision to undertake this exercise derived from the Academy's recognition that, and I quote from its records: "[t]here appears to be a vast difference of understanding and interpretation in respect of the terminology." It cannot be doubted that litigation — the process of formal determination of a dispute by a court — stands clear and positive amongst dispute resolution procedures. It is indeed well that this process, the sovereign remedy of litigation leading to judicial determination, is clearly recognisable and understood. The area of inconsistency and confusion is in the classification of other mechanisms that make up the whole spectrum of dispute resolution procedures. I have on an earlier occasion when invited to address this Institute expressed a deep commitment to regarding ADR as standing for 'Additional Dispute

Resolution.' (Chartered Institute of Arbitrators 75th Anniversary Conference, London, 4 October 1990). I venture to quote my observations from the transcript of the proceedings in relation to the acronym ADR as short for Alternative Dispute Resolution. In so doing I note that the passage relates to the domestic environment rather than international commercial disputation.

"It is not in truth Alternative. It is not in competition with the established judicial system. It is an Additional range of mechanisms within the overall aggregated mechanisms for the resolution of disputes. Nothing can be alternative to the sovereign authority of the court system. We cannot tolerate any thought of an alternative to the judicial arm of the sovereign in the discharge of the responsibility of resolving disputes between state and citizen or between citizen and citizen. We can, however, accommodate mechanisms which operate as additional or subsidiary processes in the discharge of the sovereign's responsibility. These enable the court system to devote its precious time and resources to the more solemn task of administering justice in the name of the sovereign."

I recognise that the phrase Alternative Dispute Resolution is by now far too deeply entrenched to be able to be recommitted. In making this point, however, my purpose is not to increase the element of terminological uncertainty, but rather to remove preconceptions that have tended to develop out of the use of the word 'Alternative.' These preconceptions underlie the question of whether arbitration itself is an ADR procedure. In one sense, of course, in the domestic arena arbitration can be fairly regarded as an alternative to litigation. Indeed, until the post World War II era it occupied almost the whole field of structured dispute resolving processes outside the court system. Expert appraisal constituted the remainder of that field.

With the more recent development of other structured procedures for dispute resolution, arbitration has become recognised as occupying its own particular field and enjoying the same distinctiveness and understanding as does litigation. Arbitration is a universally understood, readily definable process, recognised as such amongst the domestic and the international trading community. Indeed, in the international arena arbitration is and always has been the primary mechanism with litigation very much in second place except in the exercise of strictly limited supervisory or appellate powers and enforcement of awards. In consequence there has developed an increasing consensus in dispute resolution usage that ADR comprises the whole body of procedures not properly classifiable either as litigation or as arbitration. This degree of consensus is now such that we can and should discard any further suggestion that ADR is to be understood as including arbitration.

What, then, is comprised within the field of ADR? Once again the fog descends. For example, we frequently encounter the proposition that conciliation and mediation have separate and mutually distinguishable characteristics. It is suggested that in one of these two procedures the role of the third party facilitator is merely to guide and participate in the course of settlement negotiations between the parties, whilst in the other the third party facilitator is more actively involved in the sense of originating proposals for settlement and influencing the parties towards accepting them.

It is devastatingly significant that, amongst those who assert that the distinction exists, there is a direct reversal of polarity as to which word describes which process.

For example, Lord Wilberforce in a paper published in UNCITRAL Arbitration Model Law in Canada (Carswell, Toronto, 1987) writes at p. 7: "[c]onciliation I understand to be a process by which the parties to a dispute are helped by a neutral and independent third party, who may be either an official provided by the state or a private person, to reach a mutually acceptable settlement. It is the responsibility of the parties themselves to reach agreement. Mediation involves a further step. The mediator not only conciliates but makes his own recommendations. The parties are not obliged to accept them, but they may be accepted, or they may provide a basis for further negotiation."

On the other hand, Cornelius and Faire in their handbook on conflict resolution 'Everyone Can Win' (Simon Schuster, Australia, 1989) suggest as current usage, (p. 151):

"Recommendation: Third party gathers facts and arguments. Makes a recommendation with substantial weight. Non-binding, invites compromise. Conciliation.

Process controller: Third party has tight control over process but not contents. Forgoes power to decide or recommend. Assists parties to isolate issues and options, and to reach a settlement by consensus that jointly satisfies their needs. Mediation."

I agree with Maxwell Fulton's observation in 'Commercial Alternative Dispute Resolution' (The Law Book Co Ltd, Sydney, 1989) that there is an absence of any general consensus as to whether conciliation is an active or passive pursuit. I would go further, however, and deny the utility of attempting to introduce an active or passive element as a distinguishing feature amongst consensus-oriented ADR procedures. The extent and nature of the facilitator's involvement in order to optimise the prospects of a successful outcome of the process will inevitably be more or less active according to the nature of the dispute, the personalities involved, the stage of deterioration of relations between the parties and the stage of negotiation itself. Practitioners recognise the wisdom of the facilitator adopting a passive attitude at the outset. Likewise, they recognise both the expectations of the parties for a more active involvement as the negotiations progress, as well as the value of a positive contribution by the facilitator at the time the facilitator judges this to be propitious.

In the textured range of participation by a facilitator in structured settlement discussions, attempted distinctions between conciliation and mediation, and between active and passive, if they exist at all, could at times become extremely fine. I myself hold firmly to the view that there are no such relevant, practicable or useful distinctions: the words mediation and conciliation are, I suggest, synonymous. Conciliation seems to be the preferred choice in international and European usage; in North America and Australia mediation is pre-eminent.

Both so-called conciliation and so-called mediation have an identical genetic structure: both have three fundamental characteristics. In the first place both originate in an agreement between the disputants to call in the aid of a facilitator to assist in the structuring and conduct of settlement negotiations which will include, as part of their very essence, private consultations with each disputant. In the second place the facilitator has no authority to impose a solution on the disputants as does a judge, arbitrator or expert appraiser. And in the third place the whole process remains at all times entirely flexible and dependent upon the continuing willingness of the disputants to continue it until such time as either they themselves agree upon the terms of a settlement or one or other of them terminates the negotiations; it is, in short, consensus oriented. Of these three fundamental characteristics, I emphasise an essential aspect of the first, namely that the negotiations include private consultations with each disputant. This distinguishes negotiations of this genus from the long established and well understood interlocutory procedure of a formal or informal settlement of pre-trial conference. At such a conference both parties are present — there are no private discussions with each party behind the back of the other.

I have a clear preference for describing all such procedures conceptually as being mediations. A more cautious phrase that has some currency is conciliation/mediation, but this is capable of conveying the erroneous impression that the two words have different meanings; even worse they could be thought, equally erroneously, to suggest a sequential, combined process. The single word mediation, or its synonym in international usage conciliation, is a general conceptual description that adequately embraces all but one of the mechanisms ranging right across the ADR spectrum. These include those labelled variously as mediation, conciliation, mini-trial and the like and extend on to other special procedures used in some jurisdictions such as the summary jury trial in the United States. The other class of ADR mechanisms that, I suggest, should be recognised as distinct from mediation (the excepted mechanism I referred to in the preceding paragraph) is that comprising the expert appraisal procedure. Ancient and prestigious within this species is the 'look-sniff arbitration' commonly employed in disputes arising between participants in transactions within commodities trading associations such as the London grain trade. Although called arbitrations, these determinations lie outside modern concepts of arbitration and modern arbitration statutes (Cf Redfern and Hunter 'Law and Practice of International Commercial Arbitration', Sweet & Maxwell, London, 1986, pp. 36-37 and Bernstein 'Handbook of Arbitration Practice', Sweet & Maxwell, London, 1988, pp. 42-43). They are essentially summary determinations or appraisals owing their binding force to the pre-contract of the parties and not attended by procedural requirements of ordinary arbitrations. They share with litigation and arbitration the characteristic of the dispute being resolved by the imposition of a third party's decision. They share with arbitration and mediation the characteristic that they derive from pre-contract between the disputants. But they are themselves a separate and distinct ADR procedure described in modern usage as expert appraisal or expert determination.

I should note one further developing procedure, namely the combination of an arbitration and a mediation in a single structured process. This mechanism is short titled 'arb-med' or 'med-arb.' A simple example of arb-med is a composite single agreement to arbitrate one issue in a dispute (say liability) and mediate another (say damages), with a fall-back provision for referral of the second issue to a new arbitrator if the mediation of that issue does not succeed. This is a classic exemplification of the complementary (rather than alternative) relationship of mechanisms within the total dispute resolution spectrum. I add the cautionary observation that whilst the same person can fulfil the sequential roles of arbitrator followed by mediator (arb-med), the same person ought not to be chosen to fill both roles when the parties wish to follow the opposite sequence (med-arb). I am a firm adherent to the school of thought that denies acceptability of a person who has mediated subsequently filling the role of arbitrator, notwithstanding statutory recognition of this possibility. Such a prospect must inevitably distort and inhibit the mediation process, quite apart from its personally invidious, indeed risky, overtones so far as the erstwhile mediator is concerned. Arb-med, in that sequence, is a useful hybrid procedure in which it is permissible for the same person to be arbitrator and, later, mediator. If, as is very commonly the case, the parties wish to follow a med-arb sequence, they should not in my view select the same person for both roles — and I add the rider that it would be unwise for a person to accept appointment to both roles in that sequence.

I summarise the views I have advanced in an attempt to remove some of the confusion surrounding the language of ADR: (1) Litigation, the ultimate, sovereign dispute resolution process, stands above and apart from all other processes; (2) Arbitration has well-defined and well-understood specific mechanisms that enable it to be recognised as occupying its own clearly defined place in the spectrum of dispute resolution mechanisms; (3) Complementary to litigation and arbitration is a widely flexible and varying range of additional mechanisms commonly described as ADR; (4) There is neither utility nor validity in attempting classification or definition of ADR procedures that involve participation by a facilitator in structuring and conducting of negotiations designed to assist the parties to agree upon a resolution of the dispute, including, as part of the essence of the negotiations, private consultations with each party; all such procedures can be effectively grouped under the one title of mediation; the nature of the structure and the role of the facilitator is widely variable according to the wishes of the parties as they proceed with their negotiations towards settlement; (5) A discrete mechanism within the field of ADR is summary appraisal or summary determination; this is a quick, inexpensive and decisive procedure that is gaining in popularity as a mode of resolving commercial disputes, particularly disputes arising in the course of ongoing performance of a contract; (6) Finally, I have noted the developing use of 'arb-med' and 'med-arb' combined procedures and have offered some comments on the need to select a different person as arbitrator if the mediation fails.

THE UTILITY OF ADR IN RESOLVING INTERNATIONAL COMMERCIAL DISPUTES

In considering the utility of ADR mechanisms, that is to say mediation and expert appraisals, in the resolution of international commercial disputes it is, I believe, necessary to recognise the unlikelihood of stand-alone expert appraisal achieving widespread use. I have mentioned earlier the 'look-sniff' arbitrations currently carried out between members of various London commodities trade associations. This is a well-established and highly efficient process, but it necessarily originates within its own specialist area of international commerce. Within the general area of international trade it seems unlikely that parties to transactions would opt for an expert appraisal in place of arbitration. There are attractions of enforceability, certainty, quality and integrity in arbitrations administered by a recognised arbitral institution such as the LCIA and the ICC; these are by no means assured in an expert appraisal. Moreover, the need to select the trusted neutral to fill the role of appraiser is unlikely to be met by agreement between the parties when the initial commercial engagement is being negotiated.

At best, the prospect of expansion of the use of expert appraisal in the resolution of international commercial disputes is most likely to materialise in an ad hoc arrangement reached between the parties in the course of a mediation. For example, a wide-ranging dispute, particularly in the course of the ongoing performance of a contract, can at times involve more than one mechanism being brought into play as a mediation procedure progresses. In the course of a mediation in such a dispute it may be suggested by the mediator and agreed by the parties that the submission of a particular issue to a chosen expert for an expert appraisal, either binding or non-binding, will enable the mediation process to break out of a deadlock and to be carried forward. Within Australia case histories of this nature, although rare at present, can be forecast as likely to increase in number. Recorded cases are difficult to find but there is every reason to anticipate that similar trends are developing in other nations in the handling of domestic commercial disputes. It is likewise foreseeable that this will flow across into international commercial dispute resolution procedures, although it does not seem likely that it will achieve any significant presence in the international arena, apart from the specialist field I have mentioned earlier (London-based commodities disputes).

The current climate in the international field for mediation can be assessed against the background of its use in domestic commercial disputes. Mediation has been the clearly preferred mechanism for many years in some of the major trading nations or regions of the world, notably in Asia and the Middle East. Amongst common law and Western nations its use has in the last couple of decades been lifted to the level of academic and professional respectability in the United States. This development has extended to other common law nations and it is beginning to establish a significant presence in Western nations generally. I can speak at firsthand in relation to its use in domestic commercial dispute resolution in Australia where, in the last five years, it has been increasingly studied and practised.

An indicator of the readiness of the international community to embrace mediation is provided by the endorsement of the General Assembly of the United Nations of the UNCITRAL Conciliation Rules. I quote some portions of the General Assembly resolution of 4 December 1980: "[t]he General Assembly, Recognizing the value of conciliation as a method of amicably settling disputes arising in the context of international commercial relations, Convinced that the establishment of conciliation rules that are acceptable in countries with different legal, social and economic systems could significantly contribute to the development and harmonious international economic relations ... 1. Recommends the use of the Conciliation Rules of the United Nations Commission on International Trade Law in cases where a dispute arises in the context of international commercial relations and the parties seek an amicable settlement of that dispute by recourse to conciliation; 2. Requests the Secretary-General to arrange for the widest possible distribution of the Conciliation Rules."

I acknowledge that the General Assembly resolution refers to conciliation. So also does the ICSID formulation. This has tended to add to the terminological confusion I have already mentioned. The procedures outlined in the UNCITRAL Rules and the ICSID procedure are, however, in entire conformity with the concept of mediation as I have characterised it in this paper.

The attraction of mediation for commercial disputants is that it breaks down the existing estrangement and presents the very real prospect of achieving a more commercially attractive and a more personally satisfactory means of solving the dispute. I do not intend to rehearse the many virtues claimed for mediation by its proponents. In commercial disputes a significant attraction from the point of view of the parties is that they retain at all times their own control over the process. This is a factor that has particular relevance in the arena of international commerce. An international arbitral institution and its processes, although originally chosen by the parties for good reason as the ultimate dispute-resolving mechanism in their relationship, can at times present a degree of remoteness from the parties and insensitivity to their commercial requirements when a dispute actually emerges. Learned Hand J remarked many years ago that "it is a rare litigant who recognises his own case when he sees it in court." The same can be said of many international commercial arbitrations — perhaps with greater emphasis. A mediation, as an additional early step in exploring the resolution of the dispute, has obvious advantages in this regard. International arbitral institutions are themselves beginning to recognise the developing market for mediation services. For example, the London Court of International Arbitration as recently as 26 June 1991 announced a joint collaboration negotiated between the Centre for Dispute Resolution (CEDR) and the LCIA "with the intent of promoting more effective commercial dispute resolution." CEDR was launched in London in November 1990 "to promote mediation and other ADR techniques and services in Europe." Already it has achieved wide membership and recognition. It is likely that in the Asia-Pacific region a similar joint collaboration will shortly be announced between the LCIA and the Australian Commercial Dispute Centre in Sydney.

Moving across to North America the AAA has long been an active provider of mediation services. It can be confidently predicted that this trend of established arbitral institutions providing either directly, or through collaborative arrangements, access to mediation services in aid of the resolution of international commercial disputes will increase. The topic is interesting and challenging. Indeed, the very fact that the Chartered Institute of Arbitrators has included a segment such as this within the range of matters for discussion at this prestigious Annual Conference is indicative of the growing interest and potential of ADR processes on the international scene.

THE ROLE OF THE MEDIATOR

The mediator is a trusted, independent neutral whose task is to keep the settlement negotiations moving forward positively towards a successful outcome. Litigation lawyers often remark that it is frequently easier to litigate, than to settle, disputes. From the other side of these processes I am confident that it is frequently easier to adjudicate on, than to mediate in, disputes. The approaches are fundamentally different — most noticeably, perhaps, in the fact that it is not only permissible, but indeed it is essential, that the mediator should discuss the dispute freely and privately with each party separately. The role of the mediator is, like mediation itself, endlessly variable. Some inkling of this can be gained by listing what are said by Dr Stulberg, a distinguished US mediation teacher and practitioner, to be the 'job qualifications' of a mediator: neutral, impartial, objective, intelligent, flexible, articulate, forceful and persuasive, empathetic, effective as a listener, imaginative, respected in the community, sceptical, able to gain access to resources, honest, reliable, non-defensive, having a sense of humour, patient, persevering, optimistic (Joseph Stulbert Taking Charge/ Managing Conflict, Lexington Books, Massachusetts, 1987, pp. 37-41). Where, one might ask, does one find such a paragon? I quote the list, however, only as a useful reflection of the role filled by the ideal mediator.

Essentially the mediator's skills are people skills, coupled with some understanding of the field of commercial endeavour out of which the dispute has arisen, even if deriving only from dispute resolution experience. A prerequisite is the capacity of the mediator to command the trust of the disputants. Unless both parties trust the mediator it will be difficult for the mediator to achieve the primary purpose in the mediation process, namely freeing up communication between the parties, building a bridge of understanding and guiding or enticing the parties across that bridge to reaching a consensus. A commercial transaction is formalised in a contract the very essence of which is a consensus *ad idem* between the parties. A dispute arises out of circumstances not adequately covered by the original contract. There may arise a legal argument as to the meaning of the contract. There may arise a dispute upon the precise significance of a set of facts not clearly covered by the terms of the contract. In many cases the dispute turns upon a hotly contested argument as to what are the true facts in a situation that has developed. The dispute will be resolved only when a consensus is re-established having the effect of terminating the contest. Where that resolution is achieved by an externally binding decision (litigation, arbitration or expert appraisal) the maker of the external decision simply picks up the conflicting contentions and imposes on the parties a decision that they are bound to treat as equivalent to a consensus. Performance of the contractual relationship between the parties, even if all that remains to be performed is the payment of money, goes forward in obedience to this external determination.

In a mediation the re-established consensus is reached by the parties themselves. The mediator plays the role of a catalyst. In establishing lines of communication and building a bridge of understanding the mediator attempts to instil in each side an objective assessment of the commercial reality and significance of the dispute situation. This is often referred to within mediation circles as assessing the BATNA — Best Alternative To a Negotiated Agreement. A great deal has been written about the techniques of mediation in particular and negotiation in general. It is neither practicable nor necessary to attempt to present a synopsis. For present purposes it is sufficient to offer the view that the two essential requirements of a mediator are a capacity to earn the trust of the disputants and a capacity to guide their discussions towards full communication and understanding of the whole dispute situation both from their own, and from the other side's point of view. A good judge or a good arbitrator may well not be a good mediator. I revert to my earlier comment that mediation requires people skills. In the selection of a mediator this is the touchstone.

CONCLUSION

In Australia we are following the lead of the US in regarding dispute resolution, including as it does ADR procedures, as an integral subject for study and practice. It must be said that, within my own profession, the lawyers hidebound by the philosophies of yesterday have not found it easy to embrace the new philosophy of dispute resolution. Their more flexibly minded colleagues most certainly have. The lawyers of tomorrow will wonder why the ADR revelation was so long in coming.

* This article was originally published as L. Street, 'The Language of ADR — Its Utility in Resolving International Commercial Disputes — The Role of the Mediator', *Arbitration (Supplement)* 58, no. 2 (1992): 17-22.

CHAPTER 1

Report of the Committee on Alternative Dispute Resolution

Sir Roy Beldam

We were appointed in March 1991 with the following terms of reference: "[t]o enquire into the possibility of promoting a system of court-based alternative dispute resolution, which would encourage and assist parties to litigation to resolve their differences without resort to a formal trial." We began our work on 20 March 1991 and have met together in full session on six occasions. In addition there has been a considerable number of smaller meetings and much correspondence, in the course of which we have gathered a great deal of information and help from the various individuals and bodies to whom we refer in the text of our Report. We should like to take this opportunity of thanking them collectively for their patient help in responding to our questions and invitations. Our Secretary, John Verdin Davies, bore the main burden of organising our work and preparing drafts of our Report. We are grateful for his many excellent suggestions and for his tireless help and patience. By the end of our work we were convinced that the case was made out for the courts themselves to embrace the systems of alternative dispute resolution, which have now been well tried and tested elsewhere. We believe that ADR has much to offer in support of the judicial process, and that, in whatever system may eventually be adopted, the legal profession is likely to be called upon to play an important role.

ADR PROVISION IN ENGLAND AND WALES

We made enquiries of the various bodies currently concerned with the provision of ADR services. These included a number of voluntary members' associations, to some of whom we addressed a detailed questionnaire designed to assist us in the task of reporting on the types of ADR service which might be made available to litigants, and any limits there may be to their compatibility with a court-based system of justice. We also approached, for their general background views, the Director General of Fair Trading and some of the specialist ombudsmen dealing with particular sectors of business activity such as banking and building societies (A summary of the replies received from the five ADR-provider bodies whom we approached with specific questions about their mode of operation has been published in the journal of the Chartered Institute of Arbitrators, Volume 58, Number 3, 1992, p. 185).

The five ADR organisations included two bodies concerned in a general way with the promotion of ADR across the whole range of business and consumer activity, namely the Chartered Institute of Arbitrators and the Centre for Dispute Resolution. Of the remainder ACAS is concerned only with disputes (collective and individual) relating to employment, while the National Family Conciliation Council and the Family Mediators Association exist solely to provide help in the area of family matters. A notable common feature of all five bodies is their concern with standards and their willingness to provide training (either in-house, as in the case of ACAS, or by means of courses and conferences) in the various tasks undertaken by their members or accredited ADR practitioners. All are enthusiastic about their stated aims and about the efficacy of ADR. These bodies could not, of course, be counted upon to provide administrative support or premises for use in connection with any proposed system of court-based ADR, except upon a commercial basis. The bodies concerned are supported mainly by voluntary membership subscriptions and/or charitable funds.

Apart from the arrangements just described, a great deal of less formal machinery exists for the resolution of disputes by assisting parties in the selection of suitable arbitrators or mediators. For example, many professional bodies and trade associations are prepared to nominate arbitrators or mediators to deal with disputes within the scope of their members' activities. Sometimes the parties are encouraged to choose a mediator or arbitrator with direct experience of the profession, trade or industry most relevant to the dispute. The disadvantage is, of course, that the 'consumer' in such a case may not perceive the 'neutral' as truly impartial, particularly if, as sometimes regrettably happens, the individual chosen has no demonstrable ADR experience or knowledge of the legal framework.

OBSERVATIONS OF THE DGFT

We received some pertinent observations from the Director General of Fair Trading, Sir Gordon Borrie. After referring to the part played by the OFT in encouraging trade associations to take part in the formation of arbitration schemes, sometimes in collaboration with the Chartered Institute of Arbitrators, and indeed other forms of dispute resolution, Sir Gordon told us that the OFT would in principle have no objection to alternative dispute resolution systems being made available as part of the process of redress available through the courts, since this "would provide consumers with a wider choice and enable them to use the most appropriate system for dealing with their particular dispute." There could also be benefit to the court system itself, if such a scheme resulted in removing some cases from the lists. He raises with us, however, the following caveats. "The first", he says, "is the cost both to the courts and to consumers, a point which was raised in the 1988 Report of the Review Body on Civil Justice. Careful consideration will have to be given to the staffing and financing of any such scheme and the way in which costs are passed on to the parties. Clearly it would be self-defeating if litigants were discouraged from using any ADR systems on offer because of costs. Secondly, I note that your terms of reference include the phrase 'encourage and assist'. It is essential that the choice of system to resolve disputes lies with litigants, or rather potential litigants. The courts should not take upon themselves the task of limiting litigants' access to those courts, even on the not unreasonable grounds that the dispute would be better dealt with by other means. Finally there is always a risk that consumers or litigants will become confused by the range of choices on offer. The courts will need to give clear advice on the range of choices available and quite possibly on the relevance to the particular case." He also suggested that clear written advice on the system would be needed and that sometimes advice from court officials would be desirable. This could make some additional demands on their time. Consideration might be given to the possibility of siting independent advice centres in or near the courts. We are extremely grateful to Sir Gordon and the OFT for their help, and hope that we have sufficiently taken into account their observations in our recommendations.

OBSERVATIONS OF THE OMBUDSMAN

Soundings were taken from several of the ombudsmen appointed under the various schemes which have been established with the support of the OFT. Most of them expressed support for the idea of giving parties to litigation a formal opportunity to opt for some kind of ADR. The experience of the ombudsmen, like that of ACAS, seems to suggest that parties are often prepared to elect for a conciliatory solution, given the opportunity to do so. For example, Professor Farrand, the Insurance Ombudsman, told us that of some 40,000 enquiries received annually most were able to be settled by informal advice. Only about 10% fell to be adjudicated by the ombudsman. The success record of the ombudsmen in having their adjudications accepted by the parties appears to be uniformly good, and Professor Farrand was unaware of any case in which, after a decision by the ombudsman, parties had later found it necessary to resort to litigation. We are very grateful to Professor Farrand for his help, and also to Mr Laurence Shurman, the Banking Ombudsman, and to Mr Stephen Edell, the Building Societies Ombudsman, whose views and observations reinforced the conclusion that, where a conciliatory service is in operation, parties will generally make use of it.

OBSERVATIONS OF THE REGULATORY BODIES

Mr Mark Gore, General Counsel to the Financial Intermediaries, Managers and Brokers Regulatory Association (FIMBRA) gave us his views on the impact which court-based ADR might have upon the work of his Association. FIMBRA is required by Schedule 2 of the Financial Services Act 1986 to provide effective arrangements for the investigation of complaints against its members. To this end an arbitration scheme has been established under the supervision of the Chartered Institute of Arbitrators. Such a scheme should: (1) be cost effective since FIMBRA bears the costs of any award; (2) provide the requisite level of expertise in the arbitrator to determine difficult issues such as 'best advice'; (3) result in a high proportion of expeditious determinations on a documents-only basis, as opposed to adversarial hearings with oral evidence on both sides.

We are told that the present scheme is working well and that there is now an appreciable pool of skilled mediators and arbitrators, who welcome the opportunity to use their specialist knowledge in the public service. It is an interesting feature of the scheme that before arbitration takes place it must be certified that mediation has been attempted.

THE ACAS EXPERIENCE

As an example of the conciliation process in action, we were especially interested in the experience of ACAS. We had meetings with ACAS officials at Headquarters and at the South Eastern Regional Office. On individual conciliation cases the Service achieves an extremely high success rate for cases referred under the statutory procedure from the Central Office of Industrial Tribunals. In 1990, for example, of some 52,000 cases referred to ACAS (mainly Industrial Tribunal unfair dismissal claims) some 56% were settled at the conciliation stage; 23% were withdrawn, and only some 21% proceeded to a Tribunal hearing. It seems generally agreed that this high success rate in the individual conciliation cases is largely due to two main factors: (1) the existence of a statutory 'trigger' for conciliation actually built into the Tribunal procedure by the requirement upon the Central Office to notify ACAS upon the registration of any claim and (2) the existence of a corps of skilled conciliators whose services are free of cost to the parties. This has resulted, over time, in an expectation on the part of parties to employment disputes that conciliation will be the 'normal' procedure in such cases, thus conserving the resources of the Tribunals for the more intractable disputes. We noted with interest the relative average cost — £1,200 or so for an IT hearing, compared with about £200 for a conciliated settlement.

On staffing and training matters we were told that most conciliation officers in ACAS join as executive officers often with previous experience as job centre managers. The statutory background figured prominently in the training, but the techniques of dispute resolution also featured. All staff received a six-week induction course. They would also receive post-experience refresher courses. We are extremely grateful to the ACAS officials who spoke to us, especially to Mr Dennis Boyd and Mr Brian Atkins.

THE LAW SOCIETY REPORT ON ADR

During the period of our work (in July 1991) a working party of the Law Society, under the chairmanship of Christopher Chandler, produced a useful and wide-ranging Report on alternative forms of dispute resolution. The purposes of the Law Society Report were twofold; first to provide, in the form of a practical user's guide, information about the various ADR services which are currently available, and second to identify some issues, which call for action and wider discussion. A number of these issues will be of interest in the present context: Should neutrals be accredited to give satisfactory assurance of competence? If so, should solicitor neutrals be accredited by the Law Society, perhaps on the model of the specialist panel procedure? Should Law Society training arrangements (both pre- and post-qualification) take account of ADR developments? Should Law Society conduct rules be adjusted to take account of the roles which solicitors may be called upon to play as neutrals in the course of ADR procedures? Should legal aid and legal expenses insurance be made available for use in connection with ADR procedures? The Law Society Report also makes a number of specific recommendations on various fronts towards promoting and facilitating the ADR process.

THE OFFICIAL REFEREES' COURT

We received a most helpful submission from the Official Referees. They pointed out that litigation in their courts arising, as it frequently does, from disputes in the construction industry is often complex and between large public companies. Many disputes arise under contracts approved by the Joint Contracts Tribunal, which represents all sections of the industry. It is recognised that mediation of disputes in the construction industry is most likely to be successful if it is undertaken as soon as possible after a dispute arises. Thus recent standard sub-contracts make provision for referral to an 'adjudicator' before resort is had to arbitration and litigation. The adjudicator's decision is only binding until the matter is settled by agreement or the determination of an arbitrator or the court. It is the general view that the procedure works well. Obviously, however, in cases which reach the Official Referees' Courts the parties have failed to resolve their differences in this manner. Because the parties will have referred the issues to the adjudicator at an earlier stage, the scope for successful mediation, once litigation is commenced, is generally thought to be less.

Some years ago it was thought that the Official Referees strove too hard to persuade litigants to settle their differences and that they were unwilling to try disputes. Consequently the Official Referees stress the distinction between mediation and trial and the need for the two processes to be seen to be separate. They therefore concentrate their efforts in attempting to minimise the issues, making orders requiring the experts for each side to meet to endeavour to agree technical facts and clarify issues and to keep the parties to the dates fixed for pre-trial hearings and for trial. This approach has been successful to the extent that the parties in 80-85% of the cases commenced in the Official Referees' Court reach settlement between the summons for directions and the date fixed for trial.

It seems to us that this confirms the experience of ACAS that there is still room for mediation even though the parties may have incurred significant costs in preparing for trial. It confirms our view that the process of mediation should not be allowed to delay or impede the progress of an action once it has started, and earlier settlements would be encouraged if mediation was easily available. The Official Referees were at pains to point out that not all disputes in the construction industry were between large corporations or merited proceedings in the Official Referees' Courts. There are many disputes involving small builders and householders. These normally come before the County Court. In such cases there is often no provision for an 'adjudicator' or for arbitration and in our view such disputes would be particularly likely to benefit from the existence of a court-based system of ADR. However, as in the case of disputes in the Official Referees' Court, such cases would demand a degree of expertise and would be likely to require much of the mediator's time to study the necessary documents and to visit the site. Finally, if a court-based system of ADR were available, the Official Referees felt that it could be brought to the attention of the parties' solicitors by notices in the court building at St Dunstan's house, together with the availability of leaflets advertising ADR and giving the names and addresses of organisations who would maintain lists of trained construction mediators, such as the British Academy of Experts, CEDR, the Chartered Institute of Arbitrators, the Official Referees' Bar Association and the Official Referees' Solicitors' Association.

INITIATIVES BY DISTRICT JUDGES

A number of District Judges have, on their own individual initiative, been developing techniques designed to encourage the parties in contested civil and matrimonial cases to find their own solution with some judicial assistance. In some cases the technique results in a District Judge feeling unable to try the case himself if settlement is not achieved. This reinforces our view that generally speaking the functions of judge and mediator are best separated. This would avoid any risk of the parties feeling that their case may have been prejudiced by a failure in mediation. The ordinary progress of a case in the courts is not interrupted, and any difficulty of having to transfer it to a different tribunal is avoided. In cases within the small claims limit the preliminary hearing may often provide an opportunity for each side to consider the other's relative strength, and so to form a realistic view as to the likely outcome. A simple statement by the District Judge of the relevant law and what facts need to be proved will sometimes produce an agreed solution when both sides are litigating in person.

Matrimonial ancillary relief cases are more involved and generally the parties and their lawyers are expected to attend at Court at an early stage; they may have been required to complete a fairly detailed questionnaire prepared by the District Judge which will give particulars of their resources and liabilities. The District Judge will then see the parties and their representatives to identify the issues between them and then send them out to see if they can negotiate a solution. One or two carefully framed questions for the parties to consider will often lead them to agreement. If settlement is slow in coming, some District Judges will be prepared to express a view on the merits of the case on the basis of the information before them at this stage or on some particular question which may be causing difficulty. It is only after the completion of this process that, assuming no solution is reached, the case will be set down for a formal hearing. One of the Law Society's representatives on our Committee, Christopher Chandler, is aware that these ideas have been circulated and discussed among District Judges. We are not aware, however, of any central co-ordination in these developing techniques, which, we believe, could have a beneficial effect on the overall management of cases in the system.

BASIC REQUIREMENTS OF A COURT-BASED ADR SYSTEM

We believe that no system of court-based ADR could work successfully unless litigants were able from the outset to have a clear indication of what is being offered as an alternative to a court hearing once proceedings have been commenced. We think the key points are: (1) Subject-matter: Any restrictions or conditions on the right of parties to elect for ADR need to be made clear (e.g., in cases involving allegations of fraud or family matters affecting children); (2) Stage: The exact stage in any litigation where the formal opportunity to elect for ADR needs to be given is, in our view, a crucial matter; (3) Form: Any scheme would need to be clear about the form of procedure being recommended. Litigants might need to be warned that ADR may not be cost-free and should be given a clear idea of the costs of any available service; (4) Person: A scheme would need to make reasonable provision as to the type of person who should be selected as a neutral in the ADR process; (5) Practical considerations: accommodation, time limits, et cetera, would need to be provided for; (6) Effect: Any scheme would need to spell out, in detail, the effect of the election for ADR upon the subsequent course of the litigation.

It is, in our view, essential that parties should be assured that their legal rights will remain unaffected by attempts to resolve their dispute by mediation and that the normal progress of any claim will continue.

A NOTE ON TERMINOLOGY

It may not be surprising that in a comparatively new procedure words may be used with differing shades of meaning. Two particular problems arise. First, should ADR include arbitration? The award of an arbitrator, which is enforceable by court order under the Arbitration Acts 1950-1979, is, in one sense, part of the existing legal process, so cannot strictly be termed 'alternative'. For the purposes of our report, therefore, the term ADR includes mediation, conciliation and mini-trial, but does not extend to arbitration except where the context specifically requires arbitration to be included. A further problem concerns the use of the words mediation and conciliation. Purists argue whether mediators/conciliators should introduce their own ideas in the course of leading the parties towards a settlement. We have found it most convenient to treat the two terms as being virtually interchangeable. In practice there is little to choose between the functions of an ACAS conciliator and a CEDR mediator! So far as possible we have avoided confusion by referring mainly to mediators but adding the word 'facilitative' if the individual's task is only to facilitate rather than express his expert opinion upon the merits of each sides's case.

MANAGEMENT OF LITIGATION BY THE COURT

The Civil Justice Review catalogues (at paragraphs 237-260) demonstrate the decline in the use of the pre-trial review ('PTR') in smaller cases over a fifty-year period and despite earlier enthusiasm. It is clear that the PTR had become largely a formality where the Master or Registrar had little or no knowledge of the dispute and the parties little or no inclination to participate. In the result and with changes which have eliminated pretrial hearings in most cases, provided parties comply with procedural obligations, a case will not be reviewed by the court until it reaches trial. These changes can be compared with the diametrically opposite shift towards greater management of litigation by judicial officers which is found in the United States for example in the Judicial Improvements Act 1990. The Act recites that evidence heard by a Congress committee suggests that there should be increased management of litigation including early involvement of a judicial officer in planning the progress of a case (Section 102(5)(B)) together with the use of ADR procedures if costs incurred by the court system and by litigants is to be reduced.

We have been referred to the 'Multi-Door' scheme of the District of Columbia Superior Court. This reflects a degree of development of the role of the courthouse in the local community far beyond anything yet contemplated in England. Here, mediation is treated as an important part of the range of dispute resolution processes and made available by the court to its local community. Literature is printed (in both English and Spanish) showing parties the opportunities of alternatives to litigation. Supported by 180 volunteer lawyers, 2,377 disputes were mediated during December 1990. Of these 47% "reached some sort of resolution." This development, born out of a concern to cut delay and costs, demonstrates the usefulness of mediation as an adjunct to the traditional court process and to provide a possible target of employing court facilities to assist parties to resolve disputes in the most effective manner with a trial as the ultimate solution if compromise is unattainable.

Also in Australia we learn of similar initiatives, including a 'settlement week' to be held in New South Wales. In the Federal Court, in a scheme which is provided for by rules of the court, the Registrars have been undertaking mediation and there is pressure to permit outside mediators to participate. And in the Supreme Court a committee whose membership includes judges, lawyers and insurers all working together, picked 3,000 cases which would not reach trial before the nominated settlement week.

The Court Registry staff worked overtime writing letters to all parties asking them to volunteer their cases for mediation. In 300 or so cases the parties did agree to mediate. A procedure has been laid down requiring a one hour pre-mediation session with the mediator followed by a mediation expected to last some three hours. The parties will pay for four hours of his time. If this succeeds, it is hoped that settlement weeks will become part of a continuing court-annexed programme.

We find the success of the developments in the United States and Australia persuasive. We would hope that if a scheme does show positive results, a further review may be made of the principles of management of litigation by the court. We think that, in keeping with the spirit of the Civil Justice Review, developments overseas which have demonstrated the benefits of new techniques should be examined and tried here in England.

A PILOT SCHEME IN THE COUNTY COURT

In September 1990, the London Common Law and Commercial Bar Association put forward a proposal for a pilot scheme in the County Court. Although the scheme was not adopted by the Lord Chancellor's Department, one of our members, Philip Naughton, has had discussions with county court judges in London in the hope that it might be possible to implement a scheme on a trial basis at little or no cost. There is a willingness (in principle) to participate in such a scheme but there are problems which must be overcome.

In Lambeth County Court, where HH Judge McNair QC is the senior judge, a very high proportion of disputes concern landlord and tenant. Lambeth Council is by far the largest landlord. These disputes usually begin because rent is unpaid but may also concern complaints about the maintenance of property or neighbour disputes or arise out of unemployment or family problems. The Defendant tenant is rarely represented by a lawyer and many cases cannot easily be resolved before the hearing day. At least one conciliation scheme already exists to assist parties in these local disputes. There is rarely a need for lawyers here.

In Westminster, HH Judge Harris QC, the senior Judge, has made a number of useful suggestions and has offered to assist by selecting suitable cases for a limited period, if a pilot scheme were introduced. Westminster has a broader mix of cases but it is an old court with very limited accommodation and rooms would only be available after court hours. This would mean paying staff for working overtime.

Having approached and discussed a pilot scheme with the judges in Lambeth and Westminster and having ascertained that such a scheme would apparently be feasible, we should warmly welcome the introduction of a scheme on these lines at suitable county court centres. A suggested procedure for such a scheme has been published in the journal of the Chartered Institute of Arbitrators, Volume 58, Number 3, 1992, p. 186).

THE TENFOLD INCREASE IN THE COUNTY COURT LIMIT

The scheme put forward by the London Common Law and Commercial Bar Association envisaged mediation by lawyers of some experience but we are impressed by the achievements of the ACAS conciliators (who are not legally qualified) in assisting parties to resolve disputes. Of course, the ACAS conciliator is concerned with one field of law only, whereas the county court judge must have a familiarity with the whole breadth of the law. It may be that many county court cases, whether they involve housing, debt collection, personal injury or other small claim do not require a mediator qualified in the law but rather a mediator skilled in facilitating the resolution of disputes who has sufficient training to understand their substance. With the increase in the County Court limits from £5,000 to £50,000, it might be felt that if a pilot scheme succeeded, consideration could be given to the appointment of full-time mediators attached to the court. For more complex cases mediators with specialist qualifications could be engaged. Such a system would be analogous in some respects to that developed by ACAS in dealing with industrial disputes partly by 'in-house' conciliators and partly by external 'empanelled' arbitrators.

If a scheme were to be introduced on the lines we have suggested there would be a need for suitably experienced persons to undertake the work. A pool of experience already exists as a result of the training activities of such bodies as the British Academy of Experts, CEDR, and IDR (Europe) Limited. Clearly litigation experience would also be desirable. A panel of approved mediators could be made available in the selected county courts so that suitable mediators could be chosen on a case by case basis. To provide a statistically useful result we would suggest a target of at least 100 mediations per county court centre in the first period of operation. This would suggest a panel size of between six and ten mediators per court.

We would suggest that a pilot scheme, free of cost to the parties, should be undertaken in three or four court centres; one in a low population area, such as Exeter or Ely, one in a major provincial city, and either one or two in London. Some types of case might be excluded, for example family law cases, straight debt collection and local authority housing, together with cases involving allegations of fraud. A pilot scheme should cover all other types of case. Legal representation in the mediation process should be available at the wish of a party. We would not propose that any pilot scheme should place upon county court staff the burden of determining the needs of particular cases. Lay staff do not have the experience to assess litigation or intervene in its management. Thus, a pilot scheme, to be successful, would need largely to run itself. One of three 'triggers' would need to be chosen: (a) the scheme is entirely voluntary, triggered by a notice to litigants sent out with the originating process with a subsequent reminder containing automatic directions, or (b) suitable cases are identified by the District Judge or the Presiding judge and a letter written to the parties suggesting mediation. This would impose an additional workload but would enable a sensible number of cases to be selected in which mediation might give some benefit (excluding, for example, small cases destined for arbitration and cases where one litigant is unrepresented); (c) All litigants (or perhaps as many litigants as possible) might be contacted by the mediators themselves after pleadings have been closed.

For a pilot scheme we favour the options in (a) and (b). For a full scheme the third option, which reflects the ACAS model, might be preferable. The accommodation for a mediation should preferably be provided in or near the courthouse. The demands on court staff could be confined to taking care of the premises. Again, for a pilot scheme, evening sessions might be attractive both for the parties and for mediators who might be otherwise occupied during court hours. The mediation process offered should be that of facilitative mediation — so that the mediator would be expected to help the parties to reach solutions rather than suggesting them. The mediation would be entirely confidential and without prejudice to any party. All notes taken by the mediator, other than the terms of any agreement reached, should be destroyed after the process has been completed. The mediation process should not hold up the court timetable — otherwise it might be used by the unscrupulous to delay judgment.

THE HIGH COURT

In June 1991, Philip Naughton submitted a paper to the Official Referees Users Committee for a pilot scheme similar to that proposed for the County Court. It is still being considered. The observations we have received on behalf of the Official Referees themselves are recorded in Section 8 of our Report (above). It is our conclusion, after examining present procedure and in noting the advances made in superior courts in other parts of the English speaking world that if the encouragement of the Court is justified in the County Court it is justified in the High Court. We would like to see a pilot scheme, similar to that which we propose for the County Court, introduced in at least one Division of the High Court.

During our work we were invited to offer some observations to a working group of the Supreme Court Procedure Committee, chaired by the Rt Hon Lord Justice Neill, which was considering the possible use of a mediation procedure in connection with High Court actions for libel. We were supportive of the idea and hope that it will prove possible to use mediation in the libel context, particularly if that would lead to improvements in the position of parties who currently feel themselves to be disadvantaged by the exclusion of this class of case from the operation of legal aid.

TRAINING AND SELECTION OF MEDIATORS

Apart from ACAS conciliators, there is now a body of individuals who have received training by at least three organisations: CEDR, IDR (Europe) Ltd, and the British Academy of Experts. All three have relied heavily upon the experience of American practitioners. For a pilot scheme it may be preferable to choose the mediators from those with litigation experience who are barristers or solicitors and to arrange their supplementary training in mediation so far as may be necessary with one or more of the organisations mentioned above. Both IDR and CEDR have already offered assistance in providing training for court-based mediation. We would suggest that legal mediators should be chosen from lawyers with at least seven years' post qualification experience.

* This article was originally published as R. Beldam, 'Report of the Committee on Alternative Dispute Resolution', *Arbitration* 58, no. 3 (1992): 178-186.

CHAPTER 1

Windows on the World

Lord Goff

We live in an age of change — of change more rapid than has ever before been experienced by mankind. Of course, the rate of change in this country is not so rapid as it is in other parts of the world — notably in Eastern Europe, where the great leap for freedom has been watched by us all with astonishment, with admiration and with joy, as we extend our arms to welcome as colleagues and as friends the citizens of countries who have in the past contributed so much to the culture of mankind. Even in this country, where gradual change is preferred to revolution, the revolutions in Eastern Europe are perceived as profoundly welcome, since they constitute not so much a leap into the dark as a leap into the light, a resumption of the norm rather than a social experiment. But there have been other changes of great significance to us all in the world. There has been the enormous and continuing growth of the economies on the rim of the Pacific Ocean, which now constitute an area of economic importance as significant as those of Europe and North America. There is also the development of a single market in Europe due to come into effect in 1992; we must devoutly hope that the reality will conform to the aspirations of its progenitors, and that the deeds of the Member States will conform to the ideals which their leaders so readily proclaim. Even in the UK, we have undergone fundamental changes in the past decade — changes which have not always been pleasant for the easy-going citizens of these comfortable islands, but are no doubt very good for us all. One result of all these changes is that we find ourselves at a point in our history when the dusk is falling or has fallen, whether temporarily or permanently, upon the age of socialism, and the sun is rising again upon the age of capitalism.

There is, of course, no such thing as a capitalist system. That concept was invented by those who think in terms of systems, and who felt compelled to identify a system which was inferior to that which they themselves advocated. But capitalism is not a system: it is the absence of a system. Those who support it are those who believe that the state is fundamentally incompetent to run our affairs for us and, in particular, is incompetent to increase our material prosperity. They, therefore, believe that the state should interfere with the lives of its citizens only to the minimum extent necessary to ensure order and justice in society; to promote the physical well-being and ensure the basic necessities of its citizens, especially the elderly and the infirmed; to save the environment from desecration; and to protect society from its enemies without and within. This is the prevailing philosophy which today appears to inform governments of countries throughout the world. However, like all such philosophies, it no doubt requires some qualification in practice. There is a sense in which the idea of arbitration is a reflection of that philosophy. Of course every civilised state worthy of the description has to provide a system of laws to which all its citizens, great and small, are subject. There must also be a system of courts and of law enforcement for the implementation of those laws. For centuries, too, it has been thought right to extend those systems beyond the scope of the criminal law — to protect our lives and property; to regulate marriage and to promote the family; to prevent officers of the state from exceeding their lawful powers; and, from our point of view most important, to provide the ultimate means for the resolution of civil disputes, in the interests of the parties and in the interests of society as a whole.

I use the word 'ultimate' advisedly, because nowadays it is almost universally recognised that parties are free to create their own mechanisms for the resolution of their disputes, and that the state should only interfere with such arrangements to the minimum degree necessary in the interests of justice. The problem of how to identify that minimum degree of interference has been troubling lawyers and arbitrators much in recent years, but we are not concerned with that today. What we are concerned with is rather how we should exercise the freedom which we have to create appropriate mechanisms for the resolution of disputes; how and when those mechanisms can best be employed; and how the courts can best assist by providing support for the just and efficient working of those mechanisms, and for the enforcement of the solutions which emerge from them.

In this age of rapid change, we can perceive a far greater readiness than before to create, or at least to recognise, new mechanisms for the resolution of disputes. I refer of course to the ADR movement, the initials 'ADR' standing for the ugly but useful expression 'Alternative Dispute Resolution'. This embraces the methods of resolving disputes which are alternative to the forms of adjudication traditionally employed in court proceedings, and in many arbitrations in the past. We need not, however, trouble ourselves with definitions. We, as practical men, can leave such things to the scholars, who are free to indulge in that difficult, and sometimes fruitless, pastime. We are concerned rather with the mechanisms themselves; their virtues and defects; their use and abuse; and their suitability and unsuitability for particular disputes.

Here we all, as so often before in this world, owe much to our American friends. The readiness to experiment, and the energy and enthusiasm with which new ideas are put into practice, are laudable characteristics of the dynamic American society. In consequence, the United States of America has become the legal laboratory of the world, which usefully demonstrates to us all which ideas are worth pursuing, and which are best avoided. We in other countries, who are as a result spared to some extent the painful processes of experiment, have reason to be grateful to the Americans for the guidance which they provide for us. But another feature of American society is its fertility in the creation of new religions, and (perhaps one aspect of its great skill in marketing) the production of missionaries to spread the new gospels as they emerge. We have seen and heard the missionaries of ADR, as they spread the new gospel around the world. There are one or two countries in the old world whose citizens tend to be rather sceptical of new ideas of this kind. One of those countries is, I fear, the United Kingdom; and I entertain (perhaps unjustly) the suspicion that the beautiful country which lies just to the south of the English Channel, whose history has been so closely entwined with ours, is another. There are particular reasons for this scepticism. One is that ADR has, in a limited form, been around for a long time. In this country, and I believe in many others, the vast majority of lawyers perceive it to be part of their duty to their clients to promote the amicable resolution of disputes, and judges have taken an active part in the process, so far as is consistent with their judicial function. In civil law countries, I believe, the role of conciliator or mediator is formally conferred upon the judge. This may well result in judges in those countries taking a greater part in the process of amicable resolution than do judges in common law countries. But it is plain that ADR transcends simple negotiation, or even conciliation by the court. It presupposes the introduction of an outside agency to bring about agreement in the privacy and informality of surroundings separate and distinct from the officialdom of courts. It further presupposes the possibility of some form of attenuated trial process to draw out the parties' respective cases and expose them to the view, not only of the other party, but also of such an outside agency in the same surroundings.

In the event, as the nature of ADR has become more fully understood, it is attracting great attention in this country and, I believe, in many other countries of the world. That interest has been stimulated by the huge cost and frequent over-complexity, not only of modern court proceedings but also of the more substantial modern commercial arbitrations, fuelled partly by the intricacies of modern technology; partly by the generation of uncontrollable masses of documents; and partly also by the substantial increase in fees nowadays charged by professional men. Cost and delay have been identified as two of the principal enemies of justice in the modern world; and, since time is money, it is really cost that we are talking about.

But, in addition, formal arbitration has become to some extent afflicted by arthritis, the disease which, as time passes by, seems to attack nearly all institutions as it does nearly all human beings. ADR is seen as one means of escaping from the inflexible processes towards which substantial arbitrations seem to gravitate. ADR, if effective, may produce not only a less expensive, but also a less traumatic resolution of disputes — especially important where the parties may continue to do business together in the future. I only comment that the personality as well as the methods of a conciliator or mediator must surely be most important. Knocking people's heads together is one thing. Conciliation is another. The conciliator's fist, if made of iron, must be well and truly enveloped in a glove of the deepest velvet.

However, if all that our American colleagues tell us is correct, then ADR surely merits the most serious consideration and perhaps, dare I suggest it, not only in common law countries. At all events, we should be looking not only at ADR itself, but at some of the related problems. Let us not forget that the arrival of ADR may, with other things, have an impact upon our traditional forms of adjudication by forcing us to render them more flexible and more responsive to the particular needs of the parties. If that does indeed occur, the need for ADR may itself diminish. Let us not forget too that ADR has its vices as well as its virtues. Indeed there might, I suppose, be a domino effect if it was decided that the judges of the Commercial Court could lay aside their wigs and gowns and sit in private conducting proceedings in an informal manner, provided that both parties agreed and the public interest did not otherwise require. What, I wonder, would be wrong with that? All things are, I suppose, possible. Then the need for arbitration might diminish. But I must be careful not to exceed my brief.

The English poet Hilaire Belloc, whose name betrays his French ancestry, once wrote of the rich: "[t]he husbands and the wives of this select society Lead independent lives of infinite variety." I myself suspect that it may be said, with equal truth, that the forms of ADR may likewise be of infinite variety. Remarkable examples have occurred and are still occurring in countries throughout the world, usually as the result of the inability of the courts to provide what the citizen requires. In India there is the remarkable lok Adalat movement, a by-product of the immense delays in the Indian courts. Here distinguished judges descend, so to speak, from the bench to the public forum for a couple of days at a time, disposing on an informal basis of some hundreds of cases each. Less remarkable, though perhaps more interesting for us, is the Centre for Settlement of Traffic Accident Disputes established in Tokyo in 1978, funded by the insurance industry. More than one hundred attorneys work there on a part-time basis, giving advice and acting as conciliators in disputes. In one year, 1986, the Centre advised on over 11,000 cases. In 1,671 cases the parties reached a compromise. In this way delay is greatly reduced and costs are largely eliminated. I have been told that, in most cases, the dispute is settled after four or five visits to the Centre and that the time needed for each case is about one hundred days from accident to resolution. Here surely are lessons for us all. However, I am straying from the subject of international commercial arbitration. It is not only ADR which has hit arbitration in the past few years. We have also seen the arrival of the UNCITRAL Model

Law, which has received much attention and consideration throughout the world and has been adopted in some countries, though not necessarily without qualification. There have been one or two predictable reactions. In some countries, where the indigenous arbitration law was perceived to be less than satisfactory (perhaps because is was incomplete or scattered among diverse sources) the adoption of the model law has solved a domestic problem by providing a unified, coherent arbitration law contained in one instrument. In other countries, the adoption of the model law has been perceived as providing an attraction for overseas customers to come and arbitrate. In yet others, in particular those with highly developed laws of arbitration, the adoption of the model law has been resisted on the ground that to adopt it would create a new area of uncertainty in place of principles already defined in detail by judicial decisions. And so on.

I do not wish to comment on the various reactions, except to say this. I fully accept that, for countries without a developed arbitration law, the adoption of UNCITRAL may well provide a benefit by assuring possible customers that there are, so to speak, no hidden minefields in the arbitration law of that country. That is all to the good; but I beg leave to wonder whether the mere fact of the adoption of UNCITRAL will, in itself, provide a positive attraction. I was much impressed by a paper read by Arthur Marriott at last year's Annual Conference of this Institute, in which he expounded the thesis that the development of new centres of arbitration is likely to be dependent more on economic, cultural, political, geographic and linguistic factors. It is tantalising for us to cast our eyes around the world, and then to gaze into the crystal ball in an attempt to discern the future of arbitration. What do I see portrayed in that crystal ball? One thing I see, really because I wish to see it there, is that following the resolution of the current crisis in the Gulf, the Arab countries will not only resume but enhance their role in the world of commerce and of international arbitration. We may then see more widely deployed the legal skills which so many Arab lawyers undoubtedly possess, and we may enjoy the benefit of closer collaboration with them.

More clearly, I see competition between the various jurisdictions of the world seeking to attract commercial arbitration to their countries. For myself I can see no harm in this, provided the competition is, so to speak, customer-led. This should, in theory at least, lead to an overall improvement in the arbitration services available to businessmen everywhere. I also see a determination in all countries of the world to improve their domestic arbitration laws and practice and, for that purpose, to seek guidance and inspiration from any respectable source.

Harmonisation of laws is perhaps too much to expect, certainly in the short term. We in the European Community have seen what a difficult and painful process it can be. We have to recognise not only that diverse legal systems have their own integrity, but that there are benefits to be derived from diversity as well as from harmony. Indeed, since the Second World War, we have seen something which can almost be regarded as a crisis of confidence in some countries of the world, as each of us looks with a critical eye upon our own legal system and wonders anxiously whether other systems provide better answers. There has been talk, and perhaps more than talk, in some common law countries of moving towards a more inquisitorial system of procedure and, likewise, in some civil law countries there has been talk, and perhaps more than talk, of moving towards a more adversarial system. This, if true, is surely all to the good. Perhaps one day we shall discover that Darwin was right not only about the natural world around us but also about the legal world, as processes of natural selection weed out the defects in our respective systems of procedure. But we have, as always, to be careful. The pendulum can, on occasion, swing too far and too fast. To those who are afflicted by doubt, the grass on the other side of the fence is always greener. One disaster, even one unfortunate occurrence, can provoke a clamour by the ill-informed for the wholesale abandonment of the known and tried processes and the wholesale adoption of the unknown and untried. I speak not as the enemy of change, but as a reluctant hero. Festina lente. Let us make haste slowly but not, I trust, too slowly. Or, to adopt Goethe's motto, "Ohne Hast, aber ohne Rast" — "Without haste, but without rest."

That we are more ready to learn from each other is now surely beyond doubt. The world of arbitration is one of the great melting pots of the law. International commercial arbitration is one of the principal areas in which common lawyers and civil lawyers meet in a professional context on equal terms, not only as advocates but also sitting as members of the same tribunal. We learn of the development of procedures which are neither specifically common law nor specifically civil law, but which draw elements from each system. In the European Court of Justice, since the advent of the United Kingdom and the Republic of Ireland, there has been a graceful bow in the direction of the common lawyers, and a generous recognition of the professionalism of the advocacy which comes from these islands. But international arbitration sees a true meeting and, on some occasions at least, a true merger of the different systems in a search for an effective procedure.

In a sense, the present conference provides a special opportunity for the development of this international free trade in ideas about commercial arbitration. We in the Chartered Institute of Arbitrators naturally see this conference as the great event of our 75th anniversary year. It is however far more than that. It is a celebration of international cooperation. It is a recognition of our mutual inter-dependence. It is a search for assistance in the work in which we are all engaged, and a symptom of the desire which we all possess for our own self-improvement. The purpose is sound. The objectives are clear. And we in this country know how fortunate we are to have the benefit of such excellent guidance from so many of our distinguished colleagues from other countries.

* This article was originally published as R. Goff, 'Windows on the World: An Overview', *Arbitration* 58, no. 1 (1992): 5-8.

CHAPTER 1

ADR in Civil Law Countries

Pieter Sanders

Two speakers have been invited to speak this morning on ADR in civil law countries. Their task thus had to be divided in order to avoid repetition. The two contributions, taken together, will present a more complete picture of the situation. Consequently, I will only deal with some aspects of ADR. However, before doing so I may raise the question what ADR means: for what is ADR an alternative? This question is not answered uniformly. In most publications on ADR, arbitration is also mentioned as an alternative. ADR then means: alternative to court proceedings. Regardless of whether arbitration is to be included among the alternatives, conciliation may also take place in arbitration and conciliation is undoubtedly a form of ADR. Although conciliation may be treated separately, the link between arbitration and conciliation should not be overlooked. Therefore first of all I will deal with the relationship between arbitration and conciliation. As a second topic I will make some observations about the mini-trial. This form of ADR is receiving more and more attention, both in common and civil law countries. If successful it leads to a settlement of the dispute. This paper will therefore deal with: (1) Relationship between Conciliation and Arbitration and (2) Mini-trial. Throughout this paper I will use the term conciliation. In my opinion this term is interchangeable with the term mediation. Endeavours have been made to make a distinction between the two, based on the degree of initiatives, the third party involved in these proceedings, may take. However this is a rather vague criterion which does not lead to a clear distinction. In any case there does not exist a difference in kind between the two.

THE RELATIONSHIP BETWEEN CONCILIATION AND ARBITRATION

Statutory Regulation of Conciliation

In civil law countries conciliation has, so far, not found any statutory regulation. In those countries conciliation may take place on the basis of Conciliation Rules to which parties have referred, like the Conciliation Rules of UNCITRAL or those of the ICC. Conciliation is in those cases based on contract. On the other hand, nothing prevents parties from resorting to conciliation without reference to any set of Rules. This constitutes what I may call a free type of conciliation.

Many civil law countries revised their arbitration laws during the last decades. None of them used this opportunity to add some provisions which would govern conciliation. If they were to do so the law might, for example, contain a provision excluding a conciliator from acting later as arbitrator or taking part, if conciliation fails, in subsequent arbitral or court proceedings (unless parties agree otherwise). The law could also guarantee the confidentiality of all that occurred in conciliation and provide for the stay of arbitral or court proceedings or forbid the institution of these proceedings (exception to be made for conservatory measures) whilst conciliation is going on.

In common law countries, on the other hand, conciliation has found, at least in some of these countries, a place in the arbitration law. Bermuda's International Conciliation and Arbitration Act 1993, for example, regulates conciliation in a detailed manner in its Part II (s. 3-21), which precedes Part III International Arbitration. It states, *inter alia*, in s. 14(1) that a conciliator may not be appointed as arbitrator and cannot take part in any arbitral or judicial proceeding unless all parties agree or the rules agreed for conciliation or arbitration so provide. Hong Kong's Arbitration Ordinance 1990 states in s. 2B inter alia that an arbitrator or umpire may act as conciliator and that no objection shall be taken to the conduct of arbitration proceedings by the arbitrator or umpire solely on the ground that he had acted previously as a conciliator. Under the Arbitration Act of the Canadian province of Alberta (s. 35) arbitrators may if the parties consent, use mediation, conciliation or similar techniques during arbitration to encourage settlement and may thereafter resume their role as arbitrator without disqualification. Thus, only common law countries paid attention to conciliation and its relation to arbitration. Also the Model Law on International Commercial Arbitration of UNCITRAL 1985 is silent on conciliation although during its drafting period it was, on several occasions, suggested to add provisions on conciliation. Again, only common law countries, when adopting the Model Law, added provisions on conciliation. Bermuda, several of the common law provinces of Canada and some US States, when following the Model Law, did so. It seems worth noting the different attitude by legislators from civil and common law countries, a difference which so far has not to my knowledge been remarked upon.

Settlement in Arbitration

In civil law countries, many of the arbitration laws, however, support conciliation by permitting a settlement reached during arbitration to be recorded in an award on agreed terms. This is a special type of award which does not contain a decision of the arbitrators on the dispute, but transforms the parties' settlement into an award which can be enforced, if necessary, as any other award. The award does not contain reasons as may be otherwise required and may, in several jurisdictions, have to be signed also by the parties. The award on agreed terms is also recognised in the Model Law (Art. 30). On request of the parties their settlement will be recorded in this form "if not objected by the arbitral tribunal." Indeed, if the settlement would violate rules of public policy, the arbitral tribunal will refuse to record the settlement in an award.

May Arbitrators Assist the Parties in Arriving at a Settlement?

So far I have been discussing a settlement reached by parties during arbitration in direct negotiations between the parties themselves. The situation becomes more delicate when the arbitrators, who are fully informed about the nature of the dispute, are called upon to assist the parties in reaching a settlement. This is outside the scope of their mission which consists in rendering a decision. It could be argued that arbitrators should refrain from complying with this request of the parties as they may be influenced, in case no settlement is reached and the arbitral proceedings continue, by what is revealed during the settlement negotiations. On the other hand, arbitration is a service to the parties and the interest of the parties may best be served by settling the dispute instead of continuing costly and protracted arbitral proceedings. Why should arbitrators refuse to assist if parties, in common agreement, request their assistance? I refer to what has been observed above. Bermuda's arbitration law permits a conciliator to act as arbitrator if the parties agree or the applicable conciliation or arbitration rules so provide. Under the law of Hong Kong no objection can be taken to the way in which arbitral proceedings have been conducted solely on the ground that the arbitrator previously acted as conciliator. Alberta gives a more direct answer to the question; with consent of the parties the arbitrator may act as conciliator and may resume his role as arbitrator without disqualification. According to this law arbitrators may assist the parties in reaching a settlement and, if no settlement is reached, may continue with the arbitration proceedings. Arbitration Rules, to which the law of Bermuda explicitly refers, contain a variety of provisions in respect of the relationship between arbitration and conciliation. The rules of CIETAC (China International Economic and Trade Arbitration Commission) simply state in Art. 37 that arbitrators "may conciliate cases under their cognizance."

On the other hand, the Commercial Arbitration Rules of the AAA (American Arbitration Association) state in Art. 10 that their institute, with consent of the parties, may arrange at any stage of the arbitral proceedings a mediation conference under its Commercial Mediation Rules. Here the two proceedings are separated. The rules accordingly add that the mediator cannot be appointed as arbitrator. Similarly, we find in Art. 10 of the ICC Conciliation Rules that, unless the parties agree otherwise, a conciliator shall not act in any judicial or arbitration proceedings relating to the dispute as arbitrator, representative or counsel of a party. The same is found in the Conciliation Rules of UNCITRAL (Art. 19) without the "unless agreed otherwise by the parties." To this is added that the parties shall also not present the conciliator as a witness in any subsequent proceeding. Arbitration Rules, therefore, seem to provide different answers on the question whether the arbitrators, if requested by the parties to do so, may assist them in settlement negotiations. In fact only the CIETAC Rules give arbitrators broad freedom to assist in conciliation.

This may be regarded as typical for the situation in the Orient. In the Far East, conciliation is largely preferred to arbitration. A compromise, reached in conciliation, prevents a party from being stigmatised as a losing party. The prospects of continuing friendly business relations after the dispute has been settled by conciliation are greater than in arbitration. Could we learn something from this attitude? In the Far East, conciliation and arbitration are considered to form a combined process.

MINI-TRIAL

This form of ADR was first developed, like many other ADR techniques, in the US. There, the use of mini-trial proceedings is even promoted and supported by statutory regulations. In Europe, mini-trial has only more recently received attention and so far has only led to Rules for mini-trial by some arbitral institutes. One of the first were the Mini-trial Rules of the Zurich Chamber of Commerce, published in the 1986 Yearbook Commercial Arbitration of ICCA, 241-246 with an Introduction by Marc Blessing. In England, ADR, including mini-trial has been recently discussed on several occasions. I refer to the Report of the Committee on

ADR (Chairman: Lord Justice Beldam) published in the journal *Arbitration* of the Chartered Institute of Arbitrators 1992, 173-186 and to the comprehensive survey of the various ADR methods presently in use in England, as well as elsewhere (See H. Brown & A. Marriott, *ADR Principles and Practice*, London: Sweet and Maxwell 1993).

By submitting their dispute to mini-trial proceedings, parties intend to arrive at an amicable solution and to avoid going to court or, as the case may be, to arbitration. If successful, mini-trial leads to a settlement. It thus constitutes a species of the genus 'Conciliation'. In broad outline this method can be summarised as follows. In the presence of the parties or, in case of a corporation, the presence of a Chief Executive Officer (CEO) with the capacity to settle, the lawyers of each side give a short presentation of each party's best case before a Committee in which the parties (CEO's in case of a corporation) are represented under the chairmanship of a neutral third member. After having heard this presentation the parties attempt to reach a settlement. The third party, who acts as a conciliator, assists them in arriving at a settlement.

Mini-trial Rules should in my opinion be flexible and not go too much into detail. The Rules should guide the parties, where necessary, in their attempt to reach a settlement. They should also contain some guarantees in order to protect the parties in case no settlement is reached. By reference to such Rules parties have agreed, before entering into more cumbersome court proceedings or submitting their dispute to arbitration, that an attempt shall be made to reach an amicable settlement under some procedure. Arbitration clauses may state that arbitration will be resorted to 'if friendly settlement of the dispute cannot be reached', but these words may remain idle in case no such procedure for settlement has been provided for which in any case brings the parties around the table. Which of the parties will otherwise make the first step? And would this not be interpreted as a sign of weakness? If Mini-trial Rules apply, these questions do not arise.

The Rules, on which I may make now some observations, should be flexible. There is not much experience yet in Europe with such Rules but according to information I received from Zurich, in practice the parties once they are brought together, are inclined to deviate in many aspects from the Rules. The Rules should also not be excessively detailed and not inspired by usual arbitration practice in which extensive Memoranda may first be exchanged. Mini-trial is a more informal procedure, whilst arbitration — unfortunately — is today more and more equated to court proceedings. Nevertheless, in mini-trials some procedural provisions are required. If a mini-trial committee with a neutral third person as chairman has been provided for, his appointment should be assured if parties fail to agree on the chairman.

The procedure may lead to a settlement or not. If a settlement has been reached it could be stated that this settlement may be recorded in an award, although in practice it may be enough when the settlement agreement is signed by both parties. Transforming the settlement into an award on agreed terms needs, if at all possible under the applicable law, a more complicated regulation. If no settlement is reached, this will require some guarantees. The secrecy of all that has appeared or has been admitted in mini-trial should be guaranteed. The third person, who actually functions as conciliator, should be excluded from participating in any form to appear in subsequent arbitral or court proceedings. These and other issues as well have to be considered when Mini-trial Rules are drafted.

Mini-trial in civil law countries finds itself still in an initial stage without much experience. However, this form of ADR is in my opinion worth being considered. A settlement, which may be the result of mini-trial, may be in the interest of the parties as it not only avoids court or arbitral proceedings but also may contribute to the continuance of friendly business relations between the parties. It may also, if no arbitration has been agreed upon, be in the interest of the courts in terms of reducing the Court list — a common problem in civil and common law countries. It also gives the court, if well drafted Rules are available, the possibility of referring the parties to such rules. This may occur when courts convene a meeting of the parties for settlement as, under the CCP of civil law countries, courts are entitled to do. In such a case the position of the judge is rather delicate and not the same as the position of the chairman (conciliator) in a mini-trial. The judge is limited in expressing his opinion on the case and cannot, for example, require from the parties production of further documents. He could, however, suggest that the parties, if adequate rules exist, resort to mini-trial. A suggestion of the court might be enough to induce the parties to follow this procedure which again, if successful, would relieve the court calendar.

CONCLUSION

Only some of the aspects of ADR have been discussed in this paper. Although ADR is on the move everywhere, in civil law countries it is more discussed in theory than applied in practice. As far as conciliation is concerned it may take some time before legislators will begin to promote and stimulate conciliation, as in some common law jurisdictions is the case. This is in spite of the fact that it may be in the interest of the courts to do so.

Parties also have an interest in ADR. Mini-trial is one of the alternatives for the resolution of their dispute parties may resort to instead of going to court or arbitration. For arbitral institutes there may lie a task to provide the tools in the form of well drafted Mini-trial Rules.

REFERENCES

* This article was originally published as P. Sanders, 'ADR in Civil Law Countries', *Arbitration* 61, no. 1 (1995): 35-38.

1 International Labour Office, Study on 'Conciliation and Arbitration Procedure' (Geneva: International Labour Office, 1989), 15.

2 For the sections quoted in the text see the Annexes to the national reports of those countries published in *the International Handbook on Commercial Arbitration*, ed. J. Paulsson, (The Hague: Kluwer Law International, 1984).

3 See Annex III to National Report China in *International Handbook on Commercial Arbitration*, ed. J. Paulsson, (The Hague: Kluwer Law International, 1984).

4 Expression used by T. Houzhi in his report for ICCA Congress Series No. 4 (Tokyo 1988) in *Arbitration in Settlement of International Commercial Disputes for the Far East and Arbitration in Combined Transportation*, ed. P. Sanders, (The Hague: Kluwer Law International, 1989), 55.

CHAPTER 1

ADR:
The Civil Law Approach

Otto L. O. De Witt Wijnen

The task to speak this morning on the civil law approach to ADR is certainly not an easy one. There are two reasons. First, it is not an easy task to follow such an eminent speaker as Professor Sanders. Secondly, there is so very little to say about the topic. Let us face it: ADR is virtually unknown in the civil law countries and the main approach that I have been able to discover so far in all those countries is one of great scepticism. As Dr Gillis Wetter from Sweden once said: "mediation is the stuff dreams are made of." There is no civil law legislation with respect to ADR, as in China and Japan and, to some extent, in the US. There is virtually no literature and, obviously, no case-law either. Now of course I have to qualify this statement. First of all, the fact that there is so little to find in any established form makes it all the more exciting and challenging to think about the possibilities of this new phenomenon. Creation and development of new legal tools are often more interesting than describing what already exists. The more so as there are signals that the attitude towards ADR in the civil law countries is changing. Secondly, what I said refers not to ADR in general, but to the phenomenon of non-binding ADR only. I believe that one should always clearly make the distinction between binding and non-binding ADR. For example, in a recent definition given by the British

Academy of Experts, ADR is defined as: "any method of resolving an issue susceptible to normal legal process by agreement rather than by imposed binding decision." Decision meaning an authoritative decision imposed on the parties other than by their consent, or a judge or an arbitrator. Obviously, there is a lot of binding ADR in the civil law countries. Thirdly, what I said refers to official non-binding ADR only. In practice, there is, in all civil law countries, a lot of mediation, conciliation and the like within the framework of normal arbitral proceedings and — at least in some civil law countries — of normal state court proceedings. Also many contracts, e.g., joint venture contracts, provide for settlement routes before a binding procedure can be embarked upon. But there are no, or at least very few official, structured or institutionalised systems of non-binding ADR in the civil law countries such as in the US. Finally, what I said refers to commercial disputes. In non-commercial fields there are, in some civil law countries, more structured and institutionalised systems for mediation. I am notably thinking of family mediation, which flourishes in my own country and is growing in other countries, e.g., in Austria; and of labour disputes where mediation is used officially in various civil law countries. Additionally, in certain countries, there are mediation systems specifically for consumer disputes. Although such disputes could qualify as commercial disputes, I do not think this meeting is intended to put the emphasis thereon. Accordingly, what I will speak about from now on is the approach in the civil law countries of Europe to non-binding, structured and/or institutionalised ADR — for efficiency's sake hereafter referred to as: 'ADR' — for major commercial disputes.

SITUATION AND POSSIBILITIES IN THE CIVIL LAW COUNTRIES

Would the civil law oppose non-binding ADR? I do not think so. As I have already mentioned, there is a lot of non-official mediation within the framework of official arbitration and even of state court proceedings. There are arbitrators on the Continent, and even judges, who have a great reputation for settling disputes during hearings and even before. This confirms that ADR as such is not against the civil law or against the civil law philosophy. There is no reason why more structured and/or institutionalised ADR would not be possible. The few examples of institutionalised ADR that we have confirm this: the Zürich Mini-trial and the one or two examples that we have in this country, about which Professor Sanders has spoken.

From a more principled and dogmatic point of view, the following could be observed. One of the important features of all civil law systems is the will of the parties. Also the consensual will of the parties. Agreements between parties are paramount to whatever the positive law is, except where the positive law is mandatory and where public order is involved. Now all ADR-systems and techniques are based on what the parties want: on their consensual will. Civil law will have to respect that. Let us look, in this light, at some of the forms that ADR has developed in the US: Mediation/ Conciliation, Mini-trial, Med-Arb, Final Offer (Baseball) arbitration/ Medaloa, Court-annexed arbitration, Early Neutral Evaluation, Summary Jury Trial. There are many more techniques, but these seem the most important ones; other techniques and forms seem to be derived from these 'archetypes'. A new phenomenon is that of 'lawyerless arbitration': lawyers for both sides prepare their clients for the arbitration proceedings, but then leave the matter to arbitration without lawyers. I am not sure, as a practising lawyer, if I would strongly advocate this new form.

MEDIATION (OR CONCILIATION)

Of all the structured dispute resolution mechanisms, this is possibly the most unstructured one. The focus is on the parties' willingness to bargain, combined with the mediator's skill to arrive at a successful resolution. As I have learned in the United States, each mediator uses his own techniques and procedures. The most common one is that the parties get a possibility — rather limited in time and otherwise — to present their case to the mediator. Thereafter the mediator will engage in a discussion with the parties in order to see if a solution can be reached. He may do so in meetings with the parties together, but also in separate caucuses — shuttling back and forth from one room to another. During such meetings and caucuses, the mediator will try to clarify each party's position, help each to understand the other party's position, propose alternatives and seek possible solutions. He may, aside from the legal merits of a case, try to find out where the financial bottom line of both parties lies and, subsequently, try to bridge the gap if he feels that the gap is not too wide. I have tried this latter approach myself, with success, in one arbitration, and without success in another.

MINI-TRIAL

I can be very brief on the mini-trial which Professor Sanders has dwelt on. This is a settlement process which is more elaborate. A panel is established consisting of senior managers from the parties (one from each side) and a neutral chairman. Parties' counsel will present the case — briefly again — to the panel. Thereafter, the senior executives on the panel are supposed to try and come to a settlement which has worked quite well in a great number of cases in the United States and which seems the form most palatable, so far, for institutionalised ADR in Europe: cf. the Mini-trial of the Zürich Chamber of Commerce and the mini-trial system that has been established in the computer software field in the Netherlands.

In my view, it is imperative that senior executives of the parties are appointed to the panel who have not previously been involved in the case. How often one sees staff-members (in-house counsel and others) and executives who have been dealing with a particular dispute for a prolonged period so entrenched in their own views that they are mentally blocked to any settlement. Whereas other executives who have a fresh mind and are mainly only interested in getting disputes out of the way, as quickly as possible, may not be hampered in trying to find a settlement.

MED-ARB

This is a mixture between mediation and arbitration. The parties agree in advance to authorise the mediator to decide as arbitrator if the mediation is not successful.

BASEBALL OR FINAL OFFER ARBITRATION/MEDALOA

In the final offer, or baseball arbitration, each party writes out its own proposal for a settlement and presents it in a sealed envelope to the arbitrator, before the hearing. After the hearing, the arbitrator opens the envelopes and picks the parties' proposals which he thinks most appropriate and fair. He has no authority to render any award other than on the basis of one of the two proposals. The advantage is that the parties are compelled to propose reasonable compromises, lest the arbitrator takes the other party's proposal. Medaloa or 'mediation and last offer arbitration' is a combination of med-arb and final offer arbitration.

COURT-ANNEXED ARBITRATION

In certain states of the US, the courts will order the parties to arbitration or mediation (the same happens in Australia). The court will appoint arbitrators or mediators. In the case of arbitration, this will lead to an award which is binding in some states and not binding in others. I understand that this system is now practised in more than 70 federal district courts, authorised to the use of ADR under the Civil Justice Reform Act of 1990.

EARLY NEUTRAL EVALUATION

This is an ADR process that brings all parties and their counsel together early in the pretrial period to present summaries of their cases and receive a non-binding assessment by an experienced neutral attorney with subject-matter expertise. The evaluator also provides case planning guidance and, if requested by the parties, settlement assistance.

SUMMARY JURY TRIAL

This is a flexible, non-binding ADR process designed to promote settlement in trial-ready cases, headed for protracted jury trials. The process provides litigants and their counsel with an advisory verdict after a short hearing in which the evidence is presented by counsel in summary form. The jury's non-binding verdict is used as a basis for subsequent settlement negotiations.

COULD THESE FORMS AND SYSTEMS BE USED IN THE CIVIL LAW COUNTRIES?

Where virtually all these systems are based on the voluntary consensual will of the parties, and the civil law principally attaches much weight to such consensual wish, all these systems seem acceptable. Some observations must be made however. The first observations relates to court-annexed mediation which, in various forms, is growing in the US and elsewhere (e.g., Australia). It is my understanding that referral to court-annexed mediation, or arbitration, can either be mandatory, or based on party consent. There would seem to be no problem in civil law countries in the first case; in the latter case this would be different. Under the Constitution of my own country, no party or person may be compelled to a jurisdiction not following from the law — and mandatory arbitration would so far not follow from our law. It is my impression that the position is not different in other civil law countries. This would not be different if the mediation to which the parties are referred, or even the arbitration, is not binding in its result — as I understand is sometimes the case. It is, in this context, of course fascinating to note the totally different approach and background to this matter in a country like Japan, where court ordered conciliation is part not only of the tradition but imbedded in the court system and in the law as such (the Civil Conciliation law). However, although the referral to conciliation is binding, the procedure is not — parties can always withdraw. I understand, in the early 90s, that over 18,000 court appointed conciliators were actually engaged in conciliation in Japan and that, in 1992, of around 330,000 new court cases over 100,000 were referred to conciliators. In China, there is a long tradition of conciliation. The Chinese Civil Procedural Law provides that, in conducting civil proceedings, the courts shall carry out conciliation. However, I understand that the will of the parties is decisive: at least in court litigation. In arbitration the position is different.

The second observation is with respect to the med-arb system. Again, I think that it is acceptable also under civil law systems that parties appoint, in advance, their mediator as arbitrator should the mediation fail. But personally, I would not favour such a system. In the mediation proceedings, the mediators and the parties should feel completely free to openly discuss the merits of the case and the respective positions of the parties. And also what, ultimately, the parties' own feelings and views are and what they would be willing to sacrifice in terms of money. I doubt if the parties would feel completely free to do so if they knew in advance that their confessor might eventually also be their judge. Civil law practice and tradition might also have a problem with the private caucusing used in the mediation system and others.

I believe it is a principal feature of our civil law proceedings that there is a balance in information and enquiry. A court or an arbitrator should abstain from *ex parte* communication and the parties should exchange all information that they would like to submit to the court or the tribunal and between themselves. In the separate caucuses, this is not the case. But I think that this would be acceptable in the civil law philosophy. I have practised it myself and I have been told that such a well-known arbitrator as Professor Claude Reymond has done it — but we are not familiar with it and it would strengthen my own already mentioned difficulties with the med-arb technique.

WHY THE SCEPTICISM IN MOST CIVIL LAW COUNTRIES?

I think there is no real reason for scepticism. If the system works elsewhere and works here, in practice, on an informal and ad hoc basis, why could it not work on a more official basis? The dominant question to pose is whether there is a necessity for any institutionalised or more sophisticated non-binding ADR system in this part of the world. That, indeed, can be doubted. Whereas, for example, arbitration in Switzerland is flourishing, the Zürich Mini-trial is not. In the eight years or so of its existence, there have only been three cases. They were settled successfully although, I have been told, they were not initiated and conducted in accordance with the rules!

The questions are, I think: (1) there is a lot of non-binding ADR in actual real practice, and it works without it being institutionalised; so why the necessity of having it structured and institutionalised? (2) In general, litigation and arbitration have not got out of hand to the extent obtaining in some common law jurisdictions. More specifically, we are not victimised in this part of the world by such horrors as discovery of documents, long protracted hearings and jury trials. In civil law systems, litigation and arbitration are less cumbersome, less expensive and more predictable than, for example, in the United States. (3) In general, commercial people and lawyers are more likely to settle disputes in a friendly atmosphere than notably, again, in the US: "mediation is lunch and we love to lunch", as a French colleague told me the other day. This doubt is shared by many of my learned colleagues all over Europe: in the Latin countries as well as

Scandinavia, Austria and Germany. In the December-issue of the Journal of International Arbitration 1993, Jacques Werner, its editor, asked the question "ADR: Will European Brains Be Set On Fire?" The question turned out to be a rhetorical one. Likewise, in an article in the 'Liber Amicorum' for Professor Karl Heinz Schwab, German Professor Fritz Nicklisch concluded recently than non-binding ADR had no purpose to serve in Germany. But there are signs, nevertheless, that there is a growing awareness that non-binding ADR might be useful.

In the first place, in certain European countries initiatives have been taken to develop institutionalised ADR. In my own country, I understand that ±100 disputes have been submitted to mini-trial, and with some success. Already for more years, the road construction industry in this country has established a similar system. I understand however, that no cases have been brought before this mini-trial system so far. In France, I was told that the French ICC Committee has recently set up a committee which should investigate the possibilities of more structured/ institutionalised ADR in France. I was told that the chief legal counsel of various major French industries were enthusiastic about this initiative and have joined this committee. Also in France, the Channel tunnel construction contract had a mediation clause. Fifteen disputes were submitted to mediation with success. A year ago, the US Centre for Public Resources organised a symposium on ADR in Paris for some European lawyers. Virtually all European lawyers present had their scepticism and their doubts. However, I have met several of them since who told me that they been converted. Also, a few months after that symposium I was asked to mediate in a dispute between a major European and a major American company. This shows on the one hand that at least the European company had an interest in mediation — and it shows equally that we should not look at the possibility for mediation from an European viewpoint only: trade and commercial contacts with other parts of the world may well have a great influence.

A great advantage of ADR processes is the parties' own active involvement. In many court cases, the parties often do not recognise their own case any more after some time. Also this may well stimulate enthusiasm in civil law countries — besides the fact that, even if the court and arbitration systems have not got so much out of hand as in certain common law countries, there are justified complaints also in this part of the world about the costs, the duration and the complications notably of the court procedures and international arbitration. At meetings where mediation is discussed and European lawyers are present, I sometimes ask for a show of hands of protagonists and antagonists. A number of people who used to be antagonist have meanwhile turned into protagonist. One of them is in this room today.

CONCLUSION

Summarising, notwithstanding all the doubts that we have, I think (non-binding) ADR may have a great and interesting future in the civil law countries.

REFERENCES

* This article was originally published as O. De Witt Wijinen, 'ADR, the Civil Law Approach', *Arbitration* 61, no. 1 (1995): 38-42.

1. Marginally, it is of interest to note that there is a great interest for ADR in South Africa, which I would partly consider as a civil law country.
2. Again for the sake of efficiency, I will not distinguish between mediation and conciliation.
3. In making this overview, I have benefited from papers, recently read by respectively Robert Coulson, past president of the American Arbitration Association and Tom Arnold, a well known US mediator, at a symposium organised by the World Intellectual Property Organisation in Geneva in March 1994, from a paper read by Judge Marven Aspin, one of the US judges most involved in this field in the US at a symposium on the reform of arbitration held in London in February 1994 and from the frequent publications by the US Centre for Public Resources (CPR).
4. Cf. CPR's 'Alternatives to the high costs of legislation', March 1994.
5. In high/low arbitration certain minimum and maximum limits are put for the parties' proposals.
6. CPR's 'Alternatives to the high costs of legislation', January 1994.
7. Cf. E. Palpinger & M. Shaw, 'Court ADR: Elements of Program Design', (CPR Legal Program, CPR Judicial Project, 1992), 1-18.
8. At least in the most common arbitration in China, the CIETAC arbitration. Cf. T. Houzhi, *International Commercial Arbitration in China*, Yearbook CIETAC 1992, 87.
9. C. H. Becksche Verlagsbuchhandlung, München 1990.
10. Cf. J. Rozemond, Jonge Balie Congresbundel 1992, 58, 59.

CHAPTER 1

Dispute Resolution in the 21st Century: Barriers or Bridges

John Uff

A discussion of dispute resolution at any time during the last millennium would have been bound to include, if not to start with, consideration of the rivalry which has existed between different methods, each with its own dedicated proponents. At times this has included open conflict between different courts of the English realm which, however, have generally been united in their suspicion and even hostility towards 'private' dispute resolution, which has always depended ultimately on the courts for enforcement. While the relations between different means of dispute resolution has fluctuated, the processes themselves have, during the last century particularly, undergone great changes, which will certainly continue. A discussion of dispute resolution in the next century must encompass both the future shape of the separate branches of the dispute resolution industry and their interrelationships, which necessarily tend to circumscribe the different processes.

At the present time, the courts regard themselves not as participants in any contest, but more as the referee. They promise nothing but support to private dispute resolution processes, as exemplified in Lord Mustill's words in the *Channel Tunnel* case: "[h]aving made this choice I believe that it is in accordance, not only with the presumption exemplified in the English cases cited above that those who make agreements for the resolution of disputes must show good reason for departing from them, but also with the interests of the orderly regulation of international commerce, that having promised to take their complaints to the experts and if necessary to the arbitrators, that is where [the employers] should go. The fact that the [employers] now find their chosen method too slow to suit their purpose, is to my way of thinking, quite beside the point." The constraints formerly represented by the controls exercised by the courts are now superseded by the competition between separate bodies which promote different methods of dispute resolution, which can be seen as erecting barriers for the promotion of their own interests. Barriers may find some justification in the need to break away from the established order and to develop radical new processes. But fragmentation has its price, and this paper will examine whether the public interest would be better served by the building of bridges. It will also examine what the future might hold for arbitration, if those barriers can be broken down.

WHY DIFFERENT METHODS?

For as long as state courts have admitted private commercial disputes, two potential methods of dispute resolution have necessarily existed in the form of litigation and privatised decision-making. For most of the last millennium private dispute resolution has, despite some variety of method, generally been content to be labelled as arbitration. The past century has seen a number of significant changes, with the recognition of processes of resolution not falling within the umbrella of conventional arbitration. The past two decades have seen a rapid acceleration of activity in privatised dispute resolution and the evolution of a now significant number of different methods. This phenomenon can be linked to a broader scale of evolution. The history of all institutions shows an inevitable process of diversification and fragmentation, typically followed by the creation of restrictive rules and barriers, reinforced and exploited by those whose interests depend upon their continuation. The broader sweep of history will usually reveal a further period of change in which the rules and barriers are demolished, the old order swept away, and the process allowed to begin anew. This brief survey encompasses not merely the major instruments of power (governments and religious movements) but, more vitally, the trades and professions through which ordinary folk must seek to make their living. The legal professions, as currently regulated in different countries, can be seen as lying at different points on this scale of evolution. That in England could be characterised as presently slouching towards the third stage of sweeping away the old order, having been preceded there by some countries but still followed by others. Privatised dispute resolution, it is suggested, has recently passed through the first stage of fragmentation and is rapidly entering the second stage of the development of restrictive rules and barriers, which could be seen as aping some of the former practices of the legal professions. This paper will examine the nature of these restrictions and barriers and their effect on dispute resolution generally.

RULES AND BARRIERS

Each individual dispute resolution process now seems to have discovered a need for rules. While some form of rules may be needed for the basic operation of any process, rules also have the potential to restrict entry to the process and to define boundaries between one process and another. Rules which may be intended to facilitate can easily become barriers. Some of these are discussed later in relation to particular procedures. It is relevant at this point to ask whether it is necessary for each dispute resolution method to regard itself as holding exclusive territory, such that a dispute is to be resolved exclusively by the method chosen by, or imposed upon, the parties. This situation is indeed surprising, given that the courts are now prepared to forgo any claim to exclusivity, as explained by Eveleigh LJ in *Lloyd v Wright*: "[t]he principle that the court will not allow its jurisdiction to be ousted is at the root of the defendant's argument. However, the court does not claim a monopoly in deciding disputes between parties. It does not, of its own initiative, seek to interfere when citizens have recourse to other tribunals. The court exercises its jurisdiction when appealed to. Until then, the court is not conscious of ignominy if an arbitrator decides a question with which the court is competent to deal. Furthermore, the court will not refuse to allow the subject matter of an action already begun to be referred to arbitration, if the parties so agree ... The court, however, will not permit its assistance to be denied to a party who has invoked it except by that party's consent or by its own ruling."

To regard dispute resolution processes as exclusive may give rise to 'demarcation issues' between alternative methods, which can be seen as capable of generating prejudice. An example of this was the decision of the English Court of Appeal in the *Crouch* case where it was held the Court could not exercise the same powers as an arbitrator under particular and widely used forms of building contract. To the credit of the island of

Ireland, it was an appeal to the House of Lords from the six counties which finally laid this particular ghost to rest. The decision was that, although the parties could have created such a dispute resolution regime, clear words (which were in this case absent) would have been required to achieve such a commercially improbable result.

Another example of prejudice resulting from demarcation is the supposed need in arbitration for strict proof of any relevant fact, including the amount of any sum claimed. Most forms of alternative dispute resolution (ADR), notably including statutory adjudication, entitle or require the tribunal to provide a commercial solution which may fall far short of strict proof. When the costs involved in strict proof are considered, it is easy to see how arbitration can operate to deter bringing of claims, where no such deterrent would exist in relation to other methods. These examples reveal the potential disadvantage of being bound by one method and being unable to use the most suitable aspects of two or more procedures.

These considerations lead to one of the central questions to be addressed in this paper: may a Tribunal be appointed simply as a dispute resolver, with a mandate to make use of all or any procedures and powers that may (consensually) be conferred upon it? A second question, necessarily to be addressed, is how might this be achieved? Before addressing these questions further, however, consideration will be given to the individual methods of consensual dispute resolution currently available, in particular to examine their potential. These two central questions look to the future and should be addressed in the context of the future scope and potential of the individual processes. Before considering arbitration itself this review examines what might be regarded as the 'user's choice' — those methods which have been devised to avoid the apparent failings of arbitration.

THE ROLE OF MEDIATION

The growth of mediation, conciliation and ADR generally has amply demonstrated the response of the free market to the inability of arbitration, as presently understood, to deliver the service demanded by customers. So much has been written about these processes that another foray into their analysis would serve little purpose. An aspect which does call for comment, however, is the evolving structures of the systems currently in use, notably referred to in his Freshfields lecture by Dr Gerold Hermann as developing "dangerously increasing formalization." One aspect of this is in the 'rules' applicable to such processes which have already been touched upon in this paper. Rules are clearly perceived by the promulgating bodies as serving a useful purpose which is, however, not always apparent to others.

It is clearly important for the parties and the ADR 'facilitator' to know whether his function is limited to finding a mutually acceptable solution, or whether it may include expressing a view on the merits. Other requirements contained in rules may be counter-productive if they seek to impose a structure on the process which may be at variance with the evolving position of the parties as they are guided towards resolution. Some ADR rules give the impression of seeking to create a quasi-legal mystique, accessible only to the initiated, and providing a further example of unjustified barriers. The existence of exclusive mediation rules inhibits the combining of mediation with other dispute resolution processes. It is suggested, however, that mediation rules may have a more important and necessary role in facilitating the use of this process in combination with other processes, without causing prejudice to the status of either.

STATUTORY ADJUDICATION IN THE UK

The term 'adjudication' has now acquired, throughout the UK, a statutory meaning. The Housing Grants, Construction and Regeneration Act 1996 (HGCRA) has introduced in every construction contract an inalienable right to a statutory process of adjudication 'at any time'. Quite apart from other criticism of its efficacy, this can be seen as somewhat counter-productive in the evolution of free-market dispute resolution processes. Parties are not permitted to contract out of the right to adjudicate; this applies to construction operations carried out in England, Wales, Northern Ireland and Scotland irrespective of the governing law of the contract. An unavoidable disadvantage of statutory adjudication is that the process has become frozen in time, in terms of late 1990s' procedures, while the rest of the dispute resolution industry has moved on. As the cases progress through the English, Northern Ireland and Scottish courts, it will be several years before the adjudication revolution is fully worked out, including the latest storm cloud represented by human rights legislation, which will break in or shortly after October 2000.

The difficulty of integration of statutory adjudication with other forms of dispute resolution is well illustrated in the case of *Herschel Engineering v Breen Property* in which Dyson J had to decide whether to enforce an adjudicator's decision given in proceedings which had been commenced and concluded during the course of litigation. In this case, the contractor had brought proceedings in the county court to recover sums alleged to be outstanding under a construction contract. In order to hasten the process, the claimant entered judgment in default. This proved counterproductive, however, since the defendant had the judgment set aside and the parties then entered into lengthy appeal proceedings as to whether the defendant should be permitted to defend the action. Without any suspension of the proceedings, the claimant then decided to pursue the statutory remedy of adjudication 'at any time'. The absence of any bar on the time within which adjudication could be brought necessarily led to a potential conflict between enforcement of decisions given in separate proceedings on the same issue. Leaving aside human rights issues, enforcement proceedings following adjudication are said to have given rise to in excess of 40 court decisions to date. The only ground which seems to be firmly established as a basis for resisting enforcement is that of jurisdiction, but new cases are appearing regularly. What seems clear is that many of these cases involve relitigating issues on which extensive authority already exists in the field of arbitration. Other issues, for example the extent to which 'due process' requirements apply, should also be litigated in relation to the use of provisional procedures under the Arbitration Act (AA) 1996 s39. What seems to be fast developing is a series of different jurisprudential streams with no clear connection. Quite apart from wastage of judicial time, this can hardly add to the cause of commercial certainty and confidence.

NON-STATUTORY ADJUDICATION

It should not be forgotten that consensual adjudication, as provided for under several standard forms of contract prior to HGCRA and in international construction contracts, remains a useful and viable alternative particularly in countries which do not enjoy the benefits of statutory adjudication. Among the advantages of the consensual process, now clearly to be seen, is the ease with which the procedure can be adjusted by the promoting bodies to take into account problems, for example, relating to conflict with other dispute resolution processes. A form of temporarily binding adjudication is readily available under AA 1996 s39 (provisional relief). This section, which is considered further below, is capable of offering any remedy otherwise available through statutory adjudication and can readily be adapted, through appropriate rules, to provide for emergency relief where the nature of the dispute so requires. One of the particular advantages of s39 is that the appointed tribunal may then review its own decision in the light of further evidence, unlike the statutory adjudicator who becomes *functus officio*, and whose decision may reviewed only by a different tribunal. Various forms of non-binding adjudication are available. Non-binding dispute boards are considered below. A form of non-binding adjudication is available through the courts under the name early neutral evaluation (ENE). In my opinion, this consists of a form of 'mini-trial' in which a judge gives the parties a decision based on limited documents and arguments, which is intended to form the basis of settlement. The judge performing the ENE is not, without consent of the parties, then to be further involved if settlement is not reached. This formalised system is necessarily less flexible than the more traditional approach of simply asking the judge (or the arbitrator) for an informal 'indication' of his current view to aid settlement. Little in the dispute resolution industry is truly novel.

DISPUTE BOARDS

Dispute boards are said to be a growing area of activity, at least in the sense of their use under construction contracts. It is claimed that they can be highly successful in deterring parties from bringing forward formal disputes, perhaps on the basis that the dispute board members are intended to acquire a serious working knowledge of the contract, and will therefore be less likely to be persuaded by unmeritorious contentions. They are referred to as dispute review boards (DRB) in the US and as dispute adjudication boards (DAB) under the FIDIC forms of contract used worldwide.

DRBs and DABs differ from other forms of dispute resolution in that they are intended to be set up and to operate throughout the period of a construction contract, irrespective of whether any actual disputes materialise. Dispute boards are thus in a position equivalent to that of the nominated arbitrator found in 19th and early 20th century construction contracts, to whom any dispute that might arise was to be referred. Leaving aside the inchoate status of DRB members prior to a dispute arising, once the matter is referred to them they become either adjudicators, mediators, experts or arbitrators (in the conventional sense), depending upon the detailed terms of appointment. There is little uniformity in the process. The pattern frequently encountered in the US involves formal hearings but an award which is not binding. The DAB pattern under FIDIC involves a decision equivalent to that of the engineer/architect, which is binding until superseded by an arbitrator's award. Thus, while the dispute boards may constitute a different procedure, all of its elements are to be found embedded in other processes. What the new fashion does reveal is a continuing demand, not merely for the novel, but for something that might be better than the existing processes in terms of efficiency and cost.

USE OF SINGLE JOINT EXPERT

While not usually regarded of itself as a means of dispute resolution, a tribunal-appointed or joint expert has the potential to achieve much more than the presentation of expertise. Conventionally, such an expert takes the place (or occasionally duplicates) the party-appointed experts, fulfilling an essentially similar role to them. The appointed expert can also, with great potential advantage, be given an extended role to promote settlement of particular issues, so that the full tribunal need deal only with those matters incapable of less formal resolution. The appointed expert, after conducting his investigation of the opposing cases, will be in a position to present his opinion to the parties, who then have the opportunity to reach a much more informed settlement than through conventional ADR. Given that the parties are generally free to agree upon any procedure, the appointment of a tribunal expert as an intermediate tribunal, not bound by any formal rules, presents great scope for cost-effective resolution of all but those issues which positively require the tribunal's formal determination. The author has personal experience of the successful use of such procedures in a number of cases, where the particular procedure could be tailor-made for the disputes to be resolved. A close parallel to this procedure can be seen in the French *procédure de référé*, which is available through the courts. It is also available internationally through the ICC, in the pre-arbitral referee process. The court-based system was originally intended for emergency use in cases where the parties have not had time to issue formal proceedings. But the process can be and often is used as an alternative to the court, whereby an expert is appointed and directed by the judge, who otherwise takes no part in the proceedings until the expert has completed his mission. The court-appointed expert will conduct a full investigation of the facts and circumstances, including the hearing of factual and expert evidence from the parties, and the conducting of investigations and inquiries, including requesting documents. The French Court Rules require the submission of a formal report which is intended to be presented to, and which is generally acted upon, by the court. Frequently, however, the report leads to negotiation and mediation by the expert and eventual settlement, often without formal proceedings ever being issued.

These examples show the advantage of flexibility of procedure and the potential benefits in devising techniques which lie essentially outside the rules, which can nevertheless offer the parties what they need in terms of cost-effective resolution of disputes. Such examples also give rise to the question of why an arbitrator, given sufficient technical expertise, should not act in exactly the same role, giving opinions and encouraging settlement of issues which are capable of such resolution, while reserving other issues for a more formal determination, by the same tribunal.

INNOVATION IN ARBITRATION — TWO PROPOSED CHANGES

Arbitration has traditionally occupied a central and pivotal role in private dispute resolution. Given the considerable strides which arbitration procedure has made in the past decades there should be no doubt as to its future potential. However, it is suggested that major changes are still needed before arbitration can properly play a universal role in the field of dispute resolution. In order to demonstrate the potential of arbitration, two areas of possible change are proposed. Both depend on conventions which, it is suggested, are based upon a supposed parity with court proceedings and which may be seen as unnecessary in arbitration.

The first area of proposed change is in the present inability of arbitration, largely through self-imposed barriers, to accommodate within its procedures the process of mediation or amicable dispute resolution, for the more efficient disposal of elements of a dispute to which is more suited. The process, which became known as med-arb, was much discussed in the journals in the period 1994 to 1996, including in a collated series of correspondence following an article by Paul Newman. A re-published article by David Elliott discussed the dangers and opportunities of med-arb and concluded that, with careful management, both roles could be accommodated. A similar proposal was put forward by Professor Roy Goode in his 1997 Alexander lecture: 'Dispute Resolution in the 21st Century.' Now that the 21st century is upon us, perhaps the time has come to act.

The root of the problem lies in the assumption that an arbitrator cannot act as mediator without impairing his independent role. Examples of arbitrators who have been removed from office for attempting to act in this way are well known. It is suggested that such cases are no more than particular examples of arbitrators who have crossed the boundary of 'natural justice' and that there is no firm foundation for the assumption that an arbitrator cannot act in both roles, given proper safeguards. The use of mediation is expressly contemplated under the ICC Rules (through the process referred to as amiable composition) and is occasionally seen in domestic arbitration practice. What needs to be further explored are procedures which would allow an arbitrator, once he or she is fully involved in the issues, to take the initiative formally to propose terms of settlement to the parties on particular issues or on the whole case, while retaining the ability to continue as arbitrator in the event that no settlement is reached.

It has to be recognised at once that some aspects of mediation and amicable resolution are potentially inconsistent with the role of an arbitrator in making final and binding decisions. Thus, the process of mediation may involve receiving information unilaterally which is intended not to be imparted to the other side at all. Plainly, this imposes some limits on use of mediation within conventional arbitration, and some processes of resolution could not be adopted without restricting the future role of the arbitrator. The devising of appropriate rules of procedure will be a task of some delicacy, but one which will repay the degree of formalisation necessarily introduced.

The second suggested area of change is in regard to the conventionally assumed need to define precisely the 'dispute or difference', and therefore the arbitrator's jurisdiction, at the outset. The common law tradition has always allowed a party to give a generalised 'notice of dispute', to be refined subsequently through the parties' pleadings and particulars. The civil law approach, as reflected in the ICC Rules, requires more precise definition at the commencement of an arbitration. The ICC Rules, in effect, require pleadings and full supporting documents to be served at the outset before the appointment of the tribunal. Thus (in theory at least), further pleadings are unnecessary and the process of investigation and drawing up of an award can (again in theory) be limited to a period such as six months. Common lawyers have shown themselves extraordinarily adept at taking on board such fundamentally different procedures and should have no difficulty in accommodating a change in the opposite direction. The question now posed is whether the costly process of defining the issues in advance might, with advantage, be dispensed with in appropriate cases.

All arbitrators used to dealing with English (and other) counsel and solicitors will have had the experience of being presented with voluminous pleadings and particulars, often accompanied by procedural disputes as to their adequacy, only to find that the case eventually focuses on a relatively small part of those pleadings as requiring final determination. These experiences are often accompanied by complaints about arbitration being too costly and excessively influenced by High Court procedure, even in the post-Woolf era. Forms of procedure used in public inquiries allow the process of investigation to commence with generalised terms of reference, usually with a list of topics or questions to be considered. Only at the end of the process is it necessary to define those issues which require determination, specifically for the purpose of giving notice to persons who may be adversely affected. The same process could readily be used, in appropriate circumstances, in arbitration, where the precise issues to be decided could be identified and agreed with the parties during, or at the end of, an inquiry process. The conventional objection to such a procedure is that the parties and their advocates would not know the precise issues to be addressed. Yet this would be a small price to pay for the advantage of being able to embark on the arbitration process without the lengthy and often costly pleading process; and the parties would be entitled to address the tribunal on the issues as finally defined before any decision was reached. In the majority of commercial disputes, the parties would have a full and detailed knowledge of the dispute before arbitration was launched. In such cases, conventional pleadings might serve only to add a legal framework to the issues which were already well known. An example of the way in which such a procedure would work in practice can be seen from the French court *referée* system, already discussed. Other examples are in the field of commodity arbitration, where usually the only issue concerns the quality of goods. Such a procedure may be of benefit in many areas where the urgency of the case does not allow the time required for formal pleadings or where the sums in issue do not justify the expense. Given the availability of such a procedure, market forces can be relied on to determine its usefulness.

THE NEED FOR REGULATION

The creation of barriers in the form of the regulation of persons to be regarded as qualified now seems to be a central part of the process of diversification of dispute resolution. In some professional areas this may be justified by the need to ensure proper levels of expertise or experience. Few would challenge the need for registration of medical practitioners, and most people would be surprised to know that structural engineers, at least in the UK, are not required to be registered. Lawyers have historically acquired an unrivalled reputation for regulation and the maintenance of 'closed shops'. This has been the subject of debate for some years in the UK and has recently resulted in considerable slackening of rules as to rights of audience.

In the field of international arbitration, lawyers in many countries throughout the world have, in the past, sought to promote the employment of local lawyers through the Legal Profession Act, or local equivalent. This is, however, now generally recognised as being irreconcilable with the promotion of a country as a neutral venue for international arbitration. Consequently, countries which have formerly allowed such protectionism are now ensuring its removal, at least in the case of arbitration not subject to the local law.

Arbitration and other means of dispute resolution have traditionally been free of such attempts at protectionism. Yet there is a worrying tendency for bodies which are intended primarily to promote the interests of different forms of dispute resolution, also to act in ways which promote the interests of members of the institution or group against non-members. This may seem harmless enough until one examines the rules of membership. More than one such body is known to require attendance at its own courses as a condition of registration. Courses tend to be expensive and not subject to the degree of audit which would be expected of a mainstream academic institution, either in terms of course content or selection of course leaders. Once qualified in this way, continued practice becomes conditional upon attending and paying for refresher courses, with little regard to the experience or distinction of the person concerned. In addition, the volume of tuition required is such that those who can be found to conduct the courses may often have little practical experience of what they teach in theory. These remarks, of course, are not addressed to any organisation in particular. What seems to be in course of being created is a secondary dispute resolution industry in the regulation and training of those actually to be involved in the process. This worrying tendency needs to be tackled firmly to ensure that bona fide education and the dissemination of knowledge and expertise does not become abused.

THE FUTURE OF DISPUTE RESOLUTION

This paper now returns to its main subject: the future. Improvements in regard to individual dispute resolution methods have been suggested. But the process of fragmentation is itself the major problem which needs to be addressed in the future. The process of creating institutions which promulgate different means of dispute resolution is bound to emphasise the separate nature of the processes. Furthermore, the promotion of separate dispute resolution methods inevitably leads to rivalry as to the merits of one method to the exclusion of others. The dispute resolution 'user' surely has no interest in such antics, nor can there be any public benefit in promoting one method of resolution. The user needs whichever method or combination of methods is most efficient for his or her particular dispute.

While some institutions include both arbitration and mediation within their areas of interest, other bodies promote one process only. It is of more significance that there has been little to promote the integration of different dispute resolution procedures or their intelligent combination, or even the study of common ground between the processes. The pressure has been all in the opposite direction. Strong positive steps will be needed to bring about change. The recent change to the Charter and Bye-Laws of the Chartered Institute by which 'Arbitration' has become 'Arbitration and other methods of dispute resolution', is a significant step. The remarks of the President in his inaugural speech on 20 June 2000, which set out the benefits of that change, are particularly timely. This paper, however, suggests an alternative route to the same goal: that arbitration should be seen as including other means of consensual dispute resolution.

INTEGRATION OF PROCESSES

If the right solution to the current trend of fragmentation lies in the integration of separate processes, this must necessarily occur under the umbrella of arbitration. It has already been suggested that mediation should form part of the arbitration process. Given the conceptual leap involved in the introduction of equity arbitration clauses by AA 1996, the enlargement of arbitration to include mediation aimed at resolution of a dispute initiated through the process of arbitration, seems a small additional step. Given also that successive arbitration Acts in England and elsewhere have resisted any attempt to define the process, its notional enlargement should create no conceptual difficulty. In the light of the current emphasis on party autonomy, there would seem no reason why this small step could not be accomplished through appropriate rules. Another candidate for the process of integration is the procedure generally known as 'expert determination'. The history of this process of resolution shows that it has evolved to cover situations not amounting to a 'dispute', typically where some article or commodity is to be valued. The process has, however, also gained currency in recent years as a process which can also be applied to the resolution of disputes. Expert determination in this sense is usually intended to encompass all that arbitration offers, without particular perceived disadvantages, such as the possibility of judicial intervention. As in the case of mediation, it would require comparatively little by way of additional rules to bring the process squarely within the umbrella of 'arbitration' again, notionally widening the definition of arbitration.

Adjudication (whether statutory or consensual) is generally regarded as a summary process which may fall short of the mandatory requirements of due process. The simultaneous drafting of HGCRA 1996 and AA 1996, involving a patent lack of communication between two UK government departments, has already been commented upon in some detail. It needs to be re-stated that any relief capable of being awarded by an adjudicator could be awarded with equal facility by an arbitrator exercising powers under AA 1996 s39 (Provisional Relief). Similarly, a procedure complying with the requirements of HGCRA s108 could readily be drafted so as to fall under AA 1996. In this event, all the current difficulties concerning enforcement of adjudication decisions, which are presently taking up the time of the courts in London and Edinburgh, could be solved more readily by reference to a century of commercial law already available in the field of arbitration. The perceived difficulty, however, is that the suggested process would be branded as arbitration. The parliamentary debate over the HGCRA Bill left no doubt that arbitration was regarded, both by the government then in power and by the opposition, as offering no solution to the perceived problem of the construction industry. Adjudication, on the other hand, offering a rough and ready means of ensuring cash flow, was regarded as both appropriate and politically acceptable, apparently in ignorance of what was already (in 1995) contained in the Arbitration Bill. Both the Bill published in 1995 (which led to the 1996 Act) and the Bill published in

1994 (which was substantially superseded) contained new and groundbreaking powers enabling arbitrators to give 'provisional' relief equivalent to the summary processes previously available only through the courts. Whether it is yet appropriate to re-open the debate on adjudication is for others to judge. The time will come, however, when the increasing backlog of adjudication enforcement cases in the UK, coupled with the impact of the Human Rights Act 1998, require that a fresh look be taken at the role of adjudication. Even if the word must be retained, there is no reason why it should not be brought squarely within AA 1996, with the statutory right to invoke the procedure continuing in the case of contracts falling within the definition of construction. It might be added that, if the statutory process is as beneficial as it is presently claimed to be, it should be extended to cover other areas of trade and commerce.

TRIBUNAL AS DISPUTE RESOLVER

The question was posed earlier whether a tribunal might be appointed as a dispute resolver with power to use all appropriate methods of resolution. In the light of the above discussion, the question needs to be reformulated. What has emerged is that the process of arbitration may be understood as including all other subsidiary forms of dispute resolution, i.e., those which encompass part but not the whole of the arbitration process. In this sense appointment as arbitrator would include the power to use all means of consensual dispute resolution save where the powers of the tribunal were restricted expressly, or by implication. The parties to an arbitration could thus restrict the powers which the arbitral tribunal is to exercise in exactly the same way as the ICC Rules require it to be stated whether the arbitral tribunal is to act as amiable compositeur. Similarly, agreement that the arbitral tribunal was not to exercise the power to give relief on a provisional basis would effectively exclude the power of adjudication and impose a general requirement as to due process. Where a tribunal is to be appointed solely for the purpose of conducting a conciliation, this would involve further exclusions of the tribunal's powers including, crucially, the power to give a binding decision. There is no good reason, however, why other aspects of AA 1996 should not, with advantage, continue to apply to such a process. These might include powers of appointment and removal and the power to appoint experts, legal advisers or assessors. The tribunal, in these circumstances, might be required to deliver an award which the parties agree would not be binding. It would, therefore, not fall to be enforced or set aside, but might form a significant factor in any subsequent settlement negotiation. If conciliation and mediation are to be taken as part of mainstream dispute resolution, why should they shrink from being designated as part of the arbitration process? The answer to be given to the question, as reformulated, is that a tribunal may be appointed to resolve such disputes as are referred to it, in such manner and using such techniques as the parties may agree upon within the overall meaning and concept of arbitration. The parties should be free to restrict and confine the powers of the tribunal as they think fit. The tribunal should, equally, be free to request further powers where it thinks appropriate. All such powers should be seen as falling within the scope of arbitration.

WHAT DOES THE USER WANT?

No paper on the future of dispute resolution, whether theoretical or practical, can be of any serious value without addressing the needs of the client or 'user'. What changes would the user be prepared to sanction? Two recent sources of information concerning construction disputes may assist in addressing this question. First, statistics concerning the use of statutory adjudication in the UK have shown the incidence of referrals as running at some ten times the previous rate of cases brought before the TCC. At the same time, there is said to be a reduction of the number of TCC cases, variously estimated at between 20% and 50%. These figures must, however, be viewed in the general context of the post-Woolf 'pause' in litigation business. It is similarly reported that numbers of arbitration referrals are substantially reduced, but this may apply mainly to disputes which are suitable for statutory adjudication. While methods of dispute resolution which lead to the generation of disputes which would not otherwise exist are not necessarily to be seen as having achieved their purpose, these figures plainly indicate some preference in the field of construction for adjudication over what is alternatively on offer. The second factor, already mentioned in this paper, concerns the use of dispute resolution boards. These are claimed to be remarkably successful in deterring, or by other means avoiding, the incidence of disputes. The particular type of DRB under consideration was that which involved formal hearings subject to the requirements of due process, while leading to a decision which was non-binding. Where decisions were given, they were claimed to achieve a 99% success rate in terms of the incidence of further referrals to arbitration or the courts. A similar percentage of success is claimed in respect of adjudication, where the decision is binding but open to challenge through arbitration or otherwise. Bearing in mind that these data apply only in the limited field of construction, and that parties in construction might be regarded as more 'litigious' than in other areas of commerce, some tentative conclusion might be drawn, taking into account the review of other dispute resolution methods above.

The following conclusions are suggested as having more general application: clients are attracted to methods of dispute resolution involving less delay and less expense; customers are indifferent to the method or mechanics of dispute resolution. They have no loyalty to any established method; he availability of an impartial 'first round' decision will usually be sufficient to deter further more costly disputes.

Arbitration, with all current improvements and innovations, including those suggested in this paper, will still fall short of clients' expectations and needs. The process of reform must be kept firmly in the forefront of the Chartered Institute's objectives and those of its individual practitioners. Any changes or innovations should pay careful regard to the wishes of the user.

CONCLUSION AND SUMMARY

The changes suggested in this paper will not be brought about without full debate, the formulation of detailed proposals and their promotion (where appropriate) by a body of professional standing influence. No body other than the Chartered Institute of Arbitrators could undertake such a role. The proposals outlined in this paper are, it is suggested, squarely in the public interest rather than the sectional interest of any particular branch of the dispute resolution industry. They should also be seen as within the interest of the Chartered Institute. The proposals may be summarised as follows: (1) All means of privatised dispute resolution should be regarded as potentially included within the term 'arbitration'. This is consistent with the Chartered Institute's revised Charter and Bye-Laws; (2) Means of dispute resolution involving powers which fall short of the final and binding determination of rights should be regarded as forms of restricted arbitration, subject to AA 1996 except where otherwise agreed; (3) Parties should be encouraged by suitable arbitration agreements and rules to empower arbitrators, where appropriate, to make alternative use of forms of restricted arbitration, including mediation and adjudication; (4) Future development of all forms of arbitration, including restricted arbitration, should be harmonised, as should the approach to training, qualification and promotion of all forms of dispute resolution. Finally, it is emphasised that this paper does not advocate any restriction on the use of any particular methods of dispute resolution or of the bodies which promote them. The theme of bridge building, however, positively advocates the creation of easy access between all such methods and the promotion of their combined use under the umbrella of arbitration. Given the general acceptance of the principle of party autonomy, the difficulties involved are not theoretical but practical, in that users need to be convinced that arbitration has the capacity to change.

REFERENCES

* This article was originally published as J. Uff, 'Dispute Resolution in the 21st Century: Barriers or Bridges?', *Arbitration* 67, no. 1 (2001): 4-16.
1 *Channel Tunnel Group v Balfour Beatty Construction* [1993] AC 334, HL.

2 [1983] QB 1065.
3 *Northern RHA v Derek Crouch Construction* [1984] QB 644.
4 *Beaufort Developments v Gilbert-Ash* [1999] 1 AC 266.
5 G. Hermann, 'Does the World Need Additional Uniform Legislatio on Arbitration?', *Arbitration International* 15 (1999): 227.
6 HGCRA Section 104(6), (7).
7 2000 CILL 1616.
8 See *Homer Burgess v Shirex* [2000] BLR 124, *Grovedeck v Capital Demolition* [2000] BLR 181.
9 Following original publication of this paper in Dublin, proposals have been formulated for extension of the CIMA Rules to provide for such an emergency procedure.
10 See J. Toulmin & R. Stevenson, 'Early Neutral Evaluation in the TCC', (London, 1999).
11 However, FIDIC has deviated recently from that concept by giving preference to ad hoc DABs in its new Yellow Book.
12 See now CPR Rule 35.7.
13 See generally D. Duprey & R. Gandur, *L'Expert et l'Avocat dans l'Expertise Judiciaire en Matière Civile*, Guide des Bons Usages.
14 P. Newman, 'The MED-ARB Debate-Some Contributions', *Arbitration* 60 (1994): 173-183.
15 D. Elliott, 'Med/arb: Fraught with Danger of Ripe with Opportunity?', *Arbitration* 62 (1996): 175-183.
16 R. Goode, 'Dispute Resolution in the Twenty-First Century, *Arbitration* 64 (1998): 9-18.

17 *Turner (East Asia) v Builders Federation (HK)* (1988) 42 BLR 122; *Town & City v Wiltshier Southern* (1988) 42 BLR 109.
18 1998 ICC Rules, Art. 18.1(g).
19 The so-called 'Salmon procedure' was evolved for the purpose of ensuring compliance with natural justice requirements and the avoidance of judicial review. It will come in for further scrutiny following the coming into force of the Human Rights Act 1998.
20 See Lawler, *Matusky v A G Barbados* (1983) 2 CLYb (1995) 117.
21 Particularly in Singapore and Hong Kong during the past decade.
22 Section 44.
23 See generally J. Kendall, *Expert Determination* (London: F.T. Law and Tax, 1996).
24 E.g., as expressed in AA 1996 Section 33.
25 The then Department of the Environment having responsibility for construction and the Department of Trade and Industry having responsibility for arbitration matters.
26 J. Uff (ed.), *Construction Contract Reform: A Plea for Sanity, Contemporary Issues in Construction Law* (London: Construction Law Press, 1997).
27 ICC Rules of Arbitration 1998, Art. 18.1(g).
28 Address by R. Rubin at Anglo-American Construction Law Colloquium, 17 July 2000.

CHAPTER 1

Dispute Resolution 2020

Sir Anthony Evans

When Bruce Harris asked me to write this piece on 2020 dispute resolution, I thought that he must be referring to 20/20 eyesight, the only context in which I had heard those figures used. The far-sighted arbitrator? Perhaps, the perfect arbitrator, 20/20 sometimes being used as a metaphor for excellence. Either way, it was flattering to be asked, even to be considered as the speaker on such a topic. But then, only a few enquiries brought me down to earth. What he had in mind was how did I think dispute resolution, and arbitration in particular, would look in the year 2020 — the millennium theme with a difference. It is some consolation that any prediction about 20 years hence cannot be proved or disproved until nearer the time, and by then no one will be interested in knowing whether our forecasts were correct. Much better, I think, to concentrate on the situation as it is today and to consider in what direction things are moving, if we approve, to say so and to encourage development and change, and if not, then to issue our warnings and do what we can to keep the process on the right road.

NATIONAL OR INTERNATIONAL

I doubt whether even this limited ambition can be achieved, except from some national perspective. Even so-called international arbitration tends to be firmly rooted in some national jurisdiction or another. Where is the arbitration to be held? What law governs? Where does the arbitration have its seat? Where is the award to be enforced? Over the past few decades, the concept of transnational arbitrations and of some universal *lex mercatoria* has often been mooted, but to little practical effect. Arbitration remains subject to national laws, and state jurisdiction is stubbornly territorial. There seems to be no prospect of these basic factors changing in the next 20 years, certainly not to the extent that national laws will cease to be the first concern of arbitrators, nor even that some international convention containing uniform rules for arbitration in all its aspects will be accepted by all or even by a majority of states. So, if you want my guess, arbitration will remain solidly based in the municipal laws of individual states.

Now let me qualify that dogmatic assertion. There is undoubtedly a tendency for individual states to engage in regional groupings and to modify their own laws in the interests of regional harmony. The European Union is a prime example and the most topical for this meeting of the European Branch of the Chartered Institute of Arbitrators. We have in Vienna the offices of UNCITRAL and we know what efforts are being made there to harmonise the law of arbitration, not least from the admirable address given at the branch's last meeting at Vilnius in May by Dr Sekolec. While I take leave to doubt whether any form of truly international consensus covering the whole scope of arbitration will develop within the next 20 years, or become embodied in one widely accepted convention, nevertheless it is quite another thing to contemplate a closer degree of assimilation between the arbitration laws of individual states, and that is something I do expect to occur. The growing significance of regional cooperation was graphically made clear during the Institute's International Conference at Cancun in Mexico last year. The choice of venue and the timing both proved highly appropriate. It emerged there that almost all the nations of South and Central America had introduced arbitration laws during the previous decade. Many had adopted the New York Convention, demonstrating the practical importance of being able to enforce international awards — probably the first concern of the businessman. Some introduced substantive rules based more or less comprehensively on the UNCITRAL Model Law. There was room for debate as to the reason for this coincidence of legislation in so many different countries, but one factor certainly was the emergence of regional trade groupings which made such legislation necessary, particularly in order to encourage, or not discourage, foreign investment and trade. So here is another reason for expecting some regional if not truly international development of arbitration law.

ENGLAND AND WALES

I have said that a national perspective is essential, and so for obvious reasons which I hope you will not find overly chauvinistic I shall look next at possible developments in English (and Welsh) arbitration law and practice. Many people might say that the future or at least the immediate future is set fair — and in terms of arbitration law, 20 years or so may be regarded as immediate. The Arbitration Act (AA) 1996, it might be said, has barely settled down. It has rightly been praised for codifying the basic rules and even the principles of arbitration law, and no change should be contemplated in them. The Woolf reforms to the rules of civil litigation have had or are likely to have a significant effect on the practice of arbitration, and they are certain to be with us for at least 20 years, subject only to fine tuning from time to time. No significant changes, therefore, in arbitration law or practice during the next two decades? Speaking for myself, I am not bold or complacent enough to say this. So I should suggest what changes may take place.

ARBITRATION AND MEDIATION

Mediation, of course, is a fast-growing method of dispute resolution which some claim is bidding to replace arbitration but which I prefer to see as complementary to it. What is clear is that a new form of professional skill has been identified during the past 10 years or a little longer. This is the ability of an independent third party to assist the parties towards an agreed settlement of their dispute. That is quite different from the task of an arbitrator or judge, which is to make his or her own decision on the merits of the dispute and to announce it to the parties in his or her judgment or award. Whether the parties agree with the solution is irrelevant, and in the nature of things it is likely that only one party will do so.

Of course, as every practising judge or arbitrator knows, part of his or her function is to encourage the parties to reach an agreed settlement. Any number of anecdotes testify to this, whether of the judge who tries to clear his or her list quickly, for personal or other motives, or of the conscientious tribunal which recognises that almost invariably an agreed settlement produces a better outcome for both parties than an imposed decision can ever do. But the fact remains that the arbitrator or judge is there to decide, while the mediator does whatever he can to assist the parties towards a settlement to which only they can agree.

What does the growth in the number of mediations — perhaps I should say, of mediators and of mediation institutions — during the past 10 years signify for the development of dispute resolution techniques during the next 20 years? The answer lies, in my view, in the fact that mediation is coming to be regarded as an institution, in the sense that arbitration is an established part of the machinery for the resolution of civil disputes in the United Kingdom and elsewhere. There are professionals who practise it, and although many individuals may hold themselves out to practise both professions we should not lose sight of the fact that the two skills are inherently different, for the reasons I have suggested above. That is why I am cautious about future developments on the lines of med-arb (though here in Barcelona I can add that if the phrase means arbitration on the shores of the Mediterranean then it has my full support).

GOVERNMENT POLICY

The next feature to notice, in England and perhaps elsewhere, is that the government which provides and funds the state judicial system has become increasingly aware of the financial advantages of limiting the number of disputes which come before the courts. Those that do result in court proceedings require the attention of court staff and state-funded judges in expensive court buildings provided by the state. I am not meaning to sound cynical about this, I merely note the happy coincidence, for governments, of the advantages for the parties of an agreed settlement resulting from mediation or of an award resulting from private arbitration proceedings, with the savings in government expenditure which can result if the number of disputes coming before the state courts is reduced. These are powerful factors. They mean that there is likely to be continuing and even increasing pressure from government for both arbitration and mediation to become established forms of dispute resolution, outside the courts but regulated by the legal system. Whether this will lead to a Mediation Act in the early years of the 21st century, or at all, I do not know. But I do believe that we can expect some changes in our arbitration law and procedures partly as a result of the forces I have described. In particular, we may see some move away from the contract-based principles which so far have determined our arbitration law, towards rules which result from arbitration being recognised as what I have called an institution, a recognised part of the civil justice system. Such a development could mean that arbitration should no longer be regarded as exclusively the creature of the parties' agreement to arbitrate. The autonomy of the parties might be called in question. That sounds like a major inroad into established principles, but it is worth considering what changes there might be.

ARBITRATION: CONTRACT-BASED?

I can give two examples where changes of this sort have already taken place. First, in the County Courts in England and Wales, where a Small Claims Arbitration procedure was introduced about 15 years ago, with a low (£1,000) upper limit that has now been significantly increased. The district judge hears and decides the case as an arbitrator, not as a judge. His decision can be appealed to the circuit judge, but only on grounds which entitle the court to set aside an award. There is a requirement for the parties to agree to this form of procedure, and it has been widely popular; but the reality is that the existence of this form of arbitration and the validity of the award rests more on its statutory foundation than upon an agreement by the parties to refer their dispute to a chosen arbitrator. The contract-based theory applies only to a limited extent, if it applies at all.

Secondly, and more sophisticated, are the provisions of AA 1996 s32, which permit the arbitration tribunal, within certain limits, to determine whether or not it has jurisdiction to decide the dispute. If its jurisdiction derives exclusively from the parties' agreement, then logically it cannot decide what the scope of that agreement was. Only a court can do so, notwithstanding the manifest inconvenience and the additional expense of obtaining a court ruling if such a dispute as to jurisdiction does arise. One can also ask whether that is what the parties expected to occur. The logical difficulty is summed up in the celebrated phrase *competens competens*. I, like many other British lawyers, I suspect, have always found the concept difficult to grasp. Now, AA 1996 preserves the legal principle — ultimately, only the court can decide — but it also permits the arbitrator to make a preliminary decision which in practice may often be final. So to this extent the strict 'contract basis only' principle has been eroded.

In another context, AA 1996 stopped short of permitting arbitrators to exercise another power which convenience and even justice sometimes suggest that they should have, but which is precluded by the strict rule that their jurisdiction is conferred by the parties and by them alone. I refer to the problem of consolidation, which occurs when the same dispute, or what is for all practical purposes the same dispute, arises under two separate contracts, even where both contracts contain an arbitration clause.

Sometimes one person is a party to both contracts, as with a head contract and subcontract, but there is no power to compel the other parties — the employer and the subcontractor — to join in one arbitration. There can be such a joinder, of course, if there are two or more sets of court proceedings, and by definition, therefore, there are cases where no inconvenience or injustice results from such an order being made. To provide by statute that this was permitted in arbitrations would involve a further inroad into the principle that arbitrators derive their jurisdiction solely from the agreement between the parties. But I hope and even expect that during the next 20 years this change will come about.

Unfortunately — I am sorry to end on a pessimistic note — the contract basis principle has recently been affirmed by a majority in the House of Lords, in *Alfred McAlpine Construction Ltd v Panatown Ltd* (27 July 2000). I must declare my interest, because the judgment I gave in the Court of Appeal was reversed. A much-criticised but established rule of English common law (it has now been modified by statute, but that was too late for *Panatown*) is that only the parties to a contract can sue for breach of contract and that the party which sues can only recover damages for loss which it has suffered itself. So, when a property company had a subsidiary company and it was the subsidiary company which entered into a contract for the construction of a new building that was to be owned and occupied by the parent, the construction company was able to defend the claim brought against it in an arbitration under the construction contract by saying to the subsidiary company, the claimant in the arbitration, "it is not you but your parent company which has suffered the losses you are claiming, and if the parent wishes to make a claim, then it must do so in the courts." There was in fact a separate contract between the construction company and the parent, in the nature of a guarantee, but it did not contain an arbitration clause. This argument succeeded in the House of Lords, as it had done before the first instance judge, though not before the arbitrator. Orthodoxy prevailed, and it is disappointing that the procedural consequences of the decision — the impossibility of all claims including those by or against subcontractors being heard and decided in one arbitration, as was envisaged in the construction contract — were not given more prominence by the House of Lords.

I hope that the problems of consolidation, or rather the problems which can occur when consolidation is not permitted, will be the subject of reform during the next 20 years, as part of the increasing recognition of arbitration as part of our civil justice system. But I was too optimistic in the Court of Appeal in *Panatown*, and I must not be too optimistic now.

SUMMARY

The current tendency, which I expect to continue, is for different forms of dispute resolution processes to become recognised not only for their own particular advantages but as parts of the civil justice system provided by a modern state, and to a greater or lesser extent regulated by national laws. Arbitration is already comprehensively regulated, but there are ways in which its convenience and effectiveness can be improved, if not by judicial decision then by national legislation. Mediation is becoming recognised as a process requiring professional skills, but these are different from those of arbitrators. I am cautious about the two processes becoming merged into one, though that is a development of which some people would approve. What all practitioners should bear in mind is that none of the processes exists for its own sake, nor for the benefit of those who practise it. The object shared by all should be to resolve the dispute in the speediest and most cost-effective way, taking account of commercial considerations such as the prospect of the parties continuing to do business together. There is unlikely to be regulation of any of the processes, even arbitration, on a truly international scale, but the work done by international bodies such as UNCITRAL will continue to be invaluable in influencing and even determining the content of national laws. Put that way, there is an awful lot to do, or which can be done, during the next 20 years. I cannot promise to be here to see whether you can do it.

* This article was originally published as A. Evans, 'Dispute Resolution 2020', *Arbitration* 67, no. 1 (2001): 30-34.

CHAPTER 1

Are Trial Lawyers Bad for ADR?

Geoffrey Gibson

If you want an alternative to medicine, you do not want medicine. You want something else. If you go to a herbalist, you are not looking for brain surgery or Prozac. Perhaps you do not trust medicine, or perhaps you believe it has failed but, whatever else you want, you do not want medicine. In our world, you would be quitting western medicine for something else. Someone giving you western medicine would therefore be acting against your wishes. If doctors were involved, they would be suspected of succumbing to an intellectual bias induced by their professional training, or, worse, of being corrupted by a fear of a loss of professional fees if the patient was lost to the medical profession and left with the alternative. It is the same with alternative dispute resolution. People who seek it do so because they want to avoid litigation. Many find themselves involved in mediation because the courts have ordered it but, once they get there, they will at least try this alternative to litigation. They may not trust litigation, or they may believe it has failed them, or is likely to fail them. Whatever may be their reason, they do not want litigation, at least while they are seeking to work through the alternative. Someone giving them litigation would be acting against them. If lawyers were involved, they would be suspected of succumbing to an intellectual bias induced by their professional training, or, worse, of being corrupted by a fear of loss of professional fees if the client was lost to the legal system. Litigation lawyers — barristers or solicitors — are trained to litigate. That is, to fight. Most of them have little training in mediation or arbitration. In Australia they spend four years at university learning the law, with 12 months of articles or the like, and possibly three months or thereabouts in a readers' course if they have gone to the Bar. They may do a tax deductible course for one sunny weekend in mediation, or something similar for arbitration. Their training is overwhelmingly in litigation — the kind of dispute resolution that many want to avoid. There are not, after all, many litigants who like litigation; and those in charge of litigation, the judges, routinely order the parties to avoid litigation if they can by undergoing mediation. The question then is whether or not litigation lawyers are the right people for the job of ADR. That question is more acute if looked at from the point of view of the financial interests of the lawyers. If ADR may be bad for the lawyers, the lawyers may be bad for ADR. Just how does the mindset of lawyers affect the way they go about ADR? It is not the obvious case that, if you need a dentist, you do not want a vet; but rather, if you want to broker a peace treaty, is it a good idea to send in the commandos?

The two main modes of ADR currently used in Australia are mediation and arbitration. The two are different. Mediation involves a negotiation process that may or may not lead to an agreement that determines the dispute. Arbitration involves a decision-making process that must resolve the dispute. In mediation the parties negotiate with someone else there. In arbitration, the parties bring their own judge. One involves off-the-record without prejudice negotiations. The other commonly involves evidence and argument but given in private, unlike a court. Both processes depend on agreement. There has to be an agreement to get arbitration off the ground but, once that agreement is reached, the contract and the law relating to the conduct of arbitration will enable the arbitration to be conducted independently of any further agreement. Mediation can only resolve the dispute if the parties reach agreement. If the mediation is not entered into voluntarily but by order of the court, it can only succeed if the parties agree to participate — they will not be in contempt of court if they turn up at the mediation, tick the roll and leave. They may be open to criticism, but the courts are still chary of ordering people to negotiate. The parties do after all have what might be called, for want of a better word, a constitutional right — it is at least a Magna Carta right — to have their disputes resolved by their courts, and have them resolved decently.

It is obvious that the mind-set of a litigation lawyer may have a different effect on the ADR process depending on whether the ADR is mediation or arbitration. One involves an attempt to reach agreement between the parties. The other involves the forensic determination of issues. At first blush it might be thought that the arbitration processes were more likely to attract the kind of forensic skills learnt by a litigation lawyer in preparation for litigation, while the same skills may have little to offer for the process of guided negotiation. Is this so? Litigation in Australia is a forensic contest that derives from trial by ordeal and trial by battle. Each side usually has a lawyer. The lawyer for each side presents the case. The trial is in public. Witnesses are examined, and cross-examined, and arguments are presented.

The aim is to get through the evidence and argument in a continuing sitting and then give judgment. The judge rules on procedural issues and then weighs the case as presented. The party who wins the case is the one whose case the judge has found to be the better. Pollock and Maitland compare the function of the judge in the old days to a cricket umpire. The judges sit in court not to discover the truth but so that they may answer the question "How's that?" The analogy of a tennis referee is just as appropriate. That official sits there above the protagonists, calls the shots in or out, adds up the score, and says who is the winner — not who is the best, but who has scored the most points on the day. This process of the common law, developed in England over the course of a millennium, is said to be adversarial. That is true as far it goes. But in so far as it is said to represent a distinction from the inquisitorial, it is now misleading. The English Chancery employed inquisitorial procedures like the subpoena and discovery. They now have been abused in our procedure so that major commercial cases can now take on the air of a Royal Commission. The current trend towards judge controlled lists, and varying procedural mixes for different kinds of cases, also makes the current process more inquisitorial. The distinction is no longer worth talking about. The issue more relevant to our time is: is the adversarial position customarily adopted by trial lawyers consistent with the conciliatory position required to make ADR work? Is it simply negative against positive?

THE MIND OF THE TRIAL LAWYER

Litigation — whether you call it adversarial or inquisitorial — involves a contest. The parties are opposed to each other. Otherwise they would not be in court. Each party wants to win. It is the duty of their lawyers to try to get them over the line. The parties and their lawyers are contestants. As Sir Owen Dixon remarked: "the object of the parties is always victory, not absolute truth." Lawyers involved in trying to win these contests are likely to develop some characteristics, whether you are talking about solicitors who practise litigation, or the paradigm litigation lawyer, the trial lawyer, being either barrister or solicitor. What are the characteristics that define the trial lawyer? What are you likely to notice about them?

Combativeness

Conscientious objectors are excused, at least in civilised societies, from fighting wars. There is not much point in sending people out to fight if they will not. People regularly engaged in combat naturally become combative. If you have to go into combat yourself, you want someone to represent you who knows what to do — and who is not frightened, or at least no more frightened than is necessary. Trial lawyers have to face hostility in various ways. They may have to face a hostile judge. There is law on how to deal with a hostile witness. Very few trial lawyers would blush at the suggestion that their job in respect of a hostile witness may be to destroy the witness. Destroying people — hostile or not, witnesses or not — is not something to be entered into lightly or ill-advisedly. This tendency to hostility is one of the reasons why some young lawyers instinctively react against practice in litigation. Women are yet to get into this combat zone as much as men: a reluctance to put women in the front line is not found only in the armed forces. Trial lawyers acquire a warrior status that sets them apart. And why should it not? It is completely uplifting and honourable to be the only thing standing between someone and the powers that be or want to be. There is nothing else in the profession to match it.

Gamesmanship

The analogy between war and games seems to come easy to Anglo-Saxons, especially since someone said the Battle of Waterloo was won on the playing fields of Eton. There is a conscious exercise of skill against the interests of the other side, or the lawyer for the other side. You are trying to put the other side in hazard. This leads to a sporting, blokey attitude to the proceedings. It is in part a demonstration of the urge to win, in part the need to hide from what might be the high seriousness of the occasion, and in part the need to hide your own nerves. This sporting attitude, these exercises in gamesmanship, can be very unsettling for people who have not experienced it face to face before, and who had hoped that their destiny might be in the hands of people whose serious intent and high office may have shown themselves more beneficently.

Advocacy

Because of the manic digression of large cases into trench warfare, into wars of attrition that exhaust the parties, while at the same time satisfying the lawyers, we are breeding a generation of trial lawyers who hardly ever fight a trial. We are certainly breeding a group that do not know how it is simply to run trials day after day on the footing that you get something that looks like a statement of what a witness might say, put them in the witness box and proceed. But this falling off in trial turnover should not obscure the fact that the primary function of a trial lawyer is to persuade. It is to represent the case by persuading the judge or jury or tribunal to adopt the evidence of the witnesses and the submissions in support of those witnesses. Whether you regard advocacy as high technique or an art form, its final command is beyond teaching. As the professional coach said in the film Chariots of Fire, "you cannot put in what God left out." The successful application of the techniques in cross-examination, or before a judge, or before a jury, or in the High Court of Australia, is what gives counsel their biggest charge. It also gives their client a charge. Most lawyers would subscribe to the old proposition that out of a hundred cases, ninety decide themselves, three are won on good advocacy, while seven are lost on bad advocacy. But most litigants would not accept that view. They want to regard their counsel as their champion, and they have very high ideas of what their counsel, and only their counsel, can do for them, sometimes bad ideas which are often left uncorrected until it is too late. While counsel might sometimes apply the techniques of advocacy to try to persuade their client, or a witness, or the other side, the full panoply is left for the court. Whether those techniques of persuasion can be applied in pursuit of agreement in private is another matter. There is no doubt that successful advocates, like successful actors or singers, can develop a public *amour propre* that thrives on public acceptance, which in turn depends on public performance. It is what Osric may have called "a very liberal conceit." Again like the case of actors and singers, you may see a felt need and a felt capacity to manipulate. If advocacy as such is a tool to be deployed in settlement discussion, it will be a different kind of advocacy from that deployed before the High Court of Australia or a jury in a murder trial.

Learning

Trial lawyers have to have specialised knowledge of the rules of procedure, including those relating to the trial. Some people, for their sins, make a living out of pleadings and discovery and arguments about them. Some barristers make their living out of paper work and nothing else — they act de facto as solicitors. Lawyers are frequently called on to display this knowledge in the course of exchanges. Some trial lawyers find it harder to resist displaying their learning, or their advocacy, than lawyers whose practice does not involve a celebrated extraversion.

Snobbery

All this can lead to a degree of intellectual snobbery, as you see with some surgeons. There is a funny rollover in intellectual snobbery in our profession. The big firms at the big end of town look down on litigation with something like contempt. Litigation lawyers have to live with the suggestion that somehow or other they are not real lawyers. They are tolerated, just. They are plainly inferior. At the other end of town, at the Bar, they believe they are the only real lawyers, and the top of the pile. Most of them look on all solicitors as being inferior. But as between the kinds of litigation lawyers, there is little doubt that the Bar claims the high ground. Its members show a tendency to posture, like some football supporters: "We are the champions."

Independence

There is no doubt a level of independence at the Bar that is rarely seen, if understood, in other parts of the profession. It is vital. It is one reason why the independent Bar must and will go on. This leads to a professional approach or standing that on a good day is robust, on a bad day is brash, and on a worse day shows the nauseating arrogance of a schoolyard bully. But the fact that some get crazed by their own success, or corrupted by their own power, should not obscure the obvious need for trained, specialised and independent lawyers at something like the Bar. It is becoming daily more important as big firms are bought off from acting against big corporations and big government.

Snappishness

There is in some trial lawyers a snappishness bred from their practice. Trial lawyers are there to fight trials. If the other side do not want to behave in a reasonable way and look like they are not serious about getting a settlement, the best thing to do is to get on with it and go to court. You will meet some lawyers who after one round of negotiations will start walking off to court, and not just as an exercise in dramatics. If the other side do not want to play ball sensibly (however that is judged), then counsel can get on with what they are trained and paid to do. We will see you in court and you, sportsman, are cruising for a bruising. This attitude would not serve well in negotiations in the Middle East. You do not always see that capacity to keep a dialogue going that industrial advocates and peace brokers have. You do not always see that determination to get a deal that business may require.

Theory of Relativity

Trial lawyers understand, from hard experience, that there are no absolutes, and no certainties. Litigation is a lottery. You simply cannot assess the odds. People who think they can are deluding themselves. Your client might have all the credibility in the world and all the circumstantial evidence that one could find, and still go down for reasons that were simply not seen. The judge might just get it wrong — whatever that means. For this reason trial lawyers know that they have to suspend belief. They do not believe anything or anyone. It is not their job. Their job is to persuade someone that their case is just that much more acceptable than the case of the other side. All this leads to is a form of scepticism that is healthy and in tune with the empirical tradition in our Anglo-Saxon philosophy. Unhappy experiences in litigation — bad accidents — may lead to seasoned scars that may temper aggression and provide a healthy antidote to the insouciance of the mercenary. Trial lawyers are best placed to have a full understanding of the effects of the decision to "open the purple testament of bleeding war."

Insecurity

This part of the personality of a trial lawyer derives as much from the time spent out of court as in. Barristers will tell you that none of them knows where their next brief may come from. This is obviously true in a philosophical sense. Most barristers believe it to be true in every sense. That is why they are afraid to knock a brief back and that is why therefore their practice gets into a shambles and they let people down. There is also the insecurity that derives from not knowing what the result may be. There is nothing quite like the tension of waiting for and receiving the verdict of a jury. This leads to a certain wannishness on the part of seasoned counsel. One senior silk said many years ago that barristers are like cats: when they are born they have so many lives in their belly and each fight they have is one less fight they have left. There is no doubt most barristers feel this kind of wear and tear. That is why the Government still gets some affirmative answers to offers of a position on the bench. These generalisations have no scientific backing or standing. Unleashing the measurers on trial lawyers could be entertaining, if useless, but there is enough anecdotal support for this kind of analysis to make it worthwhile in assessing how litigation lawyers in general, and trial lawyers in particular, might approach ADR. The issue is clear in the mediation of commercial disputes. Business depends on agreement. Litigation depends on disagreement. People in business live to make deals. Litigation lawyers live to fight. The prevailing cast of mind is therefore likely to be radically different. Barristers who after years of practice come to practise at a corporate firm notice an immediate difference, putting to one side any partnership commitments they may have entered into. What they find is that they are working with lawyers whose main object is to secure a deal for their client. They are there to make things, rather than break things. The idea is to get the deal done on the best terms possible. There may be serious arguments on the way through but the object remains the same. The opposing parties have the same objective — an agreement.

The commercial approach, and indeed the forensic equipment, are radically different from those of a litigation lawyer. If you look at the characteristics of a trial lawyer set out above, you might conclude that only the last two — the theory of relativity and insecurity — might assist in the mediation process while the others — combativeness, gamesmanship, advocacy, learning, snobbery, independence and snappishness — might be unhelpful to that process, and might derail an arbitration from the process that the parties wanted. In looking at how the training or disposition of trial lawyers may affect their contribution to ADR, it is fundamental that the parties want to avoid it. In arbitration they have rejected litigation. In mediation they are trying to avoid litigation. They are therefore rejecting a process from which trial lawyers make their living. You might therefore expect friction.

ARBITRATION

The most obvious way in which the background of trial lawyers affects their position on arbitration is that most of them either pretend it does not exist or do not want to know about it. There used to be good reasons to avoid commercial arbitration. The law was obscure and encouraged intervention by judges and obstruction by a party with money. It was difficult to find arbitrators of appropriate standing in the profession. Why pay an arbitrator when you get a judge for nothing? All those things have changed. The law now firmly encourages judges to stay out of the process. You can get arbitrators of high standing; if you take the view, fairly or otherwise, that there has been a decline in the standing of certain courts, then you may also be confident of finding a lawyer as arbitrator of a standing at least as high as that on offer in the courts. You now have to pay for your day in court, and your judge, and at a substantial rate. The effect of the difference in the costs of an arbitrator and a judge has largely gone out of the window. The problems that business has with litigation need no further cataloguing. In arbitration, they can set their own pace. If they want to they can assure themselves of a decision in weeks, or less. The hearing will be in private. There may not have to be a hearing at all. They can ban discovery. They can ban appeals. The CEO does not have to worry about being called names or made a fool of in public. The shareholders need not worry about the impact on the value of the shares of some allegations being made public. They do not have to worry about the Deputy Commissioner of Taxation or the Australian Competition and Consumer Commission getting involved. They can forgo a transcript if they have not forgone a hearing. They can almost certainly count on paying less to their lawyers. They can know in advance who their 'judge' will be — they can never do this in court. The decision of their dispute might be given by a distinguished silk or a commercial partner of a large firm of standing in the business community. The decision may or may not be a monument to jurisprudence, depending on the predilection of its author, but you can be confident that those who are paying for it will not want that. They just want a decision, which they will get. Given all these advantages, and they are huge, it is sad, to put it at its lowest, that commercial lawyers do not spend more time at least discussing arbitration as an option to commercial litigation. The problem here for trial lawyers is not so much that they are biased against arbitration because it will reduce the level of fees they can charge for a given dispute — which will most often be the case. The problem is that they have not been brought up to consider commercial arbitration as an option to litigation. The result of this general communal ignorance and antipathy is that arbitration is not widely used in commercial disputes, but tends to be invoked in specific areas. The principal of these historically has been building cases. The problem here is that trial lawyers simply bring in all their attitudes and procedural learning, with the result that they are having a trial process by a different name and expressly denying to the parties what the parties promised each other, namely, a form of resolution that would not involve the procedures of litigation. You get pleadings, directions, discovery, the rules of evidence, transcripts, court books — the lot. The issue was described by Rogers C.J. (Commercial). Before referring to Mustill and Boyd for the observation that "pleadings are not the ideal way of isolating the essential issues in dispute", he said: "I would venture to suggest that one reason why parties submit to arbitration is so that they should avoid pre-trial pleadings, discovery and other procedures of the Court: This is so whether the arbitration is long and complex, or short and simple. The heart of the arbitral procedure lies in its ability to provide speedier determination of the real issues. Those aims, to a large extent, are made impossible of achievement if the procedures of a Court are mimicked. Nor is there anything in the requirement to provide natural justice which requires adoption of the pleadings and procedures of Courts. What is required is that the parties enjoy the benefits of natural justice consistently with the requirements of arbitrators for dispensing with technicalities, with discovery, and doing away with interrogatories. The proper requirement that each party have full notice of the case to be made by the other and a full opportunity to prepare and to answer that case does not require pre-trial pleadings, discovery and other procedures of the Court."

Clients are frequently told that the dispute is their dispute. The problem is that it can be hijacked by the lawyers either in arbitration or in mediation. What happens involves a form of corruption of the procedure. You can see a similar process in some statutory tribunals. They start off with the best will in the world to be informal and to keep out legal niceties but the lawyers start to creep in and a process of mutual preening takes place. Before long, you can feel people wanting to bow at the tribunal and some do. People who have spent years doing this kind of thing commence addressing the tribunal: "If the tribunal pleases." No matter how hard the tribunal members try, this has a satisfying effect on their ego. They may not be so unlike real judges after all. The takeover process is more manifest when, as commonly happens, the lawyers involved form a club so that the adherence to proper ritual is appropriately enforced. Before long you have got to a stage where you do not have a court and you do not have the tribunal that Parliament intended to set up, but you do have something that the members and the lawyers feel comfortable about. Just how the punters feel is not often studied. This process is not entirely the fault of the lawyers. There are areas where people do want their lawyers to go into bat for them, and to go for it in a lawyerly way. Parliaments of all political colours over many years have tried to get lawyers out of jurisdictions, or reduce their role, but they have to confront not only the machinations of the lawyers, but the wish of people to have some sort of protection not just against the other side, but the machinery of government including the judges.

MEDIATION

When it comes to mediation, trial lawyers should perhaps be on firmer ground than they may be with arbitration. After all, most cases do settle and lawyers get plenty of practice at it. Indeed, in some jurisdictions it is said that the settlement rate is so high that that is all the lawyers are capable of — a good fight would kill them. The paradigm trial lawyer in Australia is the barrister. Barristers are generally very good at settling cases as between themselves. They are candid, to the point, and accept the value of settlement. But when the occasion is structured so that there is an audience, even an audience of just the client, the mediator and the other side, then even though the audience is in private, some may start behaving a little like they do in court. They may take technical points. They may refer to the pleadings. They may make a speech. They may even posture. Rather than sounding like a commercial lawyer who is there to conclude a deal with the other side, they may sound like a litigation lawyer, who is there to assert a case against the other side: "Priests pray for enemies, but princes kill." You can see a trial lawyer sometimes commence a mediation with what looks like an instinctive urge to score a king hit as soon as the ball is bounced. The commitment to learning can degenerate into an uncomely arrogance. Combativeness may drive the parties apart when the idea is to bring them together. Gamesmanship can become mere point scoring and you do not often attract someone to your position by slapping them in the face. Snappishness can turn into a sclerotic tendency to pull the pin, which from a commercial perspective might involve a form of suicide. You can sometimes sense business people thinking that lawyers at a mediation who are unduly argumentative or ostentatious do not seem to have contact with the world of business. They are not committed to doing a deal. It is interesting to see how a lot of these problems have started to wear off since mediation became sanctioned, and trial lawyers have come to accept it, but they can still be seen in some lawyers, barristers or solicitors, whose practice consists mainly of fighting cases in court. These problems can be worse if the mediator shows the same warlike tendencies and pulls rank to back them up. There are some former judges who still behave as if they were judges and seek to impose their will. Some silks seem intent on developing a similar reputation for firmness that others find just demeaning. Perhaps the problem is merely generational, but it will be as well when we are rid of it. Not surprisingly, therefore, the weapons of war may not always be helpful in making the peace.

CONCLUSIONS

Some trial lawyers may not be as good at settling cases as others. It bears repeating that most cases settle. We train our lawyers primarily, if not exclusively, in one form of dispute resolution, the civil trial. This, it also bears repeating, involves a fight. Of course people have a right to have their disputes settled, and the peace preserved, by Her Majesty's judges. But we ought to do more to educate our lawyers about the settlement process. It is the right of people to go to law, but the problems of that course are notorious. Why should we therefore treat the right as being one of first recourse rather than last resort? Why should we not teach civil procedure in the law schools: mediation first, arbitration second, litigation third. There is no doubt that in the last 10 years or so the attitude of litigation lawyers in general, and trial lawyers in particular, has become more sophisticated in its reception of mediation, but the lack of education in the proper approach to it is still sometimes apparent. The failure to respect arbitration either by giving it a go or by reducing it to a mockery of a court form shows a bad lack of sophistication in commercial lawyers generally. The business community finds serious fault in the way the courts resolve commercial disputes. The profession is not doing all it should to provide and promote the alternative. Attitudes will change. They may also change on the role of lawyers as mediators or arbitrators. Judges say that the only people who are qualified to hear and determine civil trials are those brought up as trial lawyers — which means, for the most part in Australia, barristers. There is a compelling, even inexorable, logic to this proposition. But does it have a converse? If the parties agree to avoid a civil trial by going to arbitration or mediation, may it not be the case that the worst person they could get as mediator or arbitrator is someone whose whole training has been as a trial lawyer?

REFERENCES

* This article was originally published as G. Gibson, 'Horses for Courses: Warlords as Peacemakers; are Trial Lawyers Bad for ADR?', *Arbitration* 68, no. 1 (2002): 2-10.

1 F. Pollock & F. Maitland, *The History of English Law Before the Time of Edward I*, (Cambridge: Cambridge University Press, 1898).

2 O. Dixon, *Jesting Pilate* (Melbourne: Law Book Co., 1965), 131.

3 W. Shakespeare, *Hamlet* 5, ii, 150.

4 W. Shakespeare, *Richard II* 3, iii, 93-94.

5 *Imperial Leatherware Co. Pty Ltd v Macri Marcellino Pty Ltd* (1991) 22 N.S.W.L.R. 653 at 661.

6 M. Mustill & S. Boyd, *The Law and Practice of Commercial Arbitration in England* (London: Butterworths, 1989), 318.

7 W. Shakespeare, *Henry VI*, 5, ii, 71.

CHAPTER 1

ADR Developments within the European Union

Ann Brady

Trying to find ways to contain escalating costs, while providing access to justice for all within a national civil justice system, is a problem faced by many countries. As a result, it is inevitable that the "public legal system of any country represents a compromise between conflicting demands for quality, speed and cheapness of decision making." In common with many countries around the world, the last few years have witnessed increasing interest and use being made by Member States within the European Union (EU) of alternative methods of settling disputes other than resort to the courts. Appendix A to this paper sets out some common examples of ADR processes which can be found in operation within the EU and around the world. ADR processes comprise a range of private (confidential) or public processes, which can be court-annexed, court-linked or out-of-court. They can be either decisional procedures where a neutral third party makes the decision or consensual procedures where a neutral third party assists the disputing parties to reach a mutually agreed settlement. Some of these procedures are mandatory and some are voluntary. Decisional processes, such as arbitration, can have negative consequences for the disputing parties in terms of how they perceive the fairness of the process and their compliance with the decision reached.

What consensual ADR processes, such as mediation, are capable of producing is the ability to create a resolution that takes into account the varying needs, interests and concerns of the different parties and the nuances so often inherent in a complex consensual settlement. Settlement of a dispute under these conditions increases the likelihood that the parties will be able to maintain their commercial or other relationship; an indirect outcome of consensual agreements is social harmony.

This paper sets out to indicate some of the practical steps that the European Commission (EC) is taking in an attempt to establish common practice in some areas of ADR within the EU. Following the publication of the EC's Green Paper on ADR in civil and commercial law in 2002, summarised below, not all countries within the EU felt it was wise to attempt to legislate on ADR. For example, the United Kingdom's overall response to this Green Paper stated: "The UK welcomes the Commission's Green Paper on ADR, and considers that it has correctly identified the issues that need to be addressed. However, we would urge the Commission to be cautious before attempting to introduce regulation for ADR. Regulation would stifle the very aspects of ADR that make it such a valuable part of the civil justice system — its flexibility and innovation. Instead, we suggest that the Commission should, as the Green Paper suggests at paragraph 57, concentrate on initiatives that encourage best practice and facilitate the use of ADR in civil disputes in cross border matters only."

Since then, however, there have been developments. Following more negotiations between Member States, in April 2005, a proposal for a directive of the European Parliament and of the Council on certain aspects of mediation in civil and commercial matters was drafted and is being considered by Member States. The EEJ Net, a project underway even at pre-Green Paper stage, continues to thrive, and a major study on ADR processes in six countries within the European Union has been undertaken by the Centre for Judicial Studies (CeSROG) at the University of Bologna.

In the United Kingdom we now have an increasingly influential Civil Mediation Council, we continue to expand our court mediation schemes and have a Department of Constitutional Affairs and Civil Justice Council who are very active in promoting ADR and investigating its best use with the legal system. These developments are discussed below. Finally, the paper gives some brief examples of the European links which are being fostered independently of governments by commercial, professional and charitable providers of ADR services. Thus, interest and development of ADR within the EU continues apace.

ADR IN EUROPE: A PERSPECTIVE

The use of alternative methods of resolving disputes rather than resort to the courts is old within Europe, but the accelerated interest and use of such methods is also underpinned by a practical consideration. ADR is able to offer a solution to the problem of access to justice faced by citizens in many Member States due to the following factors: the volume of disputes brought before the courts is increasing; court proceedings are becoming longer and the costs incurred by such proceedings are increasing; the quantity, complexity and technical obscurity of the legislation also help to make access to justice more difficult. Furthermore, cross-border disputes within the EU tend to result in even more lengthy proceedings and higher court costs than domestic disputes. The intensification of trade and the mobility of citizens between Member States, amplified by e-commerce, have led to an increase in the number of cross-border disputes before the courts. The courts themselves, already overworked, have to deal with increasing numbers of disputes which raise complex issues involving conflicts of laws and jurisdiction as well as the practical difficulties of finance and language. The issue of access to justice for all is a fundamental right enshrined in Article 6 of the European Convention for the Protection of Human Rights and Fundamental Freedoms, and the right to valid remedies has been determined by the European Court of Justice to be a general principle of European Community Law and set out in Article 47 of the Charter of Fundamental Rights of the EU. Access to justice is an obligation which is met by Member States through the provision of swift and inexpensive legal proceedings.

THE ROLE OF THE EC IN FURTHERING ADR DEVELOPMENTS WITHIN THE EU

The role of the EC as a promoter of legislative and operational initiatives is to seek information that will assist it define the general lines of policy to be conducted in the years ahead. ADR is a declared political priority on the part of the EU institutions whose task it is to promote these alternative techniques, to ensure an environment propitious to the development of these techniques and to do what it can to guarantee quality. ADR is an integral part of the policies aimed at improving access to justice and complementing judicial procedures. Policy development within the EU is taking place against a backdrop of increasing awareness that ADR can be a means of improving general access to justice in everyday life and the widespread availability of web-based information technology. There are, however, some daunting challenges. Within the EU there are differing legal systems and a plethora of different national regulations for different types of ADR process. These range from legislation that encourages the use of mediation to extensive legislation for arbitration, which is subject to comprehensive court-linked national legislation which reflects principles of international and commercial arbitration practice.

The extent of this diversity can be seen in the recent study of ADR in European countries undertaken by the University of Bologna (CeSROG), and currently being prepared for publication by the Study's Director, Professor Francesca Zannotti. The study focuses on six Member States of the EU; Finland, France, Italy, Netherlands, Spain, and the United Kingdom and makes comparisons with some aspects of ADR practice in the United States. As will be explained below, the EC, when proposing the new ADR Directive, restricted itself to a relatively narrow area of ADR practice, that of mediation. The CeSROG Study looks at all the ADR processes which the six participating countries use and indicates how these processes are accommodated within their individual legal systems.

FACING THE CHALLENGE OF DIVERSE LEGAL SYSTEMS AND ADR PROCESSES AND PRACTICES

The EC, aiming to establish consensual agreement on ADR regulation between Member States, is thus faced with diverse legal systems, different types of domestic ADR legislation and differing approaches to the provision of ADR within individual national legal systems. The issue of the costs of mediation serves as a useful example. Whilst in some EU jurisdictions the cost is borne by the parties themselves, in others the third parties (mediators) are not paid. In some jurisdictions operating costs are paid by public authorities or by professional organisations, or one or all of the parties may be entitled to legal aid or legal representation. So how is the EC approaching this challenge? Over the years there have been numerous conferences and debates on the use of alternative means of settling disputes in areas such as cross-border disputes, consumer electronic commerce and employment. The EC was also mindful of the work on ADR being undertaken by organisations such as the United Nations Commission, international non-governmental organisations such as the Global Business Dialogue (GBDe), as well as major ADR projects undertaken in countries such as the United States, Canada and Japan. In May 2000 the EC began gathering information on the situation within Member States as regards alternative methods of resolving cross-border disputes governed by civil and commercial law. Based on this information, the EC then drew up and presented the Green (Consultation) Paper, discussed below. No Member State had detailed framework regulations on ADR, and the view was taken that the Green Paper might lay the groundwork for consensual agreement on ADR regulation between Member States.

The 2002 Green Paper on ADR in Civil and Commercial Law

The objective of this Green Paper was to initiate a broad-based consultation on a number of legal issues in relation to ADR processes. In recent years ADR processes have become increasingly common and have been the focus of more and more attention by a number of observers. Given the diversity of ADR practices within the EU, of necessity the remit for the Green Paper was set within defined limits. Some types of ADR processes and some areas of law were specifically excluded from the paper. Arbitration was excluded on the grounds that the process was closer to a quasi-judicial procedure and arbitrators' decisions (awards) replaced judicial decisions. Furthermore, arbitration was already the subject not only of widespread legislation at national level in Member States, but also at international level, such as the 1958 New York Convention.

The Green Paper also rejected the process of expert opinion on the basis that it was not a method of dispute resolution but a procedure involving recourse to an expert in support, for example, of a judicial or arbitration procedure. Complaint-handling systems made available to consumers by professionals were also deemed to be outside the scope of the paper because they were not conducted by third parties but by one of the parties to the dispute. Similarly, 'automated negotiation systems' not involving any human intervention, which were offered by providers of IT services, were excluded because it was argued these systems were not dispute-resolution procedures conducted by third parties but technical instruments designed to facilitate direct negotiations between the parties to the dispute.

Finally, the ADR processes were limited to the areas of civil and commercial matters, including employment and consumer law. Thus, it did not cover questions relating to non-negotiable rights of public policy concern, such as certain provisions of the law of persons and family, competition law and consumer law that cannot be put to ADR. The paper was designed to seek the broadest public consultation and take stock of the prevailing situations in Member States. It was also perceived as an opportunity to familiarise the broadest possible public with ADR facilities and make the initiatives taken by Member States and the Community more highly visible.

The consultation paper took the form of a series of questions put to Member States, primarily legal in nature, concerning the salient features of ADR processes, such as ADR clauses in contracts, limitation periods, confidentiality constraints, the validity of consent given, the effectiveness of agreements generated by ADR processes, the training of third parties, their accreditation and rules governing their liability.

As stated before, no Member State had detailed framework regulations on these issues. The result of the responses to this questionnaire and further negotiation is the current proposal for a directive on certain aspects of the ADR process of mediation in civil and commercial matters, and this is discussed below.

The EEJ Net

Another issue of concern to the EC was dispute resolution in consumer and electronic commerce (e-commerce) and in employment relations. It was felt that there was a need for the creation of a public information system on ADR and one of the measures underway even before the Green Paper was the creation of an internet-based information system, known as European Extra-Judicial Network (EEJ-Net). It aims to help consumers access out of court or ADR schemes in other EU Member States when they are involved in cross-border disputes with traders. A complaint form is available which can be used for national as well as cross-border disputes within the EU. The form is designed to be consumer-friendly and is available in all the languages of the EU. The system is maintained and updated by a network of national authorities. A clearing-house system operates with each Member State participating in the scheme having a national clearing house. National websites contain reports on EEJ activities and give insights into its work and the type of complaints received. The 'Euroconsumer Archive' includes items such as examples of European consumer complaints, evidence-based reports, consumer rights, campaigns, promotions and activities.

THE PROPOSED DIRECTIVE ON CERTAIN ASPECTS OF THE ADR PROCESS OF MEDIATION IN CIVIL AND COMMERCIAL MATTERS

The objective and scope of this proposed directive is to facilitate access to dispute resolution by promoting the use of the ADR process of mediation and to ensure a sound relationship between mediation and judicial proceedings. The directive, when agreed, will apply to those Member States of the EU whose law permits the ADR process of mediation to take place, and it will apply to all civil and commercial matters and to cross-border disputes. The proposed directive (Article 2) defines mediation as a process where two or more parties to a dispute are assisted by a third party to reach an agreement on the settlement of their dispute. The mediation process can be initiated by the parties, or suggested or ordered by a court, or prescribed by the national law of a Member State. Outside the scope of this directive will be attempts made by a judge to settle a dispute within the course of judicial proceedings.

The Definition of a Mediator

A mediator is defined in Article 2(a) as any third party conducting a mediation, regardless of the denomination or profession of that third party in the Member State concerned and of the way the third party has been appointed or requested to conduct the mediation.

Ensuring the Quality of Mediation

Under Article 4 Member States are urged to encourage the development and adherence to voluntary codes of conduct by mediators and organisations providing mediation services, and to encourage the training of mediators.

Referral to Mediation

Under Article 3 a court before which an action is brought may, when appropriate and having regard to all the circumstances of the case, invite the disputing parties to use mediation in order to settle the dispute. The court may, in any event, require the parties to attend an information session on the use of mediation. Any legislation passed by Member States in conformity to this proposed directive must not affect the right of access to the judicial system and in particular in situations where one of the parties is resident in a Member State other than that of the court.

Agreements Resulting from Mediation

Article 4 asks Member States to ensure that, upon request of the parties, a settlement agreement reached as a result of the mediation can be confirmed in a judgment, decision, authentic instrument or any form of court or public authority that renders the agreement enforceable in a similar manner as a judgment under national law, provided that the agreement is not contrary to European law; or the national law of the Member State where the request is made.

The Admissibility of Evidence in Civil Judicial Proceedings

Article 6 proposes that mediators shall not, in civil judicial proceedings, give testimony or evidence regarding any of the following: an invitation by a party to engage in mediation or the fact that a party was willing to participate in mediation; views expressed or suggestions made by a party in a mediation in respect of a possible settlement of the dispute; statements or admissions made by a party in the course of the mediation; proposals made by the mediator; the fact that a party had indicated its willingness to accept a proposal for a settlement made by the mediator; a document prepared solely for purposes of mediation.

However, this information may be disclosed or submitted as evidence in civil and judicial proceedings or an arbitration procedure: where disclosure is necessary to implement or enforce the agreement resulting from the mediation; where disclosure is required by law or for overriding considerations of public policy; or where the parties agree to disclosure. All other evidence used in a mediation procedure can be submitted as evidence in civil or commercial judicial proceedings. It is proposed that the above provisions apply whether or not the judicial proceedings relate to the dispute that is or was the subject matter of the mediation.

Limitation Periods

The running of any period of prescription or limitation regarding the action that is the subject matter of the mediation shall be suspended as of the date on which, after the dispute has arisen the parties agree in writing to use mediation; or the use of mediation is ordered by a court order; or an obligation to use mediation arises under the national law of a Member State. It is proposed that the suspension of the period of prescription or limitation shall cease on the date on which the mediation agreement has been concluded. Alternatively, if the mediation procedure fails to result in an agreement, on the date on which either the mediator or at least one of the parties establishes in writing that the mediation procedure is over or when one of the parties effectively withdraws from the mediation procedure.

Member States are now negotiating these issues and, once agreement is reached, the directive will come into force on the 20th day following that of its publication in the Official Journal of the European Union (Article 10).

THE UNITED KINGDOM AND THE PROPOSED DIRECTIVE

Ensuring the Quality of Mediations

In the United Kingdom there is a plethora of organisations providing the services of mediators and each has its own list of mediators, and some have their own training courses and codes of conduct. For example, the Bar Council, the controlling body for barristers, produces an annual list of barrister mediators graded according to mediation experience. It also keeps under review the code of conduct for barristers who practise as advocates at mediations and those who practise as barrister mediators. Mediators have the opportunity to join more than one mediation service-provider in an attempt to obtain mediation work. There is not as yet a national code of conduct for mediation practice or a national standard for mediator training. A relatively new national body, known as the Civil Mediation Council (CMC), is currently producing a national list of mediators. The CMC came into being in April 2003 as an unincorporated association, and its constitution embodies its objects: to be a neutral and independent body to represent and promote civil and commercial mediation and other dispute resolution options as alternatives to litigation and thereby to further law reform and access to justice for the general public. It hopes to create a culture of best practice by encouraging research, continuing education and by accrediting mediation providers. It has been an active participant in the various conferences and meetings on mediation organised by the EC. On 2 December 2004, as part of its commitment to continuing training, it organised a national seminar on the application to mediators of the Proceeds of Crime Act 2003 with presentations by officials from the Home Office, judges, mediators and representatives of the professional bodies.

Referral to Mediation

Under the United Kingdom's Civil Procedure Rules it is the duty of the court to encourage parties to co-operate with each other in the conduct of the proceedings. Furthermore, the Rules specifically set occasions during the pre-litigation and litigation stages of a dispute where there are both incentives and sanctions for parties to make and to take seriously offers to settle — thus seeking to reduce costs and delays to those bringing civil claims before the court. Case law is supporting these rules and parties who refuse reasonable requests to mediate can expect to be penalised in costs. Those wishing to pursue a prospective legal claim should first encounter the possibility of using the ADR process of mediation when they either seek legal advice or choose to conduct their own cases. Pre-action protocols for a range of civil claims include encouragement for the parties to avoid litigation by either negotiating a settlement between themselves or by the use of mediation. Even when court proceedings have started there are still opportunities for the parties to settle their dispute by way of mediation. Once a defence to the action has been submitted to the court, parties are given an opportunity, or the court may invite the parties, to temporarily stop the proceedings in order that the dispute can be mediated. There are further opportunities as the case proceeds to trial for the parties and the court to encourage the settlement of the dispute by way of mediation.

Judge-led court mediation schemes are now expanding rapidly in England and Wales. By way of example, on the Western Circuit, the Exeter Court Scheme started in 2002 has helped to pioneer additional courts schemes within the Western Circuit and elsewhere in the country. Bath County Court's Mediation Scheme which commenced in April 2005 has had the benefit of the experience gained at Exeter Court as well as an information package 'Courts Mediation Schemes — Toolkit' produced by the ADR Committee of the Civil Justice Council (CJC).

The CJC is a Non-Departmental Advisory Public Body established by statute. It was intended to be more than a mere consultative body, rather a "high-powered body representative of all the relevant interests that monitors the effects of the civil procedural rules in practice." It is charged with keeping the civil justice system under review, considering how to make civil justice more accessible, fair and efficient, referring proposals for changes in the civil justice system to the Department of Constitutional Affairs (DCA) and the Civil Rule Committee and making proposals for research. Much of its day-to-day business is conducted by sub-committees. The ADR Sub-committee is very active and, over the last few years, has drafted a number of submissions to the government, hosted a number of fact-finding and discussion workshops and forums on topics such as the EEJ and ADR in the county court. Its 'Courts Mediation Schemes — Toolkit' gives advice and information to those wishing to set up court-based mediation schemes; it is not a mandatory instruction. While the search continues for court mediation schemes which are cost effective to both the court and court user, creativity is encouraged. As stated in the introduction to this paper, "trying to find ways to contain escalating costs, while providing access to justice for all within a national civil justice system, is a problem faced by many countries."

More effective and proportionate dispute resolution is part of the DCA's strategy 2004-2009: 'Delivering Justice, Rights and Democracy.' The DCA aims to establish a dispute resolution system which provides a well sign-posted range of options for preventing or resolving disputes, with a 5% reduction in the proportion of disputed claims that are ultimately resolved by a formal court hearing. This strategy recognises that there will always remain those cases where a formal court hearing is necessary and appropriate but that the civil justice system is much wider than just judicial decisions in formal court or tribunal hearings; it encompasses a range of information, advice and legal services, and a variety of dispute resolution options (e.g., ombudsman, arbitration and mediation schemes). Action to achieve these aims will include "developing a range of court-based ADR options to help people settle their cases without the need for a formal court hearing." Much of the work of the DCA in the field of ADR to date has been to encourage greater use of mediation through the setting up and evaluation of a range of court-based mediation schemes. However, in the view of the DCA, most people using the courts still do not have ready access to mediation and most people with a dispute know little or nothing about mediation or the potential benefits it might provide. Mediation schemes that operate outside the court system and prior to the commencement of proceedings are also under scrutiny.

A recent innovation has been the launch of the National Mediation Helpline, a national telephone helpline developed jointly between the CMC and the DCA. The scheme commenced in November 2004 and will run as a pilot scheme for one year, supported by a website. The telephone helpline operator provides information about mediation and the scheme and, if the caller wishes to use the services of a mediation provider, the details are passed on to one of the providers on a rota. When a request is submitted 'on line', the details are automatically forwarded to a provider on the same rota as for the callers. The scheme is being evaluated.

Another mediation initiative, organised by the Better Dispute Resolution Team (BDRT) of the Courts Service is a proposed Mediation Awareness Week to take place in October 2005 and involving 60 county courts in England and Wales. The purpose of this campaign is to promote and increase awareness of mediation, and it will target court users, court staff, judiciary, the legal profession, local services and local press. The BDRT are to provide national promotional activities and materials. At local level, local courts and mediation representatives will decide and plan events and activities they feel are appropriate to their particular courts. Thus, referral to mediation and encouraging disputing parties to participate in mediation schemes in England and Wales is currently subject to much creativity.

Enforcement of Mediation Agreements

There is currently no statute which specifically deals with the enforcement and confidentiality of mediation agreements. Disputes in either of these areas would probably have to be dealt with under the common law rules of contract law. It is of note, however, that agreements made under court-based mediation schemes become consent orders and, if breached, the injured party may return to the court for directions from a judge.

ADR ORGANISATIONS MAKING EUROPEAN LINKS

Finally, the contribution being made by many commercial, professional, ecclesiastical and charitable providers of mediation services should not be forgotten. These organisations are fostering their own independent links across Europe in order to discuss and develop the use of ADR. Commercial mediation service-providers now offer their services on a European and even global basis. Professional bodies, such as the Chartered Institute of Arbitrators, have European branches which organise pan-European seminars and conferences on a range of topics, including ADR; Devon and Exeter Law Society (which pioneered the Exeter Court Small Claims mediation scheme with solicitor and barrister mediators) hosted a Working Day on Mediation in May 2004 as part of the Annual International Lawyers' Meeting in Exeter. Ecclesiastical organisations, such the Mennonites, hold international conferences on mediation. These organisations help to reduce the number of disputes which would otherwise go to formal court hearings, helping to reduce the workload of overworked courts and provide access to justice to those who may not be able to risk the uncertainties of a court hearing and costs.

CONCLUSIONS

Interest and development of ADR within the EU continue apace. With the expansion of mediation services across Europe, the public has the right to expect quality services from both mediators and those who provide mediation services; the proposed directive takes the first tentative steps towards ensuring this right.

APPENDIX A

Forms of ADR

Arbitration is a procedure whereby both sides to a dispute agree to let a third party, the arbitrator, decide. In some instances, there may be a panel. The arbitrator may be a lawyer, or may be an expert in the field of the dispute. S/he will make a decision according to the law. The arbitrator's decision, known as an award, is legally binding and can be enforced through the courts.

Early neutral evaluation is a process in which a neutral professional, commonly a lawyer, hears a summary of each party's case and gives a non-binding assessment of the merits. This can then be used as a basis for settlement or for further negotiation.

Expert determination is a process where an independent third party, who is an expert in the subject matter, is appointed to decide the dispute. The expert's decision is binding on the parties.

Mediation is a way of settling disputes in which a third party, known as a mediator, helps both sides to come to an agreement which each considers acceptable. Mediation can be 'evaluative', where the mediator gives an assessment of the legal strength of a case, or 'facilitative', where the mediator concentrates on assisting the parties to define the issues. When a mediation is successful and an agreement is reached, it is written down and forms a legally binding contract, unless the parties state otherwise.

Med-arb is a combination of mediation and arbitration where the parties agree to mediate but, if that fails to achieve a settlement, the dispute is referred to arbitration. The same person may act as mediator and arbitrator in this type of arrangement.

Neutral fact-finding is a non-binding procedure used in cases involving complex technical issues. A neutral expert in the subject-matter is appointed to investigate the facts of the dispute and make an evaluation of the merits of the case. This can form the basis of a settlement or a starting point for further negotiation.

Ombudsmen are independent office-holders who investigate and rule on complaints from members of the public about maladministration in government and in particular services in both the public and private sectors. Some ombudsmen use mediation as part of their dispute-resolution procedures. Ombudsmen are able to make recommendations, only a few can make decisions which are enforceable through the courts.

Utility regulators are watchdogs appointed to oversee the privatised utilities such as water or gas. They handle complaints from customers who are dissatisfied by the way a complaint has been dealt with by their supplier.

REFERENCES

* This article was originally published as A. Brady, 'Alternative Dispute Resolution (ADR) Developments within the European Union',

Arbitration 71, no. 4 (2005): 318-328.

1 J. Tackaberry & A. Marriott, *Bernstein's Handbook of Arbitration and Dispute Resolution Practice* (Lodnon: Sweet & Maxwell, 2003), Vol.1, 16.

2 Commission of the European Communities, Brussels, April 19, 2002 COM (2002) 196 final.

3 The United Kingdom's response to the Green Paper on ADR in civil and commercial law, paras 109 and 110.

4 Directives set a goal which must be reached by a certain date. Member States are responsible for making their own laws in order to reach this goal. An example of a directive is the EC Package Travel Directive, which was incorporated in UK domestic law by the Package Travel, Package Holidays and Package Tours Regulations 1992.

5 Centro Studi e Ricerche sull'Ordinamento Guidiziario, Dipartimento di Organizzazione e Sistema Politico, Universita di Bologna.

6 Commission of the European Communities COM (2002) 196 final, 7.

7 Commission of the European Communities Green Paper "Judicial co-operation in civil matters; the problems confronting the cross-border litigant," COM (2000) 51 final (Brussels, February 9, 2000).

8 Trade conducted electronically, e.g., by email.

9 Case 222/84, *Johnston* [1986] E.C.R. 1651 (judgment given May 15, 1986).

10 Commission of the European Communities, 8.

11 *Ibid.*, 5.

12 *Ibid.*, 8.

13 For example, in the United Kingdom, the Civil Procedure Rules (CPR).
14 Such as the New York Convention and UNCITRAL Model Law.
15 The author is the UK representative.
16 See Appendix A.
17 For example, in France, the justice conciliators.
18 E.g., in Ireland, the family mediation service.
19 E.g., in Sweden, damages attributable to road traffic are covered by automobile insurance companies.
20 E.g., in France, legal aid can be granted to pay the fees of advocates who conduct the transactional negotiations.
21 Commission of the European Communities, 9 and 10.
22 The United Nations Commission on International Trade Law — model legislative provisions concerning commercial conciliation. Work of the working group on arbitration www.uncitral.org/frindex.htm.
23 See www.tabd.com.
24 Commission of the European Communities, 12.
25 Council Dec.2001/470 (May 28, 2001).
26 On the basis of two recommendations of the EC throughout Europe only institutions of dispute resolution which fulfil basic principles such as transparency, independence, impartiality, legality and effectiveness are registered under the scheme.
27 Details of the process are available from Europaisches Verbraucherzentrum, Clearing House, Brennerstr.3, I-39100 Bozen. Email: info@euroconsumatori.org, www.eejnet.org.
28 www.euroconsumatori.org/16853.html.

29 For the United Kingdom: www.euroconsumer.org.uk/index/publications/other_reports/ecc_activity.htm.
30 For the United Kingdom: www.euroconsumer.org.uk/index/publications.htm.
31 Brussels, April 26, 2005 (27.04) (OR.fr).
32 Art. 1.
33 With the exception of Denmark.
34 Explanatory Memorandum 1.2 Legal basis.
35 This would include, for example, legal systems which permit judges to use mediation techniques to attempt a settlement between disputing parties.
36 The instruments referred to are Regs (EC) Nos 44/2001 (Brussels I), 2001/2003 (Brussels Ha) and 835/2004 (EEO).
37 Art. 6 Option 1, para. 2 states that this shall apply irrespective of the form of the information or evidence referred to therein. Para.3 goes on to state that such disclosure shall not be ordered by a court or other judicial authority in judicial proceedings, or during an arbitration procedure and if such information is offered as evidence, it should be treated as inadmissible
38 In particular, when required to ensure the protection of children or to prevent harm to the physical or psychological integrity of a person.
39 Art. 7. In this case, determination of the precise date on which an obligation to use mediation arises is governed by national law.
40 The directive proposes that this article shall be without prejudice to more favourable national provisions applicable to prescription or

limitation periods.

41 www.barcouncil.org.uk and legalservices@barcouncil.org.uk.
42 The Government Department responsible for this area of criminal activity.
43 CPR r.1.4(2)(a)
44 The Court of Appeal in *Halsey v Milton Keynes General NHS Trust, Steel v Joy* [2004] EWCA Civ 1651 has given general guidance on the use of mediation, ruling particularly on the circumstances when it is appropriate to penalise a party who refuses mediation.
45 In *Burchell v Bullard* [2005] EWCA Civ 358, Ward L.J. stated that reasonable requests to mediate can no longer be shrugged aside by the legal profession.
46 CPR pre-action protocols, C1-001.
47 Such as personal injury and clinical negligence.
48 At allocation questionnaire stage: CPR r.26.4(1).
49 At case management and pre-trial review stage.
50 Where I sit as a court mediator at Bath, Barnstaple, Exeter and Torquay courts.
51 Described in my World Jurist Association Congress Paper (August 2003, Australia).
52 A copy is available on www.adr.civiljusticecouncil.
53 Chaired by Professor Martin Partington.
54 Civil Justice Council Annual Report 2002, 5.
55 Civil Evidence Act 1997, Section 6.
56 This Government Department was created in 2003 as the Department for

Justice, Rights and Democracy.

57 www.dca.gov.uk/dept/strategy/dcastratch4.pdf.

58 National Mediation Helpline Information Pack (March 2005), p.1.

59 www.nationalmediationhelpline.com.

60 The mediation service-providers selected for the pilot are CEDR, Chartered Institute of Arbitrators, In Place of Strife, ADR Group, Academy of Experts, ADR Chambers UK—selected on the basis that they were supporting existing court-based mediation schemes and were covered by professional insurance, have professional regulatory bodies, have proven administrations, and have continuing professional development and supervision requirements that could provide nation-wide coverage.

61 Part of the DCA: www.hmcourts-service.gov.uk.

62 Such as CEDR, ADR Group, ADR Chambers UK.

63 www.european-arbitrators.org.

64 Described in my World Jurist Association Congress Paper (August 2003, Australia).

65 Fifth International Conference of the World Mediation Forum (WMF) (September 9-11, 2005, Switzerland), www.mediation.qualilearning.org.

CHAPTER 1

Mandatory ADR and Access to Justice

Arthur Marriott

My main subject is the increasing use of methods of ADR to resolve civil and commercial disputes, principally by mediation. This has been done in a number of ways, such as by informal court-attached schemes now offered at various courts and civil trial centres, for example in Birmingham, the Court of Appeal and at Central London; or by private arrangement in the private sector. These services have been offered by a growing number of individuals and commercial institutions who hold themselves out as expert in the field, sometimes working pro bono or for low fees, but increasingly at commercial rates akin to those prevalent in domestic arbitration. Given the increasing use of alternative dispute resolution, there have been some important decisions from the courts on the role of ADR in settling litigation, largely favourable and approving, but in one case, *Halsey v Milton Keynes General NHS Trust* and conjoined cases, with potentially disastrous policy consequences.

Adjudication, which is a form of fast track arbitration, was introduced because the construction industry was dysfunctional with its apparently entrenched adversarial and dispute-driven approach to projects. The reports of Sir Michael Latham and Sir John Egan in the mid-1990s emphasised the need for more collaborative forms of contracting and the introduction of methods and ideas drawn from manufacturing industry and the distributive services. As a consequence we now have an increasing acceptance of collaborative contracting with new forms of contract. We also have a radical change in dispute resolution by the use of adjudication in ways which were never originally contemplated. The use of adjudication is now under review. If there is one flaw in the system which I think merits change, it is the fact that it has been bedevilled by disputes over jurisdiction. This reflects in turn a conflict between public and private interests, which also affected the policy expressed in the Act, as for example on consolidation, where proposals for reform were rejected because it was said to offend the principle that arbitration was consensual, so parties should not be forced to arbitrate with those with whom they had not contracted even though their contract was back to back with others or part of a network of related agreements. Once you accept that private dispute resolution such as arbitration and adjudication are very important in the public interest, you cannot allow the private interest to dominate. If, as in the case of adjudication, the public interest dictated that there should be a mandatory scheme applicable to construction contracts, then the scope for jurisdictional disputes should have been removed. I have no doubt that adjudication in the construction industry has many lessons for other industries. We need to do far more work on developing fast track methods for use in arbitration and in the courts.

One interesting reaction to the difficulties of access to justice is perhaps the increase in the number of ombudsmen, the emphasis being on the resolution of grievances produced by public or private sector bureaucratic inefficiency and incompetence and, in some instances such as insurance and pensions mis-selling, greed and sharp practice. This is unquestionably an area which merits development as part of an effective regulatory system. Central to my case for the use of various forms of ADR in civil and commercial dispute resolution are two propositions. First, that the demands of the public, the expectations which it has of its legal profession and the entrenched power of the lawyers, mean that there is little scope to reduce the cost of access to justice and that, almost certainly, the new methods of funding which may well include contingent fees will increase the overall cost of litigation, even if the cost to an individual litigant in a particular case is reduced. My second proposition is that without the widespread use of ADR attached to formal adversarial processes, whether before courts or tribunals, no significant improvement in access to justice and its cost is to be expected. Incidentally, the same is true for arbitration. I am far from saying that these are the only reforms which are required. There are in my view other steps we can take but these are beyond the scope of this paper. Although it is dangerous to generalise, I think that different levels of the judiciary take a different approach to the role of ADR in litigation. There is no doubt that the use of ADR in litigation has been actively encouraged and promoted at senior levels. This is reflected in a number of ways. There have been public pronouncements over many years, for example, by very senior judges such as Lord Bingham and Lord Woolf, by other judges in the Court of Appeal and in the High Court, in favour of ADR. County court judges on the whole have been slower to accept that ADR has a useful role to play. This is not necessarily through antipathy or indifference, but sometimes because of an ignorance of the processes and, in particular, the lack of ADR services in the area of the county court. It is all very well to encourage county court judges to refer cases to ADR, but to whom and at what cost? Judges have been understandably reluctant to refer parties to private mediation services, the more so when in the early days there was little or no protection against the charlatan and the incompetent. These concerns ought to fade now that there are several schemes attached to civil trial centres and, with the increasing availability of mediation services, there should be more reason for county court judges to make referrals. Not all county court judges have been slow to respond to the challenges. It was the pioneering initiative of Sir Frank White and his successor Judge Butter Q.C. at the Central London County Court, which led to the ADR scheme at that court, supported by the judges and made possible by the efforts of the staff at the Trial Centre and mediators from the private sector. The history of that pilot project is well set out by Professor Hazel Genn in her seminal report in the LCD series. It is also clear that there are many district judges who, in administering the small claims jurisdiction, actively promote settlement themselves, though not to the point of separate meetings.

When Lord Irvine became Lord Chancellor in April 1997, he instituted a review by Sir Peter Middleton of the Woolf proposals. Following Sir Peter's report of September 1997, which merits re-reading today as a warning of how lawyers can ruin attempts at reform, Lord Irvine decided to implement them. He was a convert to the use of ADR in the civil justice system and gave powerful support to it, including bringing about the pledge that government departments would use ADR in disputes over government contracts. There had never been any objection in principle to this being done before; it was just never done in practice. A very important issue of policy to which the Lord Chancellor gave urgent consideration early in his term of office was whether or not it would be possible to have a national scheme of court-attached ADR. He came to the conclusion, quite rightly, that this was not possible in the then prevailing state of court administration. It was due first to a lack of resources both financial and human within the court system and secondly, that there were not enough service providers to provide a comprehensive national service. The real issue was the best use of limited public funds. Vital decisions had to be made. It would have been wrong simply to devote public money to ADR processes which were untried in this country and where the existing pilot schemes demonstrated a low rate of voluntary acceptance. It was therefore incumbent on those who advocated ADR to demonstrate its efficacy and to show that not only could access to justice be improved, but there would be better value for scarce public funds.

As various reports and research projects in the United States such as Rand and the Federal Judicial Center have shown, measuring the economic benefits of ADR is both difficult and controversial. It needs, for example, to be borne in mind that most litigation settles. There were those who said that well-tried and conventional methods of settlement negotiation well understood by experienced practitioners, particularly in personal injury and clinical negligence cases, were preferable to the imposition of court-attached schemes, which would inevitably add a layer of cost both to the judicial administration and also the litigation itself. These arguments could not simply be ignored. The yardstick, adopted by some of us connected with the pilot schemes in Central London and the Court of Appeal, was the very simple, perhaps simplistic, one of looking primarily at the savings in judicial time. We thought that this was comparatively easy to measure and would give some indication of the benefits. It would be a relatively small step from there to establishing as a matter of common sense that if cases settled earlier, costs would be saved. But few were prepared to argue that, taken overall, there would be substantial savings in the cost of the civil justice system. Rather, the argument had to be predicated on better value for money. Another consideration prevalent at the time, which I think still applies and appears to be a partial explanation for the Court of Appeal's unfortunate decision in *Halsey*, is the fear that mediation schemes, particularly mandatory or quasi-mandatory, might serve to encourage litigation and the bringing of unmeritorious claims in the belief that institutional defendants in particular would be forced to compromise in a mediation, simply to get rid of the claims. It is true that some institutional defendants and their insurers do think that by agreeing to mediation, let alone being compelled to go to it, they are exposing themselves to pressure to settle cases they might well prefer to fight. Critics of the way in which insurance companies conduct litigation argue, on the other hand, that mediation helps to stop some insurers from waging a war of attrition, postponing settlement to the last moment and thereby abusing their greater financial power.

It would be wrong to categorise the whole insurance industry as recalcitrant, for we know that there were insurers who, even before pre-action protocols were introduced in personal injury and clinical negligence cases, were prepared to mediate and to settle cases as a consequence much earlier than they would otherwise have done. Many were prepared to pay more in settlement at an earlier stage, having regard to the overall cost savings that would be made by early settlement. The more enlightened insurers saw the benefits of the system, but it seems that those engaged on both sides in resolving personal injury and clinical negligence cases are not prepared to put all their eggs in the ADR basket. It is beyond the scope of this paper but I draw attention to steps which have been taken with respect to the mediation of National Health Service cases where there is an obvious need to reduce the amount of expensive litigation. One concern about the introduction of a national scheme was the sceptical attitude of many litigation solicitors, to the point of outright hostility. It is an open secret that there was and remains strong opposition within the Law Society from many litigation solicitors who consider the introduction of ADR a direct threat to their livelihood: this clearly influenced the Law Society in its intervention in *Halsey*. This anxiety ignores two things: first, there is an overriding public interest in bringing about settlements; and secondly, many litigation lawyers now have mediation skills which clients want and for which they will pay.

Accordingly, the Lord Chancellor decided that the introduction of a comprehensive national scheme was not a practical proposition, but what he and his department then did was actively to encourage private initiatives and ADR schemes attached to civil trial centres and in the Court of Appeal. The LCD provided much useful practical encouragement by commissioning

Professor Hazel Genn to study the schemes and procedures in the Central London County Court, the Commercial Court and the Court of Appeal and to report on them. For the reasons that I have given, it was felt to be very important that there should be some statistical basis for evaluating the advantages and disadvantages of ADR and a lack of statistical evidence still applies despite the increase in the number of schemes in various parts of the country. It was unfortunate though understandable that the LCD support at that time could not have extended to the provision of court administrators to help with ADR schemes.

Experience in the United States, Australia and Canada shows beyond any doubt that such schemes only function well when there is an appropriate dedication of time and resources within the court system to their administration. An example closer to home is the experience in the initial appeal court scheme, which demonstrated dramatically improved results for the use of ADR in appeals when the scheme was administered by Caroline Morris, a judicial assistant who was financed for five months by a number of City law firms. This is borne out again by the administration of the new scheme by CEDR Solve.

Even if the decision had been to establish a comprehensive national scheme, I very much doubt that it would have been made mandatory and therefore in my view its benefit would have been very limited and arguably not worth the investment certainly in the short term. However, it is right to say that in early discussions about the use of ADR in the courts there was overwhelming objection which plainly remains to this day, to mandatory references by judges. For many judges and practitioners it was and remains a question of principle that citizens are entitled to come to the courts for a resolution of their differences and being referred to compulsory mediation as a prerequisite is an unjustified interference with access to the courts. Lord Woolf was prepared to encourage the use of ADR and his final report is notably more strongly expressed on that topic than his interim report. But he was not prepared to go so far as to recommend mandatory references. The opposition of others with responsibility for judicial administration such as the then Head of Civil Justice, Sir Richard Scott, was implacable. It is that opposition which is at the root of the single most important decision to emerge from the English courts on the use of ADR in civil litigation. *Halsey* in the Court of Appeal, while generally supportive of ADR processes, has done a serious disservice to improving access to justice and to the reform of our civil justice system. Although, as a matter of policy, no comprehensive national scheme was sought to be introduced and the imposition of mandatory requirements to refer was opposed, a practice has developed in the High Court (or certain parts of it) which borders on mandatory references. The Commercial Court, for example, had considered and reported on the use of ADR before the introduction of the Woolf reforms. A practice direction had been issued in 1996. The Commercial Court began to make adjournment orders in 1996 when 25 orders were made. The practice of the Commercial Court in making adjournment orders is well established and well understood. Sometimes, the commercial judges make them in opposition to the wishes of both parties, the judge taking the view that the case is suitable for mediation and adjourning it for that purpose. Colman J. has referred to that practice in his seminal judgment in *Cable & Wireless plc v IBM United Kingdom Ltd* in which he recognises and gives effect to an agreement to go to ADR as part of a structured dispute resolution provision in a long-term contract. One of the effects of adjournment orders has been that the Commercial Bar and solicitors have become accustomed to considering seriously whether they should agree to mediate. Practitioners now know that they will be expected to give reasonable grounds for declining to mediate, so they do consider it seriously. The requirement also has removed what is often an obstacle to the initiation of mediation, namely the fact that one party does not wish to appear to be weak in proposing it. Other judges have taken similar views of adjourning to mediate, encouraged it should be said by decisions of the Court of Appeal in such cases as *Cowl and others v Plymouth City Council* and *Dunnett v Railtrack plc*. Lord Woolf himself, who gave judgment in *Cowl*, has long seen the advantage of ADR in cases which involve appeals on administrative and social questions. He was, for example, instrumental in arranging that the first cases mediated by the initial Court of Appeal scheme were seven appeals in the false imprisonment cases where very high damages awards against the police had been given by juries at the Central London County Court. In the Chancery Division, Lightman J. in *Hurst v Leeming* made it plain that, with very few exceptions, all professional negligence cases should be mediated before coming to a judge for adjudication. Last year in *Shirayama Shokusan Co Ltd and others v Danovo Ltd*, Blackburne J., also in the Chancery Division, plainly considered that the court had the power to make a mandatory reference to mediation even if a party was wholly opposed to it, if it thought that it was in the interests of justice and the efficient conduct of the case to do so. He relied on an unreported decision of Arden J. in 1999 in *Guinle v Kirreh: Kinstreet Ltd v Belmargo Corp Ltd*. He also relied on a very robust decision of the Court of Appeal in 2000, a charity case *Muman and others v Nagasena*, in which Mummery L.J. had made in effect a mandatory reference.

It was therefore clear that, in perhaps a typically pragmatic way, practices were developing in certain kinds of civil and commercial litigation, of encouraging to the point of quasi-compulsion, parties to seek to resolve their differences with the aid of a mediator. Part of the justification for this arose because as was apparent from various judicial pronouncements such as by Brooke L.J. in *Dunnett v Railtrack*, Colman L.J. in *Cable & Wireless v IBM* and Lightman J. in *Hurst v Leeming*, judges recognised only too well that experienced mediators could bring parties to the point of settlement in ways that were beyond the powers of judges to accomplish, constrained as they are by the need to decide cases according to law and to grant the conventional remedies such as damages, injunctions or specific performance.

Some judges were also more conscious than others that they have a duty to consider the role of ADR in litigation, given the overriding objective of the CPR expressed in r.1.1 as "enabling the court to deal with cases justly." They were also conscious that r.1 also enjoined them to save expense and ensure the case be dealt with expeditiously and fairly and that the court has an obligation actively to manage cases, which by r.1.4 includes "encouraging the parties to use an alternative dispute resolution procedure if the court considers that appropriate and facilitating the use of such procedures;" also, by "helping the parties to settle the whole or part of the case."

So, not only was the rule-based power there but there was an obligation to use it, reflecting no more than the public policy that it is in the interest of the state to encourage the settlement of litigation. The rules expressed the fundamental approach of the Woolf reforms to encourage settlement of disputes before litigation and failing that as soon as possible thereafter. The judicial pronouncements until *Halsey* reflected also, I think, an increasing realisation on the part of judges, that it was not actually that difficult to identify cases suitable for mediation. The fundamental rule propounded by David Shapiro and others (with which I fully agree) is that, if a case can be settled, then it is suitable for ADR. No responsible ADR practitioner would say that ADR is suitable for all cases, for plainly there are disputes between the citizen and the state, or cases which require a decision in principle as to the operation of a market, where ADR is not practicable and will not produce the desired results. However, it should be borne in mind, as has been amply demonstrated, that once decisions in principle are made, ADR can have a role to play in their implementation.

The judges have considered ADR in litigation at three stages. The first is the enforcement of agreements to go to an ADR process, categorised often as little more than an agreement to agree and, therefore, in accordance with well-established English authority, of no binding effect. But the judges have found ways around that conceptual problem, as indeed judges have done in America and in Australia. This was the issue before Colman J. in *Cable & Wireless v IBM*. He adopted the analogy of a stay of proceedings to enable arbitration to take place. I am not sure just how far that analogy takes us, but I think it clear in the light of Colman J.'s judgment that, where parties have agreed to an ADR process particularly as part of a structured dispute resolution scheme in a long-term contract, they will be compelled to go to it as a prerequisite to further steps such as litigation or arbitration. In fact in *Cable & Wireless v IBM* the reference to mediation did not succeed, but Colman J. was entirely right to decide the case as he did. I think his approach is to be preferred to earlier judicial rulings that perhaps such agreements should not be given effect.

The second stage at which the judges have had to consider the question of ADR is at the beginning of litigation. They have had to decide whether cases were suitable for ADR and whether the parties should be encouraged to settle using ADR. It is plain, as we have seen from the Commercial Court practice and such decisions as *Hurst v Leeming*, that some judges have developed a somewhat robust view as to the type of case which should be referred. I think it could safely be said that in a pragmatic way based on great experience, many judges were demonstrating very well how the duty to encourage parties to settle and to use ADR could be performed by the use of adjournment orders. The power to adjourn is to be found in CPR r.26.4 which provides that the court can stay proceedings of its own initiative where it considers it would be appropriate to do so for a period of one month which can be subject to extension.

Henry Brown and I have criticised this power of adjournment as not going far enough. It is plain on its terms that it is designed to be operated at a preliminary stage and it contemplates that mediation is a system of ADR that should be used. There should have been provisions for encouraging ADR at later stages as well and also in different forms, such as Early Neutral Evaluation, a practice introduced in the Northern District of California in 1976 and which has proved extremely successful in the United States. Such a practice might well respond to the need perceived by Hazel Genn in her analysis of the Central London County Court scheme, that a substantial proportion (in excess of 20%) of those participating in mediation wanted some indication from the mediator as to what would happen if the case went to trial. In *Hurst v Leeming*, Lightman J. had enumerated certain criteria which he felt appropriate to deciding on the suitability of a reference to mediation. I shall refer to these when considering *Halsey*. He considered this question at the third stage when the courts have looked at the use of ADR, namely at the end of litigation when deciding on costs. The problem was anticipated by Lord Woolf's final report when considering whether ADR should be made mandatory, or should be a purely voluntary process. Lord Woolf said that he remained: "... of the view, although with less certainty than before, that it would not be right for the court to compel parties to use ADR and take away or postpone their rights to remedy from the courts, although this approach has been successfully adopted in a number of other jurisdictions. Nevertheless where a party has unreasonably refused a proposal by the court that ADR should be attempted, or has acted uncooperatively in the course of ADR, the court should be able to take that into account in deciding what order to make as to costs." That statement of policy found expression in the costs sanctions provisions of CPR r.44.5, where in assessing whether costs were proportionately and reasonably incurred, the court must now have regard to the conduct of all the parties, in particular by CPR r.44.5(3)(a)(ii): "the efforts made, if any, before and during the proceedings in order to try to resolve the dispute." Henry Brown and I pointed out in the second edition that this rule was fraught with difficulty and gave rise to the very real risk of satellite litigation and an inquiry into what had happened, which would be a clear breach of what most would regard as the fundamental requirement of the mediation process, namely complete confidentiality. An approach which we proposed in 1999 was that in very exceptional circumstances where, for example, the judge had himself adjourned a case for mediation and no principled explanation for the failure to settle had been given, without extensive enquiry he might reflect that in his cost order. We pointed out that no hard and fast guidelines can be laid down in the abstract. We thought then that there may be scope for considering compulsory disclosure of the results of negotiation prior to any automatic references and the judge could be informed of this at the end of the case. This might then help the judge to decide whether or not either or both parties genuinely tried to reach a settlement. Alternatively, we suggested that there might be scope for either party at the end of an inconclusive mediation, to summarise their proposals in a type of Calderbank letter and submit them to the other party to put it to risk as to costs.

The problems are obvious: how can a court properly assess who was uncooperative in an ADR process? Are parties, who stand firm in a principled way and do not change their position significantly, to be regarded as recalcitrant? Who is to tell the judge? Do cost sanctions, where imposed by the mediator or by a court following a mediator's report, damage the integrity of the process? I am coming increasingly to the view, as is Henry Brown, despite the attempts of Lightman J. in *Hurst v Leeming* and by Brooke L.J. in *Dunnett v Railtrack*, that this is an area in which it may be too dangerous for the courts to trespass. It may well be that we will just have to accept that, even in cases where a party may have abused the system, there should be no cost sanction, because that mischief is preferable to satellite litigation and a possible breach of confidentiality. The question of an unreasonable refusal to mediate came to be considered in *Halsey* and it is to that case to which I now turn. The Court of Appeal considered two appeals from the county court and indicated that they raised a question of some general importance namely: "when should the court impose a costs sanction against a successful litigant on the grounds that he has refused to take part in an alternative dispute resolution (ADR)?" In the cases before the court, namely *Halsey* and the conjoined case of *Steel v Joy*, there had been a refusal by the defendant in *Halsey* and by the second defendant in *Steel*, of a number of invitations to mediate. The court therefore set out to give guidance as to what it termed "the general approach that should be adopted when dealing with a costs issue raised by these two appeals." As I have indicated, the judgment of the court was in general supportive and approving of ADR to resolve civil disputes. The court said in terms that it was: "in no doubt that we should proceed on the basis that there are many disputes which are suitable for mediation. This approach is consistent with, and (we have seen) underpinned by, the Woolf reforms" for the virtues of mediation in suitable cases are also recognised in the Chancery Guide (paragraphs 17.1 and 17.3), the Queens Bench Guide (paragraph 6.6), the Admiralty and Commercial Court Guide (paragraph D8.8) and the Technology and Construction Court Guide (paragraph 6.4). As the court said: "Judges in the Commercial Court routinely make ADR orders in the form set out in Appendix 7 to the Admiralty and Commercial Court Guide." The Court of Appeal also drew attention to the Lord Chancellor's announcement of the 'ADR Pledge', to which I have already made reference, and to the July 2002 DCA report which showed the pledge had been taken seriously by government, and a number of initiatives introduced as a result of it, including the National Health Service Litigation Authorities' encouragement of the greater use of mediation.

The court also referred to *Cowl v Plymouth*, *Dunnett v Railtrack* and *Hurst v Leeming*. The court stated at [10] of its judgment that: "... if a judge takes the view that the case is suitable for ADR then he or she is not, of course, obliged to take at face value the expressed opposition of the parties. In such a case, the judge should explore the reasons for any resistance to ADR. If the parties (or at least one of them) remain intransigently opposed to ADR, then it would be wrong for the court to compel them to embrace it." The court reiterated "that the court's role is to encourage, not to compel. The form of encouragement may be robust." The difficulty with *Halsey* is not the general endorsement of the use of ADR which it is obvious that the court supports. It could hardly have done otherwise given the very strong judicial endorsement of the Court of Appeal in *Cowl v Plymouth* and in *Dunnett v Railtrack*. The court was plainly fully taking into account the success of ADR references and recognised "the value and importance of

ADR had been established within a remarkably short time." The court went on to say "all members of the legal profession who conduct litigation should now routinely consider with their clients whether their disputes are suitable for ADR."

So why do I think the decision is so seriously wrong? The first problem with *Halsey* is in its finding that parties cannot be compelled to go to ADR in suitable cases. The second problem is the narrow interpretation of what was or was not reasonable in a refusal to mediate. The court based its rejection of a mandatory reference, first of all by endorsing the guidance given by Volume 1 of the White Book 2003, para.1.4.11: "[t]he hallmark of ADR procedures, and perhaps the key to their effectiveness in individual cases, is that they are processes voluntarily entered into by the parties in dispute with outcomes, if the parties so wish, which are non-binding. Consequently the court cannot direct that such methods be used but may merely encourage and facilitate."

I observe in passing that that conclusion is wholly inconsistent with the experience in the United States, Canada and Australia, where the key to effectiveness of ADR is precisely that references are mandatory and where experience shows the same level of satisfaction with the result of the process by litigants, whether they voluntarily agreed, or were compelled to go to it. Unfortunately, the Court of Appeal in *Halsey* rested its objection on a further point, namely that no mandatory reference was possible in view of Art. 6 of the European Convention on Human Rights, because a mandatory refusal would constitute the imposition on the parties of "an unacceptable obstruction on their rights of access to the courts." This argument was advanced by Lord Lester of Herne Hill Q.C. on behalf of the Law Society. The argument had formed no part of the Law Society's written submissions to the court. Regrettably, it appears that none of those who were allowed to intervene as amicus argued in favour of mandatory reference. With the greatest respect to Lord Lester's argument and to the Court of Appeal which adopted it, it is a nonsense to say that a requirement that a party must go to mediation, not in lieu of a formal adjudication, but before a formal adjudication by a judge, is a contravention of the right of access.

If it is in the public interest to promote the settlement of cases, if the right of access is preserved and if there is a crisis in the civil justice system, which means that access to justice is being effectively denied, then it cannot be unjust to require parties to mediate before they can get a formal and binding adjudication by a judge. Human rights and access to justice are not concepts peculiar to England and Wales. The Americans, the Canadians and the Australians do not feel that human rights are being breached by mandatory references. They all have a right of access to the courts. But to the contrary, they feel that access to justice is being improved by mandatory mediation.

Professor Goode's warning has truly been ignored in *Halsey*. The parallel of arbitration and human rights relied upon by the court in *Halsey* is not apt. The courts in this country will enforce agreements to arbitrate in both domestic cases and in international cases covered by the New York Convention, retaining very limited supervisory powers. An arbitration is not considered a breach of Art. 6. It is very unfortunate that the Court of Appeal has taken this approach and the sooner this question is considered by the

House of Lords the better. However, in fairness to the Court of Appeal, it should be said that the decision does reflect the conviction of the majority concerned with litigation and ADR in this country, that references should not be mandatory. Where that conviction takes us is the continuation of the crisis affecting the civil justice system.

Unfortunately, the other line of reasoning in *Halsey* may have a more immediate effect on voluntary mediation and the view which the court is to take when encouraging parties to mediate and in applying cost sanctions in the event of abuse or a refusal to do so. In *Hurst v Leeming* Lightman J. had said "the fact that a party believes he has a watertight case again is no justification for refusing mediation. That is the frame of mind of so many litigants." The Court of Appeal in *Halsey* thought that: "... this judgment should be qualified. The fact that a party unreasonably believes that his case is watertight is no justification for refusing mediation. The fact that a party reasonably believes that he has a watertight case may well be significant justification for refusal to mediate." That is to substitute the subjective test of the litigant for the objective test of the court.

The Court of Appeal in *Halsey* seems to have believed that the subjective test was preferable, because otherwise there: "... would be considerable scope for a claimant to use the threat of cost sanctions to extract a settlement from the defendant even where the claim is without merit. The courts should be particularly astute to this danger. Large organisations, especially public bodies, are vulnerable to pressure from claimants who, having weak cases, invite mediation as a tactical ploy. They calculate that such a defendant may at least make a nuisance value offer to buy off the cost of a mediation and the risk of being penalised in costs for refusing a mediation even if ultimately successful."

In my experience the big battalions do not need this kind of protection. They are well able to look after themselves. Also in *Halsey*, I think that application of the approach as understood before *Halsey* might well have led a judge to say as the county court judge did, that the refusal to mediate was not unreasonable, though, in *Steel*, I would have exercised the discretion differently. Again unfortunately, the Court of Appeal qualified Lightman J.'s view that he considered that the critical factor in deciding whether mediation had a reasonable prospect of success was to view it objectively. Lightman J. in *Hurst v Leeming* had also said: "[t]hese words will strike a responsive chord with anyone who has any practical experience of mediating often complicated, bitterly contested and seemingly intractable disputes." However, the Court of Appeal expressly disavowed Lightman J.'s tests: "… if mediation can have no real prospect of success, a party may, with impunity, refuse to proceed to mediation on this ground. Refusal is a high risk course to take for if the court finds that there was a real prospect, the party refusing to proceed to mediation may, as I have said, be severely penalised. Further, the hurdle in the way of a party refusing to proceed to mediation on this ground is high, for in making this objective assessment of the prospect of mediation, the starting point must surely be the fact that the mediation process itself can and often does bring about a more sensible and more conciliatory attitude on the part of the parties that might otherwise be expected to prevail before the mediation, and may produce a recognition of the strengths and weaknesses by each party of his own case and that of his opponent, and a willingness to accept the give and take essential to a successful mediation. What appears to be incapable of mediation before the mediation process begins often proves capable of satisfactory resolution later.... We do not therefore accept that as suggested by Lightman J it is appropriate for the court to confine itself to a consideration of whether, viewed objectively, a mediation would have had a reasonable prospect of success. That is an unduly narrow approach ... it focuses on the nature of the dispute, and leaves out of account the parties' willingness to compromise and the reasonableness of their attitudes." This led the court to conclude: "... the burden should not be on the refusing party to satisfy the court that mediation had no reasonable prospect of success. As we have already stated, the fundamental question is whether it has been shown by the unsuccessful party that the successful party unreasonably refused to agree to mediation ... it seems to us that the fairer balance is struck if the burden is placed on the unsuccessful party to show that there was a reasonable prospect that mediation would have been successful. This is not an unduly onerous burden to discharge: he does not have to prove that a mediation would have in fact succeeded. It is significantly easier for the successful party to prove that there was a reasonable prospect that a mediation would have succeeded than for the successful party to prove the contrary." I must say this opinion bears little relation to how mediations work and how they fail; and combined with the subjective test will probably encourage satellite litigation to inquire into what actually happened.

Finally, with respect to government cases, the Court of Appeal expressly disavowed the reliance which Lewison J. in the *Royal Bank of Canada v*

The Secretary of State for Defence had put on the ADR Pledge. The Court of Appeal considered that: "... the pledge was no more than an undertaking that ADR would be considered and used in all suitable cases. If a case is suitable for ADR, then it is likely that a party refusing to agree to it will be acting unreasonably, whether or not it is a public body to which the ADR pledge applies. If the case is not suitable for ADR, then a refusal to agree to ADR does not breach the pledge. It is, therefore, difficult to see in what circumstances it would be right to give weight to the ADR pledge." This reasoning totally ignores the point of public policy that what the then Lord Chancellor and the government were endeavouring to do as a matter of sound public administration and in order to settle expensive litigation, was indicating that in disputes the state agency would be expected to mediate. If, as a result of *Halsey* for example, individual NHS Trusts and their insurers are encouraged to place no special importance on the pledge, then an important object of public policy will be frustrated. The effects of *Halsey* may have already been felt. CEDR Solve has just published last month's first report on the new Court of Appeal mediation scheme covering the first 15 months of its life. I desire simply to draw attention to the fact that according to CEDR Solve there were no referrals in July 2004, as compared with six in July 2003. This is described by CEDR Solve as "disappointing." They go on to say "whether it reflects a trend following *Halsey* ... is too early to judge." However, they conclude: "... perhaps the only disappointing note is that the referrals seem to have dropped off considerably since the end of June 2004. As noted above, this may or may not have a link with the court's decision in *Halsey* ..., though in view of the fact that this decision promoted and underlined the significance of judicial encouragement of mediation by ADR orders in commercial court form, this would be surprising. There is some sense that lawyers may perceive that the *Halsey* decision has taken some pressure off them in terms of costs risks where mediation is declined between parties without court intervention. Alternatively, it may simply be a lack of appreciation of what the CAMS scheme has managed to achieve." To adapt Napoleon's phrase, access to justice is too serious a matter to be left to the judges, let alone to practitioners. Unless the decision in *Halsey* is reconsidered, it will have deleterious effects on improving access to justice. First of all, and immediately, as we may well now be seeing, it will discourage the greater use of ADR by encouraging the recalcitrant and their advisers. Secondly, and in the longer term, it will prevent us from grappling with the central problem that, while access to justice rests on a complexity of factors which admit of no simple or single solution, ADR is an essential element of any reform.

The use of ADR in civil litigation is not a panacea. It will not make the problems disappear, connected as they are to questions of funding. My argument is, and it is based on experience elsewhere but also here, that mandatory references to ADR will significantly improve access to justice and ensure, as well, that funding, whether from the public or the private sector is more efficiently and better employed. In our second edition therefore, we came to the conclusion that mandatory references to ADR might well be appropriate as, indeed, the Americans had decided and which had prompted the US Congress to enact the 1998 legislation establishing mandatory requirements in the Federal system. We also said: "... there is no need for England to follow slavishly the course adopted in the US and other common law jurisdictions. Learning from the US experience and that of other common law jurisdictions, we can devise our own solutions. It would be arrogant and shortsighted for us to ignore what is happening elsewhere, or to dismiss the experience of others as irrelevant to the English civil justice system. Too often in this country we have been content to rest upon the laurels of past achievement."

If we were writing that now we would also have to take into account other international developments, such as the EU draft directive on the use of ADR in the courts and the UNCITRAL Model Law on Conciliation. That must wait for our third edition. But we concluded our discussion of court attached ADR, as I do this evening, by drawing attention to Professor Goode's timely warning which heads this paper. We ignore it at our own risk.

REFERENCES

* This article was originally published as A. Marriott, 'Mandatory ADR and Access to Justice', *Arbitration* 71, no. 4 (2005): 307-317.
1 Professor Sir Roy Goode QC, 1991 Freshfields lecture. See H. Brown & A. Marriott, *ADR Principles and Practice* (London: Sweet and Maxwell, 1993), xii.
2 M. Latham, *Constructing the Team* (London: HMSO, 1994); J. Egan, *Rethinking Construction* (London, 1998).
3 H. Genn, *Court-based ADR Initiatives for Non-family Civil Disputes: the Commercial Court and the Court of Appeal* (London: Lord

Chancelor's Department, 2002).

4 Peter Middleton Report to the Lord Chancellor, September 1997.
5 [2002] EWHC 316 (Comm).
6 [2001] EWHC 734 (Admin).
7 [2002] EWCA Civ 303; [2002] 2 All E.R. 850.
8 [2001] EWHC 1051 (Ch).
9 [2004] All ER (D) 61 (Aug).
10 Lawtel Reference LTL3/12/99 (unreported elsewhere) Document Number AC7200588.
11 [1999] 4 All E.R. 178.
12 *Deweer v Belgium* (6903/75) [1980] E.C.H.R. 1 (February 27, 1980) considered in *Placito v Slater* [2003] EWCA Civ 1863; [2004] 1 W.L.R. 1605.
13 [2003] EWHC 1479 (Ch).
14 The Court of Appeal Mediation Scheme: April 2003 to July 2004, A report on the first 15 months of CAMS administered by CEDR Solve, pp. 4 and 8.

CHAPTER 1

Alternative Dispute Resolution: An English Viewpoint

Lord Phillips

My professional life in the law started as a barrister 46 years ago. In England a young barrister in those days cut his teeth on small criminal prosecutions, such as infringements of road traffic legislation and small civil cases in the County Court, such as disputes between landlord and tenant. Actions in the High Court normally went to barristers of experience. One such action was down for trial in which a senior member of my chambers was instructed for the plaintiff. Then, at the last minute, he was unable to appear because a previous action in which he was appearing had overrun. Our clerk persuaded the solicitor to transfer the brief to me instead. This was my first High Court action, producing mixed emotions of excitement and terror. I read the papers with great care. My client was an elderly lady who had slipped and fallen in a vegetable shop, sustaining a nasty broken ankle. She alleged that she had slipped on a squashed plum that had been left on the floor, and that the shop was in breach of its duty to her under the Occupiers' Liability Act. The shop denied this and suggested that the old lady must have tripped over her own shopping bag. None the less, the shop's liability insurers had made an offer to settle on the basis of paying 50% of the damages. My client had refused this offer. There were no witnesses. The result of the action was going to depend on whether the judge accepted my client's version of the accident.

I met my client for the first time in the corridor outside the court on the day that the action was due to begin. She was obviously very nervous. The first thing that she said to me was, "I won't have to give evidence, will I?" I explained to her that her evidence was absolutely critical. She said that she was too frightened to go into the witness box. Try as I might I could not persuade her to change her mind. What a disaster for my first High Court case. I saw my opponent at the opposite end of the corridor. He was a very experienced counsel who regularly acted for the insurance company involved. I went up to him and explained that I had only just come into the case. I said that my view was that my client had been foolish to reject the 50% offer (but I did not tell him why). I asked whether the offer was still open for acceptance. Experienced as he was, he viewed my question with some suspicion. "Is your client actually here?" he asked. I assured him that she was and pointed her out to him. He then took instructions and returned to say that the insurance company would still settle for 50%, so I quickly clinched the deal on that basis. She was relieved to miss her day in court but I was very disappointed to miss mine.

That was my first lesson in the merits of alternative dispute resolution. It avoids the trauma of court proceedings. If, like my client, you are not prepared to undergo that trauma at any price, then there is no alternative to alternative dispute resolution, and in the first 30 years of my life in the law, the only form of ADR was negotiation. Any sensible person who finds himself party to a dispute will wish to resolve it, if possible, by negotiation. Over 90% of actions that are commenced in England end in a negotiated settlement before trial. One reason for this is the cost of litigating under the adversarial process. Resolving a dispute by adversarial litigation usually involves a solicitor on each side, a barrister on each side and the judge, whose cost is covered by the court fees that the claimant has to pay. Add to this, very often, the cost of professional expert witnesses on each side and it is no wonder that the cost of litigation is frequently disproportionate to what is at stake.

Under the English procedure, there is a principle that "costs follow the event." This means that the party who loses has to pay not only his own legal costs, but the costs of the successful party. So the detriment of losing an action is immeasurably greater than the benefit of winning. This added to the incentive to negotiate a settlement, and this used to be the only realistic form of dispute resolution that provided an alternative to litigation or arbitration. If a plaintiff refused to accept the best offer that the defendant was prepared to make, there was one way that he could attempt to protect himself against the costs of the litigation. That was to pay into court the sum that he was prepared to pay in settlement. If the plaintiff did not accept the money paid into court, but recovered less than this, he would have to bear the costs of the litigation from the time that the money was paid into court. This was a protective measure that the defendant could only take once an action had been commenced by the plaintiff.

The risk of a disproportionate liability to pay costs has been significantly increased, for defendants at least, by the legalisation of conditional fee agreements, or CFAs, under the Access to Justice Act 1999. These were introduced by the Government as an alternative to providing claimants with free legal aid. Under a CFA the claimant agrees with his lawyers that if his claim fails he will pay no legal fees, but that if it succeeds his lawyers will receive a mark-up of up to 100% on top of what they would otherwise have charged.

This mark-up is known as a 'success fee.' Where the claim is successful, the unsuccessful defendant is liable to reimburse the claimant both for his costs and for the success fee. Indeed the defendant's position may be even worse, because a CFA only protects the claimant from having to pay his own legal expenses if his claim fails. He remains liable to pay the defendant's costs in that event. But he can insure against the risk of his claim failing and thus of having to pay the defendant's costs. The premium for such insurance is often very large. If the claimant's claim succeeds, he can recover not only his own legal costs and the success fee from the defendant but also the premium he had to pay for insuring against his potential liability in costs to the defendant. So in addition to losing the action the defendant is faced with a huge bill for the claimant's costs and insurance. So the desire to avoid the risk of liability for all these costs is an additional cogent reason why a defendant may want to seek an alternative means of dispute resolution that does not involve litigation.

In this lecture I propose to concentrate on that form of ADR that is described as mediation. In 2004 the Centre for Effective Dispute Resolution, known as CEDR, published a revised definition of mediation as follows: "[a] flexible process conducted confidentially in which a neutral person assists the parties in working towards a negotiated agreement of a dispute or difference, with the parties in ultimate control of the decision to settle and the terms of resolution."

Mediation offers many attractions in addition to that of avoiding the cost and trauma of litigation. In India it may well be that it is not so much the cost of litigation as the delay involved that makes the parties anxious to find an alternative way of solving their disputes. Before this audience I suspect that there is no need to labour the other attractions of mediation. It is a private and confidential way of resolving a dispute. It is informal. It is voluntary. It is a process that those involved can understand.

I sometimes think that law is like medicine. Once you are in the hands of professional litigants they take charge of you, willy-nilly, and you find that you have embarked on a course that has no turning back and the incidents of which you cannot even understand. Mediation is not like that. You can always turn back and you have explained to you precisely what is going on. You are in control of what is happening to you. You can preserve, or restore, good relationships with the other party to the dispute — you can come to feel that you are partners in a common endeavour rather than antagonists. And the resolution of the dispute can involve a much wider range of remedies than the court can offer.

There are of course down sides to mediation. If what you are after is your just rights according to the law, then mediation is not the place for you, but you need to consider carefully the cost of seeking those rights. Above all, so it seems to me, mediation is really suited for two parties who are in genuine dispute. Sometimes it is necessary for a defendant to stand his ground and challenge the claimant to prove his case in court, because if he does not do so, he will find himself facing claims that are not made in good faith but are brought be fraudsters, relying on the fact that the defendant may think that it is cheaper to reach a settlement agreement than to fight the action, even if successful.

I started this talk with an account of a claim by an old lady who had slipped over in a shop and who was undoubtedly a bona fide claimant. But local authorities in England are familiar with claims from people claiming to have injured themselves by tripping over uneven paving stones, some of whom are not genuine claimants but fraudsters "tripping and slipping." There was one local authority, Knowsley Council, that almost always settled such claims on the grounds that this was a desirable alternative to litigation. In 1998 they dealt with 600 claims. By 2002 the number of claims had risen to 1,800. They then had a change of policy and rigorously investigated and defended claims, with the result that by 2006 the annual number of claims had reduced to below 400.

Mediation is a relatively recent arrival on the legal scene — having its origin in the United States in the latter half of the twentieth century. In the United States there are different reasons for resolving disputes without recourse to litigation. There the successful claimant does not recover his costs from the defendant, but has often agreed that his lawyer will receive a substantial percentage of any recovery he makes under a contingency fee agreement. The defendant is often faced with the fact that if he loses the action the damages will be assessed by a jury and the sky will be the limit.

Mediation has been enthusiastically embraced by a number of states, often making it a mandatory stage of the court process. I have seen a judge conducting mediation in California — admittedly some years ago now —

and it was very robust indeed. In England the courts' enthusiasm for mediation has been much more muted and the growth of what I might term "court induced mediation" has been attributable in large measure to the enthusiasm of a comparatively small number of judges.

I shall start with the greatest and most influential of these, Lord Woolf, who preceded me in the offices of both the Master of the Rolls and the Lord Chief Justice. He will be known personally to many of you. In the early 1990s there was an awful lot wrong with the civil justice system in England and Wales. Cases moved very slowly, they were beset by complex and costly interlocutory battles and, in part for this reason, they were inordinately expensive. Lord Woolf was asked to examine our civil system and to recommend reforms to it. He did so very comprehensively, tearing up and re-writing from scratch our rules of civil procedure. But, for present purposes, the interest of his reforms lies in their approach to mediation. Some urged him to follow the American example and make ADR compulsory. In his Interim Access to Justice Report in 1995 he declined to follow this course. He did not recommend court-annexed mediation. He saw the role of the court as being no more than to encourage the parties to consider ADR, without suggesting any sanction if they declined to respond to such encouragement.

As so often in English civil law, the Commercial Court was ahead of the game. The Commercial Court, of which I was a member when I was a puisne judge, is drawn from barristers who practise in commercial work, much of which is international, and they tend to be more forward looking than some of their colleagues. In 1994 the Commercial Court had published a Practice Note requiring legal advisers in all cases: "[t]o consider with their clients and the other parties concerned the possibility of attempting to resolve the particular dispute or particular issues by mediation, conciliation or otherwise."

And, "to ensure that parties are fully informed as to the most cost-effective means of resolving the particular dispute." This Practice Note may not sound very significant — but it was nonetheless valuable. One problem with mediation had been that neither side wanted to be the first to propose it, fearing that this would be taken for a sign of weakness. Now the court had made it mandatory for the parties to at least consider ADR. I shall be returning to the support given to mediation by the Commercial Court in due course. But first I want to return to Lord Woolf.

In his final Access to Justice Report, Lord Woolf recommended that, when a judge was considering how to award costs at the end of an action he should take into account an unreasonable refusal of a court's proposal that the parties should attempt to resolve their differences by ADR. When the new Civil Procedure Rules were drawn up in 1998 they contained a number of express provisions designed to promote ADR. The very first rule laid down an overriding objective of the CPR, namely that of "enabling the court to deal with cases justly." This includes "saving expense" and "dealing with the case in ways which are proportionate". Instead of leaving it to the litigants to make the running, the new Rules placed a duty of "active case management" on the court, and this includes: "1.4(e) encouraging the parties to use an alternative dispute resolution procedure if the court considers that appropriate and facilitating the use of such procedure." This was the first time that ADR was officially recognised by the rules of court.

Under the old rules, when the court was considering awards of costs, it was only entitled to have regard to how the parties behaved after the action had been commenced. The new rules radically change the position. Rule 44.5 now provides that the court must have regard to the conduct of the parties, including conduct before as well as during the proceedings, and, in particular, the efforts made, if any, before and during the proceedings in order to try to resolve the dispute.

Here then is a rule that permits the court to use liability in costs as a sanction against a party who unreasonably refuses to attempt alternative dispute resolution before the action begins. We shall see in due course what use the English court has made of that power. First, though, I want to draw attention to another novelty of civil procedure consequent upon Lord Woolf's reports, and that is the 'pre-action protocol'. These are protocols, prepared individually, for different types of litigation, that direct the manner in which the parties ought to behave before the litigation is commenced. They are endorsed by Practice Directions issued by the Master of the Rolls as my nominee. Since 2006 these have directed that every pre-action protocol shall contain the following clause: "The parties should consider whether some form of alternative dispute resolution procedure would be more suitable than litigation and, if so, endeavour to agree which form to adopt. Both the Claimant and Defendant may be required by the court to provide evidence that alternative means of resolving their dispute were considered. The Courts take the view that litigation should be a last resort, and that claims should not be issued prematurely when a settlement is still being actively explored. Parties are warned that if the protocol is not followed (including this paragraph) then the Court must have regard to such conduct when determining costs."

We shall see, in due course, to what extent the courts have made use of the costs sanction to encourage parties to resort to ADR. First let me draw attention to provisions in the Rules that enable the court to encourage ADR while the action is in progress. Early on in an action there is a stage called allocation, when the court decides on the manner in which the action is to be tried. The Rules provide that at that stage the court may, on the application of the parties or on its own initiative, stay the proceedings to enable the parties to explore ADR and the court may, where appropriate, extend that stay.

A more powerful weapon is given to the court by a Practice Direction Pt 29 PD 4.10(9), introduced in 2005, as follows: "[i]n such cases as the court thinks appropriate, the court may give directions requiring the parties to consider ADR. Such directions may be, for example, in the following terms: 'The parties shall by [the date determined by the court] consider whether the case is capable of resolution by ADR. If any party considers that the case is unsuitable for resolution by ADR, that party shall be prepared to justify that decision at the conclusion of the trial, should the judge consider that such means of resolution were appropriate, when he is considering the appropriate costs order to make.' The party considering the case unsuitable for ADR shall, not less than 28 days before the commencement of the trial, file with the court the witness statement without prejudice, save as to costs, giving reasons upon which they rely for saying that the case was unsuitable." That order was invented by a Queen's Bench master, Master Ungley. It stops short of ordering the parties to resort to ADR, but it certainly concentrates the mind and fires a warning shot across the bows of any litigant disinclined to resort to ADR. Master Ungley deals with a lot of personal injury litigation and, as you can see, he is an enthusiast for ADR.

Another enthusiast who has recently retired from the Commercial Court is Colman J. Some of you may know him, for he is not only an enthusiast of ADR but also an enthusiast of India. He is who must take most, or perhaps all, the credit for what has come to be known as 'the Commercial Court ADR Order.' This takes, more or less, the following form: "(1) On or before [Date 1] the parties shall exchange lists of 3 neutrals or identifying one or more panels of individuals who are available to conduct ADR procedures in the case prior to [Date 4]; (2) On or before [Date 2] the parties shall in good faith endeavour to agree a neutral individual or panel from the lists so exchanged or provided; (3) Failing such agreement by [Date 3] the court will facilitate agreement on a neutral individual or panel. (4) [T]he parties shall take such serious steps as they may be advised to resolve their disputes by ADR procedures before the individual or panel so chosen not later than [Date 4]; (5) If the case is not settled, the parties shall inform the court what steps towards ADR have been taken and why such steps have failed." This is a pretty punchy order. So far as I know, litigants have not objected to it and it quite often results in a mediated settlement.

We have now seen how, over the last 12 years — and it is only 12 years — rules of court, which are statutory instruments, give the court the powers to encourage ADR but fall short of entitling the court to direct that the parties actually engage in this. The rules also expressly impose on the court the duty to have regard to any unreasonable refusal to take part in ADR when considering awards of costs. In his final report on access to justice Lord Woolf had gone further and recommended that the court should have regard when awarding costs to unreasonable conduct in the course of ADR. That recommendation was not adopted and, indeed, it would be difficult to reconcile with the confidential nature of the mediation process.

I am now going to turn to see how the English courts have responded to the Woolf reports and to the powers that they have been given by the new Rules. The first case is one in which Lord Woolf was presiding as Master of the Rolls. It is particularly significant because it was not a dispute between two private parties but a public law dispute.

The case is *Cowl v Plymouth City Council*. The claimants were elderly people (the oldest was 92) who lived in an old people's home run by the Council. The Council had decided to close down their home and they were understandably upset. Some said that Council officials had assured them that they could live out the rest of their days in the home. The claimants sought judicial review to quash the closure decision. The Council made a sensible suggestion under which the claimants' complaints would be dealt with by an informal process before an independent panel, but the claimants insisted on going to court. There were proceedings that lasted several days at first instance in which psychiatric evidence was called as to the effect that closure might have on some of the claimants. The judge decided that the Council had acted lawfully and expressed the view that it was a pity that the

Council's offer had not been taken up. He observed that the offer was still open.

The claimants did not, however, take advantage of it. Instead they had a lengthy and expensive visit to the Court of Appeal, where they got Lord Woolf. He was characteristically gentle to the claimants, but he made it plain that they had been mistaken in resisting the overtures of the Council to an alternative to litigation. He observed at the outset of his judgment: "[t]he importance of this appeal is that it illustrates that, even in disputes between public authorities and the members of the public for whom they are responsible, insufficient attention is paid to the paramount importance of avoiding litigation whenever this is possible." Later on he added: "[w]ithout the need for the vast costs which must have been incurred in this case already, the parties should have been able to come to a sensible conclusion as to how to dispose of the issues that divided them."

In fact, earlier in the year, the Lord Chancellor published a pledge on behalf of all government departments and agencies that ADR would be considered and used in all suitable cases whenever the other party accepted it. The Government regularly publishes figures that purport to show that it is honouring this pledge.

Lord Woolf's judgment in *Cowl* was given in December 2001. Two months later Brooke L.J. gave the only judgment of the Court of Appeal dealing with costs in *Dunnett v Railtrack*. Sir Henry Brooke is a great jurist and I made him my deputy as President of the Civil Division of the Court of Appeal when I was Master of the Rolls. He was and is a great enthusiast for mediation. He retired from the Bench 18 months ago and has since conducted 30 mediations with a 75 to 80% success rate. His enthusiasm for ADR is apparent from his decision in *Dunnett*. It was a sad case. Mrs Dunnett kept horses in a field that abutted a railway line. Railtrack installed a new gate between her field and the line and she requested them to keep it padlocked. They declined to do so. Strangers left the gate open and three of her horses wandered onto the line and were killed by the Swansea to London express. She sued Railtrack in negligence, claiming both for the value of her horses and for psychiatric injury that she said she had suffered as a result of the accident. She lost at first instance but was given permission to appeal.

At that point the Court of Appeal offered a free mediation service. The judge who gave permission to appeal urged the parties to take advantage of this. Mrs Dunnett was prepared to do so but Railtrack turned the suggestion down flat. They offered £2,500 in settlement but Mrs Dunnett turned the offer down. She lost her appeal and Railtrack applied for an order that she pay their costs. They argued that she should have accepted their offer. Brooke L.J. was not sympathetic. He observed: "[T]his was a case in which, at any rate before the trial, a real effort ought to have been made by way of alternative dispute resolution to see if the matter could be resolved by an experienced mediator, without the parties having to incur the no doubt heavy legal costs of contesting the matter at trial."

So far as the appeal was concerned, he held that Railtrack had been wrong to turn down the offer of mediation. He said: "Mr Lord, when asked by the court why his clients were not willing to contemplate alternative dispute resolution, said that this would necessarily involve the payment of money, which his clients were not willing to contemplate, over and above what they had already offered. This appears to be a misunderstanding of the purpose of alternative dispute resolution. Skilled mediators are now able to achieve results satisfactory to both parties in many cases which are quite beyond the power of lawyers and courts to achieve. The court has knowledge of cases where intense feelings have arisen, for instance in relation to clinical negligence claims. But when the parties are brought together on neutral soil with a skilled mediator to help them resolve their differences, it may very well be that the mediator is able to achieve a result by which the parties shake hands at the end and feel that they have gone away having settled the dispute on terms with which they are happy to live. A mediator may be able to provide solutions which are beyond the powers of the court to provide. Occasions are known to the court in claims against the police, which can give rise to as much passion as a claim of this kind where a claimant's precious horses are killed on a railway line, by which an apology from a very senior officer is all that the claimant is really seeking and the money side of the matter falls away."

He added: "It is to be hoped that any publicity given to this part of the judgment of the court will draw the attention of lawyers to their duties to further the overriding objective in the way that is set out in CPR Part 1 and to the possibility that, if they turn down out of hand the chance of alternative dispute resolution when suggested by the court, as happened on this occasion, they may have to face uncomfortable costs consequences."

Practitioners certainly did take this judgment to heart. They were shocked by a decision that robbed the successful party of costs even though an offer of settlement made by that party had been refused. CEDR keeps statistics. Those statistics showed that mediations increased at the rate of 25% per annum in the two years that followed the decision in *Dunnett*. CEDR say *"post hoc ergo propter hoc"*, and I am inclined to think that they are right.

The courts have adopted the approach in *Dunnett* in a number of other cases. In *Leicester Circuits Ltd v Coats* the parties had actually agreed to mediate and appointed a mediator. The defendants then pulled out of the mediation the day before it was due to take place. Their solicitors had, apparently, insisted that they do so. The claim failed but the Court of Appeal subsequently denied the defendants the costs that they had incurred after pulling out of the mediation. This was on the basis that the mediation might have been successful and saved incurring these costs.

Royal Bank of Canada v Ministry of Defence was a landlord and tenant dispute. The Ministry of Defence was successful on most of the issues but had several times refused an offer of mediation. The court ruled that this was contrary to the Government's pledge to make use of ADR and refused to award the Ministry of Defence its costs.

Another enthusiast for mediation is Sir Gavin Lightman, who has recently retired from the Chancery Division. He has been an outspoken critic of the high cost of civil litigation and in *Hurst v Leeming* he ruled that a number of reasons given by the defendant for refusing an offer of mediation were without validity. These included that heavy costs had already been incurred, that the claimant was alleging that the defendant had committed serious professional negligence and that the defendant was confident that he had a watertight defence. He held, however, that it was reasonable to reject the request for mediation because mediation would have been doomed to failure. The facts of that case were extreme. The claimant was an obsessive litigant who was suing everyone in sight on charges of professional negligence and I do not think that it would have been reasonable to expect anyone to sit down with him at the mediation table. In general, however, it does not seem right to me to entertain an argument that the mediation would not have succeeded as justification for a refusal to mediate. Usually it is impossible to know whether a mediation may succeed until you try it.

These were all cases in which the court made, or considered making, adverse costs orders against parties who declined to attempt mediation, usually in circumstances where this had been urged by the court. There were, however, a number of early cases in which the court actually directed the parties to mediate. I have referred to the standard Commercial Court order, which comes very close to that. In one unreported case Arden J., now Arden L.J., sitting in the Chancery Division, directed that a particularly complex web of disputes be referred to mediation, over the objections of some of the parties. Blackburne J., also sitting in the Chancery Division, followed her example in making an ADR order in the face of strenuous opposition from the claimant. Whether it was appropriate for the court to act in this way came under review in what has, to date, been by far the most important English judgment about ADR. This is the judgment of the Court of Appeal delivered by Dyson L.J. in two appeals that were heard together: *Halsey v Milton Keynes General NHS Trust* and *Steel v Joy and Halliday*. In each case the relevant issue was whether it was right to deprive a successful party of an award of costs on the ground that the party had refused an invitation from the opposing party to take part in alternative dispute resolution. Dyson L.J. used the appeals, however, as a vehicle for some general observations on ADR. First he dealt with the question of whether the court had power to order ADR and, if so, whether it was a power that the court should exercise.

He said: "[w]e heard argument on the question whether the court has power to order parties to submit their disputes to mediation against their will. It is one thing to encourage the parties to agree to mediation, even to encourage them in the strongest terms. It is another to order them to do so. It seems to us that to oblige truly unwilling parties to refer their disputes to mediation would be to impose an unacceptable obstruction on their right of access to the court. The court in Strasbourg has said in relation to article 6 of the European Convention on Human Rights that the right of access to a court may be waived, for example by means of an arbitration agreement, but such waiver should be subjected to 'particularly careful review' to ensure that the claimant is not subject to 'constraint.' See *Deweer v Belgium* (1980) 2 EHRR 439, paragraph 49. If that is the approach of the ECtHR to an agreement to arbitrate, it seems to us likely that compulsion of ADR would be regarded as an unacceptable constraint on the right of access to the court and, therefore, a violation of Article 6. Even if (contrary to our view) the court does have jurisdiction to order unwilling parties to refer their disputes to mediation, we find it difficult to conceive of circumstances in which it would be appropriate to exercise it. We would adopt what the editors of

Volume 1 of the White Book (2003) say at paragraph 1.4.11: "[t]he hallmark of ADR procedures, and perhaps the key to their effectiveness in individual cases, is that they are processes voluntarily entered into by the parties in dispute with outcomes, if the parties so wish, which are non-binding. Consequently the court cannot direct that such methods be used but may merely encourage and facilitate."

If the court were to compel parties to enter into a mediation to which they objected, that would achieve nothing except to add to the costs to be borne by the parties, possibly postpone the time when the court determines the dispute and damage the perceived effectiveness of the ADR process. If a judge takes the view that the case is suitable for ADR, then he or she is not, of course, obliged to take at face value the expressed opposition of the parties. In such a case, the judge should explore the reasons for any resistance to ADR. But if the parties (or at least one of them) remain intransigently opposed to ADR, then it would be wrong for the court to compel them to embrace it.

Parties sometimes need to be encouraged by the court to embark on an ADR. The need for such encouragement should diminish in time if the virtue of ADR in suitable cases is demonstrated even more convincingly than it has been thus far. The value and importance of ADR have been established within a remarkably short time. All members of the legal profession who conduct litigation should now routinely consider with their clients whether their disputes are suitable for ADR. But we reiterate that the court's role is to encourage, not compel. The form of encouragement may be robust." Later in his judgment Dyson L.J. commented on the Commercial

Court ADR Order. He commented that this was the strongest form of encouragement but that it stopped short of actually compelling the parties to undertake an ADR. He then referred to the Order devised by Master Ungley, commenting: "[t]his form of order has the merit that (a) it recognises the importance of encouraging the parties to consider whether the case is suitable for ADR, and (b) it is calculated to bring home to them that, if they refuse even to consider that question, they may be at risk on costs even if they are ultimately held by the court to be the successful party. We can see no reason why such an order should not also routinely be made at least in general personal injury litigation, and perhaps in other litigation too. A party who refuses even to consider whether a case is suitable for ADR is always at risk of an adverse finding at the costs stage of litigation, and particularly so where the court has made an order requiring the parties to consider ADR." These comments were strictly *obiter dicta*.

The same is not true of the comments that Dyson L.J. made in relation to the use of adverse costs orders as a sanction for an unreasonable failure to resort to ADR. He said: "[i]n deciding whether to deprive a successful party of some or all of his costs on the grounds that he has refused to agree to ADR, it must be borne in mind that such an order is an exception to the general rule that costs should follow the event. In our view, the burden is on the unsuccessful party to show why there should be a departure from the general rule. The fundamental principle is that such departure is not justified unless it is shown (the burden being on the successful party) that the successful party acted unreasonably in refusing to agree to ADR. We shall endeavour in this judgment to provide some guidance as to the factors that should be considered by the court in deciding whether a refusal to agree to ADR is unreasonable." Dyson L.J. identified the following factors as being relevant to whether it was reasonable to refuse an invitation to mediate. The nature of the dispute: some disputes are not suitable to mediation — for instance a dispute where the parties want the court to set a binding precedent on a point of law. The merits of the case: Dyson L.J. said that it could be reasonable to refuse mediation where one reasonably believes that one has a strong case. He rejected the view to the contrary expressed by Lightman J. in *Hurst*. Failure of other settlement methods may make it reasonable to decline ADR. The cost of ADR may be disproportionately high. ADR may threaten to involve unacceptable delay.

Dyson L.J. agreed with Lightman J. that it was not unreasonable to refuse mediation if, by reason of the intransigence of the other party, mediation had no prospect of success. He held, however, that the burden was on the party seeking to avoid paying costs to show that mediation would have had a reasonable prospect of success, not on the party refusing mediation to show that mediation would not have had a reasonable prospect of success.

Dyson L.J.'s judgment has been controversial. Those who support ADR say that it has had a dampening effect on the willingness of parties to agree to mediation. They suggest that in some respects Dyson L.J.'s analysis was wrong. In his judgment Dyson L.J. differed in some respects from the judgment of Lightman J. in Hurst.

Lightman J. got his own back at a reception given by solicitors SJ Berwin at a summer reception given for mediators and mediation users. The reception was enlivened by a jazz and blues band but I doubt if this was any more lively than the critique Lightman J. made of Dyson L.J.'s judgment in a talk entitled 'Mediation: An Approximation to Justice.' In that talk Lightman J. drew attention to the fact that the cost of litigation and the withdrawal of legal aid have left many disadvantaged citizens without realistic access to justice in the courts. He argued that for this mediation was a necessary palliative. It could provide an approximation to justice. But if it was to do so, it required the removal of two obstacles placed in its path by the decision in *Halsey*.

The first was the finding that the court could not require a party to proceed to mediation against his will, because this would defeat his right of access to a court under Article 6 of the European Convention on Human Rights. The second was the finding that the burden of proving an unreasonable refusal to proceed to mediation lay on the party seeking a costs sanction. Lightman J. described these findings not merely as unfortunate but, in his opinion as "clearly wrong and unreasonable." As to the first proposition, he said: "(1) [t]he court appears to have been unfamiliar with the mediation process and to have confused an order for mediation with an order for arbitration or some other order which places a permanent stay on proceedings. An order for mediation does not interfere with the right to a trial: at most it merely imposes a short delay to afford an opportunity for settlement and indeed the order for mediation may not even do that, for the order for mediation may require or allow the parties to proceed with preparation for trial; and (2) the Court of Appeal appears to have been unaware that the practice of ordering parties to proceed to mediation regardless of their wishes is prevalent elsewhere throughout the Commonwealth, the US and the world at large, and indeed at home in matrimonial property disputes in the Family Division. The Court of Appeal refers to the fact that a party compelled to proceed to mediation may be less likely to agree a settlement than one who willingly proceeds to mediation. But that fact is not to the point. For it is a fact: (1) that by reason of the nature and impact on the parties of the mediation process parties who enter the mediation process unwillingly often can and do become infected with the conciliatory spirit and settle; and (2) that, whatever the percentage of those who against their will are ordered to give mediation a chance do settle, that percentage must be greater than the number to settle of those not so ordered and who accordingly do not give it a chance."

Turning to the question of the burden of proof on the issue of whether it was unreasonable not to agree to mediation he said: "[t]he decision as to onus must be guided by consideration of three factors: (1) the importance that those otherwise deprived of access to justice should be given a chance of an approximation to it in this way; (2) the commonsense proposition that the party who has decided not to proceed to mediation and knows the reasons for his decision should be required to give, explain and justify his decision; and (3) the explicit duty of the court to encourage the use of mediation and the implicit duty to discourage unjustified refusals to do so and this must involve disclosing, explaining and justifying the reasons for the refusal. All these factors point in the opposite direction to that taken by the Court of Appeal." Lightman J. ended with this conclusion: "[n]o thinking person can but be disturbed by the imposition of the twin hurdles to mediation which the decision in *Halsey* creates to achieving the approximation to justice which the institution of the mediation process may afford."

This is pretty punchy stuff by way of commentary on the decision of a superior court, but Gavin Lightman is not one to pull his punches. Is his criticism of these parts of *Halsey* well founded?

Let me first deal with the suggestion that Dyson L.J. was wrong to express the view that it would infringe Article 6 of the European Convention on Human Rights for the court to order the parties to submit to mediation. Article 6 provides, in so far as relevant: "[i]n the determination of his civil rights and obligations ... everyone is entitled to a fair and public hearing within a reasonable time by an independent and impartial tribunal established by law. Judgments shall be pronounced publicly."

Dyson L.J. referred to the decision of the European Court in *Deweer v Belgium*. He did so, however, only as supporting the proposition that any waiver of the Article 6 right to a public trial must be subjected to careful review to ensure that it was not induced by "constraint", i.e., that it really was voluntary. Some have attributed considerable significance to this reference to *Deweer*. The authors of the useful ADR Practice Guide, now in its third edition, describe it as the leading case on this topic. So let us see what the European Court had to say. In *Deweer* a Belgian butcher was facing a criminal prosecution for over-charging for pork. The Belgian authorities threatened a provisional closure of his business until the conclusion of the criminal proceedings, which might be for a period of months. Alternatively they offered the butcher what they described as "a friendly settlement", which involved payment of the relatively modest sum of 10,000 Belgian francs. Not surprisingly he chose the "friendly settlement", but he complained to the ECtHR at Strasbourg that he had been constrained to do so and thus was in reality denied the fair trial to which he was entitled. The Strasbourg Court agreed. It held that while there was nothing wrong in principle with a party waiving his right to either a civil or a criminal trial by entering into an agreed settlement, on the facts of the case the settlement had been procured by constraint, so that it was not voluntary. The consequences of having his business closed down for months were so severe that the butcher had no practical alternative but to agree to pay the 10,000 francs. What in effect had happened was that the state had inflicted a penalty on the butcher without a trial.

The facts of *Deweer* are a long way away from the imposition of a mediation order. That case demonstrates that a coerced agreement that involves waiving the right to trial will infringe Article 6. Does it follow from *Deweer* that it is contrary to the citizen's right to have his dispute resolved by a court to compel him first to try to reach an agreement by mediation? I think that it depends what you mean by "compel." This involves considering the sanctions if the litigant does not comply with the court order to attempt mediation.

It is of the essence of mediation that the parties are prepared to consider forgoing their strict legal rights. What of the litigant who simply refuses to contemplate this, who when the court orders him to attempt mediation simply says "no I won't." If you commit him to prison for contempt of court then you can truly say that you are compelling him to mediate. What if you say: "unless you attempt mediation you cannot continue with your court action?" In quite a lot of jurisdictions mediation is ordered by the court on this basis.

I think that if a litigant in Europe was subjected to such an order, refused to comply with it and was consequently refused the right to continue with the litigation, the ECtHR at Strasbourg might well say that that he had been denied his right to a trial in contravention of Article 6. The European Commission has shown support for mediation, but not compulsory mediation. Whether such a scenario is very likely is another matter. Experience shows that where a court directs the parties to attempt mediation they usually comply.

Dyson L.J. approved of the practice of the English courts of penalising a party in costs for unreasonably refusing to attempt mediation, so he plainly did not consider that the use of a costs sanction was tantamount to compelling a party to litigate. But Dyson L.J. significantly weakened the costs sanction by saying that the burden was on the party seeking costs to show that the other party had unreasonably refused to resort to mediation, rather than holding that it was on the party refusing mediation to justify his conduct. I think that there is little doubt that this finding significantly reduced the pressure on English litigants to attempt mediation. After all, parties usually resort to litigation because they believe that they are going to win and, if you win, it can be quite difficult for the loser to show that you acted unreasonably on insisting on your full legal rights.

I referred to the support given to mediation by the European Commission. Let me tell you about that. In 2002 the European Commission circulated a Green Paper seeking the views of Member States on ADR in civil and commercial disputes. The answers led the Commission to extol the virtues of mediation and to comment: "[t]he Commission believes that mediation holds an untapped potential as a dispute resolution mechanism and as a means of providing access to justice for individuals and businesses."

In 2004 the Commission published a draft Directive designed to encourage mediation. Article 3 of the aforementioned Directive provides: "(1) A court before which an action is brought may, when appropriate and having regard to all the circumstances of the case, invite the parties to use mediation in order to settle the dispute. The court may in any event require the parties to attend an information session on the use of mediation; (2) This directive is without prejudice to national legislation making the use of mediation compulsory or subject to incentives or sanctions, whether before or after judicial proceedings have started, provided that such legislation does not impede the right of access to the judicial system, in particular in situations where one of the parties is resident in a Member State other than that of the court." That Article does not explain how a court can make mediation compulsory without "impeding the right of access to the judicial system." On the face of it this is something of a contradiction in terms. Whatever European law says, the fact remains that in a number of jurisdictions the courts make orders which, on their face, compel the parties to resort to ADR, and these, as I understand it, include India.

What are the pros and cons of compulsory mediation? Strong views are expressed about this on both sides. Those opposed argue that compulsion is the very antithesis of mediation. The whole point of mediation is that it is voluntary. How can you compel parties to indulge in a voluntary activity? You can take a horse to water, but you cannot make it drink. To which those in favour of compulsory mediation reply, "yes, but if you take a horse to water it usually does drink." Statistics show that settlement rates in relation to parties who have been compelled to mediate are just about as high as they are in the case of those who resort to mediation of their own volition.

Let me end by nailing my colours firmly to the mast. I number myself with Sir Anthony Colman and Sir Gavin Lightman as an enthusiastic supporter of ADR. It is madness to incur the considerable expense of litigation — in England usually disproportionate to the amount at stake — without making a determined attempt to reach an amicable settlement. The idea that there is only one just result of every dispute, which only the court can deliver is, I believe, often illusory.

Litigation has a cost, not only for the litigants but for society, because judicial resources are limited and their cost is usually borne — at least in part — by the state. Parties should be given strong encouragement to attempt mediation before resorting to litigation. And if they commence litigation, there should be built into the process a stage at which the court can require them to attempt mediation — perhaps with the assistance of a mediator supplied by the court.

I believe that we are moving in that direction in England. In family law disputes there is now a requirement for the parties to attempt mediation and this has I believe, an 80% success rate. The Government has established a National Mediation Helpline which currently receives 7,800 calls a month.

Through this mediation can be arranged for civil law disputes on fixed fees. For those who qualify, legal aid is available. For this service there is a 15% year on year growth rate planned. At the end of last year there was at Cobham an important meeting sponsored by the Ministry of Justice, the Civil Justice Council and the Civil Mediation Council, in which the Master of the Rolls took part. It was agreed to form a Proportionate Dispute Resolution Team to consider possible reforms of the law and practice of ADR. Suggestions included a Mediation Code, an appropriate Practice Direction, mediation training for judges and lawyers, the mandatory inclusion of mediation as part of legal professional training and legislation to alter the effect of the decision in *Halsey*. In this field, as in others, India is ahead of us. I was aware before this visit of the amendment made to your procedural code by the famous section 89 and of Sabharwal C.J.'s support of mediation in *Salem Advocate Bar Association, Tamil Nadu v Union of India*. On this visit I have been learning with admiration of the progress made in instilling a culture of ADR in this jurisdiction. I hope very much that we shall follow where India is leading.

REFERENCES

* This article was originally published as P. Nicholas, 'Alternative Dispute Resolution: An English Viewpoint', *Arbitration* 74, no. 4 (2008): 406-418.

1 *Cowl v Plymouth City Council* [2001] All E.R. (D) 206.
2 *Dunnett v Railtrack* [2002] 2 All E.R. 850.
3 *Leicester Circuits Ltd v Coats* [2003] EWCA Civ 333.
4 *Royal Bank of Canada v Ministry of Defence* [2003] EWHC 1479.

5 *Hurst v Leeming* [2001] EWHC 1051.

6 *Halsey v Milton Keynes General NHS Trust* [2004] EWCA Civ 576; *Steel v Joy and Halliday* [2004] 4 All E.R. 920.

7 *Deweer v Belgium* [1980] E.C.C. 169; (1980) 2 E.H.R.R. 439.

8 K. Mackie, D. Miles & W. Marsh, *Commercial Dispute Resolution: an ADR Practice Guide*, (Haywards Heath: Tottel, 2007).

9 Salem Advocate Bar Association, *Tamil Nadu v Union of India* (2003) 1 S.C.C. 49.

CHAPTER 1

Online Dispute Resolution (ODR):
What Is It, and Is It the Way Forward?

Julio César Betancourt and Elina Zlatanska

Online Dispute Resolution (ODR) refers to the use of Alternative Dispute Resolution (ADR) mechanisms over the internet. ODR methods can be used to deal with both offline and online related disputes. The idea of using ADR mechanisms 'online', as opposed to 'offline', appears to have arisen in the 1990s. During that decade, some of the most noticeable ODR services were provided by: (1) the Virtual Magistrate Project; (2) the Online Ombuds Office (OOO); and (3) the Online Mediation Project. These projects were originally developed under the auspices of various institutions, including the American Arbitration Association (AAA) and the National Center for Automated Information Research (NCAIR). Within a short period of time, dispute resolution professionals realised that there were possibilities for considerable expansion of this burgeoning field. In 1997, Professors Ethan Katsh and Janet Rifkin founded the National Center for Technology and Dispute Resolution, which "supports and sustains the development of information technology applications, institutional resources, and theoretical and applied knowledge for better understanding and managing conflict". Four years later, the first book in the field of ODR was written. Later on, the area of ODR started to be explored by institutions such as the US Federal Trade

Commission, the US Department of Commerce, the Hague Conference on Private International Law, the Organisation for Economic Cooperation and Development, the Global Business Dialogue, the World Intellectual Property Organisation, and the European Union. In the European Union, in particular, legislative measures have tended to favour the utilisation of ODR mechanisms. Examples include the Directive on Electronic Commerce (art.17) and the Directive on certain aspects of Mediation in Civil and Commercial Matters Recitals 8 and 9. Further, in the area of consumer law, both a new Proposal for a Regulation on Online Dispute Resolution for Consumer Disputes and a Proposal for a Directive on Alternative Dispute Resolution are currently being discussed. These proposals are intended to improve the functioning of the retail internal market and enhance redress for consumers. In principle, ODR mechanisms are expected, among other things, to "facilitate access to justice", and should therefore be able to tackle some of the problems concerning the use of offline dispute resolution mechanisms. It is believed that ODR could "resolve disputes quickly and more efficiently" than the traditional methods but, to our knowledge, no research has been reliably and skilfully conducted to back up this assumption. ADR scholars have put forward various proposals aiming at developing an ODR system, and during the last 10 years an important number of ODR services have been developed. Within the vast array of ODR mechanisms, negotiation, mediation and arbitration appear to be the most commonly practised. As the legal profession has begun to modernise its working practices with the aid of several technological advances in computing and telecommunications, one may wonder whether the utilisation of offline mechanisms will eventually be replaced by the employment of the so-called ODR mechanisms. This article provides a concise explanation of the notion of dispute resolution in cyberspace. It reviews some of the recent studies on the use of ODR, especially the use of e-negotiation, e-mediation and e-arbitration, considers the issues concerning the intricacies of settling and resolving disputes in cyberspace and concludes that the idea of banishing offline dispute settlement and dispute resolution methods — in the near future — is extremely unlikely ever to come true.

E-NEGOTIATION

Negotiation is one of the most commonly practised forms of dispute resolution and, probably, "one of the most basic forms of interaction". It is believed that "people negotiate even when they don't think of themselves as doing so". Negotiation, in essence, can be defined as any type of communication between two or more people with the aim of reaching an agreement. For this, negotiation can be seen as an amicable, and perhaps as a highly desirable, way of resolving disputes. With the advent of the internet, this form of interaction, particularly within the dispute resolution arena and the legal profession, has somewhat moved off the court corridors and polished offices of a law firm on to the Web, which resulted in the advancement of the idea of electronically based negotiations (e-negotiation). The first research project in the area of negotiation via the World Wide Web (INSPIRE) came into operation in 1996. This project was "[d]eveloped in the context of a cross-cultural study of decision making and negotiation". Extensive experimentation with INSPIRE prompted the design of several other e-negotiation systems (ENSs). These systems together with decision support systems (DSSs) have been classified into several categories, including planning systems, assessment systems, intervention systems and process systems. Public awareness of both ENSs and DSSs, however, continues to be very low and, therefore, it remains to be seen whether electronically based negotiations that rely on these systems will gain widespread acceptance. The notion of e-negotiation is inextricably linked with the concept of computer-mediated communication (CMC). It is argued that CMC facilitates the interaction process through the use of computers. The internet, without a doubt, has become one of the main means of communication and information exchange. CMC through email, for example, is increasingly commonplace. In 2011, corporate users sent and received approximately 105 email messages per day, that is, 38,325 emails per year. New research would be needed to determine how many of those email messages, if any, involved negotiations of some kind, but in terms of the effectiveness of e-negotiation — via email — it is believed that it can "lead to misunderstandings, sinister attributions, and ultimately, negotiation impasse". Research shows that email negotiations "1) increased contentiousness, 2) diminished information sharing, 3) diminished process cooperation, 4) diminished trust, [and] 5) increased effects of negative attribution". Likewise, it has been proved that "resolving conflict, or reaching consensus ... is better done face-to-face than electronically". Similarly, it has been demonstrated that "[m]ore face-to-face contact produces more rapport, which in turn leads to more favorable outcomes for both parties". In a similar vein, it has been pointed out that "[c]onventions of personal interaction that would apply in a telephone call or a face-to-face [mediation] do not apply in cyberspace". Further studies have shown that "information exchanged over electronic media such as e-mail is less likely to be true". The great majority of the research in the area of e-negotiation through email cast doubt upon the perceived advantages of electronically based negotiations over face-to-face negotiations. In email communications, there is a likelihood that the parties will end up misreading each other's messages, and although one can say that further clarifications can be given, and that this means of communication continues to expand and so on, no research has been done to support the hypothesis that e-negotiations via email are — or can be — more effective than face-to-face negotiations.

E-MEDIATION

E-mediation can be defined as a system-based — as opposed to a face-to-face-based — mechanism in which an impartial third party called "the mediator" facilitates the negotiation process between two or more people. Because e-mediation is basically "[e-]negotiation carried out with the assistance of a third party", it can be said that the arguments against the deployment of a system-based negotiation can be applied, *mutatis mutandis*, to the area of e-mediation. This is true for both text-based and video-based systems. Despite this, a small minority believes that in those cases in which it would not be appropriate to mediate face to face — e.g. when both parties are emotionally charged, when it would not be cost-effective to bring both parties together, when there is a huge power imbalance between the parties, etc — e-mediation becomes an option. The first research project aimed at determining the "effectiveness" of e-mediation to resolve online-related disputes, particularly the ones that arose out of eBay transactions, was conducted towards the end of the 1990s. This project was developed "based on the premise that mediators could adapt at least some skills and tactics used in face-to-face practices to the online mediation process". Both the mediator and the parties used email as a means of communication. Of 144 cases brought to mediation, only 50 of them, that is, less than 40 per cent were mediated successfully. Not surprisingly, the project's reliance on text was considered to be one of the drawbacks of email as a primary form of interaction. The average internet user is possibly well equipped for being involved in online mediation sessions via email, chat room, instant messaging, etc. These systems have something in common — they allow people to exchange written messages with one another over the internet. Nevertheless, written language does not "always convey the complete meaning of what an individual is trying to communicate". A detailed examination of the relevant literature reveals that "the most influential linguistics of the first half of the [twentieth] century ... went out of their way to emphasize the primacy of spoken as opposed to written language, relegating the latter to a derived secondary status". Such a distinction between written and spoken language may impinge upon both the effectiveness of the levels of communication and, more importantly, the outcome of a virtual mediation.

E-ARBITRATION

E-arbitration may be defined as "an electronic version of offline arbitration". It encompasses everything from the "online arbitration agreement" to the "online arbitral award". Generally speaking, in light of the principle of party autonomy, the validity of online arbitration is not an issue. In the international context, however, a number of concerns have been raised regarding the validity of not only online arbitration agreements but also online arbitral awards, especially, within the meaning of the New York Convention (NYC). It has been posited that the NYC was adopted "at a time when the drafters could not foresee that [both arbitration agreements and arbitral awards] could take other than a physical form". Therefore, one can only speculate that the courts will — in due course — agree that online arbitration agreements and online arbitral awards satisfy the formal requirements of the NYC. At the time of writing, there are no "universally accepted rules ... governing [online arbitration proceedings]". Such proceedings are certainly taking place, although no comprehensive statistics on e-arbitration appear to have been published. In online arbitration, the parties, the arbitral tribunal, experts and witnesses are expected to make use of electronic devices to take part in the arbitral proceedings. This involves the use of sophisticated software and hardware devices. The existing systems, however, have been criticised on the basis that they can only deal with "very restricted classes of disputes, a simplified or basic arbitration process, the start of the process before variations become necessary [and] the process used by a single arbitration provider". Some argue that e-arbitration *"significantly"* reduces the transaction costs of dispute resolution" [italics added], and this might be true in some cases, but no research has been done on the costs of e-arbitration as opposed to offline arbitration. In general, it can be said that third-party decision-making is potentially more expensive than joint decision-making. Research shows that, in the area of international arbitration, for instance, most of the costs are associated with both arbitral and legal fees, and it remains to be seen whether arbitrators and legal representatives would be prepared to make a substantial reduction to their fees when conducting arbitrations online. In terms of the appropriateness of online arbitration, it has been said that it is "particularly appropriate with respect to simple fact patterns and small claims". Hence, online arbitration may appeal to the users of small claims and documents-only arbitration schemes, but definitely not to the users of "international arbitration", where complex issues and large amounts of money are at stake. This is probably one of the reasons behind the perceived "virtual arbitration's low attractiveness" within this area. It might be that e-arbitration needs to develop further before a full assessment of its efficiency can be undertaken, but it is unlikely that "international arbitration", in particular, would ever take place entirely online.

CONCLUSION

Despite some optimistic predictions about ODR's potential to coalesce — on a level playing field — with the traditional methods, it is still too early to predict what the future of ODR might be. The virtues of technological advances in the area of dispute resolution have perhaps been overestimated. ODR is just "another" option, and in some cases it might even be the best option, but it is definitely not a panacea. States' dispute resolution machinery is a complex system that cannot be replaced with "faster microprocessors and larger memory boards". Dispute resolution mechanisms, in general, are a means of maintaining social order. These mechanisms are intended to deal with conflicts and disputes — on the basis of the rule of law — and it is doubtful that such a function can be fully and effectively performed in cyberspace.

REFERENCES

* This article was originally published as Julio César Betancourt & Elina Zlatanska, 'Online Dispute Resolution (ODR): What Is It, and Is It the Way Forward?', *Arbitration* 79, no. 3 (2013): 256-264.

1 The initialism ADR, commonly and mistakenly referred to as an acronym for "Alternative Dispute Resolution", was coined by Professor Frank E.A. Sander of Harvard Law School. See Frank Sander, 'Varieties of Dispute Processing' (1976) 70 Federal Rules Decisions: Addresses Delivered at the National Conference on the Causes of Popular Dissatisfaction with the Administration of Justice 111–134; Frank Sander, 'Alternative Methods of Dispute Resolution: An Overview', *University of Florida Law Review* 37(1) (1985): 1; and Simon Roberts et al., *Dispute Resolution: ADR and the Primary Forms of Decision-Making* (Cambridge: Cambridge University Press, 2005), p. 5. ADR, in plain English, refers to the idea of settling and resolving disputes through different means other than litigation. As to the notion of ADR, see Henry Brown et al., *ADR Principles and Practice* (London: Sweet & Maxwell, 1993), p. 9; Karl Mackie et al., *The ADR Practice Guide* (London: Butterworths, 2000), pp. 8–10; George Applebey, 'Alternative Dispute Resolution and the Civil Justice System', in Karl J. Mackie (ed.), *A Handbook of Dispute Resolution: ADR in Action* (London: Routledge, 1991), p. 26 and Albert Fiadjoe, *Alternative Dispute Resolution: A Developing World Perspective* (New York: Routledge-

Cavendish, 2004), p. 2.

2. ODR encompasses a series of online means of communication, including "e-mail, Internet Relay Chat (IRC), instant messaging, Web forum discussions, and similar text-based electronic communications": in Robert Gordon, 'The Electronic Personality and Digital Self', Feb–April *Dispute Resolution Journal* (2001): 11. See also Jason Crook, 'What is Alternative Dispute Resolution (ADR)?', in Julio César Betancourt (ed.), *What is Alternative Dispute Resolution (ADR)?* (London: Chartered Institute of Arbitrators, 2010), p. 25; José Antonio García Alvaro, 'Online Dispute Resolution—Unchartered Territory', *Vindobona Journal* 7(2) (2003): 187; Jerome T. Barret et al., *A History of Alternative Dispute Resolution: The Story of a Political, Cultural, and Social Movement* (San Francisco: Jossey-Bass, 2004), p. 261; Nadja Alexander, 'Mobile Mediation: How Technology is Driving the Globalization of ADR', *Hamline Journal of Public Law & Policy* 27(2) (2006): 248. For a different view, see Rossa McMahon, 'The Online Dispute Resolution Spectrum', *Arbitration* 71(3) (2005): 218.

3. See, generally, Colin Rule, *Online Dispute Resolution for Business* (San Francisco: Jossey-Bass, 2002). See also Ethan Katsh, 'Bringing Online Dispute Resolution to Virtual Worlds: Creating Processes through Code', *New York Law School Law Review* 49 (2004): 275.

4. See E. Casey Lide, 'ADR and Cyberspace: The Role of Alternative Dispute Resolution in Online Commerce, Intellectual Property and Defamation', *Ohio State Journal on Dispute Resolution* 12 (1996): 219. See also Alejandro E. Almaguer et al., 'Shaping New Legal Frontiers:

Dispute Resolution for the Internet', *Ohio State Journal on Dispute Resolution* 13 (1998): 719.

5   For a more complete explanation of the concept of ombudsman, see Talbot D'Alemberte, 'The Ombudsman, a Grievance Man for Citizens' *University of Florida Law Review* 28(4) (1966): 545; George B. McClellan, 'The Role of the Ombudsman', *University of Miami Law Review* 23 (1969): 463; Mary Seneviratne, 'Ombudsmen 2000', *Nottingham Law Journal* 9 (2000): 13; Ian Harden, 'When Europeans Complain: the Work of the European Ombudsman', *Cambridge Yearbook of European Legal Studies*, 3 (2000): pp. 199–208.

6   For an overview of these services, see Frank A. Cona, 'Application of Online Systems in Alternative Dispute Resolution', *Buffalo Law Review* 45 (1997): 986.

7   For the purposes of this paper, the expressions "dispute resolution" and "dispute settlement" will be used interchangeably, although the authors acknowledge that they have a different meaning. The distinction is important because, terminologically speaking, the notion of "resolution" is related to the idea of joint decision-making, whereas the concept of "settlement" is connected with the idea of third party decision-making. See Tony Marks et al., 'Rethinking Public Policy and Alternative Dispute Resolution: Negotiability, Mediability and Arbitrability', *Arbitration* 78(1) 2012: 19, n.6. See also Barbara Hill, 'An Analysis of Conflict Resolution Techniques: From Problem-Solving Workshops to Theory', *Journal of Conflict Resolution* 26(1) (1982): 115. John Burton, cited by Gregory Tillett, *Resolving Conflict: A Practical Approach*

(South Melbourne: Sydney University Press, 1991), p. 9. See also Andrew Pirie, *Alternative Dispute Resolution: Skills, Science, and the Law* (Toronto: Irwin Law, 2000), p. 42; John Burton, *Conflict and Communication: The Use of Controlled Communication in International Relations* (New York: Free Press, 1969), p. 171.

8 See Ethan Katsh, 'Dispute Resolution in Cyberspace', *Connecticut Law Review* 28 (1996): 953. See also M. Scott Donahey, 'Current Developments in Online Dispute Resolution', *Journal of International Arbitration* 16(4) (1999): 129.

9 See National Center for Technology and Dispute Resolution (NCTDR), at http://odr.info/ [Accessed June 12, 2013].

10 Ethan Katsh et al., *Online Dispute Resolution: Resolving Conflicts in Cyberspace* (San Francisco: Jossey-Bass, 2001), pp. 1–240.

11 Ethan Katsh, 'Online Dispute Resolution: Some Lessons from the E-Commerce Revolution', *Northern Kentucky University Law Review* 28 (2001): 813. Similarly, working groups were set up by several other organisations with a view to studying this area. See Mireze Philippe, 'Where is Everyone Going with Online Dispute Resolution (ODR)?', *International Business Law Journal* (2002): 192. See also UNCITRAL (Commission Documents), Report of the United Nations Commission on International Trade Law (2010) a/65/17; Possible Future Work on Online Dispute Resolution in Cross-border Electronic Commerce Transactions (April 23, 2010) UNGA A/CN.9/706; Possible Future Work on Online Dispute Resolution in Cross-border Electronic Commerce Transactions, Note Supporting the Possible Future Work on

Online Dispute Resolution by UNCITRAL, submitted by the Institute of International Commercial Law (May 26, 2010) UNGA A/CN.9/710; Possible Future Work on Electronic Commerce—Proposal of the United States of America on Online Dispute Resolution (June 18, 2009) UNGA A/CN.9/681/Add.2; and UNCITRAL (Working Group III) Report of Working Group III (Online Dispute Resolution), Twenty-fourth Session (November 21, 2011) UNGA A/CN.9/739; Annotated Provisional Agenda (August 22, 2011) A/CN.9/WG.III/WP.108; Online Dispute Resolution for Cross-border Electronic Commerce Transactions: Draft Procedural Rules (September 27, 2011) UNGA A/CN.9/WG.III/WP.109; Online Dispute Resolution for Cross-border Electronic Commerce Transactions: Issues for Consideration in the Conception of a Global ODR Framework (September 28, 2011) UNGA A/CN.9/WG.III/WP.110; Report of Working Group III (Online Dispute Resolution), Twenty-third Session (June 3, 2011) A/CN.9/721; Annotated Provisional Agenda (February 24, 2011) A/CN.9/WG.III/WP.106; Online Dispute Resolution for Cross-border Electronic Commerce Transactions: Draft Procedural Rules (March 17, 2011) A/CN.9/WG.III/WP.107; Report of Working Group III (Online Dispute Resolution), Twenty-second Session (January 17, 2010) A/CN.9/716; Annotated Provisional Agenda (August 26, 2010) A/CN.9/WG.III/WP.104; Online Dispute Resolution for Cross-border Electronic Commerce Transactions (October 13, 2010) A/CN.9/WG.III/WP.105; Online Dispute Resolution for Cross-border Electronic Commerce Transactions (November 18, 2010) A/CN.9/WG.III/WP.105/Corr.1

12 Faye Fangfei Wang, *Online Dispute Resolution: Technology, Management and Legal Practice from an International Perspective* (Oxford: Chandos Publishing, 2008), p.43ff.

13 The area of consumer law has received considerable attention within the ODR literature. See, e.g. Karen Stewart et al., 'Online Arbitration of Cross-Border, Business to Consumer Disputes', *University of Miami Law Review* 56 (2002): 1111; Mohamed Wahab, 'Globalisation and ODR: Dynamics of Change in E-Commerce Dispute Settlement', *International Journal of Law and Information Technology* 12 (2004): 123.

14 See Alternative Dispute Resolution and Online Dispute Resolution for EU Consumers: Questions and Answers, Press Release (November 29, 2010), Memo/11/840.

15 Gabrielle Kaufmann-Köhler et al., *Online Dispute Resolution, Challenges of Contemporary Justice* (The Hague: Kluwer Law International, 2004), p. 68. For this to happen, it is necessary to explore, from a multidisciplinary perspective, how the internet can be used to improve access to justice through the deployment of ODR mechanisms. See Catherine Kessedjian et al., 'Dispute Resolution On-Line', *International Lawyer* 32 (1998): 990.

16 As to the perceived advantages of ODR mechanisms, see Lan Q. Hang, 'Online Dispute Resolution System: The Future of Cyberspace Law', *Santa Clara Law Review* 41 (2001): 854; George H. Friedman, 'Alternative Dispute Resolution and Emerging Online Technologies: Challenges and Opportunities', *Hastings Communications and*

Entertainment Law Journal 19 (1997): 695, 711; Laura Klaming et al., 'I Want the Opposite of What You Want: Reducing Fixed-pie Perceptions in Online Negotiations', *Journal of Dispute Resolution* 1 (2009): 139.

17 Robert Bordone, 'Electronic Online Dispute Resolution: A Systems Approach — Potential, Problems and a Proposal', *Harvard Negotiation Law Review* 3 (1998): 191.

18 See, e.g. R. Bordone, 'Electronic Online Dispute Resolution: A Systems Approach — Potential, Problems and a Proposal', Harvard Negotiation Law Review 3 (1998): 199; Joseph A. Zavaletta, 'Using E-Dispute Technology to Facilitate the Resolution of E-Contract Disputes: A Modest Proposal', *Journal of Technology Law and Policy* 7 (2002): 24; Beatrice Baumann, 'Electronic Dispute Resolution (EDR) and the Development of Internet Activities', *Syracuse Law Review* 52 (2002): 1232; Arno R. Lodder et al., 'Developing an Online Dispute Resolution Environment: Dialogue Tools and Negotiation Support Systems in a Three-Step Model', *Harvard Negotiation Law Review* 10 (2005): 287; George H. Friedman, 'Alternative Dispute Resolution and Emerging Online Technologies: Challenges and Opportunities', *Hastings Communications and Entertainment Law Journal* 19 (1997): 695; Michael E. Schneider et al., 'Dispute Resolution in International Electronic Commerce', *Journal of International Arbitration* 14(3) (1997): 5.

19 Julia Hörnle, *Cross-border Internet Dispute Resolution* (Cambridge: Cambridge University Press, 2009), p.76.

20 Haitham A. Haloush et al., 'Internet Characteristics and Online Dispute Resolution', *Harvard Negotiation Law Journal* 13 (2008): 328; Mary Shannon Martin, 'Keep it Online: The Hague Convention and the Need for Online Alternative Dispute Resolution in International Business-to-Consumer E-Commerce', *Boston University International Law Journal* 20 (2002): 151. See also Faye Fangfei Wang, *Internet Jurisdiction and Choice of Law: Legal Practices in the EU, US and China* (Cambridge: Cambridge University Press, 2010), p.156ff.

21 George H. Friedman et al., 'An Information Superhighway "on Ramp" for Alternative Dispute Resolution', *New York State Bar* Journal (1996): 38.

22 As to the notion of negotiation, see P.H. Gulliver, *Disputes and Negotiations: A Cross-Cultural Perspective* (New York: Academic Press, 1979), pp. 1–293; Howard Raiffa, *The Art and Science of Negotiation* (Cambridge, MA: Belknap Press, 1982), pp. 1–373; Roger Fisher et al., *Getting Together: Building Relationships as We Negotiate* (New York: Penguin Books, 1989), pp. 1–216; Carrie Menkel-Meadow, 'Toward Another View of Legal Negotiation: The Structure of Problem-Solving', *UCLA Law Review* 31 (1984): 754; Linda Putman et al., *Communication and Negotiation* (Newbury Park, CA: Sage Publications, 1992), pp. 1–294; Dean G. Pruitt et al., *Negotiation in Social Conflict* (Buckingham: Open University Press, 1993), pp. 1–251; Max H. Bazerman, *Negotiating Rationally* (New York: Free Press, 1993), pp. 1–196; Carrie Menkel-Meadow, 'Lawyer Negotiations: Theories and Realities — What Do We Learn From Mediation?',

Modern Law Review 56(3) (1993): 361; Robert H. Mnookin et al., *Beyond Winning: Negotiating to Create Value in Deals and Disputes* (Cambridge, MA: Belknap Press, 2000), pp. 1–354; Carrie Menkel-Meadow, 'Teaching About Gender and Negotiation: Sex, Truths and Videotape', *Negotiation Journal* 16(4) (2000): 357; Roger Fisher et al., *Getting to Yes: Negotiating Agreement Without Giving in* (London: Penguin Books, 2011), pp. 1–194.

23 Bruce Patton, 'Negotiation', in Michael Moffit et al. (eds), *The Handbook of Dispute Resolution* (San Francisco: Jossey-Bass, 2005), p.279.

24 Fisher et al., *Getting Together: Building Relationships as We Negotiate* (1989), p. xxvii.

25 Cf. Kathleen Valley, 'Conversation: The Electronic Negotiator', *Harvard Business Review* (2000): 16.

26 See Gregory Kersten et al., 'WWW-based Negotiation Support: Design, Implementation, and Use', *Decision Support Systems* 25 (1999): 135. It is important to mention that research on e-negotiation has been carried out based upon three different approaches, namely normative, prescriptive and descriptive. See Mareike Schoop, 'The Worlds of Negotiation' Proceedings of the 9th International Working Conference on the Language-Action Perspective on Communication Modeling (2004), pp. 179–196.

27 See, e.g. Jin Baek Kim et al., 'E-negotiation System Development: Using Negotiation Protocols to Manage Software Components', *Group Decision and Negotiation* 16(4) (2007): 321. See also Ernest M.

Thiessen, 'Beyond Win-Win in Cyberspace', *Ohio State Journal on Dispute Resolution* 15(3) (2000): 643, and Christopher A. Hobson, 'E-Negotiations Creating a Framework for Online Commercial Negotiations', *Negotiation Journal* (1999): 201.

28 Gregory Kersten, "E-negotiation Systems: Interaction of People and Technologies to Resolve Conflicts" UNESCAP Third Annual Forum on Online Dispute Resolution (2004), pp.2–3.

29 See Russell Spears et al., 'Panacea or Panopticon?: The Hidden Power in Computer-Mediated Communication', *Communication Research* 21 (4) (1994): 427. See also Rachel Croson, 'Look at me When You Say That: An Electronic Negotiation Simulation', *Simulation & Gaming* 30 (1) (1999): 24.

30 See Sara Radicati, 'Email Statistics Report, 2011–2015' (2011), available at http://www.radicati.com/wp/wp-content/uploads/2011/05/Email-Statistics-Report-2011-2015-Executive-Summary.pdf [Accessed June 12, 2013].

31 Janice Nadler, 'Rapport in Legal Negotiation: How Small Talk can Facilitate E-mail Dealmaking', *Harvard Negotiation Law Review* 29 (2004): 23. See also Don A. More et al., 'Long and Short Routes to Success in Electronically Mediated Negotiations: Group Affiliations and Good Vibrations', *Organizational Behavior and Human Decision Processes* 77(1) (1999): 23; Elaine Landry, 'Scrolling Around the New Organization: the Potential for Conflict in the On-line Environment', *Negotiation Journal* (2000): 133; and Jacqueline Nolan-Haley, *Alternative Dispute Resolution* (St Paul, MN: Thomson-West, 2008), p.

10.

32 Noam Ebner et al, 'You've Got Agreement: Negoti@ting via Email', *Journal of Public Law & Policy* 31(2) (2009-2010): 434.

33 Gerardine DeSanctis et al., 'Introduction to the Special Issue: Communication Processes for Virtual Organizations', *Organization Science* 10(6) (1999): 697.

34 Leigh Thompson, 'Negotiating via Information Technology: Theory and Application', *Journal of Social Issues* 58(1) (2002): 111; Aimee L. Drolet et al., 'Rapport in Conflict Resolution: Accounting for How Face-to-Face Contact Fosters Mutual Cooperation in Mixed-Motive Conflicts', *Journal of Experimental Social Psychology* 36 (2000): 26. See also Michael Morris, 'Schmooze or Lose: Social Friction and Lubrication in E-Mail Negotiations', *Groups Dynamics: Theory, Research, and Practice* 93.

35 Joel Eisen, 'Are We Ready for Mediation in Cyberspace?', *Brigham Young University Law Review* (1998): 1311.

36 Kathleen L. McGinn et al., 'How to Negotiate Successfully Online', *Negotiation* 3 (2004): 8.

37 Jill M. Purdy et al., 'The Impact of Communication Media on Negotiation Outcomes', *The Journal of Conflict Management* 11(2) (2000): 162; Janice Nadler et al., 'Negotiation, Information Technology, and the Problem of the Faceless Other' in Leigh Thompson (ed.), *Negotiation Theory and Research* (London: Psychology Press, 2006), pp. 154–155; Charles Craver, 'Conducting Electronic Negotiations', *The Negotiator Magazine* (2007), available at http://

www.negotiatormagazine.com/ [Accessed June 12, 2013].

38 See, e.g. Amira Galin et al., 'E-negotiation versus Face-to-Face Negotiation: What has Changed — if Anything?', *Computers in Human Behavior* 23 (2007): 789; Lynn A. Epstein, 'Cyber E-mail Negotiation vs. Traditional Negotiation: Will Cyber Technology Supplant Traditional Means of Settling Litigation?', *Tulsa Law Journal* 36 (2001): 840.

39 David R. Johnson, 'Screening the Future for Virtual ADR', *Dispute Resolution Journal* (1996): 118.

40 Cf. Gabrielle Kaufmann-Köhler et al., *Online Dispute Resolution: Challenges for Contemporary Justice* (The Hague: Kluwer Law International, 2004), p. 22. See also Sarah Rudolph Cole et al., 'Online Mediation: Where We Have Been, Where We Are Now, and Where We Should Be', *University of Toledo Law Review* 38 (2006):193. For an overview of the concepts of negotiation and mediation in the online environment, see Joseph Goodman, 'The Advantages and Disadvantages of Online Dispute Resolution: An Assessment of Cyber-Mediation Web Sites', *Journal of Internet Law* 9(11) (2006): 10.

41 Stephen B. Goldberg et al., *Dispute Resolution: Negotiation, Mediation and Other Processes* (New York: Wolters Kluwer, 2007), p.107.

42 Janice Nadler, 'Electronically-Mediated Dispute Resolution and E-Commerce', *Negotiation Journal* (2001): 333.

43 Llewellyn J. Gibbons et al., 'Cyber-Mediation: Computer-Mediated Communications Medium Massaging the Message', *New Mexico Law Review* 32 (2002): 33.

44 Susan Summers Raines, 'Can Online Mediation be Transformative?: Tales from the Front', *Conflict Resolution Quarterly* 22(4) (2005): 437. See also Richard S. Granat, 'Creating an Environment for Mediating Disputes on the Internet', (1996) A Working Paper for the NCAIR Conference on On-line Dispute Resolution.

45 See Jason Krause, 'On the Web', *ABA Journal* (2007): 44. It is important to mention that the vast majority of the initiatives concerning the promotion and facilitation of e-mediation are related to consumer transactions. See Louise E. Teitz, 'Providing Legal Services for the Middle Class in Cyberspace: The Promise and Challenge of On-line Dispute Resolution', *Fordham Law Review* 70 (2001): 1002.

46 Ethan Katsh et al., 'E-Commerce, E-Disputes, and E-Dispute Resolution: In the Shadow of "eBay Law"', *Ohio State Journal on Dispute Resolution* 15(3) (2000): 713. See also Richard Birke et al., 'U.S. Mediation in 2001: The Path that Brought America to Uniform Laws and Mediation in Cyberspace', *Mediation in Cyberspace* 50 (2002): 208.

47 Ethan Katsh et al., 'E-Commerce, E-Disputes, and E-Dispute Resolution: In the Shadow of "eBay Law"', Ohio *State Journal on Dispute Resolution* 15(3) (2000): 711.

48 For a different view, see James C. Melamed, 'Mediating on the Internet: Today and Tomorrow', *Pepperdine Dispute Resolution Law Journal* 1 (11) (2000): 11.

49 Cf. Bruce Leonard Beal, 'Online Mediation: Has Its Time Come?', *Ohio State Journal on Dispute Resolution* 15(3) 2000: 738.

50 Joseph B. Stulberg, 'Mediation, Democracy, and Cyberspace', *Ohio State Journal on Dispute Resolution* 15(3) (2000): 641. See also Richard Victorio, 'Internet Dispute Resolution (iDR): Bringing ADR into the 21st Century', *Pepperdine Dispute Resolution Law Journal* 1 (2001): 293.

51 Wallace Chafe et al., 'The Relation Between Written and Spoken Language', *Annual Review of Anthropology* 16 (1987): 383.

52 Cf. Susan Nauss Exon, 'The Next Generation of Online Dispute Resolution: The Significance of Holography to Enhance and Transform Dispute Resolution', *Cardozo Journal of Conflict Resolution* 12 (2010): 23.

53 See Chinthaka Liyanage, 'Online Arbitration Compares to Offline Arbitration and the Reception of Online Consumer Arbitration: An Overview of the Literature', *Sri Lanka Journal of International Law* 22 (2010): 175. For a different view, see Farzaneh Badiei, 'Online Arbitration Definition and Its Distinctive Features', (2010) Proceedings of the 6th International Workshop on Online Dispute Resolution, pp. 87–93.

54 See, generally, Hong-lin Yu et al., 'Can Online Arbitration Exist within the Traditional Arbitration Framework?', *Journal of International Arbitration* 20(5) (2003): 455.

55 Cf. Richard Hill, 'On-Line Dispute Arbitration: Issues and Solutions', *Arbitration International* 15(2) (1999): 199. See also Thomas Schultz, 'Online Arbitration: Binding or Non-Binding?', *ADR Online Monthly* (2002): 5; and Julia Hörnle, 'Online Dispute Resolution', in John

Tackaberry et al. (eds), *Bernstein's Handbook of Arbitration Law & Practice* (London: Sweet & Maxwell, 2003), pp. 787–805. Legal scholars have raised several other concerns about: distrust of the operability and privacy of internet systems, fear about the "unseen" nature and neutrality of online arbitration providers, technological and presentation imbalances, elimination of face-to-face communications and the lack of voice; see Amy J. Schmitz, '"Drive-thru" Arbitration in the Digital Age: Empowering Consumers through Binding ODR', *Baylor Law Review* 62 (2010): 214.

56 Alejandro López Ortiz, 'Arbitration and IT', *Arbitration International* 21(3) (2005): 353.

57 Paul D. Carrington, 'Virtual Arbitration', *Ohio State Journal on Dispute Resolution* 15 (2000): 673.

58 M.H.M. Schellekens, 'Online Arbitration and E-Commerce', *Electronic Communication Law Review* 9 (2002): 113.

59 United Nations Conference on Trade and Development, Dispute Settlement: International Commercial Arbitration, Electronic Arbitration (2003) UNCTAD/EDM/Misc.232/Add.20, pp. 3–55.

60 Julian Lew et al., *Comparative International Commercial Arbitration* (The Hague: Kluwer Law International, 2003), p. 48. As to the regulatory framework for ODR, in general, see Rafal Morek, 'The Regulatory Framework for Online Dispute Resolution: A Critical View', *University of Toledo Law Review* 29 (2006): 163–192. See also Tiffany J. Lanier, 'Where on Earth Does Cyber-Arbitration Occur? International Review of Arbitral Awards Rendered Online', *ILSA Journal of*

International and Comparative Law 7 (2000): 3. However, because of the widespread acceptance of arbitration, particularly within the commercial arena, it is believed that a useful first step would be the establishment of an international regulatory framework for resolving disputes through e-arbitration. Cf. Henry H. Perritt, 'Dispute Resolution in Cyberspace: Demand for New Forms of ADR', *Ohio State Journal on Dispute Resolution* 15 (2000): 677.

61 Thomas Schultz, 'Online Arbitration: Binding or Non-Binding?', *ADR Online Monthly* (2002): 2.

62 See, e.g. Dusty Bates Farned, 'A New Automated Class of Online Dispute Resolution: Changing the Meaning of Computer-Mediated Communication', *Faulkner Law Review* 2 (2011): 335.

63 Tony Elliman et al., 'Online Support for Arbitration: Designing Software for a Flexible Business Process', *International Journal of Information Technology and Management* 4(4) (2005): 447.

64 Roger P. Alford, 'The Virtual World and the Arbitration World', *Journal of International Arbitration* 18(4) (2001): 456. See also Julia Hörnle, 'Online Dispute Resolution — The Emperor's New Clothes? Benefits and Pitfalls of Online Dispute Resolution and its Application to Commercial Arbitration', *International Review of Law, Computers and Technology* (2003): 28.

65 Cf. Sara Kiesler, *Culture of the Internet* (Mahwah: Lawrence Erlbaum Associates, 1997), p. 235.

66 Chartered Institute of Arbitrators, Costs of International Arbitration Survey (London: Chartered Institute of Arbitrators, 2011), p. 2. See also

Michael O'Reilly, 'Conference Review: Costs in International Arbitration, London September 27–28, 2011', *Arbitration* 78(1) (2012): 59.

67 Daniel Girsberger et al., 'Cyber-Arbitration', *European Business Organization Law Review* 3 (2002): 626.

68 See Roger P. Alford, 'The Virtual World and the Arbitration World', *Journal of International Arbitration* 18(4) (2001): 449. See also Justin Michaelson, 'The A-Z of ADR — Pt I', New Law Journal (2003): 182.

69 Sami Kallel, "Online Arbitration" (2008) 25(3) *Journal of International Arbitration* 350.

70 Nicolas de Witt, 'Online International Arbitration: Nine Issues Crucial to its Success', *American Review of International Arbitration* 12 (2001): 441.

71 Gabrielle Kaufmann-Köhler, 'Online Dispute Resolution and Its Significance for International Commercial Arbitration', in Gerald Aksen et al. (eds), *Global Reflections on International Law, Commerce and Dispute Resolution, Commerce and Dispute Resolution, Liber Amicorum in Honour of Robert Briner* (South Africa: ICC Publishing, Publication 693, 2005), p. 455.

72 Andrea M. Braeutigam, 'What I hear You Writing is ... Issues in ODR: Building Trust and Rapport in the Text-based Environment', *University of Toledo Law Review* 38 (2006): 101. See also Benjamin Davis, 'Building the Seamless Dispute Resolution Web: a Status Report on the American Bar Association Task Force on E-Commerce and Alternative Dispute Resolution', *Texas Wesleyan Law Review* 8(3) (2002): 538;

Anne-Marie Hammond, 'How Do You Write "Yes"?: A Study on the Effectiveness of Online Dispute Resolution', *Conflict Resolution Quarterly* 20(3) (2003): 261–286, and Nicole Gabrielle Kravec, 'Dogmas of Online Dispute Resolution', *University of Toledo Law Review* 38 (2006): 125.

73 Francis Gurry, 'Dispute Resolution on the Internet', in Papers of the International Federation of Commercial Arbitration Institutions: 5th Biennial Dispute Resolution Conference (New York: AAA, 1999), p. 60.

74 Andrea M. Braeutigam, 'Fusses That Fit Online: Online Mediation in Non-Commercial Contexts', *Appalachian Journal of Law* 5 (2006): 301.

75 This system facilitates, among other things, access to justice, and it can certainly be "improved" by means of technology. See, e.g., Pablo Cortés, *Online Dispute Resolution for Consumers in the European Union* (London: Routledge, 2011), p. 95f.

76 See Michael Wheeler, 'Computers and Negotiation: Backing into the Future', *Negotiation Journal* (1995): 169 and Ethan Katsh, 'Ten Years of Online Dispute Resolution (ODR)', *University of Toledo Law Review* 38 (2006): 19.

77 Cf. Jean Sternlight, 'ADR is Here: Preliminary Reflections on Where it Fits in a System of Justice', *Nevada Law Journal* 3 (2003): 289.

78 Thomas Schultz, 'The Roles of Dispute Settlement and ODR', in Arnold Ingen-Housz (ed.), *ADR in Business: Practice and Issues Across Countries and Cultures*, Vol.2 (The Hague: Kluwer Law International, 2011), p. 140.

ADR, ARBITRATION, AND MEDIATION
A Collection of Essays

CHAPTER 2

ARBITRATION

CHAPTER 2

Arbitration — Its Future — Its Prospects

Sir Ronald Davison

An overview of the history of arbitration and of the manner in which arbitrations in many jurisdictions are presently conducted has enabled me to discern what in my view are undesirable trends in present day arbitration and what new direction arbitration may take in the years ahead. I propose to discuss these matters looking somewhat into the crystal bowl but hopefully with a practical eye, endeavouring to ascertain the likely forms which arbitration might usefully take. Arbitration has become a well-established means of resolving disputes particularly in the fields of trade and commerce and institutes and associations of arbitrators have over a period of many years promoted the education and training of arbitrators seeking to maintain high standards in the profession. One might say that the future of arbitration as an alternative means of resolving disputes outside of the judicial system is a healthy one. Arbitration, however, will only remain a popular device if it provides a real alternative to existing processes of dispute resolution and if it maintains the confidence and respect of those who use it and are likely to use it. It would be folly to deny that arbitration as presently developed and practised in many countries has disadvantages as well as advantages. It is only by constantly identifying problems and responding to them and improving arbitration techniques that the future of arbitration can be assured. Response to some disadvantages has already occurred in some countries and improvements introduced by legislative action. But improvements can come from within the profession itself quite apart from any legislative reforms. Some of the areas for such improvement will be discussed shortly. I now proceed then to discuss improvements and developments to the arbitral process under a number of heads:

ARBITRATION PROCEDURES

Conduct of Arbitrations

The early arbitrations were summary in procedure designed to provide a ready answer to a trading or commercial dispute. With the complexity of modern commerce and the value of the issues in dispute arbitrations have become more and more formalised with the result that at the present day arbitrations are virtually a mirror image of court proceedings. Arbitration proceedings have tended to become too sophisticated in nature. This is understandable. But with the growth of a body of trained arbitrators however, trained and knowledgeable in various areas of expertise, the need for court-like procedures involving instructing a judge usually unskilled in the technical implications of a dispute, may no longer be so necessary. More reliance can be placed upon the special skill and knowledge of the arbitrator. This could result in a number of changes. (1) The adversary procedures so commonly adopted in arbitrations could give way to a large extent to a more inquisitorial procedure in which the arbitrator is free to make his own inquiries and investigations into the matters in dispute. This would involve less formal hearings and would likely result in the arbitrator being able more readily to reach the kernel of the dispute rather than being left with the material presented to him in the formal adversary manner by the parties. He knows what he is looking for and it might be more expedient for him to pursue his own inquiries. It could shorten the time of the hearing and result in lower legal costs and charges and arbitrators' fees being incurred. If the arbitrator can make his own inquiries then the chances are that he will more likely reach a correct conclusion than would be the case where he has had to listen to evidence and weigh it up and decide on which to accept and which to reject in arriving at his decision. I do not suggest that arbitration should do away with evidence or a hearing of some sort. He must usually receive some evidence and hear the parties but I suggest there should be a leaning by the arbitrator toward more direct inquiry in the investigative process. If arbitrations are to be conducted more informally then the training and education of arbitrators becomes important. They should be encouraged to use and develop different techniques of arbitration which they think are more suited to the case. This will no doubt involve ensuring that any such techniques are allowed within the terms of the submission. The techniques however should be based on the overriding principle that natural justice should always be preserved; (2) A more direct inquiry in the arbitral process will involve a relaxation of the rules of evidence normally applied to arbitration proceedings. The rule normally applied in Commonwealth countries is this: "[i]n the conduct of the proceedings in his capacity as arbitral tribunal, the arbitrator or umpire must conform to any directions which may be contained in the agreement of reference itself. Subject to any such directions he should observe, so far as may be practicable, the rules which prevail at the trial of an action in court including rules as to issue estoppel but he may deviate from these rules provided that in so doing he does not regard the substance of justice." A relaxation of that rule could be based simply on the relevance of the evidence to the inquiry; (3) The right of review of an arbitrator's award by the court should be more restricted to ensure the finality of the award subject only to limited rights of review based principally on breach of natural justice. The provisions of the English Arbitration Act 1979 go a long way in this respect. That Act endeavours to achieve this object in two ways. The first is by giving the parties powers to exclude review by the High Court and the second is when such review is not so excluded, by restricting the rights of the parties to such review by requiring them to obtain leave of the court to seek the review. Some observations made by Lord Diplock in the House of Lords in *Pioneer Shipping v BTP Tioxide* indicate the new approach introduced into arbitration by the 1979 Act:

"[m]y Lords, in weighing the rival merits of finality and meticulous legal accuracy there are, in my view, several indications in the Act itself of a parliamentary intention to give effect to the turn of the tide in favour of finality in arbitral awards (particularly in non-domestic arbitrations of which the instant case is one), at any rate where this does not involve exposing arbitrators to a temptation to depart from 'settled principles of law'. Thus Section 1(1) removes a former threat to finality by abolishing judicial review (formerly certiorari) for error of law on the face of the award. Section 1(3) withdraws the previous power of an arbitrator to accede to a request to state his award in the form of a special case if such request was made by any party to the reference ... 'Except when all parties to the reference consent, the first part of s 1 (4) places an absolute bar on the grant of leave to appeal unless the determination of the disputed point of law would substantially affect the rights of one or more parties to the reference and this, be it noted, even though the point might have arisen under a standard form contract and be of outstanding importance to the trade generally ... Section 1(7) is another provision in favour of reaching finality as soon as possible; the stringent conditions imposed on a further appeal from the judge to the Court of Appeal are clearly adapted from the provisions of the Criminal Appeal Act 1968 relating to appeals to the House of Lords in criminal matters, another field of law in which speedy finality is much to be desired ... Section 3 gives effect to a reversal of public policy in relation to arbitration as it had been expounded more than half a century before in *Czarnikow v Roth, Schmidt & Co.* Exclusion agreements, which oust the statutory jurisdiction of the High Court to supervise the way in which arbitrators apply the law in reaching their decisions in individual cases, are recognised as being no longer contrary to public policy ... The classes of contracts listed in s 4 in respect of which the right to make exclusion agreements is not unfettered but is subjected to some qualifications are those in which (i) the use of standard forms of contract, in the vast majority of transactions, is a commercial necessity, (ii) English law is very widely chosen as the 'proper law' of the contract, even though the parties are foreign nationals and no part of the transaction is to take place in England, and (iii) provision is very frequently made for London arbitration. My Lords, in view of the cumulative effect of all these indications of Parliament's intention to promote greater finality in arbitral awards than was being achieved under the previous procedure as it was applied in practice, it would, in my view, defeat the main purpose of the first four sections of the 1979 Act if judges, when determining whether a case was one in which the new discretion to grant leave to appeal should be exercised in favour of an applicant against objection by any other party to the reference did not apply much stricter criteria than those stated in *The Lysland* which used to be applied in exercising the former discretion to require an arbitrator to state a special case for the opinion of the court."

If the law in the various countries is changed in line with this suggestion then arbitration will move back to the type of adjudication where it found its origins and arbitration will again be more a system of adjudication in its own right providing a parallel system of dispute resolution complementing the court system but not one which is but a mirror image of that court system; (4) Before leaving the topic of arbitration procedures it might be well to mention briefly the many standard forms of contract in use today which provide for arbitration in the event of a dispute arising. Many persons do not know what is involved in arbitration. I think there is an increasing need to inform the consumers of society of the service which arbitration can provide, and the different forms arbitration can take. The public should be told that where an investigation is conducted by an arbitrator the parties are not going to be disadvantaged just because it is not conducted like a court case. This is important where standard forms of contract are being used more frequently and where one of the parties is often given no choice but to accept the terms of such a contract. I foresee moves to involve arbitrators more and more in the resolution of consumer related disputes and facilities being provided by the State at State expense.

SMALL CLAIMS TRIBUNAL

Although the concept of arbitration tends to be associated largely with commercial and trading disputes, it has great possibilities of application to minor trade and even personal disputes. The so-called 'small claims' disputes are an example. In some countries arbitration procedures are used to prevent or alleviate the clogging up of court lists with simple and minor disputes. Parties are encouraged to submit their dispute to a third person for adjudication. Informality and low costs are a particular feature of these small claims' arbitrations where facilities and staff are provided by the State.

In New Zealand we have had such Small Claims Tribunals since 1976. They are presided over by referees appointed by warrant. Referees need not be legally qualified if they are otherwise capable by reason of special knowledge or experience. Some arbitrators have been appointed referees. The functions of the Tribunal are: (1) Primarily to attempt to bring the parties to a dispute to an agreed settlement; (2) Where an agreed settlement is reached the Tribunal may make various forms of order to implement the settlement; (3) If it appears to the Tribunal that it is impossible to reach a settlement of the dispute the Tribunal proceeds to determine the issue according to the substantial merits and justice of the case and in doing so is required to have regard to the law but is not bound to give effect to strict legal rights or obligations as to legal forms or technicalities. The current limit of jurisdiction of the Tribunals is $500 but a working party report recently published recommends an increase to $1,500 with further jurisdiction in other areas also.

In small claims tribunals the use of legally trained persons is usually kept to a minimum and in most schemes legal representation is prohibited. A large measure of informality in the proceedings exists and where the Tribunal makes its determination according to the substantial merits of the case, there appears to be a very fruitful field for the engagement of trained arbitrators to act as referees. Arbitrators are persons of standing in the community and they bring their expertise, their training, a wealth of experience and common sense to their determinations. They are persons readily accepted by the parties as proper persons to resolve their disputes. It will be noticed that especially in relation to small claims tribunals arbitration has a changing profile. It becomes more closely associated with mediation and conciliation and these techniques will be used more readily than they are commonly used in ordinary arbitrations today. Strictly speaking mediation and conciliation are quite distinct from the process of arbitration, nevertheless they can be intermingled with arbitration in the small claims/disputes area to produce a more effective and satisfactory method of resolving disputes. I foresee arbitrators being more and more involved in small claims' tribunals as referees. In New Zealand the referees are paid by the State and they are provided with the necessary facilities to enable them to carry out their duties.

PETTY CRIMINAL MEDIATION

Perhaps one of the more radical uses of arbitration in the future will be its use in community disputes. Traditionally arbitration has only applied to disputes which are justiciable as the suit of the parties in the courts. But already there are some experimental programmes that have been initiated, notably in the United States of America, to resolve minor criminal disputes. Such disputes which have resulted in probable breaches of the criminal law are likely to arise out of incidents involving neighbours, work associates family members or even complete strangers. They are ones however which police officers feel can be more appropriately dealt with by mediation than in court. The process involved is called community mediation where the mediators are trained lay persons from the community. The role of the arbitrator becomes that of mediator. Almost invariably in these petty criminal matters there are deep seated and more personal problems which underlie the 'criminal' behaviour. Criminal proceedings in court would more likely aggravate relationships between the complainant and the offender and where they have to continue living their daily lives in close proximity to each other it is important that acceptable relationships be established. Arbitration/mediation is seen as a viable alternative to court proceedings as a means of resolving a problem and minimising personal conflict. The aim is not to determine fault and punish the offender but rather to find a solution which will prevent conflict in the future.

A Philadelphia Municipal Court case reported on by James Green illustrates the type of dispute involving a criminal act which may be dealt with by the mediation procedure:

The issue concerns a domestic argument between a father and his 47-year-old daughter, who has admitted to assaulting her father by striking him on the head with a metal soup ladle — an indictable offence under the Pennsylvania Criminal Code.

Summary of Facts

Father and daughter living together — daughter unmarried, never left home — took care of the father since wife deserted him some 30 years ago. Daughter has a relationship with a male companion and brings him home to commence a *de facto* relationship. Father feels his authority has been usurped, moved into single bedroom, feels relegated to second place. Constant domestic argument between all parties, culminating in an assault on him by his daughter.

Result

Arbitrator makes an award all on the evidence presented. The award had the following terms: (a) That the daughter be bound over to keep the peace for 12 months; (b) That the daughter undergo a prescribed course of counselling through one of the supportive agencies (undisputed evidence put forward and admitted of previous violence and bouts of depression); (c) That the father be reinstated to his former position in the household — and not to be treated unfairly; (d) That contribution ($40) weekly to the household expenses be made by the '*de facto* spouse'; (e) That the father must accept that the daughter who has cared for him since her mother left home is entitled to a life of her own — whether this be under his roof or elsewhere; (f) That in the event of any further likelihood of domestic conflict happening, serious consideration be given to the daughter and '*de facto* spouse' living elsewhere.

It is not hard to foresee many other types of cases which arise within a community where arbitration/mediation procedure may be considered appropriate. In New Zealand the working party on access to law strongly supports the development of community mediation as having the potential to divert and satisfactorily resolve a considerable number of disputes which would otherwise end up in the courts at a cost to the taxpayer through the provision of legal aid and the use of court time. As a consequence of the encouraging results achieved in mediation centres overseas a centre is to be set up in Christchurch New Zealand later this year. As the trend away from the formality of the courts to a greater informality of arbitration/mediation develops, I foresee an increasing need for suitably trained and qualified persons to become available to preside over the various tribunals that are established. Arbitrators should be encouraged to move into this field where they can make a very worthwhile contribution to the resolution of matters which would otherwise involve the exercise by the courts of their criminal jurisdiction. Arbitration/mediation results in a humanising of the criminal justice system. The problems of the parties concerned become the paramount consideration for the tribunals, and not the State's desire to punish for criminal behaviour. Some would say that in many cases of minor criminal behaviour punishment is an inappropriate response and will achieve little for those involved.

STATE ARBITRATION — THE COSTS

One of the greatest disadvantages of arbitration at the present day — in New Zealand and I believe also in other countries — is the cost. Where one, or even worse, where two arbitrators and an umpire are engaged the costs can be very heavy indeed when the fees payable plus the provision of premises and the recording of evidence are taken into account. On the other hand in court litigation awards of costs — in New Zealand certainly — are usually limited and the State provides the judges and all other court facilities free of charge.

I believe that with the growing trend towards informal adjudication of disputes which is becoming apparent in many countries there is a strong case for the State to provide arbitration services at small cost as an alternative to the court systems. Facilities for hearings could be made available — not in large premises, but in quite small hearing rooms — with provision for evidence recording as required. Arbitrators could be paid by the State and could be available for the parties to choose from panels made up for the purpose or be chosen from suitably qualified persons outside of those panels even, so long as they are prepared to accept engagement on the panel terms. Provision of such facilities can be more than justified on the basis that disputes which would otherwise enter the court system can be disposed of more readily and more economically by arbitration. Arbitration would then have its place in the community not as a rival to the court process but as a complement to it. The award of the arbitrator should be virtually final with the exceptions to which I have earlier referred leaving the court to exercise its supervisory function in only a very limited number of cases.

Greater acceptance by the public of the advantages of arbitration in appropriate cases must surely lead to the State assuming the responsibility for the provision of the facilities to enable it to operate. This is already emerging in the cases of small claims tribunals and petty criminal mediation tribunals. It is but a small extension to the assumption of responsibility for all arbitrations. But acceptance by the State of responsibility for provision of facilities for all arbitrations will only come if arbitrators demonstrate that there is a sufficient demand for the services that they can provide to justify State intervention. The basis of arbitration as at present conducted is the voluntary submission of a dispute by the parties concerned. Arbitrators both personally and through their institutions must make known to the public the services they can provide, they must give to the public confidence in those services and create public demand for them. It is only then I believe that the State will feel justified in assuming responsibility for their provision at State expense.

ARBITRATORS AND THE COURTS

Arbitrators may have a role in association with the courts in the resolution of certain forms of dispute. One of the disadvantages suffered by judges in some cases — although few will admit it — is their lack of technical knowledge on some issues coming before them for decision. Parties to an action in court, where the dispute is a technical one, must produce evidence from experts to inform the judge of the matters in issue. He commonly hears expert evidence from one side then like as not conflicting expert evidence from the other side and uses his judgment to decide which evidence to accept. There is something to be said for providing courts with expert advisers or associates to assist in technical cases. There is also the possibility of courts being able to refer factual issues of a technical nature to be determined by an expert who reports back to the court his findings on such issues leaving it to the judge to determine other issues on the evidence and to apply the law. There come to mind questions relating to engineering and architectural matters in the construction industry: technical methods of manufacture and manufacturing processes; chemical processes in industry with particular reference to patent cases. Arbitrators who have the necessary technical background and professional expertise would be admirably suited to carry out such expert investigations and report their findings to the courts. I think courts have for too long been denied the benefit of technical assistance which would assist materially in the resolution of disputed issues. Perhaps the time is coming when the situation may be changed. In New Zealand in a limited way we do make use of technical expertise. In the Administrative Division, when dealing with valuation matters, we sit with one or two associate members who are registered valuers. In claims for infringement of patent, scientific advisers may be appointed to assist the court. I would like to see it made possible for the courts to use more readily the services of arbitrators to inquire into and report on technical factual matters where I am sure their services would be found to be invaluable and would speed up the judicial process.

IN SUMMARY

In my view developments in arbitration are likely to involve: (1) A greater finality of awards and more restricted grounds for review of those awards by the courts; (2) Greater use being made of arbitration in the areas of: (a) small claims tribunals; (b) petty criminal mediation services; (3) Greater State involvement in the provision and funding of arbitration facilities; (4) Greater participation by arbitrators in the court judicial process.

REFERENCES

* This article was originally published as R. Davidson, 'Arbitration — Its Future — Its Prospects', *Arbitration* 51, no. 1 (1985): 225-232.
1 Arbitration Act 1979 (UK).
2 Halsburys 4th para 592.
3 *Pioneer Shipping v B TP Tioxide* 1980 3 All ER 117, 124.
4 Small Claims Tribunals Act 1976.
5 *Ibid.*, Section 15(1) to (4).
6 *Final Report of the Working Party on Access to the Law* (New Zealand: Department of Justice, 1983), 27 and 53.
7 J. Green, *Research Report on the Philadelphia Pennsylvania USA Municipal Court Private Criminal Arbitration Programme* (June 1983).
8 *Ibid.*, 6.
9 Land Value Proceedings Act 1948 Section 3.
10 Patents Act 1953 Section 113.

CHAPTER 2

Using Arbitration to Achieve Justice

Warren E. Burger

The obligation of the legal profession is, or has long been thought to be, to serve as healers of human conflicts. To fulfil that traditional obligation means that there should be mechanisms that can produce an acceptable result in the shortest possible time, with the least possible expense and with a minimum of stress on the participants. That is what justice is all about. There is, of course, very little new that can be said about the subject of voluntary arbitration, especially to a group of sophisticated lawyers and businessmen. If there were some new or profound thoughts, I would hardly be qualified to spell them out. Before going on the Bench, I participated in eight or ten arbitration situations of a commercial nature and in one rather large international disposition that was a hybrid of arbitration, conciliation and negotiation. As a private attorney, I was no stranger to arbitration in the labour-management areas, both as an advocate and as an arbitrator. Labour unions paid me the compliment in those days of consenting to my acting as the neutral or public member of panels on interpretation disputes under labour contracts. My overview of the work of the courts from a dozen years on the Court of Appeals and now 16 in my present position, added to 20 years of private practice, has given me some new perspectives on the problems of arbitration. One thing an appellate judge learns very quickly is that a large part of all the litigation in the courts is an exercise in futility and frustration. A large proportion of civil disputes in the courts could be disposed of more satisfactorily in some other way. I will try to tell you why I think this is so. As lawyers, we generally know that litigation is not only frustrating but expensive, frequently unrewarding for litigants. If it is a personal injury case, it diverts people and entire families from their normal pursuits and sometimes makes them neurotics. Nor is it enjoyed by doctors who must set aside their normal pursuits to appear as witnesses. One of our country's greatest lawyers, Abraham Lincoln, said: "Discourage litigation. Persuade your neighbours to compromise whenever you can. Point out to them how the nominal winner is often a real loser — in fees, expenses, and waste of time. As a peacemaker the lawyer has a superior opportunity of being a good man.... Never stir up litigation. A worse man can scarcely be found than one who does this." And one of the eminent judges of our time, Learned Hand, said, "I must say that, as a litigant, I should dread a lawsuit beyond almost anything else short of sickness and death."

Large commercial litigation takes businessmen and their staffs off the creative paths of production and often produces more wear and tear on them than the most difficult business problems. Consider the costs of lost productivity in the IBM antitrust litigation, with six years of discovery leading to a trial that went on for nearly seven years. I doubt the Founding Fathers anticipated such results. That these cases are infrequent is not the whole story. In 1960, there were only 35 federal trials that took more than one month. By 1981, these protracted cases multiplied five times, and that is not the end of the story. All litigants standing in line behind a single protracted case — whether it is a one-month, a three-month or a longer case — are denied access to that court. These protracted cases not only deny parties the benefits of a speedy resolution to their conflict, but they also enlarge the costs, tensions and delays facing all other litigants waiting for access to court. Inequities flowing from such delays are particularly acute if a litigant cannot recover interest on the award or if the interest rate allowed is much less than current market rates.

Criminal cases that flood the courts produce the least — the very least — constructive results. Too many criminal cases are now protracted, with endless delays before trial, long trials and seemingly endless appeals and post-appeal reviews by *habeas corpus* or *coram nobis*. They prolong a guilty person's hostility toward society and deepen the bitterness and frustration, undermining whatever hope there may be for rehabilitation. We know the law-abiding public is appalled by the snail's pace of criminal justice. There is a common thread in all courtroom contests (1) All lawyers are natural competitors and strive to win; (2) Businessmen engaged in court battles transfer their normal drives to the immediate contest; (3) The ordinary mortal struck down by a car suddenly becomes a fierce contender at the expense of his normal pursuits; (4) The accused in a criminal case, especially if guilty, transfers his hostilities from his normal criminal patterns to the judge, the prosecutor, the opposing witnesses — even to defense counsel. When you examine this, even briefly, the wastefulness of the litigation process emerges, and one can understand the layman's lament: "There must be a better way to do this." Indeed, this lament is increasingly shared by lawyers and judges. Perhaps one factor in the changed attitude of judges is found in the congestion in all courts in the country. A few figures will suffice. At the end of World War II, 40 years ago, the Federal District Courts in the United States had roughly 30,000 new civil cases filed each year. In 1984, the figure was over 261,000 cases. The Circuit Courts of Appeals had some 3,000 appeals filed in 1944; the figure for 1984 was in excess of 31,000. The long-range solution is not to create more and more judgeships, even though that is needed now. New judgeships are costly in terms of new courthouses, staffs, libraries and equipment. For example, it costs the taxpayers more than $250,000 a year to sustain one Federal Judge, even though his salary is less than a third of the total. Today neither judges nor lawyers need worry about being 'put out of business' by arbitration. The real concern is 'How can we do it?' The anomaly is that there are 'better ways of doing it' — of resolving private disputes — and in the public interest we must move toward taking a large volume of private conflicts out of the courts and into the channels of arbitration, mediation and conciliation.

Over the years before going on the Bench, I began to observe what other societies in England and Europe have done. Jury trials are virtually unknown in Europe, and even in England juries are used only in criminal cases and a few kinds of civil cases — libel, for example. Even though these changes have sped up the litigation process, there is widespread use of private arbitration in England and on the Continent. European business people, lawyers and judges cannot understand our failure to use arbitration more widely. A host of new kinds of conflicts have flooded the courts.

There are cases with students seeking to litigate a failing mark, professors litigating a denial of academic tenure, and welfare recipients with myriad claims under the Equal Protection Clause. There is some form of mass neurosis that leads many people to think courts were created to solve all the problems of mankind. We must learn from the experience of labour and management that courts are not the best places to resolve certain kinds of claims. There are encouraging signs; let me mention a few.

THE PHILADELPHIA STORY

Many years ago the lawyers in Philadelphia worked out a plan which merits careful study, not for great commercial and business disputes, but for the common garden variety claims, currently $10,000 to $20,000. The legislature of Pennsylvania empowered the County Courts to transfer certain kinds of cases to compulsory submission to lawyers on a panel set up with the cooperation of the Bar Association. More than 3,000 lawyers make themselves available, and thousands of cases have been referred to private arbitration. I am confident that this process saves money, time, anxiety and stress for litigants and obviously spares the judges and courtrooms for larger claims.

LABOUR

The organised labour movement, going back to Bismarck's Germany, made an enormous contribution to what we loosely call 'arbitration', and it is a contribution not fully appreciated. Lawyers representing employees and unions helped to refine the techniques, but the basic contribution came from laymen who were union leaders and often relatively low-level but skilled craftsmen working in shops and factories. Many of these men knew something of the history of labour strife in Europe from which they or their fathers came. Even in the period when autocratic governments and autocratic industrialists in Europe were partners, they had discovered the secret that workers who have chronic, unresolved grievances are not good producers. The really great contribution of the labour movement is not the collective bargaining contract — important as that is — but the efficient grievance procedures, from the shop steward level up to the final and dispositive compulsory arbitration. The genius of this mechanism was reflected indirectly in the Minnesota Labor Peace Law of 1939 which now, 45 years later, remains a model. The grievance procedures developed over many years by labour and management — but with labour taking the lead — is in essence what American industrial and commercial leaders could adopt to their own internal litigation problems.

ADVANTAGES OF ARBITRATION

Let me suggest some of the advantages of private arbitration in a large, complex commercial transaction: (1) Parties can select a trier or triers by agreement, whereas they cannot select a judge even with joint consent; (2) Triers can be selected on the basis of special experience and knowledge of subject matter, of business and commercial practices and of the relevant law. Such triers can get to the heart of a case swiftly and resolve it in a fraction of the time it would take to present it to a jury of layperson; (3) A privately selected trier can conduct all proceedings in private with only the parties present, and confidentiality can be preserved where there is a valid basis for it — as in the protection of trade secrets, for example; (4) I could well mention the value of not waiting on crowded court calendars; (5) I could also mention the value of being able to submit a large volume of complex business contracts, of involved technical matters, financial statements and stipulated expert testimony which a skilled lawyer, selected because of wide commercial experience, can digest at his or her own time and pace without the burden of the whole panoply of a regular court proceeding. My own experience persuades me that in terms of cost, time, and human wear and tear, arbitration is vastly better than conventional litigation for many kinds of cases. In mentioning these factors, I intend no disparagement of the skills and broad experience of judges. I emphasise this because to find precisely the judge whose talents and experience fit a particular case of great complexity is a fortuitous circumstance. This can be made more likely if two intelligent litigants agree to pick their own private triers of the issues. This is not at all to bypass the lawyers; they are key factors in this process.

The acceptance of this concept has been far too slow in the United States. The Federal Arbitration Act is over a half-century old, and judicial decisions continue to reinforce the standing of final and binding private arbitration. Fortunately, Congress, at the request of the Judicial Conference, appropriated funds in 1978 for a pilot programme. Two districts have found court-annexed arbitration effective in reducing both the incidence of trial and the time needed to achieve settlement. In the Eastern District of Pennsylvania (Philadelphia), throughout the 71 months ended 31 December, 1983, only 1.5% of cases designated for arbitration later went to trial, whereas 8% of civil cases following traditional procedures during the same period went to trial. Additionally, the median time for cases terminated by the arbitration programme was seven months from date of issue to date of award, while the median time from date of issue to date of trial for other civil cases was 14 months. That court recently agreed both to raise the authorisation limit from $50,000 to $75,000 and to expand the type of cases going to arbitration. Similar success has been achieved in the Northern District of California (San Francisco) where, since 1978, only 34 of 2,000 cases (1.7%) designated for arbitration have later gone to trial. Last year Congress passed and the President signed Public Law 98-411 to appropriate $500,000 in fiscal year 1985 for additional pilot programmes in federal court-annexed arbitration. Eight federal districts will use this money in closely monitored experiments. This is a programme whose time has come. Experimentation and practical implementation in this area are sorely needed. I cannot emphasise too strongly to those in business and industry — and especially to lawyers — that every private contract of real consequence to the parties ought to be treated as a 'candidate' for binding private arbitration. In the drafting of such contracts, lawyers will serve their clients and the public by resorting to tested clauses the American Arbitration Association has developed to fit particular needs.

In the past 50 years, may new techniques have been developed. Administrative law has grown from an infant into a large branch of law disposing of large interests in the SEC, FTC, FCC and NLRB, and addressing the problems of energy and environment. We must now use the inventiveness, the ingenuity and the resourcefulness of American businessmen and lawyers — the 'Yankee Trader' innovativeness — to shape new tools to meet new needs. In the area of arbitration, the tools and the techniques are ready and waiting for imaginative lawyers to make use of them. If the courts are to retain public confidence, they cannot let disputes wait two, three and five years or more to be disposed of. The use of private arbitration is one solution, and lawyers should be at the forefront in moving in this direction.

*   This article was originally published as W. Burger, 'Using Arbitration to Achieve Justice', *Arbitration* 52, no. 2 (1986): 92-94.

CHAPTER 2

Arbitration: The Six F's

Peter Mason

Like a judge, every arbitrator is in a sense his own man. The law prescribes the parameters within which he must operate, but, subject to that, his style and his technique are his own. "The arbitrator has a complete discretion to determine how the arbitration is to be conducted ... so long as the procedure he observes does not offend against the rules of natural justice": Bremer Vulcan etc., (1981) 1 All ER 289 per Lord Diplock. There are, however, as it seems to me, certain qualities which the really good arbitrator will aim to develop in order to assist him dispose of the dispute in a manner satisfactory to all the parties concerned. In the case of a judge these qualities are said to be the three 'hum's' — humanity, humility and humour. The qualities of an arbitrator are similar, but slightly different, and each begin with the same letter of the alphabet. They are all aspects of style or technique, because it must never be forgotten that a party may be disappointed at the result, but satisfied with the method by which it was achieved; the arbitrator's task is not only to get the answer right (which is often difficult enough) but also to do this in the right way. First and foremost among the qualities mentioned above is fairness. This is so obvious that it almost goes without saying. An arbitrator is by definition unbiassed, but it must never be allowed to appear at any stage in the arbitral procedure that he is leaning unfairly to one side or the other. This involves, for example, never refusing to allow an advocate to cross-examine a witness: *Chilton and another v Saga Holdings plc* (1986) 1 All ER 841. It also involves giving to the side against whom an adverse point has been made, either by oral or documentary evidence, the opportunity to deal with the point in argument before any finding upon the point is made. And if, as sometimes happens, the arbitrator forms a certain view on a certain point because of his own experience in the trade or profession, he should make this view clear in order that the parties may comment on it. As the taxidriver said, 'experience is stupidity hardened by practice!' If it isn't, at least it may be! The need for everything to be done fairly, and to be seen to be done fairly, is the more important because, as is well known, the arbitrator's function can strictly be said to be to enquire rather than to adjudicate, and in this respect he is different from a judge. "The parties (to an arbitration agreement) ... shall ... submit to be examined by the arbitrator ... in relation to the matters in dispute": section 12(1) Arbitration Act 1950. In practice, of course, once the matter reaches the stage of oral argument, arbitral procedure tends to become adversarial rather than inquisitorial because that is how advocates, in the common law jurisdictions at any rate, have been brought up. But before this stage, and after it, the arbitrator has by law to display initiative in a way never required of a judge — initiative in getting the issues between the parties defined, initiative in discovering documents and making any necessary interlocutory directions, and initiative after the hearing with regard to the taxation of costs. And it is throughout, of first importance that fairness should be a steady and constant guiding light.

Chartered Institute of Arbitrators

The second quality required of an arbitrator is firmness. This is an aspect of personality which is more apparent in some than in others, but in an arbitrator it is of great consequence. It involves a reluctance to speak, and a readiness to think; a much-speaking arbitrator, like a much-speaking judge, is an ill-tuned cymbal. It also involves a great deal of hesitation before making a decision, but an absence of vacillation thereafter. It is surprising how quickly a firm arbitrator can take control of his tribunal, and how obvious it becomes that he has taken such control. Control moreover is of the essence, because without it, the proceedings can so easily degenerate into a bear-garden and the arbitrator's voice be lost in the din.

Linked with firmness is formality. I do not suggest that an arbitrator should put on airs, or act out a charade; that would ill befit the times in which we live or the spirit of consumerism (Bentham would perhaps have called it utilitarianism) which is now abroad. But it should never be forgotten than an arbitrator is dealing with serious matters which are of consequence to the parties and maybe to others too. An arbitration is not a coffee party, and the parties must not be encouraged to think it is.

No one suggests that court procedures should be imported into arbitrations lock, stock and barrel. But some elementary procedures are so helpful that nothing but good can come of making use of them — for example the use of formal pleadings (however short), orders for discovery of documents if and only if clearly needed in order to decide the dispute, and the order of speeches at the hearing. The good arbitrator will know where to draw the line and when to allow himself (and the parties) to become innovative and to leave formality behind, even if this involves a

friendliness

breach of rules of evidence or procedure.

It is in a sense a paradox to say that the next quality I wish to stress is friendliness, in which I include courtesy, at all times and to all persons — parties, witnesses, and advocates. It is easy for those clothed in brief authority to become pompous and self-opinionated. Among judges 'judgitis' is a notifiable disease which tends to develop in some cases quite soon after appointment. One hopes that no arbitrator will ever be accused of having caught something similar, because the disease does nothing to improve the performance of the advocates appearing before the tribunal, nor to promote consumer satisfaction. The advocate does his best work in my view if the atmosphere of the tribunal is relaxed, and nothing helps this ambience along more, than a courteous smile by the arbitrator, and a willingness to share the odd lighter moment. "The court is very much obliged to any learned gentleman who beguiles the tedium of a legal argument with a little honest hilarity": Erle CJ (Manson's Builders of Our Law 2nd edition 1904 p. 279). This of course is not to say that the advocate should ever be allowed to become a kind of court jester, nor that the arbitrator should tread the same path, but the occasional well-timed quip should never be discouraged; its value in removing heat and tension can be incalculable. And if the quip is very occasionally at the expense of the arbitrator he should join in the fun. I remember an occasion many years ago in the Court of Criminal Appeal (as it then was) when very junior counsel was appearing before Lord Goddard CJ and making (in his own words) "his very humble submission." The Lord Chief Justice immediately said "Mr Smith, I never humbly submitted to anyone in my life." A member of the

Chartered Institute of Arbitrators

Bar in counsel's seats whispered "[y]ou could have fooled me", a remark which the Lord Chief Justice heard and which, in fairness to him, made him smile. So let it be with the good arbitrator.

The fifth quality is flexibility. Every dispute is different, and what the arbitrator must do is to recognise the differences and to cater for them in the provisions he makes at a preliminary meeting for pleadings or documents, or at the hearing itself for the procedures to be adopted. He has a wide discretion in the methods he adopts and he must bear in mind the whole time that the object of all that he does is to achieve a solution to the problem before him with efficiency and expedition. He must also never give the impression to the parties that he has made his mind up on the pleadings or otherwise before the arbitration even begins. He must retain a willingness to listen to evidence, and to be influenced by it and by the arguments of the parties as they develop, and to follow wherever they lead. Nor should he be dismayed if he finds in the course of the hearing that his mind has been changed; this makes manifest his flexibility and is wholly a mark to his credit. He will be amused rather than depressed to recall the words of Crossman J. "I suppose Mr Sims", said the learned judge to counsel ,"that the parties in this case are sitting on the fence to see which way the cat jumps?" "No, my Lord" said counsel "they are sitting on the fence to see which side their bread is buttered."

The good arbitrator will always remember furthermore as the case proceeds, that "true justice consists of the masterful administration of the unforeseen." Finally the arbitrator must be fast. Power is given to the High Court to "remove any arbitrator who fails to use all reasonable despatch in entering on and proceeding with the reference and making an award" and an arbitrator so removed may have to whistle for his fees: section 13(3) Arbitration Act 1950. But speed is not only a matter of law, it is a matter of common-sense. What the parties require in nine cases out of ten is a speedy resolution of their dispute. It cannot be said of the arbitrator what is sometimes said of the trial judge, but none the less, the saying points a moral for both. "The trial judge" the saying goes, "must be quick courteous and wrong. That is not to say that the Court of Appeal must be slow, rude and right, for that would be to usurp the function of the House of Lords!"

There are various causes of delay, both in interlocutory proceedings and at the hearing. It is difficult to categorise such causes, but it can be said that a sure antidote to delay is an active arbitrator who keeps up so far as is possible a relentless pressure, in order to achieve finality. One common cause of delay is unfortunately the long-windedness of advocates. Dealing with this is fraught with difficulty, for to interrupt the advocate and accuse him of being repetitive or long-winded is to generate a speech lasting half an hour explaining why he is not, and after half an hour he begins again where he left off. One can understand the feelings of the Chancery Judge who in desperation, when counsel apologised after a speech lasting five hours, for trespassing on his lordship's time, said to him "Sir, you have not trespassed on my time; you have encroached upon eternity."

I suggest that there are various steps which one can take to discourage long-windedness. First look at your watch (taking it off your wrist and shaking it is perhaps going too far), next look out of the window, finally close your eyes and appear to go to sleep. If none of these work, sterner measures will be required. I can see no reason why these measures should not include the suggestion to the advocate that you propose to take his waste of your time into account when considering the question of costs. This will undoubtedly produce a reaction, and may well do the trick! It is general experience that it causes the advocate to terminate his long-winded speech or examination of the witness, but prompts him at once to seek to address the tribunal on costs. It should be suggested that such addresses may be postponed until the hearing has concluded. It may be that at that stage the suggestion can be dropped, as undoubtedly its effect will have been to increase momentum on all sides.

In my view such suggestion is no idle threat. "Costs ... shall be in the discretion of the arbitrator, who may direct to and by whom and in what manner those costs ... shall be paid, and may tax or settle the amount of costs to be so paid" section 18(1) Arbitration Act 1950. The arbitrator, should he tax the costs himself as nowadays he should always consider doing, is entitled to make such adjustment to the advocate's fees as is reasonable in the circumstances, having regard to the conduct of the advocate at the hearing and the time by which the hearing was thereby prolonged: *Perkins v Bert-Shaw* (1973) 2 All ER 924. Or if he prefers the costs to be taxed in the High Court under section 18(2) he is in my view entitled to send any observations he wishes to make on the question of costs to the taxing officer for his consideration. The taxing officer, who was not present at the hearing, will certainly give weight to them. These then are the qualities which seem to me important. Any arbitrator who succeeded in consistently practising them all would be a paragon. Our reputation in this country in this field rests perhaps on the fact that although we do not always succeed, we consistently try.

* This article was originally published as P. Mason, 'Arbitration: the Six F's', *Arbitration* 52, no. 3 (1986): 147-149.

CHAPTER 2

England's Response to the Model Law of Arbitration

Lord Steyn

England's response to the challenge of UNCITRAL's Model Law on International Commercial Arbitration has been to use it as a yardstick by which to judge the quality of our existing arbitration legislation and to improve it. After a gestation period, which has been elephantine in its proportions, a draft Arbitration Bill has now been prepared and when a consultation paper has been completed the consultation process will start. The single most important influence in the shaping of the Bill has been the Model Law. The genesis of the Model Law was the idea that trading nations would benefit by having available an international text as a basis for harmonising national legislation, by adopting the text en bloc or by revising national laws, in accordance with desirable features of it. It was an ambitious project, notably because arbitration is concerned with the procedure of dispute resolution and the relationship between arbitration and national courts. The divergences between national laws on arbitration are great. And it is usually more difficult to achieve harmonisation of national laws in procedural as opposed to substantive matters. That was the principal reason why the technique of a model law as opposed to a convention was adopted. The Model Law text was settled in 1985 after many lengthy sessions spread over several years. Thirty-two states were represented by delegations. The United Kingdom delegation included Lord Justice Mustill (now Lord Mustill). A further 20 states sent observers. So did 14 international organisations. Lord Wilberforce represented the Chartered Institute of Arbitrators. Mr Martin Hunter was the delegate of the International Bar Association. All contributed in an active way in discussions. Inevitably, there had to be compromise between common law and civil law points of view, and the concerns of other legal cultures had to be taken into account. No international text ever satisfies everybody. But the Model Law was a remarkable achievement by UNCITRAL, ranking in importance with the New York Convention of 1958. The text is arranged in logical order, and its provisions are expressed in simple language, which will be readily comprehensible to international users of the arbitration process. Substantively, the solutions adopted by the Working Group reflect a widespread consensus as to what is practical and feasible in international commercial arbitration. It is therefore not surprising that 16 states have already based new legislation on the Model Law. Germany and New Zealand may follow the same route. And other states are revising their arbitration laws in the light of the Model Law.

THE DECISION NOT TO ADOPT THE MODEL LAW

It is pertinent to ask why the Departmental Advisory Committee on Arbitration Law (the DAC) recommended that England should not adopt the Model Law? Cynical foreign observers say that the decision is in character with England's role in the process of harmonisation of international trade law. Typically, they say, England is voluble at international congresses in promoting common law solutions in the framing of a convention and, having achieved significant success in that pursuit, England then rejects the convention as being inferior to native English law. This criticism is obviously too extravagant in its scope. But it is not entirely groundless. The Vienna Sales Convention has been ratified by 34 nations, including almost all the member countries of the European Economic Community, and most of the major trading nations of the world. My understanding is that Belgium, Japan, and New Zealand will also ratify. Yet England delays. I believe the reason is to be found in the deep seated antipathy of English lawyers towards multi-lateral conventions. The purity of the common law prevails over the needs of international commerce, and our own trading position. Moreover, as Professor Barry Nicholas, a United Kingdom delegate at the Vienna working sessions, pointed out earlier this year, it is vital that the United Kingdom should ratify the convention quickly, so that the experience of English lawyers and of the Commercial Court can influence the way in which the convention is interpreted and applied. I would argue, however, that the decision of the DAC to recommend that England should not adopt the Model Law was justified on special grounds. And it is right to point out that the committee took this decision under the chairmanship of Lord Justice Mustill and after a most detailed and rigorous examination of the merits and demerits of the Model law as compared with English law. Not all the reasons put forward in 1989 for not adopting the Model Law seem as compelling today as they did then. The committee stated: "[t[he arguments in favour of enacting the Model Law in the interests of harmonisation, or of thereby keeping in step with other nations, are of little weight. The majority of trading nations, and more notably those to which international arbitrations have tended to gravitate, have not chosen thus to keep in step." That was a judgment made four years after the publication of the Model Law. Today one would have to revise that judgment. Less than a decade after its first publication the Model Law has proved popular internationally and has become a benchmark by which the quality of national arbitration laws is judged. Nevertheless, in my view the decision taken in 1989 was right for England. I say that for two reasons. First, although our principal statute, the Arbitration Act 1950, is of poor quality, England already has a well developed and comprehensive arbitration system which since the watershed of the Arbitration Act 1979 has by and large proved satisfactory domestically and popular among international users of the arbitration process. In comparison the Model Law quite understandably is more skeletal in its treatment of the arbitration process. It contains many gaps which would have to be filled. Secondly, much of arbitration law is concerned with the relationship between arbitration and national court systems, and in the English system that relationship involves greater supervision of the arbitral process than is envisaged by the Model Law. Subject to two qualifications to which I will turn later, the prevailing domestic view has been that England has found the right balance between party autonomy and judicial scrutiny of the arbitral process. In combination these two factors justified the decision taken in 1989 not to adopt the Model Law.

THE WAY FORWARD

In its 1989 report the Mustill Committee recommended that a new statute should be drafted which would "comprise a statement in statutory form of the more important principles of the English Law of arbitration, statutory and (to the extent practicable) common law." The committee advised that "[c]onsideration should be given to ensuring that any such new statute should, so far as possible, have the same structure and language as the Model law, so as to enhance its accessibility to those who are familiar with the Model Law." The government accepted this advice.

The initiative to translate the idea of a new statute into action came from Mr Arthur Marriott. It involved the privatised drafting of a new statute. It was funded by a large group of law firms, barristers' chambers and arbitration institutions. The Marriott Group engaged the services of Mr Basil Eckersley, a distinguished barrister and arbitrator. That was an inspired choice. He produced an Arbitration Bill and a Commentary. It was a tour de force and a convincing refutation of the notion that only a lawyer trained in the office of the Parliamentary Draftsman is capable of drafting a statute. Nevertheless the DAC resolved that the new statute should be drafted by somebody trained as a parliamentary draftsman. That decision puzzled many experienced observers. It was yet further testimony to the astonishing awe in which Whitehall holds Parliamentary Draftsmen. As Sir William Dale pointed out legislative drafting in England is endowed with a mystique which it does not possess in civil law countries. The decision of the DAC was the outcome of realpolitik. The DAC was advised by the Department of Trade and Industry that it was essential, in view of a crowded legislative agenda, to obtain government support for the new measure and that such support would not be forthcoming if the bill was not drafted by a lawyer trained as a parliamentary draftsman. The DAC was motivated by one desire only: that England should have the best possible new arbitration statute as soon as possible. The committee accepted the advice it was given, as it had to. The Marriott Working Group instructed a former parliamentary draftsman to prepare a Bill. Unfortunately, his draft failed the threshold requirement of following the structure of the Model Law. The committee rejected it as a basis for future work. The Group instructed another former Parliamentary draftsman. The committee accepted her first draft as a working draft. The committee then advised on successive drafts of the Bill. Until 1992 the project had been financed and directed by the Marriott Working Group. By April 1992 it had become clear to all concerned that it would be more sensible for the project to become a public one. The DAC recommended that the Department of Trade and Industry should take over responsibility for work on the Bill and that it should be carried forward as a Government Bill. The government accepted this recommendation. That is the basis on which the DAC has advised on the drafting and redrafting of the bill. Nevertheless the work of the Marriott Group, and Mr Eckersley's draft, proved of immense value in the second and public phase of the project. Without that work we would not today have an Arbitration Bill. And the DAC has been able to draw on the very extensive experience of the Marriott Group because two leading members of the Group, Mr Arthur Marriott and Mr Anthony Bunch, generously agreed to join the committee.

THE STRUCTURE OF THE BILL

The Bill looks very different from the existing arbitration legislation. The structure is different. For example, the draftsman of the 1950 statute thought it right to start the statute with a provision on the revocation of the mandate of the arbitrator, and to scatter provisions about the challenge to arbitrators across the statute. Generally, the structure of the 1950 statute was illogical and confusing. The Bill has a clear and logical structure taken from the Model Law. This is an important point because it was a prime objective of the DAC that the bill should improve the accessibility of our arbitration legislation to domestic and international users alike. The 1950 statute repeatedly uses the drafting technique of deeming provisions, which provide that 'unless a contrary intention is expressed therein, every arbitration agreement shall, be deemed to include a provision that...'. Like the draftsmen of the Model Law the DAC ultimately put its faith in simplicity. The deeming provisions have been replaced by straightforward prescriptive statements, sometimes mandatory in character and sometimes not. Another new feature is that the Bill emphasises the principle of party autonomy. It also seems to me that generally the language in which the Bill has been expressed has been improved and that it is likely to be reasonably intelligible to laymen.

SOME MAJOR ISSUES

It will not be possible to discuss the Bill in detail. But it might be useful to consider briefly a few features of the Bill, which either involve or might arguably involve important changes in the law, as well as certain major issues which are not at present affected by the Bill but nevertheless lie at the heart of the current debate. The matters which I propose to discuss are: (1) *Kompetenz/Kompetenz* and the separability of the arbitration agreement; (2) Evidence; (3) Procedure; (4) Immunity; (5) The relationship between the courts and arbitration: (a) Remission, (b) Special categories; (6) Equity clauses.

KOMPETENZ/KOMPETENZ AND THE SEPARABILITY OF THE ARBITRATION AGREEMENT

The doctrine of *Kompetenz/Kompetenz*, that is the question whether arbitrators may decide on their own jurisdiction, cause difficulties in some countries. In England the position is straightforward. Arbitrators are entitled, and indeed required, to consider whether they will assume jurisdiction. But that decision does not alter the legal rights of the parties, and the court has the last word. The new Bill does not change the law. It merely contains a provision declaratory of the common law position. Given the fact that the Commercial Court has the capacity to decide such preliminary issues speedily, the DAC took the view that the existing practice in England is probably satisfactory. Accordingly, the Bill contains no provisions comparable to Article 16 (2) of the Model Law, which requires a denial of jurisdiction to be raised not later than when the defence is served, and Article 16 (3), which require an application to court challenging the arbitrators decision to be made within 30 days. If the consultation process reveals strong support for corresponding provisions in our legislation, the committee will have to think again. Until recently the doctrine of the separability of an arbitration clause contained in an integrated written agreement was not fully developed in England. Thus it was thought that a dispute whether a written agreement reflected the true intention of the parties and can be rectified always fell outside the scope of the arbitration clause in the contract. In 1987 in *Ashville Investments Ltd. v*

Elmer Contractors Ltd the Court of Appeal finally laid to rest this absurd notion. The judgments in that case were a notable contribution to the development of the doctrine of the separability of the arbitration agreement. But there was still a problem. The orthodox view was that disputes as to whether a contract was invalid or illegal *ab initio* always fell outside the scope of an arbitration clause in that contract. Earlier this year *Harbour Assurance Co. (UK) Ltd v Kansa General International Assurance Co. Ltd* the Court of Appeal held that an arbitration agreement in a written contract could confer jurisdiction on an arbitrator to decide on the initial validity or illegality of the written contract provided that the arbitration clause was not directly impeached. I respectfully applaud the judgments in the Court of Appeal in *Harbour Assurance*. England has now adopted the approach of the Model Law. Article 16 (1) of the Model Law reads as follows: "an arbitration clause which forms part of a contract shall be treated as an agreement independent of the other terms of the contract. A decision by the arbitral tribunal that the contract is null and void shall not entail *ipso jure* the invalidity of the arbitration clause."

That provision is the most compelling evidence of the workability and desirability of a fully developed separability doctrine. Given that the relevant law has now been satisfactorily developed and settled in *Harbour Assurance*, some may think that there is no need for legislation. It is true that there will be no appeal to the House of Lords in *Harbour Assurance*. But there is the risk that the point may come before the House of Lords in another case. And the infallibles may say that it is all far more difficult than the Court of Appeal realised, and they may reverse the beneficial development of the law. That has been known to happen. In order to guard against that risk the Bill contains in section 3(2) a separability provision squarely based on Article 16(1) of the Model Law.

EVIDENCE

In recent times it has been assumed by authors that arbitrators are bound by the technical rules of evidence unless the parties expressly or implied agree otherwise. This assumption is understandable since in enacting the Civil Evidence Act 1968 Parliament assumed that the technical rules of evidence apply to arbitrations. That was, however, a mere assumption and it has no prescriptive force. If there is any such rule, it must therefore be found in the case law. Here I am fortunate. In an important paper Mr Richard Buxton Q.C., a Law Commissioner, and about to become Mr Justice Buxton, examined the relevant case law with great care. His conclusion was that, contrary to what was generally believed to be the position, there is no binding authority which holds that the technical rules of evidence are applicable in arbitrations. And there are dicta the other way. That is a view which I respectfully share.

Looking at the matter more broadly it is difficult to see why the technical rules of evidence should apply to arbitrations. A term to that effect cannot be implied in the arbitration agreement. If there is such a rule, it must therefore be a rule of positive law. But what can be the rationale for such a rule? It can only be that the rules of law governing court proceedings and arbitrations must in all respects be the same. But that is a false premise because one of the purposes of arbitration is to avoid the over elaborate procedure of court proceedings and the technical rules of evidence. It is also difficult to see why, in the thousands of domestic arbitrations conducted every year by architects, engineers, surveyors and other lay men, the arbitrators should have to master technical rules of evidence which sometimes baffle the House of Lords. Moreover, in international commercial arbitrations, where the parties have selected London as the venue because of the quality of our international arbitrators and the quality of our substantive law, it is difficult to justify the application of our technical rules of evidence. And where London is imposed on the parties by the decision of the International Chamber of Commerce, or another arbitral institution, the absurdity of applying our technical rules of evidence is even greater. It is true that most institutional rules expressly exclude the rules of evidence. It is also right that the rules of evidence are usually ignored in arbitrations. These are not, however, reasons for maintaining such a rule: these are added reasons for abolishing it. Lastly, it is relevant to note that the technical rules of evidence are under seige even in the court system. The centrepiece of the technical rules of evidence is the hearsay rule. That is the rule which led the House of Lords to conclude in *Myers* that the factory records containing the engine block numbers of cars cannot be used as evidence to identify the cars since it was hearsay evidence. The fact that such evidence was rationally superior in quality to any evidence given by employees did not help. The statutory reversal of the particular decision in *Myers* has left unaffected the impact of the hearsay rule on many classes of rationally superior evidence. Since Mr Buxton's paper was delivered, the Law Commission has convincingly demonstrated that the hearsay rule has no place in a modern court system and recommended that in civil proceedings evidence should not be excluded on the ground that it is hearsay. There is, however, a risk that a court may convert the *communis* error that the technical rules of evidence apply to arbitrations into the *ratio decidendi* of a case. It is the unanimous view of the DAC that the inapplicability of technical rules of evidence to arbitrations should be made plain by legislation. Section 11(1) of the Bill provides: "the tribunal shall determine all procedural matters including the admissibility, relevance, materiality and weight of any evidence." This provision is taken verbatim from Article 19(1) of the Model Law. If it becomes law it ought to remove any suspicion that in splendid isolation England insists on applying the technical rules of evidence to arbitrations. That leaves one loose end under the heading of evidence. The losing party in an arbitration, who can identify no true question of law, frequently applies for leave to appeal under section 1 of the Arbitration Act 1979 on the ground that there was no evidence to support a finding of fact. The argument is that such a question is a question of law under section 1. To the best of my knowledge such submissions never succeed. But does the supposed rule exist? Mustill and Boyd have argued that the rule has not survived the changes introduced by the reforming measure of 1979. I respectfully agree. But this relic from the last century, which was invented to control the decisions of illiterate juries, is still around and provides a convenient basis for attacking arbitrators' decisions on matters of pure fact. The Bill does not expressly deal with this point. One would hope that with the final demise of the idea that arbitrators are bound by the technical rules of evidence this related rule would also perish. But one can imagine counsel arguing that the rule should be adjusted to provide that the issue whether there is relevant evidential material, as opposed to technically admissible evidence, in support of a finding of fact is a question of law. In drafting legislation one cannot, however, guard against every absurd argument. On balance I am confident that, if section 11(1) of the Bill is enacted, it should put an end to all arguments that it is a question of law whether there is material to support a finding of fact.

PROCEDURE

It has been a conventional wisdom of English arbitration law that there is a rule of law requiring an arbitrator to conduct a reference in an adversarial as opposed to inquisitorial fashion unless the parties have agreed otherwise. In obiter dicta Lord Roskill and Lord Donaldson of Lymington have said so. Distinguished authors have also said so. But there appears to be no binding precedent containing a ruling to that effect. Moreover, the powers vested in arbitrators by section 12(1) of the Arbitration Act do not appear to be tied to the adversarial system. It contemplates that the arbitrator will examine the parties to the dispute, and presumably also their witnesses. Moreover, in sweeping terms, section 12(1) provides that the parties shall "do all other things which during the proceedings on the reference the arbitrator ... may require." That hardly looks like a legislative prescription for a rule requiring arbitrators to conform strictly to the adversarial model of the court process.

It seemed to me that the point should be researched. Here too I have been fortunate. I have had the advantage of meticulous historical and legal research done by Claire Blanchard. A good starting point is to ask why English civil court proceedings acquired their distinctive adversarial character. Historically, the general mode of trial was by a judge and jury. The dynamics of a jury trial required one predominantly oral hearing, and involved a relatively passive judge, who left the deployment of the evidence and arguments to the lawyers. There was no reason why this procedural framework should be imposed on arbitration as a matter of law. On the other hand, it is easy to see that historically the habits of the courtroom would often have been carried over into arbitration. Between 1694 and 1889 a number of textbooks were published on arbitration law. These books stated that the procedural powers of arbitrators are wider than those of judges; that arbitrators are not bound by rules of practice; and that arbitrators may in their discretion either examine the parties and their witnesses or leave it to the lawyers. The contemporary case law provides an inconclusive picture. One must, of course, put to one side cases concerning court arbitrators, who were the predecessors of official referees. Clearly, it was only natural that such arbitrators would follow the same procedure as the court from which it received its authority. Subject to this qualification, and subject to the further qualification that arbitrators must always obey the principles of natural justice, there is nothing in the decided cases to show that there was an established rule requiring arbitrators to adopt an adversarial procedure. In 1889 the Arbitration Act provided by paragraph (f) of its First Schedule as follows: "The parties to the reference ... shall, subject to any legal objection, submit to be examined by the arbitrators ... and shall, subject as aforesaid, produce before the arbitrators ... documents within their possession or power respectively which may be required or called for, and do all other things which during the proceedings on the reference the arbitrators or umpire may require." That provision was the forerunner of section 12(1) of the Arbitration Act 1950. It did not impose an adversarial framework on arbitrators. On the contrary, its language contradicts the notion that arbitrators are rigidly tied to adversarial procedures. Given these statutory provisions, it is not surprising that there is no binding precedent requiring arbitrators as a matter of law to follow the adversarial procedure of the White Book. It is realistic, however, to accept that throughout this century, lawyers trained in civil court proceedings in fact allowed that experience to govern arbitral procedure. And it is a fact that arbitrators and lawyers generally assume that they are bound to adopt adversarial procedures.

Under the Model Law system, arbitrators have wide procedural powers to proceed in accordance with adversarial or inquisitorial methods or in accordance with a mixture of both methods. Article 19 provides as follows:

"(1) ... the parties are free to agree on the procedure to be followed by the arbitral tribunal in conducting the proceedings.

(2) Failing such agreement, the arbitral tribunal may, subject to the provisions of this Law, conduct the arbitration in such manner as it considers appropriate."

The DAC unanimously took the view that it would benefit English arbitration to make clear that, subject to the terms of the arbitration agreement and to the overriding principles of natural justice, arbitrators may adopt inquisitorial powers. It does not at all follow that the essentially oral character of contested hearings will be dramatically changed if our proposal is adopted. On the other hand, such a provision may be a useful weapon in the uphill fight against ever longer and costlier hearings. In order to achieve this policy objective, section 11(1) of the Bill in substance enacts the Model Law provision.

Before I leave the subject of procedure, there are two qualifications which ought to be mentioned. First, if an arbitrator exercises inquisitorial powers, the risk of him committing technical misconduct will become greater. After all, it is easier for an arbitrator to hold the scales fairly if matters are left to the parties. But our arbitrators would not be assuming unique burdens. After all, the adversarial system is unknown in half of the industrialised world. Secondly, my impression is that in sectors of the construction industry the idea is gaining ground that arbitrators are entitled to exercise procedural powers contrary to the wishes of the parties. That is wrong. The principle of party autonomy requires the tribunal to respect any agreement of the parties whenever it may be concluded and however informal it may be. It is enshrined in section 11(1) of the Bill.

IMMUNITY OF ARBITRATORS

In a collection of comparative law essays edited by Dr Julian Lew it is demonstrated how widely national laws differ on the immunity of arbitrators. During the sessions of the Working Group, which led to the adoption of the Model Law, Canada proposed that the Model Law should confer immunity from liability for negligence on arbitrators. It proved to be a highly controversial proposal. The draftsmen of the Model Law were seeking common ground. It is therefore not surprising that the Canadian proposal was rejected. In England the question whether under the common law arbitrators are immune from actions in contract or tort alleging breach of a duty of reasonable care is probably still an open one. The question before the DAC was whether a statutory immunity should be conferred on arbitrators. This subject was a very controversial issue in the discussions of the DAC. The opposition to such a provision took various forms, covering outright rejection of the idea as a matter of principle, difficulties of definition and the pragmatic view that in a complex area of the law the matter is best left to development by the courts. By a very narrow majority the DAC recommended that an immunity provision should be included in the draft Bill. It seems to me that the better view might be that, under the common law, arbitrators — because of the judicial character of their duties — already have the benefit of an immunity from liability for negligence. I would also not oppose the enactment of a statutory immunity in favour of arbitrators. On the other hand, I do not regard this aspect as one of the critically important parts of the new legislation.

THE RELATIONSHIP BETWEEN THE COURTS AND ARBITRATION

The supervisory jurisdiction of English courts over arbitration is more extensive than in most countries, notably because of the limited appeal on questions of law and the power to remit. It is certainly more extensive than the supervisory jurisdiction contemplated by the Model Law. Nevertheless, the Subcommittee on Arbitration Law of the Commercial Court Committee, which was chaired by Mr Justice Mustill and reported in October 1985, recorded that in an extensive consultation process it received no representations for a change in the law. Similarly, the Mustill Committee, which was appointed in 1985 and reported in 1989, received no proposals for a change in the law. In its second report of May 1990 the DAC endorsed the earlier decision to maintain the status quo. But eventually it became clear that further thought had to be given to the so-called special categories under section 3 of the Arbitration Act 1979 and to the ambit of the power to remit under section 22 (1) of the Arbitration Act 1950.

SPECIAL CATEGORIES

Section 3 of the Arbitration Act 1979 recognises the contractual freedom of parties under non-domestic arbitration agreements to exclude at any time appeals on questions of English law to the High Court under Sections 1 and 2 of the Arbitration Act 1979. That contractual freedom is restricted by Section 4(1) of the Act. It provides that an exclusion agreement made before the commencement of the arbitration shall have no effect if the question of English law arising under the award or in the course of the reference relates to any of three special categories, namely maritime, insurance and commodities disputes. Section 4(3) of the Act provides that the Secretary of State may either limit or remove these special categories by statutory instrument.

The only justification for the restriction of the freedom of contract of commercial men engaged in shipping, insurance or commodities was that it was needed to protect the standing of our commercial law. In the debates in the House of Lords, Lord Diplock made clear that the special categories were intended to apply for an "experimental period during which it will be possible to see how the section works." After some 14 years it seemed right to review the matter. There was also considerable criticism from commentators. They argue that the standing of our commercial law is secure enough not to need the protection enshrined in the special categories provision. The DAC recently issued a consultation paper in order to invite comment on the desirability of maintaining the special categories. On this occasion that process has been specially targeted on users of the arbitration process. The DAC will want to pay the closest attention to the wishes of the markets.

REMISSION

Section 22(1) of the Arbitration Act 1980 provides in sweeping terms that the court "may from time to time remit the matters referred, or any of them, to the reconsideration of the arbitrator." On the face of it, section 22 (1) creates an entirely open textured discretion permitting a court to order the re-opening of the arbitration in circumstances where an appellate court would not be empowered to order the re-opening of High Court proceedings. Since judicial intrusion in arbitration proceedings should be less extensive than the full appellate process applicable to court proceedings such an unlimited power of remission would be surprising. And the imperative of protecting the finality of awards militates strongly against it. Not surprisingly such a wide power of remission does not exist in most countries. And the draftsmen of the Model Law rejected such a wide power of remission.

A jurisprudence grew up in England which in practice restricted the power of remission to four grounds: (1) error of law on the face of the award which is now of academic importance only; (2) "misconduct" by the arbitrator; (3) the arbitrator's request to correct an admitted mistake; and (4) material fresh evidence discovered after the award. This approach kept the power of remission in tolerable bounds. In the last four years three judgments have been given which significantly expand the power of remission. In *Indian Oil* a judge of the Commercial Court remitted an award to arbitrators to consider a point which at the hearing the applicant's legal representatives consciously and deliberately had decided not to advance. In *King v Thomas McKenna* the Court of Appeal examined the scope of the power to remit. That case also concerned an application for remission as a result of a mistake made by the applicant's lawyer. Lord Donaldson of Lymington gave the leading judgment. Lord Justices Ralph Gibson and Nicholls agreed. Lord Donaldson observed that the jurisdiction was unlimited. Turning to the way in which the jurisdiction is to be exercised, Lord Donaldson stated: "[i]n my judgment the remission jurisdiction extends beyond the four traditional grounds to any cases where, notwithstanding that the arbitrators have acted with complete propriety, due to mishap or misunderstanding some aspect of the dispute which has been the subject of the reference has not been considered and adjudicated upon as fully as or in a manner which the parties were entitled to expect and it would be inequitable to allow any award to take effect without some further consideration by the arbitrator. In so expressing myself I am not seeking to define or limit the jurisdiction or the way in which it should be exercised in particular cases, subject to the vital qualification that it is designed to remedy deviations from the route which the reference should have taken towards its destination (the award) and not to remedy a situation in which, despite having followed an unimpeachable route, the arbitrators have made errors of fact or law and as a result have reached a destination which was not that which the court would have reached. This essential qualification is usually underlined by saying that the jurisdiction to remit is to be invoked, if at all, in relation to procedural mishaps or misunderstandings. This is, however, too narrow a view since the traditional grounds do not necessarily involve procedural errors. The qualification is however of fundamental importance. Parties to arbitration, like parties to litigation, are entitled to expect that the arbitration will be conducted without mishap or misunderstanding and that, subject to the wide discretion enjoyed by the arbitrator, the procedure adopted will be fair and appropriate." These two cases concerned mistakes of a party's lawyers. Given the terms of Lord Donaldson's judgment, logically the next step was to allow remission in the event of a mistake of a party. That is what happened in *Breakbulk Marine v Dateline*. A judge of the Commercial Court decided that he had jurisdiction to remit an award in circumstances where the applicant had failed to find a material letter before the award, although such letter was in no sense fresh evidence.

For my part, I regard this development as a retrograde step. In the field of international commercial arbitration it will be regarded as an excessive judicial intrusion in the arbitral process. I would respectfully suggest that in the light of the conflicting state of the authorities a re-examination of the scope of the power to remit is not precluded. In the meantime the DAC was faced with a difficult problem. On the one hand, there was something to be said for spelling out in the Bill the circumstances in which a court may exercise a power of remission. It is, however, an exceptionally difficult exercise. And the DAC did not want to enshrine the effect of *King v*

Thomas McKenna in a statutory provision. On balance the best course appears to be to retain the language of section 22(1) in the Bill in the hope that developing case law will confine the power to remit more narrowly.

EQUITY CLAUSES

Article 28(3) of the Model Law provides as follows: "[t]he arbitral tribunal shall decide *ex aequo et bono* or as amiable compositeur only if the parties have expressly authorised it to do so." As a broad generalisation that provision mirrors a type of arbitration which is quite common in civil law countries. States in the common law family of nations are usually less comfortable with motions of good faith, and that type of arbitration is less common. It is necessary to consider whether English law at present recognises such a form of arbitration. Equity clauses are common in reinsurance contracts made in England. On the other hand, such clauses have been given only a limited effect. If an equity clause is expressed to involve a power in arbitrators to disregard the rules of substantive law, the orthodox view is that English law does not at present recognise the concept of arbitrators acting in this way. This is, however, a complex subject and it is not impossible that the courts may liberalise our arbitration law. The fact that distinguished commentators such as Sir Michael Kerr, Mr Stewart Boyd Q.C. and Mr V. V. Veeder Q.C. have argued in favour of such a development guarantees that the prospect must be taken seriously. But in our case law the supporting planks for such a development are as yet insecure.

Protagonists of a *lex mercatoria* were encouraged by the important decision of the Court of Appeal in *Deutsche Schachtbau v Ras al Khaimah*

National Oil Co. The case concerned a Swiss arbitration and a Swiss arbitration award. The arbitrators recorded that they were applying "internationally accepted principles of law governing contractual relations." The issue was whether an English court should enforce the award under the New York Convention of 1958. The Court of Appeal held that the award was enforceable. The critical point is that the court held that there was no head of public policy militating against the enforcement of the award. A contrary decision would, of course, have placed England beyond the pale among the signatories of the New York Convention. But the judgments do not tell us what the position would have been if the arbitration had taken place in England and if it had been an English award. In *Home and Overseas Insurance v Mentor Insurance Co (UK) Ltd* the validity of an equity clause was again considered by the Court of Appeal. Lord Justice Parker made clear that he regarded an arbitration clause allowing arbitrators to decide according to good conscience as invalid. Since Lord Justice Balcombe agreed with this judgment I regard Lord Justice Parker's view as the *ratio decidendi* of the case. In a lengthy judgment Lord Justice Lloyd commented on *DST v Rakoil*. He said: "[Counsel for the Plaintiffs] argued that *DST v Rakoil* was concerned only with the enforcement of a foreign award, and that it has no bearing on the present case, where the contract calls for arbitration in London. But why not? If the English courts will enforce a foreign award where the contract is governed by 'a system of law which is not that of England or any other state or is a serious modification of such a law', why should it not enforce an English award in like circumstances? And if it will enforce an English award, why should it not grant a stay? [Counsel] argued that it would be impossible for the court to supervise an arbitration unless it is conducted in accordance with a fixed and recognisable system of law; he even went so far as to submit that the arbitration clause in the present case is not an 'arbitration agreement' at all within the meaning of the Arbitration Acts 1950-1979. It is sufficient to say that I disagree. I would only add (although it cannot affect the argument) that if [he] is right, no ICC arbitration could ever be held with confidence in this country for fear that the arbitrators might adopt the same governing law as they did in *DST v Rakoil*."

I share Lord Justice Lloyd's instinctive reaction. But it seems to me that we are dealing with a complex and fundamental problem which will require further analysis. If a wide equity clause is invalid, it must be because it is subversive of a head of public policy governing arbitrations conducted in England and awards made in England. About that point *DST v Rakoil* can in truth tell us very little. On the other hand, some seventy years after *Czarnikow v Roth Schmidt & Co.*, it may be arguable that there is no longer such a head of public policy. That issue may turn on an historical review of the swing of the pendulum from excessive judicial scrutiny to a better recognition of the imperative of party autonomy. It may be possible for a court to rule that an award made under an equity clause is nevertheless an arbitration award governed by our arbitration statutes. Conceivably, a court might also rule that such an award is not subject to the limited appellate jurisdiction under section 1 of the Arbitration Act 1979. On the other hand, even if a court regarded such a development as beneficial, the court might take the view that it is a matter for reforming legislation.

Uncharacteristically, I will not express any concluded view on the point. But I am firmly of the view that the issues have not yet been comprehensively debated in an English court and that *stare decisis* ought not to preclude a re-examination of this question.

Lastly, if the consultation process shows that there is a widespread desire on the part of commercial men to be able to arbitrate in England under fully effective equity clauses that might be a factor which could conceivably weigh with a court seized with the problem. After all, while our courts do not have the advantage of Brandeis briefs, judges do like to have a window to the real world. And, if such a development is beyond the capacity of the courts, a widespread desire for such a liberalisation of our arbitration system may have to be considered by Parliament.

CONCLUSION

In conclusion I would only say that, while I have sketched some of the policy objectives of the DAC, it will be essential for the DAC to examine the whole Bill in the light of the responses to the consultative process. There will be ample scope for further improvements of the Bill. But something broadly like the Bill represents the best attainable arbitration legislation in England. And it would represent an enormous improvement of our arbitration legislation.

REFERENCES

* This article was originally published as J. Steyn, '1993 Freshfields Arbitration Lecture England's Response to the Model Law of Arbitration', *Arbitration* 60, no. 3 (1994): 184-193.

1 Legislation based on the Model Law has been enacted in Australia,

Bermuda, Bulgaria, Canada, Cyprus, Hong Kong, Mexico, Nigeria, Peru, Russian Federation, Scotland, Tunisia and, within the United States of America, California, Connecticut, Oregon and Texas.

2 The United Kingdom and the Vienna Sales Convention: Another case of splendid isolation? March 1993, Centro di studi e ricerche di diritto comparato e straniero, No. 9. In a paper under the heading The Vienna Sales Convention: A Kind of Esperanto? which was presented at an All Souls seminar in April 1993 I considered the arguments for and against England ratifying the Vienna Sales Convention.

3 2 par. 89.

4 Par. 108.

5 *Ibid.*

6 W. Dale, *Legislative Drafting: A New Approach* (London: Butterworths, 1977), 339.

7 In the course of his lecture 'The Competitive Society', the 1993 Combar lecture given on 18 May 1993, the President of the Board of Trade explained the Government's approach as follows: "We do very well in the arbitration field. But our law, built up over years, is becoming incomprehensible to the people who want to use it. Other countries have updated and clarified their law. Others are in the process of doing so. If we do not do the same, and keep abreast of them, we will lose business. I am pleased to be able to say that, having had the arguments put to me, I was able to agree to my Department taking on responsibility for preparing a new Arbitration Bill. This is being done in full cooperation with the Committee and others with direct interest."

8   [1988] 2 All ER 577.
9   [1993] 3 All ER 897.
10 M. Mustill & S. Boyd, *Commercial Arbitration* (London: LexisNexis Butterworths), 352; F. Russell, A. Walton & M. Vistoria, *Russell on Arbitration* (London: Sweet & Maxwell, 1982), 273.
11 Section 18(1) (b).
12 R. Buxton, 'The Rules of Evidence as Applied to Arbitrations', *Arbitration* 58 (1992): 229-234.
13 [1964] 2 All ER 881.
14 Law Commission., No. 216 (Cm 2321).
15 Mustill & Boyd, *Commercial Arbitration*, 596.
16 In *the Baleares* [1993] 1 Lloyd's L.R. 215, at 228 and 231-232 I explained in some detail why in my view this supposed rule should now be rejected.
17 *Bremer Vulkan v South India Shipping* [1981] AC 909.
18 *Chilton and Another v Saga Holidays PLC* [1987] 1 All ER 841, at 844.
19 Mustill & Boyd, *Commercial Arbitration*.
20 A barrister practising in 4 Essex Court, Temple, London EC4, my former chambers.
21 R. Wilberforce, 'Written Briefs and Oral Advocacy', *Arbitration International* (1989): 348.
22 Cleeve, *The Law of Arbitration* (1694), 18; S. Kyd, *A Treatise on the Law of Awards* (1799), 96; J. Caldwell, *A Treatise on* the *Law of Arbitration* (1825), 53; W. Watson, *A Treatise on* the *Law of Arbitration and Awards* (1846), 117; J. Redman, *A Concise Treatise on the Law of*

Arbitrations and Awards (1903), 88; F. Russel, *A Treatise on the Power and Duty of an Arbitrator and the Law of Submissions and Awards* (1864), 183.

23 The Immunity of Arbitrators, 1990.

24 H. Holzmann & J. Neuhaus, *A Guide to the UNCITRAL Model Law on International Commercial Arbitration: Legislative History and Commentary (*Kluwer Law and Taxation Publishers, 1989), 1148.

25 *Arenson v Arenson* [1977] A. C. 405.

26 House of Lords debates, 15 February 1979, 1477.

27 Article 34(4) of the Model Law does, however contain a narrow point of remission. It reads as follows: 'The court, when asked to set aside an award, may, where appropriate and so requested by a party, suspend the setting aside proceedings for a period of time determined by it in order to give the arbitral tribunal an opportunity to resume the arbitral proceedings or to take such other action as in the arbitral tribunal's opinion will eliminate the grounds for setting aside.'

28 Mustill & Boyd, *Commercial Arbitration*, 549 et seq.

29 *Indian Oil Corporation v Coastel (Bermuda) Ltd* [1990] 2 Lloyd's Rep. 407.

30 [1991] 2 QB 480.

31 491 C-F.

32 19 March 1992; unreported.

33 V. Veeder, 'Remedies Against Arbitral Awards: Setting Aside, Remission and Rehearing', *Yearbook of the Arbitration Institute of the Stockholm Chamber of Commerce* (1993): 125 et seq.

34 *Orion v Belfort* [1962] 2 Lloyd's Rep 257; *Eagle Star Insurance Co. v Yuval Insurance Co.* [1978] 1 Lloyd's Rep. 357; *Home Insurance Co. v Administratia* [1983] 2 Lloyd's Rep. 674; *Overseas Union Insurance Ltd. v A.A. Mutual International Insurance Co.* [1988] 2 Lloyd's Rep. 63.

35 M. Kerr, 'Equity' Arbitration in England, *American Review of International Arbitration* 2 (1992): 377.

36 *Arbitration International* 6 (1990): 122.

37 British Insurance Arbitration Lecture 1992.

38 [1987] 2 Lloyd's Rep. 246.

39 [1987] 2 Lloyd's Rep. 473.

40 [1987] 2 Lloyd's Rep. 489, Col. 1.

41 [1992] 2 K. B. 478.

CHAPTER 2

The Problems Facing Arbitration in the European Union

Karl-Heinz Böckstiegel

Let me first of all say that it is a pleasure indeed to participate here in this Annual Conference of the Chartered Institute of Arbitrators together with a number of distinguished colleagues and friends from the Institute, other arbitration institutions, and the arbitration community at large. My own relation to the Institute is, if I may say so, both an internal and an external one. I have been a Fellow of the Chartered Institute for many years and now, in my function as President of the London Court of International Arbitration, I also cooperate with the Institute as one of the three constituent bodies of the LCIA. I also recall attending very successful meetings and discussions of the Institute, both in London and abroad such as the one in New Orleans last year.

Under the task given to me here to present an introductory paper on the problems to be faced on the future of arbitration in the European Union and in view of the limited time available, obviously all I can do is to mention a few problems that I expect to be of specific relevance in the near future. If any of these are then considered to be of particular interest, they could be raised in detail during the discussion. Even more than any other presentation of this kind, a perspective of the future depends on one's own subjective experience. Let me therefore indicate that my own subjective perspective will, no doubt, be influenced by my own background as a former partner in a law firm and now by my work as a practising arbitrator and other functions in various arbitral institutions as well as finally my academic work at my Chair for International Business Law at Cologne University where international arbitration is one of our continuing major subjects.

MAJOR FUTURE PROCEDURAL AND SUBSTANTIVE ISSUES

As this conference is focusing on the future development of dispute resolution and particularly arbitration in the European Union, let me start with a few remarks on the specific European aspects of our topic. Let us recall that the law and practice of arbitration as its stands today in Europe is the result of a long European tradition in arbitration. The origins go back to Ancient Greece and Ancient Rome; the Middle Ages revived the Roman tradition and developed it further. When a few years ago we celebrated the 600th Anniversary of the University of Cologne, I was able to point out in introducing our colloquium with the German Institute of Arbitration that Albertus Magnus, the famous philosopher and jurist to whom we owe the major initiative for the foundation of the University, was also a famous arbitrator in his time. And more than 200 years after the French Revolution, it may also be interesting to point out that the Revolution not only considered all obligations, statutes, and society as founded on the will of the people and the idea of contract (*'contrat social'*, Jean-Jacques Rousseau); as a consequence arbitration was also considered a *'droit naturel'*. At that time, of course, England already had its Arbitration Act of 1697 to which a number of enactments were added over the years until the new Arbitration Act of 1889 came about. In the same period the new Code of Civil

Procedure was enacted in Germany which included a separate chapter on arbitration. Other states in continental Europe show similar developments. All these traditions will continue to play a role in the present and future development of arbitration in Europe. The growing presence and impact of the European Union in the practical life and legal framework of Europe will also have a continuing influence on the law and practice of arbitration in Europe. Specific aspects of this influence are discussed today in many arbitration proceedings of which we will certainly hear more during this conference. My own most recent experience in this regard was an arbitration which I had to chair in Stockholm and in which issues of European competition law became relevant regarding which the parties, with the consent of the arbitral tribunal, asked the European Commission in Brussels for an opinion which the arbitral tribunal may then have to take into account. However I feel it is very important not to lose sight of the fact that, with the growing interdependence and globalisation of international trade and investment, international arbitration likewise as a worldwide instrument for dispute settlement with its major developments and perspectives will not be limited to a particular region of the world. This is already confirmed by the fact that the major institutions used in international arbitration represented here, namely the ICC and the LCIA, are available and used not only by European business enterprises, but those from all over the world.

Let me now mention a few procedural issues which I believe will be of major relevance in the near future. As no arbitration can take place without prior consent of the parties and party autonomy continues to be the predominant basis for all modern arbitration rules, and for all procedural decisions by the arbitrators, let me first turn to arbitration clauses. As many practitioners of arbitration will confirm, arbitration clauses are often already sources of difficulty once the arbitration starts. Arbitration clauses are often drafted by inexperienced parties or inexperienced lawyers which later can turn out to be disastrous. In this context, the Chartered Institute has a major role to play by its many educational activities to spread knowledge and advice to those participating in international business transactions. While most of the time it is sufficient to include a standard arbitration clause, as suggested by the major international arbitration institutions, in practice one often finds efforts by inexperienced lawyers to amend such clauses to achieve what they consider to be improvements the effects of which they do not foresee but which cause many problems once the arbitration starts. On the other hand, certain clarifications may be suggested by the arbitration institutions, such as the decision on the place of arbitration, the applicable law or, if the parties so wish, exclusion agreements for arbitrations in certain countries.

The often repeated truism that arbitration can only be as good as its arbitrators challenges the selection procedure for arbitrators. With the growing number and diversity of international arbitration cases it will become increasingly difficult to find the best possible arbitrators for each individual case. Probably also in national arbitration, but certainly in international arbitration, it is not sufficient merely to select a good lawyer or a good jurist or a good engineer. If one wants to ensure the specific advantages of arbitration and that the particular arbitration procedure does not become the practice ground for a new arbitrator to the detriment of the interest of the parties, acquaintance with and experience in the particular demands of international arbitration are indispensable. This does not mean that the same old faces must always appear. Educational activities, such as those of the Chartered Institute and other institutions, are highly important in this context. But before somebody can be expected to be an efficient arbitrator, in addition to this education he needs some practical experience in other aspects of arbitral procedures. If the criteria of specific experience and qualification are recommended here for parties, in their selection of arbitrators, they certainly apply even more for arbitrators and particularly chairmen of arbitral tribunals nominated by arbitration institutions. Though for well intended reasons certain arbitral institutions try to implement a policy of appointing more arbitrators from what they consider to be underrepresented regions or countries, I see little room for compromise as far as a very thorough examination of the qualification of such an institution -appointed arbitrator is concerned. Parties, if they have been frustrated by an incompetent arbitrator, will have little understanding for hearing from an institution that it was 'that country's turn' to have an arbitrator appointed. As the number and diversity of cases, parties and arbitrators will grow and contribute their varying traditions for the relationship between party and arbitrator, the independence and ethical behaviour of arbitrators will continue to present important and difficult issues in the foreseeable future.

Regarding the usual options between institutional and ad hoc arbitration, I would expect both options to remain relevant in the future though for good reason probably the present trend will continue that, by far, more arbitration clauses will contemplate institutional arbitration than ad hoc arbitration. With the growing market in international arbitration we may see the establishment of new arbitral institutions seeking their share of the work load. To what extent the arbitration rules of such new institutions will be chosen in the international business contracts of the future remains to be seen. I would expect the well established major institutions of international arbitration to continue to receive the major share of arbitration cases at the international level. The arbitration rules of such bodies are already very similar today including the UNCITRAL Arbitration Rules which primarily exist for ad hoc arbitrations. As these similarities between the arbitration rules are the result of recent updatings on the basis of experience gained in many international cases, I would hope that as little as possible fundamental changes are affected to these rules because predictability and stability for a foreseeable number of years is important to parties when they include arbitration clauses in contracts which may run for a lengthy period and lead, perhaps, to disputes at a much later stage.

Regarding state arbitration laws, there is still not only room but often a need for improvement in many countries. Present efforts to adopt the UNCITRAL Model Law in England and in Germany are examples, while a number of other European countries has recently introduced arbitration laws. The experience in some countries indicates that the adoption of a new national arbitration law, or the ratification of the New York Convention, are of little practical value so long as the court system and the judges do not implement the new legal framework and accept the limitations of national courts in relation to arbitration. In the former socialist countries in Eastern

Europe the creation of an efficient court system may still take some time to establish which on the one hand leaves arbitration as the only alternative for effective dispute resolution and on the other hand leaves question marks regarding the availability of necessary court support for arbitration.

Regarding the practice of international arbitration proceedings, I would expect also here a growing harmonisation to take place as more and more parties, lawyers, and arbitrators share common experiences in arbitration publications, meetings, and practical cases. Also, in the future, a good arbitration procedure will have to be as much as possible tailor-made to the agreed wishes and needs of the parties concerned. And insofar as no specific agreed procedural decisions are reached, predictability of the procedure for the parties and their lawyers must be a major concern for the arbitration institutions and the arbitrators so that the parties can prepare themselves early enough to give a full presentation of their respective cases.

The method how this is done may differ widely depending on the parties, lawyers, and arbitrators involved. A procedure in which all parties, lawyers, and arbitrators come from a common law background may vary widely to one where all come from a civil law background. Where such different backgrounds exist, compromises will often be necessary, particularly regarding the presentation of submissions, written and witness evidence; the preparation, conduct and role of the oral hearing; and the more, or less active, role of the arbitrators during that hearing. Especially in these inter-system international arbitrations, it is important that the arbitrators at a very early stage of the proceedings clarify, in detail, the 'rules of the game' to avoid misunderstandings and surprises for the parties and their lawyers. If, as we invariably hear, one of the reasons to prefer arbitration to national courts is a faster procedure to reach the final award, more effort by the parties, the arbitrators, and the institutions are needed to speed-up the procedure. As 'lean production' and 'lean management' have permitted certain improvements, in appropriate cases flexible tailormade 'lean arbitration' or 'fast track arbitration' may more often then hitherto replace normal routine procedures while still remaining in the area of real arbitration, and not turning into alternative dispute settlement. After I had mentioned 'lean arbitration', as one of the future concepts in my presentation to the Centenary Conference of the LCIA last September, I noted with interest that this term has now been picked-up in a recent article in the journal *Arbitration International* in more detail.

The issue of multi-party arbitration will continue to be a challenge in the future in spite of the many meetings and publications that have dealt with this topic, because satisfactory procedural arrangements have not yet been found for general application. They will have to be found in the future in view of the growing number of multi-party disputes. As there is a variety of multi-party situations, no single solution presents itself. Respective provisions may be made either by parties in their arbitration clauses, or by amendments to present arbitration rules, or by specific procedural arrangements at the onset of a case if agreement is achievable. As I have experienced myself, when I had to chair a recent arbitration, even if the parties have agreed to join in a multi-party procedure, very little guidance has been developed, so far, as to how to prepare and conduct such a procedure. Like it or not, abuse of procedural options, as well as manipulated delay and disruption of the procedure, will continue to remain a common feature of international arbitration with the growing diversity of legal and cultural backgrounds involved in international arbitration exacerbated, perhaps, by present difficult economic conditions. More effective means will have to be found, in the near future, to deal with this development if the effectiveness of international arbitration is to be maintained. A very complete study of this phenomenon was presented at the Stockholm ICCA Congress but often national laws and arbitration rules still lack effective means to prevent such abuse. I also feel that the chances and legal framework for settlements between the parties before and during arbitration proceedings can and should be improved. There is still great diversity between national laws as to what role arbitrators may play with regard to agreed settlements. While in some jurisdictions arbitrators take an active role, and more than half of all arbitration procedures are finally settled by agreement between the parties, other jurisdictions forbid or at least reduce the role of the arbitrator in this regard. Though there can be no doubt as to the arbitrator finally having to decide on the basis of the facts and the law, and not entering into the role of conciliator or mediator, it would often be in the interest of the parties both for the present dispute and particularly for their future business relations if, with the help of the arbitral tribunal, an agreed settlement could be reached. It may therefore be desirable to clarify and facilitate that option, either in national laws or in arbitration rules.

Future challenges in international arbitration may also arise as either the traditional fields develop further or new fields come up. I would expect in the future international trade and international investment still to contribute the greatest number of cases to international arbitration. Indeed, with the general growth of international trade and international investment despite the recession in many countries, it would seem that the number of arbitration clauses and arbitration cases in these well defined areas will still increase in the future. Increasingly state and state institutions can be expected to be involved in international commercial arbitration because of active participation in an increasing number of international contracts and international business transactions.

In the former socialist countries the state monopoly on foreign trade has disappeared; the actual number of arbitrations, accordingly may well increase as a reliable system of courts with experience in commercial matters may not yet be available: and as legal and economic changes lead to new contracts by arrangements and possible disputes. For the present, I would not regard the creation of the United Nations Compensation Commission in Geneva for claims against Iraq as an arbitration machinery as final decisions rest with the United Nations Security Council. But the experience of the almost 4,000 cases before the Iran-United States Claims Tribunal in The Hague, with a procedure based on the UNCITRAL Arbitration Rules, shows that even in politically delicate and highly complicated relationships arbitration may be a valuable option.

As to likely areas of arbitration, it can already be seen that contracts and disputes arising from the supply of hardware material, the construction business, and the erection of large plants are decreasing in comparison to contracts and disputes concerning services. The extension of the General

Agreement on Tariffs and Trade (GATT) to services is an indication of this shift in international business relations which will also have its effect on the number and types of international arbitration cases. In this context it might be expected that areas like the transfer of technology, genetic engineering, entertainment and sports, sponsoring and similar fields will be more represented in arbitration cases than before. And it is not accidental that recently the first international arbitration of the space industry was held in London. Arbitration is not only used regularly in the shipping and aviation industry but is increasingly used for the settlement of disputes regarding space activities. The trend in moving international arbitration to new areas is also illustrated by the growing use of arbitration clauses in international loan agreements and in international financial transactions.

New challenges and options for international dispute resolution can also be expected from the present growing interest in the use of Alternative Dispute Resolution (ADR). Many of the missionary presentations for ADR that we see increasingly in publications and conferences seem to forget, or overlook, that negotiations, conciliation, and mediation have been used for decades by companies and lawyers in international business relations to settle their disputes, either before or during proceedings before national courts or arbitral tribunals. Stemming from the United Sates, various kinds of ADR are getting wider attention and use both at the national and international level. Specific institutions for ADR have been created supported by their own procedural rules. My own experience as a mediator in several cases confirm that in appropriate cases ADR may indeed be an efficient and preferable method of dispute settlement. Fresh developments in the field of ADR creates new practical and legal issues regarding arbitration which will need more detailed examination in the future.

FINAL PERSPECTIVE

I now close with a few final remarks. The future development of arbitration in Europe will be highly conditioned by future changes in society at large. In spite of efforts to collect and evaluate objective criteria for future development, there remains a wide range of speculation. My own first prediction is that international arbitration will become more international in the future. I hope and expect that national laws applicable to the procedure and substance of international arbitration will become less parochial and more internationally harmonised. And with the growing number of international arbitration cases and the increase in the lawyers and arbitrators involved in international arbitration, there should be less dependency on specific national particularities with a more open and flexible approach towards the specific needs of disputants in the European and international spheres.

Regarding the legal framework, both changes are desirable in certain national laws whilst I would not foresee, or suggest, major changes in the existing arbitration rules of the major institutions active in international commercial arbitration. Such arbitration rules have already recently been adapted to the modern needs of international trade and investment so that, now, stability and predictability for the parties should be maintained.

As arbitration proceedings can only be as good and efficient as the people involved, efforts to provide for the education of newcomers and continuing exchanges between established practitioners are highly important. The many efforts in this context of the Chartered Institute of Arbitrators, as well as other institutions such as the ICC and the LCIA, are most valuable. But they could be rendered more efficient for the development of international arbitration if the better coordination of meetings and seminars could be achieved in the future.

* This article was originally published as K. Böckstiegel, 'The Problems Facing Arbitration in the European Union', *Arbitration* 61, no. 3 (1995): 191-195.

CHAPTER 2

The Arbitration Act 1996 and its Effect on International Arbitration

Lord Saville

The Arbitration Bill received the Royal Assent on 17th June and is now the Arbitration Act 1996. The new Act is not yet in force but during the course of its progress through Parliament, the Government gave an assurance that it would use its best endeavours to try and ensure that at least most of the provisions of the Act would be brought into force at the beginning of next year. This commitment, which I wholly support, means that those concerned with institutional rules for arbitrations as well as those concerned with the rules of court for arbitration matters have had to work hard and fast to meet that deadline. The work of recasting the relevant Rules of Court is well underway. It involves completely rewriting Order 73 so as to provide Court rules that complement the new Act. With great assistance from, in particular, His Honour Judge Diamond QC, we have prepared and published for consultation entirely new draft Rules of Court to deal with arbitration applications to the Court. I have, of course, had much in mind Lord Woolf's proposals for civil justice reforms, so as to ensure so far as is possible that we can devise court rules and procedures for arbitral matters that are consistent with his overall suggestions for civil justice. The new Woolf proposals will not be ready to be brought into force at the beginning of next year, and since I am anxious that the Arbitration Act comes into force without further delay it will not be possible to include them as part of his draft scheme, but what we are doing is our best to ensure that our new arbitration rules tackle delay and expense in the same way, so that they can be readily adapted when the Woolf proposals are implemented. I want a court system for dealing with arbitration matters which complements the philosophy behind the Arbitration Act; a subject to which I shall return a little later in this address. Section 105 of the Act contains provisions enabling arbitration court work to be allocated among different courts, since it seemed to us that there was at least some work which could be properly given to County Courts, including the Patents County Court, thus avoiding the expense of a High Court proceeding whenever possible. However, this in turn means that we have to design and draft an allocation system. We are also working on transitional provisions which we hope to publish very shortly, since there are a number of cases where these will be necessary; though of course the basic starting point for the new Act is that it will apply to arbitral proceedings commenced after the Act comes into force, even if the agreement to arbitrate is made earlier. This was the method adopted for the Arbitration Acts 1889 and 1934 and avoids as far as possible having two parallel regimes operating indefinitely into the future. In July we published a paper asking for public responses to some questions we raised about these and other matters. We have considered the responses and made a number of recommendations to the Government. In the next few weeks the results of all our endeavours should be published; and at present I am confident that we can get the new Act up and running by January 1997. This talk is focused on the question whether the new Act significantly affects international arbitration in this country. My short answer is that I very much hope it does, by improving and clarifying the major elements of our arbitration law, as well as making some changes in that law. To give a longer answer I would like to explain how the Act came into being, and what specifically we have tried to achieve.

London is the acknowledged centre for international arbitration. Our arbitration laws have been developed over many years and provide a complete code available for those engaged in international trade and commerce who are minded to use arbitration as their chosen method of dispute resolution. In addition we have a highly developed system of commercial law which can also be chosen by the parties as the law to be applied by the arbitrators in deciding the substantive rights and obligations of the parties. We have built up an unrivalled reputation for the fair and impartial resolution of international trade and commercial disputes. We cannot, however, rest on our laurels. In 1985 the United Nations Commission on International Trade Law (UNCITRAL) adopted a Model Law on International Commercial Arbitration. This in turn led a number of countries to consider whether they should adopt this Model Law in place of their own arbitral laws and procedures. In this country, that task was undertaken by a Committee of the Department of Trade and Industry chaired by Lord Mustill. That Committee produced a Report in 1989. This Report advised against adopting the Model Law in place of our existing laws. The Report pointed out that while there were a number of things in the Model Law which we could usefully adopt, in other respects the Model Law contained provisions which were considered to be inferior to our existing laws. The Model Law was also not a complete Code and would have in any event to be supplemented. In my view the reasons the Committee gave for not adopting the Model Law wholesale are convincing. However, this Committee did not simply produce this negative conclusion. Instead it pointed to what was undoubtedly a defect in our existing law. This was not a defect of quality or content; but one of presentation. Our law had built up over a very long time indeed. In the main the developments came from cases, but in addition, from as early as 1698, Parliament had passed legislation dealing with the law of arbitration. To a large degree this legislation was reactive in nature, putting right perceived defects and deficiencies in the case law. Thus it was not easy for someone new to English arbitration to discover the law, which was spread around a hotchpotch of statutes and countless cases. This meant that arbitration often involved unnecessary expense, in the form of employing lawyers who were expert in intricacies of our arbitration law and where to find it. I think that there is little doubt that the position of London as the leading centre for international arbitration was being put at risk by the fact that our arbitration laws were not easily accessible. What Michael Mustill's Committee did was to address this problem by making a number of proposals. What in effect these amounted to was a recommendation that we should replace the hotchpotch with a new statute, comprising "a statement in statutory form of the more important principles of the English law of arbitration, statutory (and to the extent practicable) common law." The Committee also recommended that the statute should be set out in a logical order, and expressed in language which is sufficiently clear and free from technicalities to be readily comprehensible to the layman; that it should apply to both domestic and international arbitrations; that it should not be limited to the subject matter of the Model Law, but that it should, so far as is possible, have the same structure and language as the Model Law. These recommendations were made in 1989. After this the Department of Trade and Industry took over the task of preparing a Bill and this was produced in February 1994. It was a great disappointment. What the draftsman had done was to attempt to consolidate the existing statutes i.e., the Arbitration Act 1950, the Arbitration Act 1975 and the Arbitration Act 1979. The result was to perpetuate the defects in these statutes and to compound the very problems that had led Michael Mustill and his Committee to make the recommendations to which I have referred. The Bill, not unnaturally, was not well received. However, it produced one great benefit, in the form of a very large number of carefully considered responses, containing the most helpful suggestions, while pointing out, more or less politely, that the draft signally failed to incorporate any of them or to carry out the proposals of the Mustill Committee. It was at this point, in the late autumn of 1994, that I took over the chairmanship of the Committee from Johan Steyn who had in turn taken over from Michael Mustill. I started with great advantages not enjoyed by my predecessors. We had the DTI draft and most importantly the responses to that draft carefully and comprehensively analysed by Toby Landau, a barrister from my old Chambers who has since played a vital part in what has happened. In addition I had the advantage of another draft Bill, prepared earlier by Basil Eckersley for what has been known as the 'Private Group' whose leading light was Arthur Marriott. This draft had been put on the back burner while the DTI draft was being prepared, but it provided me with another approach to the problem. I should at this point like to pay tribute to Arthur Marriott. He it was above all who kept alive the idea that we could and should improve upon our existing legislation, and whose wise advice and constant support for what I then set out to do proved quite invaluable.

In the circumstances as I found them when I became Chairman of the Departmental Advisory Committee it seemed to me that what had to be done was obvious. The DTI draft was not acceptable, but the responses showed the way to go. What was needed was an entirely new start. At the end of January 1995 the Committee agreed with this view. The Committee also agreed that the best way to proceed was to produce a draft ourselves, not in any way as a final draft Bill, but to illustrate the sort of Bill that we would like to see. Accordingly, I retired from judging for three weeks in March 1995 and with considerable assistance from, in particular, Toby Landau, prepared what has since become known as the 'illustrative draft'. This we published in April 1995 as part of an Interim Report. We then had our next stroke of good luck, for Geoffrey Sellers, one of the most respected of Parliamentary draftsmen, agreed to turn our efforts into a Bill and to do so in a matter of weeks. It was our good fortune that we had with Geoffrey a draftsman who was ready and willing to take our draft as the basis for a Bill, and with his extraordinary skill, to alter and improve it in consultation with us. It is those last words which are of great significance, because Geoffrey was prepared to take and build on our efforts, rather than ignoring them, which had been the experience in the past. He was a delight to work with and the result was a draft Bill which we published at a Conference held at King's College London, in July last year. That Conference showed that we seemed to be on the right track, though again a number of points of detail were raised then as well as over the next two months while we were seeking responses to what we had done. In late September we considered these responses. There followed a full Committee meeting at which a number of the most important points were discussed and a number of decisions made. After that it was a matter of detailed drafting and drafting conferences which I had with Parliamentary Counsel, accompanied always by Toby Landau, without whom there is no doubt that we would never have got to where we are. We went through numerous drafts, always under pressure of time, because I had set an ambitious timetable in March to produce a Bill that could be introduced by the end of my first year as Chairman of the Committee. Too long had gone by since the UNCITRAL Model Law and the Mustill Report to allow for any further avoidable delay.

We just succeeded, and in December 1995 the draft Bill was introduced in the House of Lords. Those days in December were fairly hectic, for I was judging during the day and working on the draft in the evenings and weekends. Over Christmas we were able to stand back a little; and read and reflect on what we had done. So did others, with the result that when we wrote a Report on the Bill in January and February 1996 we made a number of recommendations for changes to the Bill. I am told that this is not unusual, and that the amendments made during the course of a Bill's progress through Parliament can often run into the hundreds. We got by with only a few; some prompted by the debates in the House of Lords;

while others were the result of further and better thoughts on our part or the result of consultation with others. In due course we shall be publishing a further Report, which will explain in detail the changes we made to the original Bill and why we made them.

We have tried to do a number of things. The basic task we set ourselves at the beginning of 1995 was to try and restate the law of arbitration in simple English, adopting a logical format which proceeds from arbitration agreements through the appointment of arbitrators, the conduct of the proceedings, to awards, so that it is easy to turn to that part of the legislation which is of particular interest to the reader. Where helpful, we have inserted cross-references to other Sections, so as to put the reader on notice that these may have to be considered. For example, where the Act deals with challenges to the jurisdiction of the arbitrators, we remind the reader that the right to challenge jurisdiction may be lost by failure to take the point in due time. This change in presentation will I hope have a significant beneficial effect on international arbitration here. Unlike the past, it is now possible to read the legislation and to learn about what arbitrating in this country entails. Indeed, the three principles which we have set out in section 1 of the Act, and to which I shall return shortly, seek to encapsulate the basis of our law of arbitration. A great deal of time and effort was spent in an attempt to depart from the usual legalese of statutes of this kind and instead to speak in plain English. You will not find any Latin, dog or otherwise, in the Act. We have also, for example, avoided the word 'taxation' when talking about the costs of the arbitration, since to someone who is not an English lawyer, this is a baffling expression. My information is that many from abroad who were considering arbitrating here were put off by their inability to discover precisely what it entailed. I hope our efforts will go some way towards providing such people with a clear exposition of our law of arbitration. They were also put off by some parts of that law.

The power of the Court to order security for costs is a prime example. Under our existing law, the arbitral tribunal does not have power to award security for costs unless the parties have expressly agreed otherwise. In 1934 the Court was given power to award security for costs in arbitrations. The theory behind this was that it is the duty of the tribunal to decide the substantive merits of the dispute referred to it and that it would not be performing its duty if it made an order for the provision of security, since the merits of the dispute could be determined without such an order. I do not subscribe to this theory, which seems to me to entail a very narrow view of arbitration. When the parties choose this form of dispute resolution, they are indeed agreeing that arbitration will be the means to resolve their dispute. To my mind, though, it does not follow that the dispute will necessarily be decided on its merits, but rather that it will be resolved by the application of the agreed arbitral process. If one party then fails to comply with that process, then it seems to me that it is entirely within what the parties have agreed that the tribunal can resolve the dispute on the basis of that failure, given that it is serious enough to carry this consequence. The theory has, in fact, already been abandoned by Parliament, which has legislated to give arbitral tribunals power to strike out claims for want of prosecution. Such a power (now to be found in the new Act) is clearly inconsistent with the notion that the tribunal's only job is to decide the merits of the dispute. The *Ken-Ren* decision in the House of Lords (reaffirming that the Courts could award security for costs in international arbitrations) was met with widespread dismay by those in the international arbitration community who had at heart the desire to promote this country as a world centre for arbitration. It was viewed as confirming the widely held suspicion that the English Courts were only too ready to interfere in the arbitral process and to impose their own *dictat* on the parties, notwithstanding the agreement of those parties to arbitrate rather than litigate. We have accordingly removed the power of the court to award security for costs in arbitrations. We did consider whether to exclude security for costs altogether from arbitrations, but concluded that the best option was to give the power to award security to the arbitral tribunal, though of course the parties can agree that their tribunal shall not have this power. In our view, the power to award security is a useful tool, which if properly exercised helps to do justice. It will be noted that in the Act there are no specific principles laid down to guide arbitrators on how to exercise this particular power, save that we have made expressly clear that the fact that the claimant or counterclaimant comes from abroad is not a ground for ordering security. To our minds, the fact that the courts could order a foreign claimant to provide security for costs in an arbitration was doubly off-putting; for not only was the court interfering in the arbitral process, but it was doing so in effect by discriminating against foreigners arbitrating their claims here. Now those from abroad arbitrating under the new Act will not suffer from this disadvantage. We did consider giving some general guidance to arbitrators over awarding security for costs. Indeed the Bill as introduced into Parliament enjoined them to apply the same principles as the Court. However, on reflection we decided that this was simply not 'user friendly' especially to people from abroad, who would not have ready access to the many cases dealing with this topic, or even to the Supreme Court Practice where these are summarised. We then considered whether to set out some specific principles in the Act; but really found this impossible to do. For example, the impecuniosity of a claimant corporation is generally regarded as the prime example of a case where security should be ordered. However, this is not necessarily always the case. In the end, it seemed to us to be sufficient to rely on the general duty of the tribunal set out in Section 33 to exercise this (and all its other powers) fairly and impartially. Thus, in a case where an order for security is sought, on the basis of the impecuniosity of the claimant, the tribunal will have to decide whether this is the fair (i.e., just) thing to do. If, for example, it can be shown that the respondent contracted with the claimant in the knowledge that the claimant had little or no money, the tribunal might well conclude that it would not be fair to stifle the claim by making an order for security, since the respondent should be taken to have accepted the risk of irrecoverable costs, having selected an impecunious claimant as a party to his contract. Each case will depend on its own circumstances; and as in any other aspect of an arbitration, upon the skill and wisdom of the arbitrators in striving to reach a just result by just means.

In this context I would like to mention another change which we have introduced and which to my mind could usefully be introduced into our Courts. This is in Section 65 of the Act, which provides as follows: "(1)

Unless otherwise agreed by the parties, the tribunal may direct that the recoverable costs of the arbitration, or of any part of the arbitral proceedings, shall be limited to a specified amount. (2) Any direction may be made or varied at any stage, but this must be done sufficiently in advance of the incurring of costs to which it relates, or the taking of any steps in the proceedings which may be affected by it, for the limit to be taken into account."

This is power to fix a cap on the costs recoverable from the other side. A party can continue to spend as much as it likes, but cannot blackmail the other party into giving up or making an unfavourable compromise by the fear of being subjected to a costs order which they could not sustain. To my mind this is a most useful power for arbitrators performing their Section 33 duty to adopt procedures suitable to the circumstances of the particular case, "avoiding unnecessary delay or expense." This particular power is also a good demonstration of something else we are trying to bring about through the new Act; namely to clarify the role of arbitrators. All too often in the past arbitrators have seen their role as reactive i.e., as responsive only to initiatives of the parties in an adversarial contest, with only the added task of announcing the result at the end of the day. We have tried to dispel this idea, and instead to make clear that (in the absence of agreement to the contrary by the parties) it is the duty of arbitrators to manage and control the arbitral process; and indeed that an adversarial as opposed to an inquisitorial or other process is only one of the options open to them in performing that management task. This duty is now expressly laid on the tribunal by Section 33 of the new Act. I cannot emphasise too strongly that part of that duty is, as I have already mentioned, to avoid unnecessary delay and expense. Thus in the context of the power to cap the recoverable costs, the tribunal will have to get a proper grip of the case from the outset, so as to be in a proper position to assess whether a cap should be imposed and if so in what amount. They will need to get such a grip anyway in order to perform their general Section 33 duty. In other words, arbitrators must stop thinking of themselves as only referees in an adversarial match between the opposing parties, and as only responsible for seeing that the players play by the rules and for announcing the result at the end of the day. They must be managers of the arbitration. In the context of litigation, this is the path which Lord Woolf wants to follow. In the context of arbitration it is much easier to follow that path; for there is an ad hoc tribunal which exists for the purpose of resolving the particular dispute, so that it is much easier for the tribunal to adopt procedures suitable for the resolution of that dispute. This indeed is one of the chief advantages of arbitration. It is also one of the features of the body of international jurisprudence which has grown up in recent years relating to the proper conduct of such arbitrations, as Sir Michael Kerr pointed out in a recent lecture. I hope the new Act reflects internationally accepted thinking on this subject.

Another feature of our existing law which has caused disquiet abroad and which many regard as detracting from arbitrating here is the ability to seek leave to appeal to the Court from the substantive award of the arbitral tribunal. What is said is that to allow an appeal of this kind is to frustrate the agreement of the parties to resolve their disputes by arbitration, since the result of a successful appeal is to substitute a court resolution for an arbitral resolution. There is substance in this view. Indeed we considered whether to recommend the abolition of any right of appeal on the substantive merits of the dispute. In the end we decided not to do so. However, we have further limited the right of appeal (unless of course the parties have agreed that there can be an appeal) so that, in my view at least, it can be regarded as a supportive rather than an interfering function of the court. In this connection we have made it clear that an appeal in this country will only be considered on a point of English law. A point of English law does not, under the new Act, include the question whether there was sufficient evidence to support the findings of fact. This is achieved in the sub-section which only allows the court to give leave to appeal if satisfied that "on the basis of the findings of fact in the award" the decision of the tribunal was obviously wrong or, if the point is one of general public importance, at least open to serious doubt; see Section 69(3)(c) of the new Act. Thus we have, as I trust, blocked off attempts (not infrequently made) to seek rehearings in Court of the evidence put before the arbitral tribunal by dressing up the application as one concerning a point of law. In addition we have required the Court, before granting leave to appeal, to be satisfied: "[t]hat, despite the agreement of the parties to resolve the matter by arbitration, it is just and proper in all the circumstances for the court to determine the question." We have thus in the new Act not only spelt out our understanding of what are presently called "the *Nema* guidelines" for appeals under the 1979 Act, but made further limitations on appeals as well. As to the former, those from abroad reading the 1979 Act (and indeed Lord Goff when a first instance judge) could be forgiven for thinking that that Act gave an unlimited right of appeal to the

Courts. *The Nema* taught us that this was not so; but the further lesson was that the 1979 Act could hardly be described as user friendly, since it took the House of Lords to explain what it really meant and to correct the view of as eminent a judge as Lord Goff! The new Act makes clear that the right to appeal only arises in cases where it is apparent that the tribunal has erred (or in cases of general public importance), where its conclusion is at least open to serious doubt. By this means it seems to me that it is well arguable that this limited right of appeal can properly be described as supportive of the arbitral process. Where the parties have agreed that their dispute will be resolved in accordance with English law, and the tribunal then purports to reach an answer which is not in accordance with English law, it can be said with some force that unless the Courts correct this error, the tribunal itself will have failed to carry out the bargain of the parties. In addition the Court will have to apply the provision I have just quoted; and will, as I trust, use this provision so that appeals from arbitration awards on questions of law arising out of the substantive dispute between the parties will be very much the exception rather than the rule.

I now turn to a different topic. In the context of international arbitration it is in my view vital that the parties (and indeed their arbitral tribunal) know in advance which courts in which countries have jurisdiction over the arbitration. There are some countries which seek to claim jurisdiction over arbitrations which really have little or nothing to do with the arbitral process in question, sometimes on the grounds only that one of the parties is a national of the country concerned, or that it is their law which is to apply to determine the substantive dispute between the parties. Under our existing law there is some doubt about the application of the English law of arbitration. For example, if the parties agree to hold their arbitration in Paris but according to English law, which Courts have jurisdiction over the arbitration? Is it the French Courts, since after all France is where the arbitration is, or is it the English Courts, since the parties have chosen English law? Is it both, which would give rise to difficult problems over competing jurisdictions? When the parties chose English law, does this mean the law to govern the resolution of their dispute, or the law to govern the meaning and effect of their agreement to arbitrate, or the law to govern the procedures of the arbitration? My very first observation to the Committee at the first meeting I chaired in January 1995 was that the Bill should make it clear to what arbitrations it applied. In the course of preparing the Bill we sought to grapple with the problem of drafting a 'scope of application' clause. This was a task which we found to be exceptionally difficult. The version we published with the Bill in December last year was, I think, a masterpiece of sophistication, because it in fact dodged all the really difficult points while at the same time pointing (we hoped) the way to where we wanted (perhaps) to go. It was, in fact, over-sophisticated, as we realised after a meeting at the International Chamber of Commerce last winter in Paris with a number of those interested in this topic from the international point of view. We came back and had another go, which is the form you will find in Section 2 of the Act, for our Parliamentary Draftsman accepted our efforts, which are based, as you will see, on the concept of the 'seat' of the arbitration. The 'seat' of an arbitration is a legal concept accepted internationally. It means in effect the juridical place of the arbitration, or in other words, where the arbitration will be regarded in law as taking place. The 'seat' will often be the place where the arbitration actually takes place, but this is not necessarily so. A number of international arbitrations may take place in a number of different countries, but only one country will be the 'seat.' How the 'seat' is to be ascertained is set out in Section 3 of the Act.

Section 2(1) states the basic rule. If the seat of the arbitration is here, then Part 1 of the Act (i.e., all the rules and principles relevant to arbitral proceedings generally) applies to that arbitration. Section 2(2) has to go further than this, for otherwise we would be in breach of our Treaty obligations under the New York Convention, for these obligations extend to any arbitration, whether or not it has a seat and whether or not the seat is here. Thus this provision applies the parts of the Act concerned with Convention matters to any arbitration, wherever its seat and even if there is as yet no seat. For example, under the Convention, which has been part of our law since 1975, we have agreed that if someone starts legal proceedings notwithstanding an agreement to arbitrate, those legal proceedings will be stayed unless there is something fundamentally wrong with the agreement to arbitrate. Thus this sub-section gives the court power to stay the legal proceedings; and it does not matter that the seat of the arbitration is elsewhere or even if there is no seat. Sub-Section 3 deals with those parts of the Act which ought, at least in some circumstances, to be made available in support of arbitral proceedings where the seat is abroad i.e., the attendance of witnesses who are in this country and similar matters. We have, however, made clear that these powers are not to be exercised automatically by the court, but only if appropriate, so as to avoid the risk of competing jurisdictions. Sub-Section 4 covers cases where no seat has yet been designated but where there is a connection with this country which makes it appropriate for the court to exercise a power. A good example would be a case where there is a breakdown in the appointment procedure in a case where, if the arbitration got under way, it would be likely that the seat would be in this country. Sub-Section 5 is necessary because of the way English law has developed. The problem arises in cases where there is no seat or the seat is abroad. Without this provision, if the parties had agreed that English law was the law applicable to their arbitration agreement, that law would be the English common law, not the law contained in this Act or its predecessors, for Section 2(1) would not apply and the other sub-sections have limited scope. Thus it could be argued that 'separability' of the arbitration agreement from its accompanying 'substantive' agreement (Section 7), or the effect of the death of a party were different from the rules expressed in the Act. This would certainly be the case for the death of a party, since the common law is that an arbitration agreement is discharged by such a death. For many years this common law rule has been reversed by statute, but since we are repealing these statutes, the common law would revive unless we had put in this provision. I have mentioned Section 2 because it is obviously of great importance in an international context. We were very anxious not to seek to arrogate to this country a jurisdiction over cases which properly belong to another forum. In my view it would not be right for this country to claim a jurisdiction over arbitrations abroad, since by choosing a foreign seat the parties must be taken to have chosen such laws of that place as apply to arbitrations taking place there. Thus the fact that the parties have chosen English law as the law to govern their substantive rights and obligations would not lead without more to the application of the Arbitration Act, unless of course the seat was here or one of the special circumstances I have outlined brings other parts of Section 2 into operation.

So far as arbitral institutions are concerned, I hope the Act will be regarded as an enfranchising measure. Arbitral institutions play a very significant role indeed in both domestic and international arbitrations. They are expressly recognised in the Act, their appellate functions (where they have them) are, I hope, given due weight, and we have provided them with a degree of immunity. Above all, we have provided arbitral institutions, and others in a similar position, with the freedom to make best use of the advantages of arbitration as a system of dispute resolution, by enshrining party autonomy as the second basic principle in Section 1 of the Act. This second principle states: '[t]he parties should be free to agree how their disputes should be resolved, subject only to such safeguards as are necessary in the public interest." Since the rules of arbitral institutions come into play by forming part of the agreement between the parties who incorporate them in their contracts or otherwise agree to employ them, the opportunity is there to formulate rules which really are adaptable to the particular case, rather than court procedures, which by and large have to be framed to suit all-comers. In Section 33 we have expressly stipulated that the tribunal must seek to do this. Slavish adherence to a set method of procedure, whatever the case or issue, is calculated to add to delay and expense and thus inconsistent with the first of the principles set out in Section 1 of the Act. I shall return to that principle shortly.

The Mustill Committee also recommended that the new Statute should be limited to those principles whose existence and effect were uncontroversial. This, however, has proved to be a recommendation that we have more honoured in the breach than in the observance. Even the basic proposal of the Mustill Committee, not to adopt wholesale the Model Law, remained a matter of controversy, and indeed for some still does so. We have had to make a number of decisions in the course of preparing this Act, weighing up the arguments as carefully as we could but finally reaching a view, often a compromise between positions which, at their extreme, were irreconcilable. The reason we were able to reach a compromise view was that all concerned on my Committee were at one in concluding that new legislation was vital, to the extent that they were prepared to compromise rather than obstruct progress.

Those who read the Act will note that over and over again we have adopted the principles set out in the Model Law, often using the language of that Model. Thus although the Act is designed to be used for all kinds of arbitrations, both domestic and international, we trust it reflects generally accepted international rules and principles and will not only maintain but enhance the reputation of this country as one offering to the international community a first class service in the resolution of disputes by arbitration.

I have already mentioned the second of the general principles set out in Section 1 of the Act, namely the principle of party autonomy. The three principles in Section 1 are an attempt to set out what we considered to be the philosophy on which we have based what we have done. The first principle seeks to define the object of arbitration as being "to obtain the fair resolution of disputes by an impartial tribunal without unnecessary delay or expense." We saw no purpose in trying to define arbitration itself, which is anyway a very difficult thing to do, but we thought that setting out the object of the exercise might be of value to parties, arbitrators and indeed courts. So far as arbitrators are concerned, this principle is reflected in Section 33 of the Act, to which I have already referred. Section 34 and the following Sections set out the things that the tribunal can do, all of which are subject to the Section 33 duties. I have heard it said that this part of the Act spells the end of what is described as 'the amateur arbitrator'. As we said in our Report on the Bill published last February, if by this is meant the end of arbitrators who are unable or unwilling, or both, to conduct the proceedings with what most would regard as self-evident rules of justice, then indeed we hope that this will be one of the results. But these self-evident rules of justice are generally accepted in our democratic society, and are not merely theoretical considerations that concern lawyers alone. It is not necessary to be a lawyer to appreciate, for example, the need in justice for all parties to be given an opportunity to put forward their respective cases and to answer those of their opponents, nor the need to avoid unnecessary delay and expense. In our view the Act will in fact encourage those who may not be lawyers, but who are ready, willing and able to apply the basic rules of justice, to act as arbitrators. For the first time their duty is clearly spelt out; as are their powers. We think the Act will assist such arbitrators to make up their own minds on how best to proceed and to resist the blandishments or indeed threats of some lawyers, which are often employed against non-lawyer arbitrators in order to gain some advantage for their clients, or indeed themselves. Arbitrators will have one simple question uppermost in their minds throughout the proceedings, namely "is what I am minded to do, or what I am being asked to do, a proper performance of my duty under Section 33?" If it is, then that course of action can be adopted; if it is not, then it must be rejected and any alternative must be subjected to the same 'quality control' test. Having said this, I wholly support and encourage the training courses for arbitrators which are now available. Those of the Chartered Institute of Arbitrators are of a very high standard. These courses introduce those minded to be arbitrators to the real world of arbitration, dealing with and providing the solutions to the sort of problems that arise over and over again in practice. Those who take these courses will find that they are much better equipped to deal with such problems; and this will mean that such problems will be solved more quickly and cheaply, which in turn, of course, means proper performance of the Section 33 duties.

The third of the general principles is that in matters governed by Part 1 of the Act, the court should not intervene except as provided by this Part. As I have said, one of the criticisms made from abroad, and indeed by some in this country, is that in the past the courts have been too ready to intervene in the arbitral process. I have already dealt with the two main aspects of this, namely security for costs and the right to apply for leave to appeal from an arbitration. We have borne this point in mind in all the cases where we have given the court a role to play. Our basic principle has been to provide the court only with powers that can properly be said to be supportive of the arbitral process; and to exclude others. We have tested each clause which concerns the courts against this principle. For example, we have removed from the provision dealing with staying legal proceedings brought in disregard of an arbitration agreement a proviso which allowed the court to refuse a stay if satisfied that there was not in fact any dispute between the parties. That qualification does not appear in the New York Convention or its predecessors, and was inserted so that notwithstanding the existence of an arbitration clause, the court could give summary judgment if satisfied that there really was no defence to the claim. To my mind, not only is this a case of the court usurping a function which the parties have agreed should be performed by their chosen tribunal, but it also leads to logical absurdities, as I endeavoured to explain in the case of *Hayter v Nelson* [1990] 2 Lloyd's Rep. 265.

It would of course be impossible to exclude the courts wholly from the arbitral process. The Model Law recognises this and so do we. Parties (when on the defence in a dispute) are often only too ready to do anything to frustrate or delay the progress of an arbitration, by failing to appoint an arbitrator, by disposing of their assets and so on. In many of these cases, without the support of the courts, the arbitration agreement would indeed be frustrated. Again, if an arbitrator fails to act impartially, it would offend our sense of justice if there was no means (which can only be the court) for the party suffering the injustice to seek to put things right. Questions of the jurisdiction of the tribunal cannot be left (unless the parties concerned agree) to the unchallengeable decision of the tribunal itself, for what would be a classic case of pulling oneself up by one's own bootstraps, so that the power we have given arbitrators to decide their own jurisdiction is made subject in the Act to challenge in the Courts. However, we have also made clear that such challenges will not be allowed to delay the progress of the arbitration, which can continue while they are pending. I have heard it said that the Act still provides the Court with too much scope for interfering with the arbitral process. As you would expect, I disagree with this comment. I do not know, and would be interested to hear, whether those of this view have in mind any particular Section or Sections, or which provisions they regard as unnecessary for the support of the arbitral process.

Going back to the other provisions of the Act where the court may play a role, I would draw your attention to Section 44, which gives the court powers to make orders in support of the arbitral process, but only where the tribunal has no such power or is for the time being unable to act effectively. Subsection (6) of this Section gives the court a new power, which is to direct that the tribunal (when able to act) shall itself have power to direct that any order made by the court under the section shall cease to have effect, in whole or in part; thus to hand back the particular matter to the tribunal. This, I hope, provides a good illustration of our attempt to cast the courts in a supporting rather than an interfering role. There is still a lively discussion over one aspect of court interference. The existing law draws a distinction between domestic and international arbitrations. The former are those where all parties are, in effect, English. In domestic arbitrations it is not possible to contract out of the right to apply to appeal from an arbitration award until after a dispute has arisen. Furthermore, in domestic arbitrations, the Court is not bound to stay legal proceedings under the New York Convention, but has a much wider discretion. This discretion is often exercised where there are a number of parties involved, but where they have not all agreed to arbitrate in the same arbitration. For example, in many construction contracts, there will be the main contract with an arbitration clause, and sub-contracts with other arbitration clauses, or indeed some of these contracts may have no arbitration clause at all. A dispute arises. The building owner blames the contractor who in turn blames one or more sub-contractors. It would obviously be best if all the parties involved were made party to the same proceedings, so that the matter could be sorted out between them all. However, if the arbitration clauses are given full force and effect, this cannot happen. The sub-contractors are not party to the agreement between the building owner and the contractor to arbitrate their disputes and the building owner is not party to any arbitration agreements there may be between the contractor and sub-contractors. In these circumstances, one party often ignores the arbitration clause and brings legal proceedings; and the court in domestic cases often refuses to stay those proceedings, so that all the parties concerned can fight out their differences in court, joining everyone as additional defendants or third parties. This, as a matter of common sense, has something to commend it, but it does mean that the court is refusing to acknowledge and indeed is overriding the respective parties' agreement to arbitrate rather than litigate.

In my view we should abolish this distinction and apply the international rule (which comes from the New York Convention) to all arbitrations. This requires the Court to stay legal proceedings brought in breach of an arbitration clause unless satisfied that "the arbitration agreement is null and void, inoperative, or incapable of being performed." It seems to me that those who are responsible for drafting standard forms of contract for such activities as construction, could easily include provisions that would enable all the disputes between all the parties to be arbitrated in one arbitration; which would bind the parties by agreement and which would avoid the Court having to override arbitration agreements. Such agreements are expressly sanctioned by Section 35 of the new Act. There is a further and equally important consideration, which is that our present law, by drawing the distinction I have mentioned between English nationals and others, is to our minds breaking European law, and is probably even now ineffective for that reason, since other EC nationals who make arbitration agreements have less recourse to our Courts, and are thus being discriminated against. It is this European law point which will in all probability in any event require us to abandon the distinction between domestic and international arbitrations.

We appreciated this question last year, but since we did not have time for a full consultation on this point, we put the provisions about domestic arbitrations in a special part of the Act, with power to repeal that part by Statutory Instrument. We have now considered these responses and have recommended to the Minister that he should abolish the distinction between domestic and international arbitrations. As I have said, I hope that the three principles in Section 1 will help all concerned to read and apply this legislation in the spirit in which we have prepared it. I hope that those from abroad who read the Act will be persuaded that this jurisdiction is an ideal place to hold an international arbitration, since they can now understand what this is likely to entail, and can see that we have tried to reflect generally accepted international views on the proper conduct of the arbitral process. I also hope that institutions such as the ICC and the LCIA, which to my mind offer a first class arbitration service, will benefit from the new legislation since it will, as I trust, enable them to offer an even better service so far as arbitrations in this country are concerned. Only time will tell whether we have succeeded in our objective to retain and enhance the reputation of this country as the leading place for the form of dispute resolution known as arbitration, and to carry into effect those three principles. Whether my hopes will be realised I can only wait and see.

* This article was originally published as M. Saville, 'The Arbitration Act 1996 and its Effect on International Arbitration in England', *Arbitration* 63, no. 2 (1997): 104-112.

CHAPTER 2

Why Arbitration Will Be With Us Always

Albert Jan Van den Berg

Like most people, I view the coming of the new millennium as a time to reflect on the past and ponder the future. The nearly irresistible impulse to do so is a natural consequence of the turning of the year — particularly when the new one ends with a lot of zeros — and so lately my thoughts have turned to the past and future of international arbitration, and particularly to the question of whether our craft will still be practised when the next millennium comes around. My conclusion is that it will be, for reasons which I will describe. Let me begin with the past. Arbitration is a dispute resolution mechanism with a long and venerable history. There are reported examples of arbitration since ancient times, and I am sure that some day one of my British barrister colleagues will have occasion to place reliance on the case of *Tower of Babel Ltd v Citizens of the World et al.* (Celtic Bench Division, c.2500 BC) in a construction arbitration. It has been in this century, however, with the explosive growth in cross-border trade, that international commercial arbitration has come into its own. The founding of the International Chamber of Commerce (ICC) Court of Arbitration in Paris in 1923, the adoption of the New York Convention in 1958, the promulgation of the United Nations Commission on International Trade Law (UNCITRAL) Arbitration Rules in 1976 and the Model Law in

1985 are the well-known mileposts in the march of international commercial arbitration. Case filings with the major arbitral institutions are ever increasing, and all of us in the field are fully engaged in the practice of international arbitration. And so, if the past is any guide, the future of our profession looks bright indeed. But let us not become too smug too soon. For as any good investment adviser will tell you, 'past performance is no guarantee of future performance'. Markets rise and fall, and so too do the fortunes of professional endeavours. And so the questions arise: Is there reason to believe that international commercial arbitration will be as successful in the next millennium as it is today? Will it continue to be the dispute resolution mechanism of choice for commercial men and women in international transactions? I suggest that these questions can best be answered by following the classic *Getting to Yes* approach: look at the 'best alternatives' to arbitration, and see whether any of them has the capacity to surpass or displace arbitration as a method of international dispute settlement. In other words, let us examine the perceived competitors of arbitration and attempt to assess how good they really are.

ALTERNATIVE DISPUTE RESOLUTION

The most-often suggested alternative to arbitration is alternative dispute resolution (ADR), a deceptively short acronym for a panoply of devices ranging from mediation and conciliation to rather esoteric procedures like 'Partnering' (which I must confess to having initially mistaken as a family law concept). The proponents of ADR contend that arbitration has become too formalised, too expensive and too 'court-like.' The answer, they say, is to employ approaches that promote compromise and settlement in preference to litigation. The more esoteric forms of ADR have been roundly (and, in my view, rightly) lampooned by Gerold Herrmann in his own inimitable way, with which I dare not attempt to compete. Suffice it to say that in my view mechanisms such as 'Early Neutral Evaluation', 'Rent-a-Judge', 'Shadow Mediation' and 'Partnering' are the pop songs of the legal world: catchy but inevitably ephemeral. They are no more a threat to the future of arbitration than the Spice Girls are to Beethoven's Ninth. More serious potential alternatives to arbitration are mediation and conciliation. But here again I find myself ultimately underwhelmed, for the simple reason that if parties really want to settle a dispute, they can do that for themselves without the benefit of a special (and costly) procedure. This is certainly the case for sophisticated parties represented by competent legal counsel. And so, at least for the vast majority of cases, I doubt whether the game is worth the candle so far as mediation and conciliation are concerned. Furthermore, there is obviously no incompatibility between arbitration and the voluntary settlement of disputes. Parties in arbitration settle cases all the time, either *sua sponte* or with a little push from the panel. The latter circumstance is particularly common in my country, where certain pragmatic Dutch arbitrators will suggest that the lawyers take a long walk down the hall and return with an award on agreed terms. Whatever the merits of that approach — which I personally do not favour, and which understandably comes as a shock to some foreign practitioners in Holland — it illustrates the point that arbitration is no enemy to the settlement-minded party. My ultimate concern about ADR is that it is unlikely to provide value for money to the parties themselves. I would venture that a lawyer does his client a disservice by recommending a mandatory mediation or conciliation clause. He does an even greater disservice when, perhaps overwhelmed by the novelty of it all, he recommends a so-called 'compound dispute settlement clause' requiring exhaustion of a mandatory negotiation period, followed by a mandatory mediation and/or conciliation procedure, before an arbitration can be commenced. In my experience, exhaustion of the client (or his money) is likely to precede the exhaustion of such a remedies scheme by a wide margin. All of this leads me to doubt that ADR is capable of displacing arbitration as a dispute resolution mechanism. So let me now move on to the next challenger.

THE NATIONAL COURTS

A second obvious alternative to arbitration is litigation in the national courts. The strengths of the national courts are several: they are omnipresent, can mostly be used free of charge, and are largely staffed by intelligent and experienced judges. These doubtless advantages notwithstanding, the national courts are unlikely to become serious challengers to arbitration in the future. The difficulty (in many circumstances) of enforcing judgments abroad will continue to weigh against the national courts. Furthermore, no matter how fair and professional their judges may be, the fear of local bias will remain, in the world at large and even within Europe itself. Should any doubts persist on this score, simply witness the US court system — where, due to ongoing concerns about regional bias even after 200 years of nationhood, diversity of state (with a small 's') citizenship remains a jurisdictional basis for removing a case from local courts to the federal courts. To put it differently, an English party is likely to react no more happily in the 21st century than today upon learning that its case will be heard by a Texas jury — and vice versa for the Texans. Arbitration will therefore remain a necessary and popular alternative to the national court systems. An interesting caveat concerns the role of national judges themselves. In recent years the judges in most jurisdictions have become increasingly arbitration friendly — largely as a result of the mandates of the New York Convention, but also no doubt due to the desire to reduce overcrowded dockets by sending litigants somewhere else whenever possible. One wonders whether national court judges might one day become concerned that too many interesting cases are being lost in this manner and start to take a more restrictive approach on referrals. This may well remain only a theoretical question, because arbitration practitioners are not infrequently known to 'co-opt' the best national court judges by appointing them to panels. In this way international arbitration — and the national court judges themselves — benefit from the best of both worlds.

AN INTERNATIONAL COMMERCIAL COURT

A third alternative to arbitration sometimes proposed is an international commercial court. Such a court could provide a neutral, international forum for the resolution of disputes in cross-border commercial cases. Presumably operating under the UNIDROIT Principles or some form of *Lex Mercatoria*, it might even develop a body of published case law that could be referenced by practitioners in advising their clients and negotiating resolutions to disputes in the making. This is undeniably an interesting and forward-looking idea, but it suffers from at least two detractions that are, in my view, either semi or fully fatal. The first is what I would call the 'reality check': is it likely that such an institution can really be established, maintained and accepted as legitimate and useful by the international business community? My own answer is 'probably not.' Second, such an institution would inevitably entail a loss or diminution of several of the characteristics that make international arbitration attractive, including in particular the critical feature of party autonomy reflected in, for example, the ability to nominate arbitrators and fashion a procedure tailor-made for the particular dispute. Thus even if an international court could be established in our lifetimes (or those of our successors), which I doubt, the bottom line is that it would be unlikely to offer the same combination of attractive features that has made international commercial arbitration such a success.

EVALUATION

It follows from the foregoing that, at least in my view, there are no serious challengers to the ascendancy of arbitration waiting in the wings as the next millennium approaches. Alternative dispute resolution will remain a sideline — sometimes useful, occasionally wacky and too often a poor investment of the parties' time and money. The national courts are unlikely to become more attractive as a forum for international cases than they are today — European integration and harmonisation notwithstanding — and in any event the cream of the judicial crop can be (and are being) integrated into the arbitral system as arbitrators. The dream of an international commercial court is likely to remain only that, due to the intense practical and political obstacles that would impede its establishment, as well as the undesirable formalisation of the dispute resolution process that such an institution would inevitably entail. The simple fact is that in the next millennium, as in this one, commercial men and women will continue to desire a flexible, a-national, quasi-judicial forum in which to resolve disputes arising from international trade and commerce. The current international arbitral regime — certainly with some fine tuning, but without a major overhaul — will continue to be well suited to fulfil that need. The future prospects of international commercial arbitration are enhanced by the quality of its current practitioners. We are blessed in our field with some of the best lawyers in the world, and behind them a new generation — sometimes facetiously referred to as the 'junior mafia' — stands ready to carry on when the time comes for the current generation to turn its attention from prehearing conferences to post-golfing cocktails.

A CAVEAT

Having painted a rather rosy picture of the future, I must hasten to add that there remains an important caveat, which has to do with the very practitioners whom I have just lauded. The caveat is that this picture can quickly fade if those of us who are active in the field allow ourselves to become too complacent, too confident or simply too lazy. The practice of law is after all a business, and commercial arbitration will thrive only so long as it continues to serve well the ultimate consumers of the product, i.e., the parties who choose counsel and appoint arbitrators in international cases. Providing a top quality product entails several things. First, as arbitrators, we must always keep quality, efficiency and cost in mind. This does not mean flying in the back of the aeroplane or dining only at

McDonalds (although such eventualities can never be excluded). It does mean taking the time at the outset of a case to organise an efficient and sensible procedure in close consultation with the parties' counsel; intervening quickly and decisively when procedural disputes arise; providing a 'hot bench' by preparing fully before the hearing; and issuing a thorough and well-reasoned award as soon as possible after the hearing is completed. When acting as counsel the same basic precepts apply. Good practitioners must ensure that their clients are fully informed of the prospects, risks, costs and likely duration of the arbitration. This should occur at the outset of the relationship (i.e., after the retainer cheque clears, but before spending it all). Once the case is initiated, it should be prosecuted with all possible speed and all possible vigour, while at the same time keeping an eye open for settlement opportunities that might ultimately save the client money. Finally, as colleagues, all of us who practise arbitration must remember that good relations between opposing counsel benefit everyone by laying the groundwork for a smooth and efficient proceeding. Too often these days one sees counsel in international arbitrations employing the rule that if the other side proposes something, that is reason enough to object to it. Such 'scorched earth' tactics may stroke the egos of the litigators but ultimately disserve the interests of the litigants on both sides. The foregoing is simply to say that we who practise in the field must always be on guard against becoming our own worst enemy. International commercial arbitration is a highly successful system today precisely because it serves the needs of the ultimate end-users so well. So long as the present and future standard bearers of the system maintain that thought as a lodestar, I feel confident that international commercial arbitration will still be with us the next time the millennial clock chimes.

REFERENCES

* This article was originally published as A. Van der Berg, 'Why Arbitration Will Be With Us Always', *Arbitration* 65, no. 4 (1999): 248-250.

1 R. Fisher, W. Ury & B. Patton, *Getting to Yes* (New York: Penguin, 1991), Chapter 6.

2 G. Herrmann, 'Does the World Need Additional Uniform Legislation on Arbitration?' (The 1998 Freshfields Lecture), *Arbitration International* 15 (1999): 211.

3 See 28 United States Code § 1332.

CHAPTER 2

Achieving the Potential of Effective Arbitration

Julian D. M. Lew

In 1985, at the Inaugural Conference of the School of International Arbitration, Centre for Commercial Law Studies, Queen Mary and Westfield College, University of London, I put forward the following proposition: "Truly effective arbitration requires willing participants: businessmen, lawyers, arbitrators and national laws. This necessitates a willingness and desire to overcome the political, legal, economic and cultural differences which divide the nations of the world, and to transcend the national and parochial distinctions between the systems, views and concepts. This proposition was put forward in the context of the then recent promulgation by the United Nations Commission on International Trade Law (UNCITRAL) of its Model Law on International Commercial Arbitration.

The aim, design and commitment behind the Model Law was to promote uniformity in the area of international arbitration. This was to take place both in countries that had existing arbitration laws and those that did not but wanted, at least on the international level, to adopt an internationally accepted model. The absence of uniform national laws on arbitration was seen as an important factor preventing truly effective international arbitration. At least after 1985, a model at last existed."

ACHIEVEMENT OF EFFECTIVE INTERNATIONAL ARBITRATION

Two of the four essentials to which I referred in 1985 have been largely achieved. The business world and national laws have embraced international arbitration with the necessary pragmatism and realism to make it work. Both domestically and internationally, businessmen have accepted that arbitration has a vital role in the effective resolution of commercial disputes. Accordingly, the activities of the domestic arbitration institutions, for example, the Chartered Institute of Arbitrators in the UK and the American Arbitration Association, have increased significantly. Internationally, the business world has recognised an inherent preference for arbitration compared to national courts as a forum for resolving disputes between parties from many different countries and arising from many types of international commercial transactions. Hence, the International Chamber of Commerce (ICC) case load has increased from 250 in 1980 to 466 in 1998. The London Court of International Arbitration, which had only a handful of cases in the early 1980s, had 70 new cases in 1998. Similar increases were experienced by many other international arbitration centres. This is also influenced by the growth in the number of arbitration institutions and other organisations offering specialist and general arbitration services in the 1980s and 1990s. All this was to satisfy the perceived needs of the business community. National laws too have adapted to meet the new demanding world of the international business community. The traditional arbitration venues were concerned not to lose their place of preference. Nonfavoured venues saw this as an opportunity to become an arbitration venue with the benefit that this allegedly brings to both the local legal community and the local economy.

To date some 30 states and territories have adopted the Model Law without substantial amendments. A number of countries have revised their arbitration law with express consideration given to the Model Law. The Model Law went through an enormous number of drafting stages and is said to reflect acknowledged standards for international arbitration. Moreover, a significant proportion of countries chose to overhaul and/or modify their domestic arbitration law to reflect some of the key principles of the Model Law. Equally important to the implementation of the Model Law in national laws is the extent to which it has influenced both the practice of arbitrators and the attitude of national courts. The emerging commonly accepted practices in international arbitration, e.g., the form and content of agreements, the appointment and independence of arbitrators, procedural approaches and enforcement, have all been influenced by the UNCITRAL Model Law. To help this international organisation of arbitration further, in 1996 UNCITRAL also adopted a set of Notes on Organising Arbitration Proceedings. The UNCITRAL Notes should greatly assist, and could become a significant influence for, further harmonisation of international arbitration procedure. The harmonisation of international arbitration law as a result of the UNCITRAL Model Law has been slow but relatively successful. Certainly on the international level, governments have been willing participants in the drive to harmonise their national arbitration laws. With the acknowledgement of the majority of the Model Law's key principles by the governments which make up the world's major trading nations, national governments have given their stamp of approval on the use and development of modern international arbitration law and procedure. Underpinning modern arbitration procedure is the demand for the procedural independence of the tribunal from state courts, coupled with the express prescription of procedural powers to the arbitrators, except where the parties agree otherwise. This is supported internationally by 120 countries signing the New York Convention on the Recognition and Enforcement of Foreign Arbitral Awards 1958.

CONTINUING LIMITATIONS TO EFFECTIVE ARBITRATION

The other two ingredients for effective arbitration referred to in my 1985 paper, i.e., lawyers and arbitrators, have not been as pragmatic or proactive. Lawyers have increasingly seen arbitration as another playing field in which to exercise litigation skills, rather than as a forum for dispute settlement. They view the objective as 'beating' the other party rather than determining the meaning of the agreement out of which the dispute has arisen and the rights and obligations of the parties. The attempts by lawyers from one jurisdiction to impose their own procedural system on the tribunal and the other party in the name of 'fairness' can undermine the international arbitral process. Tactical issues, such as challenges to arbitrators, raising jurisdictional issues, demands for additional time, lengthy hearings, additional submissions, excessive witnesses and challenges to the procedural directions of arbitrators, have all contributed to make arbitration more contentious. All that matters is for the client to win! As a result of these factors, the original twin merits of arbitration, i.e., speed and inexpense, are no longer really true. It is too early to see whether, following the Arbitration Act 1996, arbitrators in England now see themselves as required or more empowered to be proactive. If the intention is for arbitrators to manage and improve the procedure in order to provide a better service to its willing users, the power to do so can be derived from both the 1996 Act and most sets of arbitration rules (international and domestic). If the contentious character of the arbitral process is to be controlled, it is for the arbitrators in each case to manage the arbitration and direct the lawyers' energies to the specific issues in the case. This will include identifying the issues, form and timetable for presentation of the case to the tribunal. Of course arbitrators must be willing participants in this process. In fact, in order to call themselves and accept appointments as willing and able arbitrators, these individuals owe a duty to the parties to resolve the real dispute as quickly and as inexpensively as possible. The possibility of effective arbitration is therefore, above all, in the hands of the arbitrators, who should never forget that they are paid for this service. It is well recognised in the 1996 Act that power and responsibility over procedure was passed to the arbitrators. Thus, s. 33 provides as follows:

"(1) The Tribunal shall (a) act fairly and impartially as between the parties, giving each party a reasonable opportunity of putting his case and dealing with that of his opponent, and (b) adopt procedures suitable to the circumstances of the particular case, avoiding unnecessary delay or expense, so as to provide a fair means for the resolution of the matters falling to be determined.

(2) The Tribunal shall comply with that general duty in conducting the arbitral proceedings, in its decisions on matters of procedure and evidence

and in the exercise of all other powers conferred on it."

This paper explores several ways in which arbitrators could control the arbitral process and which will in turn lead to more effective arbitration. These include: (1) Defining issues at an early stage; (2) Imposing clear procedural directions at the outset; (3) Reacting and making decisions quickly; (4) Recognising and upholding the arbitral agreement, including the making of decisions concerning jurisdictional challenge. First, however, I refer briefly to the need further to exclude and limit the jurisdiction of national courts and the primordial role of party autonomy in the arbitral process. These two fundamentals reflect the classic conflict between the 'jurisdictional' and 'contractual' legal natures of arbitration.

EXCLUSION OF THE NATIONAL COURT'S JURISDICTION AND AUTONOMY

In the search for effective arbitration one must not lose track of the reason behind the need for arbitration as a legally binding alternative dispute procedure: it is the alternative to national courts. The Model Law prescribes the principle of arbitration as a legally binding route for enforceable dispute resolution outside the jurisdiction of the otherwise appropriate national court. The Model Law enhances the jurisdictional competence of the arbitrator, as does the 1996 Act. The power of arbitrators to determine the extent of their own jurisdiction (*compétence-compétence*) is a marker for the future role of arbitrators in a world where they are increasingly (if not totally) independent of a national court's supervisory jurisdiction and in control of their own and the parties' destiny. The acceptance of the doctrine of *compétence-compétence* makes it more difficult for all parties to opt out of arbitration. It gives extra force to the arbitration agreement and the effectiveness of the arbitration procedure. By raising the profile of the arbitrators as self-determining powers, the incorporation and express adherence to the principles of *compétence-compétence* can only enhance that power.

Although the arbitrator's jurisdiction can only be derived from the parties' consent, i.e., the arbitration agreement, this does not decrease the power or responsibility of the arbitrators. The 1996 Act and various arbitration rules empower the tribunal to do what is necessary to manage and control the arbitral process. This is to make the arbitrator's role more effective. However, this power cannot be separated from the contractual foundation of the arbitration. In assessing any new powers given to the arbitrators, or the effectiveness of any arbitration procedure, party autonomy contains a degree of control or even veto on both the procedure and powers of the tribunal itself, as well as the overall supervisory jurisdiction of any national law. To recognise the power of 'party autonomy', the 1996 Act uses the words 'unless otherwise agreed' throughout as a limitation to the otherwise extensive powers given to the tribunal. Party autonomy must, at the end of the day, rule supreme. It underpins the election made by the parties to take themselves and their dispute outside of the jurisdiction of the otherwise appropriate national courts. The choice of autonomy is there for all disputes which are, as a matter of public policy, arbitrable. Once that choice has been made, the parties should be free to organise themselves and their tribunal as they see fit in order to resolve their dispute; after all they are the ones paying for it.

However, once appointed and within the authority of the applicable rules and arbitration law, arbitrators have the duty and responsibility to control and manage the arbitral process.

NATIONAL COURT INVOLVEMENT MUST BE LIMITED

The involvement of national courts in the arbitral process must be further reduced to a supportive role; 'supportive' in that the court supports the parties' agreement to solve their dispute privately without judicial interference. The court should not be directly concerned with the supervision of the arbitration proceedings. This is now well recognised in practice and law. The question really is whether national court judges will restrict their involvement, and uphold the principle of non-intervention, resisting the temptation to make *ex post facto* value judgments of the work and conclusions of the arbitrators. The outward test of any procedure is whether or not the award will be enforced. This is particularly so in light of the operation of the New York Convention. The balance between interference and supportive supervision was the subject of much debate in the drafting of the Model Law and the 1996 Act. The Departmental Advisory Committe (DAC) Report states at paragraph 21: "… there is no doubt that our law has been subject to international criticism that the Courts intervene more than they should in the arbitral process, thereby tending to frustrate the choice the parties have made to use arbitration rather than litigation as the means for resolving their disputes." The role of the English court is now limited under the 1996 Act to a largely complete list of what is recognised in arbitration circles as necessary and desirable court support. Namely: (1) Appointment and removal of arbitrators; (2) Appointment and removal of arbitrators; (3) Securing the attendance of witnesses or production of evidence; (4) Preservation of property; (5) Injunctive relief/ remedy; (6) Ancillary interlocutory injunctive relief.

ARBITRATORS MANAGING THE ARBITRAL PROCESS

Arbitrators Should Determine All Jurisdictional Issues

As noted above, under the 1996 Act arbitrators now have the power to determine their own jurisdiction. A limited right to apply to the court to determine any question as to the substantive jurisdiction of the tribunal has, however, been preserved. Such an application is only possible with either the agreement of all the parties, or the permission of the tribunal and only where 'there is good reason why the matter should be decided by the court'. An appeal will be possible only where the question in issue "involves a point of law which is one of general importance and is one which for some other special reason should be considered by the Court of Appeal." A good reason could be where one party fails, for whatever reason, to take an available point on jurisdiction. The other party may, if the tribunal consents and the court permits, apply for a declaration that the tribunal has jurisdiction, in order to proceed with the arbitration without fear of a subsequent challenge but the "basic principle is, however, not affected by the very narrow exception contained in s. 32." Until the tribunal has reached its final determination, the court's involvement with the substance of arbitration is limited to the very narrow exception of the determination of a preliminary point of law by the court. The right of appeal is limited to: (1) Points of law in specific circumstances only (that is to say where the decision of the tribunal is obviously wrong or the question of law is of general public importance); and (2) Where the tribunal's decision is clearly open to question. This right of appeal will rarely be allowed and cannot be used to undermine the agreement to arbitrate or the authority of the arbitrators. It is important that every national court should resist the temptation to accept issues for appeal where they feel that they, subjectively, might have reached a different view to that which the tribunal has reached. The limits to the situations where it is possible to 'run to the court' to determine issues which the parties have in the first instance more properly referred to arbitration for determination, do not affect those applications which are more akin to the supervisory role of national courts, for example, the powers of the court in relation to challenges to the award on the basis of the lack of jurisdiction of the tribunal, or serious irregularity. Nor do the limits detract from the overall non-interventionist approach of the English courts when asked to uphold procedural regularity and fairness in arbitration under the 1996 Act. The need to enforce an award acts as an international regulator of the arbitration procedure. Accordingly, the operation of the New York Convention is an international check on the application of internationally accepted mandatory rules of procedure. Any proliferation of ideal models for effective arbitration must be set against this background of international regulation.

Defining and Determining the Issues at an Early Stage

The earlier a tribunal is able to consider the issues the more likely it can assist with, or direct the management of, the dispute resolution process. The emphasis should be on the question: 'The parties are in dispute, but what is there to resolve?' All too often the fact that the parties are in dispute takes precedence over the real issues that are to be resolved. Often the parties become subsumed in their agreement to arbitrate, turning the process into a lengthy, expensive and time-consuming process of resolution within an all too often combative framework. If it were possible to define the true issues at the outset or early on in the process, a more effective, cheaper and quicker arbitration may be possible. With a little understanding of the respective claims and contentions of the parties a tribunal is in a better position than the parties and their lawyers to undertake this task and identify these issues. This is the first occasion when arbitrators need to exercise a management and directing role. When informed about the different and specific issues to be resolved, decisions can be properly made about the necessary preliminary and subsequent stages of the arbitration. It is then possible for the arbitrators to issue appropriate timetables for the arbitration as well as the more traditional directions, such as orders concerning the procedure for and the production of relevant documents and the factual/expert evidence. This was the aim of the Terms of Reference under the ICC Rules. It can, however, be greatly abused by both parties and arbitrators.

Early exchange and agreement of lists of issues can also result in clarity with regard to the determination of preliminary issues. These can then be dealt with easily and quickly; they can be either determinative of the whole dispute, or will assist the parties to settle their differences. It has been an increasing feature of international arbitration for a panel to try and manage the resolution by 'hiving-off' key issues for determination at a preliminary stage. The 1996 Act recognises the importance of preliminary issues. The tribunal is therefore empowered, at its own discretion, to make more than one award at different times and on different aspects of the matters submitted for determination. The skill of experienced arbitrators is exercised in the selection of issues that should be dealt with as preliminary issues. Regard should be had not only to what will be legally determinative but also commercially. There may be issues which, once resolved, may not produce finality as regards the relative legal stance taken by the parties, but may produce an outcome that vitiates the need for the arbitration to continue. Equally, there are many instances where the parties need a forum in which to vent their anger or air their grievances. After this stage, settlement will often become possible. If arbitrators are to undertake this role properly it will be necessary for them to become actively involved in reviewing, trying to understand and considering the parties' written submissions at an early stage and at the very least must do so well before any hearing.

Use of Experts

The appointment of an expert or assessor by the tribunal is another mechanism for expediting the arbitral process and reducing costs — if properly managed. The move does not preclude parties arguing certain points of expertise (foreign law, technical expertise) to the arbitrators. It could, however, if used properly by the tribunal, significantly rationalise arbitral practice, procedure, cost and time. The 1996 Act allows the tribunal to appoint its own experts or assessors. Similar provisions exist in Articles 27 and 12 of the UNCITRAL Rules and LCIA Rules respectively. The use of a single expert could mark the demise of, or at least a substantial reduction in, the adversarial style still employed in many arbitrations (especially involving common law lawyers and arbitrators) to determine matters of a technical nature. All will agree that expert opinion needs to be tested. However, the need for this to be done by two party-appointed experts, rather than a single expert appointed by the tribunal, can often be academic, provided the opportunity is there for the expertise (as opposed to the expert) to be subjected to careful examination.

A reasonable opportunity to question the tribunal's expert must of course be provided to the parties. Failure to allow such reasonable opportunity will in any event be a limit on the enforceability of any award rendered as a requirement of due process in any jurisdiction. The parties should be allowed the opportunity to put issues to the tribunal's expert and at the hearing to examine the expert about his or her report. This has been criticised by some as promoting further cost rather than a reduction in the overall costs of the arbitration procedure. This is on the basis that the parties still require their own expert, in order to understand some of the issues, to cross-examine that expert or provide comment on the tribunal's expert report or evidence.

To some extent perhaps the duplication of experts must be expected. It will not be necessary where parties have their own internal experts. However, if the arbitration process is properly managed, the need for additional party-appointed 'independent' experts could be avoided or at least limited in the majority of, if not all, typical commercial disputes involving technical expertise. Just as in international arbitration the tribunal would be expected to know the law (in accordance with civil law traditions), so too with expert knowledge. It is well recognised that in many cases the parties' so-called 'independent' experts present the case to maximise the arguments of 'their clients', despite the expectation of neutrality. Therefore, the tribunal is invariably trying to identify the experts' expert and 'real' opinion, as opposed to argument. It is worth noting that a recent refusal by a tribunal in a London Metal Exchange arbitration to allow a respondent to submit expert evidence was held not to be a serious irregularity under s. 68 of the 1996 Act.

Witnesses

The use of too many and irrelevant witnesses can also often undermine the cost-effectiveness of arbitration. This is particularly so where the witness evidence is oral and the parties and their witnesses are based in various jurisdictions, frequently different from the chosen seat of the tribunal. Although many national laws recognise the ability of the tribunal to be flexible to the needs of the parties by moving certain hearings from the 'seat' without infringing any national arbitration law provisions, parties can often be reluctant to move from a strict reliance on the provisions of the arbitration agreement. It requires firm direction from the tribunal to reduce the unnecessary cost.

Reducing Orality

The idea of documents-only arbitrations is not a new one, but it is underutilised in international arbitrations. In appropriate cases they can save a considerable amount of time and cost. The 1996 Act is clear that, in the absence of agreement by the parties, the tribunal may decide 'whether and to what extent there should be oral or written evidence or submission'. The emphasis on documents-only determination is even stronger in the ICC

Rules which provide that "the Arbitral Tribunal may decide the case solely on the documents submitted by the parties unless any of the parties requests a hearing." Too often parties (or their lawyers) feel their case will not be properly understood and determined by the arbitrators if they do not make an oral presentation to the tribunal.

Consideration by the tribunal at an early stage of the nature and extent of oral evidence to be called is vitally important. Of course, the tribunal may quite legitimately refuse to hear oral evidence in appropriate cases, even though it may be insisted upon by one of the parties. It is also not necessary to present numerous witnesses to say the same thing. Just because the same evidence is said by several people does not necessarily make it stronger, more relevant or truer. Evidence is, in all cases, considered by the arbitrators in its context. With the lawyers preferring 'to assist' the tribunal, the witness statements are drafted in impeccable and well-reasoned English, making all the points which support the case of the party putting forward the particular witness statement. These statements are often viewed with some scepticism by arbitrators.

It is now normal for direct evidence to be given in writing as 'evidence in chief'. By the time of the hearing, the other party knows the case it faces. There should be no surprises which are likely to lead to adjournments and delays. The hearings are limited to examining witnesses, to testing recollections, accuracy, veracity and reliability. It is not necessary — and most experienced international arbitrators (should) make this clear — to respond to every point made by the other party's witnesses. Much of the case may be irrelevant to the real issues.

Reception of Evidence

Reference must be made to the efforts of the International Bar Association (IBA), through Committee D of the Section on Business Law, which issued, in 1983, Rules on the Presentation and Reception of Evidence in International Commercial Arbitration. These Rules are aimed at bridging differences between civil and common law approaches. Like the Model Law, these IBA Rules formed part of the strive for the harmonisation of law seen during the early 1980s. In June 1999, the IBA published revised Rules on the Taking of Evidence in International Commercial Arbitration (The IBA Rules of Evidence). These Rules are solely concerned with the presentation and reception of evidence in arbitration. Even if not specifically adopted by agreement between the parties they have often been used as a guide by international arbitrators, particularly where the parties to the arbitration agreement are resident in both common and civil law systems.

The key focus of the IBA Rules of Evidence, perhaps not in fashion as much in the 1980s as it is now, is the wide powers similar to those existing in civil law systems that they give to the arbitrator. The powers cover both the way in which the tribunal wishes the evidence to be presented as well as its proactive and investigatory powers (which may be adopted by the parties on the adoption of the Rules). For example, the arbitrator can order a party to produce any relevant document within such party's possession, custody or control. Clearly the intention is that the arbitrator shall at all times have complete control over the procedure in relation to a witness giving oral evidence, including the right to limit or refuse the right of the party to deny, cross-examine or re-examine a witness when it appears to the arbitrator that such evidence or examination is unlikely to serve any further relevant purpose. In addition, the IBA Rules of Evidence allow the tribunal to rely on its own expert knowledge and to appoint experts to assist it or to give expert evidence or reports in the arbitration. Unfortunately the IBA Rules of Evidence have not, to date, been used to any great extent. They were, of course, intended to be used in international arbitration. In fact they are supplemental to not only any institutional rules agreed to by the parties, but also ad hoc arbitrations subject only to national arbitration law, applied by choice or as the *lex arbitri* of the seat of the arbitration. The legitimate refusal to hear oral evidence in appropriate cases, even though it may be insisted upon by one of the parties, is a real issue in terms of case management. There is an overriding duty under English law for the arbitration to be conducted speedily and in the most cost-effective manner. This duty is placed on both the tribunal and the parties. The skill and indeed responsibility of the arbitrator is to allow sufficient though not excessive time to the parties. The week- (sometimes several weeks) long hearings that we hear about so often are unnecessary. They are often an indication of the abdication of control and responsibility of the arbitrators in favour of the lawyers. Arbitrators can read and prepare for the hearing in advance and in so doing manage the case effectively. However, by limiting the scope of evidence and argument, the tribunal may bring itself in conflict with the wishes of the parties. The production of oral evidence in particular may be something which the parties insist upon in terms of 'having their day in court'. However, the same arguments cannot and should not apply to the provision of expert evidence; a solution can be found in the role of arbitrator as inquisitor.

Investigation by the Tribunal

The impression that there are always two sides to a dispute rather than a search for the truth is something which has shackled the development of the more proactive tribunal where the panel and representing lawyers derive their key dispute resolution experience from litigation. In England, arbitrators now have the power to decide for themselves 'whether and to what extent the tribunal should take the initiative in ascertaining the facts and the law'. This authority exists under other laws and arbitration rules. The real question is whether individual arbitrators have the strength of character to take control and determine the case themselves. This is their duty and responsibility; if the arbitration is quickly resolved, if the arbitrators hear or read the arguments of the parties and consider and determine the issues, they will have performed their obligations. Would it not be more efficient if the arbitrators were to collect the evidence themselves including, in some cases, meeting and talking to witnesses and experts directly? This may make the evidence collected less subjective or partial and more poignant to the case. Accordingly, where a specific issue arises, arbitrators could ask to speak to the witnesses on both sides directly without prior witness statements and preparation by the parties. For example, a witness confrontation may well help the arbitrators to determine the facts. The only down-side is that the parties and their lawyers will lose control. This alone should not deter a tribunal where it believes this is the best way forward.

Recoverability of Costs

Money tends to focus the mind of even the most hardened adversary. To be cost-effective is also now regarded, quite rightly, as an important influence and indeed duty of the tribunal to be weighed against other factors influencing arbitration procedure. The suggestions for managing arbitration and making it more effective as discussed above have the potential of achieving more cost-effective arbitration. Expensive tactical battles may often be directed by financially stronger parties against the weaker party (part of the 'beat the other party' philosophy). For example, a financially strong party may require the financially weaker party (but one who has a stronger legal case) to go through the arbitration rather than make payment of moneys due in the hope of a more favourable settlement, or that payment will become unnecessary if the weaker party should become insolvent and be wound up during the process. Arbitrators can make it clear that they will penalise the parties in the final award if this type of 'financial abuse' is discovered to have taken place. One way for arbitrators to pressurise parties is to warn them of the maximum amount the tribunal will order to the successful party by way of costs. This is a unique power given to the tribunal on a non-mandatory basis by the 1996 Act. By imposing an upper limit on what essentially should be a reasonable costs expenditure in the arbitration, the aim of the tribunal will be to encourage the parties to keep costs to a minimum. Thus, where no agreement exists between the parties as to which party shall pay all or part of the costs, the tribunal could take a proactive approach where it is clear that either or both of the parties may be tempted to indulge in excessive costs as a way of putting the other side under pressure. The parties may urge, on application, the tribunal to use its power to limit recoverable costs, but it is also open to the tribunal itself proactively to step in to limit the costs of any part of or the entire arbitration at any time on its own motion, provided it does so in line with its duty to ensure a fair arbitral procedure. To ensure this is done on an informed basis, the tribunal may first want to order the parties to provide information as part of its directions in the arbitration on anticipated costs and disbursements. Used as part of the overall case management of arbitration by the tribunal, this power is potentially an extremely useful tool in the quest for effective dispute resolution.

CONCLUSIONS FOR THE FUTURE

For arbitration to become an even more effective procedure, arbitrators must take control of the proceedings. It is for them to manage, direct and investigate the issues between the parties. This will necessitate arbitrators reading all of the documents and giving thought to how the case should best proceed at a much earlier stage. In view of the international nature of arbitration, with parties from different jurisdictions, there can be no hard and fast rules. In each case it will be for the parties ultimately to determine themselves how best to manage each particular case. What is important is that arbitrators should not only identify issues, but also what exactly is required from the arbitration procedure to resolve each of them. On that basis it is possible to determine early on what factual and expert evidence is necessary for each point. This allows the tribunal the opportunity to decide whether it should collate the relevant evidence itself or allow the parties (with the necessary instructions) to do so. Arbitrators are the 'masters of their own procedure'. They should consider carefully, in every case, how their considerable discretion can be used to best effect. They should use this discretion to collate evidence and investigate, wherever possible and practicable, all areas with a view to finding the true facts with fairness, expedition and with a mind to reducing expense. It will always be a balancing act and although it is undoubtedly important to determine the intent of the parties and listen to both them and their lawyers, ultimately it must be for the arbitrators to control the arbitral process. By doing so tribunals can increase the potential of effective determination of the issues between the parties.

REFERENCES

* This article was originally published as J. Lew, 'Achieving the Potential of Effective Arbitration', *Arbitration* 65, no. 4 (1999): 283-290.

1 J. Lew (ed.), *Contemporary Problems in International Arbitration* (London: Kluwer Law International, 1986), 5.

2 United Nations document A/40/17, Annex I; as adopted by the United Nations Commission on International Trade Law on 21 June 1985.

3 For example, the membership of the Chartered Institute of Arbitrators in 1981 was around 5000 and is now approximately 9500.

4 Recognising the value of arbitration, the Department of Trade and Industry in England has attempted, unsuccessfully, to conduct research into the economic value of arbitration to the UK, both in terms of arbitrations conducted there and also the use of English lawyers as representatives or arbitrators abroad.

5 At the close of the Commission's 18th Annual Session, the General

Assembly, in its Resolution 40/72 of 11 December 1985, recommended 'that all States give due consideration to the [Model Law], in view of the desirability of uniformity of the law of arbitral procedures and the specific needs of international commercial arbitration practice'.

6   For example, England and Wales.

7   Finalised at UNCITRAL's 29th Session, New York, June 1996. Reproduced in the UNCITRAL Yearbook, Vol. XXVII: 1996. UN Doc a/51/17. Hereinafter 'the UNCITRAL Notes'.

8   The Model Law clearly provides the tribunal's competence to rule on its jurisdiction in Art. 16. Similar provisions are found in Article 186 of Chapter 12 of the Swiss Private International Law Statute (1987) which applies to international arbitrators that 'the arbitral Tribunal shall decide on its own jurisdiction' and the French Civil Code, Art. 1466, which provides that upon being presented with a jurisdictional challenge '... it is for the arbitrator to decide on the validity or scope of his mission'. See also LCIA Rules (1998), Art. 23(1): 'The Arbitral Tribunal shall have the power to rule on its own jurisdiction'. See further ICC Rules (1998), Art. 6(4).

9   Departmental Advisory Committee on Arbitration Law, Report on the Arbitration Bill (February 1996).

10 See 1996 Act, Sections 42 to 45 and 48.

11 1996 Act, Section 30.

12 *Ibid.*, Section 32.

13 *Ibid.*, Section 32(2)(b)(iii).

14 M. Hunter & T. Landau, *The English Arbitration Act 1996: Text and*

Notes (London: Centre for Commercial Law Studies, 1998) n. 50 at 30.

15 1996 Act, Section 45.
16 See similar restrictions in Article 190 of Chapter 12 on International Arbitration in the Swiss Private International Law Statute (1987).
17 1996 Act, Section 67.
18 *Ibid.*, Section 68.
19 See ICC Rules (1998), Art. 18.
20 Terms of reference arguably can operate as the equivalent to lists of issues. However, as they are normally confined to listing the parties' contentions descriptively or defining the dispute being referred to the tribunal (i.e., the ambit of jurisdiction of the tribunal) (see ICC Rules. Art. 18(c) and (d)), they often do not refine the issues in any useful detail. It is suggested that an agreement of a list of issues at an early stage in any dispute resolution procedure, and particularly arbitration, would add to the effectiveness of any procedure thereafter.
21 1996 Act, Section 47.
22 A similar power is found in the LCIA Rules 1998, Art. 26(7).
23 1996 Act, Section 37.
24 See in particular Art. 27(4) of the UNCITRAL Rules, which provides that if the tribunal appoints an expert, all parties have an automatic right to be heard at any hearing where the expert is present. Article 20(3) of the 1998 ICC Rules allows the tribunal to hear witnesses or experts without the presence of the parties but 'provided they have been duly summoned'. See also n. 16 of the UNCITRAL Notes.
25 See criticism of partisan experts by the Commercial Court in *National*

Justice *Compania Naviera SA v Prudential Assurance Co. Ltd*, The Ikarian Reefer [1993] 2 Lloyd's Rep 68 at 81.

26 *Egmata AG v Marco Trading Corp* (unreported, 25 November 1998). The arbitrators decided not to grant the request on the basis that the respondent did not need it as it was more than well qualified to deal with the issues on its own experience of the trade.

27 1996 Act, Section 34(2)(h).

28 ICC Rules 1998, Art. 20(6).

29 See *Egmata AG v Marco Trading Corp.*

30 The IBA Rules on the Presentation and Reception of Evidence in International Commercial Arbitration 1983, can be found in International Commercial Arbitration, E. Bergsten (ed.), Binder 2, at III.8 (Oceana Pub. Inc. New York). See also UNCITRAL Notes (1996), particularly nn. 15-17.

31 The 1999 IBA Rules of Evidence are published in Arbitration and ADR, Newsletter of the IBA SBL Committee D, vol. 4, no. 1, p. 23. Editorial note: for a commentary on the new IBA Rules on the Taking of Evidence in International Commercial Arbitration, see, in the present volume, the contribution by V. Veeder, 'Evidential Rules in International Commercial Arbitration: From the Tower of London to the New 1999 IBA Rules.' The new rules are appended thereto.

32 See Art. 3.

33 *Ibid.*, Art. 8

34 *Ibid.*, Arts. 6 and 7.

35 1996 Act, Section 33.

36 *Ibid.*, Section 34(2).
37 Section 65 of the 1996 Act provides that the tribunal may direct that the "recoverable" costs in the arbitration, or indeed of any part of the arbitral proceedings, shall be limited to a specific amount (i.e., 'capped').
38 1996 Act, Section 60.

CHAPTER 2

Client-Friendly Arbitration

Andrew Bartlett

In England within the last three years there have been major developments in the landscape of dispute resolution. The Arbitration Act 1996 has endorsed a modem and flexible approach to arbitral procedures. The Civil Procedure Rules 1999 (CPR) have introduced a revolution in the conduct of civil litigation in the courts. The combined effect of these developments has been to make arbitration more attractive and to provide an impetus for a new appreciation of what may be called 'client-friendly arbitration'.

THE PHILOSOPHY OF THE ARBITRATION ACT 1996

For many years before 1996 there had been a sustained campaign by leading figures in the Chartered Institute of Arbitrators and other interested parties to induct both arbitrators and lawyers into the philosophy that arbitration proceedings need not ape proceedings in court, but could be adapted to suit the needs of the particular dispute. On all too frequent occasions judges criticised the very idea that arbitrators might take cost-effective short cuts, such as admitting evidence that would not be strictly admissible in a court of law. Many English judges and lawyers had not been educated into the distinctive advantages of flexible arbitral process. They expected arbitrations to be conducted as if the Rules of the Supreme Court

(RSC) applied. It was necessary to overcome a traditional hostility of the courts towards arbitration. Needham recently reminded readers of Arbitration that this hostility went back a long way, into the 18th and 19th centuries, if not earlier. He drew attention to the candid explanation given by Lord Campbell in 1856: I know that there has been a very great inclination in the courts for a good many years to throw obstacles in the way of arbitration. I wish to speak with great respect of my predecessors the judges; but I must just let your Lordships into the secret of that tendency. There is no disguising the fact that as formerly the emoluments of the judges depended mainly or almost entirely upon fees and they had no fixed salary, there was great competition to get as much as possible ... into Westminster Hall, and a great scramble in Westminster Hall for the division of spoil, and hence ... They had great jealousy of arbitrations ... Therefore, they said that the courts ought not to be ousted of their jurisdiction ...

The Arbitration Act 1979 tinkered with the law, restricting the circumstances in which judges could interfere with arbitral awards. The old outlook was finally discarded by the 1996 Act, which ushered in a new philosophy of flexibility, and placed a new emphasis on adapting the procedure to suit the kind of dispute. Some arbitrators had been making such adaptations for years, but the impetus of statutory change was required in order to try to get rid of the lingering effects of the more hidebound regime that had previously prevailed. In practical terms the heart of the 1996 Act is found in s. 33 and 34. Section 33 imposes on the arbitrator a duty to adopt procedures suitable to the circumstances of the case. Section 34 makes clear the width of the flexibility that is available. It extends to whether there is to be anything like pleadings, whether there is to be any mutual disclosure of documents, whether any rules of evidence are to apply and whether there is to be a hearing. The 1996 Act has applied to arbitral proceedings commenced since 31 January 1997. It is still early days to make a long-term judgment about the effect of the Act. The potential certainly exists for radical and lasting changes.

THE CIVIL PROCEDURE RULES

Hard on the heels of the new arbitration regime came a revolutionary change in English litigation procedures, which is likely to provide a strong impetus for the development of client-friendly arbitration. The CPR have knock-on effects on the practice of arbitration which work in both positive and negative ways. Positively, the CPR have an educative effect. They introduce case management techniques and (at least in theory) a greater procedural flexibility. They place emphasis on the idea that the legal costs and effort expended on a case should be proportionate to its importance and the amount in dispute. By bringing about a change in the climate, they will help arbitrators have confidence to be more proactive, and more attuned to the need for efficient and cost-effective conduct of arbitrations. Negatively, there are features of the CPR which will tend to drive disputants to choose arbitration rather than subject themselves to the process of the courts. At the present time litigation conducted under the CPR suffers from uncertainty caused by novelty. The CPR are still in their first year of operation. Many aspects of the brave new world remain unclear in practice. Some clients may choose arbitration because of fears about what litigation under the CPR might involve. This is a temporary effect. In the course of time the uncertainties about the rules will be clarified and settled practices will emerge.

There are two characteristics of the CPR which are likely to have more permanent effects in driving parties out of litigation and into arbitration. These are the lack of party control and the clear insistence that the interests of the court override the interests of the parties. These features are enshrined in the "overriding objective" set out in rule 1.1, which the court and the parties are required to adhere to. In the CPR the purpose of the courts and the nature of justice have been redefined. The overriding objective includes "dealing with the case in ways that are proportionate', 'ensuring that it is dealt with expeditiously", and "allotting to it an appropriate share of the court's resources, while taking into account the need to allot resources to other cases." Spelled out, this means that expediency overrides the importance of arriving at an inherently just result, and that cases must be dealt with quickly, whether that is what the parties want or not. In effect, judges are required to keep public expenditure down by refusing to allocate resources to cases on the basis of what the cases need. In pursuance of this new philosophy, the judges have draconian powers to require adherence to stringent timetables, to strike out claims and defences, to refuse to hold a proper trial of the issues, and to dispose of them summarily instead. They also have powers to force the parties to participate in alternative dispute resolution (ADR). The litigant no longer has a right to his 'day in court.' This is all very different from the philosophy expressed when the RSC were introduced as part of the reforms of the late 19th century. The RSC were originally scheduled to the

Judicature Act 1875, and enlarged and reissued in 1883. Bowen LJ said in 1883, in relation to exercising judicial discretion under the RSC: "[i]t is a well established principle that the object of the court is to decide the rights of the parties ... Courts do not exist for the sake of discipline, but for the sake of deciding matters in controversy." Those relaxed remarks are a far cry from the new system, which punishes parties who fail to comply with timetables laid down by the court. Under the old system, if the plaintiff and defendant did not want to rush ahead with the case, they did not have to. Under the new system, the courts will force the parties to go full speed ahead, will frequently mete out discipline, and are entitled to refuse to decide the rights of the parties. This is not client friendly.

WHAT DO CLIENTS WANT?

Of course clients do not want excessive costs. The CPR have the laudable aim of trying to keep costs down. Whether that will be achieved in practice remains to be seen. Tight timetables may have a tendency to put costs up. But there are other things that clients want. A major desideratum is that there should be some flexibility in the pace of legal proceedings. Very often both sides have businesses to run. There is useful work that they need to get on with. They do not want to have to drop everything and devote themselves full time to an old dispute. Resolving the old dispute may be important, but securing the next deal and implementing the next contract are nearly always more important. Clients want some understanding of the pressures under which they work. They do not want to be subjected to onerous timetables laid down by a judge who is duty bound to be unsympathetic to their priorities. Clients also sometimes want time to try to negotiate a settlement with the other party, without the tribunal knowing that the negotiations are taking place.

If settlement is impossible, then they want to have their day in court, in the sense of a proper hearing, where their evidence and their point of view are fully heard and fully considered, and their rights are decided. What they are unlikely to want in a substantial case is an unsatisfactory short form of hearing, from which significant relevant evidence is excluded, and where the judge decides the parties' rights by a superficial examination of incomplete material. Procrustes was a legendary Greek robber, who stretched or cut his captives' legs to make them fit the bed on which he bound them. Most clients do not want their legs cut off, even if legal costs are thereby saved. Most clients are incensed if they are not allowed to have their side of the dispute properly presented and considered. The CPR may work extremely well for consumer claims and other small cases, but the Procrustean bed is likely to be problematic for more substantial disputes.

HOW ARBITRATION CAN MEET CLIENTS' NEEDS

One of the cornerstones of the Arbitration Act 1996 is the principle of party autonomy: "parties should be free to agree how their disputes are to be resolved ..." (section l(b) of the Act). Section 34 refers to "the right of the parties to agree any matter." This puts the clients in control. Legitimate questions may be asked about the extent of this control. Section 40(1) imposes on the parties a positive duty to "do all things necessary for the proper and expeditious conduct of the arbitral proceedings." Section 33(1) imposes on the arbitrator a mandatory duty to avoid "unnecessary delay or expense." These provisions might be thought to introduce the same regime of expedition as is found in the CPR. But there is a vital difference. The proceedings are not in the hands of a judge wielding the coercive powers of the state. Instead, they are in the hands of a private arbitrator chosen directly or indirectly by the parties. What happens if both parties have limited time to devote to their dispute and want to postpone dealing with it so that they can get on with their respective businesses meanwhile? If the parties agree (as they are entitled to do) on a slower timetable than the arbitrator thinks is necessary, there is nothing the arbitrator can effectively do about it. He must either accept it or resign. This situation is unlikely to arise often in practice. Most arbitrators want repeat business. (Conscientious arbitrators can comfort themselves with the thought that, if both parties want to delay, there are probably good reasons which make the delay 'necessary.')

Section 33 and section 34 of the Act are in conflict with each other. Section l(b) and section 34(1) lay down the principle of party autonomy, which gives the parties the right to control the procedure, and hence the speed at which the arbitration is conducted. As noted, however, s. 33 imposes a mandatory duty on the arbitrator to avoid unnecessary delay. If the parties go slow, the arbitrator should in theory crack the whip and speed them up. The DAC report indulged in considerable verbal gymnastics, seeking to argue that there was no conflict. It is more realistic to accept that there is a conflict, but that it matters not, because in practice s. 34 takes precedence. Section 33, although mandatory, is toothless when faced with a united front put up by the parties. The real usefulness of s. 33 lies in the power that it gives to the arbitrator when faced with recalcitrance on the part of one party only. By choosing arbitration rather than litigation, the parties have the best of both worlds. When both parties agree that the arbitration should not proceed at an inconvenient pace, that is what will happen. They will not be subjected to unreasonable timetables which require them to abandon useful work in order to give priority to the needs of the arbitral proceedings. On the other hand, if one party unreasonably indulges in delay, the arbitrator has ample power to spur that party into prompt action. These advantages of arbitration over litigation are not merely theoretical. In several recent cases the courts have imposed on the parties draconian orders which neither of them wanted. The orders were so inconvenient that the parties responded to them by entering into arbitration agreements, so as to take their disputes beyond the control of the courts. The judges were powerless to object.

WHAT MAKES FOR CLIENT-FRIENDLY ARBITRATION?

Some advantages of arbitration are inherent in the rules of the process. One of the chief advantages for business people is that arbitration is conducted in private. In a small proportion of arbitrations there is an application or appeal which goes to the courts, and is therefore heard in public, but in the majority of arbitrations confidentiality is maintained. Other advantages depend upon the skill and outlook of the particular arbitrator.

Some of the necessary qualities in the arbitrator are axiomatic, such as integrity and fair-mindedness. These are required for any arbitration. There are other qualities which should be looked for as being of particular use in making arbitration a client-friendly process: (1) A belief in party autonomy, coupled with the confidence to act decisively when needed. The wise arbitrator knows when to allow the proceedings to drift, because the parties are not in a hurry and have more important things on their minds. He is the servant of the parties. He will not make their lives more difficult by imposing unrealistic timetables on them. But if one party is unreasonably dragging its feet, the arbitrator will crack the whip and make whatever stringent orders are needed to get the recalcitrant party moving; (2) Legal competence. A complaint frequently levelled against arbitration is the unpredictability of the result. To some extent this is inherent in any kind of contentious proceedings. All litigation or arbitration is unpredictable to some degree. This is particularly the case when facts are in dispute. What evidence will emerge? What will the witnesses say? Whose evidence will be believed? But the legal aspects ought to be more predictable. The parties should be able to have confidence that the arbitrator will understand and apply a known body of law. They should not be put in the uncomfortable position of discovering, when it is too late, that the arbitrator does not understand the relevant law; (3) Ability to understand technical issues. For some disputes the best choice of arbitrator is the person who possesses established technical competence in the field of activity which is the subject of the dispute. Often, however, this is unnecessary. There are frequently experts engaged on each side, who between them will supply all the technical competence that is needed. (The arbitrator's own technical knowledge can even be a drawback, if it leads him to approach the evidence with a preconceived viewpoint.) What is needed in all cases involving technical elements is the ability to handle technical evidence and to understand the issues that are presented; (4) Procedural flexibility.

Procedural flexibility can make for client-friendly arbitration. This requires on the part of the arbitrator a full understanding of the extent of the flexibility available under the 1996 Act, the boldness to make use of it, and the skill to do so without straying into unfairness or contravening the rules of natural justice. The flexible arbitrator is concerned with substance rather than form. He is not concerned with whether statements of case have been given the correct heading. He does not require amendments to be shown in red. He is happy to receive the parties' statements or submissions by e-mail;

(5) Willingness to use s. 65. An arbitrator committed to client-friendliness will be willing in appropriate cases to make use of the provisions of s. 65 of the 1996 Act. Under this section the arbitrator has power (unless otherwise agreed by the parties) to direct that the recoverable costs of the arbitration shall be limited to a specified amount. Arbitrators should certainly use this power when both parties request it. A s. 65 limit may also be appropriate in circumstances where one party requests it because there is a risk of injustice owing to an extreme imbalance in the respective financial resources of the parties.

The CIArb has recently launched a new set of rules designed to take advantage of s. 65. The Cost Effective Arbitration Rules limit recoverable party costs to 10% of the amount in issue. They limit total costs, including the arbitrator's own fees, to 20%. These provisions are attractive to claimants who believe they have a good case but cannot take the financial risk of losing and having to pay full costs to the respondent. They are also attractive to respondents who are unsure of their position and do not want to be exposed to the risk of paying full costs to the claimant.

CONCLUDING REMARKS

Case-managed litigation under the provisions of the new rules of court in England is unattractive to parties who would prefer to cooperate with each other in the conduct and resolution of their dispute rather than be dictated to by the court. The Arbitration Act 1996 provides all the powers needed for a suitably equipped arbitrator to provide them with a client-friendly arbitration service.

REFERENCES

* This article was originally published as A. Bartlett, 'Client-Friendly Arbitration', *Arbitration* 66, no. 1 (2000): 2-5.

1 E.g., *Re Enoch and Zaretzky, Bock & Co.* [1910] 1 KB 327, CA, still cited as good law in M. Mustill & S. Boyd, *Commercial Arbitration*, (London: Butterworths, 1989), 352.

2 M. Needman, 'Appeal on a Point of Law out of an Award', *Arbitration* 65 (1999): 210.

3 *Scott v Avery* (1856). This passage was edited out of the report at 5 HLC 811 (see D. Roebuck, 'The Myth of Judicial Jealousy', *Arbitration International* 10 (1994): 404-5).

4 CPR 1.2, 1.3

5 CPR 1.4.

6 Rule 1.4 refers to "encouraging" the parties to use ADR, but it means 'coercing', for a party that does not cooperate with ADR is at risk of adverse costs consequences, see rule 44.5(3)(a)(ii).

7 The removal of this right brings to fulfilment a trend that became evident, in proper protest against excessive cost and delay, some ten

years ago: see *Banque Financière de la Citè SA v Westgnre Insurance Co. Ltd* [1990] 2 All ER 947 at 959, *Ashmore v Corporation of Lloyd's* [1992] 2 All ER 486 at 493. Interesting questions may arise on the validity of the rules when the Human Rights Act 1998 comes into force. Article 6 of the Convention for the Protection of Human Rights and Fundamental Freedoms gives everyone the right to a fair hearing for the determination of his or her civil rights and obligations.

8   *Cropper v Smith* (1883) 26 Ch D 700, 710-11.

9   The same is true, incidentally, of solicitors and experts who are involved in litigation. It is seldom that they can devote their full time and attention to a single case. Experts have their ordinary professional work to attend to. Solicitors have other cases running concurrently.

10 Departmental Advisory Committee on Arbitration Law, Report on the Arbitration Bill, February 1996.

11 See paras 154-63 of the report.

CHAPTER 2

Appeals from Arbitral Awards: Should Section 69 be Repealed?

Roger Holmes and Michael O'Reilly

The Arbitration Act 1996 is generally clear and succinct, perhaps even "brilliant." The formulation of the legislation was not, however, without controversy. Many hoped that the United Kingdom would adopt the UNCITRAL Model Law in its entirety. The act that emerged was something of a compromise, following many of the precepts of the Model Law, but retaining some peculiarly English features. One is the procedural apparatus enabling a party to apply for leave to appeal on a point of law arising out of an award. When the Draft Bill was put out for consultation, the question arose whether or not to retain a limited right to appeal on a question of law. Many considered that there ought to be no appeal but in the end it was decided to retain the appeals procedure. In this article, we evaluate the operation of s.69, with reference to the decided cases. It is our view that s.69 adds little to the cause of justice or the development of the law. As well as being contrary to the spirit of party autonomy as expressed in s.1(b), it is a source of cost and inefficiency. Repealing s.69 is likely to enhance both the attractiveness and effectiveness of English arbitration.

HISTORICAL BACKGROUND

The English courts have traditionally been keen to supervise the performance of arbitrators. In 1865, Campbell L.J. advanced the theory that this arose from a desire by judges to get cases into Westminster Hall. Even as late as 1922 Scrutton L.J. was highly indignant at the suggestion that the parties to an arbitration might, by agreement, put their chosen arbitrator beyond judicial scrutiny. During the middle years of the 20th century, judicial attitudes to arbitration changed and the Commercial Court began to support the autonomy of the arbitral process. Nevertheless, until 1979, the court was heavily involved in supervising arbitration through the "special case" procedure, whereby an arbitrator — who was presumed likely to make an error of law — could be required to state a case on a question of law for the opinion of the court.

As a result of concerns about the effect of the special case procedure on the attractiveness of London as a centre for international arbitration, that procedure was replaced by a restricted right of appeal in the 1979 Act s.1. The scope of the appeals procedure it established was not clearly delimited. In *The Nema*, the Court of Appeal attempted to restrict the scope. Lord Denning set down a series of restrictive guidelines. Robert Goff J. refused to follow the superior court, declaring that: "[I] do not feel free to apply these principles in deciding whether or not to give leave to appeal under the Act, because I am unable to discover any basis for them in the Act itself." Goff J.'s liberal interpretation threatened to reintroduce the special case procedure, albeit in a slightly altered form. The House of Lords gave leave to appeal *The Nema*. Lord Diplock — following Lord Denning's earlier lead — carried out a "breathtakingly purposive interpretation of section 1(3)" resulting in the now familiar "Nema Guidelines" setting out the type of factors that needed to be present before leave might be given. Lord Diplock said: "there are, in my view, several indications in the Act itself of a parliamentary intention to give effect to the turn of the tide in favour of finality in arbitral awards (particularly in nondomestic arbitrations of which the instant case is one) ..." Lord Diplock — following Lord Denning's view — distinguished between a 'one-off' point and one of more general importance. In relation to one-off points, Lord Diplock said: "leave should not normally be given unless it is apparent to the judge upon a mere perusal of the reasoned award itself without the benefit of adversarial argument that the meaning ascribed to the clause by the arbitrator is obviously wrong." Where the point was of more general importance, a less stringent test might be applied. Lord Diplock decided that: "[a] rather less strict criteria [were] appropriate where questions of construction of contracts in standard terms are concerned ... But leave should not be given even in such a case, unless the judge considered that a strong prima facie case had been made out that the arbitrator had been wrong in his construction." Despite these clear indications, it seems that High Court judges still gave leave to appeal liberally for some time, prompting the House of Lords to give leave to appeal in a second 'test case' — *The Antaios*. Lord Roskill made an impassioned plea for judges to clamp down on grants of leave to appeal: "The resultant abuse was notorious. Hence the demand for the abolition of the special case successfully accomplished in 1979. But if the restricted appellate system substituted for the special case ... is to be operated in such a way as to make appeals to the High Court ... readily available, not only are the worst features of the system now abolished restored but the additional, albeit not unrestricted autonomy, of arbitral tribunals which the

1979 Act was designed to establish, [is] seriously hampered." The number of successful applications for leave to appeal reduced dramatically.

When it was decided to overhaul the arbitration legislation in the 1990s, the opportunity arose to consider whether or not to abolish the right to appeal. As Lord Saville made clear in his Bernstein Lecture, there were those who contended for abolition. In the end the 1979 Act s.1 was re-enacted but with the Nema guidelines codified.

THE APPEAL PROVISIONS

Unless the parties have agreed that the court shall have jurisdiction to hear an appeal, s.69 merely provides a right to make an application for permission to appeal on a point of law arising out of an award. There are two sets of tests that must be met: (1) jurisdiction tests — the seat of the arbitration must be England and Wales and the relevant question must arise under English law; (2) the s.69(3) hurdles.

The Jurisdiction Tests

The jurisdiction tests demarcate those cases where an appeal is possible from those where it is not. Commercial lay parties may find the demarcation tests difficult to understand. Consider, for example, two arbitrations being heard in adjacent rooms in London. Coincidentally, the same question of law arises in both arbitrations. One contract is governed by the law of England, whilst the other is governed by the law of India, but the lawyers in the latter have agreed to work on the principle that the law of India and England are identical on the issues that arise. Yet only one arbitration is subject to s.69 because a question of law under Indian law is a question of fact under English law — and questions of fact cannot be appealed. Indeed, the very distinction between a question of law and a question of fact is one which causes great confusion, even to lawyers. "It is never easy to define what is meant by a question of law in the context of an arbitration appeal." In many instances, we can only feel safe in characterising a question as one of law or fact once a court has laid down a precedent. But even then we must take care: "what is a question of law in a judicial review case may not necessarily be a question of law in the field of consensual arbitrations." The judiciary too has not been consistent even within the context of consensual arbitrations. For instance, Lord Saville has said (extra-judicially) that "A point of law does not, under the new Act, include the question whether there was sufficient evidence to support the findings of fact." Judge Thornton says, on the other hand: "[t]here is no reason why, in an appropriate case, it should not still be possible in an appeal under section 69 of the Act to raise as a question of law the question whether or not there was any evidence to support a material finding of fact."

Commercial parties might reasonably ask whether these distinctions, about which even judges seem to be confused, ought have any place in a system of law which is ostensibly — and certainly should be — designed to facilitate trade and enterprise.

The Section 69(3) Hurdles

Section 69(3)(a) to (d), sets out four specific criteria. All four must be met before leave is given. (3) Leave to appeal shall be given only if the court is satisfied that (a) the determination of the question will substantially affect the rights of one or more of the parties, (b) the question is one which the tribunal was asked to determine, (c) on the basis of the findings of fact in the award (i) the decision of the tribunal on the question is obviously wrong, or (ii) the question is one of general public importance and the decision of the tribunal is at least open to serious doubt, and; (d) that, despite the agreement of the parties to resolve the matter by arbitration, it is just and proper in all the circumstances for the court to determine the question.

Little guidance is given as to the way in which the tests should be approached, but the Departmental Advisory Committee, who were responsible for the text that went to Parliament, say in their report: "We have attempted to express in this clause the limits put on the right to appeal by the House of Lords in ... *The Nema*."

In subs.(3)(c) a key distinction is drawn between cases of "general public importance" and other cases. If the case is not of "general public importance" then, in order to get leave to appeal, nothing less than an obviously wrong decision will suffice. What does "general public importance" mean? As the draftsman sought to codify the Nema guidelines it is reasonable to suppose that Lord Diplock's own formulation remains valid, *viz* that the decision "would add significantly to the clarity and certainty of English commercial law ...". The test set out in s.69(3)(d) is new to the 1996 Act. In some ways this can be seen as further restricting the scope for granting leave to appeal. As Tuckey J. has said: "Finally before leave is given under s.69 the Court must be satisfied that it would be just and proper in all the circumstances to do so. This is a long stop provision which underlines the need for the Court to respect the decision of the tribunal of the parties' choice."

A CRITICAL REVIEW OF SECTION 69

This review touches on two main questions. First, we ask, does s.69 provide an avenue which the parties want? We then ask whether the aims of s.69 are met in practice.

Does Section 69 Provide What the Parties Want?

The Arbitration Act 1996 s.1(b) provides: "the parties should be free to agree how their disputes are resolved, subject only to such safeguards as are necessary in the public interest." Does s.69 support that basic principle? A number of commentators have attempted to justify s.69 on the grounds that this is what the parties would have expressly agreed had they considered the matter. The DAC Report suggests that this can be inferred in a case where the arbitration agreement contains an express choice of law clause. Lord Saville also expressed this view: "it seems to me that it is well arguable that this limited right of appeal can properly be described as supportive of the arbitral process. Where the parties have agreed that their dispute will be resolved in accordance with English law, and the tribunal then purports to reach an answer which is not in accordance with English law, it can be said with some force that unless the courts correct this error, the tribunal itself will have failed to carry out the bargain of the parties." We doubt whether the normal tests of contract interpretation would admit of this extrapolation; and if they did, would this not also be an argument for ensuring that any contract with an express choice of law clause, whether English or Ruritanian, be allowed an appeal — after all, why should parties under an English contract be held to their bargain, but parties under a Ruritanian contract be allowed to avoid it?

In many — indeed, probably in most — cases, however, there is no express choice of law clause. Accordingly, the suggestion that s.69 expresses what the parties have agreed is tantamount to the assertion that the appeal provisions — or something akin to them — would be implied. We suggest that the tests normally applicable to the implication of a term would rarely be met; in effect, we would have to imagine the parties testily suppressing the officious legislator with a common "Oh, of course we meant to include a limited right of appeal to the High Court." In reality, we suggest, the parties ordinarily submit disputes to arbitration, knowing that an arbitrator, like a judge, is fallible. Frequently, it is understood that the question referred to the tribunal will be a difficult question; but the parties nevertheless need to have a final resolution and choose to refer it to an arbitrator. The argument that the parties would support the limited right of appeal if they thought about it seems to us also to give insufficient regard to the negative aspects of an appeals procedure. It is frequently said — and indeed Saville L.J. himself mentions this in the quotation at the head of this article — that overseas parties do not want appeals. Indeed, there are good reasons why parties generally would not want an appeals procedure imposed on them. They are expensive, time consuming, create uncertainty as to the enforceability of awards and involve exposing private, commercially-sensitive matters in the public courts.

Has Section 69 Achieved Its Goals?

It is never easy to identify the specific goals that a piece of legislation is designed to achieve. We suggest, however, that there are clear indications that s.69 was designed to achieve two principal goals: (1) to safeguard the parties against capricious arbitral decisions which would otherwise result in serious injustice; (2) to allow cases of "general public importance" which will add significantly to the clarity and certainty of English commercial law. The success or failure of s.69 must be judged by its performance measured against these aims. This test involves examining the empirical evidence. In order to do this, we briefly surveyed the cases reported in Lloyd's Law Reports to provide a reasonable cross-section of the output from cases resulting from the s.69 procedure. The results of this survey are set out below.

A Survey of Section 69 Cases Reported in Lloyd's Law Reports

Egmatra AG v Marco Trading Corporation [1999] *1 Lloyd's Rep. 862.* (Application for leave. Application dismissed on grounds that applicable law was Swiss law, not English law), *Sanghi Polyesters Ltd (India) v International Investor (KCFC, Kuwait)* [2000] 1 Lloyd's Rep. 480. (Application for leave. Application dismissed on grounds that applicable law was Sharia law, not English law), *Merit Shipping Co. Inc. v TK Boesan A/S, The Goodpal* [2000] 1 Lloyd's Rep. 638. (Appeal brought pursuant to leave granted by another judge. Appeal failed), *Dubai Islamic Bank PJSC v Paymentech Merchant Services Inc* [2001] 1 Lloyd's Rep. 65. (Application for leave. Application dismissed on grounds that seat was not in England and Wales), *Whistler International Ltd v Kawasaki Kisen Kaisha, The Hill Harmony* [2001] 1 Lloyd's Rep. 147. (Leave to appeal was given. The first instance judge overturned the award. He was supported by the Court of Appeal. The House of Lords, however, restored the arbitrators' award), *Bayoil SA v Seawind Tankers Corporation, The Leonidas* [2001] 1 Lloyd's

Rep. 553. (Appeal brought pursuant to leave granted by another judge. Appeal failed), *China Offshore Oil (Singapore) International Pte v Giant Shipping Ltd, The Posidon* [2001] 1 Lloyd's Rep. 697. (Appeal brought pursuant to leave granted by another judge. Appeal failed), *Losinjska Plovidba v Valfracht Maritime Co Ltd, the Lipa* [2001] 2 Lloyd's Rep. 17. (Case turned on meaning of bespoke terms written into a charterparty. Appeal succeeded, but it is submitted that the arbitrator's decision was itself entirely respectable), *Brandeis Brokers Ltd v Black* [2001] 2 Lloyd's Rep. 359. (Application for leave dismissed), *Reliance Industries Ltd v Enron Oil and Gas India Ltd* [2002] 1 Lloyd's Rep. 645. (Application for leave dismissed on grounds that applicable law was Indian law, not English law. The judge said that even if the contract had been subject to English law the application would have failed), *Athletic Union of Constantinople v National Basketball Association* [2002] 1 Lloyd's Rep. 305. (Application dismissed on grounds that applicable law was Greek law, not English law), *Stolt Tankers Inc. v Landmark Chemicals SA* [2002] 1 Lloyd's Rep. 786. (Appeal brought pursuant to leave granted by another judge. Appeal failed), *North Range Shipping Ltd v Seatrans Shipping Corporation, The Western Triumph* [2002] 2 Lloyd's Rep. 1 (CA). (This appeal was principally about the impact of Human Rights Act 1998. But, at the end of its decision, the Court of Appeal decided as an appeal from Steel J.'s refusal to grant leave, the substantive point — whether leave to appeal should be given. Leave to appeal granted and appeal dismissed), *Glencore Grain Ltd v Flacker Shipping Ltd, The Happy Day* [2002] 2 Lloyd's Rep. 487 (CA). (Court of Appeal heard this appeal from the decision of the first instance judge.

Judge's decision set aside and the arbitrator's original award restored). This brief survey yields a number of conclusions: (1) The number of appeal cases worthy of publication is relatively small compared to the very great number of arbitrations; (2) In very few cases — *The Lipa* was the only example that we located — was the arbitrator's award overturned permanently; (3) Where first instances judges have overturned an award, the appellate courts have restored the arbitrator's award on several occasions.

Does Section 69 Act to Safeguard Commercial Parties Against Capricious Decisions which Would Otherwise Result in Serious Injustice?

This survey, brief and narrow though it may be, casts serious doubt upon the assertion that s.69 acts to safeguard the parties from capricious arbitrators — or, indeed, that there are many capricious arbitrators. Very few cases were overturned on appeal. Indeed, measured by that same test, the judges got it wrong more often than the arbitrators. Before dismissing s.69 as largely irrelevant, however, it is important to consider its possible psychological effect. Perhaps s.69 focuses the arbitrator's attention on the need to apply the law and thus has a beneficial effect. We have no way of testing that. But, whatever may have been the position in the past, we suggest that the typical arbitrator in practice today is highly trained and rigorously professional and strives to do his or her duty to apply the law. If this observation is accurate, s.69 will have little, or no, psychological effect.

Does Section 69 Promote the Clarity and Certainty of English Commercial Law?

To what extent have the reported cases furthered the development of English commercial law? No doubt some light has been shed on a number of important points. For example, the judge at first instance considered important the point raised in *The Happy Day* concerning the rights of owners to demurrage and of charterers to despatch, when the notice triggering the start of laytime is invalid. The Court of Appeal's decision must therefore be welcomed. Likewise, in *The Hill Harmony*, the House of Lords dealt with a point of potential importance arising where the ship's master disregards the charterer's instructions as to route and follows another course. In other cases, too, points of some importance were raised. But the point in issue is not whether these decisions are useful to the commercial community, but whether their value outweighs the cost of the appeals apparatus. Appeals increase the cost of arbitral dispute resolution generally, not just in those cases which are actually appealed. Moreover, many of the most important cases decided on appeal since 1979 have been about the appeal system itself. *The Nema*, for example, is possibly the most important case of all, measured in terms of its impact on the commercial community. There is clearly potential for circular reasoning about the value of an appeals procedure designed to facilitate the development of arbitration and commercial law when the most important decisions are about the appeals system itself.

CONCLUDING REMARKS

More empirical evidence could be collected to inform our evaluation of the effect and operation of s.69. For example, an improved feel for the cost of s.69, both in reviewing awards and in pursuing appeals would be of value. Furthermore, better evidence as to the degree of hostility (if any) of domestic and overseas parties to English appeal procedures would enable this aspect of the evaluation to be carried out less speculatively. From our survey, however, we are able to make provisional recommendations. We suggest that consideration ought to be given to the repeal of s.69 because: (1) It conflicts with the principle of party autonomy and (2) It increases the cost of commerce, e.g., reviewing awards with a view to considering an appeal and, where so advised, on pursuing the appeal, without generating any corresponding benefit. There is no evidence that s.69 has either avoided injustice or added significantly to the development of commercial law. Even if not repealed, s.69 and its associated guidelines ought to be reframed. The "question of law" test is confusing. The definition of "general public importance" also needs to be clarified and more rigorously applied. Some of the decisions in which leave has been given on that ground cannot be justified.

REFERENCES

* This article was originally published as Roger Holmes & Michael O'Reilly, 'Appeals from Arbitral Awards: Should Section 69 be Repealed?', *Arbitration* 69, no. 1 (2003): 1-9.

1 M. Saville, 'The Arbitration Act 1996 and its Effect on International Arbitration in England', *Arbitration* 63 (1997): 108.

2 In *Groundshire v VHE Construction* [2001] B.L.R. 395, Judge Bowsher Q.C. spoke of "the brilliant draftsmen of the 1996 Act."

3 Adopted by the United Nations Commission on International Trade Law (UNCITRAL) on June 21, 1985. General Assembly, Resolution 40/72 of December 11, 1985, recommended "that all States give due consideration to the Model Law ... , in view of the desirability of

uniformity of the law of arbitral procedures and the specific needs of international commercial arbitration practice". CPR 1.2, 1.3

4   See e.g., Lord Fraser of Carmyllie, Hansard, HL Vol. 574, written answer on behalf of H.M. Government at WA 53, July 16, 1996.

5   Arbitration Act 1996 Section 69.

6   Departamental Advisory Committee report, February 1996, Department of Trade and Industry, para.284.

7   See generally M. Mustill & S. Boyd, *Commercial Arbitration*, (London: Butterworths, 1989), Chapter 29: 'Judicial control: a historical survey', 431-458.

8   *Scott v Avery* (1856) 5 HLC 811.

9   *Czarnikov v Roth, Schmidt & Co.* [1922] 2 K.B. 478 at 487, 488: "There must be no Alsatia in England where the King's writ does not run."

10 *BTP Tioxide Ltd v Pioneer Shipping Ltd, The Nema* [1982] A.C. 724 (HL).

11 *The Nema* [1980] 2 Lloyd's Rep. 339 (CA), per Lord Denning M.R. at 344-345.

12 *Schiffahrtsagentur Hamburg Middle East Line GmbH v Virtue Shipping Corpn Monrovia, The Oinoussian Virtue* [1981] 1 Lloyd's Rep. 533 at 538.

13 *The Nema* [1982] A.C. 724 (HL).

14 J. Dyson, 'Finality in Arbitration and Adjudication', *Arbitration* 66 (2000): 291.

15 At 739H.

16 *The Nema* at 742H.

17 *The Nema* at 743D; 743F.

18 Arguably, the guidelines were to some extent obiter (see e.g., *BVS SA v Kerman Shipping Co SA* [1982] 1 W.L.R. 166, at 169) and when re-endorsed by the Court of Appeal in *Italmare Shipping Co v Ocean Tanker Co Inc, The Rio Sun* [1982] 1 W.L.R. 158, Lord Denning said at 162: "It must be remembered that they are only guidelines. You can step over guidelines without causing any harm. You can move them, if need be, to suit the situation."

19 *Antaios Compania Naviera SA v Salen Rederienrna AB*, The Antaios [1985] 1 A.C. 191 (HL).

20 At 208.

21 A question of law is defined in s.82(1) as a question of the law of England and Wales.

22 In *Reliance Industries v Enron Oil & Gas India Ltd* [2002] B.L.R. 36, the seat was in London, although the substantive law was that of India. The parties had made the working assumption that the law of England coincided with the law of India. The unsuccessful party sought to appeal under s.69. Held, despite the working assumption, the arbitrators applied the law of India and there was no question of law to be appealed.

23 *Fence Gate Limited v NEL Construction Ltd TCC*, December 5, 2001 per Judge Thornton Q.C. at para. 38.

24 For example, The Solholt [1983] 1 Lloyd's Rep. 605, CA, per Sir John Donaldson M.R. at 608, is frequently cited as authority for the proposition that questions of mitigation are questions of fact.

25 Steyn L.J. in *Geogas SA v Tramno Gas Ltd, The Baleares* [1993] 1

Lloyd's Rep. 215 at 231 (CA).

26 M. Saville, 108. This view is supported by M. Mustill & S. Boyd, *Commercial Arbitration 2001 Companion Volume*, (London: Butterworths, 2001), 357.

27 *Fence Gate Limited v NEL Construction Ltd*, TCC, December 5, 2001 at para.42.

28 DAC Report para. 286(iv).

29 *The Nema* [1982] A.C. 724 at 743E.

30 *Egmatra AG v Marco Trading Corporation* [1999] 1 Lloyd's Rep. 862 at 865.

31 DAC Report para. 285.

32 M. Saville, 108.

33 Paraphrasing MacKinnon L.J.'s graphic test in *Shirlaw v Southern Foundries* [1939] 2 K.B. 206 at 227.

34 It would be useful to carry out some empirical research into the real cost of s.69. When a party loses an arbitration of any size, it is now virtually obligatory to scan the award with a view to appealing it. This is a surcharge on every arbitration, even if the decision is not to appeal. Then, of course, there are all the cases where an unsuccessful application for leave is made.

35 It will typically take four months from award to hearing an application for leave. As the time from issue of arbitration notice to award is frequently less than a year, the delay is proportionately significant.

36 Lord Diplock in *The Nema* [1982] A.C. 724 at 743E.

37 [2001] 2 Lloyd's Rep. 17.

38 *The Hill Harmony* [2001] 1 Lloyd's Rep. 147 (HL); The Happy Day [2002] 2 Lloyd's Rep. 487 (CA).

39 In *The Nema* [1980] 2 Lloyd's Rep. 339 (CA), Lord Denning predicted at 344 that when it came to interpreting general contract clauses "the arbitrator is just as likely to be right as the judge — probably more likely."

40 [2001] 1 Lloyd's Rep. 755 (CA).

41 [2001] 1 Lloyd's Rep. 147 (HL).

42 This is reinforced by the fact that a significant number of the reported decisions concern procedural aspects of appeals. For example, time limits *Aoot Kalmneft v Glencore International* [2002] 1 All E.R. 76; appeals to the Court of Appeal arising from an arbitration application *Henry Boot Construction (UK) Ltd v Malmaison Hotel (Manchester) Ltd* [2000] 2 Lloyd's Rep. 625 and *Inco Europe Ltd v First Choice Distribution* [2000] 1 Lloyd's Rep. 467 (CA); whether a judge is required to give reasons for refusing leave *Mousaka Inc. v Golden Seagull Maritime Inc.* [2002] 1 W.L.R. 657 and *North Range Shipping Ltd v Seatrans Shipping Corpn, The Western Triumph* [2002] 2 Lloyd's Rep. 1 (CA).

CHAPTER 2

Commencement of Arbitration and Time-bar Clauses

Andrew Tweeddale and Karen Tweeddale

This article considers how English courts construe time-bar clauses and whether there is an advantage in having an arbitration clause in a contract where there is a time-bar clause. It is now common to find time-bar provisions in many of the major forms of construction contracts. They appear in NEC 3, in the FIDIC suite of contracts and the ICE forms. Sub-clause 20.1 of the FIDIC forms of contract, for example, creates a time-bar that gives a Contractor just a mere 28 days to put in a notice of a claim for additional cost or an extension of time. Given that the effect of a failure to issue a 28-day notice is an apparent bar on any claim, it is unsurprising that time-bar clauses have been the subject of much consideration and review. Recent decisions in the courts show that these clauses are being construed strictly. This has led one leading English lawyer, in a paper on the FIDIC forms of contract, to comment that quite possibly there are no ways round a sub-clause 20.1 notice.

TIME-BAR CLAUSES AND THE COURTS

Recent cases have focused on whether time-bar clauses are valid where the employer has caused the delay but the contractor then fails to submit a notice within the prescribed period in which to bring the claim. In such cases the issue has been whether the employer should be able to deduct liquidated damages. Litigants challenging the validity of a time-bar clause have argued that the employer should not be able to rely on such a clause, because to do so would result in the employer taking advantage of its own wrong. The opposing argument was that the employer did not prevent the contractor from giving the notice and therefore the time-bar provision should be enforced.

In *Alghussein Establishment v Eton College* the House of Lords held that a party may not benefit from its own breach of contract. This is often referred to as the 'prevention principle' and was applied to construction contracts by the Court of Appeal in *Peak Construction (Liverpool) Ltd v McKinney Foundations Ltd*, which held that: "[a]n Employer cannot hold the Contractor to the contractual completion date, if the Employer has by its act or omission prevented the Contractor from completing by that date. Instead, time becomes at large and the obligation to complete by the contract date is replaced by an implied obligation to complete within a reasonable time."

There is an isolated Australian authority which supports the view that a contractor can rely on the prevention principle in order to avoid the effects of its own failure to give notice of a claim for additional time. In *Gaymark Investment Pty v Walter Construction Group* the parties entered into a contract which contained a time-bar clause. The arbitrator found that there were delays to completion which were due to acts of prevention caused by the employer. The arbitrator further held that, although the contractor had failed to give the requisite notices for an extension of time, the "acts of prevention" by the employer rendered time at large. The arbitrator then went on to conclude that the contractor had a reasonable time to complete the works and that it had in fact completed within that reasonable time. Bailey J. in the Supreme Court of the Northern Territories upheld the arbitrator's conclusions.

Courts in other jurisdictions have taken a different approach. In *City Inn Ltd v Shepherd Construction Ltd*, the Scottish Court of Session held that the giving of the notice was a condition to the right to claim an extension of time and money. The contractor had elected not to give the notice and was therefore not entitled to either time or money. The reasoning of the court was that the instruction might not have delayed the works or have had a financial implication. It was for the contractor to decide whether the instruction would have a time and cost implication and if so it was obliged to give a notice. The Inner House of the Court of Session was not, however, asked to and did not consider the prevention principle and its application.

Recently the English High Court in *Multiplex Construction v Honeywell Control Systems* endorsed the view that time-bar clauses are valid and should be upheld. Jackson J. held that contractual terms requiring a contractor to give prompt notice of delay served a valuable purpose as they enabled matters to be investigated while they were still current. He also regarded such terms as valuable because they sometimes gave the employer the opportunity to withdraw instructions when the financial consequences became apparent. He doubted that *Gaymark* represented English law: "[i]f *Gaymark* is good law, then a contractor could disregard with impunity any provision making proper notice a condition precedent. At his option the contractor could set time at large." Jackson J.'s analysis was adopted by

Davies J. in *Steria Ltd v Sigma Wireless Communications Ltd*: "[g]enerally, one can see the commercial absurdity of an argument which would result in the contractor being better off by deliberately failing to comply with the notice condition than by complying with it." Davies J. concluded that the prevention principle did not mean that the failure by Steria, the sub-contractor, to comply with the contractual notice requirement for an extension of time put the time for completion at large. These cases were considering time-bar clauses where the claims were litigated. However, the position is different where the claim is arbitrated and under both the Arbitration Act 1950 and Arbitration Act 1996 there are provisions which entitle a court to extend time for commencing an arbitration where a party has failed to commence a claim in breach of a contractual time-bar clause.

TIME-BAR CLAUSES UNDER THE ARBITRATION ACT 1950

The Arbitration Act 1950 s.27 was entitled 'Power of the Court to Extend Time for Commencing Arbitration Proceedings': "[w]here the terms of an agreement to refer future disputes to arbitration provide that any claims to which the agreement applies shall be barred unless notice to appoint an arbitrator is given... or some other step to commence arbitration proceedings is taken within a fixed time by the agreement, and a dispute arises to which the agreement applies... [then] notwithstanding that the time so fixed has expired, may, on such terms, if any... extend the time for such period as it thinks proper." Whether s.27 could be used to extend time depended on the terms of the contract. In *Crown Estate Commissioners v John Mowlem* the court recognised that there was a distinction between a clause which barred the commencement of an arbitration and one which made a final certificate issued by an architect or engineer conclusive as to matters relating to standards and quality of work. The distinction arises because s.27 only applies to situations where there is delay in giving a notice to appoint or other step to commence the arbitration. It does not apply, and the courts cannot extend time, where a clause extinguishes a claim; for example, where the clause states that by not serving the claim in a prescribed time the potential defendant is discharged from any liability under that claim. Therefore in *Babanaft International Co SA v Avant Petroleum Inc* a time-bar operated where no claim in writing supported by documents was received within 90 days of a prescribed event. Donaldson L.J. noted that such a clause might be "a source of injustice or even oppression" but "as the law stands, that will be the position."

EXTENDING TIME FOR COMMENCING AN ARBITRATION UNDER THE ARBITRATION ACT 1996

The Arbitration Act 1996 increased the court's powers as to when it could extend time for commencing an arbitration. As stated by Mustill and Boyd, the new bases for extending time "are different from the old law, the numerous decisions on which must now be regarded as largely if not wholly irrelevant." The Arbitration Act 1996 s.12(1): "[w]here an arbitration agreement to refer future disputes to arbitration provides that a claim shall be barred, or the claimant's right extinguished, unless the claimant takes within a time fixed by the agreement some step to begin arbitral proceedings, or to begin other dispute resolution procedures which must be exhausted before arbitral proceedings can be begun, the court may by order extend the time for taking that step."

The main changes are that s.12(1) applies where the claimant's right will be extinguished, not just barred; and not only to commencing an arbitration but also commencing some other dispute resolution procedures which must be exhausted before arbitral proceedings can be begun. The changes are not merely semantic. Babanaft would probably now be decided differently and *Crown Estate Commissioners v John Mowlem* might be reversed.

In *Monella v Pizza Express (Restaurants) Ltd* the High Court had to consider a rent review clause. The relevant terms were in clause 8: "[w]henever the Revised Rent in respect of a Review Period has not been agreed between the Landlord and the Tenant before the relevant Review Date and the Landlord has not made any application to the President for the time being of the Royal Institute of Chartered Surveyors as hereinbefore provided the Tenant may serve on the Landlord notice in writing containing a proposal as to the amount of such Revised Rent not being less than the rent payable immediately before the commencement of the relevant Review Period and the amount so proposed shall be deemed to have been agreed by the parties as the Revised Rent for the relevant Review Period and sub-clause (D)(i) hereof shall apply accordingly unless the Landlord shall make such application as aforesaid within one month after service of such notice by the Tenant." The time-bar provision therefore had nothing to do with commencing the arbitration. The rent was deemed to be agreed unless it was referred to the President of the RICS for a decision. Morritt V.C. held: "I have no doubt, and I so hold, that s.12(3) is applicable to clause 8." It is implicit that he saw the referral to the President of the RICS as part of the dispute resolution procedure. It should be noted that he made no reference to *Crown Estate Commissioners v John Mowlem*. There are, however, strict requirements that a Claimant needs to overcome before a court will make an order under the Arbitration Act 1996 s.12; s.12(3) states that the English court, where the seat of the arbitration is in England and Wales or Northern Ireland, may extend a contractual time-bar provision if it is satisfied: "(3)(a) that the circumstances are such as were outside the reasonable contemplation of the parties when they agreed the provision in question, and that it would be just to extend the time, or (3)(b) that the conduct of one of the parties makes it unjust to hold the other party to the strict terms of the provision in question."

The courts have been reluctant to grant extensions of time save in exceptional cases as this has been seen to be contrary to the principle of party autonomy and would be an interference with the parties' contract. In *Harbour & General Works v Environment Agency* the claimant entered into a contract with the respondent based on ICE Conditions of Contract, 6th edition. The claimant issued a notice to refer a dispute to arbitration but it was eight days late. The Court of Appeal refused to extend time for the commencement of the arbitration. Waller L.J. stated: "[t]he sub-section is concerned with party autonomy. Its aim seems to me to be to allow the Court to consider an extension in relation to circumstances where the parties would not reasonably have contemplated them as being ones where the time bar would apply, or to put it the other way round, the section is concerned not to allow the Court to interfere with a contractual bargain unless the circumstances are such that if they had been drawn to the attention of the parties when they agreed the provision, the parties would at the very least have contemplated that the time bar might not apply; it then being for the Court finally to rule as to whether justice requires an extension of time to be given.... it would appear quite impossible to characterise a negligent omission to comply with a contractual time bar, however little delay was involved, as, without more, outside their mutual contemplation."

In *Gibson Joint Venture v The Department of Environment of Northern Ireland* the parties entered into an ICE, 5th edn, form of contract. Disputes arose and the engineer issued a decision and thereafter the contractor and engineer entered into negotiations to discuss the claims. The negotiations broke down and the contractor issued a notice of arbitration 23 days late. The contractor referred to these negotiations between him and the engineer and argued that this was "conduct of one of the parties [which] makes it unjust to hold the other party to the strict terms of the provision in question" as provided by the Arbitration Act 1996 s.12(3)(b). The court, although having sympathy for the contractor, disagreed. Furthermore, the court found that the engineer, though agent to the employer, was not one of the parties to the arbitration agreement and therefore the engineer's conduct was irrelevant when considering s.12.

In *Korbetis v Transgrain Shipping BV* the court had to consider whether an error in sending the notice of arbitration by fax to a wrong number was a circumstance outside the reasonable contemplation of the parties. The court concluded there was no basis for extending time. Toulson J. equated s.12(3)(a) with all sorts of events that may occur which the: "parties would not ordinarily expect to occur, but which they know might conceivably occur. I have in mind the sort of extraneous things which in other contexts might be considered force majeure or frustrating events."

In *Monella v Pizza Express (Restaurants) Ltd* the court had to consider whether a change in the law which affected the time-bar clause was an event under s.12(3). The court concluded on the facts that the change in the law, which made the dates specified in a rent review clause of the essence, was not an unforeseeable event. However, in *Borgship Tankers Inc v Product Transport Corp* Cresswell J. stated that, if parties had acted on a mistake as to law, "there would be significant arguments available in support of the contention that s.12(3)(a) might be engaged."

The issue in *Thyssen Inc v Calypso Shipping Corp SA* was whether the court should extend time where the claimant had commenced proceedings in the courts of the United States within the contractual time limits but had not issued a notice of arbitration. The court concluded that this was not a basis for extending time under s.12. Steel J. held that it was not enough for the claimant to commence proceedings. The claimant had to commence proceedings correctly. The proposition that by instituting proceedings in any jurisdiction in the world this would have the effect of preventing discharge of liability by passage of time was, Steel J. noted, absurd. However, *Van Oord ACZ v Port of Mostyn Ltd* illustrates that there are circumstances in which the courts will exercise their discretion and extend time. The Notice to Refer was sent not to the principal place of business of Van Oord ACZ, as required by the contract, but to a subsidiary office. It was sent in time, but Van Oord ACZ then waited and notified the Port of Mostyn of its error after time had expired and then sent it to its head office. Counsel admitted that the conduct of Van Oord ACZ was "commercially savvy." Judge

Kirkham described this admission as "an acknowledgment of conduct which was unlikely to be viewed with favour by the court." The court concluded that the conduct of the applicant was such that it would be unjust to hold The Port of Mostyn to the strict terms of the service provision. However, there is a tension between *Van Oord ACZ and Cathiship SA v Allanasons Ltd (The Catherine Helen)*, where Jeffrey Brice Q.C. held: "[m]ere silence or failure to alert the claimant to the need to comply with the time-bar cannot render the barring of the claim unjust."

The Arbitration Act 1996 s.12 may in very limited circumstances be relied upon to circumvent a time-bar provision. The approach of the courts is that the parties have agreed the terms and conditions of their contract. If the parties agree that, as a condition precedent to bringing arbitration proceedings, certain steps should be taken by certain dates, then they will be held to their bargain. As Waller L.J. stated in *Harbour & General Works v Environment Agency* this is just the application of the principle of party autonomy. A party to a contract would therefore be unwise to think that s.12 is a "get out of jail card" where it has missed a time-bar clause.

FIDIC TIME-BAR PROVISIONS

In the FIDIC 1999 forms of contract the obligation to give a notice of claim is set out in sub-clause 20.1: "[i]f the Contractor considers himself to be entitled to any extension of the Time for Completion and/or any additional payment, under any Clause of these Conditions or otherwise in connection with the Contract, the Contractor shall give notice to the Engineer, describing the event or circumstance giving rise to the claim. The notice shall be given as soon as practicable, and not later than 28 days after the Contractor became aware, or should have become aware, of the event or circumstance. If the Contractor fails to give notice of a claim within such period of 28 days, the Time for Completion shall not be extended, the Contractor shall not be entitled to additional payment, and the Employer shall be discharged from all liability in connection with the claim. Otherwise, the following provisions of this Sub-Clause shall apply." The giving of the notice under sub-clause 20.1 is considered to be a condition precedent to the right to claim time or money. The question, however, is whether the Arbitration Act 1996 s.12 can defeat this provision? In this regard it should be noted that s.12 is a mandatory provision and cannot be excluded by the parties. Therefore, irrespective of what is stated in the contract, the section will apply to an arbitration whose seat is in England and Wales or Northern Ireland.

The next point is whether the referral to the engineer is part of "some other dispute resolution procedures which must be exhausted before arbitral proceedings can be begun"? In all probability the answer is yes. It is irrelevant that there are other tiers of dispute resolution which are more formal in the contract and the engineer is required to make a "fair determination" pursuant to sub-clause 3.5 of the contract.

The third point is whether the reference to the employer being discharged from all liability defeats the claim (the *Babanaft* issue). As stated in this article, the new wording in s.12(1) referring to the claimant's right being extinguished is likely to mean that the employer would not be discharged if the claimant can justify an extension under the Arbitration Act 1996 s.12(3).

CONCLUSION

Mustill and Boyd suggested that it was irrational for there to be a distinction between clauses barring claims in arbitration and those in legal proceedings. However, there is a distinction which became more pronounced when the Arbitration Act 1996 was enacted. To date the battle lines regarding s.12 have been drawn around the interpretation of s.12(3) and when the court should extend the time limits. At present the attitude of the courts is that a party who has failed to comply with the time-bar clause will have to persuade a court that something akin to frustration or force majeure has prevented it from complying with the time bar or that the conduct of the other party makes it unjust to uphold the time-bar provision. This will never be easy and case law indicates that only in exceptional circumstances have the courts permitted an extension of time under s.12. However, if there are onerous time-bar clauses in a contract, then there may be a benefit in having the matter resolved by arbitration rather than the courts and, while it will be difficult to circumvent a time-bar clause, it is incorrect to say there are no ways round it.

REFERENCES

* This article was originally published as Andrew Tweeddale & Karen Tweeddale, 'Commencement of Arbitration and Time-Bar Clauses', *Arbitration* 75, no. 4 (2009): 481-487.
1. J. Glover, FIDIC an Overview: The Latest Developments, Comparisons, Claims and Force Majeure, <http://www.fidic.org>, 10 September 2009.
2. *Alghussein Establishment v Eton College* [1988] 1 W.L.R. 587.
3. See *Roberts v Bury Improvement Commissioners* (1870) L.R. 5 C.P. 310

at 326; *Holme v Guppy* (1838) 3 M. &W. 387 at 389; and *Ludgate Administration No.1 Ltd v Northern & Shell Media Ltd* [2002] EWHC 1023 (Comm).

4 *Peak Construction (Liverpool) Ltd v McKinney Foundations Ltd* (1970) 1 B.L.R. 111.

5 *Gaymark Investment Pty v Walter Construction Group* (2000) 16 B.C.L. 449; [1999] NTSC 143.

6 *City Inn Ltd v Shepherd Construction Ltd* [2003] B.L.R. 468.

7 *Multiplex Constructions (UK) Ltd v Honeywell Control Systems Ltd* [2007] EWHC 447 (TCC); [2007] B.L.R. 195.

8 *Multiplex Constructions* [2007] EWHC 447 (TCC); [2007] B.L.R. 195 at [103].

9 *Steria Ltd v Sigma Wireless Communications Ltd* [2008] B.L.R. 79; 118 Con. L.R. 177 at [95].

10 *Crown Estate Commissioners v John Mowlem* (1994) 70 B.L.R. 1 CA.

11 In Scotland the courts took a narrower view of the conclusive effects of a final certificate: *Firholm Builders Ltd v McAuleym* 1983 S.L.T. (Sh. Ct.) 105 and *Belcher Food Products Ltd v Miller & Black*, 1999 S.L.T. 142; and see *MacRoberts on Scottish Building Contracts* (London: Wiley-Blackwell, 1999), 93.

12 *Babanaft International Co SA v Avant Petroleum Inc* [1982] 1 W.L.R. 871.

13 See also *Tradax Export SA v Italcarbo Societa di Navigazione SpA (The Sandalion)* [1983] 1 Lloyd's Rep. 514 at 517 and *British Gas Trading Ltd v Amerada Hess Ltd* [2006] EWHC 233 (Comm).

14 *Babanaft International Co SA v Avant Petroleum Inc* [1982] 1 W.L.R. 871 at 886C.
15 M. Mustill & S. Boyd, *Commercial Arbitration and 2001 Companion* (London: Butterworths, 2000), 275.
16 *Monella v Pizza Express (Restaurants) Ltd* [2003] EWHC 2966 (Ch); [2004] 1 E.G.L.R. 43.
17 *Harbour & General Works v Environment Agency* [2000] 1 W.L.R. 950; [2000] 1 Lloyd's Rep. 65.
18 *Harbour & General Works* [2000] 1 W.L.R. 950; [2000] 1 Lloyd's Rep. 65 at 81.
19 *Gibson Joint Venture v The Department of Environment of Northern Ireland* [2001] NIQB 48.
20 *Korbetis v Transgrain Shipping BV* [2005] EWHC 1345 (QB).
21 *Korbetis* [2005] EWHC 1345 (QB) at [25].
22 *Monella* [2003] EWHC 2966 (Ch); [2004] 1 E.G.L.R. 43.
23 *Borgship Tankers Inc v Product Transport Corp* [2005] EWHC 273 (Comm); [2005] 1 Lloyd's Rep. 565.
24 *Borgship Tankers* [2005] EWHC 273 (Comm); [2005] 1 Lloyd's Rep. 565 at [49].
25 *Thyssen Inc v Calypso Shipping Corp SA* [2000] 2 All E.R. (Comm) 97; [2000] 2 Lloyd's Rep. 243.
26 *Van Oord ACZ v Port of Mostyn Ltd* Unreported September 10, 2003.
27 *Van Oord ACZ* Unreported September 10, 2003.
28 *Cathiship SA v Allanasons Ltd (The Catherine Helen)* [1998] 3 All E.R. 714; [1998] 2 Lloyd's Rep. 511.

29 *The Catherine Helen* [1998] 3 All E.R. 714 at 729.
30 Mustill & Boyd, *Commercial Arbitration*, 275.

CHAPTER 2

Mediation in Arbitration in the Pursuit of Justice

Lord Woolf

John Cock, Chairman of the East Asia Branch of the Chartered Institute of Arbitrators, welcomed the speaker, the Rt Hon. Lord Woolf of Barnes, and special guests Andrew Li C.J., Hartmann J., Alan Limbury, Chair of the CIArb Practice and Management Committee and Mercedes Tarrazon, Mediation Representative on the CIArb Board of Management.

Colin Wall introduced Lord Woolf: It is a great pleasure that we are going to hear a talk tonight on the use of mediation in arbitration. Many people questioned, is this right? Is this the use of mediation and arbitration? I said: "[n]o, no." I checked twice because people were querying that, because there is nobody I think worldwide who has done more to promote the pursuit of justice by making mediation a tool, which people now are looking at to use. In Hong Kong it is particularly relevant because next year mediation is going to be introduced into the litigation system. But those of us at the CIArb who arbitrate may want to think about the use of mediation within arbitration.

Lord Woolf: Chief Justice, a Patron of the Chartered Institute, Colin Wall, fellow members of the Institute, ladies and gentlemen, it is a great pleasure for me to be here with you this evening. It is always reassuring to be asked back after you have been a speaker before, and in my case surprising. I did receive a letter once after I had given a talk at a Law Society dinner. I did my best at the Law Society, but next year I got a letter from the president and he reiterated his thanks for my giving the dinner lecture the previous year and went on: "[w]e are having a dinner again this year and we would very much like you to come as our guest, but we are hoping it is going to be a light-hearted, amusing evening so you will forgive us if we don't ask you to speak." I am going to talk about the same time that Colin and I met initially, which was 10 years ago. I was launching the changes to civil procedure. Those changes were a cultural shock to many of those involved in the English legal system, but I believe now they are really firmly rooted and people are comfortable with them. I say that because I know that under the leadership of the Chief Justice you are about to introduce your changes. They have been very carefully thought through. They aren't identical to what we have in England but they are similar. I particularly note that whereas we have "overriding principles", here they are "underlying principles." I don't know what the distinction is. I am waiting to be told in due course, but I think it shows a rather more Hong Kong attitude to civil justice, rather more gentle in effect. But whether there is any distinction to be drawn they both have the same object in mind and that is that judges should become more proactive in the delivery of justice, and in particular that they should have in the forefront of their minds the need to assist the litigants before them to resolve their dispute if this is at all possible at the first and earliest stage. Nobody who is sensible enjoys litigation and therefore, if the court can assist them to resolve their dispute without the need for going through the process, that must be beneficial to them. My thesis tonight is that litigation in the courts is very similar to litigation through the process of arbitration. They both have the same objective of obtaining a decision which resolves a dispute and brings it to an end. It is an imposed decision but, whereas now judges will regularly consider whether they can assist parties by suggesting some form of ADR, that just does not happen in arbitration. My argument is that it should, and it is indeed my belief that it will, and that arbitrators will have to recognise the importance of their matching the courts by offering the same sort of services.

There is great concern in relation to international arbitration, indeed in relation to all types of arbitration, that it is becoming an increasingly expensive and complex and drawn out process. These are exactly the same complaints that those who were going to the courts in England before 1998 were making and no doubt make still in many cases today. People do not want to be diverted from their normal activities in trying to resolve their disputes if that can be avoided. Litigation can be hugely destructive. In many situations the parties will ultimately resolve the dispute themselves but this happens at such a late stage. Judges have always, when the mood takes them on the bench, from time to time tried to ask a question or two to facilitate a resolution. They can see the litigants really are behaving absurdly in fighting in the way they do and they could so easily avoid it.

I used to think when I was at the Bar that some of the insurance companies were approaching matters in a way that could only possibly be justified if they were determined to be my charitable benefactors; they realised that I enjoyed earning the brief fees and wished me to continue, because it was obvious that the cases could be settled but they did not do this. It was obvious that they were going to end up by making a payment, yet case after case after case they ignored the obvious because for some reason the claims manager thought it was more convenient to pay in a year's time, or two years' time, or three years' time, rather than straight away. And the same no doubt is happening in arbitration. I don't believe that anybody benefits from that, and certainly as part of my process of reforms, when I met and talked to insurers they realised the absurdity of what was happening and were able to agree with me processes which would avoid this happening quite as frequently as it did. What we have got to find out is ways in which arbitrators can play a part in at least facilitating mediation and by encouraging mediation.

I have made enquires and, insofar as my personal experience goes, it doesn't happen here that arbitrators ask the parties: "Do you want me to help facilitate mediation?" It happens I believe regularly in China, and it happens in many other jurisdictions, but not in the common law jurisdictions. It seems to me if you are being involved by the parties at their request in this process and you know, as you must usually know, that their problems could probably largely be resolved by a consensual process of mediation, they should be encouraged to do that. With my recommendations for my reforms, I had a picture in my mind of a particular court. What would happen is that those who wanted to litigate would come through the doors and there would be a table with someone there to welcome them who would provisionally ask them: "Well, what sort of dispute is yours?" And when they said what sort of dispute it was they would direct them to the best place to go to have the dispute resolved. Many of the disputes could be resolved so much better outside the courts than in the courts. The same is exactly true of arbitration because if arbitration goes through its process it ends with a judgment. Now, quite apart from the fact that a judgment is a way of resolving a dispute which drives the parties usually further apart, it is also a judgment which has to fit within the confines of a process which lacks flexibility, because its source is usually statutory in part but consensual and contractual as well. That is the framework that governs what happens in the arbitration.

Now, in mediation all possibilities are open. The mediator can find sometimes that there is a way of positively helping the parties resolve their disputes which results in a remedy which is not connected with the dispute at all. If they had had a long relationship, for example, supplying motorcar parts to a motorcar manufacturer, what is most important to the supplier is the continuity of that relationship. Without the relationship it is going to be no use winning the case because his business is going to be destroyed by other pressures; if a way could be found of his getting an order which he found was attractive then he would much prefer that than the matters which are driving the parties apart. I just cite that as one obvious example.

Two years or more ago I gave up my job of judging and I went off and became an accredited mediator and it was, although I had always been an enthusiast for mediation, eye-opening as to what the potential was. I have conducted a variety of mediations which have ended up in the most satisfactory way and with results which a court could never possibly give. I have never yet been involved in a mediation, with one exception, where at the end of the mediation the parties were not grateful for the process. That is no compliment to me, it is just the reality which happens after a well-conducted mediation, and I hope my mediations are well-conducted. The one exception where that didn't apply was where there was a substantial sum in issue. As a result of the mediation, one of the parties realised that he had underestimated his claim by about 1,000% and he immediately told me as the mediator to tell the other side that. As the other side were thinking of paying 10% of what he was then claiming, they weren't very enthusiastic and the mediation didn't last very long because everyone had to adjust to this new situation. Try as I might I wasn't able to bring them together. But, on the other hand, I can refer to situations where we had difficulty getting the parties in the same room, never mind mediating, but once they started the process they became involved and the process ended up satisfactorily.

Sometimes the most important thing is for somebody to be there to say sorry. That can change the whole atmosphere. I had, and as this is already in the public arena I don't need to be confidential, the task of arbitrating between Iraqi citizens and the Ministry of Defence in relation to quite frankly outrageous behaviour that occurred in the treatment of those Iraqi citizens. Initially they would not take part in the mediation, but eventually about 12.00 we started, which was a great relief. There was present a very senior British soldier, the third most senior in the British army and his task was just to say how desperately ashamed he was of what had happened on this occasion, and immediately he had done that the atmosphere was transformed. He said what he felt and there was a lieutenant colonel from the Iraqi Army who said how he felt, and once that was out of the way they came down to the real business, which was to work out the compensation, and it was relatively easy. Before we parted that day the case was settled. The British Army realised they had to pay. They wanted it to be as soon and as quick as possible. They had gone to great trouble to get the Iraqis to London and it all worked so well. I can only say to you that my belief was if that case had gone on, it would have ended up in the House of Lords on the very, very difficult issues which have not yet been determined. But from those citizens' point of view, the mediated agreement was so much better than the alternative long drawn out process. That is just one example.

If arbitrators are going to play a role in mediation what is that role going to be? How is this going to be achieved? One way it could be done is the arbitrator also being a mediator. The benefits of the arbitrator being the mediator is that of course he should know about the dispute. If he knows about the dispute the mediation hasn't to start right at the beginning. The second thing is he can time his intervention as mediator appropriately. If you are an experienced arbitrator you know when the parties are probably ready to negotiate and at that stage he can decide to call them together and try and negotiate. This is something which I think most arbitrators would be very cautious about. Certainly any common law arbitrator would be cautious about doing this, because they would be worried about whether this could result in their being seen as not being objective. But it is interesting to know that now the International Bar Association has given guidance which says it can happen if it is properly and appropriately structured without that being the result, and indeed the International Bar Association Code of Ethics also makes the same thing clear.

However, there are very real difficulties if the mediation does not work, because then the mediator has to revert to his role of an arbitrator, and I accept there will be situations where that just will not be practical because there will have been discussions with one party absent the other party in the ordinary process of mediation. Now, in Germany and Switzerland they manage to do it, and indeed I am now on a Commission with a very distinguished Swiss mediator where we are trying to draw up a code. It is a code which is going, we hope, to be able to be used internationally and, although she believes we are wrong, she does understand there will be very real resistance if the code envisages the mediator being formerly an arbitrator, becoming a mediator, and then going back and being an arbitrator again.

I don't think that is a practical proposition, but what if, as she points out, the parties both agree beforehand that it should be all right and they will take the risk of that happening. Perhaps because they have faith in their arbitrators being able to put matters out of mind, even though they may have heard things that they would not normally have heard if the arbitrators had remained as arbitrators and not become mediators.

All I can say about this is that it is trite for it to be said that judges can learn things in the course of a trial and then put them out of their mind. I know after my own experience that judges *bona fide* try to do that. Whether you can do it I think very much depends upon what has been told and the circumstances. I think that, even if the parties say that they are prepared to take the risk, a wise mediator/arbitrator will say: "Well, it is not possible for you to know how I will feel if I have to reverse the process, and I must reserve the right to say I am afraid I can't go on." There will be cases of that sort and, if you have a mediator/arbitrator of integrity, you should be able to rely upon him to do that.

There can be all sorts of information that an arbitrator receives during a hearing which he considers is inappropriate or unduly prejudicial; he has to perform the same sort of exercise I have indicated. However, there is a very real difference, for the process to be joint. Then it would mean, in the case of mediation, caucusing with the individual parties as is usually part of the process of mediation. It may just be a cultural inhibition, but I think to begin with it would be wise to avoid that. But the arbitration could be adjourned and a mediator employed in the same way as in courts. It could be possible for there to be an arrangement, if there is more than one arbitrator, whereby one arbitrator, who will thereafter withdraw from the process of arbitration, mediates on behalf of the arbitration process. That process should be sufficiently flexible to be capable of adapting to circumstances so it can happen properly; and in one form or another it can be made to work. If you have the arbitrators bring in a mediator, the sort of problem to which I have just referred won't arise. There will, however, be a certain extra expense and there may be certain duplication of work, but in the case of any matter of substance that should be able to be accommodated so as to get the benefit of mediation.

What I am urging tonight is that arbitrators should see it as part of their role to help facilitate a settlement, and if they see their role as involving facilitating a settlement they will also encourage the parties to go to mediation if their feeling is that that will assist. I suspect of course that part of the problem is that arbitrators, unlike judges, have not the same interest and responsibility in the well-being of the system as a whole. They have been engaged as individuals. They are earning their living every day that the arbitration takes place and they have not got the same commitment in the majority of cases to how arbitration generally works. But there are of course very many arbitrators who are totally committed to arbitration in a similar way to that in which I am committed to mediation. They want arbitration to be as good as possible. They are unhappy about the way it is working at the moment and they want to see improvements. Committees of bodies such as the Chartered Institute this evening are working at improving standards all the time. However, you have to admit that at the moment they are not making the progress they should and what is needed is for a step forward. Here they could bear in mind what is contained in Pt 1 of the Civil Procedure Rules of England and Wales, and what is going to be in Pt 1A of your Civil Procedure Rules here in Hong Kong. There they will see set out in simple language what the alternatives are and what can be done to make the system work better. It is not really for me to do more than draw your attention to that and say, whether you think mediation is the answer or whether you think something else is the answer, your management of the arbitration, just in the same way the judge's management of the case, should be directed to resolving the dispute by bringing the parties together until ultimately in many cases they are able to resolve that dispute without having a decision forced upon them. The sort of situation that can arise so often is that in the end the arbitration is over who shall go into liquidation, and unfortunately so often it can be both sides that end up in liquidation. This cannot be the sort of result that lawyers, and engineers, or whatever other profession they do, want to produce as a result of their involvement in the process. So that is what I will put before you. I hope I have left plenty of time for questions, and I would be very happy to answer any questions that anyone has. The chair then asked for questions.

Paulo Fohlin: I am a Swedish lawyer. According to the Swedish Code of Judicial Procedure, in litigation, the judge in charge of the preparation of the case before the main hearing, before the trial, is obliged to try and work for settlement, but he also has the possibility to appoint a separate mediator if the parties consent.

Lord Woolf: What about in relation to arbitration?

Paulo Fohlin: It happens now and then in court cases in Sweden that the judge in charge of the preparations appoints a separate mediator. He might be a judge or a lawyer or somebody else connected to the court or not connected to the court and, if the case is a substantial one, the judge in charge of the preparations would ordinarily not take part in the case as a mediator himself. He would appoint a separate mediator. If we compare that with arbitration, even if you have guidelines providing that an arbitrator who steps into the role of a mediator is presumed not to be biased if the mediation fails and can thus continue as an arbitrator, isn't the problem that the mediation is never going to be as efficient as in the court system where the judge can appoint another separate mediator? Because even if I know that there are rules to the effect that he is not supposed to be presumed to be biased, I will not act as freely in my conversations with that person as if I know that he will leave the case.

Lord Woolf: I think there is great force in what you say. Either it is going to affect the arbitration or it is going to affect the mediation, or both. My complaint against the present situation is that the arbitrators don't do what the Swedish court does, which is in an appropriate case suggests to the parties mediation. Now, I raised the possibility of the mediator being one of the arbitrators. I did see that there were real disadvantages in that, but the fact that there are those disadvantages doesn't mean that other more appropriate ways cannot be found and, as arbitration is a consensual process, the parties themselves can decide how they want to do it. The important thing is that at an appropriate stage somebody does the job of conciliating between the parties, because experience shows that an independent person can do what the parties and their lawyers are incapable of doing themselves, and that is to facilitate a settlement.

Colin Wall: My question is do you think that it would be helpful for arbitrators to be trained in mediation skills? For example, in the preliminary meeting where things get agreed by consent and the arbitrator is supposed to design the process to fit the nature of the dispute and maybe several disputes, if you are flexible some of them could well be hived off to separate mediation. Where the parties really have had advice so that they genuinely believe they are both right, that can go off to be decided by a decision maker, but other matters are mediated. So we should give some training to arbitrators in people skills to point them in the right direction?

Lord Woolf: You are absolutely right. At the moment in Hong Kong a number of judges are going through mediation training. The idea behind the mediation training, as I understand it, is exactly what you are indicating. It is so easy for lawyers who have spent their whole lives negotiating to think they know all about negotiating, but with the practical experience you only find out as a result of the mediation that it is hugely beneficial to understand the negotiation process which is most likely to produce results. It has got to be tailored to the dispute and then it works. Judges need to know that just as the lawyers need to know that, and I am very glad that those who are responsible for these things in Hong Kong have made it part of their responsibility to promote mediation as a preliminary step to the introduction of the reforms. It is not extensive training. It is relatively short and therefore relatively economical and not demanding. I think that every lawyer and every judge who is involved in commercial work should actually make sure that he becomes trained and regularly refreshes his skills after he has been trained. It will help him or her in all the things that they do. It is part of the life skills in fact and, you know, mediation now is moving into many more fields than litigation. Large companies are finding that the presence of a mediator to help them resolve matters like reducing staff can be hugely advantageous, that within their board they can have disputes that have to be resolved where the presence of a conciliator can make a very significant contribution. And I can only say to those who are here who haven't had the advantage of training, if they have the opportunity to do so, do take advantage of it because you will not regret it. You will find it fun and you will find that it improves your skills.

Mark Sutherland: You mentioned mediation in an informal sense. How would you see the agreement of terms of reference between the parties and the mediator, and indeed the payment of fees in the event that an arbitrator had first been appointed? How would you see the interlinking of those two matters?

Lord Woolf: I don't think it really creates any particular difficulties at all. The mediator will be employed as he is employed in regard to any dispute. Often the parties will agree that in any event his fees will be divided between them. If the settlement is reached the agreement can say the settlement should include the costs of the mediator. This is a completely flexible process, not subject to legislation, and they can agree exactly how they want it done. The arbitrator is there to serve them and he will put that into effect. Of course, to have mediation in conjunction with arbitration has one great advantage, at the end of the mediation if there is a settlement and if it is of an appropriate type, it can be then the basis for an award. That award then becomes enforceable as any other decision in the arbitration and that can be a huge benefit.

I have at the moment the responsibility for setting up a court to deal with commercial and civil disputes in Qatar. The model that we are in the process of bringing into effect is one where the mediation and the arbitration should be all part of the court which is going to be a dispute-resolving court, and all three processes will work together to support each other. If we see it as centrally organised, then we can get the best of all worlds for those who choose because they have to choose to submit to the jurisdiction of the commercial and civil court of Qatar. In a country like Qatar, which is seeking to attract financial services, it is important there should be the infrastructure to support those financial services, as they would find, if they had the wisdom to come to Hong Kong, that there were ample resources here.

Andrew Aglionby: I am a solicitor in Hong Kong but occasionally I go to China and I have been involved in CIETAC arbitration.

Lord Woolf: Yes, and they have special provisions for dealing with this.

Andrew Aglionby: But they have different rules. They are slightly different in many ways. For instance, the mediation concept as I understand it as taught in Hong Kong and in the United States, and I think in the United Kingdom, is a win/win concept. It is the concept that the parties are brought to realise that when they discuss issues they can both have an outcome which is an improvement. But negotiation in China, from my experience, starts from the prospect that it is a win/lose, that it is a zero sum negotiation and perhaps that feeds through into the CIETAC mediation, or conciliation as they call it, where the arbitrators act as conciliators but really talk about the outcome, the rights and the obligations of the parties in the context of a particular dispute, the legal remedies, if you like, not the commercial wider interests. I guess the question that comes out of that is, how does one take account in all of this in international arbitration of the very different cultures which meet, perhaps in violent misunderstanding of each other's motives, and do those different cultures meeting in that forum lend themselves to the sort of mediation process that you have been talking about?

Lord Woolf: Well, you are absolutely right about the fact that there are different approaches. My understanding of the Chinese approach, and I am afraid it is only secondhand, is that in a Chinese arbitration routinely they ask the parties whether they want a conciliation. That is one of the first things that is asked, and if that is right they are already in a different league from what happens in the majority of international arbitrations today which aren't in China. They have a particular model; in different parts of Europe there are other models; and, of course, there is a different model in the United States. It is my belief that in all aspects of civil justice there is a process of harmonisation taking place. It doesn't happen overnight, but it is again the task of bodies such as the Chartered Instituted to try and promote forms of carrying out activities that we are discussing this evening in a way which is attractive to the majority of users, whatever their cultural background. The different cultural backgrounds will no doubt be taken into account in the appointment of the arbitrators, but there usually can be sufficient give-and-take within the process to meet the different cultural background. Once arbitrations are taking place accommodating the different approaches, then we all learn from the process, and it is so much easier the next time to devise a system which will serve those interests better than we did on the previous occasion. So I think it is an evolving situation and it is by evolving, taking into account the experience in different jurisdictions, that we will get the best results.

Alan Limbury: I am the Chairman of the Chartered Institute of Arbitrators' Practice and Standards Committee. That committee has set up a working group to devise a protocol for med-arb. The idea is that the parties would get full advantage of the opportunity to have private caucuses with the mediator and, if that is not successful, that same person arbitrates. We have taken as one discussion model the Australian Commercial Arbitration Act, which provides for med-arb, but it has not been very well used. I think the reason is that, in order for it to happen, the parties have first to agree that the arbitrator will mediate. Then at the beginning they have to waive any objection that they might have on procedural fairness or apparent bias grounds. The model that we are now looking at in order to try to make it more attractive is that there should be the opportunity not merely for the parties, but also for the mediator, to opt out after the mediation phase. So, depending upon what has happened, not only could the mediator say, "well, thank you very much, I don't feel comfortable arbitrating", but the parties could say, "well, even if you do feel comfortable, we don't", in which case they would have to have somebody else appointed, in the hope that it might tempt more people to try it, knowing that they could opt out, as it were, halfway through.

Lord Woolf: I think you were not here when I was trying to explain a similar sort of position. I was saying that whereas there are those countries — Switzerland and Germany are two — which very much go down the idea of med-arb, there are real handicaps. I, therefore, think it is very ambitious. It seems to me that your approach is much more likely to lead to a model which will be more acceptable to both the user and those who practise arbitration and mediation. But the great thing is to get over the hurdle that people have now of thinking about mediation when they are involved in arbitration, and for the life of me I just don't understand that. Had they been in litigation they would have been told by the court, encouraged by the court, to go off and try the mediator.

Bob Vart: I am a consultant and engineer. I have given evidence recently at a number of arbitrations, LMAA in London in maritime disputes, and it has been my experience that the tribunal has effectively ordered a meeting of experts, which I think has always resulted in some progress, at least in narrowing the issues. Would it not be possible for a tribunal also to order a mediation?

Lord Woolf: I think it is possible. I query the use of 'order.' I think it is much better to keep it, especially for mediation, as a consensual process. So I would say 'encourage' rather than 'order', but that is my particular view. When I was doing my report on civil procedure reform, I visited Australia and I visited the United States. In both jurisdictions they were keen on ordering people to mediate, and they have had great success using that. They said, "[y]ou will never get many people mediating unless there is a power to order", and I think that probably is right. Nonetheless, I think it comes at a cost, and the cost is the consensual nature of mediation. If I may say so, asking two experts to meet and to agree where they are in agreement and agree where they differ is quite a different process from mediation, and the court is in charge there and can enforce orders, but I don't see how you can really satisfactorily enforce mediation on people who don't want to mediate. They just won't play the proper role. Albeit that there are sanctions, the sanctions will take you into satellite litigation, and satellite litigation can be even more frustrating and expensive than the original litigation, so one has to be a little bit cautious.

John Cock: Thank you. Lord Woolf has given us an interesting talk tonight about an area that everybody is always talking about, the introduction of mediation into litigation and other areas of dispute resolution. I think there are probably very few people in this room who have got experience of mediation in arbitration, but it is certainly an area ripe for discussion as is obvious from the questions raised from the floor and the interest in the talk and the topic. May I ask you to join with me in thanking Lord Woolf in the usual way?

* This article was originally published as H. Woolf, 'Mediation in Arbitration in the Pursuit of Justice', *Arbitration* 75, no. 2 (2009): 169-176.

CHAPTER 2

Universal Arbitration — What We Gain, What We Lose

Jan Paulsson

The words 'what we gain, what we lose' might suggest that we have a choice — that if we are losing more than we gain we can turn our backs on universal arbitration and return to a more comfortable existence. That would be wrong. It is interesting to take stock, but there is no choice. For better or worse, universal arbitration is here to stay. So we must deal with it, and if possible rescue those things of value which belong to the world we seem to be leaving behind. I am inviting you to consider the word 'universal' not as a legal term. That is why I'm avoiding the word 'international'. I am not referring to arbitrations between states — 'international' — or arbitrations entirely governed by a treaty (such as the Washington Convention of 1965 that created ICSID), or arbitrations defined by an arbitration act as 'international' due to an abstract characteristic — for example if parties are non-nationals of the forum. I am talking about something that we might think of as sociological, namely the convergence of the way disputes are resolved, so that disputants and advocates and arbitrators of any nationality can be found everywhere, doing the same thing in the same way — with an ever-decreasing number of linguistic barriers. English is dominant, Spanish is in the ascendant; Mandarin, German and Arabic are holding their own in particular contexts; French has plummeted in a few decades — but that is about it. A hundred other languages are out of the running, and if one of them is yours and you want to participate, you must retool. Perhaps the key to thinking about our changing arbitral industry is to observe that no legal system can be superior to the community it is intended to serve. The best community produces the best arbitral process. But is there anything like a universal community? As we widen our horizons, the picture becomes messy and disorientating. In this universalist context, no participant, whether advocate, arbitrator, or expert, is necessarily a member of a regulated profession. Nor does anyone seem to know what rules of conduct apply — do we have one code per arbitration, or one code per participant? Unique constellations of arbitrators emerge; I have sat on three-member tribunals comprised of nationals of seven countries. (There is such a thing as treble nationality.) Even if we limit ourselves to the conventional case of single-nationality arbitrators, most of us can still cite instances of tribunals comprising very unusual combinations of nationalities having in common only the fact that each arbitrator was grappling with the relevant applicable law for the first time in his life. It's enough to make us lose our bearings, and perhaps more than that. We have to operate outside our comfort zone. We find that communication becomes more difficult, that our interlocutors' expectations and intentions are inscrutable, and above all that the process, which looks more like a kaleidoscope than a flow chart, can be unpredictable. The confusion begins with language. English is universal, but it is not necessarily that spoken by native English speakers. Every participant may use correct English and have a proper dictionary understanding of words, but suddenly all important nuances are gone. In the context of a particular case, an arbitrator's impassive comment that "I don't think, Mr Smith, that I need any further assistance from you on that point" may be perfectly understood and have a very beneficial effect in an environment where everyone truly speaks the same language, but in universal arbitration some people in the room are likely to react to such a statement with bewilderment, if not suspicion or dismay. Nothing can be taken for granted, even when the English meet with such close and familiar colleagues as their cousins from the United States. I'm thinking of such matters as the permissible scope of cross-examination of witnesses who have provided a written statement; Americans tend to assume that questions will be limited to matters dealt with in the written statement, while the English tend to assume that "once you give me the witness, he's mine". We can live with either rule, but not with both; it is acutely problematic when each side comes prepared on a different premise. As for the strictly legal foundation of universal arbitration, what is one to say about the extreme inconsistency of the reactions of judges when they are asked either to decline to hear a case in deference to arbitration, or to enforce an arbitral award, when one compares, let us say, France and Saudi Arabia, two countries which both long since became signatories to the New York Convention? France routinely respects foreign arbitration clauses and awards, while no lawyer in Saudi Arabia can show you a single instance when a local court has done either in two decades of supposed obedience to the treaty. As professionals, we abhor unpredictability because it makes our advice less valuable. As business managers, our clients equate unpredictability with uncertain returns on investments, and therefore build legal risk premiums into their price. Transactions are inhibited and the temptation of corruption grows. This is all rather discouraging. Why didn't we say no to the universalisation of arbitration while there was still time? But of course we should have done no such thing. Universal arbitration holds great promise, and its costs are worth the pursuit. Just think of the things we gain! I shall mention three. We can overcome the clash of cultures. We can bring people together under a big tent. We can even save the world! Only that ...

WE CAN OVERCOME THE CLASH OF CULTURES

Let us not too quickly accept that there is culture shock in international arbitration. Do arbitrants really have different expectations? I would venture that those for whom the international arbitral process has been designed really want the same thing. To begin with, they have an equal lack of appetite for arbitration. So they wish to avoid it, but they know they may have a problem, and wish it to be solved properly, with minimal disruption. (These are of course *ex ante* objectives, not the tactics that may be employed once a dispute has erupted.) Whether government officials or business managers, they do not want their international relations to be marred by disputation; they all desire — in principle — that justice come quickly, fairly and effectively, at no cost to the deserving party. And so business managers from Sweden who operate in the international marketplace are likely to share more common assumptions about the objectives of dispute resolution with other business managers from Costa Rica than with the members of a Swedish ski club, or a Swedish tenants' association.

How about the lawyers? Might one not suspect that they will, for self-serving reasons, resist and condemn processes in which their own habits and methods are marginalised, even if their clients might benefit from the different approach? Perhaps so, in isolated cases. Yet this suspicion is powerfully contradicted by modern phenomena such as the UNCITRAL Model Law for International Commercial Arbitration, the International Bar Association's successive Rules on Taking of Evidence in International Commercial Arbitrations and the remarkable procedural commonalities to be observed even in politically sensitive arbitrations between states. Whatever turf wars may have been fought by past generations intent on securing ownership of the process by imposing their exceptionalisms, modern practitioners have adopted a universalist approach which converges in shared practices. These observations are not intended to minimise the challenges, but rather to suggest that they are misunderstood. At the level of abstract principles, there is no lack of shared values. Now when we get into an actual dispute, we find that the claimant wants speed and finality, while the respondent wants deliberateness and reconsideration. One might thus speak of "the culture of claimants" versus "the culture of respondents". This of course is not the subject with which we started, namely the concern that permanent and irreducible differences of expectations may be inherent in the national origins of the arbitrants. A final possibility deserves our full attention, because this is an opposition which may be categorical and chronic, with the result that some groups permanently reject arbitration. I am speaking of those who perceive themselves as outsiders, lacking resources — skills, influence and information — which they suspect are at the disposal of their opponents. This is not a clash of culture, since both sides share the same values and assumptions about decent justice, but rather a failure of confidence. It is a serious problem, but quite a different matter. Clashes of culture would be hardwired and intractable. Failures of confidence, on the other hand, can be redressed by concrete measures of intelligent institutional design allowing for transparency, appraisal and participation — while taking effective measures against entrenchment. I shall return to that topic at the end of my remarks.

WE CAN MAKE PEOPLE COME TOGETHER

Arbitration is unlikely to prosper if it is seen as the exclusive domain of a group of inward-looking specialists. Arbitration obviously cannot endure if those asked to consent to its authority are mystified and disaffected. The process will be rejected if it is perceived that while the arbitrants come from the four corners of the world, rights of advocacy and the power to decide are reserved to mandarins or high priests operating in a few dominant cities. The stakes are great. Fortunately, there is solid ground for optimism. It seems unlikely, at least in arbitrations involving matters of private law, that international arbitration will suffer a lack of inclusiveness. The arbitration institutions that matter have understood that their future is universalism, with open entry into decision-making organs. Inclusiveness means not only cosmopolitan recruitment to leadership positions, but also methods of governance that avoid entrenchment. After all, the networks that facilitate trafficking in influence easily cross borders. This is perhaps best combated by term limits and transparent, verifiably meritocratic processes of replacement. Inclusiveness may well be inspired by idealistic impulses, but fortunately does not depend on them. It is more fundamentally a matter of success and indeed survival; the increasingly sophisticated global environment is incompatible with closed shops. If this is true of those who run arbitral institutions, and of arbitrators who purport to issue non-appealable awards, it is also true of advocates. In this respect one may observe remarkable changes, with effects that are only beginning to be perceived.

Those whose professional ambition is to design the intellectual infrastructure of economic activity, in terms of corporate organisation, mobilisation of finance, contractual devices and optimal legal risk management, will be left behind unless they can operate in the international dimension. New generations, preparing for their entry into the arena, readily understand this. Individual investment in education today follows astonishing patterns. The days of French or German law students spending a year of graduate studies in an English-speaking country — perceived as a new wave only a quarter-century ago — now seem almost quaint. The new paradigm does not feature only the children of such students, but also Asians, Middle Easterners, Latin Americans and Africans committing themselves to full cycles of studies leading to professional qualification abroad. The mobility of young talent creates new flows of fundamental importance. True, some individuals may be part of a brain drain. But as new economies flourish, they create ever more opportunities for a new professional elite whose mobility sunders the struts of privilege and exclusivity. In the field of arbitration, the first generational change was the replacement of genial part-time artisans by dedicated professionals. The third generation is one of professional cosmopolitanism and mobility, rapidly creating an environment of shared methods and values — and in turn self-confidence and irresistible participatory demands. The importance of the Vis Moot competition, known to all arbitration specialists, is more than anecdotal. From its modest beginnings in 1993, providing a venue in Vienna for competitive mock arbitrations intended to stimulate and educate law students from around the world, the Vis Moot has enjoyed spectacular success. In 2012, the event drew no fewer than 285 teams from 71 countries, in all around 2,500 persons. These teams, typically comprised of at least half a dozen competitors selected by their law schools and coached over the course of a full academic year, are all given the template of a problematic international commercial transaction. They argue their assigned cases by reference to common rules (invariably those of the UN Convention on the International Sale of Goods). They proceed in accordance with a common set of procedures: well-known arbitration rules complemented by familiar texts relating to the reception of evidence, enforcement of arbitration agreements and awards, and ethics. The effect of these annual waves of highly motivated young scholars, all trained to view the legal problems of international trade through the same prisms of norm and method, later to be found as 'Vis Alumni' practising all over the world, should be acknowledged as a sociological phenomenon. Their common notions of principle and process will likely have a greater impact than decades of scholarly debate about the nature and function of *lex mercatoria*. They are not a tiny vanguard, but a new community of practitioners. The Vis Moot has spawned scores of imitators. All over the world, there are pre-

Vis competitions, Spanish-language competitions and regional competitions with names such as the Serbian Open or the Brazil Moot. The Vis Moot Alumni Association is now well established, with its Vindobona Journal of International Commercial Law and Arbitration (named after the legendary "last outpost" of the Roman Empire near Vienna). In sum, a new generation has created something of an Olympic movement of international trade law, and the standard of performance of its participants, one surmises, will attain ever more impressive standards, just as successive generations do in the stadium. The mobility, ambition and educational attainments of students is not an isolated phenomenon. Similar dynamics are at work in the legal profession, where the model of multinational and polyglot firms has made significant inroads. It is no longer surprising to find senior lawyers prospering in countries which only a few decades ago seemed to be prisoners of their remoteness from the great centres of practice. Australians as leading members of Korean firms; Europeans occupying similar positions in Cairo, Dubai or Dar-es-Salaam; Latin American and Chinese lawyers in great numbers reaching prominence in the leading global firms — none of this is surprising today. The old, once exclusive citadels have become cosmopolitan, and the new citadels are cosmopolitan from the start. It is a fundamental and constructive development; inclusiveness leads to the promise of engagement and consensus with respect to objectives and practices in the industry of dispute resolution.

WE CAN SAVE THE WORLD

For humanity to feed itself, international co-operation is indispensable. Co-operation does not mean gifts and subsidies. Co-operation means macroeconomically significant behaviour, from innovation and investment to transportation and distribution. All of this presupposes that it is reasonable to extend credit, that laws and contracts and institutions are reliable. That is how a poor country can access technology or infrastructure to increase agricultural yields, using future revenues from anticipated surplus harvests to pay for it. Ultimately, if there is no faith in the legitimacy of adjudication — which we all surely accept as better than violence or corruption — suppliers of goods, services and know-how will prefer to disengage, or to increase their prices. Now consider the spectre of war. For humanity to avoid destroying itself fighting over scarce resources, conciliation is indispensable. The ultimate reconciliation, when all else fails — and assuming once again that we reject violence and corruption — is the peaceable acceptance of an adverse decision, for example the location of a boundary or the existence of water rights. If there is no faith in adjudication, what will inhibit the urge to fight on? Such faith begins with the belief that one will be given a fair chance. Concerns about being given a fair chance — an equality of arms — become more acute the moment one crosses a border. Will an English party get a fair hearing in Paris? The question is not limited to a fear of chauvinism. The doubt is there even if the opponent is not French. Will the attitudes and methods of the French tribunal favour a Spanish opponent, who shares the civil law tradition, or a Senegalese opponent, who shares not only that tradition but also a common language? Just as the English party worries about Paris, so would French parties worry about London, and the Spanish and Senegalese parties worry about either Paris or London. These concerns multiply as we venture further abroad.

What confidence do we have that a foreign environment will not corrode our rights, whether by urbane but poisonous influence-peddling or brutal xenophobia and corruption? How can one get a fair hearing if one's opponent's means of communication are superior in every way? The idea of comparative resourcefulness merits careful attention. The argument is sometimes advanced that the very cost of legal proceedings is a form of serious inequality whenever the parties' financial resources are strikingly disparate. The point is not trivial, but it has less specific resonance in arbitration than may be assumed. It is simply impossible to assert that arbitration is more expensive than court proceedings. Indeed arbitration is designed to achieve the opposite result, and often does. A study conducted by the International Chamber of Commerce for cases resolved in 2003 and 2004 revealed that the parties' individual costs of presenting their cases (mostly legal fees) represented more than 82% of the overall cost of an arbitration taken to the end. Such costs are of course also incurred in presenting cases before ordinary courts, where there may moreover be one or more appeals.

There is a dearth of meaningful empirical studies of the relative cost-effectiveness of particular types of arbitration as compared to that of the national courts which would otherwise have dealt with the matter. The true inequality of arms, as a feature specific to arbitration, cannot therefore be said to be one of financial resources, but rather the disadvantages of being an outsider. In any given national environment, attitudes evolve as experience of international arbitration deepens — from a starting point of likely rejection of the unknown through a succession of phases culminating in full and confident participation in the system. Consider the past half-century, as new, post-colonial nations have encountered the international process.

The Initial Stage of Defensiveness and Defeatism

At first, the process is perceived as dominated by the capitalist First World, which made the rules and controls the institutions. It is a period of vicious cycles: "[P]resuming this is a game we cannot win, we will not make the investment necessary to learn it. We will send out our unprepared national lawyers to represent us, we will appoint our inexperienced and uninfluential national arbitrator, and when things do not go our way we will at least have the sullen satisfaction of saying 'we told you so' — this was a game we could not win."

The Stage of Pragmatic, Incidental Engagement

At some point, the cost of truculent defeatism becomes too great, and those potentially affected by a significant conflict are sufficiently motivated to apply themselves to secure more favourable outcomes. Upon closer examination, they see that the record of decided cases reveals that non-Western parties have not in fact fared too badly in international arbitrations. Upon consideration of the stakes involved and after due diligence as to what needs to be done to prevail, experienced counsel are engaged and reputable arbitrators are appointed — even if they are foreigners. Political sloganeering is put to the side; the phenomenon of international arbitration is recognised as a reality to be managed.

The Stage of Constructive Engagement

In due course, the realisation dawns that international institutions are permeable; the doors to their decision-making chambers may be opened. New entrants perceive their power, and its proportionality not only to the economic resources they command, but also to the skills and determination which their nationals develop and deploy. This is the road to ensuring not only continued successful participation in the process as arbitrants, but also to acquiring the stature of effective advocates and respected arbitrators. It is a long road of long-term efforts and substantial investment in human resources and institution-building.

The Stage of Equal Status

The sustained efforts of a variety of actors bear fruit over time. In major Asian and Latin American capitals highly effective arbitration specialists have emerged. (They are less prevalent in Africa.) Their experiences often include substantial educational and professional qualifications earned at leading institutions around the world. Many Asian law firms are now giving competitive employment opportunities to Western law graduates, and indeed induct Western partners. Non-Western law firms have made their mark as *dominus litis* in major arbitrations. Inevitably, it seems, the time will come when significant cohorts of eminent non-Western arbitrators will be selected by institutions, or by the joint nomination of arbitrators, to decide cases having no connection with their home countries. This will be a watershed, allowing us finally to jettison, as an image of the past, that of non-Western arbitrators having no place at the table except as the unilateral nominee of their own nationals. Such recognition and achievement must be earned, not imposed, but there is evidence that these transformations will not tarry much longer.

DESIGNING A LEGITIMATE SYSTEM FOR 'A NATION OF DEVILS'

Transparency

Parties are asked to entrust important affairs to the final judgment of a tribunal appointed by an institution. They are surely entitled to know how that institution goes about selecting, monitoring, policing and remunerating the arbitrators who are chosen in a given case. Just who identifies arbitrators and determines their fitness to serve, on what basis and in accordance with what process? It is no longer sufficient (if it ever was) to affirm in the abstract that a legal entity makes the relevant decisions. Whether they are 'chambers of commerce' or 'foundations' or 'non-profit corporations', institutions act by human agents. So it is legitimate to ask who owns an institute; who hires and fires its personnel; who establishes its functional organs; and who ultimately sets its policy. The arbitrants' entitlement to transparency may seem to go without saying — but that is not how many arbitral institutions seem to have developed. The rather absurd presumption seems to be that as long as the arbitrators are subject to disclosure requirements and as long as they are qualified to serve — or should one say not disqualified from serving — the process can rest on their shoulders alone, and the institution can intervene, as it were, anonymously. That simply is not good enough. Transparency alone, moreover, may be insufficient when there is an asymmetry of information. To know who decides what may not be enough for a party which perceives, rightly or wrongly, that its adversary has far greater access to qualitative knowledge of or contacts with the individuals concerned. For such information to be available only to a few initiates is redolent of practices in small locales dominated by local notables, and has no place in a process intended to be inclusive, and willing to ensure equal justice to friendless foreigners. It is difficult to solve this problem. Databanks on arbitrators come to mind, but would likely be useless, unreliable or both. In the US, where employment disputes are typically arbitrated, labour unions and business managers keep tabs on individual arbitrators, with the predictable result that the latter pay heed lest they be branded as pro-labour or pro-management. Such simplistic tools are undesirable for many obvious reasons. Nor are more probing qualitative assessments at hand; if the input is provided by different observers who have witnessed different proceedings it would be near impossible to devise a serious methodology for appraisal of performance. Still, smaller steps may yield helpful results. Prospective arbitrators' docket of pending cases and reserved dates should not be a secret; the ICC now routinely demands this information of nominees. Nor should it be outlandish for arbitrators to keep and reveal data about the number of days that pass between the last word from the arbitrants — spoken or written — and the delivery of the final award. The availability of such objective information would not only make parties' choices better informed, but also create healthy incentives.

Engagement with the Community of Users

The degree of insistence with which doubts are raised is directly proportionate to any arbitrant's self-perception as an outsider. This explains why it is preposterous for local organisations run by nationals to seek to masquerade as 'international' simply by attaching that adjective to their name. This does not mean that a formally national entity cannot acquire a credible international persona. The London Court of International Arbitration by statute limits UK nationals to one-fourth of its membership; in the 2008 election to fill seven vacancies, the new members were of the following nationalities: India, Korea, Iran, Egypt, Argentina, Russia and Sweden. The Stockholm Chamber of Commerce has an international advisory board which convenes by regular telephone conferences to discuss arbitral appointments. The Singapore International Arbitration Centre is presided over by an Australian. No one lifted an eyebrow when an Austrian was selected to chair the board of the Hong Kong Centre. Credible institutions are sensitive to the importance of renewal of their decision-makers — i.e., term limits and transparent recruitment of replacements — to avoid perceptions of entrenchment and possible capture by special interests. Still, to achieve universal legitimacy requires considerable resources in terms of management, networks, information and outreach. This is far beyond the capacity of the vast majority of purportedly international institutions. Most of you are, I imagine, aware of the clarion call of Sundaresh Menon, then still the Attorney General of Singapore but just about to become his country's Chief Justice, when last May he gave the hour-long keynote address to the ICCA Congress. One of the central concerns of his unsparing analysis of the weak spots of the arbitral process was the absence (or asymmetries) of information about the arbitrators selected by institutions. To some extent this problem is alleviated by the emergence of a universal bar of advocates who are well acquainted with eminent arbitrators, but that is not an adequate answer for a system intended to work for routine cases as well, with an even playing field for newcomers.

The AAA's Employment Due Process Protocol, which sets forth a series of criteria to be met before the AAA will agree to administer cases, contains a requirement that parties should have sufficient information to be able to contact parties who have participated in cases handled by any arbitrator being considered for appointment. While that requirement may be valuable in the course of arbitrants' due diligence, institutions as well as arbitrators also need to provide more meaningful specific information as a matter of course.

Barriers to Entrenchment and Conflicts of Interest

We would hardly entrust the preparation of a penal code, no matter how excellent, to Ali Baba and the 40 thieves. Nor did the joint study prepared by 'international experts', commissioned by Henry VIII in order to demonstrate his divinely ordered right to disregard the edict of Pope Clement; to divorce Catherine of Aragon; and to declare the royal supremacy of the Church in England, constitute a lasting contribution to ecclesiastical legal theory. We want to know who pulls the strings and pays the piper. What is one to think of arbitral panels limited to persons agreeable to industrial associations who then insist on the exclusive authority of such persons as a condition of consumer sales? Or arbitral institutions established by and financed by a government, and insisted upon as a condition of tender for public contracts? Or institutions created with the sole raison d'être that a small group of would-be arbitrators is disaffected from an existing institution around the corner because it does not give them sufficient appointments? Since arbitral institutions appoint arbitrators, their own legitimacy is fundamental; the process cannot be trusted if the choice of decision-makers is not. Even when institutions are wholly independent of public or private bodies, the possibility arises for other types of connections between their staff and the other protagonists of the process. It is of course natural for individuals who play different roles in the same environment to communicate in a manner that can foster better practices. (The judiciary and the bar, for example, should not live on different planets.) But to avoid the perceptions of undue influence, institutions likely need to police not only issues of conflict of interest on the part of advocates and arbitrators acting under their rules, but also such matters as the personal and professional relations which quite understandably emerge between their staff and the law firms which have been or may become their employers. As arbitral institutions aspire to ever-enhanced inclusiveness, the problem of unilateral appointments will be exacerbated. Arbitrants from ever more diverse backgrounds will insist on equal treatment and thus make their own appointments of arbitrators from a correspondingly more diverse pool. An institution based in a particular city may well have excellent knowledge of local professionals, but if it purports to have national legitimacy how can it endorse unknown arbitrators from other cities? And if it purports to have international legitimacy, how can it confirm unknown nominees from a country far away? The problem is surmountable, but only with determination and a constant sense of concern. Practitioners become ever more sophisticated; their demands to understand the process increase apace, as does their intolerance for asymmetries of information. Who appoints arbitrators, removes them, determines their compensation? By what criteria are these decisions made? What information is available with respect to nominees, including their availability, their expertise, their experience and, above all, factors relevant to an evaluation of their aptitude to fairness in the context of a particular case? Are there credible safeguards against cronyism, understood as ways for parties or their representatives to assert personal influence on their decision-making? Arbitrants today are ever less willing to accept that important decisions are matters of opaque discretion taken behind a curtain. The uninitiated can only guess that the most serious institutions protect their integrity with internal protocols that ensure the incorruptibility of staff members who routinely become privy to sensitive information; how they deal with parties, arbitrators, lawyers, third parties and the media; what undertakings they make as to ongoing post-employment restrictions. Equally, one surmises that many institutions ignore these matters entirely. This may be a crucial challenge for arbitration in the coming years. The good institutions have a common cause, and it is in their interest to distinguish themselves from less punctilious organisations. This can be achieved with transparent practices established and adjusted in permanent consultation with all who have an interest in the process.

Standards and Sanctions

Arbitrants naturally want to know whether administering institutions have any meaningful way to hold arbitrators accountable. Are they accredited in any way? Are they monitored for compliance with standards? What are the sanctions, if any — disaccreditation, forfeiture of fees, suspension of eligibility? Is there a serious attempt to address the disquiet that may arise from the personal familiarity that might develop among leading arbitrators and advocates — some of whom wear either hat on different occasions — in a manner which is foreign to the more distant relations between advocates and judges? How do institutions review arbitrators' fees and costs to ensure that they do not take advantage of their position vis-à-vis the parties? Is there a sensible way to provide access to qualitative data about arbitrators so as to reduce asymmetries of information? How, finally, do institutions evaluate themselves — entirely by internal reviews, by peer review, or by some form of audit? Alexis Mourre has put his finger on a danger inherent in the kind of reforms implicitly suggested by these questions. To ensure the independence of arbitrators by abolishing unilateral nominations would, for example, "create a distance between the arbitral community and the users of arbitration. Arbitrators would look less at the parties and more at the institutions, which all have their own degree of internal politics and their bureaucracy. The risk would exist that arbitrators progressively move from their current culture of services providers, close to the needs and requirements of the users, to a culture of arbitral public servants or, even worse, of arbitral politicians." Mourre's point is powerful; unless caution is exercised, the arbitral process may be suffocated by bureaucratic controls. Regulators may be empowered to license, monitor and evaluate arbitrators in accordance with ever-expanding policy directives that trump party autonomy. Other officials may step in to establish performance standards as they — not the parties — perceive them. In the end, we might thus end up with purely bureaucratic innovations such as a rule that certain types of contract may be subject to arbitration only by arbitrators appointed by ministerial decree, to be selected for individual cases by lot or simply by rotation. This is very far from arbitration as we know it — rather a new form of judicial outsourcing, masquerading as arbitration and passing on the cost to the litigants while avoiding the burden of judges' salaries, benefits and pensions. As often, it is important to proceed with caution lest the cure be worse than the malady. Arbitral self-regulation is plainly the best hope to avoid imposed dystopias. Instructive examples come from the US, where the American Arbitration Association has led the way in devising a series of "due process protocols" for different types of arbitration, intended to ensure legitimacy, especially by controlling the effects of over-reaching by parties in a superior negotiating position. (The AAA refuses to administer cases if the contractual process does not comply with the relevant protocol.) A key element of the development of these protocols has been the significant involvement of interested groups, anticipating the criticism which might otherwise arise if such self-regulatory efforts remained a purely internal process. The cause of arbitration is championed by predictable cohorts of supporters: specialist lawyers, professional arbitrators and arbitral institutions. They all have important insights derived from experience, but will be seen as subject to a professional bias. More valuable endorsement would come from those whose appraisal of the process is seen as neutral: arbitrants themselves, who seek other solutions if their legitimate demands for cost efficiency and fairness are not met; public officials, who set the limits of arbitral freedom in light of the general interest; and members of the academy and civil society, who examine the advantages of private justice as a complement to public institutions. Arbitration would be better understood if such outside observers were more engaged in assessing and improving the process. Given that their interest is only intermittent and contingent, it behoves the arbitration community to solicit their views, and to provide them with information useful to their judgment. To seek to escape their scrutiny would be a serious error. As I conclude, I should admit that the expression 'universal arbitration' did not pop into my mind out of the blue. I had come across this passage from Tennyson's long and melancholy poem 'Locksley Hall', published a century and a half ago. Well, a hundred and fifty years have not been enough to get us there, and universal law still seems to be around a very distant corner. But we do have occasions to move toward that corner, and in the absence of universal law can at least, in some civilised sectors of our troubled world, engage in a meaningful dialogue that patiently aspires to universality.

REFERENCES

* This article was originally published as J. Paulsson, 'Universal Arbitration — What We Gain, What We Lose', *Arbitration* 79, no. 2 (2013): 185-194.

1 A. Mourre, 'Are Unilateral Appointments Defensible?' (On Jan Paulsson's Moral Hazard in International Arbitration), originally a debate on the Kluwer Arbitration Blog and subsequently published in Stefan Kroll, Loukas A. Mistelis, Pilar Perales Viscasillas and Vikki Rogers (eds), *International Arbitration and International Commercial Law: Synergy, Convergence and Evolution — Liber Amicorum Eric Bergsten* (Alphen aan den Rijn: Kluwer, 2011), Ch. 20, p. 385.

ADR, ARBITRATION, AND MEDIATION
A Collection of Essays

CHAPTER 3

MEDIATION

CHAPTER 3

The Central London County Court Pilot Mediation Scheme

Dame Hazel Genn

In 1996 judges in the Central London County Court (CLCC) established a pilot mediation scheme for non-family civil disputes with a value over £3,000. The scheme's objective was to offer virtually cost-free court-annexed mediation to disputing parties at an early stage in litigation, involving a three-hour session with a trained mediator assisting parties to reach a settlement, with or without legal representation. The scheme's purpose was to promote swift dispute settlement and a reduction in legal costs through an informal process that parties might prefer to court proceedings. It was also thought that mediation would achieve savings in Legal Aid. This report is an evaluation of the CLCC mediation scheme based on: (1) data collected from hundreds of court files of mediated and non-mediated cases; (2) interviews with litigants, solicitors and mediators; (3) observation of mediation sessions. The data collection system for the evaluation has been in place since the beginning of the scheme and has continued throughout its two-year life. The evaluation offers an assessment of: (1) the demand for mediation and causes of the prevalent rejection of mediation offers; (2) the kinds of cases for which mediation is an appropriate form of dispute resolution; (3) the extent to which mediation can promote settlement in civil cases; (4) the extent to which mediation can reduce the time taken to settle civil cases and reduce the cost of resolving disputes; (5) the extent to which mediation succeeds in achieving acceptable and lasting settlement of disputes; (6) the extent to which mediation is perceived by parties and their representatives as a satisfactory method of dispute resolution.

DEMAND

The rate at which both parties accepted mediation offers remained at about 5% throughout the life of the scheme and despite vigorous attempts to stimulate demand. Demand was virtually non-existent among personal injury cases, although these comprised almost half of the cases offered mediation. Contract, goods/services disputes and debt cases had the highest levels of demand although the joint acceptance rate was less than 10%. The joint demand for mediation was lowest when both parties had legal representation.

Acceptance of mediation was highest among disputes between businesses. Interviews with solicitors rejecting mediation revealed: lack of experience and widespread ignorance of mediation among the legal profession; apprehension about showing weakness through accepting mediation within the context of traditional adversarial litigation; evidence of litigant resistance to the idea of compromise, particularly in the early stages of litigation.

OUTCOMES

The majority (62%) of mediated cases settled at the mediation appointment and this settlement rate remained constant between case types, indicating that mediation can be used across a wide spectrum of cases.

Other findings on outcome were that: where the plaintiff had legal aid the settlement rate was lower than average; the settlement rate at mediation was highest (72%) when neither party had legal representation at the mediation; mediated cases had a much higher settlement rate overall than non-mediated cases, whether or not settlement occurred at the mediation appointment, supporting the contention that mediation promotes settlement even after an unsettled mediation.

Plaintiffs settling at mediation appointments appear to be prepared to discount their claims heavily in order to achieve settlement, with average levels of settlement in mediated claims being about £2,000 lower than in non-mediated settlements.

TIME AND COST

Even on a very conservative estimate, mediated settlements occurred several months earlier than among non-mediated cases. Most parties whose cases settled at mediation believed that the mediation had saved time, although those whose cases did not settle often felt that the mediation had involved them in extra time. Solicitors felt strongly that mediation saved time. There was much more equivocation on the question of cost savings. Only half the plaintiffs settling at mediation believed they had saved costs. Solicitors tended to be more likely to think that costs had been saved. There was a common view that failure to settle at the mediation appointment led to increased costs.

EVALUATION OF MEDIATORS AND MEDIATION PROCESS

The overwhelming motivation for mediating was to save time and legal costs. Few parties or solicitors had any experience of mediation or any knowledge of the process. The vast majority of litigants and solicitors made positive assessments of the mediation process. Confidence in mediators was generally high, although less so when cases failed to settle. The characteristics most valued by litigants were: (1) the opportunity to state their grievance and focus on the issues in the disputes; (2) fully to participate in a process relatively free from legal technicality; (3) the qualities of the mediators.

Solicitors particularly welcomed: (1) the speed of the process; (2) the opportunity to review the case with a neutral party; (3) the concentration on commercial realities; (4) the opportunity to repair damaged business relationships.

Most mediated settlements were perceived by litigants to have been fair, although fairness was often assessed against the cost and time of continued litigation. Negative assessments by parties centred on: (1) deficiencies in mediators' knowledge of the law and issues in dispute; (2) undue pressure to settle and bullying by mediators; (3) mediators being 'insufficiently' directive.

MEDIATORS

Mediators in civil disputes require a wide repertoire of interpersonal and professional skills as well as sound legal knowledge. Flexibility and adaptability are crucial qualities. A 'counselling' or 'therapeutic' approach, stressing communication and reconciliation, seems less well-suited to non-family civil disputes than a more directive, interventionist approach emphasising the value of settlement. There was great variation in the skill displayed by mediators and many were very inexperienced. Some of the most successful mediators were barristers, many of whom were prepared to be explicitly evaluative during the course of mediations. Mediators exert considerable power in mediation, controlling the flow of information, the use of evidence and the architecture of settlements. There was no consistent view among mediators on the question of ethics or the nature of the mediator's responsibilities in mediation.

CONCLUSIONS

Mediation is capable of promoting settlement in a wide range of civil cases when parties have volunteered to accept mediation. Personal injury cases are amenable to mediation even when both liability and quantum are in issue. Mediation offers a process that parties to civil disputes on the whole find satisfying. Conflict can be reduced and settlements reached that parties find acceptable. Mediation can promote and speed up settlement. It is unclear to what extent mediation saves costs and unsuccessful mediation can increase costs. Mediation can magnify power imbalances and works best in civil disputes when there is some rough equality between the parties or in representation. Mediators require special personal qualities, good training and experience. Demand for mediation is very weak and the legal profession has a crucial role in influencing demand.

Issues requiring attention are, for example, the impact on weak demand of an increase in mediation fees to an economic level; mediation procedures, especially in relation to the use of documentary evidence; training of mediators; quality control of mediators; accountability and ethics of mediators. Mediation currently operates in the shadow of normal litigation procedures and the disadvantages of those procedures provide much of the incentive for parties to settle during mediation. Procedural changes could strengthen or weaken the existing low level of demand. Education of the profession and a change of litigation culture could also strengthen demand. In seeking to stimulate some enthusiasm among the grass roots of the profession, it is important for mediation proponents to focus on the value that mediation adds to normal settlement negotiations between solicitors, rather than simply setting up mediation in opposition to trial. The experience of the profession is that most cases are not, in the end, tried. Mediation can add value to the normal claims settlement process in civil disputes. It offers a cathartic pseudo 'day in court' to parties; it gets cards on the table and all the parties around the table; and, with the help of a skilled mediator, it introduces some authoritative objectivity into the assessment of the strengths and weaknesses of the parties' claims.

* This article was originally published as H. Genn, 'The Central County Court Pilot Mediation Scheme Evaluation Report', *Arbitration* 67, no. 1 (2001): 109-112.

CHAPTER 3

The Historical Background to the EU Directive on Mediation

Elizabeth Birch

The European Council stressed the importance it attached to alternative means of settling cross-border disputes at Vienna in December 1998 and then in Tampere in October 1999 at a meeting devoted to the creation of an "area of freedom, security and justice within the European Union." At the Lisbon European Council in March 2000 devoted specifically to 'Employment and the Information Society', the Council invited the "Commission and the Council to consider how to promote consumer confidence in electronic commerce, in particular through alternative dispute resolution systems." This objective was reaffirmed at the European Council at Santa Maria da Feira in June 2000 when the 'e-Europe 2002 Action Plan' was approved. In the employment relations field, the Brussels (Laeken) European Council in December 2001 "stresses the importance of preventing and resolving social conflicts, and especially trans-national social conflicts, by means of voluntary mediation mechanisms." In the draft Brussels I Regulation in September 2000, the European Parliament proposed going further and making agreements to use ADR binding as a system of extrajudicial dispute resolution and to make enforceable the settlements obtained within the framework of such ADR schemes. In fact, the proposal was not adopted by the Council in the Regulation in December 2000.

However, at the time of the adoption of this Convention, the Council and the Commission highlighted the useful complementary role of ADR, in particular with regard to electronic commerce.

THE EU GREEN PAPER ON ADR

The EU Green Paper was published in April 2002. It recited the fact that UNCITRAL has model legislative provisions concerning commercial conciliation and that the United States has a long and rich experience of ADR in various forms, which have been able to develop because they were supported by the court system. Most US States have adopted Mediation Acts in different areas. Reference was made to developments in Canada also. In general, ADR has been proceeding in Europe with considerable diversity of approach and generally unregulated. The Green Paper expressed the need for common codes of conduct applying on regional or global levels and offering a number of procedural guarantees in ADR schemes available throughout the community. Consultation followed with ADR organisations in the United Kingdom and elsewhere and with the law societies and representatives of the Bar. The Green Paper indicated that there was growing interest in ADR for three main reasons: increasing awareness across Europe; ADR had become the subject of legislation in certain Member States; and the EU's interest in ADR was fuelled by a desire to set the background for access to justice, where justice was becoming too expensive even for commercial parties in most European countries and to enhance the goal of "social harmony." The Green Paper recites: "[i]t is worth highlighting the role of ADRs as a means of achieving social harmony. In the forms of ADR in which the third parties do not take a decision, the parties do not engage in confrontation but rather in a process of rapprochement, and they themselves choose the means of resolving the dispute and play a more active role in this process in such a way that they themselves endeavour to find the solution best suited to them. This consensual approach increases the likelihood that, once the dispute is settled, the parties will be able to maintain their commercial or other relations. ... ADRs are an integral part of the policies aimed at improving access to justice. In effect, they complement judicial procedures, insofar as the methods used in the context of ADRs are often better suited to the nature of the disputes involved. ADR can help the parties to enter into dialogue where this was not possible before, and to come to their own assessment of the value of going to court."

This was not a measure directed only at consumer disputes. The Paper emphasised that cross-border disputes tend to result in even more lengthy proceedings and higher court costs than domestic disputes: "[w]ith the completion of the internal market, the intensification of trade and the mobility of citizens, irrespective of the importance of the issue or the monetary value involved, disputes between citizens from different Member States and between persons residing in different Member States, amplified by the expansion of cross-border e-commerce, are steadily increasing, and the number of cross-border disputes being brought before the courts is increasing correspondingly. In addition to the practical problem of overworked courts, these disputes often raise complex issues which involve conflicts of laws and jurisdiction and practical difficulties of finance and language."

Defined as "out-of-court dispute resolution processes conducted by a neutral third party", excluding arbitration proper, the Green Paper sought to address all forms of ADR whether conducted by a court, or through the institution of the court or whether by a third party privately engaged. It also sought to sweep up (probably spreading itself a little too widely) partially-binding decision-making processes such as Ombudsman processes and Consumer Complaint Boards operating in Scandinavian countries. The Green Paper posed a series of questions: Should ADR be compulsory? Should the period of ADR result in a suspension of court proceedings for the purposes of limitation? What should be the training, quality and ethical standards for the neutral and whether these can be uniformly defined for all countries in all fields of dispute? Should the legislation of the Member States be harmonised so that the confidentiality of ADR is guaranteed in each Member State? Most controversially, should there be a period of reflection or "cooling-off" period at the end of the mediation process, during which either party can withdraw from the settlement agreement reached. So the EU set itself the task to promote alternative techniques and to "ensure an environment propitious to their development and do what it can to guarantee quality." Although initially concerned with regulating the mediation process, after consultation it was recognised that mediation is a flexible process which is not suited to over-regulation. The emphasis has now switched to self-regulation and encouragement of best practice.

THE CODE OF CONDUCT

The draft Code of Conduct for Mediators as proposed by the Green Paper was refined over a period of time and controversial issues such as the introduction of compulsory mediation or a compulsory cooling-off period were removed. The end result is a short and fairly uncontroversial (if not anodyne) code covering: competence and training; independence and neutrality — continuing duty to disclose relevant information as to independence or conflicts; impartiality; procedure — mainly covering the need for a mediation agreement (but not requiring it to be in writing unless the parties request), conducting the proceedings in an appropriate manner and providing that the parties may agree on the manner of proceedings by reference to a set of rules or otherwise (the mediator may see the parties separately if he/she deems it useful); fairness of the procedure; provisions for termination of the procedure by the mediator; no requirement for a settlement agreement to be formalised in writing; confidentiality.

The Code of Conduct is a voluntary code but it has already been endorsed by the major ADR Service Providers in the United Kingdom. Many of the new entry countries (because of the timing) have already adopted the Code of Conduct into their constitutions, although the Directive has not yet been put in place. The preamble to the Code makes it clear that adherence is subject to national legislation and rules governing specific professions and also envisages that service-providers may want to develop more detailed codes for the type of services they offer. It represents, therefore, a "gentle toe in the water" in the mediation scene.

EU DIRECTIVE ON MEDIATION IN CIVIL AND COMMERCIAL MATTERS

The draft Directive was published in September 2004 and is now the subject of negotiation between the EC and Member States. It is due to be implemented by September 2007. The objective of the draft directive is to facilitate access to dispute resolution across the European Union (whether in domestic or cross-border disputes) by promoting the use of mediation and by ensuring a sound relationship between mediation and judicial proceedings (Art. 1). The intention is that there should be some uniformity of approach and standards across the EU that will be to the benefit of litigants in both domestic disputes and those with an international element.

There is a broad definition of mediation in Art. 2 as "any process, however named or referred to, where two or more parties to a dispute are assisted by a third party to reach an agreement on the settlement of the dispute." The draft Directive contains provisions to establish procedure and to provide the necessary tools for the courts of Member States to actively promote the use of mediation. It is left to Member States to decide how the rules and tools should be implemented.

By Art. 3 a court may, in appropriate cases, invite the parties to use mediation to settle their dispute. While the draft Directive obliges Member States to give courts the power to suggest mediation to the parties, it stops well short of making mediation compulsory (although it does not prevent Member States from making it compulsory, or subject to incentives or sanctions, provided that this does not impinge upon parties' right to access to the courts). The intention is to encourage parties to consider the possibility of using mediation as a method of dispute resolution. To encourage parties to use mediation, courts would have the ability to require the parties to attend an information session on mediation (the content of which is left to Member States to decide).

Article 4 provides for the EC and Member States to promote the development of voluntary codes of conduct for mediator and service-providers. The emphasis is on self-regulation in that it is left to Member States to encourage mediator training.

The enforceability of settlement agreements reached through mediation is the subject of Art. 5, which provides that such settlement agreements may, at the request of the parties, and subject to European law and relevant national law, be confirmed in a judgment or other instrument by a court or public authority, in the same way as a judgment. This would mean that a settlement agreement could be recognised and enforced in another Member State, for example under the Brussels and Lugano Conventions, without the need for separate enforcement proceedings. It would be up to Member States to decide which court or courts had jurisdiction to deal with requests for "confirmation" of mediated settlement agreements.

Under Art. 6, confidentiality becomes a basic principle of mediation, prohibiting mediators from giving subsequent evidence regarding the mediation, except in specific instances (including for the purpose of implementing or enforcing a settlement agreement). While confidentiality within the mediation process is now without doubt in England, many mainland European countries do not have the concept of confidentiality and this has probably inhibited the growth of mediation in those countries to date.

Article 7 provides for the suspension of the limitation period when the parties agree to use mediation, the court orders mediation or an obligation to use mediation arises under the national law of a Member State. If a settlement is not achieved at the mediation, the limitation period starts running again when the mediation is terminated by one or both of the parties or the mediator. This feature is likely to act as a further encouragement to parties to use mediation.

Article 9 envisages that Member States will be required to implement the necessary laws and regulations to comply with the Directive by September 1, 2007 at the latest.

CONCLUSION

While ADR, and mediation in particular, have developed to a relatively sophisticated level in the United Kingdom, the same is not necessarily so everywhere in the European Union. Even in the United Kingdom, the feature of the suspension of time running for limitation purposes is a matter not yet covered by legislation. In many countries, embracing confidentiality will be a major hurdle in laying the ground for an increased uptake of mediation. The uniformity of approach on enforcement will be a very important matter in cross-border disputes.

It may take longer for a common approach to develop of the methods used within the mediation process, but this is a matter that could hardly be grasped at this stage. Indeed, the success of mediation is due to the flexibility of the process and any attempt to harness this is likely to stifle, rather than enhance, the use of (and success of) mediation. In any event, some types of disputes will lend themselves to a particular format and others to a different one. Indeed, it can even be said that every case requires an individual approach. The only disappointment in the Directive is its concentration on mediation at a time when other forms of ADR such as early neutral evaluation (ENE) are in a state of growth in the United Kingdom. It would have been good if it had embraced, a little more clearly, non-binding forms of dispute resolution outside mediation.

REFERENCES

* This article was originally published as E. Birch, 'The Historical Background to the EU Directive on Mediation', *Arbitration* 72, no. 1 (2006): 57-61

1 Presidency Conclusions, para. 83: http://ue.eu.int/en/Info/eurocouncil/index.htm: "The European Council endorses the Council and Commission action plan on how best to implement the provisions of the Treaty of Amsterdam on an area of freedom, security and justice" [1999] O.J. C19/1. Paragraph 41(b) of the action plan states: "examine the possibility of drawing up models for non-judicial solutions to disputes with particular reference to transnational family conflicts. In this context, the possibility of mediation as a means of solving family conflicts should be examined." Conclusions of European Councils can be found at http://ue.eu.int/en/Info/eurocouncil/index.htm.

2 Presidency Conclusions, para.30: http://ue.eu.int/en/Info/eurocouncil/index.htm : "Alternative, extrajudicial procedures should also be created by Member States."

3 Presidency Conclusions, para. 11.

4 Presidency Conclusions, para. 22 and the e-Europe action plan: http://europa.eu.int/information_society/eeurope/action_plan/index_en.htm.

5 Presidency Conclusions, para. 25 [2001] O.J. C146/94. See also the reactions of the Commission to these different points in its amended

proposal presented on October 26, 2000, COM(2000) 689 final.

6 Joint declaration of the Council and the Commission concerning Arts 15 and 73 of the Regulation in the minutes of the Council meeting of December 22, 2000 which adopted this Regulation: http://europe.eu.int/comm/justice_home/unit/civil_en.htm.

7 Work of the working group on arbitration: www.uncitral.org/fr-index.htm.

8 On these questions, see in particular the information in the Commission Green Paper of February 9, 2000, "Judicial Co-operation in Civil Matters: the Problems Confronting the Cross-border Litigant", COM (2000) 51 final.

9 This definition results in excluding the following procedures from the scope of the Green Paper: expert opinions, which are not a method of dispute resolution, but a procedure involving recourse to an expert in support, for example, of a judicial or arbitration procedure; complaint-handling systems made available to consumers by professionals. These procedures are not conducted by third parties, but by one of the parties to the dispute; "automated negotiation systems", which do not involve any human intervention, which are offered by providers of IT services. These systems are not dispute resolution procedures conducted by third parties but technical instruments designed to facilitate direct negotiations between the parties to the dispute.

10 See *Halsey v Milton Keynes General NHS Trust* [2004] EWCA Civ 1274.

11 In France and Slovenia neither the law, nor professional rules, grant

protection of confidentiality to the mediator. In Germany, professional secrecy or confidentiality is limited to lawyers. Italy recently reformed its company law to introduce the concept of confidentiality.

12 Although, interestingly, failure to comply with a settlement agreement reached in mediation does not appear to be a prevalent problem. This is, no doubt, largely due to the extent to which the parties "buy into" the settlement by their personal involvement in the process.

CHAPTER 3

The Future of Mediation in Europe

Wolf Von Kumberg

Over the past decade I have developed a keen interest in ADR as a business model for resolving disputes, outside of the traditional state court system. This has been a view developed because of my own experience first as a litigator and for the past 18 years working in industry. Large multinational companies today are turning increasingly to alternative means for resolving their disputes be it mediation, forms of expertise, adjudication and arbitration. The legal profession has been too slow to react to this need. This is particularly true in Europe, where firms have been reluctant to offer their clients alternatives to the traditional court systems that lawyers are familiar and comfortable with. Even in the United Kingdom, where arbitration and mediation have now been common for many years, the legal profession and in particular litigation practitioners have felt that these alternative methods of dispute resolution would cut into their profits. In the end it is, however, the user that will dictate the product that it wants delivered. Those firms that offer a strong ADR practice group are where the customer will go.

THE BUSINESS CASE FOR ADR

I have been involved in industry associations and corporate counsel forums for many years. A consistent message has been the cost of traditional state-based court litigation. This is particularly true in the United Kingdom, but has also become a complaint on the Continent, where the process is not burdened by discovery, but preparation of lengthy briefs and several levels of appeal usually result in an equally costly process. It is not only the financial cost of traditional litigation but other factors as well that have contributed to the institutionalisation of ADR as the preferred means of dispute resolution for multinationals. In my discussions with the general counsel for companies like Nestlé, GE Europe and British American Tobacco, these companies have actually put policies in place requiring ADR to be used whenever possible.

It is important to understand the reasons for this development. I have developed the following list based on my own experience and discussions with my business colleagues: (1) More important than the direct financial cost of litigation is the cost of internal resources. Business is in the business of conducting business, rather than litigation. Senior business managers, key personnel and engineers are needed to develop future business, not deal with past mistakes. There is little advantage to a business in using these valuable resources in months of preparation, trial and appeals. It is difficult to keep these individuals motivated and effective participants in the traditional litigation process. This use of resources adds nothing to future business growth; (2) The traditional litigation process is poorly understood by business managers and is often perceived as being prolonged for the benefit of the lawyers. Even where a party is successful, the true success for the business in a tangible form is difficult to measure; (3) Business relations are key to the future of a business. The relationship with customers, suppliers, teaming partners are crucial to future business growth. It is simply not possible to engage in lengthy aggressive litigation and keep those relationships intact. This requires business to look to ADR to provide viable alternatives; (4) Brand names and reputation are valuable assets of any business, particularly those with a strong consumer link. Litigation once unleashed cannot be controlled. It is uncertain what damaging information can result from litigation that will hurt the reputation of a company in the market place. Private confidential dispute resolution, rather than public proceedings, is a major draw of ADR; (5) Certainty is essential in the business environment. The process that is to be followed in the event of a dispute should be as clearly mapped out as possible. ADR due to its contractual nature permits parties to mould the process to their own needs. This simply cannot be said for a one-rule-fits-all national court system; (6) The ability to deal with a dispute using the most skilled and knowledgeable persons available is also appreciated by business people. That is how they handle their other business issues. You bring in the best professionals for any particular task. Choosing the right expert, an adjudicator, mediator or tribunal member instils confidence in the process. This is important because it means that acceptance of the outcome, even where one loses, is easier. Business relationships can continue, without costly and bitter appeals; (7) Finality of the outcome is another clear business reason for choosing ADR. There is little scope for appeals. While doing away with the appeal process poses some risk if the outcome is not favourable, in most cases for the reason given in 6 above, business managers can normally accept the decision. The process will have been more understandable to them and they will in most cases have had more faith in the decision-maker; (8) A clear advantage for an arbitration process that falls under the New York Convention is the enforceability of the award in member states where assets reside. This is a huge advantage over trying to enforce a foreign judgement in another state, where the scope for challenge and further years of litigation can be the outcome. Try explaining this outcome to a board of directors that have already spent years on costly litigation just to get the judgment. Business will invest in dispute resolution, but only if there is a return given a successful outcome; (9) ADR is the only means for multinational companies to do business in less-developed legal jurisdictions. This is in fact the model when doing business outside Western Europe and North America. Companies operating in these jurisdictions are loath to subject themselves to underdeveloped and corrupt legal systems. The only alternative is to choose ADR in a neutral forum. Foreign customers and business partners understand this and, except in the case of some direct state procurements, it is usual to negotiate such ADR clauses.

THE FUTURE FOR STATE COURT LITIGATION

I am not ignoring the fact that there will always be good reason for multinational companies to litigate matters in state courts. This will be necessary where the interpretation of a key legal principle deemed necessary to the health of a business or industry sector, is in question. There will also be situations where state litigation will be used for tactical or strategic reasons against other companies. These situations will, however, become the exception for international commercial disputes and no longer be the norm. What this means is that traditional litigation practices will have to adapt from litigation to ADR. The requirements for an ADR practice, while complementary to existing litigation practices, require a different skill base, approach and mindset. The key to a successful ADR practice is to develop individuals who have the knowledge, skills and training to deal with a variety of dispute resolution alternatives to litigation. This requires lawyers with an appreciation of business requirements and the ability to create dispute resolution techniques to meet the practical needs of business management.

THE IMPORTANCE OF THE EU MEDIATION DIRECTIVE

It is my view that the Directive would enhance the use of mediation as an ADR tool throughout the EU. The Directive as drafted would facilitate greater access and uniformity of mediation practice and thereby promote its use for cross-border disputes. Some of the key elements of the Directive are: Article 1 general promotion for the use of mediation; Article 3 power given to national courts to invite parties to mediate; Article 4 setting out voluntary codes of conduct; Article 5 power of Member States to enforce settlement agreements without separate enforcement proceedings; Article 6 enshrining confidentiality in the mediation process; Article 7 suspension of limitation periods while mediation takes place. If the Directive were adopted, combined with the sound business arguments for attempting mediation as a means to settle commercial disputes, one could only see the increased use of this valuable ADR tool across the EU.

* This article was originally published as W. Von Kumberg, 'The Future of Mediation in Europe' *Arbitration* 72, no. 1 (2006): 62-64.

CHAPTER 3

Mediation and Its Future Prospects

Sir Brian Neill

It is a pleasure and a privilege to be asked to come here tonight to say something about the prospects for mediation. I will be speaking about civil mediation because I do not feel qualified to say anything useful about family mediation. But I firmly believe that the two disciplines, if one can so describe them, need to keep in close touch because they have many common features. And I think one should look forward to the day when all types of mediation, including community mediation, come under one umbrella. In order to consider the future it is useful to examine, though as shortly as possible, the past. Ever since I became interested in the use of mediation and other forms of ADR as means of tackling disputes and conflicts I have been surprised that these processes have taken so long to come to the fore. Other civilisations embraced mediation long ago. You will find references in Justinian, and before that historians speak of the Phoenicians using mediation in commercial disputes. In Greece a mediator was termed a *proxenetes*. In China there has been a long tradition of compromise and those of you who are familiar with the works of Confucius will know that he favoured persuasion rather than coercion. There are other traditions where a neutral third party has helped disputants reach an accord — the Quakers, as merely one example, have played a distinguished role.

The history of mediation in England has been traced by Professor Roebuck in his very interesting article 'The Myth of Modern Mediation', from which it is apparent that in mediaeval times and later the courts played a role in promoting mediation. Indeed, when the creation of the new county courts was being considered before the enactment of the County Courts Act 1846, Lord Brougham suggested that the judges of these new courts should be able to conduct both mediation and arbitration. But in general mediation was dormant in the nineteenth century and the early part of the twentieth century.

Towards the end of the nineteenth century, however, conciliation procedures began to spring up in industrial relations, notably in the cotton industry and in 1896 the Conciliation Act was passed. Not long after in the United States the Department of Labor set up a panel of Commissioners of Conciliation to handle management/labour disputes. But I think it is generally recognised that it was not until the last third or so of the twentieth century that serious attention was given to the settlement of disputes by mediation. Some academic work on conflict resolution helped to point the way. About 1970 there were publications by two cultural anthropologists — Laura Nader and P. H. Gulliver — and from an even earlier date the Harvard Law School began its work of examining techniques for use in conflict resolution.

The bibliography on mediation is now very extensive and there have been important recent works by leading figures in the field. Names that spring to mind include Paul Randolph, Allan Stitt and Professor Mackie. The search for new ways of solving conflicts has been spurred on by other developments. One may mention three of these. First, the cost of court and indeed arbitration proceedings has soared. The photocopier and the increasing complexity of the law have taken their toll. I well remember in my very early days at the Bar writing in an advice on evidence that at the trial we should have copies of all the letters between, let us say, A Co and B Co, and being telephoned by a rather annoyed solicitor to ask if I realised all the work this would entail for a copy typist.

I sometimes wonder whether some semi-legible sixth carbons may not be more cost effective than the serried ranks of beautifully produced but little used bundles. Secondly, the unhappy policy that decrees that all civil litigation should be self-financing does little to help ready access to the courts. Thirdly, one cannot fail to notice a change in the scope of civil legal aid since the days following the Rushcliffe Report of 1945 when the Civil Aid and Advice Act 1949 seemed to usher in a new dawn. Enough of the past.

WHERE ARE WE NOW?

Let me start by listing some of the favourable developments of the last 20 years and more particularly of the last three years. We now have a substantial number of organisations that provide mediation and other ADR services. These are not only in London, but in the North, the Midlands and the West. The pioneers like CEDR, the ADR Group, the Academy of Experts and the Chartered Institute of Arbitrators are well known. But there are other important groups, some just providers of services, but some who also teach. In addition, there is a growing body of individual practitioners whose work is wholly or mainly in the field of ADR. As a result we have available many hundreds of trained mediators whose services can be called upon when needed. The recent establishment of the Civil Mediation Council (CMC) has provided some structure for what I think one can call an embryonic profession. The CMC is a focal point for discussions between the providers of mediation services and a focal point too for individual practitioners. It also has the invaluable support of the two branches of the legal profession — the Law Society and the Bar. In addition, it is capable of providing a link with the judiciary and with the Department of Constitutional Affairs as well as with other government departments.

I should also mention that we are beginning to be recognised in a wider field. Two weeks ago Lord Slynn and I were invited, by courtesy of the ADR Group, to go to Guernsey to talk to the Bailiff (the head of the judiciary there) and the Mediation Group that has been formed in Guernsey. Also, just before Easter I was telephoned by a judge of the Court of Session who wanted to know about our work.

I must mention next the Department of Constitutional Affairs (DCA) and the Court Service. The Proportionate Dispute Resolution Team of the DCA under the inspiring leadership of Robert Nicholas has made immense strides. You will all know about the court schemes for mediation in the county courts and the National Helpline that in time, I hope, will bring mediation into the mainstream.

Most important too is the support for ADR that comes from the Civil Procedure Rules and notably from the 41st amendment, which three weeks ago introduced a general pre-action protocol. The higher judiciary as well as many county court judges lend enormous strength to the concept of mediation and I am delighted to see that the Master of the Rolls is here tonight. As you know, the Judges' Council has its own ADR sub-committee and I have had many useful discussions with Professor Martin Partington who until recently chaired that sub-committee. I must mention too the academic community. The CMC is fortunate in having an academic group chaired by Linda Mulcahy of Birkbeck College and the present and future generations of law students will enter the profession with a much greater understanding of mediation and ADR than their predecessors.

CHALLENGES AND PROBLEMS

May I turn to some of the challenges for the future and the problems that must be faced. An important challenge is to find a kite mark for mediators. This raises the question of how tight any control should be. Many people are fearful of too much centralised control, but if the courts encourage and indeed recommend mediation, the judges must have confidence in the quality of the mediators who will undertake the task.

The CMC has started, as a pilot scheme, a system of accreditation of the organisations that provide the mediators. It can be said that this is not an ideal scheme because it is the individual mediator whose competence is in issue. But I am very hopeful that the scheme will work well. The providers are carefully vetted and it is then up to them to ensure that individual mediators are trained and equipped for the task entrusted to them.

Another problem can be stated thus: if the courts can apply costs sanctions to support recommendations to mediate, how are the sanctions to be enforced? An outright refusal to mediate may not give rise to any difficult problems. But as a mediator I have known of at least one case where, as far as I could judge, one party was not taking part in the process with any real intention of reaching a settlement, but was merely trying to fish for information. This was not a mediation recommended by a court, but had it been I would have had no means of making my suspicions known because the process is and must be completely confidential. Should the court have the power to order mediation? This topic was recently debated in the City and by a substantial margin the idea of compulsion was rejected. But those who favour a discretionary mandatory power will not go away and an argument based on proportionality has force. Speaking for myself, however, I am not yet convinced that a case for compulsion has been made out. The Commercial Court has developed a useful system of what may be termed strong nudges.

There is another problem with mediation that can cause difficulty: the problem of authority. Where individuals are the parties, the problem of authority does not loom large. But where a settlement involves the payment of money and in the background there are figures such as insurers or reinsurers, or officials in public authorities who have to satisfy some value for money criteria, there can be difficulties. It is one thing for a senior official in central or local government to be faced with a judgment or award that is enforceable at law. The official cannot be blamed and can place responsibility for an unwelcome expenditure of funds on the foolish judge or arbitrator. It is another thing when officials themselves have to authorise or approve a mediated settlement. This brings me to the most important challenge. The real challenge for the future, if mediation is to fulfil its potential, is more fundamental. One needs what one can describe as a culture change. When I was at the Bar one prepared for a case in court as for a battle. After a certain stage, to suggest a settlement was usually a sign of weakness — a white flag — but an agreed compromise may be a blessing to both sides. One thinks of courts as being very powerful, but the powers of courts are very circumscribed. In most cases, a court can only award or decline to award a sum of money. Occasionally a court will grant or withhold an injunction or make a declaration.

At present people still think in terms of conflict. The words "I am putting it in the hands of my solicitor" are heard too often. Worse and even more depressing is an announcement by a business executive or a government official: "[i]t is now in the hands of the legal department." I remember at an ABA conference talking to a very experienced American mediator, Ms Betty Murphy, who is in practice in Washington DC. She said much of her work came from presidents of large corporations who by-passed their legal departments. Dismayed by writing large quarterly cheques for legal fees they turned to her for help to find a business solution. I am hopeful that as time passes it will become a natural reaction when a dispute reaches an apparent impasse to say: "[l]et us see if a neutral person can help." It is a big jump for a solicitor or officials who consider themselves to be skilled negotiators to turn to an outsider, but anyone who has been engaged in mediation knows that so often disputes involve misunderstandings or misconceptions or personal animosities.

I have heard many stories, and witnessed one or two cases myself, where in a mediation a duel at dawn has led eventually to a shared bottle at nightfall. The advocate seeks to highlight differences and to emphasise legal rights. The mediator seeks to explore common ground and possible pragmatic solutions. There is at present a lack of awareness of mediation as an available process. I sometimes wonder if one could introduce a mediation into a television or radio soap. A little while ago a friend of mine told me of a family dispute between two brothers about the ownership of a farm. Both of them had gone to solicitors and they had run up legal costs amounting between them to about £20,000. Someone suggested mediation. They both jumped at it and the solicitors said what a good idea. A happy ending, but for a modest farm what a waste. Perhaps there is a script writer for *The Archers* in the audience.

THE FUTURE PROSPECTS

I think the prospects are good. I do not expect a surge in mediation in the next two years, but taking a longer view I think the good sense of mediation will ensure its success. There are a number of points to watch. (1) We want to take care that the standards of mediators are maintained. (2) We want to avoid exaggerated claims for mediation. Mediation is not a panacea. There are some cases that require the ruling of a court. But on the other hand there are few cases where the assistance of a skilled neutral will not help to isolate the real points at issue. (3) We want to make mediation known to the public at large and it is important to make it known to the business community. I cannot stress this second point strongly enough. On our visit to Guernsey we learned that the local chamber of commerce was keenly interested. We need to bring the Confederation of British Industries and the chambers of commerce and other like organisations in from the cold. The Institute's links with the CDP may be a good omen, and some organisations like In Place of Strife and InterResolve are already establishing firm links with the insurance industry. (4) We need to think of new areas where mediation may help. The Barker Committee is currently examining the law and practice of planning. I wrote a short memorandum the other day to draw attention to the fact that so often planning disputes cry out for compromise. (5) We need to be aware of what is happening in other jurisdictions. Australia, Canada and the United States are leaders and we can learn from them. The EU countries are lagging behind us, but the International Chamber of Commerce in Paris has now published a guide to ICC ADR. (6) There is always a real possibility of legislation and some measure of control exercised from Brussels, but I hope that any legislation avoids being too prescriptive. Mediation and ADR are at a stage of development and it is important to retain flexibility. (7) We also need to develop the other forms of ADR and in particular early neutral evaluation (ENE). I believe that ENE has a valuable part to play to enable parties to make realistic assessments of their strengths and weaknesses.

At present there are too many trained mediators for the available work, so that after training, individual mediators have insufficient opportunity to practise their skills. I hope and am confident that this will change when people really begin to embrace mediation. One should remember that it was not until 1819, less than 200 years ago, that the old procedure of trial by battle was finally abolished.

Anyone who has time to spare might like to turn to *Ashford v Thornton* (1818) 1 Barnewall & Alderston 405. I anticipate that in 2020 I shall be able to look down, or perhaps up, at a country where mediation is the first and preferred option for settling all disputes.

* This article was originally published as B. Neill, 'Mediation and Its Future Prospects', *Arbitration* 73, no. 1 (2007): 2-5.

CHAPTER 3

The Myth of Modern Mediation

Derek Roebuck

Mediation needs its own history, not because there are now enough practitioners to sustain a sense of belonging to a profession, but because the myths about its development threaten to skew the debate on its future. If, as some believe, mediation sprang to life in the mid-twentieth century United States, either for the first time or after a long slumber, then it is a creature of clever and well-intentioned lawyers, concerned to ameliorate the worst evils of litigation. It would be proper to debate its future within that context, with no need to bring in other disciplines or knowledge of the world or tougher ethical criteria. However, what if it is found everywhere at all times, the most natural and pervasive means that humans have devised for managing disputes? These few pages are not a start to the writing of that history; they intend to do no more than dispel some myths. To do that, I will present an assortment of evidence, mostly drawn from primary sources, of the use of mediation in many times and places, leaving it to speak for itself, with the minimum of commentary. Wherever I have looked, I have found proofs that mediation was normal and widespread. To make my point, I have set out the evidence not as historical argument but mere annals, just one thing after another. The only order is chronological and that is approximate.

THE ANCIENT WORLD TO AD500

There is no room here for the anthropological evidence, but it would show that: "[i]n pre-capitalist societies, people of high as well as low status invest extraordinary amounts of time in mediation, an investment that (proportionately) far exceeds the resources devoted to the adjudication of disputes in our society." Everywhere in the Ancient Greek world, including Ptolemaic Egypt, arbitration was normal and in arbitration the mediation element was primary. However formal the procedure, mediation was attempted first and a mediated settlement was preferred, so that even an adjudication might, where possible, be incorporated in an agreement. Conversely, a settlement might be converted into an award, for easier enforcement. The processes of mediation and arbitration often intermingled, but they were conceptually distinct, as shown by the precision of terminology and the formal step of swearing an oath before moving to adjudication.

From Ancient Rome there is a surprising dearth of direct evidence of mediation, perhaps because public arbitration was quick and cheap, and private ad hoc arbitration cost nothing. It was the duty of every decent citizen, *bonus homo*, to participate. Yet it is clear that some of our modern problems had already arisen and were the topic of scholarly debate. Favorinus, the philosopher, said in the second century AD: "[i]t is often asked whether it is fit and proper for a *judex* after the case has been heard, if there seems to be a chance to settle, to postpone his adjudicatory function for a little while and play the part of a mutual friend and a kind of peacemaker." These early examples of the sophisticated use and knowledge of mediation are enough to dispel the myth that mediation, even court-ordered, is an invention of the twentieth century. But what of the centuries of development in England?

AD500 TO 1100

There were no courts as we know them in England before the Norman Conquest. Justice was done in assemblies, without professional judges or lawyers. There was litigation, of course, and arbitration, public and private. From the time that the first written sources survive, there is evidence of mediation, though not surprisingly it is of only the most important disputes. Bede tells how Theodore of Tarsus, Archbishop of Canterbury c.668-90, mediated a settlement between the Northumbrians and the Mercians in 679, ending a conflict in which the brother of the Northumbrian king had been killed.

A better example of the ordinary mediation of a civil dispute comes from the second half of the eighth century. It had its origin in a transfer of land at some time between 670 and 676 by Cenred, King of Wessex, to Abbot Bectun, and confirmed by a charter. Bectun was succeeded by Catwali, who transferred part of the land, let us call it Fontmell for convenience, by charter to Abbot Wintra. Generations later, the successors of Catwali and Wintra each claimed Fontmell and produced those charters as evidence of ownership. In later times, the sale to Wintra would have been recorded on the original grant, showing the subtraction of Fontmell from Catwali's title, but this all took place long before that practice had been invented. There was no one left who remembered the transactions 90 years later when a dispute came before Bishop Cyneheard. He mediated a settlement: "I, Cyneheard, unworthy bishop, have impressed this sign to confirm and strengthen this charter which I declare to have been drawn up as follows: the successor of the above-named Abbot Bectun, called Catwali, sold the land of ten hides described above to Abbot Wintra for money, and he wrote another deed confirming the sale and the possession described above. But he retained the charter of the original gift, and the subscriptions of the kings, bishops, abbots and leading men, because it could not be easily separated, because this part of the land had been enrolled among the other testimonies of their lands, and it still cannot be. And so, after the original witnesses were dead, a lengthy dispute arose between the communities of the two monasteries and it still continues. From the time it was given to Wintra by the above-named abbot his successors have held this land. But the successors of the other community kept the original deed, confirmed by the hands of the witnesses named above.

So now I and our king and all the others who bear witness and subscribe below have brought about a peaceful reconciliation between them, partly by means of the payment of money and partly by the making of an oath, so that the successors of Abbot Wintra, namely Ecgwold and his community of the monastery called Tisbury, with the permission of the other community of which Abbot Tidbald is head, shall henceforth have and hold for ever the land over which there has been a dispute for a long time. I have transcribed this present deed and made excerpts from the one which was originally given to Abbot Bectun, with the agreement of Abbot Tidbald and his community. I have given this document to Abbot Ecgwold, with the consent and confirmation of the witnesses named below, but I have rejected the other documents that have been prepared concerning this land. These things have been done 759 years from Our Lord's incarnation, the twelfth interdiction.

Cynewulf the king

Herewold the bishop ... [and other witnesses]"

The clarity and confidence of this document do not look like the product of an unpractised mediator-arbitrator.

Anglo-Saxon assemblies preferred the dispute to be mediated to a settlement. Sometimes the process seems contrived. A charter drawn up in 1023 by Wulfstan at King Aethelred's command recites that Leofric had sold land at Inkberrow to Bishop Aethelstan, with a full title: "unopposed and unquestioned, to give and to transfer in his lifetime or at his death, to kin or friends however he wished." Many years later, a different Wulfstan and his son Wulfric claimed part of the land. Bishop Aethelstan took the matter before the assembly of the shire at Worcester. There Earl Leofwine presided and he and Leofric and "the whole shire" granted him full title to the land because he had taken it "unopposed and unquestioned" and they set a date for the boundaries to be inspected and confirmed by those who had confirmed them in the first grant. Bishop Aethelstan took Leofric with him and Wulfstan and Wulfric and "their friends" joined them and inspected the boundaries. Then Leofric and all who were there held that Bishop Aethelstan was the rightful owner. However, that was not the end of it; negotiations continued: "Then Leofric's friends and Wulfstan's friends said that it would be better if they were to come to an agreement rather than to keep up any dispute between them. So they worked out this settlement.

Leofric was to give one pound to Wulfstan and his son. Leofric and two thegns were to swear an oath that Leofric would have been satisfied with that amount if the decision had gone against him as it had for Wulfstan. This was the agreement of all of us. Wulfstan and his son then transferred to Leofric full title to the land; and Leofric and Wulfstan and Wulfric gave full and unquestioned title to the bishop to grant in his lifetime or at his death to whomever he wished."

Of particular interest is the winner's affirmation that he would have accepted the compromise if he had been in the loser's place. That saved face. Aethelred legislated to ensure that such mediated settlements had the force of law, equating an agreement with an adjudication, 'love' with 'law': "[w]here a thegn has two choices, love or law, and he then chooses love, that stands as fast as a doom."

An agreement of 1046, between the bishop and religious community of Sherborne, and Care, son of Toki, disposes of their different interests, but may have arisen without the parties having fallen into an open dispute. It fits well the latest modern category of 'dispute management': "[h]ere it is made known in this writing how the agreement was worked out at Exeter before Earl Godwin and before the whole shire, between Bishop Aelfwold and the community at Sherborne and Care, Toki's son, about the land at Holcombe. That was that they would settle it that all the brothers should leave the land but one, called Ulf, to whom it was devised, and he should have it for life and that on his death the land should pass just as it was, with produce and men, undisputed and without conflict, to the holy church at Sherborne." There was no adjudicated award here, but a mediated settlement. This was soon after Edward the Confessor had become king. A little later, about 1053, a mediated settlement allowed Wulfweard a life interest in land at Hayling Island at an agreed rent and so that it would pass without contest on his death to the Old Minster, Winchester. In 1060, Edward himself became involved in mediating a settlement rather than adjudicating, as presumably he had the power to do, though in the circumstances he was wise not to do so. Leofgifu had made a will before setting out on a pilgrimage to Jerusalem, on which she died. She left land to Peterborough Abbey, whose abbot Leofric, learning of her death, claimed the land and offered to prove the will by witnesses. Edward's queen Edith, however, claimed that Leofgifu had left the land to her. She was the sister of Harold (later the king who died at Hastings) and Tostig. Her husband and brothers mediated. They got Edith to give up her claim to the land in return for 20 gold marks and the same value of church ornaments. The settlement was formally incorporated in a grant by Edward and Edith to the abbey.

There is evidence from western France at about the same time, showing not only the prevalence of mediation, but that women acted as mediators.

TWELFTH CENTURY

Van Caenegem's researches have shown: "[w]hat was usually expected of a law court was not a clear-cut decision ... but ... an effort to bring about a settlement ... by the mediation of the court or the good offices of some doomsmen or various people present at the session, or jurors from the neighbourhood or arbiters, accepted or even elected by the parties..." Furthermore, he provides the evidence. At some time between 1111 and 1117, Ermenold failed to pay the rent for land just down the road from where I am writing in Oxford. His landlord, the abbot of Abingdon, took the land back. Ermenold gave sureties that he would appear in the abbot's court. None of them did. So, at the next sitting, the sureties mediated an agreement with the abbot and Ermenold's other creditors. Fifty years later, a dispute in which Thomas Becket got involved was resolved, "the mediators being Geoffrey de Mandeville the younger, Earl of Essex, Richard de Lucy and other friends of either party."

THIRTEENTH CENTURY

The court could always take a hand in mediating a settlement. In 1202, the claimant brought an action in debt before the king's court at Westminster; the parties were mediated to an agreement to payment by instalments. In a dispute between two abbots in 1234, the court ordered that, if the mediated settlement agreed in court broke down, any dispute should go to six named arbitrators. Arbitrators appointed by courts of Equity were often charged to mediate and if unsuccessful to come back to the court and "advertise" who was at fault. In 1234, one party chose three men, the other chose two, and the archdeacon was added; the six were to work towards peace between the parties and if they could not come to an agreement then the six would take a seventh, whose decision was to prevail in default of their agreement and their arbitration would stand. There are many more examples from the end of the century like this from Coventry : "that dispute (about an encroachment of a wall) has been settled by the intervention of mutual friends in this form." Papal judges made similar orders in the ecclesiastical courts, instructing arbiters to mediate disputes to an amicable settlement if they could.

FOURTEENTH CENTURY

From this time there are many examples of the rules of guilds of various kinds, religious or of town or craft, which provide for mediation and arbitration of disputes between their members. One will suffice, from the guild of St George, Norwich, of 1385, which I have put into modern English: "[a]lso it is ordained that whatever brother or sister feels themselves aggrieved in any manner of cause one with another ... they shall complain to the alderman and the masters of their causes and grievances ... and then the alderman and the masters shall busy themselves as much as they can within fifteen days of the complaint being made, to hear and examine both parties and to set them at peace and rest if they in any way can. And if the alderman and masters cannot bring them to unanimity and accord within the aforesaid time, then by consent of the alderman and masters they may sue at Common Law, but not otherwise."

A typical example of an action brought in the Court of Common Pleas was met by the defence that the claim had been settled by mediation: "... and he says that on the same Friday a certain agreement was made by mediation, *per mediacionem facta*, between him, John, and the aforesaid Philip in London." John's case was that Philip never owned the land and that, even if there had been a settlement, he should recover.

FIFTEENTH CENTURY

In a detailed study of disputes among the gentry of Cheshire in the fifteenth century, particularly in the Bucklow hundred, David Tilsey found: "[t]he gentry of the hundred were certainly well represented in the ranks of those Cheshire gentlemen who resorted to the mediation of a third party in the event of a dispute."

John P. Dawson's study of the Privy Council shows that: "... the large-scale use of laymen to conduct examinations of witnesses outside London opened opportunities for mediation through spontaneous suggestions from the examiners themselves." Parties had already learned that one way to persuade their opponents to talk about settlement was to start court proceedings. That might even lead to the compromise, with the judge's approval, of a prosecution for murder.

SIXTEENTH CENTURY

A hint from the awesome Council was usually enough to persuade a party behaving inequitably to make a fair settlement, as when the Council suggested to Abraham Tournour that he should give reasonable time to two debtors, as other creditors had done, for fear that their Lordships would be "constrained to take that course against him as otherwise they would be lothe to do." Few mediators have had such powers of persuasion at their disposal, that is imprisonment. "It is therefore of some interest that the Elizabethan Council undertook to organise the work of mediation by commissions of a more permanent character, and to invest them with wider powers. The first of these commissions was appointed in 1576, headed by the two Chief Justices."

By the end of the sixteenth century, the courts were regularly sending matters to arbitrators, whose first task was to mediate. "There was one general theme that constantly recurred — the desirability of settlement by consent as a means of avoiding strife and promoting peace. The recitals in a decree of 1596 are characteristic: 'It was moved and thought meete by this cowrt that some indifferent gentlemen who are of understanding and dwell in the county where the controversy groweth and may thereby knowe the partyes and credytt of the witnesses' should be asked to call the parties and bring them to a 'frendly and a quyett end ...' Often the Chancellor or Lord Keeper himself persuaded the parties to submit to his own mediation."

Mediation did not always work. Sir Edward Coke, the champion of the Common Law, as counsel might stymie it by insisting on a trial. He could fail when appointed mediator, although he "showed himself to be a persistent and effective negotiator, earning the Lord Keeper's gratitude."

SEVENTEENTH CENTURY

During the Commonwealth, there were arguments to restore the old assemblies of the Anglo-Saxons at the expense of the Common Law courts and that mediation should take the place of civil litigation: "Winstanley proposed that officials known as peacemakers and overseers should endeavour to settle civil disputes ... Peters wanted every parish and hundred to choose three men to act for a year as peacemakers or friendmakers."

The most explicit example I know of mediation being subsumed in the process of arbitration, even to the extent of making an adjudication abnormal, does not come from England. It is provided by Alexandre de la Roche, a lawyer in Paris in the seventeenth century, whom I wrote about in Charitable Arbitrator. De la Roche's belief in the role of the church as universal mediator is made clear not only in his text, but in the accompanying plates: "The Good Bishop Saint Augustine: In his Diocese. He settles suits and disputes. He says that he would give everything else up for this; that it is one of the most important functions of the episcopate. The

Gospel and the Fathers require this of the pastors, Philip 3; John 14; Paul, Romans 12, Corinthians 1; Leo, Epistle 82. The Eastern Church has retained this holy practice. The Councils so order all bishops: it must be the concern of bishops to exhort brethren who have differences, whether they be clergy or lay, towards peace rather than to litigation. Carh 4 c26. Our kings in the past have exhorted the bishops to excommunicate those who refuse to settle their differences following the thundering Councils of Worms 15 c41, Agath c31. The majority so agreed that whosoever were in hatred, or were in dispute in long drawn out litigation among themselves, and were unable to be brought together in peace, should first be challenged by the priests of their communities to say why, if they were not willing to put an end to their enmities, they should not be excommunicated from the most righteous fellowship of the Church. C ad 4 c31."

The same arguments applied to lay as to ecclesiastical mediation. The system of charitable arbitrators which the next plate portrays may never have been implemented, but there is no doubt about Henry IV's intention, prevented by his assassination: "The Good Advocates and Procedures and Charitable Arbitrators: There were some established in Provence who took care of the suits of the poor for nothing, and brought almost all of them to an amicable conclusion, following the intention of the Ordinance of Henry IV of 6 March 1610. The first President at that time, and the King's men in this Parlement of Provence, put this Ordinance promptly into Practice. That good Prince had resolved to bring it into operation throughout France after the example of Venice, but death prevented that." De La Roche sets out the qualities of the good mediator: "[h]e does not need ability nor eloquence, nor the grand manner; all he needs is goodwill. He should not put himself to the trouble of preparing fine harangues to persuade the litigant to make peace. His own miseries are persuasion enough ... if the curé wants to get help, he should take someone from his parish who has a reputation for probity and is prudent. This mediator will be able to settle most of the peasants' differences when they are of little consequence. We know from experience that in the parishes where this is established, the parties will go before him and ask him themselves, to avoid them having to look for arbitrators from a long way off. But to be a good mediator you need more than anything patience, common sense, an appropriate manner, and goodwill. You must make yourself liked by both parties and gain credibility in their minds. To do that, begin by explaining that you are unhappy about the bother, the trouble and the expense that their litigation is causing them. After that, listen patiently to all their complaints. They will not be short, particularly the first time round. You must have the wisdom and discretion not to say anything to upset the one you first talk to, however poor his case seems ... the mediator ought to have an inexhaustible supply of goodwill ... Those who act on these principles bear with patience the complaints, the disgruntlement, the grievances, even the ingratitude of those to whom they have rendered services."

It would not be difficult to replicate examples from elsewhere in western Europe, particularly from Italy, to show how widespread the practice was.

EIGHTEENTH CENTURY

James Oldham's scholarship has shown Lord Mansfield's "relentless efforts to get parties to settle their disputes". He quotes him: "I tried all I could to have the whole referred and settled, but Plaintiff would agree to nothing." Arbitration included preliminary attempts to mediate. The Commissioners of the Courts of Requests could do their own mediation: "it seems that courts of requests used their wide discretionary powers to resolve disputes amicably and to achieve a genuine blend of communal justice and situation equity. For example, Hutton attempted mediation from the bench."

After the Revolution, France set up a system of *juges de paix* which lasted until 1958. They have survived in Belgium and parts of Switzerland. These judicial appointments, at first amateur, were charged with mediating more minor disputes.

NINETEENTH CENTURY

By the beginning of the nineteenth century, voices began to be raised for reform, including suggestions for 'Judges of Reconcilement.' Lord Brougham proposed the creation of new county courts, whose judges might conduct mediation and arbitration, but had to remove that suggestion from his bill that became the County Courts Act 1846. Yet 30 years later he was still pressing for mediation in the courts: "[t]he profession have an incurable prejudice against every such means ... not unconnected with motives of interest ... With the profession I will compound; they shall have ... no more law amendment to do them injury, no more of costs reduced, no more of litigation prevented. Let them give me this, and I will lay down my head in peace and comfort." Perhaps the reason why so many have assumed that mediation was dormant in the nineteenth and early twentieth centuries was the hostility of the lawyers which hid it from view. Mediation continued nonetheless but the public outcry was for legislative improvements in formal arbitration, too big a topic to be treated here.

TWENTIETH CENTURY

The century began with the first sociological enquiry into the nature of mediation, by Georg Simmel, who spelled out an important distinction. The mediator may be, and always is in modern mediations of all kinds, a 'neutral.' That was not always so. Many societies have preferred what the Greeks called a "*koine*", someone common to both parties, equally the friend of both, or, as Pope Clement VI declared himself to be as mediator between Edward III and Philippe VI of France, *persona privata et amicus communis.*

It is not just among the lawyers of the United States, the United Kingdom and some western European jurisdictions that mediation lives on. Late twentieth-century societies of all kinds have made use of mediation: "The mediator may be an institutionalised neutral, such as the Nuer leopard-skin chief, or he may be a person of acknowledged prestige, such as the Ifugao go-between. The *burgermeister* of rural Bavarian villages and the *mukhtaar* in Lebanese villages are examples of mediators in small-scale societies ... Nader's work on the Zapotec *presidente* illustrates how a single person, the *presidente*, may be mediator, adjudicator and arbitrator all in one day." The same volume shows how mediation can work in a small and isolated community of fisher people in the United States.

The second half of the century saw the creation of the profession of neutral mediator. The century ended with at least three problems unresolved: should there be public control and certification of mediators;

should mediation ever be compulsory and, if so, in what circumstances; and should judges and arbitrators be allowed, even encouraged, to act as mediators during the course of litigation or arbitration and, if so, should they, if their attempts fail, be allowed to continue and adjudicate.

CONCLUSIONS

In conclusion: "[t]here are societies in the world (even if none can be seen to have existed in Europe in historical times) without formal procedures for judgment, but there are none without legitimate procedures for mediation." That is all I have set out to show. Mediation existed before there was litigation of any kind whose excesses it could ameliorate. It was an integral part of the arbitration process long before "med-arb" was coined. No such word was necessary, because, although all knew the distinction between mediation and adjudication, in ordinary usage arbitration included both. That is why mediation is sometimes hard to find, particularly in indexes. Moreover, it was not just ad hoc and informal. The courts ordered it regularly, in Cleopatra's Egypt and Elizabeth I's England and at most times and places between and after.

The need for deeper thinking about the future of mediation demands greater care in assessing its past. There have been warning voices for more than a quarter of a century, for example Richard Abel's: "[s]ometimes one mode of conflict can so dominate the others that the latter are reduced to little more than a façade. Thus 'mediation' in the contemporary United States often is merely a more palatable name for processes that reflect economic power, as in the Better Business Bureau, or state domination exercised through the courts, as in some landlord-tenant disputes."

There is room for much more research into all aspects of mediation. It needs to be conducted at a scientific level if we are not to go round in circles. Much that is now published is repetitive in a way that would not be accepted in other disciplines. This argument is not new. Sociologists have been saying it for 30 years: "[n]o theorist to date has elaborated a theory of society in such a way as to construct a theoretical object (concept) of dispute. On the contrary, the concept of dispute has typically been constructed inductively, by the method of abstracted empiricism ... research questions and problems may be posed by a theory, or for a theory, by changes in the material world. Thus we are arguing not that the concept of dispute be jettisoned, but that it be refined and given a historically and materially specified place in theory."

It is the "historically and materially specified place" that these few pages have tried to establish. I almost conclude with an anecdote from my wise old friend De La Roche: "[o]n the other hand, sometimes everything seems fine with a mediator, when in fact there are faults. I know of another important matter, between eminent persons, where the mediator, who was not of their station in life, negotiated between them for a long time but made some big mistakes. They told him so, at least they complained to him often. Nevertheless they forgave him everything. He was always welcome, eating and drinking with all the parties. At last he was the cause of their settlement, really because he always acted on the lofty principles of goodwill and love for one's neighbour." Incompetence in a mediator can be a blessing, it seems, so long as goodwill all round produces trust. The last word must be given to Shakespeare, speaking through Lucrece for violated women at all times and showing mediation's limits:

Out idle words, servants to shallow fools!

Unprofitable sounds, weak arbitrators!

Busy yourselves in skill-contending schools,

Debate where leisure serves with dull debaters;

To trembling clients be you mediators.

For me, I force not argument a straw,

Since that my case is past the help of law.

Can anyone, after that, believe that ours are the first generations to understand what mediation is all about?

REFERENCES

* This article was originally published as D. Roebuck, 'The Myth of Modern Mediation', *Arbitration* 73, no. 1 (2007): 105-116.

1 Could there be a better testimony than Sarah Rainsford's report, which follows next?

2 Much of the research on which this paper draws has been published: D. Roebuck, *Ancient Greek Arbitration* (Oxford: Holo Books, 2001); D. Roebuck, *The Charitable Arbitrator: How to Mediate and Arbitrate in Louis XIV's France* (Oxford: Holo Books, 2002); D. Roebuck & B. de Fumichon, *Roman Arbitration* (Oxford: Holo Books, 2004), D. Roebuck 'Sources for the History of Arbitration', *Arbitration International* 14 (1998): 237-343; D. Roebuck, '"Best to Reconcile": Mediation and Arbitration in the Ancient Greek World', *Arbitration* 66 (2000): 275-87; D. Roebuck, 'L'Arbitrage en Droit Anglais avant 1558', *Revue de l'Arbitrage* (2002): 535-77; and D. Roebuck, 'Customary Law before the

Conquest', *Amicus Curiae* 68 (2006): 7-16. D. Roebuck, *Early English Arbitration: Dispute Resolution before the Common Law* is due in 2007. I have not tried to deal with mediation in the history of Islam, but: "incentives to settle rather than litigate were built into the tahkim system ... It is a general rule in all schools of the Shari'a as well as in the statute laws of most modern Arab states that disputes that cannot be conciliated cannot be arbitrated. Thus, the possibility of conciliation must always remain open in tahkim", G. Sayen, 'Arbitration, Conciliation and the Islamic Legal Tradition in Saudi Arabia', *University of Pennsylvania Journal of International Business Law* 9 (1987): 234. For the position in China: M. Palmer, 'The Revival of Mediation in the People's Republic of China I and II' in W.E. Butler (ed.), *Yearbook on Socialist Legal Systems* (London: Transnational Books, 1998 and 1999).

3 R. Abel, 'Mediation in Pre-Capitalist Societies', *Windsor Yearbook of Access to Justice* (1983): 181.

4 Roebuck, *Ancient Greek Arbitration*, 158.

5 Aulus Gellius, *Attic Nights*, 14.2.13-16; Roebuck, *Roman Arbitration*, 69.

6 The story is told by R. Stacey, 'Texts and Society' in *After Rome*, T. Charles-Edwards, (Oxford: Oxford University Press, 2003), 247-249.

7 D. Whitelock, *English Historical Documents* (London: Eyre and Spottiswoode, 1955), 441-442, on which this translation is closely based.

8 A. J. Robertson (ed.), *Anglo-Saxon Charters* (Cambridge: Cambridge University Press, 1939), 162, no. LXXXIII. It cannot be entirely

fortuitous that the Britons in contemporary Brittany followed similar processes, 500 years after they had emigrated there: W. Davies, 'People and Places in Dispute in Ninth-Century Brittany' in *The Settlement of Disputes in Early Medieval Europe*, W. Davies & P. Fouracre (eds)., (Cambridge, Cambridge University Press, 1986), 76. The essays in this collection give many examples of mediated settlements, from fifth-century Gaul to sixteenth-century Scotland.

9   III Aethelred 13.3 and 13.4.

10 For the history of the expression "love-day": M. T. Clanchy, 'Law and Love in the Middle Ages' in *Disputes and Settlements*, J. Bossy, (Cambridge: Cambridge University Press, 1983), 47-67; and J. W. Spargo, 'Chaucer's Love-Days', *Speculum* 15 (1940): 36-56.

11 Robertson Anglo-Saxon Charters no.CV; P. H. Sawyer, *Anglo-Saxon Charters: an Annotated List and Bibliography* (London: Royal Historical Society, 1968), no. 1474. Care and Toki are Scandinavian names.

12 Robertson no. CXIV; Sawyer no. 1476.

13 Sawyer no.1029. For the position in France: S. D. White, '*Pactum ... Legem Vincit et Amor Judicium:* the Settlement of Disputes by Compromise in Eleventh-Century Western France', *American Journal of Legal History* 22 (1978): 281-308.

14 White, *Pactum ... Legem Vincit et Amor Judicium'*, 293. "Faced with the fact that Matilda of Tuscany and other women mediated between their subjects, the decretist Stephan of Tournai reasoned that while women did not really have the power of judgment, they did seem able to

make comparisons", Linda Fowler, "Forms of Arbitration" in Stephan Kuttner (ed.), Proceedings of the Fourth International Congress of Medieval Canon Law 1972 (Biblioteca Apostolica Vaticana, 1976), pp.133-147, 136. But then Matilda (1046-1115) was a general whom Stephan would not have dared to look at.

15 R. C. Van Caenegem, 'Royal Writs in England from the Conquest to Glanvill', *Selden Society* 77 (1959): 42. J. Hudson (ed.), *Historia Ecclesie Abbendonensis: the History of the Church of Abingdon II* (Oxford: Oxford University Press, 2002), xciii & 204-207.

16 R. C. Van Caenegem, 'English Lawsuits from William I to Richard I Vol 1', *Selden Society I* 106 (1990): 178, no. 209.

17 Van Caenegem, "English Lawsuits" II, 414-419, no. 415. (1949) 68 Selden Society 259, no. 878.

18 *Cerne v Middelton*, Curia Regis Rolls (CRR) XV 1277.

19 CRR XV 1471; also (in 1207) CRR V 55-6.

20 P. R. Coss, *The Early Records of Medieval Coventry* (Oxford: Oxford University Press, 1986), 314, no. 691.

21 J. E. Sayers, *Papal Judges Delegate in the Province of Canterbury 1198 -1254* (Oxford: Oxford University Press, 1971), 105.

22 T. Smith (ed.), *English Gilds* (London: Oxford University Press, 1870), 450-451.

23 YB 11 Richard II Ames Foundation 98-100 (1387); YB 6 Richard II Ames Foundation 115 (1382) is about another mediation.

24 D. Tilsey, 'Arbitration in Gentry Disputes: the Case of Bucklow Hundred in Cheshire, 1400-1465' in *Courts, Counties and the Capital in*

the *Later Middle Ages*, D. E. S. Dunn ed., (Stroud: Sutton, 1996), 55.

25 J. P. Dawson, *A History of Lay Judges* (Boston, Harvard University Press, 1960); and 'The Privy Council and Private Law in the Tudor and Stuart Periods I', *Michigan Law Review* 48 (1950): 423-28.

26 E. Powell, 'Arbitration and the Law in England in the Late Middle Ages', Transactions of the Royal Historical Society Fifth Series 33 (1983): 49-67; and 'Settlement of Disputes by Arbitration in Fifteenth-Century England', *Law and History Review* 2 (1984): 21-43.

27 Dawson, 'The Privy Council', 414, fn.62-415-16.

28 Dawson, *A History of Lay Judges,* 168 and the cases he cites in p. 164, fn.115, e.g., *Lovet v Chamberlen* 1583; *Longe v May* (1597).

29 Dawson, *A History of Lay Judges*, 165-66.

30 D. Veall, *The Popular Movement for Law Reform 1640-1660* (Oxford: Oxford University Press, 1970), 170.

31 Roebuck, *The Charitable Arbitrator,* 110.

32 *Ibid.*, 210.

33 *Ibid.*, 197-99.

34 Fabrizio Marrella and Andrea Mozzato, Alle Origini dell'Arbitrato Commerciale Internazionale: l'Arbitrato a Venezia tra Medioevo ed Età Moderna (Padua: CEDAM, 2001).

35 J. Oldham, *The Mansfield Manuscripts and the Growth of English Law in the Eighteenth Century* (University of North Carolina P, Chapel Hill, 2 vols, 1992 I), 155.

36 *Ibid.*, 154.

37 H. Horwitz & J. Oldham, 'John Locke, Lord Mansfield, and Arbitration

during the Eighteenth Century', *Historical Journal* (1993): 137-59.

38 H. W. Arthurs, *"Without the Law": Administrative Justice and Legal Pluralism in Nineteenth-Century England* (Toronto: University of Toronto Press, 1986), 29.

39 *Ibid.*, 39, citing T. W. Snagge, *The Evolution of the County Court* (London: Clowes, 1904).

40 Arthurs, 42.

41 K. Wolff (ed.), *The Sociology of Georg Simmel* (Free Press, Glencoe Illinois, 1950), 149-50, extracted by S. Roberts & M. Palmer, 159, who follow with a pertinent extract from P. H. Gulliver, *Disputes and Negotiations: a Cross-Cultural Perspective* (New York: Academic Press, 1979), 214-17.

42 E. Déprez, "La Conférence d'Avignon (1344): l'Arbitrage Pontifical entre la France et l'Angleterre" in *Essays in Medieval History Presented to Thomas Frederick Tout, Manchester for the Subscribers 1925*, A. G. Little & F. M. Powicke (eds.), 301-20.

43 L. Nader & H. F. Todd Jr (eds), *The Disputing Process: Law in Ten Societies* (New York: Columbia University Press, 1978), 10. However, the best and latest proof is in Sarah Rainsford's BBC 4 "From Our Own Correspondent" piece, which immediately follows this, showing that mediation is used regularly and effectively by Kurdish communities in Turkey today, with no official involvement, to manage feuds.

44 Davies & Fouracre, *The Settlement of Disputes in Early Medieval Europe*, 237.

45 R. Abel, "Mediation in Pre-Capitalist Societies", *Windsor Yearbook of*

Access to Justice (1983): 179.

46 M. Cain & K. Kulcsar, 'Thinking Disputes: an Essay on the Origins of the Dispute Industry', *Law and Society Review* 16 (1981): 385, 399.

47 See now S. Roberts & M. Palmer, *Dispute Processes: ADR and the Primary Forms of Decision-Making* (Cambridge: Cambridge University Press, 2005), reviewed below, especially Ch. 6.

48 Roebuck, *Charitable Arbitrator*, 199.

49 The Rape of Lucrece, lines 1016-22.

CHAPTER 3

Mediation:
Big Bang, Steady State or Black Hole?

Tony Willis

Some provocative questions about mediation. Is it a profession, if so what are the consequences, what are the drivers, what is the relationship with the civil justice system, is that relationship healthy, what is the external climate, what are the current issues, providers versus independents, training sufficiency or oversupply, regulation, the role of the Civil Mediation Council, judges as mediators, will we see more growth and if not why not and a mediator's tentative manifesto.

INTRODUCTION

I would like to speak to you of mediation. Not arbitration. Not ADR, a particularly silly acronym. Mediation is not alternative, it is complementary and most American practitioners and many elsewhere think ADR includes arbitration. But plain, simple, vanilla-wrapped mediation. I would like to do that by asking some questions that I believe are pertinent and venturing some possible and possibly iconoclastic answers. I will do my best to avoid the MEGO syndrome and I am also conscious of the Canadian humourist Stephen Leacock's warning: "[m]ost people tire of a lecture in ten minutes; clever people can do it in five. Sensible people never go to lectures at all." Good omelettes are not made without breaking a few eggs. I am not here to praise mediation (and of course not to bury it), to teach or sell mediation or to explain mediation. It follows that, more than usually, I should caution you that these views are my own, not those of the Chartered Institute of Arbitrators, of the Civil Mediation Council, of CEDR, the ADR Group, In Place of Strife, the International Academy of Mediators, the Panel of Independent Mediators, CPR, the ICC, WIPO, the American Arbitration Association or any of the good institutions I sometimes work with or for and the many others for whom I have much admiration.

If you do not disagree with me at least a third of the time, I have obviously not made myself clear. Only narcissists cannot stand disagreement. It is the stuff of life, of progress and intelligent conversation. It is what leads to agreement, which is ultimately the entire and only basis on which we can live on this fragile planet.

BIG BANG, STEADY STATE OR BLACK HOLE?

As I sometimes say to excuse making some blindingly obvious comment, you can always rely on me to make the cosmic suggestions. But what do I mean by giving you these alternatives?

Big bang is the currently-favoured theory of how the universe emerged from its largely agreed beginnings in an immensely hot and dense state about 13.7 billion years ago by explosive exponential expansion. Applying that theory to the state of mediation as it is today would suggest we are in a state of exciting and ever increasing expansion. It is indeed the mantra of most of the mediation institutions and has been so for at least the last 15 years. The competing claims fall over themselves with excitement. This programme, that programme, this initiative, that initiative, this conference, that conference. Training bodies churn out hundreds of mediators regardless of the amount of work available for them. If you believed only 10% of the claims made for the mediation big bang enthusiasts, your head would spin. They are all in the messianic phase. Even the Economist, that most valuable temple of iconoclasts, has been seduced. In 2002, it reported that mediation was new and fast growing, indeed booming. I respect some of the motives (and I want to go on to examine some of the economic drivers) but I believe the messianic approach is doing us all a disservice because a false picture is being painted of exponential growth accompanied by widespread public acceptance and enthusiasm.

Steady state is the competing theory of the universe advanced most prominently by Sir Fred Hoyle in the 1940s, 1950s and 1960s, which argued that new matter is being created continuously as the galaxies move away from each other. In this theory, the universe is in a steady state at any point in time. The theory is no longer accepted by most scientists. Applying that theory to the state of mediation as it is today would suggest that while there are developments going on to fill the void and expansion might be going on largely unnoticed all about us, the observable universe remains pretty much the same except in the margins. I believe this is closer to the state of mediation in England at this time if it is properly described.

Black holes have achieved notoriety despite their necessarily theoretical characteristics but the characteristic I apply to mediation is that of invisibility. If you doubt that mediation is virtually invisible to most of the population, Professor Hazel Genn in her excellent study with the National Centre for Social Research published in 1999 'Paths to Justice, What People Do and Think about Going to Law' made it absolutely plain based on extensive research. She found that: "[q]uite simply, current ADR activity in the context of civil and family disputes appears to be negligible. The reasons for this are lack of knowledge about ADR services amongst the general public and to some extent among advisors and the legal profession; suspicion about what is a relatively new development in this country; and also principled objections to the compromise of legal rights and entitlements."

Much has happened since, some of it (such as the state-funded National Mediation Help Line which started operating last year) being really excellent and it would be surprising if knowledge of mediation has not increased to some extent since — but all the evidence is that Professor Genn's conclusion in 1999 remains true today. We do not have any comprehensive statistics showing the total number of mediations conducted in England and Wales every year. It would be difficult to obtain completely reliable figures although some attempts ought to be made to collect data of this kind on a rather more systematic basis.

We do, however, have the information produced over a number of years by, for example, CEDR showing the number of mediations CEDR conducts every year. In 1999-2000, CEDR arranged a total of 550 mediations (including those arranged through bulk schemes). In 2000-2001, CEDR's numbers were only slightly higher and that trend has continued since but the increase has not been dramatic. In the published results of the second mediator audit from November 2005, CEDR estimated that the current size of the civil and commercial mediation market may be in the range of 2,500 to 2,700 per annum. That figure was based on their internet-based survey which attracted 416 individual responses — most of those involved in significant numbers of mediations. While necessarily approximate (and the figures probably underestimate the true size of the market to some extent) that is a tiny (and I would argue virtually invisible) economic activity, which confirms Professor Genn's finding from 1999. I say 'tiny' by comparison with the 150,000 or so claims lodged in the county courts every year and the thousands of claims lodged in the High Court every year — not to mention the hundreds of thousands of disputes which occur every year but which never go near a court.

IS MEDIATION A PROFESSION?

The question needs to be asked because a good deal depends on the answer. A profession in the work sense can be defined as an occupation that requires training and the mastery of specialised knowledge, usually with a professional association, ethical code and process of certification or licensing. George Bernard Shaw characterised all professions as conspiracies against the laity. Sociologists have tended to define professionalism as "self-defined power elitism" but although you would expect me to distance myself from sociologists on my profession, some of the characteristics identified by that gloomy discipline hold true to this day, although somewhat unfashionable such as altruism, self-governance, esoteric knowledge, ethical behaviour and special skills. Altruism is usually given expression by a commitment to do good through one's profession, even in cases where the buyer of the service cannot afford it but is in strong need. Hence, the pro bono ethic is, I suggest, an integral part of a professional career.

What I suggest is that professionals are always individuals. As such, they are unusually vulnerable to those who might wish to exploit their services, sometimes for good reasons, sometimes for understandable economic reasons but sometimes for ill. (If you doubt this, consider the effective nationalisation of the medical profession in Britain after the Second World War in the formation of the National Health Service.) Given the gross imbalance between numbers of mediators and numbers of available mediations, it means that providers are in a powerful (and in competition terms dominant) position; a position that can be abused. If you accept that self-governance is an essential ingredient of a profession, you would expect there to be a professional organisation to put it in place. Moreover, the existence of professional organisations (sometimes regarded as an indicator of professionalism in itself) is always likely to be a much better means of training and discipline than externally-imposed regulatory models.

Sir Brian Neill, the first Chairman of the Civil Mediation Council — who in that role has done so much for the organisation of mediation in recent times — in a thoughtful and interesting speech to the London Branch of the Chartered Institute of Arbitrators earlier this year concluded that mediation was an 'embryonic profession.' I respectfully disagree that we are embryonic. In my view, mediation is a profession. New, certainly and small in numbers but until mediators see that that is the case and draw the conclusions that follow concerning organisation and the responsibilities that go with it, we will continue to be seen as embryonic and we will all be the worse for it as will those who rely on us.

IF SO, WHAT ARE THE CONSEQUENCES FOR MEDIATORS?

First, mediators need to recognise the need to organise. We have a responsibility to ourselves and those we serve to so arrange our affairs that our professionalism can be given more effective expression and so that we can be protected to a greater extent from those with different (frequently benign and intrinsically valuable in themselves but very still very different) motives and drivers. By protected I mean giving ourselves the ability and power to be heard and to influence policy as well as in the sense of not allowing ourselves to be exploited where that is undesirable. Secondly, mediators need to recognise the need for greater excellence. This is likely to be achieved not just (and arguably not at all) from quantitatively greater training courses and CPD programs (although they are likely to form part of a bigger whole) but from collegial activities dedicated to spreading knowledge and best practice, allowing for mentoring and thought leadership. Thirdly, mediators need to stand up and make their voice heard on matters of policy that affect what we do and that affect the civil justice system which is our partner in the commercial field.

Until we do those things, we will continue to be invisible, the agenda will continue to be made by others with sometimes very different interests and little or no knowledge of what we actually do and the true value of what that is and we will not be able to grow our special skills sufficiently to make a difference now and in the future.

WHAT ARE THE DRIVERS FOR MEDIATION?

The roots of mediation are not really in doubt. They lie in methods and systems of social organisation that go back into history and prehistory.

Whether you rely on Confucius, Roscoe Pound in 1906 with his powerful call for civil justice reform in the United States, or on Frank Sander's multi-door court house, on Professor Simon Roberts' wonderful book describing dispute processes and thinking from round the world or that wonderful burst of common sense by Andrew Acland from 1990, there is no doubt that there are endless powerful streams of thought and human behaviour that underpin what we do. But those are not in doubt. What have not been sufficiently examined are the economic, political and policy drivers and their consequences. This is a subject that would justify at least a couple of doctoral theses and I am conscious of the MEGO factor but I will try to summarise what in my view has in recent times generated work for mediators.

Experimentation, Research and Training

The literature is voluminous and it reflects much very high quality research and teaching. The Program on Negotiation at Harvard stands out with the seminal work of the likes of Roger Fisher and William Ury and many others up to the current leaders of the Program on Negotiation such as Bob Mnookin, Larry Susskind from MIT and the younger generation such as Daniel Fisher and Erica Fox who leads the Harvard Negotiation Insight Initiative. There are others such as the work being done at Pepperdine School of Law in Malibu, California and Bond University in Queensland. British universities have been much slower into the academic subject but work is being done and courses now being offered here too, such as the Oxford Saïd Business School's Programme on Negotiation. There are many others.

The main focus in Britain started with the formation of CEDR led then and now by the remarkable Professor Karl Mackie. Karl and I don't always agree but we could not have done without him and all the work he and others at CEDR have done and continue to do. As a driver of our profession, these are all benign, highly regarded and vitally necessary.

Professional Institutions

Starting with CPR in New York in 1979, CEDR in Britain in 1990 and LEADR in Australia and New Zealand a little earlier and then followed by the likes of the International Academy of Mediators (IAM) based in the United States, these bodies, each rather different in scope and ambition, have done an enormous amount to take the research and theory out into the business and public world. In the case of CEDR in particular, its mission has always been not just to teach and promote mediation but to do it and so it has the CEDRSolve mediation business offering high quality mediation services. CPR in the United States has been a catalyst for change in Fortune 500 companies at general counsel level and has more recently been active in Europe. The IAM is interesting because it is becoming the first properly recognisable collegiate body of purely professional mediators and while it remains overwhelmingly peopled by North Americans, I and some others outside the United States are fellows as full-time mediators and I gain a great deal from that contact with like-minded mediators every time we meet. Less formal groupings such as the twice-yearly Lamport Hall meetings in England are no less important. As drivers of our profession, these Institutions are wholly benign and have been critically important in the growth of mediation worldwide.

Providers of Mediation Services

I have already mentioned CEDR as a non-profit provider but a number of highly professional and well-organised mediation businesses have sprung up in the last decade and a half such as the ADR Group (which actually pre-dated CEDR), In Place of Strife and now many others in Britain and JAMS in the United States to name but a few. As drivers of our profession, we need these institutions to grow and thrive but their respective business models will inevitably conflict with our economic interests as mediators. So the attempts to form exclusive mediator panels (which have largely failed with the exception of JAMS in the United States) tying mediators to sometimes quite high-cost operations and restrictive conditions and the failure at least until now to unbundle the services actually performed by the provider are generally a problem for the mediation community. Those problems may resolve themselves, particularly if we as mediators work together to achieve sensible solutions.

Defensive Mediation Providers

More recently, a number of previously exclusive arbitration providers have climbed on board. So, the Chartered Institute of Arbitrators, our hosts this evening, has in the last few years taken an interest and set up a good training scheme and has some good mediation schemes up and running. If I am frank, such providers in their present form are not likely to be attractive homes for professional full-time mediators since they are and have always been run as a home for the completely different discipline of adjudicative dispute resolution and it shows. They may change but it will be difficult to accommodate such different animals in the same pen.

The ICC, which has had a conciliation procedure that sounds a bit like mediation on its books for many years and reformed in 1998 but with very little take up and reformed again as ICC ADR, has started again promoting the ICC brand of conciliation. So far as I am aware, it has little contact with the mainstream of mediation thought and practice elsewhere and so may have little impact.

In my view, until these defensive moves involve themselves in the mediation mainstream, they are unlikely to be a major driver of mediation. Moreover, activities that fail to recognise and involve themselves in the mediation profession as it exists run the risk of diversion of resources, some confusion and possible schism.

Civil Justice Reform

As in the United States, civil justice reform in England has been the most powerful driver in favour of mediation. The Woolf reforms, following the earlier practice in the Commercial Court, have had a profound effect. The most recent change to the Rules, the 41st Amendment, has introduced a General Pre-action Protocol requiring any party to litigation to consider the suitability of mediation and other forms of dispute resolution.

I was and am a firm admirer of Lord Woolf both personally and as an outstanding judge. His reforms have had many good results, not least the creation of a new profession that is unlikely to have seen the light of day without his energy and determination to improve a broken civil justice system. The problem is that they have in the end fallen prey to the old English vice of complexity. The result of front-loading the costs has been to increase the cost of litigation significantly in the early stages. Moreover the reforms have provided the state with an excuse (I must be frank, it is an excuse) to underfund the civil justice system. It is nothing but a disgrace that the Government has forced the courts to be self-funding on a simple cash flow basis, completely ignoring the absolute imperative of providing the citizens of this rich country with adequate access to justice and the real cost benefits that would flow from that. More than ever, it is impossible for most people to contemplate their own civil litigation. The filing fees are now very high and the system is now organised round numerical targets designed to force litigation away from the courts. The system is run on a calculated scarcity principle and, for such a critical constitutional entitlement, it simply will not do.

It is a bit of a puzzle, frankly, that the Civil Justice Council does not have some hands-on professional mediation representatives on it — but no. It has an excellent ADR (that discredited acronym again!) Subcommittee with at least two front-rank mediator members but it appears to work to policy set elsewhere including espousing targeted reductions in access to the courts.

I yield to no one in my admiration for the individual judges and also for the excellent work being done by Robert Nicholas and others at the Department of Constitutional Affairs in their work to popularise mediation and make it widely available. The problem is that mediation is being treated as an alternative to adjudication when properly analysed it is not. Any court system that uses mediation as a means to fix its inability to respond effectively to users (litigants and their lawyers) is ultimately doomed. Mediation works because, unless parties agree (and they have the absolute right not to agree), the judges are waiting for them, promptly and at reasonable cost. The court system should work because of the range of options available to litigants, each of them professional and affordable. In that way, litigants will have true alternatives. They either settle or they have a judge settle the matter for them.

As a mediator I frequently worry a good deal when I see parties burdened with extraordinarily high costs and very significant delays that I believe should not really occur. To mediators, I say that the present position under which the civil justice system is very costly and slow and mediation is touted as the answer cannot be sustained because one day the small boy at the back of the crowd will notice what the state has done to the civil justice system and the citizenry will cry enough. It is well said that one should never put one's trust in governments. That is not because the individuals are necessarily bad people. Most are trying hard to do the right thing — but they march to a very different drum and it is not ours. No thought ever seems to be given to the law of unintended consequences.

Mediators should therefore be cautious about the possibility of continued mass growth in mediation driven by government policies. It may work for some time but it is in my view unsustainable. Even if it works for a considerable time, the experience in the United States is instructive. Where the courts have been most coercive in favour of mediation, for example northern California, Texas, Florida, the growth has been exponential (although dominated by personal injury and employments cases, areas in which mediation has made only small progress in England — in itself a real puzzle). Moreover, the mediation profession there is still very pyramid shaped with a few at the top with very handsome practices but the mass of mediators under considerable cost pressure. In other parts of the United States, contrary to what you might have expected, mediation is not widely known, carried out if at all largely by retired judges with uncertain results.

F. E. Smith is reported to have once described the Bar as a profession of about (then) 2,000 members with work for 1,000 — all of it done by 500. That is the reality of a very competitive profession. There will always be lots of work for the best mediators who work hard and bend every sinew towards all the components of professionalism (particularly in the major matters of the kind that inhabit the Commercial Court and the Technology and Construction Court and some other parts of the High Court) but my best guess is that it will continue to be a minority profession, very important in places but never a mass movement of many thousands earning a living.

The External Climate

The world we inhabit is based on adversarial principles. In sport, that new religion, there is always a winner and a loser and draws are frankly a nuisance. Political opinion is frequently averse. Popular opinion is rightly suspicious of deals cobbled together in smoke-filled rooms. "To me", said Margaret Thatcher, "consensus seems to be the process of abandoning all beliefs, values and policies. So it is something in which no one believes and to which no one objects." Margaret Thatcher was always astute in her reading of the popular mind and although that was a long time ago, it says what many of the population would say if prompted today. It does too exemplify the parliamentary model of life. My conclusion has always been that mediation will continue to be considered with scepticism.

A COUPLE OF CURRENT ISSUES

Regulation

Nowhere in the world has a well developed system for regulating mediators, not even the United States. The Civil Mediation Council (CMC) (I should declare an interest because I am an elected, independent, mediator member and I am responsible for parts of the drafting of the Provider Accreditation Scheme now in place) wearing one of its hats has put in place a pilot scheme for accrediting mediation providers.

The scheme is voluntary and a pilot is to run for two years so that the results can be analysed and lessons learnt. It is designed (and in this respect I take the brickbats or the kudos depending on your point of view since this was my idea) to be quite different from the ordinary model of "you apply, we decide and don't ring us, we'll ring you if you passed." It requires providers to pass over some relatively simple thresholds and then to provide detailed information about themselves, so that the CMC can publish it all on its website. This is to enable the public to decide for themselves on choice of provider.

Although not a scheme for accrediting mediators, I hear increasing concern from the mediation community about the proposals — reflecting rejection of the idea that providers should be the gatekeepers. I also hear all round me the siren voices of those who seem to regard quite complex and intrusive regulation as intrinsically good whatever its results. More respectable is the understandable concern on the part of the judiciary (and state funding agencies if involved) that they do not know the quality of the mediators their cases might come before. In a speech to the Academy of

Experts given by Professor Martin Partington, Law Commissioner and Chair of the Civil Justice Council ADR Committee a couple of years ago, he set out his concern to build judicial confidence and so reasons for imposing common standards for mediators. They were: constitutional objections from those who say that the judges are there to decide cases, not settle them; lack of understanding about ADR (sic), causing the judges to pause before accepting the concept still less embracing it; lack of confidence in the providers of ADR (sic); practical concerns about adding to the cost of litigation; uncertainty about the type of case suitable for mediation; procedural reform — the judges wanted more direct guidance as to when to order mediation.

I believe there are many answers to these concerns but we have to face the fact that we need the judiciary to accept that we are not a bunch of amateurs who will simply waste time and damage the system. The CMC initiative is interesting. It will be more so when we have the result of the two-year pilot of accrediting providers. But consistent with my views about mediation as a profession and the responsibilities that follow from acceptance of that view, I believe the time has come for mediators themselves to address this issue.

It is not for providers to impose some form of common standard for mediators, nor is the CMC in its present shape able to do that. It is down to the mediators to take up that challenge. I believe that need is here and now and needs to be addressed as a matter of urgency. If we do not pick up this gauntlet, then others will do so and the result will be much worse than acceptable.

TCC Judges as Mediators

You will know of this scheme. It was met with strong opposition when announced but is going ahead as a pilot. I have an interest in that David Miles included me in a small faculty of four teaching the TCC judges some of the rudiments of mediation. I will be very interested to see the result of the scheme. It is unclear what the take-up will be. Judges as mediators in other parts of the world (for example, Israel and Quebec) have a chequered history. In the United States, retired judges are used regularly with uncertain results. The law reports include some cautionary tales. Consistent with my belief that the civil justice system needs more resources and should be allowed to become quicker and more responsive to litigants, I believe judges should judge and mediators should mediate. But let us see.

A MEDIATION MANIFESTO

If you have accepted some of what I have argued, I hope you will understand my call for the following: (1) Mediators need to organise as befits a group of professionals; (2) Mediators should start to exert a degree of control over training standards; (3) Mediators should, as a matter of urgency, work up an acceptable set of common standards so as to move quickly to a certification scheme for mediators that will enhance confidence amongst the judiciary, government and other stakeholders; (4) Mediators should work hard to improve practising excellence — preferably by emphasising collegiate means of spreading best practice; (5) Mediators should learn the lessons of their own craft in all that they do — striving through dialogue and negotiation to reach agreed solutions; (6) Mediators should work to enhance the standing of mediation as a profession.

REFERENCES

* This article was originally published as T. Willis, 'Mediation: Big Bang, Steady State or Black Hole?', *Arbitration* 72, no. 4 (2006): 339-347.
1. MEGO, "my eyes glaze over", a useful phrase I have purloined from May LJ.
2. The term first used by the late Sir Fred Hoyle (1915-2001), the British Astronomer Royal in a programme broadcast on the BBC Third Programme on March 28, 1949 by way of criticism ("this big bang idea") of the theory competing with his own theory of the steady state universe.
3. "Law Reform, Don't Sue", Economist, October 26, 2002, p. 34.
4. Some very laudable and interesting.
5. A black hole is a region of space time from which nothing can escape, even light.
6. Professor Stephen Hawking has more recently asserted that it might be possible for messages to be received from within a black hole — a rather dubious comfort to those within.
7. Hart, Oxford 1999, funded by the Nuffield Foundation.
8. See the Department for Constitutional Affairs Website at www.dca.gov.uk/civil/adr/index.htm. The National Mediation Helpline is on 0845 60 30 809.
9. www.cedr.co.uk.
10. Compared to the estimate given in their 2003 first mediator audit of between 1,800 and 2,000.
11. A definition loosely cribbed from Wikipedia.

12 For barristers see the Bar pro bono unit (www.barprobono.org.uk) and for solicitors the solicitors' pro bono group now re-named LawWorks (www.lawworks.org.uk).

13 M. Palmer & S. Roberts, *Dispute Processes, ADR and the Primary Forms of Decision Making* (London: Butterworth, 1998).

14 A. Acland, *A Sudden Outbreak of Commonsense, Managing Conflict through Mediation* (Hutchinson, 1990).

15 Founded by the great Bob Creo and led by some remarkable mediators like Teresa Wakeen from Baltimore, Eric Galton from Texas, Pat Coughlan from Florida and Maine, Jeff Krivis from California (who has done some teaching in London recently for CEDR) and John Wagner also from California and last year's excellent president Tracy Allen. See the IAM website at www.iamed.org.

16 The last meeting I attended at Harvard at the end of April this year conducted with the Harvard Negotiation Project was an excellent example generating thought leadership in many directions. Of the 110 members of the IAM, 105 were present at that meeting from countries as far apart as the UK and New Zealand.

17 It is arguable that the CMC will ultimately have to decide which of its incompatible roles it wishes to fulfil: regulator or promoter/ representative.

CHAPTER 3

The Role of the Mediation Advocate: A User's Guide to Mediation

Craig Pollack

Mediators often express the view that the parties' lawyers — the mediation advocates — are the reason why some mediations fail. As seen through the eyes of the mediator, mediation advocates are apparently guilty of a multitude of sins in mediation, ranging from 'falling in love with their own case' to 'being uncommercial' to simply 'advising their clients badly.' Such criticism tends to assume, wrongly, that the role of the mediation advocate is to assist the mediator in reaching the common goal of settlement. That is too simplistic an approach, since it ignores the obvious fact that not all settlements are equal in the eyes of the parties. Accordingly, not only are mediators unrealistic if they expect mediation advocates to assist them in their task, but mediation advocates are equally misguided if they assume that mediators are working with their clients' best interests in mind. Indeed, I would go so far as to argue that mediation advocates who rely on mediators to resolve their clients' disputes are guilty of misplaced faith since mediators are not in the business of advancing a particular side's interests. This article is an attempt to explain the peculiarities of the relationship between mediators and mediation advocates from the perspective of a party lawyer and to examine the nature of the interaction between them. Its primary thesis is that mediation advocates are well advised to view mediators as 'settlement junkies' who are prepared to feed their habit (settlement) by almost any means. Recognising this fact should help mediation advocates in their dealings with mediators and enhance their clients' prospects of achieving better settlements in mediation than might otherwise be the case.

THE ADVERSARIAL RELATIONSHIP BETWEEN THE MEDIATOR AND THE MEDIATION ADVOCATE

Listening to some of the propaganda about mediation, one might assume that it has undone centuries of human behaviour and has introduced a framework of negotiation which is non-adversarial. Not so. The fact that mediation is most often a successful means of negotiation (the statistics for settlement consistently being in excess of 85%) should not mask the reality that this is an adversarial framework in which the parties are each trying to advance their own position at the expense of the other. There is no difference in this regard to without prejudice party-to-party negotiations. The added ingredient in the mediation is the introduction of the so-called 'neutral', the mediator.

What is perhaps not sufficiently recognised is that the mediator and the mediation advocates are also in an adversarial position. There is an inherent conflict of interest between the mediator's interest and the mediation advocate's. The mediator's sole ambition in the mediation is settlement (hence the term 'settlement junkie'). By contrast, the mediation advocate's interest is settlement on the best possible terms for the client. The difference is critical and therein lies the conflict between them. How then should mediation advocates approach their dealings with mediators? A successful mediation depends on the willingness of the parties and the parties' lawyers to co-operate with the mediator and perhaps to entertain ideas that are unpalatable to the party, for the purpose of exploring the alternatives to litigation. Nevertheless, the need to co-operate openly has to be tempered with a degree of wariness by the mediation advocate based on a clear understanding of the mediator's tools of trade and the mediator's goal.

THE MEDIATOR'S TOOLS OF TRADE (AND WAYS OF RESISTING THEM)

The most powerful tool of trade employed by the mediator is reality testing. This is the process whereby the mediator forces the parties to consider and assess the risks that they face in continuing with the litigation. The specific purpose of undertaking reality testing is to encourage the parties to choose to close out those risks by settling. This is why you hear some mediators describe themselves as insurance salesmen; they are selling insurance against the risk of an adverse outcome at trial. Mediators tend not to be subtle in this respect. Indeed, there is little point in being subtle if the objective is to force the parties metaphorically to look into the abyss (the 'lottery of the trial', the costs consequences of losing, etc.) so as to lower their resistance to the idea of settlement on terms less than outright surrender by the other side. As a mediation advocate, it also makes no sense to resist engaging with the mediator in the 'reality testing' if your clients are truly interested in a settlement. However, this needs to be managed carefully. The mediator's goal is to create a framework in which the 'reality gap' between the parties has narrowed sufficiently so that settlement can take place on a realistic basis. Indeed, mediators are extremely interested in the process reaching a point at which the parties, through aggressive reality testing, conclude that settlement is the only viable option for them and that it has to take place then and there. I describe this as a 'settlement frenzy.' The mediation advocate's response to this should be that it is not generally a rational reaction for a client to believe that settlement at the mediation that particular day is the only option available. It is the mediation advocate's role to ensure that the client is not sucked into a settlement frenzy. In the final analysis, mediators have no vested interest in whether a settlement is achieved at £1 or £100 million. Their only real goal is settlement. However, from a client's perspective it is the level of settlement which is paramount and mediation advocates have to ensure their clients do not experience the equivalent of buyer's/seller's remorse the day after the mediation when, after a good night's sleep, clients are extremely unhappy about the deal they did at the mediation at a time when they felt under huge pressure to reach a settlement. The reality is that settlement at any cost is rarely a client's best or only alternative. Furthermore, most often the mediation is not the only opportunity the clients will have to settle. So for the mediation advocate the mantra is generally 'settlement yes, but not at any price.'

DEALING WITH THE MEDIATOR

Mediation advocates have at least two elements within their control which can assist in steering their clients through the "reality testing" phase. The first is the benefit of in-depth knowledge of the case. The best mediators will read the mediation bundle carefully. However, they also tend to be busy and cannot have as deep an understanding of the case as the mediation advocate who has been leading the case. Preparing for a mediation with the same rigour as you would prepare for a mini-trial or at least a hotly contested interlocutory application, means being best prepared to deal with the questions which the mediator will pose during the mediation, whether it is by way of testing your case theory, your legal analysis of the merits, your damages theory or your cost-benefit analysis of continuing with the litigation. Preparation extends to preparing your client's negotiating strategy. In this regard, it is senseless to concentrate only on your client's 'best case scenario.' Most mediation advocates will attest to the fact that, more often than not, you spend your time in the mediation negotiating the other side either up or down (depending on whether your client is the paying party or not) to your client's 'worst case scenario.'

The second control available to the mediation advocate to deal with the mediator's 'reality testing' is access to the clients both before and during the mediation. Prior to the mediation, clients should be told that they will most likely be dissatisfied to some degree with the outcome of a successful mediation; that is the nature of a compromise. If they are entirely happy, then the process has not worked as intended because it means that the other side is likely to be extremely unhappy. While mediators talk of 'win-win' situations, examples where both sides are entirely happy with the commercial result are in the minority. What 'win-win' often means in the majority of cases is that both sides manage to extract themselves from the dispute at a level of discomfort they can live with.

During the mediation, the role of mediation advocates, when not arguing their client's position with the mediator, is essentially one of damage control; namely to ensure that the clients maintain perspective on the case (both its strengths and weaknesses) despite the rigorous reality testing which the mediator is putting it through. Mediation is often tiring and tedious, with the parties left with their own team in a room for long periods of time. This can mean the clients spending significant periods of time reflecting alone on the merits of their position. Clients invariably come into the mediation believing strongly in their case. Through the process they are forced to confront the fact that their case has certain problems (which is exactly what the mediator will keep emphasising). The rational response to this by clients is to accept that there is a level of risk in litigating, which is why they are at the mediation, but at the same time to maintain perspective. Clients should also recognise that the other side is being put through exactly the same process; that their claim/defence is also being subjected to severe scrutiny by the mediator and that they too will be feeling less optimistic about their prospects.

WHAT PLACE HAS PERSUADING THE MEDIATOR ON THE MERITS?

There tend to be two approaches to arguing the merits of the case with the mediator. One approach assumes that it is necessary to persuade the mediator of the merits of your client's case. That is a misconception, since the mediator is not the arbiter of the dispute and is not tasked with making a judgment or an award. Indeed, the mediator has no brief to do justice between the sides. The other approach assumes that mediation is all about a commercial negotiation and therefore the merits have no part to play in the process and can be largely ignored. That is equally wrong. Mediations take place in the shadow of the law. The objective of mediation is to achieve a negotiated settlement agreement. In this regard, there is a role for arguing the merits, but perhaps not for an obvious reason. The merits count to the extent that a party is able to use them to undermine the other side's clients' confidence in their case. Because mediators tend to keep the parties apart for the majority of the time, the opportunity for mediation advocates to argue the merits to their client's advantage one on one with the other side are limited. That is where it can help if mediation advocates are able to persuade the mediator that the merits lie with their client. The more ammunition mediation advocates can provide to the mediator to undermine the other side's confidence in its case when the mediator undertakes "reality testing" with it, the better it is for their client.

WHY MEDIATION WORKS

The focus of this article has been to redress the balance of criticism which mediators make against mediation advocates, by stripping away some of the mystique which surrounds mediation based on the writer's own experiences. Having regard to the above, you might think that the writer is a mediation sceptic or a reluctant participant at mediations. On the contrary, experience has taught me that mediation can work in settling seemingly intractable disputes.

So why does it work? I will highlight a few of the reasons that have become clear to me. The first is the set-up. There are certain built-in mechanisms in the mediation process which are designed to maximise the prospects of success. Mediation is essentially a process in which a third-party neutral (the mediator) is engaged to help the parties reach a negotiated settlement. Simply introducing a respected "neutral" into some disputes assists resolution. Mediation is conducted on a 'without prejudice' basis. This is critical as it allows the parties the freedom to offer compromises without the fear of a judge or arbitrator being informed as to the level of compromise offered. More importantly, and in contrast to bilateral negotiations between the parties, mediation has a mechanism whereby the mediator can be told a party's bottom line confidentially, without being authorised to disclose that bottom line to the other side. Such disclosure to the mediator of each of the parties' actual level of settlement has the effect of transforming the mediator into the proverbial 'one-eyed man in the land of the blind.' That facility cannot be underestimated in terms of creating the groundwork for settlement.

A second aspect which helps to explain why mediations are generally successful is the psychology at play. Whilst I do not hold myself out as an expert in psychology, having gone through dozens of high value mediations, I can attest to the fact that the process introduces a psychological dynamic which tends to develop so as to point the parties towards settlement. In some disputes, particularly those in which commercial common sense long exited the arena, the emotional aspect is often the real obstacle to settlement. The 'venting' process, by which the clients are encouraged to get off their chests all of the frustrations and anger which they might harbour towards the other party or the situation in general, can be very cathartic for them. Mediation is unique in dispute resolution frameworks in offering a structured outlet for this venting. There is another psychological element which is brought into play simply by forcing the parties to spend a minimum period of time together in the same location, off-site, for the specific purpose of resolving the dispute, where each party is asked at the outset to confirm to the other that it has authority to settle the case. The 'atmospherics' in a mediation differ significantly in this regard from those in direct party-to-party negotiations.

Finally, in my experience mediations tend to be successful where mediators know their business. One of the difficulties we face in the United Kingdom is the proliferation of trained mediators. The problem, however, is that simply having the badge of a mediator does not mean that the person is an effective facilitator of the resolution of disputes. It can be extremely counter-productive if the chosen mediator is not up to the job, as parties can leave a failed mediation with their positions having become more entrenched and less inclined to settle.

In the final analysis, therefore, the mediator is critical. However, the view of some mediators that lawyers get in the way in a mediation is misconceived. The role of mediation advocates is to achieve a settlement on the best possible terms for their client. This is simply not the mediator's goal and any mediator-driven view that the process would be easier without undue interference by the mediation advocate is wishful thinking.

* This article was originally published as C. Pollack, 'The Role of the Mediation Advocate: A User's Guide to Mediation', *Arbitration* 73, no. 1 (2007): 20-23.

CHAPTER 3

Mediation:
An Approximation to Justice

Sir Gavin Lightman

When the Government gave statutory effect to the European Convention on Human Rights in the form of the Human Rights Act, the Government proudly boasted "human rights have come home." The Government's welcome in words was blunted by the Government's actions. For at the same time the Government continued the process of withdrawing the protection of citizens' rights (human and otherwise) by emasculating civil legal aid at a time when the costs of enforcing or defending such rights had reached heights beyond the reach of all but the very rich and the legally aided. As a fig leaf the Government proffered as an alternative to legal aid statutory provision for the conduct of litigation on the basis of a conditional fee. The statutory provision recognises two essential components of the conduct of litigation on this basis. The first is the acceptance by the legal advisers of instructions on terms that they receive a fee below what they would ordinarily charge (or indeed nothing at all) if the action fails, but an uplifted fee up to 100% above their normal charges if the action succeeds, and this uplifted fee may be recoverable from the losing party. The second component is that the client is protected by insurance against any liability under any adverse order for costs made in case his action fails, with the premium likewise recoverable if the action succeeds from the losing party.

The Government was made aware that there were the most serious legal and ethical problems raised by the conditional fee — in particular, why should the losing party be exposed to paying more in costs merely because his successful opponent finances his litigation in this manner? And how could the lawyer's conflicts of interest be resolved when agreeing with his client the uplift and determining whether to agree terms of settlement? Going beyond these problems, the inherent limitations of the conditional fee are obvious and they have later proved critical in practice; legal advisers will only agree to accept instructions on this basis and the insurer will only provide insurance if the prospects of success in the action are very high — above 80%, indeed often 90%. Otherwise, it is not financially worthwhile for them to provide the required services and insurance to the client. The Government has been willing to spend millions on luxuries such as wallpaper, the Dome and the Olympics but has been unwilling to provide funds on essentials such as affording access to justice. In this situation others have had to focus on alternatives to the resolution of disputes by the court. Resolution of disputes by arbitration could not provide an answer. Arbitration can prove as expensive as, and indeed more expensive than, court proceedings, for arbitrators charge and judges are for free. As an aside, I may record the suggestion that the reason for this difference regarding the pricing of the services of arbitrators and judges is that in terms of quality you get what you pay for.

The dilemma has been accordingly how to provide the protection of the law where the citizen does not have the means to pay for it or cannot afford the risk of losing and in consequence incurring the risk of incurring liability for the opponent's costs and of consequent bankruptcy. Where can you find the wherewithal to provide protection? Advocates do it every day in court, but in the real world you cannot make bricks without straw. Mediation cannot provide such protection. But mediation affords a palliative. What it can do and does do is to open previously locked doors to a settlement. What it can afford is a mechanism through the efforts of trained intermediaries for opening the eyes of parties to the merits of the opponent's case, the issues involved, the risks and costs of litigation and the attractions of a settlement.

The practice of mediation was given a hefty boost by CPR r.1.4 which provides that the court must further the overriding objective of: (1) dealing with cases justly by encouraging the parties to use ADR if the court considers that appropriate; and (2) facilitating the use of that procedure and helping the parties to settle. In accordance with this rule the courts have played their part in encouraging the taking of giant strides forwarding the wide and effective use of the mediation process, but they (like the Duke of York) have also on occasion themselves unfortunately taken giant strides backwards. The giant strides forward include (amongst others): (1) the abandonment of the notion that mediation is appropriate in only a limited category of cases. It is now recognised that there is no civil case in which mediation cannot have a part to play in resolving some (if not all of) the issues involved. Indeed on the Continent mediation between the accused and the victim has now a substantial part to play in criminal cases, and this development yet may find its place here; (2) practitioners (and in particular litigators) generally no longer perceive mediation a threat to their livelihoods, but rather a satisfying and fulfilling livelihood of its own; (3)

practitioners recognise (or should recognise) that a failure on their part without the express and informed instructions of their clients to make an effort to resolve disputes by mediation exposes them to the risk of a claim in negligence; (4) the Government itself adopts a policy of willingness to proceed to mediation in disputes to which it is a party; (5) judges at all stages in legal proceedings are urging parties to proceed to mediation if a practical method of achieving a settlement and imposing sanctions when there is an unreasonable refusal to give mediation a chance; and (6) mediation is now a respectable (indeed fashionable) subject of legal study and research at institutes of learning.

We have to recognise today that under the prevailing circumstances the disadvantaged citizen for economic reasons is all too often without legal redress or protection, that this leads to a social divide between the advantaged who enjoy the protection of the law and the disadvantaged who do not and this in turn leads to understandable loss of confidence in the law and the legal system. Do not believe that justice can be readily achieved by litigants acting in person. Quite the reverse. They cannot generally distinguish what is and what is not arguable, what course serves their interest and what risks they run as to costs. Their liability for their opponent's costs so often renders the perceived injustice which prompted proceedings a mere pinprick in comparison with the final (self-inflicted) pain. This state of affairs has brought to the fore the crucial need for mediation as a palliative — as the only available recourse of those who cannot afford the costs and risks of litigation, the chance of the approximation to justice which it affords.

As I have repeatedly said on occasions such as the present since the decision of the Court of Appeal in *Halsey v Milton Keynes*, the achievement of this approximation requires the removal of two obstacles placed in its path by the Court of Appeal decision in that case. The court there held that: (1) the court cannot require a party to proceed to mediation against his will on the basis that such an order would contravene the party's rights to access to the courts under Art. 6 of the European Convention on Human Rights; and (2) to impose a sanction (and in particular a sanction as to costs) on a party who has refused to give mediation a chance, the burden is upon the party seeking the imposition of the sanction to establish that the party who refused to proceed to mediation acted unreasonably. The burden is not on the party against whom the sanction is sought to prove that his refusal was unreasonable. Both of these propositions are unfortunate and (I would suggest) clearly wrong and unreasonable. Turning to the first proposition regarding the European Convention my reasons for saying this are twofold: (1) the court appears to have been uninformed about the mediation process and the distinction between an order for mediation and an order for arbitration or some other order which places a permanent stay on proceedings.

An order for mediation does not interfere with the right to a trial: at most it merely imposes a short delay to afford an opportunity for settlement and indeed the order for mediation may not even do that, for the order for mediation may require or allow the parties to proceed with preparation for trial; and (2) the Court of Appeal appears to have been left in the dark as to the practice of ordering parties to proceed to mediation regardless of their wishes is prevalent elsewhere throughout the Commonwealth, the United States and the world at large, and indeed at home in matrimonial property disputes in the Family Division. The Court of Appeal refers to the fact that a party compelled to proceed to mediation may be less likely to agree a settlement than one who willingly proceeds to mediation. But that fact is not to the point. For it is a fact: (1) that by reason of the nature and impact on the parties of the mediation process parties who enter the mediation process unwillingly often can and do become infected with the conciliatory spirit and settle; and (2) that, whatever the percentage of those who against their will are ordered to give mediation a chance do settle, that percentage must be greater than the number to settle of those not so ordered and who accordingly do not give it a chance.

I turn to the second proposition regarding the onus of proof of reasonableness or unreasonableness. The decision as to onus must be guided by consideration of three factors: (1) the importance that those otherwise deprived of access to justice should be given a chance of an approximation to it in this way; (2) the common-sense proposition that the party who has decided not to proceed to mediation and knows the reasons for his decision should be required to give, explain and justify his decision; and (3) the explicit duty of the court to encourage the use of mediation and the implicit duty to discourage unjustified refusals to do so and this must involve disclosing, explaining and justifying the reasons for the refusal. All these factors point in the opposite direction to that taken by the Court of Appeal. A thermometer of the health of mediation today reveals its worldwide spread and appeal. It permeates the US insolvency system. Training courses are given throughout Eastern Europe. A European Directive on Europe-wide mediation is on the cards. (I should add that the directive has been 'imminent' for a long time.) I am and have been for some years the UK Board Member of GEMME, an organisation of European Judges committed to mediation, an organisation recognised and partly financed by the European Union. Its purpose and activities are directed to promoting the use and understanding of and training in mediation within Member States.

Developments ahead (as I see them) include the following: (1) increasing efforts to secure public awareness of the benefits and availability of mediation; (2) increasing provision of public funds, facilities and trained mediators to facilitate mediation in all courts and tribunals; and (3) increased insistence (indeed pressure) on litigants to give mediation a go.

I come now to my conclusion. I see often in court the price paid by parties who have not (for any of a variety of reasons) proceeded to mediation and have in consequence picked up the heavy tab of the litigation. I have seen litigants and their families broken by the process and by the cost of litigation. Plainly it is the duty (in particular) of the law and lawyers to avoid this scenario and at the same time to afford to those who on grounds of means have been deprived of access to justice the chance of the approximation to justice that may be available through mediation. I suggest that: (1) no thinking person can but be embarrassed by the lack of provision by the State of the means for access to the court; and (2) no thinking person can but be disturbed by the imposition of the twin hurdles to mediation which the decision in *Halsey* creates to achieving the approximation to justice which the institution of the mediation process may afford. The removal of the first hurdle is a matter for the legislature and the second is for the courts. The removal of the second by the courts may be made easier by a greater familiarity with the mediation process and by the recognition that in practice the hurdles are regularly sidestepped or overlooked without occasioning any shock waves causing tremors to the scales of justice.

REFERENCES

* This article was originally published as G. Lightman, 'Mediation: An Approximation to Justice', *Arbitration* 73, no. 4 (2007): 400-402.
1 [2004] 1 W.L.R. 3002.

CHAPTER 3

Mediation and ADR: A Judicial Perspective

Sir Anthony Colman

It is always a pleasure and a privilege to attend a Chartered Institute of Arbitrators gathering — particularly on a subject which I hope I understand. As many here will know, I have been closely associated with the relationship between the courts and alternative dispute resolution (ADR) for the last 11 years. I have to say, however, that when the couple first met it was hardly love at first sight! But with the passage of time they have become endeared to each other and the prospects for future marriage seem encouraging. Although there have been some major changes since we in the Commercial Court first developed and started handing down ADR orders, the foundations of the jurisdiction, as it is presently exercised, remain what they were at the end of 1996. Fundamental to this jurisdiction was that ADR orders were not mandatory. This is important. Those of us who developed the forms of order now still in use considered that, whereas those who invoke the Court's jurisdiction to obtain a judgment or pursue a defence should not be subjected to any order that required them to settle or which had the effect of penalising them for failing to do so, they should at least be persuaded to try to settle their disputes. The Working Party Reports of 1996 and 1998 were firmly of the view that it was not open to the courts to force the parties to do more than, as it is said in the standard form of the order set out in Appendix 7 of the Commercial Court Guide, to "take such serious steps as they may be advised to resolve their disputes by ADR procedures." Failure to resolve those disputes was not in itself disobedience to the order, for the duty to take steps in the mediation was conditional upon what the parties had been advised. Just as in *Walford v Miles* it had been conclusively determined by the House of Lords that an agreement to negotiate in good faith was unenforceable in English law because of the lack of objective criteria, so it was considered by the judges and the Commercial Court Users Committee that if analogous orders were made to that effect, it would be impossible for the courts to administer them.

In the second Working Party Report in 1998 we not only reviewed the way in which ADR Orders were working, but also considered an issue, which was beginning to emerge, as to whether the court should apply a costs sanction against a party who simply refused to participate in a mediation. This idea was firmly rejected for three main reasons. First, those cases where litigants simply walked away from ADR, where the court had made an order, were very few and far between. Secondly, there was a perceived inconsistency between the imposition of sanctions for failing to take part in a mediation and the essentially voluntary nature of the whole exercise. Finally, the imposition of costs sanctions would be a derogation from the availability of the courts for the correct resolution of civil litigation. If a party had enforceable civil rights and invoked the jurisdiction of the courts for the purpose of obtaining a judgment that reflected those rights, why should that party be deprived of his costs because he had insisted on pursuing his rights in the courts rather than giving up part of them in the course of a mediation for which he would have to pay the fees of the lawyers and the mediator?

As the success rate of ADR orders in the Commercial Court became widely known, other parts of the court system began to introduce various forms of encouragement towards the use of ADR. In the course of preparing the Access to Justice reforms, otherwise to become the Civil Procedure Rules (CPR), Lord Woolf was distinctly cool about the introduction of ADR, but he soon became a strongly committed convert. The CPR opened up a whole new procedural jurisprudence founded on the Overriding Objective of enabling the court to deal with cases 'justly.' But that expression was crucially defined in CPR r.1.1(2) as including, so far as practicable, various objectives, notably "allotting to the case an appropriate share of the court's resources, while taking into account the need to allot resources to other cases." So dealing with cases justly included at least one matter which was quite intrinsic to the substance of the rights and obligations of the parties and their ascertainment.

Starting with *Dunnett v Railtrack*, decisions in the Court of Appeal supported the proposition that adverse costs orders would in some cases be justified where the winning party to the litigation had previously refused to submit the dispute to mediation. The most comprehensive consideration of such a course is in *Halsey v Milton Keynes General NHS Trust*. Relevant considerations were there identified as: (1) the nature of the dispute; (2) the merits of the case; (3) the extent to which other settlement methods have been attempted; (4) whether the costs of the ADR would be disproportionately high; (5) whether any delay in setting up and attending the ADR would have been prejudicial; (6) whether the ADR had a reasonable prospect of success.

The form of orders normally made in the Commercial Court was expressly approved in *Halsey* and it was clearly indicated that to fail to attempt mediation in the face of one such order might well be one of those cases which would justify an adverse costs order against a winning party. But this conclusion raises difficult questions. It is firmly established that the public policy underlying the usual costs order whereby the winning party recovers his costs unless his conduct at or before trial justifies a contrary order, because, for example, he has pursued bad points or acted in abuse of process, is that the costs should, by adverse costs orders, discourage the taking of bad points or abusive conduct by the losing party or by the winning party if he has had only a partial victory. If that regime is to be displaced or superseded, that can only be because there is a countervailing public policy. But with regard to ADR what can that be? One is left with the distinctly uncomfortable impression that here we have a new *raison d'état* — the public policy of encouraging litigants to assist in the conservation of judicial resources by entering into negotiations only likely to be successful if they relinquish, to some extent, their true legal rights by trading them off to settle the case.

I have to say that this comes uncomfortably close to the policy of the present so-called Minister of Justice of letting out of prison those who have been given carefully thought-out sentences in the criminal courts because the Government did not have the foresight to provide enough prison places to accommodate its own law and order policy.

The seventh and most recent edition of the Commercial Court Guide has been amended to warn litigants of the risk of adverse costs orders. So where does all this leave the ADR policy of the Commercial Court in relation to arbitration? It has to be remembered that the Commercial Court is the tribunal primarily vested with the function of supervising the operation of the Arbitration Act 1996. As such it entertains many different kinds of application ranging from applications to appoint arbitrators to applications (under s.67) to determine whether the tribunal has jurisdiction to applications to set aside awards for serious irregularity in procedure (s.68) and applications for permission to appeal against awards (s.69). Apart from this last area of jurisdiction, the Court's function is not to determine the substantive rights of the parties in relation to their underlying dispute, but to determine their rights and obligations as participants or potential participants in an arbitration. But these rights and obligations, although ancillary to the resolution of the underlying dispute, all emanate from the arbitration agreement and its connected remedies. That being so, I can see no reason why the courts should not also make ADR orders in the course of entertaining at least some applications under the 1996 Act.

Let me give some examples. We sometimes get applications under s.17(3) of the 1996 Act to set aside the unilateral appointment of a sole arbitrator under s.17(2) on the grounds that the respondent was never a party to an agreement to arbitrate. Although these applications are necessarily founded on the lack of an agreement to arbitrate, the real dispute is invariably about whether there was ever any underlying agreement between the parties at all and, therefore, whether the claimant can establish any underlying substantive rights against the respondent. Similar questions may arise where there is an application under s.32 for the courts to determine a question as to the substantive jurisdiction of the tribunal by consent of both parties or with the tribunal's permission or where under s.67 there is an application to set aside an award on grounds of lack of substantive jurisdiction.

In this kind of case the issue of jurisdiction is inseparable from a major issue going to the substantive rights of the parties which, were there a binding agreement to arbitrate, had been agreed by the parties to it to be determined by arbitration. Take a case like *AZOV Shipping v Baltic Shipping No.2*. The issue arose between Baltic, a party to a multi-party agreement for the use of containers entered into between former Soviet Union shipping companies and which contained an arbitration agreement referring disputes to London arbitration, and Azov, which applied under s.67 in order to establish that the arbitrator had no substantive jurisdiction, and adduced fresh evidence, including expert evidence on the Ukrainian law of agency and notification. I decided that there was no assent to the original agreement and no authority to sign an addendum to it; therefore Azov was not party to the arbitration agreement and the arbitrator had no substantive jurisdiction. Thus, in concluding whether there was a binding agreement to arbitrate, the court was really deciding the key feature of the underlying issue between the parties. This unusual jurisdiction was inserted into the 1996 Arbitration Act as something of a compromise between, on the one hand, respect for the *kompetenz-kompetenz* principle and, on the other, the belief that it should be open to a party who, in truth, as a matter of fact and law had not referred the dispute to arbitration, to avoid a decision on this issue by the very tribunal he had never agreed to.

In such a case if the court's decision may differ from that of the tribunal, there is a good deal to be said for the court adjourning the application so that the parties can try ADR, even over the objection of one of the parties. As I see it, there is no reason in principle why such an order should not be made. Another type of case which may well call for an ADR order is where the court is asked to set aside an award under s.68 for serious irregularity by the tribunal. In such cases one may find that the parties have already subjected themselves to a complicated and costly hearing before the arbitrators which has been misconducted through no fault of their own to such an extent that the arbitration has to be started again. In such a case a court might justifiably feel that it is time to say enough is enough and to send the parties off to ADR.

Now I have to say that such a course ought to be sparingly adopted. This is so particularly because the parties have only invoked the court's jurisdiction for a limited and ancillary purpose and secondly because there is only likely to be a vestigial public interest in encouraging settlement of the underlying dispute; vestigial because it is highly improbable that the matter will ever again be before the courts, even if the parties fail to settle before another arbitration takes place. But each case has to be evaluated on its own particular facts. What is the proportion of costs to the amount in issue? Does the previous inter-party relationship bode ill for compromise? Are there experienced commercial solicitors on either side? What is likely to be the delay factor? Is there real evidence of prevarication by the respondents? So far I have been discussing the Court's use of ADR orders. But is there a case for arbitrators themselves acting analogously with the judges of the Commercial Court and making such orders? I am very firmly of the view that, unless both parties confer such a power on the arbitrators, there is absolutely nothing in the Arbitration Act which vests in the tribunal any power to make such an order. Any attempt to do so without being thus consensually empowered could amount to an irregularity in the conduct of the proceedings.

The arbitrators' function is to provide the parties with what they honestly consider to be the right answer on the issues of fact and law and not to emulate in every detail the overriding objective under the CPR. Such considerations as the efficient use of arbitral resources by analogy with the efficient use of judicial resources have no part to play. Apart from that, even with mutual consent to such power being vested in an arbitrator, he could find himself in acute difficulties were he to exercise it.

REFERENCES

* This article was originally published as A. Colman, 'Mediation and ADR: A Judicial Perspective', *Arbitration* 73, no. 4 (2007): 403-406.

1 [1992] 2 A.C. 128.
2 [2002] EWCA Civ 303.
3 [2004] EWCA Civ 1740.
4 [1999] All E.R. 476; [1999] 1 Lloyd's Rep. 68.

CHAPTER 3

The Future of Civil Mediation

Lord Clarke

It gives me great pleasure to be here at the Civil Mediation Council's second national conference. It is perhaps always a worry for nascent organisations when they hold their first conference as to whether it will be the first of many or the one and only. Today's proceedings put any such worries to rest. And rightly so. It is plain to me that, as the importance of mediation grows in the years to come, conferences such as this will grow both in stature and importance. They will help to shape the development of mediation, explore the issues it raises and how best it can be implemented for the benefit of all those who have the misfortune to become entwined in civil disputes.

This afternoon's session is entitled 'The Future of Civil Mediation'. Its focus is how the quality and standards of mediation, and mediators, can be improved over the coming years. Karl Mackie is going to look at the issue from the perspective of accreditation, before David Richbell, Mark Jackson-Stops and Richard Schiffer look at whether the use of codes of good practice is the answer. Before placing you in their capable and very knowledgeable hands I thought I might take this opportunity to make some general comments, some of which you may well wish to revisit in the open debate session which is to follow this one.

Alternative Dispute Resolution — ADR as it is more commonly known — has been around now in one form or another for a number of years. Since its effective rebirth in America in the 1970s it has steadily grown in importance. That importance was recognised in England (or I should say England and Wales) in the Heilbron/Hodge Report which preceded and informed the two Woolf reports and through them the CPR. Lord Woolf saw it as playing a crucial role in shaping our civil justice system's future. He put it this way: "[In future]... parties should: (1) whenever it is reasonable for them to do so settle their disputes (either the whole dispute or individual issues comprised in the dispute) before resorting to the courts; (2) where it is not possible to resolve a dispute or an issue prior to proceedings, then they should do so at as early a stage in the proceedings as is possible. Where there exists an appropriate alternative dispute resolution mechanism which is capable of resolving a dispute more economically and efficiently than court proceedings, then the parties should be encouraged not to commence or pursue proceedings in court until after they have made use of that mechanism."

The CPR introduced a number of mechanisms to give effect to this. Pre-action Protocols, for instance, were introduced so as to facilitate the settlement of disputes before the parties resorted to the courts. They all now stress the importance that is placed on parties considering whether "some form of alternative dispute resolution would be more suitable than litigation and, if so, endeavour to agree which form to adopt." Once litigation has been commenced the court and the parties place themselves in the hands of the overriding objective. They are both encouraged to utilise ADR, of which mediation is a key part, under the duty imposed on the court to actively manage cases in order to further the overriding objective (CPR r.1.4(1)(e) and (f) and 3.1) and the duty imposed on parties and their lawyers to assist the court in so doing (CPR rr.1.3 and 26.4). Active pursuit of ADR is further encouraged by CPR r.26.4(1), which enables parties to make a written request with their allocation questionnaire for, or the court of its own initiative to order, a stay of proceedings while settlement via ADR is attempted, and by CPR r.44.5(3)(a)(ii) and the guidance given by the Court of Appeal in *Halsey v Milton Keynes General NHS Trust*. I wish to return to *Halsey* in a moment. ADR is further encouraged by a number of court-based mediation schemes, such as the one operated by the Court of Appeal.

With all the support ADR in all its many forms has had, from Heilbron/Hodge to Woolf to the CPR and in recent times its tireless support by Lightman J., it came as a real surprise to me to hear at a recent joint meeting in Surrey between Her Majesty's Court Service, the Civil Justice Council and the Civil Mediation Council that so few solicitors had been asked to or had taken part in a mediation. I also very recently went to the Association of Personal Injury Lawyers' annual conference and people there were saying the same thing. Experience thus shows even now that far too many people know far too little about mediation. I think we can all agree that this has to change. ADR in general and mediation in particular, where it is the appropriate ADR mechanism, must become an integral part of our litigation culture. It must become such a well established part of it that when considering the proper management of litigation it forms as intrinsic and as instinctive a part of our lexicon and of our thought processes, as standard considerations like what, if any, expert evidence is required and whether a Part 36 offer ought to be made and at what level.

This will require education; education on the part of litigants, lawyers and the judiciary. Lawyers and judges will need educating so that mediation becomes part of the culture; so that it becomes second nature to us all. The onus lies on you and me to ensure that litigants appreciate mediation's many benefits: its informality, its confidentiality, the possibility it holds of enabling the parties to reach a consensual resolution to their dispute and to do so more quickly and at lower cost than might well be possible in the zero-sum game which is litigation. Equally, the onus lies on us to highlight its drawbacks as well as its benefits. There are to my mind few disadvantages but they may include the fact that, for example, it does not produce a judgment of the court setting out the individual litigant's rights. Education is the key to this. Training, accreditation and the creation of Codes of Good Practice are all I think useful tools to that end.

Over and above education what can the judiciary do? What we certainly cannot do is sit back and do nothing. Those days are now long gone. Active case management and the overriding objective very properly put paid to the days of the passive judge. One thing we can do is to render mediation part of the normal pre-trial case management process. There is of course a potential problem here, of which you are all well aware. I refer to the Court of Appeal's decision in *Halsey*, although it is to my mind much maligned. Dyson L.J., giving the judgment of the court, in that case held that compulsory ADR would breach the right to fair trial as it would amount to an unacceptable constraint on the right of access to the court. He concluded that while the court could and should encourage ADR robustly it could not compel the parties to engage in it. This decision has been understood to rule out the possibility that the court can require parties to proceed to mediation unless they wish to do so. That is certainly the view taken by many to the effect of this aspect of the *Halsey* judgment. Lightman J. for one has taken this view of its effect. He has criticised it on a number of grounds: first, that the Court of Appeal's judgment failed properly to appreciate the difference between arbitration, which places a permanent stay on proceedings, and mediation which does not interfere with the right to fair trial but simply imposes a short delay on the trial process; and secondly that a number of other jurisdictions have compulsory mediation processes. On the second point he is clearly right. A number of European states such as Belgium and Greece, both signatories to the Human Rights Convention, have introduced compulsory ADR schemes without, as far as I am aware, any successful Art. 6 challenges. Equally, Germany's federal states can legislate to require litigants to either engage in court-based or court-approved conciliation prior to the formal commencement of litigation. The European Union itself acknowledges in Art. 3.2 of its Directive on Mediation that the encouragement it offers to mediation is made: "[w]ithout prejudice to national legislation making the use of mediation compulsory or subject to incentives or sanctions, whether before or after judicial proceedings have started, provided that such legislation does not impede the right of access to the judicial system."

Equally, compulsory ADR schemes have been introduced in a number of US jurisdictions. For instance, New York has established mandatory arbitration in claims coming before a trial court where an official arbitration programme has been established for claims of a certain value. Similar schemes have been introduced in other states, for instance California. The federal district courts can also require parties to mediate disputes under a power granted by the Alternative Dispute Resolution Act (28 USC) s.652. Taken together, what could be described as the European and US approach to ADR, appears to demonstrate that compulsory ADR does not in and of itself give rise to a violation of Art. 6 or of the equivalent US constitutional right of due process. This suggests, admittedly without hearing argument, that the *Halsey* approach may have been overly cautious. This was not a point that was investigated in detail in *Halsey* and (who knows) may be open to review — either by judicial decision or in any event by rule change.

Turning to Lightman J.'s first point, is there any support for the view that the Court mistakenly confused mediation with arbitration? The Court relied on the decision of the European Court of Human Rights in *Deweer v Belgium* in arriving at its decision. That case was reported in *Halsey* as having established that 'the right of access to a court may be waived, for example by means of an arbitration agreement, but such waiver should be subjected to a "particularly careful review" to ensure that the claimant is not subject to "constraint ." What was the context of *Deweer*?

The claim arose out of an alleged infringement of a Belgian Ministerial Decree which required butchers to reduce the price of retail pork and beef in accordance with the terms of the decree. As a consequence of the breach the butcher's shop was closed and he became liable to imprisonment. The butcher was however given the option of paying a fine fixed at 10,000 francs (BFR) by way of what was described as a "friendly settlement". If he paid, his shop could reopen and the criminal proceedings against him would be barred. On the face of it this is far away from mediation, which both parties enter as equals.

What did the Strasbourg Court have to say about this? It said this at [49] of its judgment: "[b]y paying the 10,000 BF[R] which the Louvain procureur de Roi 'required' by way of settlement... Mr Deweer waived his right to have his case dealt with by a tribunal. In the Contracting States' domestic legal systems a waiver of this kind is frequently encountered both in civil matters, notably in the shape of arbitration clauses in contracts, and in criminal matters in the shape, inter alia, of fines paid by way of composition. The waiver, which had undeniable advantages, does not in principle offend against the Convention... Nevertheless, in a democratic society too great an importance attaches to the 'right to a court' ... for its benefit to be forfeited solely by reason of the fact that an individual is party to a settlement reached in the course of a procedure ancillary to court proceedings. In an area concerning the public order... of the member States of the Council of Europe, any measure or decision alleged to be in breach of Article 6 calls for careful review." This statement is a long way away from declaring that mediation is contrary to Art. 6 ECHR. It acknowledges that agreements waiving the right to fair trial are compatible in principle with Art. 6. It does however call for caution where that right is waived in proceedings ancillary to court proceedings, such as where parties enter into arbitration agreements. Such caution is clearly justified in the situation identified in *Deweer*.

Is it as clearly called for in mediation proceedings? Does mediation require parties to waive their right to a fair trial? The answer is surely no. Mediation and ADR form part of the civil procedure process. They are not simply ancillary to court proceedings but form part of them. They do not preclude parties from entering into court proceedings in the same way that an arbitration agreement does. In fact all a mediation does is at worst delay trial if it is unsuccessful and it need not do that if it is properly factored into the pre-trial timetable. If the mediation is successful it does obviate the need to continue to trial, but that is not the same as to waive the right to fair trial. If it were, any consensual settlement reached either before or during civil process could arguably amount to a breach of Art. 6, which clearly cannot be the case.

The arguments can of course be developed much further than this and it is not my place today to do that. That will have to await a future occasion when the Court of Appeal may have to grapple with this issue and do so after full argument rather than the sketch I have given here. What I think we can safely say though, without prejudicing any future case, is that there may well be grounds for suggesting that *Halsey* was wrong on the Art. 6 point.

But what of the present time? Lightman J. expressed the view that district judges are at present bound to follow *Halsey* on this point. It seems to me that that is a pessimistic reading. The substantive issue in *Halsey* had nothing to do with compulsory mediation. The issue before the court then was: "[w]hen should a court impose costs sanctions against a successful litigant on the grounds that he has refused to take part in an alternative dispute resolution (ADR)?" Whatever the Court of Appeal held in *Halsey* in answer to that question, its comments regarding compulsory ADR were surely what we used to call obiter dicta, although I note that they have subsequently been summarised in, for instance, *Hickman v Blake Lapthorn* as establishing that compulsory ADR is contrary to Art. 6 ECHR. But again that summary contained no more than obiter dicta. With that in mind it seems to me at any rate, that despite the *Halsey* decision it is at least strongly arguable that the court retains a jurisdiction to require parties to enter into mediation. How might this happen? It seems to me that the court has sufficient powers at present routinely to direct the parties to take part in a mediation process or attend a mediation hearing during the course of the pre-trial stage of any proceedings. I think of it like this. It could not be seriously argued that the case management judge could not direct the parties, say, to meet in the first week in June in order to discuss settlement. I would like to see such a direction as routine, if it is not already routine. No one could sensibly refuse to meet the other side to discuss settlement in almost any kind of case. The great advantage of directing such a meeting would be to ensure that both parties prepare for a discussion on the case at the same time. One of the bugbears of any system is cases which settle at the door of the court. The reason they do so is partly (as it were) the clang of the prison gates but partly the fact that it may well not be until then that both parties are thinking about the case at the same time. It seems to me to be but a small step from an order that the parties meet to an order that they meet in the presence of a mediator. Such orders could surely be made either routinely on allocation as anticipated by CPR r.26.4(1) or at the first case management conference. They could easily be factored into and become an integral part of standard directions. To my mind the power exists under a combination of the court's case management powers under CPR r.1.4(2)(e) which specifies: "[e]ncouraging the parties to use an alternative dispute resolution procedure if the court considers that appropriate and facilitating the use of such procedure," and CPR r.3.1(2)(m), which enables the court to take any step in managing a case to further the overriding objective. It seems to me that furthering the overriding objective in this sense calls for the case management power to be applied consistently with the duty under CPR r.1.1(2)(e) which requires the court to take account of the needs of all litigants and the court in furthering the overriding objective; to further access to justice for all. Equally, it is surely part of the parties' duty to assist the court in the furtherance of the overriding objective that they should take active steps to take part in mediation (CPR r.1.3).

This is not to say that the courts should penalise parties for not taking part in mediation, save perhaps in exceptional circumstances. The bane of civil litigation is what I call satellite litigation, that is, disputes which are not about the underlying merits. I would certainly not like to see a new type of satellite litigation in which complaints about the parties' approach to mediation are investigated in detail and at great expense. I note that in a case which rejoices in the title Carleton, *Seventh Earl of Malmesbury v Strutt & Parker*, Jack J. extended the *Halsey* principle, that if parties unreasonably refuse to mediate that may sound in costs against them, to the situation where a party acted unreasonably in a mediation. The actual decision in *Halsey* was that a successful party should only be penalised in costs on grounds of his refusal to take part in mediation if that refusal was unreasonable. Moreover the burden of showing unreasonableness is on the losing party. I see nothing wrong with that approach. Such cases should be very few and far between. All depends upon the circumstances of the particular case. One can understand the position of a party who says, "I have a cast iron case and I decline to mediate because there is no point", and who subsequently wins at trial and is appalled when it is suggested that he should be penalised in costs for refusing to mediate.

However, such cases must be very rare indeed. We all know that a cast-iron case is a very rare bird indeed; so that for the most part only a madman does not want to settle. None of this is to say that parties must settle claims through mediation. It is simply to say that parties must assist the court in furthering the overriding objective by taking proper part in the mediation process. Some complain about the costs of mediation but why not have a general principle that the costs of a mediation will ordinarily be treated as costs in the case. The person with the strong case will then be protected against the costs of a failed mediation if the action subsequently succeeds. Is this a good idea and, if not, why not?

In conclusion, it seems to me that the power exists for the courts to regularise mediation and to make it an integral part of the litigation process. That is not to say that in every case it will be desirable. The court must be sensitive to this when assessing whether to make a standard direction with a mediation order in it. There is no reason why it cannot do this. Equally it is not to say that it will or ought to succeed in every case. It is of course a cliché that you can take a horse to water but whether it drinks is another thing entirely. That it is a cliché does not render it the less true. But what can perhaps be said is that a horse (even a very obstinate horse) is more likely to drink if taken to water. We should be doing more to encourage (and perhaps direct) the horse to go to the trough. The more horses approach the trough the more will drink from it. Litigants being like horses we should give them every assistance to settle their disputes in this way. We do them, and the justice system, a disservice if we do not.

REFERENCES

* This article was originally published as A. Clarke, 'The Future of Civil Mediation', *Arbitration* 74, no. 4 (2008): 419-423.
1 Woolf Report (1995), Ch. 4. 7.
2 *Halsey v Milton Keynes General NHS Trust* [2004] 1 W.L.R. 3002.
3 G. Lightman, 'Mediation: Approximation to Justice' (June 28, 2007) (speech given to SJ Berwin); 'Access to Justice' (December 5, 2007) (speech given to The Law Society).
4 *Halsey* [2004] 1 W.L.R. 3002 at [9]-[11].
5 G. Lightman, 'Mediation: Approximation to Justice', para.8.
6 See Art. 214 of the Greek Civil Code.
7 See now Directive 2008/52/EC OJ L136/3 (of May 21, 2008) recital 14 and Art. 3(a): "This process may be ... suggested or ordered by a Court" [Editor].
8 *Deweer v Belgium* [1980] E.C.C. 169; (1980) 2 E.H.R.R. 439.
9 *Hickman v Blake Lapthorn* [2006] EWHC 12 (QB).
10 *Hickman* [2006] EWHC 12 at [21].
11 Carleton, *Seventh Earl of Malmesbury v Strutt & Parker* [2008] EWHC 424.

CHAPTER 3

A Word on 'Halsey v Milton Keynes'

Lord Dyson

Good morning everybody. I was asked if I would express a few thoughts about the *Halsey* decision six years on, do I wish to recant or am I obstinately sticking? I am delighted to see my former colleague Sir Henry Brooke in the audience. In light of some of the press that I received since the *Halsey* decision which was way back now in 2004, you might be forgiven for thinking that I am not mediation's greatest zealot, and that word: 'zealot'. It is amazing how it seems to crop up and, indeed, I heard your President use it only a few moments ago. There is something about mediation which does attract very considerable keenness. One of the more colourful accusations levelled against me was that I am an ADR non-believer, or at least an ADR sceptic, that is Professor Hazel Genn. I am quite happy to admit that I am not an evangelical about mediation. I didn't think, and I still don't think that it is necessarily appropriate for every dispute, but I do not consider that either of those epithets used by Hazel Genn accurately reflects my views about mediation. Far from indulging in ADR atheism, I in fact am a strong believer in its merits although I don't think that it is necessarily appropriate for every dispute.

Halsey has been the subject of many a speech and many an article. What I will attempt in the few minutes that are available to me this morning is to reflect on that judgment of six years ago and to respond to, to take account of some of the comments that have been made extra judicially during the last six years. I am sure you all know that *Halsey* was regarded, in some circles, as a rather controversial judgment — it certainly had a mixed press. Some were suggesting that we were attempting to turn the tide back and indeed close the door on ADR. That in my view is complete nonsense. The main point that we were addressing was how a refusal to mediate should be viewed by the courts when deciding the question of costs at the end of the day and, in particular, whether a successful party who would normally be awarded his costs should be deprived of some or all of those costs on the grounds of refusal to mediate. It was certainly not an attempt to thwart or sabotage the development of mediation as a supplement to the judicative process. So where do I stand six years on? Well I am afraid if anyone came here expecting some sort of *Halsey* recantation on my part then they will be disappointed. I am still of the view that the *Halsey* decision was on the whole correct (I will deal with the Art. 62 point shortly) and that the guidance in relation to costs was sound. This may sound complacent, I hope it doesn't, but I will explain why I am still of that view in a moment. There are three main propositions that I think one can extract from *Halsey* and I still agree with all of them. First, mediation is important and should be used in many cases but it is not a universal panacea. Secondly, parties should not be compelled to mediate if they are truly unwilling to do so, and thirdly that adverse costs orders are an appropriate means of encouraging parties to use mediation. As for the first of these points — that mediation is positive but not a panacea — I share the general view that recourse to the informality of

ADR can reduce cost, delay and the emotional strain associated with litigation and is often a very effective way of resolving disputes more effectively than traditional litigation. I don't think there is much doubt about that these days and I think that the mediation fraternity, if I may use that word, have been hugely successful in promoting mediation and putting it very firmly on the map. But there is another side. Mediation can be expensive. Some mediators are expensive, I don't imagine any of you are, but I imagine some are and mediations often involve lawyers and some of them can be very expensive. I don't suppose there are any of those here today either, but the fact is that mediation can be expensive and if it proves to be unsuccessful then of course the total costs of the dispute will have just been increased and that's why one should be wary of forcing mediation onto parties who really do not want it. As I said in *Halsey*, the fact that parties say they don't want it shouldn't necessarily be taken at face value by a court. But there are some cases where the parties simply do not want it or generally one party is simply unprepared to countenance it. So, as I say, and as I mentioned a few moments ago, there are some cases which are inherently unsuitable for mediation. They may be very few. I expect most people in this room think they are so few that one can almost discount them as a category. I accept entirely that family disputes are undoubtedly suitable for mediation — it's difficult to imagine a family dispute which is not. Personal injury, clinical negligence claims, all those sorts of claims are inherently suitable, as indeed are many, if not most, contractual disputes. But there are some cases where parties who wish to have a court or an arbitrator decide a point of law and should, in my view, be entitled to do so.

I refer to Hazel Genn on this point when she says that there is a public interest in the courts being there to promote the proper development of the law.

Should the parties ever be compelled to mediate even if they really do not want to? As I have said, I am still of the view today that I expressed in May 2004 that truly unwilling parties should never be compelled to mediate. Cajole them, yes. Encourage them, yes. But compel them, no in my view. What I would now say, however, is that ordering parties to mediate in and of itself does not infringe their Art. 6 rights. I rather regret, (and I wasn't alone, my two colleagues were with me) that I was tempted by the Law Society to embark upon something which it was unnecessary to embark upon, and venture some views upon Art. 6. What I said in *Halsey* was that to oblige truly unwilling parties to refer their disputes to mediation would be to impose an unacceptable obstruction to their right of access to the court in breach of Art. 6.

I think those words need some modification not least because the European Court of Justice entered into this territory in March this year in the case of *Rosalba Alassini*. The Court entertained a preliminary reference from Italy. The question for the Court arose out of a dispute between two telephone companies and their customers who had brought proceedings, seeking damages for breach of contract, under the EU directive on the Provision of Electronic Communications Networks. The telephone companies contended that the actions were inadmissible as the applicants had not first attempted mediation in accordance with the Italian implementing law. The Italian law made such legal actions conditional on a prior attempt to achieve an out-of-court settlement. If the parties declined to submit to mediation then they would forfeit their legal right to bring proceedings before the Court. Quite a strong law. The ECJ held that there was no contravention of Art. 6. In particular, the Court recognised that the right to effective judicial protection is not granted unconditionally and that every judicial procedure requires rules and conditions governing admissibility. In order not to infringe Art. 6, any such restrictions must correspond to objectives in the general interest and must not be disproportionate. The Court found that the Italian provisions did pursue legitimate objectives in the general interest in the quicker and less expensive resolution of disputes. It also held that the measure was proportionate as no less restrictive alternative existed to the implementation of a mandatory procedure since the introduction of an out-of-court settlement procedure, which is merely optional, is not as efficient a means of achieving those objectives.

The Court analysed the Italian rules from the perspective of EU principles of effectiveness and found that the rules did not make it impossible or excessively difficult to exercise the right derived from the Directive. This was because the parties were coerced to mediate, not to settle, so if the parties failed to settle a case they could then bring the action before the courts. The delay to bringing proceedings was minimal as the time limit for completion of the mediation procedure was 30 days and, during this period, time was stopped for limitation purposes and there were no fees involved in the mediation process. The EU legislator appears to agree with the Court because Art. 5 of the Mediation Directive adopts a similar position to that taken by the ECJ.

Article 5.1 does not prescribe that compulsory mediation must be adopted by Member States. Article 5.2 permits Member States to use compulsory mediation provided that it does not prevent parties from exercising their right of access to justice. So it is clear that in and of itself compulsory mediation does not breach Art. 6. Whilst six years on I agree with the EU legislator and the judiciary on the Art. 6 point, I am still less convinced that compulsory mediation is more effective than when it is voluntary. I remain of the view I advanced in *Halsey* that, if the court were to compel parties to enter into mediation to which they objected, that would achieve nothing except to add to the cost to be borne by the parties. It would also possibly postpone the time when the court determined the dispute and damaged the perceived effectiveness of the ADR process.

So what has happened in England since 2004? Well I think the first thing to say is that, leaving the Art. 6 point aside, the decision in *Halsey* remains good law. It has been followed and applied in a number of cases. It has, as I'm sure you're aware, been the subject of considerable extra judicial writing. In his well-known speech at the Second Civil Mediation Council National Conference in Birmingham in May 2008 the then Master of the Rolls, now Lord Clarke, discussed the Art. 6 point on the *Halsey* judgment; he said "we can safely say that there may well be grounds for suggesting that *Halsey* was wrong on the Article 6 point." He put that in a typically restrained way, but it is interesting to see that he based that conclusion on two points; the first was a European point that compulsory mediation existed in other Member States, and secondly an understanding of mediation, unlike arbitration, as forming part of court proceedings. I see the force of these points which have now been reinforced as I say by recent developments in Europe. It is undoubtedly true that compulsory mediation exists in the legal order of the Council of Europe Member States and indeed other common law jurisdictions, but this is not in itself proof that ordering parties to mediate or forfeit their access to the court would not breach Art. 6 and I emphasise, "or forfeit their access to the court." That would be a very strong thing to do. As far as I am aware this issue has not been litigated in other jurisdictions. As regards the second point made by Lord Clarke, that mediation is an integral part of the civil procedure rights process, I would say that it all depends on the nature of the court's order for mediation. In his view, at worst, an order to mediate delays the trial if mediation is unsuccessful. I think that the form of compulsory mediation which Lord Clarke appeared to be describing, namely where courts order parties to mediate, but do not penalise them for not taking part in the mediation (so that at worst the trial is delayed) would certainly not fall foul of Art. 6. If Lord Clarke was suggesting that mediation does not breach Art. 6 because it is an integral part of civil procedure process. I would say that this does not necessarily mean that an order for mediation involves no breach of Art. 6. It all depends on the terms of the court order for mediation. In any event I remain of the view that I expressed in *Halsey* that, whatever the Art. 6 position may be, the real question is not whether a power exists to order mediation. It is rather whether the court should exercise that power. In my view the court should not exercise that power if it is satisfied that the parties are truly unwilling to embark upon a mediation. That view has been endorsed by the Jackson review on costs published in January this year. The review devotes Ch.36 to ADR. Whilst recognising that mediation is a highly effective means of achieving a satisfactory resolution of many disputes, it also recognises that it is not a universal panacea, and that the process can be expensive and on occasions result in failure: "[i]t is clear ... that mediation should never be compulsory although courts should in appropriate cases encourage mediation by pointing out its benefits, by directing parties to meet and or discuss mediation and by using the Master Ungley form of order in the field of clinical negligence." That seems to me 'pure' *Halsey* if I may say so. As I explained in my judgment in *Halsey*, this has been happening in the Admiralty and Commercial Courts since 1993 where in cases identified as suitable for mediation judges may make an order directing the parties to attempt ADR.

So I remain six years on where I was six years ago. As I have said, it is one thing to compel parties to consider mediation, it is quite another to frogmarch them to the mediation table, specifically, if the result of a refusal to be frogmarched is to deny them access to the courtroom. The judgment of the ECJ in *Rosalba Alassini* does not rule that compulsory mediation will never breach Art. 6. I am of the view that in some circumstances where, for example, the costs of mediation were very high (and it is interesting that in the *Rosalba Alassini* case the compulsory mediation was free) compelling a party to mediate could still perhaps be considered a denial of access to justice. But perhaps there is another more overarching point to be made here. It seems to me that forcing individuals who truly do not wish to mediate, does raise a moral question: can it be right that a person who has exercised his constitutional right to go to court should be forced to sit down with the individual he believes to have wronged him to try and find a compromise which will probably leave him worse off than he would have been if he had had his day in court? You may say that's a rather tendentious way of putting it because it begs the question whether it would leave him worse off. What I have in mind is those cases where the parties truly do not want to compromise because they are adamant that they wish to go to court. It doesn't seem to me that it is the role of a court of law to force compromise upon people who do not want compromise. Parties who have a strong case and wish to vindicate that case rather than compromise should not, in my view, be denied their day in court.

I turn to the third point raised in *Halsey* namely that adverse cost orders are an appropriate way to deal with parties who unreasonably refuse to mediate. In my view this is an appropriate midway point between those who advance a sanction-based solution and those who favour incentives. It acts as a future threat of financial penalty on a party who unreasonably refuses to mediate. In the *Halsey* case we confirmed that a court may make an adverse cost order if a party has unreasonably refused mediation and then we set out the guidelines as to the circumstances in which refusal would be considered to be unreasonable. Compared to what has been said about the Art. 6 point, this aspect of the decision, which is really what the case was all about, has received comparatively little discussion as far as I am aware. I hope that I am not overly optimistic in considering that the reason for this was that we were largely right. I am encouraged in this thinking by the Jackson review, which agrees that parties who have unreasonably refused to mediate should be penalised in costs. I would emphasise that I had no part in writing this part of the Jackson report. Jackson said that the form of any cost penalty must be at the discretion of the courts.

What I want to do in the short time that I have left is to comment briefly on some of the issues on this part of *Halsey* that have come to light following the decision. First the situation where a party agrees to mediate but then behaves unreasonably during the mediation was not discussed in *Halsey*, but it has received the attention of the High Court in the case of *Carleton v Strutt & Parker (A Partnership)*. In giving judgment in that case Jack J. extended the *Halsey* guidelines to cover this situation. He held that the situation where the party takes an unreasonable position during mediation is not dissimilar to an unreasonable refusal to mediate. I see the force of this reasoning but I would enter a serious note of caution, allegations of unreasonableness in conduct of mediation or indeed in any traditional interparty negotiation are easy to make but they may be highly contentious, and I think that the courts should be very slow indeed to embark on a detailed exercise of fact finding to find out the rights and the wrongs in such circumstances. There are real dangers of costly satellite litigation here and I am not sure I would agree with the approach suggested by Jack J. But I think that question will have to be considered at some point, I hope, by the Court of Appeal.

Finally there is the issue of the burden of proof. In *Halsey* we ruled that the burden was on the party seeking costs. In other words the unsuccessful party had to show that the other party, the successful party, had unreasonably refused mediation. The alternative would have been to make the party who had refused mediation, the successful party, prove that his or her conduct was reasonable. Our approach was criticised by Lord Phillips in a speech that he gave in India (2008). It's very interesting that Lord Clarke in his speech did not agree with what we said about Art. 6 but did agree with what we said about the burden of proof. Lord Philips agreed with what we said about Art. 6 but disagreed with what we said about the burden of proof. He argued that our ruling on the burden of proof had significantly reduced the pressure on English litigants to attempt mediation. His reasoning was that parties will generally insist on litigation when they believe that they are going to win. Accordingly once a party has won it can be difficult for the loser to show that the winner acted unreasonably in pursuing litigation over ADR. I appreciate that proving that the successful party acted unreasonably in insisting on his or her right to a trial is no simple task. But in my view as a matter of principle the burden of proof must be on the unsuccessful party which is making the allegation. To force the party who refused ADR to justify him or herself is wrong in principle. It is usually the party who applies for an order for costs other than the normal order who should bear the burden of substantiating it.

So all in all, six years on from *Halsey*, not all that much has changed. The ECJ has settled the Art. 6 issue for cross-border cases. Its decision has not settled the question of whether compulsory mediation coupled with a denial of access to the court would breach Art. 6. But I accept that it would appear to have settled the Art. 6 issue in a case where there is merely a preliminary step which the parties are required to go through which, if unsuccessful, would leave them free to litigate; and as I said earlier, I would no longer adhere to what I said about Art. 6.

For the time being though, the English courts, so far as I can see, will continue to follow the *Halsey* guidance on the impact of a refusal to mediate on orders for costs. As to where "we" or "you" go from here, well, we are awaiting changes to the CPR due to implementation of EU Directive and, in the meantime, I would endorse the conclusions of the Jackson report; and, as the dust settles on *Halsey*, there are many challenges facing mediation. But there is no question that it is well and truly on the map and if what I've said over the last 20 minutes has confused you by giving certain conflicting signals, I hope that I leave you with message that I am firmly of the view that mediation is extremely important, occupies now a central part in our dispute resolution system, but the role of the court should never be underestimated. At the end of the day, parties do have a right to have their disputes resolved in court or if they have agreed to arbitration, by an arbitrator. Thank you very much.

REFERENCES

* This article was originally published as J. Dyson, 'A Word on *Halsey v Milton Keynes*', *Arbitration* 77, no. 3 (2011): 337-341.
1 *Halsey v Milton Keynes General NHS Trust* [2004] EWCA Civ 576; [2004] 4 All E.R. 920.
2 European Convention on Human Rights Art. 6.
3 *Alassini v Telecom Italia SpA* (Joined Cases C-317-320/08) [2010] 3 C.M.L.R. 17 ECJ.
4 Directive 2002/22/EC on universal service and users' rights relating to electronic communications networks and services (Universal Service

Directive) [2002] OJ L108/51.

5 Directive 2008/52/EC on certain aspects of mediation in civil and commercial matters (Mediation Directive) [2008] OJ L136/3.

6 A. Clarke, 'The Future of Civil Mediation' (speech delivered to a conference of the Civil Mediation Council, May 8, 2008).

7 R. Jackson, *Review of Civil Litigation Costs: Final Report* (London: TSO, 2010).

8 *Carleton v Strutt & Parker (A Partnership)* [2008] EWHC 616 (QB).

9 N. Phillips, 'Alternative Dispute Resolution: An English Viewpoint', (speech delivered to a conference at the International Centre for Dispute Resolution, New Delhi, March 29, 2008).

CHAPTER 3

Mediation 2020

Sir Vivian Ramsey

In about eight and a half years we look forward to 2020, and my central message today is that in all dispute resolution methods there is always pressure for change. The reason for this is that many enthusiasts find it tedious to have the same thing going on time and time again. There is always the pressure of change and my underlying theme is that people should keep an eye on the fundamentals rather than looking to change things.

A MEDIATION ACT?

Let us imagine that we are now in 2020 and those who want to change things have succeeded. You will therefore be glad to know that yesterday, November 2, 2020, Royal Assent was given to the Justice, Mediation and Dispute Resolution (Miscellaneous Provisions) Act 2020. That is a statute which is building on a number of European Directives which have come out over the past 10 years since the fourth symposium of the Chartered Institute of Arbitrators. What does this hypothetical new statute do? First, it makes mediation compulsory before any claim can be commenced in the courts or arbitration. It establishes the Mediation Authority which is responsible for giving qualified mediators Chartered Mediator status, for making mediation rules and for administering all mediations. It requires any settlement entered into after a mediation to be the subject of an award by the Mediator certifying that the settlement was fair and reasonable and entered into by the parties of their own free will. It provides for applications to the High Court to set aside any Mediation award on the basis of serious irregularity in the course of the mediation process. It also introduces a schedule of conflicts for mediators preventing mediators from acting in a wide range of circumstances, with the Director of the Mediation Authority having power to change those rules.

Now, what is wrong with that? Is that really where mediation should be in 2020? Do we want to move down the regulatory route for mediation and do we need regulation about those matters? People may have seen the European cross-border Directive which is six pages long and also now the domestic Regulations made to bring it into effect, which are 23 pages long. I think that this provides a good example of a fairly limited incursion into mediation by way of statutory regulation. However, it shows how it breeds further regulations. What I would like to do is look at what would be wrong with the Mediation, et cetera Act 2020 and see whether, in fact, that regulatory route is needed. I will deal with a number of topics.

Voluntary or Compulsory Mediation

The first point is whether mediation should be voluntary or compulsory. That is always a good topic and, given the difficulties they had to make it compulsory in California, it can be seen that compulsory mediation is not straightforward. There is now, it would seem, a move toward making mediation compulsory and I believe that this is an undesirable way to move. The courts in *Halsey* gave parties encouragement to mediate because if they unreasonably refused to mediate they would have an adverse cost order. That certainly had an effect. Everybody wrote letters saying "would you please mediate?" and when they did not receive an answer they would say "you are unreasonably refusing to mediate. We refer you to *Halsey* ...". Then the other party would write a long letter setting out why under *Halsey* they did not need to mediate.

I would suggest that the essence of mediation is that it should be voluntary. One of the difficulties with *Halsey* is that it may be unreasonable to refuse to mediate in terms of starting a mediation but how many times have we seen a party in the mediation acting unreasonably? If you go down the route that the court starts to look at the reasonableness of the parties' actions in mediation, then you take away the whole basis for mediation. I would suggest that a provision of the 2020 Act which made mediation compulsory is not what is wanted.

Mediation: A Process in Its Own Right

The second point is that mediation has, to some extent, a name for being the 'best of a bad bunch.' In other words, because litigation or arbitration takes so long, because other dispute resolution processes are expensive, people choose mediation because it is better than those other alternatives. I think it is important that mediation is seen as a dispute resolution process in its own right, and not one which is only used in the face of the enormous costs of the alternatives of litigation or arbitration. It is a process by which the parties come to an agreement rather than using somebody to make a determination of their dispute. Too often parties who are in litigation or arbitration look to mediation as a way out of their dispute resolution process rather than looking at it as a dispute resolution process which they might have undertaken in the first place as a process in its own right. My second point would therefore be to have mediation recognised more as a process in its own right rather than being the 'best of a bad bunch' of dispute resolution processes.

The Litigation Approach to Mediation

The third point is that, in my experience of commercial mediation, it is starting to be turned into a process akin to litigation and arbitration. Arbitration, as we know, was once a process where the parties went before somebody in the trade who would resolve a dispute between the parties by saying what his view was and then seeking to resolve it. Arbitration then suffered through the impact of the courts and then through statutory intervention and it is now a process which is very different to the process which started. I think that if there was a Mediation Act, the danger would be that mediation would go down the same track of making it another formalised process of dispute resolution. In my experience it is becoming more common for a team of lawyers — solicitors, Leading Counsel, Junior Counsel — to be involved and then for the person put forward on behalf of the client to be a trained negotiator brought in to negotiate for the purpose of mediation. When that happens, it seems to me that one is losing an important aspect of mediation, being a negotiation between reasonable people on both sides rather than involving two vast legal teams. Sometimes the position papers have attached to them a lot of documents, reports and even witness statements, converting it into a quasi-arbitral process. When this happens it can lead to stalemate through experience.

Free Choice in Mediation

I next want to look at pressure and free choice in mediation. Those of us who have acted for parties in mediation will recall that discussion which I call the 'morning-after effect.' The party will ask: "did we settle at the right figure?" or "should we have obtained more out of the other party?" or "what would have happened if we had gone on with the arbitration or litigation?" Those questions form part of the management process of mediation. But care has to be taken that there is a free choice in entering into the agreement at the end of the mediation. There is obviously commercial pressure because of the window of opportunity in mediation, but one has to be careful, particularly where you have parties of non-equal bargaining strengths. It is a conflict between free choice in entering into the agreement and pressure. There has to be pressure, but I think one has to notice that pressure as a mediator and know how to deal with it.

Regulation of Mediation

The next point is regulation of the process. The more regulation, the less I consider you have the flexibility or confidentiality of the process. The more you have people wanting to regulate the process, the more you have to disclose whether in terms of statistics on mediation or otherwise. In international mediation, in particular, there is often a need for some degree of transparency because a party which is a government in a third world country may be unhappy about having a settlement in a secret mediation. There may be allegations of "why did you settle at that figure?" and suspicions of corrupt practices in the settlement because there is not a full, transparent process. Therefore, transparency is important as is confidence that the settlement has been fair and reasonable. One mediator in Australia always writes a letter confirming that the parties have settled on a fair and reasonable basis and of their own free will. This may be a difficult thing for a mediator to do but for parties in countries where there might otherwise be suspicion, this enables the person acting in the mediation to give something to their superior to show that someone independent has certified the correctness of the settlement. Otherwise, if the 2020 Act included provision for some type of 'award' by a mediator this would, I suggest, be a move too far in regulation of the process. The balance between transparency and secrecy needs to be kept under control.

Conflicts for Mediators

The next item looking ahead to 2020 is the question of conflicts and the pool of mediators. The important thing about mediators is to choose one who is going to mediate the dispute to a satisfactory settlement. Conflicts of the type seen in the international arbitration community would start to erode that freedom of choice. The fact that a mediator comes from a law firm where a partner has advised one of the parties on tax matters need not be a conflict in mediation. If such conflicts are taken into account, it could lead to parties objecting so that the mediator might be one neither party would have chosen. I would suggest that what is most important is the quality of the mediator rather than the potential for conflicts. I had a mediation in Singapore some years ago where there were a large number of parties and it was discovered that there was a common director for some of those parties. That director was chosen as the mediator and was able to bring enormous commercial experience to bear and reached a settlement. That is why I would suggest that you have to look at the mediator, and the more one looks at conflicts, the less you are likely to get the mediator you really want to help resolve a dispute.

Creative Use of Mediation

I now turn to two final themes. I think it is important that mediation is not seen as just being of use in resolving intractable disputes in arbitration and litigation. Mediation and the power of a neutral are important in a number of fields of human endeavour and I know some mediators are now involved in mediations where, for instance, at the end of a franchising agreement between parties, the mediator is used to help the parties negotiate new terms. The parties in those agreements may have a commercial relationship and they do not want to negotiate face-to-face the renewal terms. They then use a mediator who mediates the resolution of those terms. Equally in the economic downturn it has been found that parties are prepared to negotiate to avoid financial hardship. For instance, if you are a tenant of commercial property you are more likely now to be able to enter into a negotiation with your landlord to have some rent-free period or a reduction of rent and mediators have been used to help those parties to reach an agreement. This prevents litigation for rent arrears and overcomes the potential for voids in commercial premises. In addition I have used a mediator in the course of an arbitration where we had engineering experts on each side who were unable to produce a sensible joint statement. I therefore arranged for the parties to appoint a professional engineering neutral and within a short time there was a sensible experts' joint statement. I would therefore suggest that mediation should not be seen as just a process to resolve intractable disputes but also as a way of reaching creative solutions in other areas through the use of neutrals.

The Courts and Mediation

My final theme is the role of the courts. The courts have a role to support mediation agreements, both to support those who want to go to mediation under mediation agreements and to support the enforcement of agreements which come out of mediation. But worldwide the courts are now also taking part in mediation by using judge mediators and, indeed, the Directive refers to judicial mediation.

Over the next few years to 2020 it may be that here, as has happened in a number of other countries, we will move towards mediation not only of civil cases, but also of criminal cases. In criminal cases, judges are often asked to give *Goodyear* indications of the maximum sentence which would be passed if someone pleaded guilty. On the other hand, there is often discussion of whether a defendant would plead guilty to a lesser charge. That process really, in my view, could do with some structure being given to it, so it could form the basis of mediation of criminal disputes. This is not new because many other parts of the world have mediation of criminal matters. I would suggest that that would be a much better way of dealing with a lot of minor offences.

CONCLUSION: THE AVOIDANCE OF REGULATION

My overall view of this is that what we must avoid before 2020 is someone saying we must have a Mediation Act. Despite the pressure on change and regulation, those involved in mediation should adhere to the fundamentals of mediation which I have reviewed and which I believe would be eroded by going down a statutory approach to the mediation process.

REFERENCES

* This article was originally published as V. Ramsey, 'Mediation 2020: A Presentation to the Chartered Institute of Arbitrators, 4th Annual Mediation Symposium, October 9, 2011', *Arbitration* 78, no. 2 (2012): 159-162.
1 Directive 2008/52/EC on certain aspects of mediation in civil and commercial matters on certain aspects of mediation in civil and commercial matters.
2 The Cross-Border Mediation (EU Directive) Regulations 2011 (SI 2011/1133).
3 *Halsey v Milton Keynes General NHS Trust* [2004] EWCA Civ 576.
4 *R. v Goodyear* [2005] EWCA Crim 888.

Lightning Source UK Ltd.
Milton Keynes UK
UKOW04f2256200214

226873UK00002B/26/P